MW00634295

The **Outer Banks** Gazetteer

The **Outer Banks**

Gazetteer

The History *of* Place Names *from* Carova *to* Emerald Isle

Roger L. Payne

THE UNIVERSITY OF NORTH CAROLINA PRESS

Chapel Hill

Published with the assistance of the Blythe Family
Fund of the University of North Carolina Press.

© 2021 Roger L. Payne
All rights reserved

Designed by Richard Hendel
Set in TheSans
by Tseng Information Systems, Inc.
Manufactured in the United States of America

The University of North Carolina Press has been a
member of the Green Press Initiative since 2003.

Cover photograph: *Manteo Lighthouse on Dock at
Sunrise* (Roanoke Marshes Lighthouse); © iStock/
bookwyrmm.

Library of Congress Cataloging-in-Publication Data
Names: Payne, Roger L., 1946– author.
Title: The Outer Banks gazetteer : the history
of place names from Carova to Emerald Isle /
Roger L. Payne.
Description: Chapel Hill : The University of North
Carolina Press, 2021. | Includes bibliographical
references.
Identifiers: LCCN 2020033426 |
ISBN 9781469662275 (cloth) |
ISBN 9781469662282 (pbk ; alk. paper) |
ISBN 9781469662299 (ebook)
Subjects: LCSH: Names, Geographical—North
Carolina—Outer Banks. | Outer Banks (N.C.)—
Gazetteers. | Outer Banks (N.C.)—History. |
North Carolina—History, Local.
Classification: LCC F262.O96 P388 2021 |
DDC 975.6/1—dc23
LC record available at https://lccn.loc.gov
/2020033426

This book is dedicated to
Irvin L. Payne, my father,
who first introduced me
to the Outer Banks,
and to the memory of
Gladys Binkley Payne,
my mother.

Contents

Maps

Preface

Work on this gazetteer began many, many years ago with my first trip to the Outer Banks. While waiting for the ferry at Oregon Inlet (before the bridge), I asked my dad, "Why is this inlet called Oregon Inlet?" He hesitated, thought for a while, and responded, "That's a good question." It seemed an unlikely name to be on the Outer Banks of North Carolina. After all, what does Oregon have to do with North Carolina? Thus began my interest in geographic names of the Outer Banks and in geographic names in general. On this and subsequent trips I began to keep records of unusual names on the Outer Banks. Later, while attending East Carolina University, I continued my interest in the Outer Banks and its place names.

In the late 1970s I began to organize my accumulated notes and launched a serious systematic study of the place names of the Outer Banks. The work was done sporadically, in my spare time, until about two years before I decided to publish the results of my efforts as *Place Names of the Outer Banks* (1985).

Upon retirement in 2006 I turned my attention again to names on the Outer Banks, but reemployment and other projects and priorities took precedence until the past five years, when I began a much-needed revision and expansion of *Place Names of the Outer Banks*. I was aware, when publishing, that all of the known names of places and features would not be included. Absolutely every name will never be compiled because names are dynamic and will continue to be added to the Outer Banks' lexicon.

This greatly expanded gazetteer yields the fruits of these efforts, with almost four times the number in *Place Names of the Outer Banks*. The advent of the digital age has allowed almost unlimited access to vast amounts of source material, both primary (digitized) and secondary. Also, maps have been updated and have increased in number as a result of digital mapping, with a wide array of maps and charts for thematic application and at ever larger scales (which show more detail), digital and conventional. This increased availability of all types of source material has allowed for a comprehensive volume, with almost all known names for geographic features on the Outer Banks and neighboring islands. To be sure, some names (mostly small features) are still not included, as it is not possible to find every name ever used; this volume contains almost all known names. Furthermore, with access to additional material came the ability to analyze name origins critically and histories in more depth, which yielded some startling conclusions. Finally, unlike *Place Names of the Outer Banks*, this volume has an extensive annotated bibliography, and bibliographical citations are referenced in the gazetteer entries.

The purpose of this volume categorically is to include names for as many geographic entities on the Outer Banks as possible, because it is most important to preserve the original Outer Banks culture. The collection and analyses of a place's name(s) is a proven method of accomplishing this preservation. Recording the place names, and particularly their meaning, or determining the name origin and meaning through informed analysis and research based on years of toponymic investigation, publicly and privately, adds to the literature of the Outer Banks. Additionally, meaningful research can help to dispel myths created by folk etymology, which sometimes invents reasons for meaning when the original meaning is unknown or forgotten (see, e.g., entries for Jockeys Ridge and No Ache). Even so, many names and their meanings have been forgotten even by older residents, stressing the need for this work.

I hope those interested in names and name origins find this work interesting, informative, and enjoyable to read as I did to compile. The study of Outer Banks' place names is truly dynamic and should be expanded and updated periodically. The process is continuous, and any name contributions will be appreciated and researched accordingly. Please direct all suggestions, questions, and other reference materials to Roger L. Payne (yadkinv@gmail.com or OBX.placenames .com).

Roger L. Payne
Williamsburg, Va., July 2020

Abbreviations

Agencies and Organizations

ACE	U.S. Army Corps of Engineers
C&GS	U.S. Coast and Geodetic Survey
CCC	Civilian Conservation Corps
CHNS	Cape Hatteras National Seashore
CS	U.S. Coast Survey
Currituck DB	Deed books, Currituck County Register of Deeds
F&WS	U.S. Fish and Wildlife Service
GNIS	Geographic Names Information System, U.S. Board on Geographic Names
NCDOT	N.C. Department of Transportation
NOS	National Ocean Service
NPS	National Park Service
PC HOA	Pirates Cove Home Owner's Association
PKS	Pine Knoll Shores History Committee
USBGN	U.S. Board on Geographic Names
USGS	U.S. Geological Survey
WPA	Works Progress Administration

Directions and Measurements

e	east, eastern, eastward
ese	east-southeast
est.	established
ft.	feet
lat.	latitude
mi.	mile and miles
ne	northeast, northeastern
n	north, northern, northward
no.	number
nw	northwest, northwestern
se	southeast, southeastern
sq.	square (with unit, e.g., sq. mi.)
s	south, southern, southward
ssw	south-southwest
sw	southwest, southwestern
w	west, western, westward

The **Outer Banks** Gazetteer

Introduction

The Outer Banks of North Carolina have been studied by researchers in almost every discipline. There are books on Outer Banks history, geography, geology, land use, and folklore, but a toponymic study—study of place names—was lacking until I completed *Place Names of the Outer Banks* (1985). Incomplete or highly localized lists have appeared in magazines and papers, but no complete or systematic study of the named features of the Outer Banks existed until 1985, and now, with publication of this gazetteer, it is available in greatly expanded and enhanced form.

The Nature of Names and Naming

Establishing, determining, and assigning names take various forms, from established methodology to random actions. The names of natural features are subject to the rules and policies of the U.S. Board on Geographic Names (USBGN) and the N.C. Board on Geographic Names, but man-made features are not. After decades, most forget the true meaning and origin of certain names, and it becomes natural to invent or develop meanings (based on parts and pieces of information), known as folk etymology (see, e.g., the entries for Jockeys Ridge and No Ache). Through research and analysis based on decades of professional experience, most of the real and forgotten meanings and name origins have been discovered and uncovered for presentation in this volume.

The Outer Banks Defined

For this study, the Outer Banks includes the barrier complex of North Carolina from the North Carolina–Virginia boundary in Currituck County, generally southward to Cape Lookout, and then westward to Bogue Inlet in Carteret County. This delineation is believed logical, both physically and culturally. Beyond Bogue Inlet, the barriers cease to be true barriers and are often attached to the mainland at low tide or comprise many broken marsh islands just off the mainland. Cultural activities are generally similar in the study area (although might differ locally), but clear cultural differences are apparent beyond Bogue Inlet. Also included are four large islands, Knotts Island, Colington Island, Roanoke Island, and Harkers Island, as well as many smaller islands in the system of sounds or lagoons, because they are culturally part of the Outer Banks.

Physically, the Outer Banks is a complex barrier system known as a barrier chain. This barrier system is narrow, varying from as little as 0.5 mi. on Core Banks to almost 5 mi. at greater Cape Hatteras. There has been much debate over the years as to how barriers form. It has been suggested that many causes are at work in barrier formation, and this is the case on the Outer Banks.

Sounds and Inlets

Characteristics of any barrier system are lagoons (locally called sounds) and inlets. The sound system of the Outer Banks is extensive and includes Pamlico Sound, the largest inland water body on the U.S. East Coast. From north to south, the sounds are Currituck, Albemarle, Croatan, Roanoke, Pamlico, Core, Back, and Bogue. The meaning of "sound," originally from the Saxon or Norse word *sund*, meaning to separate, indicating narrow water bodies separating land masses, was later expanded and applied generally to inland water bodies, especially as reference to sounded or sounding, because these water bodies are shallow, requiring soundings to be taken (before electronic sounding) when navigating. The term has persisted in place names.

The names of all known inlets recorded since the beginning of the European discovery of the Outer Banks are included (for quick reference, see "Current and Historic Inlets"). Some inlets were open before 1585 and are shown on some maps in specific reports, but without names, so were given labels used as referents in scientific studies. Such references as South Core Inlet Number 1 and Bogue Banks Inlet Number 2 are not included here. Kill Devil Hills Inlet, while of questionable existence, is included for the reasons given in the entry.

Native American (Indigenous)–Derived Names

Native American names are part of the history and toponymic evolution of the Outer Banks. Unfortunately, early colonists infrequently kept records. Little is known about the Native populations and especially their place names. Fortunately, from their initial visits, noted artists Thomas Harriot and John White made copious drawings with descriptive notes and some maps, but almost no place names. By the middle of the 18th century, when the first accurate maps appeared, the indigenous influence had become minimal.

The Indian population on the Outer Banks was never significant. Wars and exposure to European diseases, for which they had no immunity, soon reduced their numbers. By the mid-18th century Native populations had all but disappeared. Many Native-derived place names were lost by inadequate mapping and records prior to the disappearance of the Indians; only about 7 percent of the Outer Banks place names are of Indian origin. However, this percentage includes some of the most colorful and interesting names. No Native American place names likely exist in their original pronunciation form (throughout the Americas, indigenous peoples had no written languages) but have become anglicized through phases of use and morphing. Many possibilities exist, but records are incomplete and true origins might never be known for words of the indigenous languages along the East Coast. Care should be used in analysis, and no assumptions should be made. For example, the root "accomic" can be seen in the place names of Maryland, Delaware, and Virginia and on the Outer Banks (e.g., Chicamacomico) and probably refers to a dwelling or campsite, or might also mean "land on the other side." "Kitt" is found to mean big, and "hakki" to mean land. Not much imagination is needed to obtain Kitty Hawk. Another possibility is "moskitu-auke," reportedly meaning grassland (see Musketo Inlet). This could evolve etymologically to "mosquito hawk" and then to Kitty Hawk. These are seemingly possibilities, but caution should be used when studying origin and etymology of place names because many meanings are lost or were never known, and the same or similar words could have different meanings. Also, since these languages were not written, the colonists transcribed them as they heard them, in the English of the time. For example, the above-mentioned terms are coincidental and not the origin of the name Kitty Hawk, which actually evolved from Chickehauk, the indigenous name for that area.

Subdivisions, Neighborhoods, and Communities

The names of all communities or community-like features are presented, including the names of traditional communities, which have been established and developed over many decades (some historical now). The names of relatively recent communities (referenced as subdivisions, housing developments, or neighborhoods) were compiled but, because of the high number and length of entries, could not be included. A small number of communities that began as housing subdivisions are quite large and well established, becoming

mapworthy and so are included. Mobile home sites and camp sites for tourists are not included. Similarly, timeshare units, although named, represent a transient situation so are not included. Also, names of camps of the Civilian Conservation Corps (CCC) and the Works Progress Administration (WPA), while historically important, are not included because they were not permanent and the residents were transitory.

Post Offices and Influence on Community Names

It is an almost universal concept and belief that the Post Office Department (now U.S. Postal Service) named communities, or actually changed the name of a community that already had a name on the Outer Banks, and throughout the United States. This is the impression unwittingly (or by design) conveyed by every author writing about the Outer Banks. Rodanthe and Corolla are examples. The Post Office Department did not ever, nor does it now, have the authority to name any community or to change the name of any community. The Postal Service only has authority to name the post office (building) and the postal zone (ZIP code area). The Postal Service has (and had) three basic rules for naming the post office and postal zone: (1) the name cannot repeat an existing postal name in the same state, (2) the name should not be cumbersome to spell or pronounce, and (3) the name should not create any confusion. Further, the Postal Service does not want to decree a name. In fact, the Postal Service wanted a locally chosen and accepted name, so when a post office was to be established, the community was asked to submit three choices, and one would be chosen in accordance with established procedures. Sometimes, the three choices submitted were not acceptable, or the community could not agree on a name, in which case the Post Office Department chose a name. Unfortunately, in many cases on the Outer Banks the reason was not provided or, as with many other instances, the postal records were lost or destroyed. If the name of the post office was different from the name of the community, for whatever reason, after some amount of time it was natural that the community identified with the post office name. The post office was a means of communicating with the outside world, and the community name then became or assumed that of the post office, and the original community name usually fell into disuse.

U.S. Board on Geographic Names and N.C. Board on Geographic Names

The U.S. Board on Geographic Names (USBGN) is a federal body created in 1890 and established in its present form by public law 80-242 in 1947 to maintain uniform geographic name usage throughout the federal government. The USBGN is reactive, meaning it does not initiate cases on which it makes decisions but only responds to problems and controversies proposed to it. Since 1890, there have been only 62 actions from the USBGN regarding names on the Outer Banks and adjacent islands. Similarly, the N.C. Board on Geographic Names is a standing committee of the Statewide Mapping Advisory Committee, operating under authority of the N.C. Geographic Information Coordinating Council. The N.C. Board on Geographic Names is the state authority recognized by the USBGN for consultation and making recommendations concerning geographic names.

How to Use the Gazetteer

In order to preserve history, it is important to capture place names that are quickly becoming lost and to record the history of as many names as possible. The function of names is to serve as a referent to a particular landmark, object, person, and so forth. For place names, name and circumstances of naming reveal valuable insights into culture and history, becoming markers that preserve and protect culture. Names establish landmarks in an otherwise undifferentiated spatial environment. Information provided connects names to historical events and/or geographical function and name origin; however, it is not possible to provide complex and detailed analyses of historical events, and indeed, entire volumes are dedicated to certain topics. While relevant details are provided here, additional reading on individual topics will be necessary for complete details.

While many names are old and well established, a small number are more recent and have been subject to the process of "reversed usage." This process begins when a man-made feature, such as a subdivision or a road, is established at or near a natural feature, and the name of the subdivision or road subsequently is recorded as official in tax records or other documents and signage is erected. New owners, transient population, and even older residents begin to associate the new subdivision or road name with the natural feature, and the name originally used for the natural feature is replaced, or is transferred to a previously unnamed natural feature. Numerous examples of this practice exist on the Outer Banks (see, e.g., entries for Schooner Ridge in Currituck County and Osprey Ridge in Dare County).

In this volume, all categories of natural features are included, along with certain categories of cultural or man-made features, including communities and some subdivisions, harbors or marinas, landings, wharves, anchorages, canals, channels, transportation entities serving as a focal point, causeways and intersections, and camps and forts of historical significance. Not included are churches, cemeteries, schools, shopping centers, commercial establishments, and similar categories.

The concept of univocity (one official name per feature) is followed by the U.S. government and in this volume. In a few cases, names are included that can be reasonably determined to be accurate but there is some disagreement among those familiar with the area. If more than one name was uncovered for a single feature, one official name was decided on, based on research and preponderance of evidence, with the remaining names presented as "Other names" within the main entry. Some of these are cross-referenced to another main entry if different in form (e.g., for Mirlo Breach, *see* Rodanthe Breach). A few names have been found in reliable and reputable sources, directly or indirectly, but without specific location, and subsequent research has not been able to pinpoint the location. These are included for historical interest.

Main entries are arranged alphabetically and, in cases of multiple locations with the same name, by county and then by township. Names in *italics* indicate that the feature is historical, meaning it no longer exists. In some cases, a name is described as "associative." Such features might be of varying types yet are in close proximity and, as such, might be associated with each other. Examples include Chinquapin Ridge and Chinquapin Ridge Pond, and Dancing Ridge, Dancing Ridge Pond, and Dancing Ridge Swamp.

Additional information, especially regarding the Roanoke voyages, is available at the website for this book: OBXplacenames.com.

A

Aaron Harbor. *See* Black Dog Harbor.

A. Baums Landing, former landing, Currituck County, Poplar Branch Township (*see* Kennekeet Township for explanation) (C&GS 1852). On Currituck Banks just w of Piper Hill, 6.7 mi. s of Corolla.

Abbeys Nole, former small hummock, Currituck County, Fruitville Township (Currituck DB 23, 1841, 156). On s Knotts Island at Indian Creek 2.5 mi. sw of Knotts Island (village). Jesse Nole, Long Nole, and Whites Nole also here, according to deed, where named are "in Knotts Island . . . at an angle of Indian Creek." Only distinctive angle today is halfway between Indian Pond and Sandy Cove, no knolls or hummocks there. Topography could change considerably over 200 years, and features might no longer exist or could be short distance ne on e side of Indian Pond where some hummocks exist. "Nole" is a variation of "knoll."

Abes Creek, water passage, 0.5 mi. long, Currituck County, Fruitville Township (Cox 1923). N-s trending separating Big Bird Island from Middle Marsh 4 mi. se of Knotts Island (village). *Other names:* Muddy Creek (Cox 1923).

Abes Island, island, 0.1 mi. long, less than 0.1 mi. wide, Currituck County, Fruitville Township (Cox 1906). At nw end of Fresh Pond Bay, at entrance to Abes Island Cove, 2.2 mi. e of Knotts Island (village).

Abes Island Cove, cove, 0.3 mi. across, Currituck County, Fruitville Township (Cox 1906). N extension of Fresh Pond Bay, 3 mi. e of Knotts Island (village).

Academy Green, former area, Carteret County, Portsmouth Township (White 2012, 75). At former school, Portsmouth (village) just s of The Crossroads, formerly main intersection in Portsmouth (village). Maintained for school activity and gatherings.

Academy Pond, lake, Carteret County, Portsmouth Township (White 2012, 77). At former school, Portsmouth (village) adjacent to Academy Green, just s of The Crossroads, formerly main intersection in Portsmouth (village).

Adams Pond, pond, 0.3 mi. long, 0.1 mi. wide, Currituck County, Fruitville Township (USGS 2013: Knotts Island Overedge East). Just w of historical Deals (village) at Wash Woods, 3 mi. s of Carova. "Pond" used in n Outer Banks referring to coves or water surrounded by ever-changing marsh, sometimes with small water passages, sometimes not.

Aibonito, former subdivision, Carteret County, Morehead Township (PKS 2016). Former planned community in center of original Pine Knoll Shores (halfway between two entrances of Pine Knoll Waterway) 4.5 mi. w of Atlantic Beach. Oscar Kissam purchased 82 acres (1908) at what is now Pine Knoll Shores with intention of developing. He built no infrastructure, and surveyed lots were sold as raw land. By 1915 one-fourth had been sold with limited seasonal usage, but by 1915 Kissam abandoned his scheme (PKS 2016). Recorded as Aibonito (map and deed [bk. 8, Nov. 15, 1909, 18] presented by PKS 2016). Later deeds issued on lots sold use "Abonit*a*." "Aibonito" (masculine form initially recorded) only form not perpetuated at Pine Knoll Shores (maybe because feminine form is easier for speakers of English). "Aibonito" name of town, river, and pass in Puerto Rico; not Spanish but Spanish version of a Taíno (division of Arawak Indians who inhabited the Caribbean) word, perhaps a Taíno chief. Kissam had a relative who participated in Battle of Aibonito Pass in Puerto Rico during Spanish-American War, and as an attempt to honor that service at that battle, Kissam named this real estate venture Aibonito. *Other names:* Aibonita (PKS 2016), Abonita (PKS 2016), Abonito (PKS 2016), Albonito (Zaenker 2014).

Aires Shoal, former small shoal, Carteret County, Portsmouth Township (Price 1795, 630). Just inside Ocracoke Inlet near Wallace Channel 1 mi. nw of Portsmouth (village). Only encountered in Price 1795 and associated with Rimus Shoal (q.v.). Possibly name of a ship that ran afoul in or near inlet (such names occasionally used—*see* Vera Cruz Shoal), but name not found in lists of shipwrecks. A ship by this name was known to operate along the Outer Banks during Civil War (well after Price's map) initially as a blockade runner and then as a patrol ship after being captured by Union forces. No mention of action at Ocracoke.

Albacore Point. *See* Power Squadron Spit.

Albemarle, The, region; controversy regarding extent but included present counties of Currituck, Dare, Camden, Pasquotank, Perquimans, Chowan, Gates, Tyrrell, Washington, Bertie, and Hertford. Continues to have some regional significance today, especially when referring to agricultural activity. *See* Albemarle Sound.

Albemarle County, former civil division, included ne portion of "New Province" of Carolina containing 1,600 sq. mi. Est. 1664, divided into Chowan, Currituck, Pasquotank, and Perquimans Precincts 1668. Precinct as a division ceased to exist 1689. *See* Albemarle Sound.

Albemarle Sound, estuary, 50 mi. long, 15 mi. wide, Currituck, Dare, Camden, Pasquotank, Tyrrell, Perquimans, Bertie, and Washington Counties. Nontidal or small tide, freshwater body into which Chowan River and Roanoke River flow, then drains s through Roanoke Sound and Croatan Sound into Pamlico Sound. Since earliest settlement, Albemarle Sound provided outlet for agricultural products of Albemarle region. Today important for transportation, fishing, and recreation. Named for George Monck, first Duke of Albemarle and one of the eight Lords Proprietors of Carolina (*see* Carolina). *Other names:* Abbaramal Saund (Wimble 1733), Albemar Sound (Currituck DB 9, 1807, 307), Albemarle Bay (historical sources), Albemarle River (Moll et al. 1708), Albemarl River (Schroeter 1859), Albemarl Sound (Sauthier 1769b), Arlbemarle Sound (Imlay 1795), Bahia de Magdalena (Keulen 1690), Baye d'Albemarle (Bellin 1757), Bay of Albemarle (Stick 1958, 5), Carituck River (Crisp 1711), Carolina River (historical), Chowane River (colonial references), Chowan River (misapplication), Colleton River (Moll 1729), Detroit de Albemarle (Frédéric 1807), Great River (Oldmixon 1708), Occam (Haklyut 1589), Occam River (Haklyut 1589, 6:127), Occom (Austin 1984), Oceana (Burke 1958, 6 — apparently mistaken interpretation of Occam), River Roanoke (Keulen 1682), River van Weapemeoc (Blaeu 1640 — Weapemeoc indigenous name on mainland n of Albemarle Sound for Indian

tribe there), Roanoake Sound (Comberford 1657), Roanoke Sound (misapplication), Rolli Passa (Ferrar 1657 originally Magna Passa [1651] — might be attempt at phonetic spelling of Raleigh Pass), Sea of Rawnocke (historical), Sound of Albemarl (Lawson 1709, 74), Sound of Weapemeoc (historical), Sound of Weapomeiock (historical), Sound of Weapomeiok (historical), Sound of Weopemeiok (historical), Stretto di Albemarle (Tardieu, ca. 1800).

Alberts Pond, cove, Currituck County, Fruitville Township (Cox 1923). N-s–trending cove 1.5 mi. nne of Currituck Bay, 4.3 mi. se of Knotts Island (village). *See* Adams Pond.

Alder Branch, small stream, 1 mi. long, Dare County, Nags Head Township (local informants and research reports). Begins just n of Sunny Side, meanders w to Weir Point 3 mi. nw of Manteo. Use of generic term "branch" on the Outer Banks is limited and appears sparingly on Roanoke Island. Feature larger 19th century and before; reportedly (no proof) used by Lost Colonists. Doughs Creek (q.v.) also reportedly used (no proof). Subdivision named for feature. *Other names:* Alder Creek (some local use), Aulder Branch (Currituck DB Miscellaneous, 1763, 39–40).

Alfords Point. *See* Shellbank Point.

Allen Slough, cove, 0.2 mi. wide, Carteret County, Morehead Township (USGS 2013: Beaufort). In Bogue Sound at e end Bogue Banks, 1.1 mi. e of Atlantic Beach. "Slough," "slue," or "slew" indicates (Outer Banks) tidal water passage ranging from open channel to restricted water passages through dense marsh. "Slough" (or "slogh") from Middle English refers to muddy or mucky area where one might become mired. Additionally, "slew," originally a nautical term used extensively (1700s) referring to twisting and turning (mast movement), might have been applied to normally irregular and twisted course of these water passages. Sloughs at the Outer Banks can range from free-flowing water passages to those clogged with mud and shoals, often spelled "slue" and "slew."

Alligator Gut, tidal stream, 0.2 mi. long, Carteret County, Morehead Township (USGS 2013: Mansfield). At White Ash Swamp, 2.2 mi. w of Hoop Pole Woods. Origin not documented but appears on earliest maps and presumed named for alligators found there during colonial period (disappeared, but some say making a comeback). "Gut" commonly used throughout U.S. for small tidal water passage, though less so on the Outer Banks. Outer Banks usage was mostly in Kitty Hawk (Ocracoke historically), mostly in colonial period.

Amity Shoal, former shoal, Carteret County, Portsmouth Township; and Hyde County, Ocracoke Township (CS 1857b). Was at sw entrance Ocracoke Inlet 5 mi. sw of Ocracoke (village) before becoming part of Portsmouth Island then later inundated. No one recalls name origin. Could be name of a wrecked ship here, but no record of ship by this name wrecking here or even visiting. A ship by this name in this time period after refitting recorded as whaling in the Atlantic, but no mention of Ocracoke. Vague references to two other ships in 1600s named Amity, no record of visiting the Outer Banks coast. Sketchy records exist of two French ships in 1700s named *L'Amitié*, but no interaction with the Outer Banks. *Other names:* Amity Shoals (White 2014, 23).

Amity Shoal Point, former point, Carteret County, Portsmouth Township (House of Representatives 1895). Was e point of Amity Shoal before shoal became part of Portsmouth Island then later inundated, 5.2 mi. sw of Ocracoke (village center).

Anchorage Marina, harbor, Carteret County, Morehead Township (signage). Soundside just e of Atlantic Beach, just se of Money Island 2 mi. s of Morehead City (mainland).

Anchorage Marina, harbor, Hyde County, Ocracoke Township (signage). N shore Silver Lake in Ocracoke (village) 4 mi. nw of Ocracoke Inlet.

Andersons Island, former island, Dare County, Croatan Township (Currituck DB 25, 1810, 393–94). Exact location unknown, was in s Croatan Sound offshore at n entrance Ship Channel (Dare County) near Roan Oak Narrows. With scores of other islands in former Roanoke Marshes (q.v.), inundated over 75 years when Roanoke Inlet closed 1811 and water forced s through Croatan Sound.

Angel Island. *See* Baum Point Island.

Arcadia, historical area. Applied to Nags Head and Kitty Hawk by early English explorers. Use short-lived and limited to historical significance. *See* Outer Banks.

Archer Creek, cove, 0.5 mi. long, Carteret County, White Oak Township (USGS 2013: Swansboro). In Bogue Sound just s of Archer Point 6.3 mi. ese of Swansboro (mainland). Original application to open cove and short creek to this cove from w to e. Over time and with subdivision development, application extended along canalized marsh 2 mi. to Bogue Sound through Emerald Plantation subdivision just e of Langston Bridge. Subdivision name uses "Archers" while names of creek and point use "Archer." Local residents refer to w extension as The Canal. Piney Creek (sometimes Piney Island Creek) often confused with Archer Creek; Piney Creek (q.v.) applied to former cove on Piney Island short distance n of Archer Creek. Piney Creek was misapplied until mid-20th century and still used in some applications. *Other names:* Archers Creek (local use, street sign), Arthurs Creek (Stephens 1984, back cover map—could be original name, but now Archer), Piney Creek (USGS 1952: Swansboro), Piney Island Creek (C&GS 1915a).

Archer Point, point, Carteret County, White Oak Township (USGS 2013: Swansboro). On w Bogue Banks, n point at Archer Creek, 6.5 mi. ese of Swansboro (mainland). Sometimes name applied to entire peninsula created by Archer Creek, 1 mi. long. Piney Point often confused with Archer Point; Piney Point (q.v.) applied to point on Piney Island just n of Archer Creek and misapplied until mid-20th century. Subdivision named for feature but uses "Archers" while names of creek and point use "Archer." *Other names:* Archers Point (some local use), Arthurs Point (Stephens 1984, back cover map—could be original name, but now Archer), Holly Point (occasional recent use from nearby subdivision), Piney Point (USGS 1952: Swansboro).

Archers Ridge, sand ridge, 1 mi. long, Carteret County, White Oak Township (diminished local use). Extends e-w along peninsula between Archer Creek and Bogue Sound in w Emerald Isle, 2.5 mi. e of Langston Bridge. Not recognizable because of development.

Around Creek ('Round Creek), area, Hyde County, Ocracoke Township (local sources and Howard 2016). One of three major areas in Ocracoke (village) defining historic parts within the village. Each generated a mild form of competition first half 20th century (and a bit beyond) as there were three major focal points of dwellings: w side of

Silver Lake (Cockle Creek q.v.), Pointers (*see* Springers Point); around s, n, and e sides Silver Lake, Creekers (this entry); and ne part near Pamlico Sound, Trenters (*see* Up Trent).

Asa Gray Harbor, former landing, Dare County, Kinnakeet Township (Garrity-Blake 2010, 492). Was soundside just s of Aunt Phoebes Marsh just n of Waves, 1.5 mi. s of Rodanthe.

Asbury Beach, small beach, Carteret County, Morehead Township (Stanford 2015, 5). In Atlantic Beach (town) just e of Money Island Beach, 2 mi. sse of Morehead City (mainland). Acquired separate name (1922) during period establishing bathing houses along beach across from Morehead City when beach became destination for African Americans. Street nearby named Asbury Avenue, small subdivision here, but name rarely used today. Named for V. Asbury, developer, or someone in his family.

Ashbee Harbor, harbor, 0.1 mi. wide, Dare County, Nags Head Township (USGS 2013: Manteo). In Croatan Sound at Roanoke Island just w of Skyco 2.1 mi. s of Manteo. Ashbee or Ashby, surname here, harbor named for Solomon Ashbee. Late 19th and early 20th centuries was stop along Old Dominion Steamship Company route to Norfolk and therefore sometimes referenced as Old Dominion Docks. Nearby Skyco (q.v.) originally known as Ashbees Harbor, but Post Office Department used Skyco (q.v.) when post office opened 1892. A "settlement" (Old Field) noted here (or near Sand Point) on Maule 1718. Union Army landed most troops here (almost 10,000), first 4,000 landed just n of here at Hammonds Landing (q.v.) because Confederate troops were lying in wait at Ashbee Harbor. After brief Battle of Roanoke Island nearby (*see* Battery Defiance), Union troops took possession of the island and effectively all the Outer Banks (1861). Made official by USBGN as form most used and recorded in Office of the Register of Deeds. Subdivision named Ashby Harbor nearby. *Other names:* Ashbees Harbor (some local use), Ashbys Cove (USBGN staff), Ashby Harbor (Wise 2010, 12; also subdivision), Ashbys Harbor (USBGN staff), Ashley Harbor (Cram and Worret 1861—typographical error or misinterpretation), Old Dominion Docks (steamship records), Old Dominion Wharf (Dunbar 1958, 209), Old Field (Maule 1718—general vicinity predating Ashbee Harbor),

Roanoke Island Wharf (occasional from steamship stop serving Roanoke Island), Solomon Harbor (colonial deeds—original land owner).

Ash Swamp, small swamp, Dare County, Atlantic Township (Town of Kitty Hawk 2007). Just e of Sage Swamp 1 mi. ene of Sound Landing 2 mi. nw of original Kitty Hawk. Nw-most swamp in Kitty Hawk Woods Swamps (q.v.). Applied since late 1800s. *See* Kitty Hawk ridge-and-swale system.

Askins Creek, tidal stream, 0.4 mi. long, 0.1 mi. wide, Dare County, Kinnakeet Township (USGS 1950: Buxton). In Pamlico Sound 1.9 mi. s of original Avon, named for Thomas Askins, colonial landowner. Subdivision named for feature. Former North Hunt Club soundside just n. *Other names:* Deep Creek (early use).

Askins Hill, linear sand dune, Dare County, Kinnakeet Township (Currituck DB 3, 1736, 236). On Hatteras Island at Askins Creek 3 mi. s of original Avon. *See* Askins Creek. *Other names:* High Hill (early deeds).

Atlantic Beach, beach, 1 mi. long, Carteret County, Morehead Township (USGS 2013: Beaufort). On Bogue Banks at Atlantic Beach (town), 1.9 mi. s of Morehead City (mainland). Early 20th-century application extended w and sw to Pine Knoll Shores (town). *Other names:* Circle Beach (Holland, 2006, 5—proximity to Atlantic Beach Circle).

Atlantic Beach, town, Carteret County, Morehead Township (USGS 2013: Beaufort). On e end Bogue Banks 1.6 mi. ssw of Morehead City (mainland). Development by Royal and Chadwick began 1887 based on original concept by Appleton Oaksmith first developed in 1870s. Development increased considerably (1928) when a bridge from Morehead City was built allowing vehicle access, replacing facilities at Money Island Beach. Town was chartered and incorporated 1937, tourist area s end of the Outer Banks (e end Bogue Banks). During past 50 years (especially w along Bogue Banks) experienced high degree of growth. Post office opened 1936. *Other names:* The Atlantic City of the South (tourist poster, Holland Consulting Planners 2006, 4).

Atlantic Beach Causeway, area, Carteret County, Morehead Township (signage). Connects Atlantic Beach to Atlantic Beach

Bridge leading to Morehead City (mainland). Alteration of this somewhat natural causeway began 1926 to support the road from the new bridge completed 1928. A swing bridge (1953) replaced old bridge, causeway route altered slightly, drawbridge replaced (1987) by high-rise bridge creating additional improvements to causeway. *Other names:* The Causeway (local use).

Atlantic Beach Channel, channel, 1 mi. long, Carteret County, Morehead Township (local use). N-s from middle e Bogue Sound to just ne of Money Island 1.5 mi. s of Morehead City (mainland).

Atlantic Beach Circle, former area, Carteret County, Morehead Township (local references). Large traffic circle at s terminus of Atlantic Beach Causeway allowing visitors access to primary beach facilities at Atlantic Beach 2 mi. across bridge from Morehead City (mainland). Built 1928 after development of Atlantic Beach provided access to new Pavilion. Intense development occurred from 1960s though 1990s. Shortly after 2000 effort made to refurbish deteriorating structures, but 2004–5 many structures removed and reconfigured. Today, little resemblance to its original look throughout 20th century, configuration is actually a triangle. *Other names:* The Circle (Holland Consulting Planners 2006, throughout document).

Atlantic Ocean, sea. N.C. coast extends generally n-s approx. 330 mi. Atlantic Ocean lies between North America and Europe and South America and Africa from Arctic Ocean to Southern Ocean at Antarctica and equator divides it into North and South Atlantic Oceans. Name is Latin origin referring to Atlas and probably means "water body w of the Atlas" range of mountains in nw Africa (mostly Morocco). *Other names:* Atlantick Ocean (17th-century texts and Barnwell-Hammerton 1721), The Western Ocean (Lawson 1709, map), The Great Western Ocean (Angley 1984, 84—from Quinn 1955, based on Haklyut 1589 maps).

Aunt Easters Creek, small cove, Dare County, Kinnakeet Township (Garrity-Blake 2010, 492). In Pamlico Sound at n edge Clarks Bay in s Salvo, 4 mi. s of Rodanthe. Specific part of name is given name of a local woman. "Easter," in this case, could be a variation of Esther based on local pronunciation, and

Smith (2001, 18) confirms Esther and Easter are same name at least on nearby Roanoke Island.

Aunt Marys Hill, sand dune, Carteret County, Morehead Township (Stephens 1984, 146). In Salter Path reportedly near Headens Landing (exact location not known).

Aunt Phoebes Marsh, swamp, 0.2 mi. wide, Dare County, Kinnakeet Township (USGS 1983: Rodanthe). Is 0.2 mi. s of North Drain, 0.8 mi. n of Waves. Reportedly named for Phoebe Scarborough Midyett (Midgett).

Aunt Winnies Gut. *See* Big Gut.

Austin Creek, cove, 0.02 mi. wide, Dare County, Hatteras Township (USGS 2002: Hatteras). Docking basin in Pamlico Sound for Hatteras-Ocracoke Ferry 1.1 mi. sw of Hatteras (village). Austin is Outer Banks surname, especially in Hatteras and Ocracoke. Original creek dredged at terminus to accommodate ferry boats operated by state (Hatteras-Ocracoke Ferry). Historically, Austin Creek drained from ne into Clubhouse Creek (q.v.), mostly what is now ferry basin, but Austin Creek now more used. *Other names:* Clubhouse Creek (historical local use).

Austin Reef, shoal, 0.5 mi. long, Dare County, Hatteras Township (USGS 2013: Cape Hatteras). In Pamlico Sound, 1.5 mi. ne of Pelican Shoal 3.2 mi. w of Hatteras (village). "Reef" in Outer Banks geographic names usually refers to oyster colonies. Made official by USBGN in 2000. *See* Austin Creek. *Other names:* Austin Shoal (NOS field crews), Austins Reef (Weslager 1954), Austins Shoal (NOS field crew notes 1981), Bulk Head (CS 1857a), Cross Shoal (C&GS 1928).

Avalon Beach, beach, Dare County, Atlantic Township (USGS 2013: Kitty Hawk). In Kill Devil Hills (town) 2 mi. se of original Kitty Hawk at e shore Kitty Hawk Bay. *See* Avalon Beach subdivision.

Avalon Beach, subdivision, Dare County, Atlantic Township (USGS 2013: Kitty Hawk). Kill Devil Hills (town) subdivision 5.3 mi. nnw of original Nags Head. Subdivision est. 1950s now soundside to oceanside, though only soundside originally. Some believe a venture of Frank Stick (noted artist and Outer Banks enthusiast) and Avalon in New Jersey 85 miles s of Interlaken where Stick lived (1920s). Also, not for Avalon, mythical place where King Arthur's sword Excalibur was forged as some believe (folk etymology).

However, actual developer was family named Young. Name suggested by Clarence York (partner in the development), who held a fondness for Avalon Beach in Florida; two places named Avalon Beach in Florida, beach at Avalon State Park just n of Fort Pierce in Saint Lucie County and small subdivision in Santa Rosa County known as both Avalon and Avalon Beach. Records do not indicate and is unknown for which place in Florida Avalon Beach in Kill Devil Hills was named; speculation is Avalon Beach just n of Fort Pierce since the place in Santa Rosa County has no real beach, is urban, and is not well known. There are three additional annexes. *Other names:* Avalon (original name early 1950s), Avalon Bench (map error USGS 2013: Kitty Hawk; and "bench error" prevalent on 2013 USGS maps for elsewhere on the Outer Banks), Moores Shore (Stick 1958, 270), West Avalon (sometimes used w of US 158 Bypass—Downing 2013, 79), West Lower Avalon (Downing 2008, 79).

Avery Isle, peninsula (not island), Dare County, Atlantic Township (subdivision name here). In n Kitty Hawk Landing subdivision just n of Shellbank Point 2.5 mi. w of original Kitty Hawk. Altered and enhanced by man, example of reversed usage, natural feature acquiring name of man-made feature (subdivision).

Avery Pond, cove, Dare County, Atlantic Township (census block maps). In w Kitty Hawk Landing subdivision just n of Shellbank Point 2.5 mi. w of original Kitty Hawk, dredged and altered by man.

Avon, village, Dare County, Kinnakeet Township (USGS 2013: Buxton). On Hatteras Island 7 mi. n of Cape Hatteras, 20 mi. s of Salvo. Post office est. 1873 as Kinnakeet and serving Kinnakeet (Big Kinnakeet) and Little Kinnakeet but changed to Avon 1883 with confusion over spelling Kinnakeet. Name gradually changed from Kinnakeet (*see* Kinnakeet) to post office name, Avon. Name is thought selected for River Avon in England (reason unknown), but name origin is really unknown since most post office records are lost. Some authors propose there was also an Indian village in Avon, though no documented proof and might be confused with the village in Buxton (*see* Indian Town) or semipermanent camp.

Original village (Kinnakeet or Old Avon settled early 19th century) often divided into two sections: Cat Ridge (q.v.) and Dog Ridge (q.v.). Cat Ridge was n side of The Creek (*see* Peters Ditch—now Avon Harbor after dredging), and Dog Ridge was s side of The Creek. The notion locally (jokingly) was families on either side "fought like cats and dogs" (NPS 2005B: NPS 1, 166).

Some consider Avon as really two parts (especially historically): Old Avon, original village known as Kinnakeet or Big Kinnakeet, and new Avon, developed around Mill Creek (q.v.; Old Creek—originally two features until development) and Spencer Creek (q.v.), latter being 1 mi. n of original village. N part around Mill Creek (Old Creek) was known as The North'ard (q.v.) (or Spain: Garrity-Blake 2010, map, 169—reason lost; *see also* Scarboro) and early 20th century through today has developed considerably. *Other names:* Big Kennakeet (historical local use), Big Kinekeet (schooner *Lonia Buren*, 1903, online), Big Kinnakeet (Stick 1958, 154—NCDOT 1951 highway map uses this name and Avon mislabeled just s of correct label for Avon), Chicomicomico (Foster 1866a—misinterpreted), Kennekeet (Hill 1983, 11—same spelling as township name from Buxton to Oregon Inlet used until late 20th century), Kennekut (Colton 1857), Kennikeet (Rollinson 1884), Kinekeet (historical local use), Kinnakeet (Stick 1958, 175), Kinnakeet Village (deliberate usage since late 20th century reflecting historical name), Kinnekeet (Post Office Department), Kinneket (Rand McNally 1890), Kinnekett (historical not standardized), Old Avon (original of two-part community—*see* Mill Creek and The North'ard), Old Kinnakeet (spoken references), South Kinnakeet (Bishop 1878), The Village (local use).

Avon Beach, beach, 2 mi. long, Dare County, Kinnakeet Township (local use and media). At Avon (both sections), extends n-s from Black Pelican Beach to just e of Askins Creek.

Avon Channel, small channel, 1 mi. long, Dare County, Kinnakeet Township (local use). Approach from Pamlico Sound to Peters Ditch entrance Avon Harbor 5.5 mi. n of Buxton.

Avon Harbor, harbor, Dare County, Kinnakeet Township (signage). At original Avon entered by passing through Peters Ditch 6.2 mi. n of Buxton. Used sparingly since settled as

Kinnakeet 19th century but difficult to use until ACE dredged (1946—before large fish houses on stilts in sound for transferring cargo); harbor has been continuously improved over years. Kinnakeet, original name (*see* Avon), and Peters Ditch is entrance. *Other names:* Kinnakeet Harbor (still some local use), Old Harbor (occasional local use), Old Town Harbor (occasional brochures), Peters Ditch (still some local use), Port Avon (some local use mostly 1970s from subdivision name), The Creek (Garrity-Blake 2010, 166), The Harbor (Garrity-Blake 2010, 169).

Ayers Rock, rock, Hyde County, Ocracoke Township (USGS 1950: Portsmouth). In Pamlico Sound just w of Wallace Channel 3.7 mi. sw of Ocracoke (village). *Other names:* Eyers Rock (CS 1856).

B

Baby Graves. *See* Bell Cove (former community).

Back Bay, bay, 1.3 mi. across, Carteret County, Cedar Island Township (USGS 2013: Atlantic). Separates Hog Island and unnamed marsh (sometimes considered part of Hog Island) from Cedar Island 1.5 mi. e of Cedar Island Ferry landing 11 mi. sw of Ocracoke (village). "Back," often used with water bodies that are parts of larger bodies or "arms" of other bodies, mostly enclosed signifying the back portion of water.

Back Bay. *See* Croatan Sound.

Back Bay Point. *See* Northwest Point.

Back Creek, tidal stream, 0.4 mi. wide at mouth, 2.5 mi. long, Currituck County, Fruitville Township (USGS 2013: Knotts Island, Barco). Empties into North Landing River at s end of Great Marsh just n of Mackay Island, 2.6 mi. w of Knotts Island (village). Named since early 1700s. Creek has filled in considerably and s portions canalized and extended s between Mackay Island (w) and Knotts Island (e) to Buck Island Bay. *See* Back Bay.

Back Creek, water passage, 0.5 mi. long, Dare County, Hatteras Township (local use). E-w trending in n Hatteras (village) flowing into

Muddy Creek 4.5 mi. ne of Hatteras Inlet. *See* Back Bay.

Back Landing, former landing, Currituck County, Fruitville Township (historical reference). Was general vicinity se Sandy Cove just n of Currituck-Knotts Island Ferry Dock 2 mi. sw of Knotts Island (village).

Back Landing Creek, cove, Dare County, Hatteras Township (Brooks 2010; Currituck DB 7, 1763, 301–2). In Pamlico Sound just s of Bald Point 1.7 mi. e of Buxton. Name mostly historical use; with changing topography, most people now indicate part of Cape Creek. Also remnant of Chacandepeco Inlet (q.v.), during storms subject to overwash and sound surge. *Other names:* Landing Creek (Currituck DB 7, 1793, 50).

Back Landing Creek. *See* Cape Creek.

Back Landing Creek Marsh, marsh, Dare County, Hatteras Township (Brooks 2010). Just s of Cape Creek formerly known as Back Landing Creek 1 mi. s of Bald Point, 1.5 mi. e of Buxton. *Other names:* Goose Marsh (early maps).

Back Marsh, marsh, Dare County, Nags Head Township (Currituck DB 8, 1799, 207). Believed to be marsh and swamp w and sw of Thicket Lump as described in deed.

Back of the Beach, historical. Designated oceanside of barrier island and almost totally unknown today. Use indicates original Outer Banks settlements on more protected soundside, in wooded areas providing additional protection, therefore opposite from its sense today. Little interest in exposed beach until tourist trade began in earnest (1920s) with construction of first real roads. Mainland families and hunters came to the Outer Banks as early as revolutionary times and especially in 19th century both to vacation and to avoid the miasma (foul-smelling vapor or swamp gas) thought to cause illness, but really mosquito-borne malaria; organized tourist industry did not really begin until early 20th century.

Back Sound, lagoon, 8.2 mi. long, 2 mi. wide, Carteret County, Harkers Island Township (USGS 2013: Harkers Island). Separated from Atlantic Ocean by Shackleford Banks and trends nw-se from Core Sound to Bogue Sound. *See* Back Bay and Albemarle Sound. *Other names:* Back Sound Channel (historical local use), Core Sound (Wimble 1738), The Great Sound (Mackay 1756).

Baggala Inlet, canal, Dare County, Atlantic Township (local use). At Colington Harbour, 2.5 mi. wsw of Kill Devil Hills (town). "Inlet" not used in traditional sense on the Outer Banks as barrier island breach, because indicative of dredging allowing water inward for access by boats to open water (Albemarle Sound). Canal naming scheme at Colington Harbour is ships or nautical terms. "Baggala" refers to a two-masted boat used for trading in Indian Ocean.

Bahia Della Madalena, former bay, Dare County. Appears to reference former bay between Nags Head and Kitty Hawk (Dudley 1647); exact referent is unclear, as with many place names given on early maps. Reportedly applied initially by Ēcija (Francisco Fernández de Ēcija, Spanish pilot) on his 1609 voyage looking for English colonies and especially the Roanoke Colony (Lost Colony) specifically to Trinety Harbor and as only the label Magdalen as it was Magdalen Day. Possibly the application was noted by later mapmakers and given a wider application. Certain authors indicate an inlet, but the name was more likely applied to the convergence of what are now Albemarle, Currituck, and Roanoke Sounds (indigenous name, Occam). Blaeu (1640) labels Port Ferdinando as off Bahia della Madalena, suggesting the name applied to Roanoke Sound or extreme e Albemarle Sound. Maps until late 17th century sometimes included a place name followed by name of feature from which it issued or with which it was associated by using the reference "off." "Madalena" is Portuguese form of Magdalene, a religious reference for Mary Magdalene. Portuguese and Spanish explorers liberally applied place names with religious (Christian) reference. *Other names:* Bahia de Magdalena (Keulen 1690).

Baileys Hammick. *See* Ourdsleys Hammock.

Baileys Hammick. *See* Round Hammock.

Balance Hill, large sand dune, Dare County, Hatteras Township (Brazier 1833). On Inlet Peninsula 2 mi. sw of Hatteras (village), 2 mi. ene of Hatteras Inlet. Changes size, but approx. same location as early 19th century. Balance or Ballance (and other variations), surname here appearing in numerous early deeds.

Balance Point Bay. *See* Goat Island Bay.

Bald Beach, small beach, Dare County, Kinnakeet Township (Colton 1860). On n Hatteras Island just n of former Little Kinnakeet 4.7 mi. n of original Avon. Example of description becoming a name. *Other names:* Naked Bald Beach (colonial maps—descriptive term initially; Currituck DB 15, 1761, 367).

Bald Hill, sand dune, Carteret County, Harkers Island Township (USGS 2013: Harkers Island). On Shackleford Banks just w of Bald Hill Bay 4.2 mi. nw of Barden Inlet.

Bald Hill Bay, cove, Carteret County, Harkers Island Township (USGS 2013: Harkers Island). In Back Sound just e of Bald Hill 3.9 mi. nw of Barden Inlet.

Bald Point, point, less than 5 ft. high, Dare County, Hatteras Township (USGS 2013: Buxton). N point of marsh island in Pamlico Sound 0.5 mi. n of Cape Creek 1.1 mi. ne of Buxton. Descriptive, lack of vegetation.

Bald Sand Hills, sand dunes, 1.5 mi. long, Dare County, Atlantic Township (miscellaneous deeds, 1719). Just e of Kitty Hawk Bay between Kitty Hawk (n) and Kill Devil Hills (s), historical reference altered significantly by development. Remnants of five distinct dunes with two n-most dunes connected by a semicircular sand ridge. Each named dune has a separate entry: N-most dune was historically Jacks Cabin Hill (40 ft.), occasionally known today as Keepers Hill, same name as subdivision here. Second dune is First Flight Ridge (same name as subdivision—40 ft.) connected to Jacks Cabin Hill (Keepers Hill) by sand ridge known as Bay Ridge (25 ft.) for subdivision by that name associatively for nearby Kitty Hawk Bay. Third and fourth dunes might be considered as one dune connected by a saddle (lower part) historically referenced as Hill of the Wreck (40 ft. and 35 ft.). The fifth and smallest dune (20 ft.) is apparently unnamed. *Other names:* Sand Hills (Foster 1862).

Ballances Hill. *See* Round Hammock.

Ballast Bay, bay, 0.2 mi. across, Currituck County, Poplar Branch Township (USGS 2013: Mossey Islands). In Currituck Sound just se of Indian Gap, 8.3 mi. s of Corolla. Ballast is any heavy substance (usually rocks, especially before 20th century) giving weight and stability to a ship in water traveling without cargo, loaded or unloaded as needed. *Other names:* Ballast Point Bay (C&GS 1852).

Ballast Point, point, Currituck County, Poplar

Branch Township (recent local use). Small, distinct point just w, s end Pine Island Airport Runway 5 mi. nw of Duck. No evidence historic or otherwise for ballast use here in shallow water and marsh. Name likely applied from street name just e.

Ballast Point, point, less than 5 ft. high, Dare County, Nags Head Township (USGS 2013: Manteo). On Roanoke Island at se entrance Shallowbag Bay 1.3 mi. e of Manteo. Points at entrance to Shallowbag Bay used to leave ballast rocks, and rocks here are foreign origin. Named since 18th century. Subdivision in Pirates Cove named for feature. *See* Ballast Bay. *Other names:* Balast Point (Joshua Judson Davis Papers, 1888, from Smith 2001, 95), Ballas Point (Brazier 1820—recording error).

Ballast Point Canal, canal, 0.7 mi. long, Dare County, Nags Head Township (PC HOA 2016). One of seven named canal segments interconnected throughout Pirates Cove, named portions corresponding with limits of adjacent named subdivisions. Trends n-s 1.2 mi. se of Sandy Point at Roanoke Island Festival Park, 3.3 mi. w of Whalebone Junction. *See* Ballast Bay.

Banana Island. *See* Crab Claw Spit.

Bank Channel, short channel, 1 mi. long, Carteret County, White Oak Township (Stephens 1984, 26). E-w separating Bell Cove from Bean Island and Long Island, 6 mi. w of Salter Path.

Bank Creek, narrow tidal creek, 1 mi. long, Currituck County, Fruitville Township (Cox 1906). Trends s-n to junction with Hanes Creek and Inlet Creek at sw point of Hanes Thicket, 2.5 mi. e of Knotts Island (village).

Banks Channel, channel, 0.7 mi. long, Carteret County, White Oak Township (USGS 2013: Swansboro). In Bogue Sound trending e-w as branch of Main Channel at w end Bogue Banks 2.3 mi. sw of Swansboro (mainland). *Other names:* Bank Channel (USGS 1948; Swansboro).

Banzai Landing, implied landing, Dare County, Kinnakeet Township (local use). Soundside in Rodanthe 0.5 mi. n of Blackmar Gut, 12 mi. s of Oregon Inlet. A small tidal creek here altered by development, not an actual landing and name is most likely whimsical. Applied originally only to a house here; though private, through extended use applied around this small tidal creek. Since surfing is nearby, tantalizing to suggest association with surfing term "Banzai Pipeline," originating on North Shore, Oahu Island, Hawaii. Surfing occurs from Carova to Ocracoke; however, little association here for Banzai or pipeline surfing.

Bar, The, former shoal, Hyde County, Ocracoke Township; and Carteret County, Portsmouth Township (Hooker 1850). Was at entrance Ocracoke Inlet 3.5 mi. se of Ocracoke (village). No longer exists in original form.

Barbage Island. *See* Harbor Island.

Barbers Island. *See* Harkers Island.

Barden Inlet, water passage, 1.2 mi. long, Carteret County, Harkers Island Township (USGS 2013: Harkers Island). Trends ne-sw connecting Lighthouse Bay, Back Sound, Core Sound to Atlantic Ocean separating Core Banks from Shackleford Banks 5 mi. sse of Harkers Island (village). Named for Graham Arthur Barden, U.S. congressman from North Carolina, who was instrumental obtaining military bases for e North Carolina and funds used to dredge the inlet. Open partially (mostly swash or overwash) 1770–1860, reopened or widened and deepened 1933. Relict remnants, various adjacent sites. Relatively unimportant because shallow and continues to "shoal up" or fill in with sediment and shifting sand even though dredging continues. Locally and historically was (still is) known simply as The Drain until renamed officially Barden Inlet by USBGN 1948. *Other names:* Bardens Drain (short-term local use combining new name Barden [1948] and original name, The Drain), Bardens Inlet (local use), Borden Inlet (possibly typographical error on some 19th-century maps, perhaps not, much of what is now Bogue Banks was known as Borden Banks [q.v.] in 18th century), Bordens Inlet (*see* previous name), Cape Inlet (local usage and Fisher 1962, 88), Cape Look Out Inlet (Wimble 1733), Lookout Bight Channel (local usage), Old Topsaile Inlet (Wimble 1733), The Ditch (limited local use and some brochures), The Drain (local usage and C&GS 1947), The Haulover (historical local usage before Barden Inlet reopened 1933, haulover or trickle at best).

Barefoot Canal, canal, 0.5 mi. long, Carteret County, Morehead Township (Carteret County GIS 2019). Central canal s of Willis Canal in Atlantic Beach Isles subdivision

(w part of Canals at Atlantic Beach q.v.), 1.3
mi. s of Morehead City (mainland).

Baregrass Island, island, 0.2 mi. long, less than
5 ft. high, Carteret County, Harkers Island
Township (USGS 2013: Harkers Island). In
Back Sound 0.5 mi. w of Sheep Island Slue,
3 mi. s of Harkers Island (village). Descriptive,
lack of grass or marsh. *Other names:* Bare
Grass Island (C&GS 1931).

Bare Hill, sand dune, Dare County, Hatteras
Township (USGS 2013: Cape Hatteras).
On s Hatteras Island, 1.5 mi. e of Hatteras
(village). *Other names:* Blue Hill (limited local
use—reason unknown).

Bare Inlet. *See* Swash Inlet.

Bare Sand Beach, beach, Carteret County, Sea
Level Township (Carteret County GIS 2019).
On n end North Core Banks between Ophelia
Inlet (ne) and Sheep Islands (sw). Descriptive,
used as place name because beach is devoid
of any other feature references. Much of
low-lying and narrow Core Banks is flat and
sandy, but this particular beach and another
(*see* Bare Sand Beach, Carteret County, Stacy
Township) acquired use of descriptive term
as names.

Bare Sand Beach, beach, Carteret County, Stacy
Township (USGS 2013: Horsepen Point). Just s
of Hogpen Bay, just e of Gunning Hammock
Island, 8 mi. s of Davis (mainland). *See* Bare
Sand Beach (Carteret County, Sea Level
Township).

Barkentine Inlet, canal, Dare County, Atlantic
Township (local use). At Colington Harbour,
2.5 mi. wsw of Kill Devil Hills (town). "Inlet"
not used in the traditional sense on the
Outer Banks as barrier island breach,
because indicative of dredging allowing
water inward for access by boats to open
water (Albemarle Sound). Canal naming
scheme at Colington Harbour is ships or
nautical terms. "Barkentine" is a sailing ship
with three or more masts.

Barland Pond, pond, 0.2 mi. long, Currituck
County, Fruitville Township (USGS 2013:
Knotts Island). In unnamed marsh islands
between Bank Creek (w) and Cedar Snag
Cove (e), 2.4 mi. e of Knotts Island (village).

Barleys Bay, large bay, Currituck County,
Fruitville Township (F&WS 1984, map, 74).
Just n of The Causeway between Great
Marsh (e) and Morse Point (w) 2.5 mi. wnw of
Knotts Island (village). Original name, Barls
Island Bay, was misinterpreted by F&WS

map maker, but appears that way on map,
so Barleys Bay has become the name. *Other
names:* Barls Island Bay (early local use), Biels
Island Bay (early local use).

Barnes Landing, former landing, Currituck
County, Fruitville Township (historical). Was
at s end Knotts Island between Knotts Island
Ferry Dock and Knotts Island Landing 2.5 mi.
s of Knotts Island (village). Road still named
Barnes and Barnes Hunting Lodge here, but
landing no longer exists and area is private.

Barnes Mill, former mill and windmill, Dare
County, Kinnakeet Township (CS 1852).
Reportedly in original Avon between Peters
Ditch and Uncle Bates Ditch, 6 mi. n of
Buxton. Might be same windmill as Zeb
Millers Windmill (q.v.) as locations are almost
identical. Dunbar (1958, 87) and Bishop (1878)
indicate only two windmills in Avon—this
one and Farrow Scarboroughs Windmill 1 mi.
n. Barnes Mill as a name confirmed by Covey
(2018, 13), though Zeb Millers Windmill is
most remembered, with no mention of a
landing named Barnes Landing. *See* Farrow
Scarboroughs Windmill and Zeb Millers
Windmill. *Other names:* Askins Creek Mill
(Covey 2018, 111).

Barney Slue, channel, 3 mi. long, Dare County,
Hatteras Township (USGS 2013: Cape
Hatteras). Trends sw-ne connecting Hatteras
Inlet to Rollinson Channel just w of Hatteras
(village). Part is now used for Ocracoke-
Hatteras Ferry Route (U.S. Coast Guard 2015).
See Allen Slough. *Other names:* Barney
Slough (local hand-made sign), Barney
Slough Channel (NOS notes), Barn Slue
(occasional), Long Slue (older local use).

Barn Pond, pond, Currituck County, Poplar
Branch Township (local use). On n Dews
Island just s of North Pond connected to
n Dews Island Bay, 5.7 mi. nw of Duck.

Barracuda Beach. *See* Whalehead Beach
(subdivision).

Barra San Ijago, former shoal, Dare County,
Atlantic Township (Blaeu 1640—likely
location), or Currituck County, Fruitville
Township (Keulen 1690). At entrance of
now closed Trinety Harbor or near entrance
of now closed Musketo Inlet, 12.5 miles n
of Trinety Harbor. Shown on only a few
earliest maps variously placed at entrance
to these two inlets. Particular application
is elusive, though Musketo Inlet was open
about 10 years longer than Trinety Harbor,

both of which closed before some maps were published depicting the shoal, but often status of such changeable data was unknown to mapmakers using second-hand information. The English name would be Saint James Bar, and San Ijago is an earlier form of what became Santiago. *Other names:* Barra de San Ijago (Blaeu 1640).

Barrel Beach, small eroding beach, Dare County, Nags Head Township (NPS 2010). On n shore of Roanoke Island at Albemarle Sound adjacent to site of Fort Raleigh (Lanes Fort) 2.5 mi. nw of Manteo. Erosion with just a bit of sand against a bluff. Named by archeologists who discovered and authenticated a barrel here from Lane's military colony (first colony), White's Lost Colony, or both.

Barrel Head, beach, Dare County, Nags Head Township (historical maps). At s end of Bodie Island (no longer an island) 1.5 mi. n of Oregon Inlet, 6 mi. se of Wanchese. Historical and not generally known today. "Head" or "headland" refers to curvature or gentle bend in a coast less pronounced than a cape, the case here just n of Oregon Inlet. Name could be derived from archeological finds here (Port Ferdinando), remnants of barrels used for collecting rainwater known to be at this outpost of Lane's military colony (first colony), White's Lost Colony, or both. *Other names:* Barel Beach (Currituck DB 8, 1801, 262).

Bars Head Island, former island, Currituck County, Poplar Branch Township (C&GS 1852). Formerly in Currituck Sound near n entrance to Big Narrows just w of Bay Tree (Bay Tree Island), 5.5 mi. ssw of Corolla. Possibly a relationship between this island's name and point named Bearhead applied on Northwest Island. Since Bars Head Island no longer exists, name could have been transferred short distance to Northwest Island to a point and changed over years through pronunciation (difference in local pronunciation of "bear" and "bar" often not discernable).

Basnett Landing, former landing, Dare County, Hatteras Township (local use). Formerly in Frisco 0.7 mi. ne of Joe Saur Creek, 4 mi. ne of Hatteras (village). Basnett, with variations, surname in Frisco appearing in numerous early deeds.

Batleys Gap, deep, Carteret County, White Oak Township (Stephens 1984, 127). In Bank Channel between Long Island and Point of Marsh just e of Bell Cove 6 mi. e of Salter Path. Small area where cows had to swim when driven (historically) from mainland to Bogue Banks to graze.

Bats Beach, beach, Dare County, Kinnakeet Township (Currituck DB 6, 1792, 230–31). Probably between Kinnakeet (Avon) and New Inlet. Meaning unknown now, and name not encountered in any other sources, though is likely for Nathaniel Batts, who explored here in mid-1600s.

Battery Defiance, former fort, Dare County, Nags Head Township (Civil War maps). Small Confederate gun emplacement hastily constructed near center of Roanoke Island at Suples Hill n part of The Causeway (just s of US 64 and US 264; *see* The Causeway, Roanoke Island, and Suples Hill) through marshes and swamps connecting n and s portions of Roanoke Island (Click 2001, 27). Makeshift battery hastily erected with three guns to thwart advancing Union forces landed at Ashbee Harbor, abandoned with little resistance after short battle and renamed Battery Russell by Union in honor of officer who fell in the battle. "Battery," arrangement of cannon strategically placed to protect or repel advancement. *Other names:* Battery Russell (Click 2001, 27), Fort Defiance (Army Historical Register), Fort Russell (Wise 2010).

Battery Monteil, former fort, Dare County, Nags Head Township (Click 2001, 27). Hastily erected by Confederates at Ballast Point to protect Shallowbag Bay entrance just e of Manteo at n terminus of what is today Pirates Cove subdivision. Battery did not have a Confederate name (none discovered). Named for a Union officer who fell during Battle of Roanoke Island. "Battery," an arrangement of cannon strategically placed to protect or repel advancement. *Other names:* Ballast Point Battery (Confederate use), Battery de Monteil (Army Historical Register), Fort Ellis (original Union reference), Fort Monteil (battle reports), Fort Shallowbag Bay (occasional), Shallow Bag Bay Battery (secondary use, Union and Confederates).

Baum Bay, cove, 0.2 mi. wide, Dare County, Atlantic Township (USGS 2013: Kitty Hawk). Just e of Colington Creek, 1 mi. sw of Wright Brothers National Memorial, 3.9 mi. nw of

Nags Head (town). Old established surname on Roanoke Island and n Outer Banks. Three subdivisions named for this feature. The very occasional use of Bermuda Bay (not normally by older residents) is from a condominium development named Bermuda Bay (Cambridge Cove, Devonshire Place, and Hamilton Cay with Spring Arbor) 0.3 mi. e of Baum Bay. The e-w road sometimes referenced as Bermuda Bay Boulevard (Bermuda Bay Condominiums), though name of the road is often used as Ocean Bay Boulevard. Usage is nonlocal because n-s road to here from Colington Road is actually named Baum Bay Drive. Condominiums are named Bermuda Bay as an attractive name, supposedly evoking images of Bermuda. The only known occurrence of "Bermuda" as an Outer Banks place name is Bermuda Island, not so well-known today as these former two islands are now one and mostly inundated in Kitty Hawk Bay 2.5 mi. n of the condominiums. Early, limited use of Walker Bay associative with Walker Island, a large marsh island just w of this bay. *Other names:* Bermuda Bay (erratic new local use-condominium name), Walker Bay (some early use), Ocean Bay (street sign).

Baum Bay Harbor, small harbor, Dare County, Atlantic Township (local use). Private subdivision Baum Bay Harbor at this small harbor in Kill Devil Hills (town) just ne of Baum Bay, 4.5 mi. sse of original Kitty Hawk. From same name subdivision, named for nearby Baum Bay.

Baum Creek, cove, 0.4 mi. long, 0.2 mi. wide, Dare County, Nags Head Township (USGS 2013: Wanchese). At Croatan Sound at sw Roanoke Island, 1.4 mi. w of Wanchese. Raums Creek, transcribing error and was applied to the incorrect feature at Ashby Harbor (*sic*) based on misinformation received by Union forces. *See* Baum Bay. *Other names:* Baum Bay (some local references based on size perception), Baums Creek (CS 1852), Raums Creek (Abbott 1866—misinterpretation).

Baum Hole, area, 2 mi. long, 1 mi. wide, Dare County, Atlantic Township; and Currituck County, Poplar Branch Township (NOS 2014g). Deeper water, relative to surrounding depth in Currituck Sound, 2 mi. wnw of Duck. Currituck Sound is shallow, average depths of 1–5 ft., but here 6–10 ft. *See* Baum Bay.

Baum Landing, former landing, Dare County, Nags Head Township (historical local use). Formerly just w of Baumtown, at Baum Creek 1.5 mi. nw of Wanchese. *See* Baum Bay.

Baum Point, point, Dare County, Atlantic Township (USGS 2013: Kitty Hawk). Nw point of Baum Point Island, 1.2 mi. nw of Colington. *See* Baum Bay.

Baum Point, point, less than 5 ft. high, Dare County, Nags Head Township (USGS 2013: Manteo). On Roanoke Island at nw entrance Shallowbag Bay 0.9 mi. ene of Manteo. According to local interviews, variant names Dolby, Dolly, and Duffy are unknown as given names associated with families locally and not found in early school records of Roanoke Island or census lists, maybe added by cartographers without access to proper information. Named for Moris [*sic*] Baum (1760s). *See* Baum Bay. *Other names:* Baums Point (local use and historical sources, including Fulton 1820 and ACE 1843), Dolbys Point (C&GS 1860), Dollys Point (C&GS field notes), Duffys Point (C&GS field notes), Point of the Creek (small tidal creek enters Shallowbag Bay here).

Baum Point Island, irregularly shaped marsh island, 0.9 mi. long, 0.3 mi. wide, Dare County, Atlantic Township (USGS 2013: Kitty Hawk). Separates Kitty Hawk Bay and Blount Bay just w of Colington Creek, 2.8 mi. s of original Kitty Hawk. *See* Baum Bay. *Other names:* Angel Island (early local use), Braum Point Island (transcribing error), Bum Point Island (USGS 2010, 1940: Kitty Hawk; Google Maps/GNIS–perpetuated error).

Baums Beach, small beach, Currituck County, Poplar Branch Township (C&GS 1852). Soundside Currituck Banks 1 mi. nw of Piper Hill, 5.5 mi. s of Corolla. *See* Baum Bay.

Baums Creek, water passage, 0.8 mi. long, Currituck County, Poplar Branch Township (USGS 2013: Mossey Islands). Tidal area between Pine Islands and marshes and Currituck Banks, 7.3 mi. nnw of Duck. Some applications extend Baums Creek into Salt House Bay. *See* Baum Bay. *Other names:* Baums Lead (some local use—*see* Buzzard Lead), Josephus Baums Creek (C&GS 1852), Thorowfare Creek (Currituck DB 5, 1785, 223–24).

Baums Mill, former mill and windmill, Currituck County, Poplar Branch Township (historical local use). On Currituck Banks 1 mi. s of

Poyners Hill (former community), 8 mi. nnw of Duck. *See* Baum Bay. ***Other names:*** Baums Wind Mill (CS 1856), J. Baums Windmill (C&GS 1852).

Baums Upper Marsh, former small marsh, Currituck County, Poplar Branch Township (C&GS 1852). On s edge of Corolla just w of Currituck Beach Lighthouse just e of Great Beach Marsh. Remnants remain, but name has fallen into disuse. Directional "upper" because historical features named Baum (windmill, landing, and creek) 5–7 mi. s. *See* Baum Bay.

Baums Wharf. *See* Sound Landing.

Baumtown, former community, 5 ft. high, Dare County, Nags Head Township (USGS 2013: Wanchese). On sw Roanoke Island 1 mi. nw of Wanchese with only a few scattered houses. *See* Baum Bay. ***Other names:*** Baum (Cram and Worret 1861).

Baumtown Canals, canals, area 1 mi. wide and long, Dare County, Nags Head Township (N.C. Marine Fisheries 2019 H2, map 5). About 20 canals omnidirectional in Baumtown divided equally by Baumtown Road, 4.5 mi. s of Manteo (center).

Bayberry Bluffs. *See* Powder Ridge.

Bay Hammock, small hummock, Hyde County, Ocracoke Township (local informants). On n shore soundside of Sound Shores subdivision in n Ocracoke (village) between Cuttin Sage Lake (e) and Northern Pond (w). ***Other names:*** Bay Hummock (Garrity-Blake 2010, 356—an error transcribing or attempt at presumed correction: unusual to find "hummock" in any source referring to the Outer Banks instead of local form, "hammock"—*see* Black Hammock).

Bay Landing, former landing, Carteret County, Portsmouth Township (NPS 2018, 136). Was in Middle Portsmouth (Middle Community) at Casey Bay and s terminus of Baymarsh Thorofare serving as landing for this portion of Portsmouth.

Bay Marsh, swamp, Carteret County, Portsmouth Township (USGS 1950: Portsmouth). Just w of Portsmouth (village), 6.8 mi. sw of Ocracoke (village). USGS persistently labels marsh incorrectly as Sheep Island (USGS 1950: Portsmouth). ***Other names:*** Baymarsh (local maps).

Bay Marsh Bay, cove, 0.1 mi. wide, Carteret County, Portsmouth Township (USGS 1950: Portsmouth). Just n of Casey Bay, just wsw of Portsmouth (village), 6.6 mi. sw of Ocracoke (village). Use of repeated generic term occurs occasionally when associative name derived from descriptive name of nearby feature. Descriptive term applied to marsh (became name) with proximity to bay; adjacent bay named for marsh (associative).

Baymarsh Thorofare, water passage, 0.6 mi. long, Carteret County, Portsmouth Township (USGS 1950: Portsmouth). In Pamlico Sound, separates Bay Marsh from Portsmouth Island, connects Casey Bay and Pamlico Sound just w of Portsmouth (village), 6.3 mi. sw of Ocracoke (village). Note combining two generic terms (bay and marsh) often occurs in such situations. ***Other names:*** Bay Marsh Thorofare (NPS 2007, map, 35–36).

Bay Point, point, 0.4 mi. long, 0.3 mi. wide, Currituck County, Fruitville Township (USGS 2013: Barco). Se point of Knotts Island on Whites Neck, 2.3 mi. s of Knotts Island (village). ***Other names:*** Kings Point (occasional 18th-century use), Neck Point (occasional usage), Whites Neck (road sign).

Bay Point, point, Dare County, Kinnakeet Township (Garrity-Blake 2010, 493). Soundside 0.7 mi. s of Kennigees Pond, 5.5 mi. s of Salvo.

Baypole Cove. *See* Marsh Cove.

Bay Ridge, small sand dune, Carteret County, Morehead Township (local use). Offshoot of Ocean Ridge (q.v.), trends s-n just w of Hoop Pole Bay on w end Atlantic Beach, 3.5 mi. w of Pine Knoll Shores. Named for location just w of Hoop Pole Bay, with street sign. Subdivision named for feature or vice versa. Unclear if name is or is not of recent origin; if so, a case of reversed usage, natural feature acquiring name of man-made feature.

Bay Ridge, semicircular sand ridge, 25 ft. high, 0.2 mi. long, Dare County, Atlantic Township (local use). Trends n-s in Bald Sand Hills (q.v.) in original Kitty Hawk. Connects Jacks Cabin Hill (n) to First Flight Ridge (s), 3.5 mi. s of Southern Shores. Subdivision named for feature.

Bay Ridge, former small ridge, Hyde County, Ocracoke Township (historical use). Was in Oyster Creek subdivision e part of Ocracoke (village). Was also road name here historically; today ridge no longer exists and name is unknown.

Bay Shoal, shoal, 0.5 mi. wide, 1.5 mi. long, Dare County, Kinnakeet Township (local use).

Culminates in point into Pamlico Sound, just e of Gull Island, 3.5 mi. s of Salvo.

Bay Tree, island, 0.1 mi. across, Currituck County, Poplar Branch Township (USGS 2013: Mossey Islands). In Currituck Sound at w end Big Narrows, 6.2 mi. ssw of Corolla. Occasionally a natural feature name has no generic term (describing feature) or has a generic term embedded in one-word form often as reference to some aspect of the feature. In spoken language, definite article is usually included, becoming part of the name (e.g., The Causeway, The Beach) but not in this case. Generic term "island" was used originally with this name but had been dropped in spoken language by end 19th century and this form now used on maps. Here, "bay" is not used as a generic term, refers to tree type found here: Sweet Bay, Loblolly Bay, or Red Bay, with numerous other localized coastal names for these trees. *Other names:* Baytree (unknown, ca. 1900), Bay Tree Island (C&GS 1852).

Bay Tree Point, point, Currituck County, Fruitville Township (F&WS 1984, map, 74). Distinctive point protruding into North Landing River from nw Mackay Island, 4 mi. w of Knotts Island (village). *See* Bay Tree.

Bayview Harbor Marina, linear approach harbor, Carteret County, Harkers Island Township (N.C. Marine Fisheries 2019, E7, map 27). N part Harkers Island 6.5 mi. ese of Beaufort (mainland). *Other names:* Ervins Marina (NC Marine Fisheries, 2019, E7, map 27).

Bay Villa Marina, dock, Currituck County, Fruitville Township (signage). Small facility e-central Knotts Island at s entrance Knotts Island Channel 10 mi. nw of Corolla.

Beach, The, beach, Hyde County, Ocracoke Township (local use). Was oceanside opposite Ocracoke (village) 1.5 mi. distant. Descriptive but with use and time became a name, in Ocracoke usually applied specifically to just beach opposite village, whereas elsewhere on the Outer Banks was more general application. *Other names:* Bald Beach (older local use), Piney Beach (Weslager 1954, 43 — use must have been historical when stands of trees present).

Beach, The, historical. Was used by residents of Hatteras Island and Pea Island as general reference to barrier islands n of Oregon Inlet.

Actual limits vague, but usually to Kitty Hawk, sometimes to Duck and beyond. Could indicate just about any beach because most villages were in protected places soundside.

Beach Creek, bay, 0.4 mi. long, 0.1 mi. wide, Currituck County, Poplar Branch Township (USGS 1982: Jarvisburg). In Currituck Sound 0.8 mi. s of Doxeys Salthouse, 5.2 mi. nw of Duck.

Beach Creek. *See* Horse Island Creek.

Beach Lake, small lake, Dare County, Kinnakeet Township (signage). In Waves just e of Davids Point just w of Bold Dune, 2.5 mi. s of Rodanthe. Subdivision named for feature.

Beach Pond, lake, Currituck County, Fruitville Township (Cox 1923). Open water almost completely surrounded by marsh 1 mi. n of e terminus North Channel, n channel former New Currituck Inlet 11 mi. nnw of Corolla. Known historically by variations of the original name Fresh Pond and associative names exist as Fresh Pond Bay, Fresh Pond Hill, Fresh Pond Island, and Little Fresh Pond Island nearby. The name, in forms of Fresh Pond, was referenced scores of times in historical deeds (1760–1850) to large fresh pond on (upper) Currituck Banks (not to be confused with large feature named Fresh Pond in Kill Devil Hills and Nags Head). This well-established historical name morphed into Beach Pond for some reason, as descriptive name (as was original name). *Other names:* Fresh Pond (historical records), Grate Fresh Pond (numerous historical deeds), Great Fish Pond (Currituck DB 25, 1849, 387), Great Fresh Pond (historical deeds).

Beach Pond Creek, former drainage, Currituck County, Fruitville Township (former use). Issued from sw Beach Pond (s North Swan Beach) trended w to Doe Island (probably) 3.5 mi. se of Knotts Island (village). Feature barely discernable; name was never used much.

Beach Ridge, sand ridge, Dare County, Atlantic Township (Harris 2017; unknown, 1779–83). According to Harris (2017) somewhere in Kitty Hawk ridge-and-swale system (q.v.), w of original Kitty Hawk. By virtue of the name, could have been closer to oceanside Kitty Hawk. Harris does not provide additional information, and as a named feature (either form) does not appear in early deeds. *Other* names: Beech Ridge (Harris 2017, source unknown—beech tree here, not prevalent today).

Beach Slue, cove, 0.7 mi. long, 0.2 mi. wide, Dare County, Kinnakeet Township (USGS 2013: Pea Island). Former water passage just w of former New Inlet, trends e-w 5.4 mi. n of Rodanthe. Between 1950 and 1970, e end filled with sediment changing tidal water passage to cove, but slue remained with name. *See* Allen Slough.

Beacon Hill, sand dune, Currituck County, Poplar Branch Township (limited local use). Just e of Whale Head Bay just s of Whale Head Hill, 1.5 mi. s of Corolla. Subdivision here named by developer (usually the case) and beacon was selected for proximity to Currituck Beach Lighthouse (0.7 mi. n). Reportedly, no name for sand dune prominent here considerably altered by man during development. Before development, sand dune was 0.5 mi. long trending nw-se 20 ft. high. Dunes of this size and distinction usually had a name. Reverse usage, natural feature acquiring name of man-made feature (subdivision).

Beacon Island, island, 0.3 mi. long, 5 ft. high, Carteret County, Portsmouth Township (USGS 1950: Portsmouth). In Pamlico Sound at w end Ocracoke Inlet between Wallace Channel and Blair Channel, 3.8 mi. w of Ocracoke (village). Name originated from two large beacons on the island used by pilots to guide ships through Ocracoke Inlet during 18th and early 19th centuries. Sometimes considered in Oyster Rocks (q.v.) complex. *Other names:* Bacon Island (Stick 1958, 77—probable transcribing error), Beacon Castle (CS 1852), Beacon Islands (Brazier 1833).

Beacon Island Fort, former fort, Carteret County, Portsmouth Township. Somewhere on Beacon Island; no trace has been found nor any reference on any map. In 1799, John Wallace and John Gray Blount, owners of Beacon Island, sold the island to the federal government to build a fort there. Question if fort was ever built, but according to some historians evidence suggests Beacon Island Fort was built (appears in U.S. Army records) and location would likely have been s tip, higher ground, best perspective to cover Ocracoke Inlet. A small fort was built on Beacon Island during Civil War and named Fort Ocracoke (q.v.), later Fort Morgan. *Other names:* Beacon Island Reservation (Army Historical Register), Fort Morgan (Stick 1958, 304), Fort Ocracoke (Stick 1958, 304).

Beacon Island Roads, historical anchorage, Carteret County, Portsmouth Township. Formerly in Pamlico Sound at Beacon Island, 3.7 mi. w of Ocracoke (village). Late 18th and early 19th centuries ships would ride at anchor here before delivering or obtaining cargo from economic concerns on Beacon Island. Eventually Beacon Island Roads referenced in and around Ocracoke Inlet. Usage for name disappeared during early 19th century. "Roads," a generic term used 17th, 18th, and 19th centuries as place where ships could anchor, but less enclosed than a harbor. While not used extensively today, some vestigial use can be identified found in Tidewater Virginia (Hampton Roads). *Other names:* Beacon Island Harbour (historical), Beacon Island Road (Goerch 1956; Price 1795, 632), Lower Roads (Hooker 1850), The Port of Beacon Island (Stick 1958, 79).

Beacon Island Shoal, shoal, 5 mi. long, Carteret County, Portsmouth Township (local use). In Pamlico Sound between Beacon Island and Wallace Channel, from former Drum Shoal to North Rock, 4.4 mi. w of Ocracoke (village). Named for proximity to Beacon Island, much smaller now than 18th century when it occupied much of Ocracoke Inlet. *Other names:* Beacon Island Shoals (McGuinn 2000, 212).

Beacon Island Slue, former channel, 0.5 mi. long, Carteret County, Portsmouth Township (historical local use). Was in Pamlico Sound just s of Beacon Island connected Wallace Channel and Blair Channel, 3.3 mi. wsw of Ocracoke (village). *See* Allen Slough. *Other names:* Beacon Island Slough (Angley 1984, 47).

Beacons Reach, subdivision, Carteret County, Morehead Township (signage). Large community, 1.5 mi. long, on Bogue Banks, 3 mi. w of Pine Knoll Shores. Last of former property owned by Roosevelts (*see* Pine Knoll Shores) to be developed; begun around late 1970s when Roosevelts repurchased this large tract of land. Composed of 13 separately named subdivisions, some with numbered sections: Coral Ridge, Coral

Shores, Egret Lake, Fiddlers Ridge, Forest Dunes, Forest Dunes East, Maritime Place, Maritime Place West, Ocean Grove, Ocean Grove West, Pelican Point, Westport, and Westport Woods. Name is reportedly from farthest "reach" of the light (beacon) from Cape Lookout Lighthouse, 20 mi. e. "Reach" is also a hydrographic term used occasionally with geographic names, referring to straight and uninterrupted portions of a stream and occasionally other water bodies, not applicable or used on the Outer Banks. *Other names:* West Pine Knoll Shores (PKS 2016).

Beals, former settlement, Dare County, Atlantic Township (NCDOT 1963). Was just n of Duck, 8.5 mi. nnw of original Kitty Hawk. Name used only from mid-1960s to mid-1980s.

Bean Island, elongated island, 0.02 mi. wide, 0.05 mi. long, less than 5 ft. high, Carteret County, Davis Township (USGS 2013: Davis). In Core Sound 0.2 mi. s of Great Island, 3.7 mi. ese of Davis (mainland).

Bean Island, island, 0.2 mi. long, Carteret County, White Oak Township (USGS 2013: Salter Path). In Bogue Sound, 6.9 mi. w of Salter Path. *Other names:* Piney Island (19th-century misapplication), Wood Island (19th-century misapplication).

Bearhead, island, 0.2 mi. wide, Currituck County, Poplar Branch Township (USGS 2013: Mossey Islands). In Currituck Sound just n of Lone Oak Channel, 3.8 mi. ssw of Corolla. Generic term "head" (point) with specific part of name, one-word form. *See* Bay Tree. *Other names:* Bear Head (some applications use two-word form).

Bear Island, elongated island, 0.5 mi. long (formerly 3 mi. long), Carteret County, White Oak Township (USGS 2013: Swansboro). In Bogue Sound 10 mi. ne of Bogue Inlet.

Beasley Bay, bay, 1.2 mi. wide, Currituck County, Poplar Branch Township (USGS 2013: Mossey Islands). In Currituck Sound just w of Currituck Banks, 6.7 mi. s of Corolla. *Other names:* Beasleys Bay (C&GS 1879), Beastley Bay (several commercial mapmakers—a misinterpretation error), Hicks Bay (limited 18th-century use), Selleys Bay (Currituck DB 2, 1769, 247).

Beaufort Bar, shoal, Carteret County, Beaufort and Morehead Townships (Williamson 1992). Primary shoal at entrance to Beaufort Inlet around which shipping must navigate, 3.5 mi. se of Morehead City (mainland port). *See*

Beaufort Inlet. *Other names:* Old Topsail Bar (Kell, 1777).

Beaufort Channel, channel, 1 mi. long, Carteret County, Beaufort Township (USGS 2013: Beaufort). Leads from just n of Beaufort Inlet to Beaufort (mainland) just e of Radio Island to junction Taylor Creek and Gallants Channel. Recorded and used as Bulkhead Channel (n part), but on recommendation of the North Carolina Port Authority, name and application included former Bulkhead Channel (q.v.), changed by USBGN in 1986. *See* Beaufort Inlet. *Other names:* Beaufort Harbor Channel (U.S. Coast Guard 2015, 307), Bulkhead Channel (q.v.; in part NOS 2014f—still used), Ship Channel (Kell 1777).

Beaufort Inlet, water passage, Carteret County, Beaufort and Morehead Townships (USGS 2013: Beaufort). Connects Back Sound and Bogue Sound to Onslow Bay and Atlantic Ocean, separates Shackleford Banks from Bogue Banks, 2 mi. s of Beaufort (mainland). Beaufort Inlet, Bogue Inlet, and Ocracoke Inlet are only inlets open continuously since before 1585. Name originates from Duke of Beaufort, England; several heirs were loyal to King Charles II, who granted Carolina to the eight Lords Proprietors (a descendent) (*see* Carolina). *Other names:* Alte Topsail Einfahrt (Lucas 1826—*einfahrt*, inlet in German), Beaufords Entrance (Holland 1794), Beaufort Entrance (USBGN staff and mostly 19th-century charts), Beaufort Harbor (Mast, Crowell and Kirkpatrick 1890), Beaufort Port (Bowen 1767), Bulkhead Channel (Johnson 1872), Cape Lookout Inlet (Wimble 1738), Core Sound (Mouzon and La Rouge 1777), Core Sound Inlet (Stick 1958, 312), Detroit de Core (unknown, 1806—*detroit*, strait in French), Entré de La Voile du Peroquet [*sic*] (Nolin 1783—*voile du perroquet*, literally parrot's sail, (old) French idiom meaning topsail), Gore Sound (Holland 1794), Gore Sound Entrance (mislabeled), Harbor Entrance (ACE 1891), Old Topsail Inlet (Price et al. 1808), Old-Topsail Inlet (18th-century shipwreck reports), Passe Topsail (Bellin 1757), Port Beaufort (Moseley 1733), Port Beaufort Inlet (Stick 1958, 312), Porto de Principe (Keulen 1690), Topsaile Inlett (Barnwell-Hammerton 1721), Top Sail Inlet (18th-century shipwreck reports), Topsail Inlet (Lawson 1709, map), Top Sayl Einfahrt (Huber 1711).

Beaufort Inlet Batteries, former batteries

(gun emplacements), Carteret County, Morehead and Harkers Island Townships (Army records). Three batteries from WWII to protect Beaufort Inlet shipping: Battery Atlantic Beach on Bogue Banks 2.5 mi. w of Atlantic Beach; Battery Macon outside Fort Macon on Bogue Point; and Battery Cape Lookout at Cape Lookout. *See* Beaufort Inlet.

Beaufort Inlet Channel, channel, 1.3 mi. long, Carteret County, Beaufort Township (USGS 2013: Beaufort). In Onslow Bay at entrance to Beaufort Inlet, 5.5 mi. s of Beaufort (mainland). Main approach channel for shipping to Beaufort Inlet, entrance to Port of Morehead City, with large docks for processing phosphate and (formerly) used in menhaden (*Brevoortia tyrannus*) fishing industry, declined considerably to almost nothing. Wimble (18th-century chart maker) labeled Cape Look Out Channel on his 1738 chart between Cape Lookout and entrance to Beaufort Inlet, referring to what is now Beaufort Inlet Channel, though hydrography has changed since 1738. *See* Beaufort Inlet. *Other names:* Beaufort Channel (local use), Cape Look Out Channel (Wimble 1738), Gallants Channel (confusion with nearby channel).

Bee Ridge. *See* Pine Ridge.

Bell Cove, cove, Carteret County, White Oak Township (Stephens 1984, map back cover). Located by various authors between Salter Path w to Archer (Arthurs) Creek. Actual location 1 mi. sw of Long Island, 6 mi. w of Salter Path. Stories abound name refers to large bell erected in community here to announce availability of fish catch or other activities (folk etymology). That story likely arises from large bell mounted on a post on community church grounds well after community founded, heard for some distance (church moved to Bogue on mainland in 1904). Cove reportedly named from surname of family from mainland (several families there named Bell; today community of Ocean area) who drove their cattle across the sound to graze semiannually. Today small subdivision of Bell Cove Heights is here, as is Bell Cove Cemetery with six "baby graves" and 1 adult said to be loner (Alfred Bavis) who lived on Long Island and preached periodically at the community here. *Other names:* Belco (Stephens 1984, 6).

Bell Cove, former community, Carteret County, White Oak Township (Stephens 1984, 6). Was at Bell Cove (q.v.), 6 mi. w of Salter Path. Various reports including reproduced newspaper article (no dates or credit) indicate Bell Cove and Yellow Hill same, but separate 2 mi. apart. As with small communities w of Salter Path, families eventually moved to Salter Path by early 20th century for several reasons (vacated by 1920). Community named for Bell Cove (q.v.). *See* Bogue Banks historical communities.

Bellows Bay, cove, 0.9 mi. wide, Currituck County, Fruitville Township (USGS 2013: Barco). In Currituck Sound at s end Mackay Island, 10.2 mi. nw of Corolla. *Other names:* Balles Bay (Currituck DB 6, 1791, 184), Ballows Bay (Currituck DB 10, 1809, 66–67), Bellisses Bay (early 18th-century spelling using "ſ" [long "s"] within words, common in formal printing until middle 18th century but had completely disappeared by beginning 19th century).

Bells Island, marsh island, Carteret County, Harkers Island Township (Mason 2000; NPS 1987, map, 38). In a collection of marsh islands in Back Sound between Winsors Lump and central Shackleford Banks separated from Shackleford Banks by Cabs Creek 1.7 mi. sw of Harkers Island (village). Location determined from Mason (2000) and NPS (1987, map, 38); no scale provided and location probably this large marsh island, but name placement could also apply name to Jacks Island or Shooting Hammock. Responses from local interviewees mixed, ranging from "yes, that's the area," to "maybe yes," to not familiar. Mason's (2000) map is only occurrence encountered for Bells Island.

Bells Island, marsh island, 0.5 mi. long, 0.1 mi. wide, Dare County, Nags Head Township (USGS 2013: Roanoke Island NE). In Roanoke Sound between Roanoke Island and Bodie Island just s of Headquarters Island, 1.9 mi. sw of Whalebone Junction.

Bells Island. *See* Jacks Island.

Bells Island. *See* Shooting Hammock.

Bells Shoal. *See* Mullet Shoal.

Ben Dixons Creek, cove, 0.05 mi. wide, Carteret County, Portsmouth Township (USGS 1950: Portsmouth). Just wnw of Portsmouth (village), 6.2 mi. sw of Ocracoke (village).

Bennies Landing, former landing, Dare County,

Kinnakeet Township (Garrity-Blake 2010, 169). Was on s side of Uncle Bates Ditch halfway between Peters Ditch (Avon Harbor entrance) and First Creek, 7 mi. n of Buxton. Landing Road there today.

Ben Peters Creek, small tidal stream, Dare County, Kinnakeet Township (NPS 2005b: NPS 1, 154). On n shore Midgett Island halfway (1 mi.) from Waves (n) and Salvo (s). Probable location from existing information but not verified.

Ben Pughs Landing, former landing, Dare County, Kinnakeet Township (Garrity-Blake 2010, 493). Was soundside just s of Kennigees Pond, 5 mi. s of Salvo.

Bens Point, point, Dare County, Atlantic Township (USGS 2013: Manteo). S point Colington Island, 1.2 mi. s of Colington (community). Originally Bordens Point, after many generations locally contracted to Bens Point. *Other names:* Bordens Point (surname), Raptor Point (recent use, for osprey [*Pandion haliaetus*; raptors] here, road sign).

Bermuda Bay. *See* Baum Bay.

Bermuda Island, former island, 0.1 mi. across, Dare County, Atlantic Township (historical local use). Was in Kitty Hawk Bay 1 mi. s of original Kitty Hawk; appears on early 19th-century maps but name origin is undocumented. Even older residents do not know a name origin for Bermuda Island, barely visible today. The following explanation is believed to represent name origin and supported by associated circumstantial evidence: maybe for Bermuda Island in Atlantic Ocean 500 miles e of the Outer Banks, named for Juan Bermudez, Spanish discoverer not known to visit the Outer Banks. A business making shingles locally for houses, early in Outer Banks history, was believed to have exported to Bermuda (*see* Shingle Landing). Kitty Hawk Bay is shallow, and possibly Bermuda Island in center Kitty Hawk Bay was used as a lightering point (switching cargo to and from small draft boats for use in shallow water) in support of shingle industry.

Additionally, Lawson (1709, 106) refers to "Bermudas Currants grow in the woods on a buʃh" ("ʃ" is long "s"—*see* Bellows Bay variant Bellisses Bay). However, Lawson (nor anyone else) makes no mention of Bermuda Island in connection with currants; the island is rarely mentioned because it

was minor and no longer exists, except as a temporary shoal during low water. Originally two islands, hence occasional plural form, but by 20th century only one island (often inundated). *Other names:* Bermuda Islands (historical maps and charts).

Betseys Marsh, large marsh, 1.7 mi. long, 0.7 mi. wide, Currituck County, Fruitville Township (Cox 1923). Between North Channel and South Channel, 9 mi. nnw of Corolla. Named on historical maps in former New Currituck Inlet and another smaller marsh in former Currituck Inlet (Old Currituck Inlet). Possibly confusion over location occurred, especially with early mapmakers, and may refer to only one feature, but information is vague so two entries are maintained (*see* Betsys Marsh). Unknown if named for same individual, given different spelling.

Betsys Marsh, marsh, Currituck County, Fruitville Township (historical local use). At former Currituck Inlet (Old Currituck Inlet) 3 mi. ene of Knotts Island (village). Historically, reportedly a tavern here. *See* Betseys Marsh.

Bias Landing. *See* Station Landing.

Bias Shores, historical area, Dare County, Atlantic Township (historical use and subdivision signage). Was sound-to-ocean just sse of Duck (center), 2 mi. nnw of Southern Shores. Originally in 1930s–50s designed as vacationing destination for African Americans. Eventually sold, but name (as often) remained. Named for John Henry Bias, principal of three developers from Elizabeth City, with Henry Hargraves and Charles Jenkins. Includes Hargraves Beach (q.v.) and subdivision named for Henry Hargraves, and Ocean Crest subdivision with Charles Jenkins Lane named for Charles Jenkins. *See also* Station Landing.

Big Bird Island, crescent-shaped island, Currituck County, Fruitville Township (Cox 1923). Just n of Currituck Bay just e of Middle Marsh, 9 mi. nnw of Corolla.

Big Colington, historical island reference, Dare County, Atlantic Township (local use). W portion Colington Island. In 1760s, stream with source near center of Colington Island, trending n to Kitty Hawk Bay, was manually extended s to Roanoke Sound, dividing Colington Island into two segments: larger segment is Big Colington, and smaller segment Little Colington. Canalized stream appropriately named Colington Cut, but known historically and locally as The Dividing Creek. *See* Colington Island. *Other names:* Big Colington Island (some local use), Big Collington (Currituck DB 13, 1814, 52–55), Grate Collinton Island (Currituck DB 5, 1784, 4), Great Colenton (Stick 1958, 266), Great Colington (limited references), Greate Collenton Island (Currituck DB 12, 1813, 364–65).

Big Deep Marsh Island, marsh island, 0.2 mi. long, Carteret County, Smyrna Township (USGS 2013: Horsepen Point). In Core Sound 0.5 mi. nw of Hogpen Bay, 3.5 mi. e of Harkers Island (village). *Other names:* Long Deep Marsh Island (C&GS 1947).

Big Foot Island. *See* Dredge Island.

Big Foot Slough Channel, channel, 1.8 mi. long, Hyde County, Ocracoke Township (local use). In Pamlico Sound 1.4 mi. w of Howard Reef, 1.5 mi. n of Ocracoke (village). Unusual for generic terms "slough" and "channel" used in same name since they mean essentially same thing, though use of "channel" often signified dredging and importance to navigation, and this channel used by ferry service. *See* Allen Slough. *Other names:* Big Foot Slough (Angley 1984, 50), Bigfoot Slough (local media), Big Foot Slue (ACE 1893).

Big Gut, former short tidal stream, 0.3 mi. long, Hyde County, Ocracoke Township (Weslager 1954—confirmed by interviews with Ballance [2017, 2018] and Howard [2017, 2018]). Was at se Silver Lake (then Cockle Creek) in Ocracoke (village) joined with Little Gut to form The Gut. This creek (w creek in Old Guts complex) with The Gut and Little Gut were filled in by ACE when Cockle Creek was dredged into Silver Lake. The Gut, Big Gut, and Little Gut comprised Old Guts (q.v.) complex. *See* Alligator Gut. *Other names:* Aunt Winnies Gut (Aunt Winnie Blount lived nearby— interviews with Ballance [2017] and Howard [2017]).

Big Hill, sand dune, 10 ft. high, Carteret County, Portsmouth Township (USGS 1950: Portsmouth). On s Portsmouth Island just s of Portsmouth (village), 6.6 mi. sw of Ocracoke (village).

Big Hill, hill, Dare County, Atlantic Township (local use). On Big Point 0.8 mi. s of Sanderling.

Big Island, small marsh island, 0.2 mi. wide, Carteret County, Davis Township (USGS 2013: Davis). In Core Sound just e of mainland, 2.3 mi. ne of Davis (mainland). Naming this island is whimsical because quite small. *See* Piney Point Shoal.

Big Island, island, 0.2 mi. long, Dare County, Atlantic Township (local use). In n Colington Creek just w of Kill Devil Hills (town), 2.1 mi. s of original Kitty Hawk.

Big Island, marsh island, 0.2 mi. long, 0.2 mi. wide, Dare County, Kinnakeet Township (USGS 2013: Buxton). In Pamlico Sound near mouth Mill Creek, 1.2 mi. n of original Avon. *Other names:* Lookout Island (CS 1852).

Big Island, marsh island, 0.6 mi. long, 0.3 mi. wide, Dare County, Nags Head Township (USGS 2013: Wanchese). At sw Roanoke Island, 1.3 mi. sw of Wanchese, more prominent 17th and 18th centuries when Roanoke Marshes existed. Name likely transferred from island approx. 3 mi. w of here (*see* Big Island—historical) when that island disappeared late 19th century.

Big Island, former island, Dare County, Nags Head Township (C&GS 1883). Was in Roanoke Marshes 5 mi. sw of Wanchese. Roanoke Marshes now flooded by Croatan Sound, and island was remnant of Roanoke Marshes. Disappeared completely, likely name transferred to Big Island 3 mi. e of this former location.

Big Kill Devil Hill. *See* Kill Devil Hill.

Big Kinnakeet. *See* Avon.

Big Marsh, marsh island, 0.4 mi. long, Carteret County, Sea Level Township (USGS 1951: Styron Bay). Separated from Core Banks by Gutter Creek, 3.9 mi. s of Atlantic (mainland). *Other names:* Big March (NOAA 1988 typographical error).

Big Marsh Point, point, Carteret County, Sea Level Township (USGS 2013: Styron Bay). Nw point of Big Marsh, 3.8 mi. s of Atlantic (mainland).

Big Morgan Island, island, Currituck County, Poplar Branch Township (C&GS 1913a). Larger of two islands (ne most) in group named Morgan Islands (q.v.) in Currituck Sound at nw tip Mossey Islands complex, 4.5 mi. sw of Corolla. *See* Morgan Islands.

Big Narrows, narrow water passage, Currituck County, Poplar Branch Township (USGS 2013: Mossey Islands). In Currituck Sound 2 mi. sw of Mossey Islands complex, 6.5 mi. sw of Corolla. *Other names:* Currituck Narrows (Currituck DB 7, 1794, 108–9; Brazier

1833), Grate Narrows (Currituck DB 3, 1802, 229), Great Narrows (Currituck DB 3, 1801, 181), Narrows (local usage), The Narrows (Comberford 1657).

Big Otter Cove, small cove, Dare County, Nags Head Township (local use). Just s of Mann Point 1.3 mi. w of Jockeys Ridge, 2.2 mi. w of Nags Head (center). North American river otter (*Lontra canadensis*) indigenous to and common here. *Other names:* Big Otter Gut (colonial use when gut was more popular).

Big Penguin Island, island, 0.1 mi. long, 0.2 mi. wide, Dare County, Nags Head Township (USGS 2013: Roanoke Island NE). In Roanoke Sound 0.9 mi. nw of Whalebone Junction. *See* Penguin Islands. *Other names:* Penguin Island (Graham 1843), Penguins Island (Fulton 1820), Penguin Isle (some recent local use, former nearby restaurant used name associatively, never used on maps).

Big Perch Island, marsh island, 0.1 mi. across, Currituck County, Fruitville Township (USGS 2013: Knotts Island). Marsh islands (Perch Islands) at n end Knotts Island Channel just se of Little Perch Island, 2.2 mi. ne of Knotts Island (village). Perch refers to yellow perch (*Perca flavescens*), fish native to Atlantic Basin. *See* Perch Islands. *Other names:* Perch Island Number 2 (Cox 1923).

Big Point, point, Dare County, Atlantic Township (local use). From barrier island into Currituck Sound, 0.8 mi. s of Sanderling.

Big Pond, water area, 0.2 mi. across, Currituck County, Fruitville Township (Cox 1923). Ne Walk Island, 2 mi. ene of Knotts Island (village). *See* Adams Pond.

Big Pond, lake, Currituck County, Poplar Branch Township (USGS 2013: Mossey Islands). On unnamed marsh island 3.5 mi. sw of Mossey Islands complex, 7 mi. sw of Corolla. *See* Adams Pond.

Big Pond, lake, Dare County, Atlantic Township (local use). In sw Kitty Hawk ridge-and-swale system (q.v.) at Kitty Hawk Landing subdivision, 1.6 mi. sw of original Kitty Hawk. *See* Adams Pond.

Big Raccoon Island, island, Currituck County, Poplar Branch Township (Currituck DB 24, 1842, 104). Largest island in Raccoon Islands (q.v.) complex in Raccoon Bay, n-most island, 0.7 mi. nnw of Corolla.

Big Raymond Island. *See* Crow Island.

Big Rock, large rock, Carteret County, Harkers Island Township (ACE 1895). About 50 mi. se of Cape Lookout near Ten-Fathom Ledge.

Big Sheep Marsh, shoal, Currituck County, Fruitville Township (C&GS 1913a). Southern Sheep Marsh on e approach to entrance Knotts Island Bay just nw of Swan Island, 2.3 mi. se of Knotts Island (village). More shoal than marsh, though more marsh mid-19th century. *See* Sheep Marsh.

Big Shoal Marsh, island, 0.2 mi. long, Carteret County, Harkers Island Township (USGS 1997: Harkers Island). In Back Sound 0.9 mi. s of Middle Marshes, 3.1 mi. wsw of Harkers Island (village).

Big Skinner Island, large marsh island, 1 mi. long, 0.8 mi. wide, Currituck County, Fruitville Township (Cox 1923). Just nnw of Little Skinner Island, 6 mi. se of Knotts Island (village). *Other names:* Sassafras Island (18th century), Skinner Island (occasional local use).

Big Slough, small natural channel, Dare County, Atlantic Township (local use). In Currituck Sound 1.5 mi. s of Sanderling, disappearing, not as defined as 50 years ago; could be remnant of former inlet, Trinety Harbor (just sw of former inlet's location) more likely Caffeys Inlet, more recent (closed 1810), channel only 1 mi. s of former Caffeys Inlet site.

Big Tim Island, marsh island, 0.1 mi. long, 0.5 mi. wide, Dare County, Nags Head Township (USGS 2013: Oregon Inlet). In Roanoke Sound, 0.2 mi. ne of Little Tim Island, 5.9 mi. se of Wanchese.

Big Yankee Pond, cove, 0.2 mi. long, Currituck County, Poplar Branch Township (USGS 2013: Jarvisburg). Just n of Little Yankee Pond, 6.3 mi. nw of Duck (center). Name origin unknown. *See* Yankee Ponds and Adams Pond. *Other names:* Yankee Pond (local use).

Bild Island, former island, Dare County, Kinnakeet Township (USGS 1943: Oregon Inlet). Mostly shoal by 1980 with only remnants remaining. Was just inside Oregon Inlet 12 mi. s of Nags Head. *Bild* is German meaning picture, drawing, etc., but no relation to this name, and believed by local historians to be misrecording of "bird" for Bird Island. Also could be corruption of "bilge," referring to rounded or lower portion of ship's hull, often contained water, hence "bilge water." Disappeared late 1940s, most not aware of its previous existence.

Bill Salters Creek, cove, 0.1 mi. long, Carteret County, Portsmouth Township (USGS 1950: Portsmouth). Joins Willis Creek in se Casey Bay just sw of Portsmouth (village), 7.1 mi. sw of Ocracoke (village).

Bills Point, point, Carteret County, White Oak Township (Stephens 1984, map back cover). Soundside 1.5 mi. ese of Wood Island, 2 mi. w of Indian Beach (town). *Other names:* Flagstaff Point (CS 1852).

Bills Point, small former settlement, Carteret County, White Oak Township (Stephens 1984, 50). Was between Rice(s) Path e 1 mi. and Yellow Hill w 1 mi., 2 mi. w of Indian Beach. As with small communities w of Salter Path, families eventually moved to Salter Path by early 20th century for various reasons. *See* Bogue Banks historical communities.

Billys Woods, woods, Dare County, Nags Head Township (local use). On Bodie Island just n of Bodie Island Lighthouse, 2.8 mi. nw of Oregon Inlet, 4 mi. ese of Wanchese, more extensive in 19th century.

Birch Island, marsh island, Dare County, Nags Head Township (local informant). Just sw of Roanoke Island, 1.5 mi. sw of Wanchese. Probable location, description provided not exact, location could be slightly different. Birch trees are known in e North Carolina but not prevalent here; recent name and reason for naming unknown.

Bird Island, island, Carteret County, Beaufort Township (local use). Exposed Bird Shoal in Beaufort Inlet, 1 mi. ssw of Beaufort (mainland), existed since earliest maps but often inundated at high water. *Other names:* Birds Island (ACE 1891).

Bird Island, former island, Carteret County, Portsmouth Township (C&GS 1916a). Was in Ocracoke Inlet near entrance, 3.7 mi. sw of Ocracoke (village). Original form no longer exists (mostly disappeared 1921), has become a shoal usually covered with water, sometimes attached to former Vera Cruz Shoal at low tide until late 20th century, when Vera Cruz Shoal became completely inundated.

Bird Island, shoal, Hyde County, Ocracoke Township (Sorrie 2014, 109). In Hatteras Inlet, exposed part of Pelican Shoal 5 mi. wsw of Hatteras (village). Formerly several exposed parts that occasionally bare.

Bird Island, small island, Hyde County, Swan Quarter Township (C&GS 1899b). Just off nw tip of Great Island, 6 mi. se of Swan Quarter (mainland).

Bird Island Channel, channel, 2 mi. long, Carteret County, Beaufort Township (USGS 2013: Beaufort). Separates Bird Shoal from marshes, 1.2 mi. s of Beaufort (mainland).

Bird Islands, islands, 1.4 mi. long, Dare County, Hatteras Township (USGS 2013: Hatteras Overedge North). Chain of 12 sand bars in Pamlico Sound, exposed parts of Clam Shoal (q.v.), 6 mi. n of Hatteras (village). *Other names:* Bird Island (used at high tide), Birds Island (error on USGS 2016: Hatteras Overedge North).

Bird Islands, islands, Dare County, Nags Head and Kinnakeet Townships (ACE 2013). Seven spoil or disposal islands in arc 3 mi. long, 1 mi. e of Oregon Inlet, 10 mi. s of Whalebone Junction. Exposed parts of Bulkhead Shoal (q.v.) maintained certain size for protected nesting for birds against predators, hence name. *See* Parnell Island and Wells Island.

Bird Pond, small lake, Hyde County, Ocracoke Township (local use). Just s of Ocracoke-Hatteras Ferry Landing just n of Styron Hills, 13.5 mi. ne of Ocracoke (village).

Birdshit Shoal, man-made shoal, Hyde County, Ocracoke Township (local informants). In inner Ocracoke Inlet, spoil (sand and gravel) piled up from dredging channel used by Cedar Island–Ocracoke Ferry, 1.5 mi. wnw of Ocracoke (village). Coarse reference to presence of numerous birds.

Bird Shoal, shoal, 2 mi. long, less than 0.1 mi. wide, Carteret County, Beaufort Township (USGS 2013: Beaufort). Between Bird Island Channel and Town Marsh Channel at n end Beaufort Inlet, 1 mi. s of Beaufort (mainland), much wider 19th century. Most of island usually inundated except for this small portion. *Other names:* Bird Island Shoal (C&GS 1889b), Bird Shoals (N.C. Marine Fisheries 2019, E5, map 29).

Bitter Swash, marsh, Hyde County, Ocracoke Township (local use). Just ne of The Great Swash, bounded sw by South Bitterswash Creek and ne by North Bitterswash Creek, 6 mi. ne of Ocracoke (village). Note two-word form while two associated creeks one-word combined form, often the case in such naming situations, known as process of concatenation, common in English.

Examples are "blue" and "bird" becoming "bluebird" and "foot" and "path" becoming "footpath"; meanings of original separate terms might or might not remain same upon concatenation. *See* Daniel Swash.

Bitterswash Creeks, tidal streams, Hyde County, Ocracoke Township (local use), 2.5 mi. sw of Green Island, 10.5 mi. ne of Ocracoke (village). Collective reference to North Bitterswash Creek (q.v.) and South Bitterswash Creek (q.v.) used more today than names separately.

Blackbeards Point. *See* Springers Point.

Black Bottom, former area, Dare County, Kinnakeet Township (local use). Former sparse vegetation just e of former Cow Pasture just ne of Midgett Cove, 3 mi. s of Rodanthe. Legend indicates so much fighting here during Civil War not much grows— folk etymology, since practically no fighting here; detritus and stumps from a historical maritime forest, hence name. Area not as swampy now.

Black Dog Harbor, harbor, Dare County, Kinnakeet Township (signage). In Salvo 4 mi. s of Rodanthe. In 2015, subdivision (same name) developer requested a change to land use permit, in this request was also to change subdivision name from Aaron Hill Harbor to Black Dog Harbor. Dare County commissioners approved name change October 5, 2015. Aaron Hill Harbor still used in real estate brochures with Black Dog Harbor perhaps because Dare County records were not changed for a year or so. Street also renamed from Aaron Hill Harbor Lane to Black Dog Lane ("Harbor" not included). Both names used though sign is Black Dog Harbor. *Other names:* Aaron Harbor (local usage originally), Aaron Hill Harbor (original name—former and current local use).

Black Duck Cove, cove, 0.1 mi. wide, Currituck County, Poplar Branch Township; and Dare County, Atlantic Township (USGS 2013: Jarvisburg). Just n of se end Great Gap, 5 mi. nnw of Duck (center).

Blackhall Bay, cove, 0.6 mi. wide, Dare County, Nags Head Township (Brazier 1820). In Croatan Sound just n of Pork Point, 1.6 mi. w of Manteo (center). Used since 18th century; however, of scores of people asked (government officials included), none knew name origin, most were not aware of the name. Occasionally 18th century, "hall"

used to reference a home (if substantial, or whimsically if shack-like), might have been used whimsically here. Currituck DB 14 (1816, 19) references a dwelling here but does not provide details. *Other names:* Black Hall Bay (USGS 2013: Manteo).

Black Hammock, marsh, 1.7 mi. long, 0.3 mi. wide, Dare County, Kinnakeet Township (USGS 2013: Buxton). On Hatteras Island between original Avon and Askins Creek, 1.1 mi. s of original Avon. "Hammock," variation of generic term "hummock," used throughout se U.S. Further corruption, "hamlet" was used very locally in Hatteras (village), though this specific reference to these hummocks or hammocks supporting at least one tree has fallen into disuse. "Hummock" is a rounded hill and might be on land or in water. Originally, "hummock" is a corruption of "hillock" and applied to any upward protuberance in swampy or tidal areas. *Other names:* Black Hammock Marsh (some local use).

Blackmar Gut, canalized channel, 0.2 mi. long, 0.05 mi. wide, Dare County, Kinnakeet Township (USGS 2013: Rodanthe). Trends e-w from Rodanthe Harbor into Chicamacomico Channel in Pamlico Sound, 0.3 mi. w of Rodanthe, entrance to Rodanthe Harbor. Coast Guard dredged (1936) to provide access to Chicamacomico Life Saving Station (only federal government dredging at the Outer Banks, not by ACE). Coast Guard records have no indication for naming (existed before dredging). "Blackmar" is from old English "black more," meaning black marsh or bog. Also, "mar" has occasionally been used for marsh at the Outer Banks mostly through spoken use. Also a surname, unknown here. Reason for naming is simply reference to appearance of marsh here and merely misrecording local pronunciation for "blackmire." Given credence by use of three-word forms Black Mar Gut and Black Mire Gut early 20th century. Two other names nearby descriptive of such coloration: Black Hammock and Black Bottom. *Other names:* Back Mar Gut (occasional misprints; *see* Alligator Gut), Black Mar Cut (some original use), Black Mar Gut (Garrity-Blake 2010, 78), Black Mire Gut (early use), Rodanthe Harbor (Garrity-Blake 2010, 492), The Creek (1930s and 1940s).

Blackmar Gut. *See* Chicamacomico Channel.

Black Pelican Beach, beach, 1.5 mi. long, Dare County, Kinnakeet Township (signage). At Ramp 34 Cape Hatteras National Seashore, 2 mi. n of original Avon. NPS has parking and beach access ramps variously placed and a few have acquired names.

Blair Channel, channel, 1 mi. long, Carteret County, Portsmouth Township; and Hyde County, Ocracoke Township (USGS 1950: Portsmouth). In Ocracoke Inlet just e of Wallace Channel, 2.2 mi. sw of Ocracoke (village). *Other names:* Blairs Channel (C&GS 1900), North Channel (occasional historical use when comparing to Wallace Channel), Pamlico Creek (Mallinson et al. 2008, 11), Ship Channel (descriptor became limited-use name), Ships Channel (Whisnant and Whisnant 2010, 125).

Blair Channel Reef, linear shoal, Hyde County, Ocracoke Township (Weslager 1954). N-s trending, follows Blair Channel e side 2 mi. from just n of Ocracoke Inlet and just w of Teaches Hole Bar n to Nine Foot Shoal Channel. "Reef" in Outer Banks geographic names usually refers to oyster colonies.

Blind Ridge, sand ridge, Dare County, Atlantic Township (Currituck DB 1a, 1763, 147–48). Exact location unknown but described on "Bank Land on Kitty Hawk Bay," so was most likely one of numerous ridges in Kitty Hawk ridge-and-swale system (q.v.) just w to 3 mi. w of original Kitty Hawk. Could be reference to lack of good view, usual from ridges here. Use of "blind" often refers to numerous blinds used throughout the Outer Banks (especially n part) for camouflage when hunting, but probably not here. *Other names:* Smith Ridge (Harris 2017; unknown, 1763).

Blinds Hammock, marsh islands, 0.2 mi. long, Carteret County, Harkers Island Township (USGS 2013: Harkers Island). At nw corner of Blinds Hammock Bay just w of Great Marsh Island, 3.5 mi. sse of Harkers Island (village). Reference to "blinds" or shacks and lean-tos used as camouflage while hunting. *See* Black Hammock.

Blinds Hammock Bay, cove, 0.4 mi. wide, Carteret County, Harkers Island Township (USGS 2013: Harkers Island). In Back Sound just s of Sheep Island Slue, 3.8 mi. sse of Harkers Island (village). *See* Blinds Hammock.

Blinds Hill, sand dune, Carteret County, Harkers Island Township (Stick 1958, 309). Was reportedly highest point in Cape Hills, considerably higher in mid-19th century, topography of Cape Lookout and environs changed greatly over past 100 years. Location reportedly was near first lighthouse at Cape Lookout (NPS 2004b, 13). Name meaning not remembered, could be reference to blind for hunting (though usually in water); lack of a view is doubtful because noted as a high point. *Other names:* Blinds Hills (some references).

Blockade Shoal, shoal, Dare County, Nags Head Township (historical local use). In Croatan Sound at nw Roanoke Island, 5 mi. nw of Manteo (center). Acquired name from makeshift blockade of pilings and old sunken ships placed by Confederates during Civil War to defend Roanoke Island, now mostly covered with sediment, creating a shoal.

Blossie Creek, water passage, 0.4 mi. long, Dare County, Nags Head Township (USGS 2013: Oregon Inlet). Separates Off Island and Bodie Island trending nw-se, 5 mi. se of Wanchese. Made official by USBGN 1980 to avoid confusion with Clubhouse Creek. *Other names:* Clubhouse Creek (NOS and C&GS charts, named for nearby hunting club).

Blount Bay, cove, 1.1 mi. long, 0.6 mi. wide, Dare County, Atlantic Township (USGS 2013: Kitty Hawk). At n end of Colington Island just s of Kitty Hawk Bay, 3.3 mi. s of original Kitty Hawk. *Other names:* Blounts Bay (local use), Brunts Bay (mispronunciation), Colington Bay (occasional local use).

Blowfish Island, probable island, Carteret County, Atlantic Township (Burkholder et al. 2017, 178). Burkholder et al. (2017) report associated with Ophelia Inlet (q.v.) but provide no other locative information. Limited discussion with locals indicates no knowledge of feature. Northern puffer (blowfish, *Sphoeroides maculatus*) occurs here.

Blubber Island Number 1, island, 0.3 mi. long, Currituck County, Fruitville Township (Cox 1923). N island of Blubber Islands at se entrance Fresh Pond Bay, 2 mi. ese of Knotts Island (village). *See* Blubber Islands. *Other names:* Little Blubber Island (local use).

Blubber Island Number 2, island, 0.3 mi. long, Currituck County, Fruitville Township (Cox 1923). S island of Blubber Islands at se entrance Fresh Pond Bay, 2.2 mi. ese of Knotts Island (village). *See* Blubber Islands. *Other names:* Big Blubber Island (some local use).

Blubber Islands, elongated marsh islands, together 0.7 mi. long, Currituck County, Fruitville Township (Cox 1923). Two n-s islands at se entrance Fresh Pond Bay, 2.1 mi. ese of Knotts Island (village). Unknown if name connected to whaling efforts during 18th and 19th centuries, but this was practiced more on s Outer Banks (generally only n to Cape Hatteras area). *See* Cape Lookout Grounds and Try Yard Creek.

Blubber Pond. *See* Plover Pond.

Blueberry Ridge, ridge, 0.75 mi. long, Dare County, Nags Head Township (signage). Trends n-s in Nags Head Woods, s Round-About Hills just n of Jockeys Ridge.

Blue Fin Canal, canal, Dare County, Nags Head Township (Town of Nags Head 2000, 91). Main and largest canal in Old Nags Head Cove subdivision, 2 mi. n of Nags Head Island, 9 mi. s of original Kitty Hawk. *See also* Nags Head Cove.

Blue Heron Pond, small pond with two sections, each 0.1 mi. long, Dare County, Atlantic Township (HOA official). Ponds with two distinct sections on either side of N.C. Route 12 in s Sanderling, 3.5 mi. n of Duck (village center); e pond n-s and w pond e-w with drainage to Currituck Sound. Enhanced and named by developer.

Blue Hill. *See* Bare Hill.

Blue Water Pond, man-made lake, Dare County, Nags Head Township (local informants). At entrance to Pirates Cove, 2.2 mi. sw of Manteo (center). Those interviewed are split 50/50 whether named for adjacent restaurant, or restaurant named for pond. Impossible to determine, pond and restaurant created about same time.

Bluff Point, former point, Currituck County, Fruitville Township (Byrd 1728, 40, 42). Was at n side Currituck Inlet just s of North Carolina–Virginia boundary, 3.5 mi. ene of Knotts Island. Existed only during early colonial period because Currituck Inlet closed 1731 and point disappeared. *Other names:* Cowpenpoint (Stick 1958, 23), High Land (Byrd 1728).

Bluff Shoal, large shoal, 20 mi. long, Hyde County, Lake Landing and Ocracoke Townships (NOS 2014b). In Pamlico Sound from mainland to Royal Shoal, 10.5 mi. nnw of Ocracoke Inlet. Very large shoal existing almost unchanged since early colonial mapping. *Other names:* Bluff Shoals (Wimble 1733), Bluff Shole (early 18th-century spelling), Bluf Shole (Wimble 1738), Machapunga Bluff (Collet et al. 1770; early-use name—*see* Machapunga Shoal).

Bluff Shoals Slough, small channel, Hyde County, Lake Landing Township (White 2012, 165). At halfway point in Bluff Shoal (officially no "s") near former Bluff Shoal Light, 7.5 mi. nnw of Silver Lake, Ocracoke (village). Not dependable, but provided e-w break in Bluff Shoal. *See* Allen Slough.

Boat Channel, channel, 1.3 mi. long, Carteret County, Davis Township (local use). Approach to Great Island Landing (q.v.) 2.5 mi. se of Davis (mainland). Descriptive term became name.

Boat Creek, cove, Carteret County, Atlantic Township (N.C. Fisheries 1923, 48). Just n of Horse Island (Atlantic Township), n side of Long Point, 5 mi. e of Atlantic (mainland). Remnant of former Long Point Inlet.

Boat Creek, tidal stream, Dare County, Kinnakeet Township (Garrity-Blake 2010, 493). Just s of former Little Kinnakeet, 3 mi. n of original Avon. Not to be confused with Boat Creek 5.5 mi. s at former Big Kinnakeet Coast Guard Station. Confusing, two tidal streams with same name at two nearby former Coast Guard Stations but suggestive of function. Possibly confused application, but documentation suggests both names correct.

Boat Creek, cove, 0.1 mi. wide, Dare County, Kinnakeet Township (USGS 2013: Buxton). In Pamlico Sound just s of Askins Creek at site of former Big Kinnakeet Coast Guard Station, 2 mi. s of original Avon. Not to be confused with Boat Creek 5.5 mi. n at former Little Kinnakeet Coast Guard Station. Confusing, two tidal streams with same name at two nearby former Coast Guard Stations but suggestive of function. Possibly confused application, but documentation suggests both names correct.

Boat Island, former island, Currituck County, Poplar Branch Township (C&GS 1852). Was in Lone Oak Channel between North Burris Island (s) and Porpoise Marsh (n), 4.5 mi. ssw of Corolla.

Boatswain Inlet, canal, Dare County, Atlantic Township (local use). At Colington Harbour, 2.5 mi. wsw of Kill Devil Hills (town). "Inlet" not used in traditional sense on the Outer Banks as barrier island breach, because indicative of dredging allowing water inward for access by boats to open water (Albemarle Sound). Canal naming scheme at Colington Harbour is ships or nautical terms. "Boatswain" is noncommissioned officer responsible for rigging and boats on a ship and who "pipes" commands to seamen ("swain" means dependable male, usually rural).

Bobs Cove, small cove, Carteret County, White Oak Township (Stephens 1984, map back cover). In w original Emerald Isle, just e of Montgomery Point 4.5 mi. w of Salter Path.

Bobs Cove, former community, Carteret County, White Oak Township (Stephens 1984, 6). At Bobs Cove just e of Montgomery Point between former communities Bell Cove e 1 mi. and Yellow Hill w 1 mi. Named for Robert Willis, original settler. As with small communities w of Salter Path, families eventually moved to Salter Path by early 20th century for various reasons. *See* Bogue Banks historical communities.

Bobs Island, marsh island, 0.2 mi. long, Dare County, Atlantic Township (USGS 2013: Jarvisburg). In Currituck Sound, 5 mi. nw of Duck. *Other names:* Bobby Island (rarely used diminutive reference).

Bockle Point. *See* Yaupon Point.

Bodens Point. *See* Rhodoms Point.

Bodie Island, former island, 10 mi. long, Dare County, Nags Head Township (USGS 2013: Roanoke Island NE, Oregon Inlet). Now connected at n end to Currituck Banks, e of Roanoke Island. Nw from historical Chickinacommock Inlet to former Roanoke Inlet just s of original Nags Head. Matthew Midgett (Midyett) acquired island from Lords Proprietors 1722. Name appears on maps early 18th century as Body Island, with first appearance of name Bodie in Mouzon and La Rouge (1777) map. Origin of "Bodie" (pronounced body) unclear, often presented as surname by some researchers (probably not), or from bodies strewn on the beach from a ship wrecked on the island, as folk etymology. No clear evidence of any shipwreck having occurred resulting in this name. Also reported spelling was changed from Body to Bodie to avoid confusion with reference to human body, but this, too, is folk etymology.

The word "body" referred to ship hull 17th through 19th centuries. Another source suggests descriptive name, it was the practice in deeds in early Virginia to refer to certain units of land as a "body of land," and many early maps labeled this island Body Island. Original cartographic application might have been merely an attempt to record description of land grant or unit of land.

Original s limit was Chickinacommock Inlet but varied over years with shifting inlets. Many early 20th-century charts showed s end as far s as New Inlet, closed 1945 and reopened 2011. Today s boundary is Oregon Inlet. N end has varied and extended occasionally and erroneously n to Kitty Hawk and beyond, agreed at former Roanoke Inlet. Subdivision named for feature.

Bodie Island made official by USBGN 1891 to clarify name most commonly used. *Other names:* Boddie Island (old deeds), Boddies Island (Joshua Judson Davis Papers, 1888, from Smith 2001, 99), Bodeys Island (historical documents), Bodie Island Spit (NCDOT 2013, 2–14—"spit," long narrow peninsula, used because Bodie Island no longer an island after Roanoke Inlet closed 1811, now terminates at Oregon Inlet), Bodies Island (Collet et al. 1770), Bodie Spit (Garrity-Blake 2010, 19), Bodyes Island (Currituck DB 3, 1803, 409), Body Island (Lawson 1709, map), Body Island Spit (scientific reports), Bodys Island (Currituck DB 8, 1799, 228), Brodie Island (19th-century typographical error), Cow Island (Moll 1729), Dugs Island (Moseley 1737—*see* Dugs), Essex Ile (Smith 1624, map—probable gesture to Earl of Essex, England, but as with names used by Smith, not used elsewhere), Essex Island (*see* Essex Ile), Etacrewac (late 17th-century maps—indigenous reference), Isle de Michard (Nolin 1783), Isle Micher (Bellin 1757), Michards Island (Wimble 1738), Micher Island (Stick 1958, 277), Misher Island (Stick 1958), Nags Head Island (N.C. Fisheries 1923, 62—from unidentified letter November 19, 1870; descriptive misinterpretation), North Bank (Maule 1718; also subdivision), The Flats (local descriptive use early 20th century).

Bodie Island Beach, historical beach, 10 mi. long, Dare County, Nags Head Township (local use from subdivision). Originally nw from former New Inlet or Chickinacommock Inlet, now considered Oregon Inlet to former Roanoke Inlet just n of Whalebone Junction. Popular late 18th and early 19th centuries and, while rarely used today, is experiencing reuse. Subdivision named for feature. *See* Bodie Island. *Other names:* Bodys Island Beach (Currituck DB 27, 1855, 296), Hollywood Beach (sizable subdivision, s-central part).

Bodie Island Beach. *See* South Nags Head.

Bodie Island Lighthouse Pier, former landing, Dare County, Nags Head Township (Hitchcock 2014, 50). Was at Cedar Point, 0.5 mi. w of Bodie Island Lighthouse. Built 1871 to service lighthouse, by early 1900s only remnants, today no trace.

Bodie Island Lighthouse Pond, large man-made lake, 1 mi. long and 0.5 mi. wide, Dare County, Nags Head Township (Sorrie 2014, map, 72). On Bodie Island (no longer island) just e of Bodie Island Lighthouse, 3.5 mi. n of Oregon Inlet. Marsh pond enhanced by Bodie Island Gun Club 1920s. *See* Bodie Island. *Other names:* Lighthouse Pond (local use).

Bodie Island Marshes, marsh, 0.5 mi. across, Dare County, Nags Head Township (Outer Banks Visitors Bureau Brochure 2016). Soundside Bodie Island just s of Whalebone Junction, 3.5 mi. e of Manteo (center). *See* Bodie Island.

Bodie Island Marsh Pond, pond, Dare County, Nags Head Township (Boone 1988). On former Bodie Island 1.8 mi. n of Bodie Island Lighthouse Pond, 5.5 mi. n of Oregon Inlet.

Bodie Island ponds, marshes, and dunes, area, 4 mi. long, 1.5 mi. wide, Dare County, Nags Head Township (Sorrie 2014, map, 76). On Bodie Island (no longer island) 5 mi. nnw of Oregon Inlet. Not actual geographic name per se but defined for scientific study of flora and fauna. Included because useful identifying this complex natural area. Complex of fresh to brackish marshes, shallow ponds, and mostly stable sand dunes. Most of natural area covered with marshes, with number of man-made and natural ponds intermixed. Marshes are brackish soundside, some are freshwater interior. *See* Bodie Island.

Bodies Island Anchorage, former anchorage, Dare County, Nags Head Township (CS 1883). Was in n Pamlico Sound 6 mi. w of Oregon Inlet and s Bodie Island. Used as temporary place to anchor and wait on appropriate tides entering and exiting Oregon Inlet during middle to late 19th century. *See* Bodie Island.

Bodines Cove. *See* Marsh Cove.

Bog Channel, former channel, Dare County, Kinnakeet Township (CS 1852). Was in Pamlico Sound just w of Little Kinnakeet, 3.2 mi. n of original Avon.

Bog Opening, elongated marsh, 0.7 mi. long, Dare County, Kinnakeet Township (local use). On n Hatteras Island just s of Little Kinnakeet, 3.7 mi. n of original Avon.

Bogue Banks, barrier island, 25 mi. long, Carteret County, Morehead and White Oak Townships (USGS 2013: Beaufort, Mansfield, Salter Path, Swansboro). Trends e-w from Beaufort Inlet to Bogue Inlet, separates Bogue Sound from Atlantic Ocean. Plural form still used because of divisions (inlets) in past, though today is one continuous unit. Most of Bogue Banks was originally granted to Christopher Gale 1720. His descendants sold most holdings in different-sized parcels to numerous people. In 1910 John A. Royall (*sic*) purchased w end, from Bogue Inlet to Rice(s) Path (now partially Royall Oaks subdivision).

Bogue is one of the oldest names along the Outer Banks. Certain authors (including Bright 2007) believe Bogue might derive from *bok*, American Indian Choctaw word stream or water passage. Numerous place names in Mississippi, Alabama, and Louisiana also use Bogue; some scholars believe "bogue" entered French and Spanish via Choctaw. Could be matter of coincidence in form and sound, however; some believe was imported much earlier into French and Spanish via Occitan (language formerly spoken in s France, Catalonia in n Spain, and n Italy), itself drawn from Latin *boca* (mouth), which in Spanish means "mouth," so possible the Spanish applied Bogue to an inlet resembling a mouth of a stream. Use of the term in U.S. Gulf area conversely could indicate an earlier Spanish nautical term referring to movement toward the leeward or side opposite the wind. Spanish frequently visited and raided places along the Outer Banks. Here the barrier islands are oriented e-w (sharp contrast to those elsewhere), conceivable this Spanish reference to "land to the leeward" found its way onto contemporaneous maps and charts given its importance in navigation. Whatever the source and original meaning, evolved as reference to a marshy or swampy area (bog). In addition to North Carolina, Mississippi, Alabama, and Louisiana, "Bogue" can be found in 11 other U.S. states, but these applications are transfer names or merely applied to marsh as a result of evolution of meaning of the word. Two further possibilities are that the name derives from Scottish surname reportedly brought here (suggestion local genealogists discuss), but name precedes this settlement. Could relate to European fish with same name, not supported by documentation.

Together with Shackelford Banks, e Bogue Banks was known as Stanford Islands (q.v.) in colonial period. Today, local residents report they are wholly unfamiliar with that name, not surprising since that name appeared only on a few 18th-century maps. Some maps applied Borden(s) Banks to much of e Bogue Banks, Borden family of Beaufort owned a large portion early 1800s.

Other names: Banc Bogue (Bellin 1764), Bogue Bank (brochures and CS 1857a), Bogue Banks Island (Rivers and Ball 1961), Bogue Beach (Colton, 1870), Bogue Island (Tompson and Albert 1854), Bogue Isle (local references, 1800s, especially in Salter Path), Borden Bank (historical), Bordens Bank (Price *et al* 1808), Bordens Banks (Tanner 1855), Bordens Island (Meyer and Tanner 1849), Borg Island (early 18th-century maps from PKS 2016, pronunciation), Boug Bank (Wimble 1738), Burdens Island (Moseley 1733 inset), Cape Lookout Banks (occasional misapplication), Isle Bogue (Bellin 1757), La Frondfriere (*sic*) (Bellin 1764—*fondrière*, quagmire in French), Sanford Island (mentioned in PKS 2016 appearing on maps early 1700s, but likely is Stanford), Stanford Banks (Mouzon 1775), Stanford Island (Wimble 1738), Stanford Islands (Romans 1776).

Bogue Banks Beach, beach, 21 mi. long, Carteret County, Morehead and White Oak Townships (scientific papers). Entire length of Bogue Banks. *See* Bogue Banks.

Bogue Banks historical communities, Carteret County, Morehead and White Oak Townships (Stephens 1984). Scattered settlements in 19th and early 20th centuries generally between Salter Path and Archer (Arthurs) Creek, from e to w: Rice(s) Path, Hopey Anns Hill, Bills Point, Yellow Hill, Bobs Cove, and Bell Cove. There was also small settlement at Hoop Pole Creek (q.v.), but not usually related to those w of Salter Path. Additionally, Roses Path was farther

w near entrance to Langston Bridge (not normally associated with other settlements w of Salter Path). From late 1800s to early 1900s most residents of these settlements (except possibly Roses Path and Hoop Pole Creek) moved to Salter Path (q.v.) for various economic reasons (*see* each entry separately). In these settlements kunners, hollowed-out log-boat (more than dugout), often with sail, used well into late 1800s (Stephens 1984, 10–11); not used (referenced) much past Civil War on n Outer Banks (*see* Piliauga Creek).

Bogue Banks historical paths, areas, Carteret County, Morehead and White Oak Townships. Use of path for routes was common on the s Outer Banks (Bogue Banks). Some incidental use on n Outer Banks 1700s, especially in Kitty Hawk (*see* Jacks Cabin Path), but these references are few and only to footpaths that never developed into the specific "paths" used by people from mainland or soundside on Bogue Banks for activities on the barrier island and beach. In some cases developed into small communities (most no longer exist, with people moving to Salter Path, mainland, and elsewhere). *See* Lowenberg Path, Oglesby Path, Rice(s) Path, Roses Path, Sage Path, Salter Path, and Uncle Johns Path. No doubt there were others, but these were recorded. *See also* Bogue Banks historical communities.

Bogue Inlet, water passage, 0.6 mi. wide, Carteret County, White Oak Township; and Onslow County, Swansboro Township (USGS 2013: Swansboro). Trends n-s from Bogue Sound to Atlantic Ocean, separates Bogue Banks from Bear Island, 3.3 mi. s of Swansboro (mainland). Bogue Inlet, one of three inlets open continuously since before 1585 (also Beaufort Inlet and Ocracoke Inlet). *See* Bogue Banks. *Other names:* Bogue Einfahrt (Lucas 1826—*einfahrt*, inlet in German), Bogue Inlett (Barnwell-Hammerton 1721), Bouge Inlet (Purcell 1788), Boug Inlet (Wimble 1738), Bougue Inlet (Blunt 1857, 346), Entré de Bogue (Nolin 1783), Passe Bogue (Bellin 1757), Topsail Inlet (misapplication from Beaufort Inlet [q.v.]).

Bogue Inlet Bar, shoal, Carteret County, White Oak Township (local use). At entrance Bogue Inlet, 4.5 mi. sw of Langston Bridge, 3.5 mi. s of Swansboro (mainland). *See* Bogue Banks.

Bogue Pines, area, Carteret County, Morehead Township (local use). Generally between Hoop Pole Creek (e) and Pine Knoll Shores (w). Recent term with subdivision development, includes street name and small marina.

Bogue Pines Boat Basin, harbor (private), Carteret County, Morehead Township (N.C. Marine Fisheries, 2019, E3, map 1). In w Bogue Pines area 3.2 mi. w of Atlantic Beach.

Bogue Point, point, 0.5 mi. across, Carteret County, Morehead Township (History of Fort Hampton). Entire e end point of Bogue Banks at Fort Macon, 1.5 mi. sw of Beaufort (mainland). *See* Bogue Banks. *Other names:* Core Point (Brazier 1833), Fort Macon Point (Stick 1958, 312), Lands End (some use), Macon Point (CS 1850a), Point Macon (Blunt 1857, 345), West End (subdivision same name).

Bogue Shores, area, Carteret County, Morehead Township (local use). Applied around shore of Hoop Pole Bay, 2 mi. w of Atlantic Beach (town). *See* Bogue Banks.

Bogue Shores Channel, channel, 3.5 mi. long, Carteret County, Morehead Township (Carteret County GIS 2019). Trends e-w in Bogue Sound just n of Bogue Shores and Hoop Pole Bay, 2.3 mi. w of Atlantic Beach (town).

Bogue Sound, lagoon, 25 mi. long, 2.5 mi. wide, Onslow County, Swansboro Township; and Carteret County, Morehead and White Oak Townships (USGS 2013: Beaufort, Mansfield, Salter Path, Swansboro). Trends e-w from Back Sound at Beaufort (mainland) to White Oak River at Bogue Inlet, separates Bogue Banks from mainland. *See* Bogue Banks. E end Bogue Sound spanned by Atlantic Beach—Morehead City Bridge, third such bridge: first was plank bridge built 1928, replaced by drawbridge 1953, then by high-rise bridge 1980s. W end Bogue Sound spanned by Langston Bridge, opened 1971, named for B. Cameron Langston of N.C. Highway Commission in recognition of efforts to procure a bridge for this part Bogue Banks. *Other names:* Core Sound (Finley and Young 1827—misapplication), Gore Sound (Holland 1794—misinterpretation of "Core" and misapplication, accounts for use of Gore Sound Entrance for Beaufort Inlet), Newport Sound (early 18th-century misapplication of Newport River, flows into junction Core

Sound and Bogue Sound), Rouge Sound (J. H. Colton 1856), The Bay (Sauthier 1770), The Sound (Sauthier 1770).

Bogue Sound Canal, canal, 0.6 mi. long, Carteret County, White Oak Township (Collette 2017). Trends e-w beginning just w of Montgomery Point to 0.5 mi. s of w tip of Long Island on n shore Bogue Sound subdivision in original Emerald Isle, 5 mi. w of Indian Beach (town). Canal this size would seemingly have an official name, but numerous interviews with residents varying in age indicate feature known simply as The Canal, though Carteret County GIS Office indicates Bogue Sound Canal is often used. Further, those interviewed and GIS Office confirm 0.6-mi.-long island created by The Canal is unnamed, though sometimes the descriptive reference Bogue Sound Island is used. *See* Bogue Banks. *Other names:* The Canal (occasional reference).

Bogue Sound Channel, small channel, Carteret County, Morehead Township (Williamson 1992, 173). Connects Morehead City Channel and Bogue Sound, 3.5 mi. se of Morehead City (mainland). *See* Bogue Banks.

Bogue Sound Ferry Dock, former dock, Carteret County, White Oak Township (NCDOT 1960). Was near where Langston Bridge leaves Bogue Banks in s Emerald Isle and provided service from the mainland from 1962 to 1971, when Langston bridge opened.

Bogue Sound Island, island, Carteret County, White Oak Township (local reference). In original Emerald Isle, trends e-w 0.5 mi. from just e of Montgomery Point to point 0.5 mi. s of w tip Long Island, 5 mi. w of Indian Beach (town). Created by Bogue Sound Canal but is really an unofficial name, initially merely descriptive given by land developers. No recorded name for the island with the county government, but this name used as the reference. *See* Bogue Banks. *Other names:* The Island (some references).

Boiler, The. *See* Pea Island Beach.

Bold Dune, prominent sand ridge, 1 mi. long (some consider it 2 mi.), Dare County, Kinnakeet Township (local use). In Waves (occasionally s to Salvo), 2 mi. s of Rodanthe.

Bonito Street Beach. *See* Whalehead Beach (subdivision).

Bonneys Store, former community, Currituck County, Fruitville Township (historical local use). Was at intersection of roads just ene of Knotts Landing, 1.7 mi. s of Knotts Island (village). Bonney surname appearing in early deeds. *Other names:* Bonnys Store (transcribing error).

Boor Creek, tidal stream, Dare County, Nags Head Township (Currituck DB 6, 1789, 68–69). Somewhere on Roanoke Island, reference deed (1768) provides no clue to exact location. Name suggests possibility of s Roanoke Island. Unusual name with no other known occurrence of its application. Probably no relation to use by present definition of "boor" (an uncultured person) or to original Dutch, meaning boring into something. Could be peculiar spelling of "bore," a rapidly moving tide pushing up a wave in front. Even so, this too seems an unusual application, as tidal bores are rare at the Outer Banks, especially around Roanoke Island. Boor is a rare surname but was not here, though could be a derivative of Burrus, surname here. Name and use remain a mystery.

Bordens Banks, former barrier island, 20 mi. long, Carteret County, Morehead and White Oak Townships (Price and Strother 1798). Was most of what is now Bogue Banks, from former Cheeseman Inlet to Bogue Inlet. Name applied short time to this part of Bogue Banks because most then owned by Borden family (probably William Borden) of nearby Beaufort (mainland). Burden Channel and Burden Reef are legacy names in Bogue Sound at w end Bogue Banks remaining from this early application. *Other names:* Borden Banks (PKS 2016), Burdens Island (Moseley 1733 inset).

Bottle Run Point, point, Carteret County, Harkers Island Township (USGS 2013: Harkers Island). On small marsh island in Back Sound 4.9 mi. nw of Barden Inlet. Point of sand island so not likely for flowing stream as "run" was applied occasionally on n Outer Banks. Named since early 19th century. According to variety of residents of Beaufort (mainland), name refers to rum running throughout 19th century, and especially later during U.S. Prohibition (1920–33). Also alludes to one story of a "booze yacht" running aground here; these were used for smuggling alcohol and parties. Rum-running origin is believed most by local folk. Also might reference bottlenose dolphins (*Tursiops truncatus*).

Bowers Old Field, former area, Dare County, Atlantic Township (Currituck DB 13, 1814, 52–55). Exact location unknown but was on Big Colington and believed to be at nw part, historical area and reference no longer used. Probable variation and reference to surname, Bowser, known here since colonial period with vague references to s Colington Island once known as Bowsers. *Other names:* Bowsers (might be original, surname used for other nearby features).

Bowser Island, narrow elongated island, Dare County, Nags Head Township (local use). Sandbar oriented n-s in Roanoke Sound 1 mi. sw of Tommy Hammock, 4.5 mi. sw of Whalebone Junction. Local opinion divided over location. Most indicate location given here, but some indicate Bowser Island is actually just s of The Causeway between Pond Island (nw) and Headquarters Island (se), 1 mi. sw of Whalebone Junction. Bowser, surname here since colonial period (*see* Bowers Old Field).

Bowsertown, area, Dare County, Nags Head Township (signage). This "community" is in Manteo, not an officially named place, name used locally because surname prevalent along this particular street, bearing name Bowsertown Road. Surname known here since colonial period. *Other names:* Bowser (some usage), Bowsers (occasional local usage).

Bragg Dock, former landing, Carteret County, Portsmouth Township (NPS 2018, 94). Was in Portsmouth at Styron-Bragg House in Core Sound just n of Baymarsh Thorofare (n end).

Braggs Dock, former dock, Hyde County, Ocracoke Township (Howard, July 21, 2012). Was in Ocracoke (village) near Gary Bragg's decoy house near Cedar Grove Inn (location not exact). Listed as "Gary Braggs dock gone" (photograph of hurricane board a method of displaying in houses the destruction by hurricanes).

Braggs Mill and Windmill, former mill and windmill, Hyde County, Ocracoke Township (Howard, January 21, 2013). Believed to be in Cat Ridge area of Ocracoke just n of Springers Point near Ocracoke Lighthouse 0.5 mi. sw of Ocracoke (village center).

Brant Island, former small island, Carteret County, Beaufort Township (U.S. Navy 1839). Was just se of Morehead City (mainland), 3 mi. sw of Fort Macon. Created from dredge material from work on port at Morehead City between 1930s and 1950s. Incorporated into Elijah Lump, no longer exists. *See* Brandt Isle, Brant Island (Pamlico County). *Other names:* Brandt Island (historical use).

Brant Island, elongated marsh island, 0.7 mi. long, Currituck County, Poplar Branch Township (USGS 2013: Mossey Islands). Extreme nw extension of Mossey Islands complex, 3.5 mi. ssw of Corolla. Name origin could be a surname, but is for gray-bellied brant geese (*Branta bernicla bernicla*) migrating to Outer Banks in winter. An intriguing observation is "brant" originally in Old English meant high or steep and since settled in late 1600s and early 1700s might have relevance: Brant Island is large and higher than the general marsh island with some small high spots. Moss Island has become attached to Brant Island. *Other names:* Brant Marsh (C&GS 1852), North Pine Island (C&GS 1852—mistaken application, in Mossey Islands complex not Pine Islands complex few miles s).

Brant Island, former island, Pamlico County, Township 4 (CS 1865). Was a portion of much larger Brant Island Shoal in w Pamlico Sound just w of mainland 25 mi. w of Ocracoke (village). Was prominent (often two islands) during 19th century, by mid-20th century former island mostly inundated, with bare sand shoal at low tide. Named for gray-bellied brant geese (*Branta bernicla bernicla*) migrating here in winter. Additionally, an intriguing observation is "brant" originally in Old English meant high or steep, area always islands or shoals since colonial times so might have relevance. Use of Brant in names here could also be surname but not likely. *Other names:* Brandts Island (Walton 1867), Brants Island (NPS 2012, 16), Gull Island (Holland 1794).

Brant Island. *See* Elijah Lump.

Brant Island Pond, cove, 0.4 mi. wide, Currituck County, Poplar Branch Township (USGS 2013: Mossey Islands). At e side Brant Island just w of Sanders Bay, 3.6 mi. ssw of Corolla. *See* Brant Island (Currituck County) and Adams Pond. *Other names:* Brant Marsh Pond (C&GS 1852).

Brant Island Shoal, shoal, 7.3 mi. long, Carteret County, Cedar Island Township; and Pamlico County, Township 4 (NOS 2014i). In Pamlico

Sound 20.3 mi. wnw of Ocracoke (village). Name in different forms since early 1700s, also applied between Ocracoke Inlet and Royal Shoal (Moseley 1733). *See* Brant Island (Pamlico County). *Other names:* Brandt Island Shoal (Blunt 1857, 343), Brant Island (CS 1883), Brant Island Shoals (Stick 1958, 83), Brant Island Shole (Wimble 1733), Brant Shoal (Wimble 1738), Brant Shole (early 18th century).

Brant Shoal, former small shoal, Carteret County, Portsmouth Township (CS 1857b). Was at w inside Ocracoke Inlet ne of Portsmouth (village), 5 mi. sw of Ocracoke (village). One of many named historical shoals associated with ever-shifting Ocracoke Inlet, still bares at low tide occasionally. *See* Brant Island (Pamlico County).

Brant Shoal Channel. *See* Horse Island Channel.

Brant Shoal Marsh, former marsh, Carteret County, Portsmouth Township (NPS 2007, map, 35 and 36). Was just s of Brant Shoal just e of Portsmouth (village), 5 mi. sw of Ocracoke (village). S of Brant Shoal formerly on section Dry Sand Shoal, which changed configuration continuously, by 21st century disappeared. *See* Brant Island (Pamlico County).

Brant Shoal Point, point, Carteret County, Portsmouth Township (Williamson 1992, 128). Most exposed point of small Brant Shoal just ne of former Portsmouth Life Saving Station in Portsmouth (village), 4.7 mi. sw of Ocracoke (village). *See* Brant Island (Pamlico County).

Brant Shoal Rocks, rocks, Carteret County, Portsmouth Township (C&GS 1866). Three to six exposed rocks depending on tide level just s of Brant Shoal, just ne of Portsmouth (village), 5.7 mi. sw of Ocracoke (village). *See* Brant Island (Pamlico County). *Other names:* Brandt Rock (NPS 2006, 51), Brant Rock (NPS 2006, 28).

Bread and Coffee Ridge, small sand ridge, Dare County, Hatteras Township (Garrity-Blake 2010, 292). In sse Hatteras (village), just ne of Deering Ridge (sometimes considered part of Deering Ridge) 4.5 mi. sw of Frisco. Descriptive name of an activity, obviously whimsical. Most local residents not aware of name.

Breakwater Point. *See* Power Squadron Spit.

Brick Creek, small tidal stream, Dare County, Kinnakeet Township (Garrity-Blake 2010, 492). Soundside just s of Midgett Island, 1.4 mi. s of Waves. Name origin unexplained in source, and name or its location not remembered by anyone. Probably descriptive with rumors of a kiln here or nearby, but no proof.

Briery Hills, sand dunes, Carteret County, Stacy Township (Stick 1958, 308). Descriptively named hills, n portion South Core Banks just s of former Cedar Inlet, 3 mi. ssw of Ophelia Inlet. Smaller now than 18th and 19th centuries. *Other names:* Brier Hills (Stick 1958, 308).

Brigand Bay, marsh, 0.5 mi. across, Dare County, Hatteras Township (local use). Just e of Brigands Bay subdivision, 2.6 mi. w of Buxton. Name came into use with establishment of Brigands Bay subdivision (note plural), case of reversed usage, natural feature acquiring name of man-made feature. *Other names:* Robbs Salt Marsh (historical, in part), Davis Salt Marsh (historical, in part).

Brigand Bay Canal, short canal, 0.3 mi. long, Dare County, Hatteras Township (Dare County Planning Department 2009, map 12E, 71). Trends e-w from s Brigands Bay subdivision into Pamlico Sound, 3 mi. w of Buxton. *See* Brigands Bay subdivision. Entrance access canal to Canals at Brigands Bay (q.v.).

Brigands Bay, subdivision, Dare County, Hatteras Township (signage). On Hatteras Island, 3 mi. w of Buxton. "Brigand" means bandit, a robber often associated with sea. Has become colorful, less offensive, hence its choice of name, developed during early 1960s as subdivision. Made official as Brigand Bay (for federal usage—singular) by USBGN, recommendation of NOS. However, signage and local use clearly are plural form. *Other names:* Brigand Bay (USGS 2013: Buxton; real estate brochures).

Broad Creek, water passage, 1 mi. long, Currituck County, Fruitville Township (Cox 1923). Trends n-s separating Bush Island and Mary Island from the barrier island (Currituck Banks), 3 mi. se of Knotts Island (village).

Broad Creek, cove, 3.2 mi. long, 0.5 mi. wide, Dare County, Nags Head Township (USGS 2013: Wanchese, Manteo). Trends nw-se in Roanoke Sound just ne of Wanchese, 5.8 mi. se of Manteo (center). Subdivision named for feature. *Other names:* Town Creek (Maule 1718).

Broad Creek Point, peninsula, l mi. long, Dare County, Nags Head Township (USGS 2013: Oregon Inlet). On se Roanoke Island at ne entrance mouth of Broad Creek, 2 mi. nne of Wanchese. Sometimes name application only to extreme point of peninsula (usually state maps).

Broad Ridge, short sand ridge, Dare County, Atlantic Township (Harris 2017). In Kitty Hawk just e of extreme s Kitty Hawk Ridge, 2 mi. nnw of Kill Devil Hill.

Brock Basin, harbor and marina, Carteret County, Morehead Township (PK Association 2016). In Pine Knoll Waterway (w portion), Pine Knoll Shores, 4.7 mi. w of Atlantic Beach (town). Harbor and marina completed with second (w section) of Pine Knoll Waterway 1971. Named for Don Brock (surveyor) by the Roosevelt family (inheritors and developers Pine Knoll Shores), which with A. C. Hall were instrumental in completing Pine Knoll Waterway. *Other names:* Pine Knoll Shores Marina (Carteret County GIS 2019).

Brock Bay. *See* Sanders Bay.

Brocks. *See* Peters Quarter.

Brocks Sand, beach, 1 mi. long, Currituck County, Poplar Branch Township (Codman, Crowninshield, and Lawrence 1925). Straight and regular soundside beach in Peters Quarter at n end Sanders Bay just n of Monteray Shores, 4.7 mi. s of Corolla. Name Brock Bay known to be in limited local use for short time for Sanders Bay. Unusual form for beach name where generic "beach" usually used, not "sand"—only known such occurrence.

Brooks Creek, cove, 0.1 mi. wide, Carteret County, Harkers Island Township (USGS 2013: Harkers Island). In Back Sound at nw Harkers Island, 4.1 mi. e of Beaufort (mainland).

Brooks Creek, cove, 0.3 mi. long, 0.1 mi. wide, Dare County, Hatteras Township (USGS 2013: Buxton). Between Brooks Point (q.v.) and Kings Point 7.2 mi. nne of Hatteras (village). *Other names:* Clarks Creek (Covey 2018, map 34), Kings Creek (Covey 2108, 41).

Brooks Creek Marina, harbor, Carteret County, Harkers Island Township (signage). At nw corner of Harkers Island between Harkers Point subdivision (n) and Harkers Village (s), 1.8 mi. wnw of Harkers Island (village center). *Other names:* Knuckles Harbor (N.C. Marine Fisheries 2019, E7, map 27—not known nor used).

Brooks Ditch, water passage, Dare County, Hatteras Township (local use). At Brigands Bay, formerly was narrow ditch separating Brooks Island from Hatteras Island, but now more flooded and wider No longer displaying ditch-like characteristics.

Brooks Island, island, Dare County, Hatteras Township (local use). In Pamlico Sound at Brigands Bay just n of Brooks Creek, 3 mi. w of Buxton.

Brooks Point, point, Dare County, Hatteras Township (USGS 2013: Buxton). At n entrance to Brooks Creek at Brigands Bay on n shore of s Hatteras Island, 7.4 mi. nne of Hatteras (village). Named since 1717 mention in a deed of Henry Gibbs. *Other names:* Brooke Point, Long Point (short-usage descriptive name).

Browns Island, island, 1.6 mi. long, 0.8 mi. wide, Carteret County, Harkers Island Township (USGS 2013: Harkers Island). In Core Sound 1.1 mi. s of mainland, 1.7 mi. ne of Harkers Island (village) separated from Harkers Island by Westmouth Bay and Eastmouth Bay. Connected to Harkers Island off and on until early 20th century.

Browns Point, point, Hyde County, Ocracoke Township (ACE 1896 or 1897). On Ocracoke Island, was much closer to Ocracoke Inlet 19th century (inlet migrated se), 0.5 mi. s of Springers Point, 1.5 mi. s of Ocracoke (village). Name fallen into disuse.

Browns Point Shoal, former shoal, Hyde County, Ocracoke Township (House of Representatives 1895). Was in Ocracoke Inlet at Browns Point just n of First Grass, 0.5 mi. s of Springers Point, 1.5 mi. s of Ocracoke (village center).

Brughs Ridge, small sand ridge, 0.5 mi. long, Hyde County, Ocracoke Township (local use). Higher ground (as is Ocracoke village), 0.5 mi. e of Silver Lake. Named for Doward and Jackie Overton Brugh (Howard, July 22, 2018). *Other names:* Brughts Ridge (old street sign).

Bryant Shoal, small shoal, Hyde County, Ocracoke Township (local use). In Pamlico Sound just e of Green Island just w of Tar Hole Inlet, 2.5 mi. w of Hatteras Inlet. Occasionally bare, but usually covered by 1 ft. of water. Name not well known; a few folk indicated they had "seen it on a map," but not on official maps. Possibly could have been originally Brant (*see* Brant Shoal [Pamlico County]).

Buccaneer Canal, canal, 0.3 mi. long, Dare County, Nags Head Township (PC HOA 2016). One of seven named canal segments interconnected throughout Pirates Cove, named portions corresponding with limits of adjacent named subdivisions. Trends nw-se 1.5 mi. se of Sandy Point at Roanoke Island Festival Park, 2.5 mi. w of Whalebone Junction. *See* Canals at Pirates Cove.

Buck Island, island, 0.1 mi. wide, Currituck County, Fruitville Township (USGS 2013: Barco). In Buck Island Bay at s end Mackay Island, 3.2 mi. sw of Knotts Island (village). Name is related to male deer. *Other names:* Hoskins Island (occasional early use), Hoskinses Island (Currituck DB 6, 1789, 15).

Buck Island Bay, cove, 0.7 mi. wide, Currituck County, Fruitville Township (USGS 2013: Barco). In nw Bellows Bay at s end Mackay Island, 2.9 mi. sw of Knotts Island (village). *See* Buck Island. *Other names:* Duckpond (n part—USGS 1943: Back Bay 1:62,500 scale).

Buckle Island. *See* Mon Island.

Buck Ridge, sand ridge, 0.5 mi. long, Dare County, Atlantic Township (Currituck DB 7, 1794, 133). S tip of Kitty Hawk Ridge just e of Kitty Hawk Woods Swamp (q.v.) complex just n of original Kitty Hawk. "Buck" normally refers to male deer but could here also mean stark, an antiquated term from bare of vegetation used occasionally in colonial era (c.f. "buck-naked"—meaning all but forgotten even in dictionaries and today "butt naked" is substituted).

Bulk Head, The, former shoal scarp, Carteret County, Portsmouth Township (Price 1795, 628). At nw scarp Bulk Head Shoal when the latter was largest, just e of former Ship Channel just e of Bulkhead Channel just nnw of North Rock 4.5 mi. w of Ocracoke (village). *See* Bulk Head Shoal and Bulkhead Shoal. *Other names:* Bulk Head (Hooker 1850), Bulk Head Shoal (Blunt 1809).

Bulk Head, The, former steep-sided shoal, Hyde County, Ocracoke Township (CS 1853). Was at n terminus of primary channel for Hatteras Inlet 19th century, 2 mi. n of Point of Beach, the e terminus of Ocracoke Island, 6 mi. w of Hatteras (village). Hydrography changed since mid-19th century, no longer exists in original form. *See* Bulkhead Shoal. *Other names:* Bulkhead (Foster 1866a).

Bulkhead Channel, channel, Carteret County, Beaufort Township (USGS: 2013 Beaufort). Trends n-s, separates Radio Island from Bulkhead Shoal just sw of Beaufort (mainland). Officially part of Beaufort Channel (since 1986), but name and application still used.

Bulkhead Channel, former channel, Carteret County, Portsmouth Township (historical local use). Was in Pamlico Sound, connected Flounder Slue to open sound, 5.5 mi. w of Ocracoke (village). *See* Bulkhead Shoal.

Bulkhead Shoal, shoal, Carteret County, Beaufort Township (C&GS 1953). Trends n-s between Radio Island and Town Marsh just sw of Beaufort (mainland). Today joined with Bird Shoal w end.

Bulkhead Shoal, shoal, Dare County, 3 mi. long, Nags Head and Kinnakeet Townships (1882 Oregon Inlet Survey from Angley 1985, 11). Shoals in crescent shape n side and w side Old House Channel, leads to Oregon Inlet; center of shoal 2 mi. w of Oregon Inlet, 3.5 mi. se of Wanchese. Developed after Oregon Inlet opened 1846 and changeable with varying levels of water but essentially in same area as when formed. Descriptive name indicating wall-like nature of the shoals ("bulkhead" is any wall anywhere on a ship and a wall to "shore up" a shoreline), meaning usually steep edge of a shoal, used mostly from Oregon Inlet to Ocracoke Inlet throughout 19th century. One-word and two-word forms used, though two-word form appears more late 18th and early 19th centuries while one-word form appears later by process of concatenation, as often occurs in English (c.f. "blue bird" vs. "bluebird"). *Other names:* Sand Shoals (ACE 1948).

Bulk Head Shoal, former large shoal, Hyde County, Ocracoke Township; and Carteret County, Portsmouth Township (Coles and Price 1806). Considerable former presence after passing through Ocracoke Inlet from Teaches Hole in nw curving arc to just n of North Rock at The Bulk Head, 3.5 mi. w of Ocracoke (village). No longer exists, exhibiting changeable nature of Ocracoke Inlet, where features were created and destroyed often in short time periods, especially after violent storms, so many

of these shoals overlapped one another during different time periods. *See* Bulkhead Shoal. *Other names:* The Bulkhead (House of Representatives 1895).

Bulkhead Swash, former shoal, Hyde County, Ocracoke Township; and Carteret County, Portsmouth Township (McGuinn 2000, 22). At former Bulkhead Shoal, 3.5 mi. w of Ocracoke (village). Was swash at massive Bulk Head Shoal (late 18th and early 19th centuries). *See* Daniel Swash. *Other names:* North Channel Swash (occasional historical use), North Swash (McGuinn 2000, 135).

Bull Island. *See* Bush Island.

Bullocks Creek, stream or water passage, Currituck County, Fruitville Township (Currituck DB 1a, 1766, 190–92). Somewhere on Knotts Island, probably n Knotts Island. Name probably was applied to Capsies Creek, but no documentation. Bullocks mentioned vaguely in 1700s deeds near Indian Creek, so could have been anywhere. *See* Bullocks Neck.

Bullocks Neck, peninsula, Currituck County, Fruitville Township, (Currituck DB 5, 1787, 291). Somewhere on Knotts Island, though exact location is unknown. Name could have applied to Simpson Neck or Whites Neck, though Whites Neck is on s Knotts Island and this feature likely on n Knotts Island. Could also have applied to short, blunt peninsula, the n-most extension of Knotts Island into Virginia. Named for (or by) George Bullock, a very early settler here, and no relation to cattle. No extant documents when Bullock arrived at Knotts Island; however, in a Virginia–North Carolina boundary case (1711) Bullock made the statement, "the surveying began 1711 but failed, and then resumed 1728." In his deposition, Bullock indicated he had been at Knotts Island for about 50 years, which would be around 1661. Deed simply indicates Bullocks Neck as "on Knotts Island."

Bull Ridge, short sand ridge, Dare County, Atlantic Township (Currituck DB 5, 1785, 40). Just e of Broad Ridge in original Kitty Hawk, 1 mi. n of North Cove (ne Kitty Hawk Bay), 3.2 mi. s of Southern Shores. *See* Kitty Hawk ridge-and-swale system. *Other names:* Bull Rige (Currituck DB 5, 1785, 40).

Bull Ridge Islands, islands, Dare County, Atlantic Township (Harris 2017; unknown, 1825). According to Harris (2017), islands somewhere in Kitty Hawk ridge-and-swale system (q.v.), w of original Kitty Hawk or possibly in Kitty Hawk Bay. Harris associates islands with Bull Ridge but does not provide additional information, and as named feature does not appear in early deeds. No islands, now or historically, were near Bull Ridge or anywhere in Kitty Hawk Bay or North Cove. Far-fetched, this name could have been applied to Kitty Hawk Bay Islands or any islands grouped in Kitty Hawk Bay Islands and still be associated with Bull Ridge. So, name and its application remain a mystery.

Bull Ridge Marsh, marsh, Dare County, Atlantic Township (Currituck DB 5, 1787, 272; N.C. Division of Coastal Management 1998, 19). Just w of Bull Ridge in original Kitty Hawk, 3 mi. s of Southern Shores (*see* Kitty Hawk ridge-and-swale system). Associative name from Bull Ridge. *Other names:* Bool Rig Marsh (Currituck DB 10, 1809, 106—spelling not standardized until early 19th century), Bullridge Marsh (Currituck DB 7, 1795, 274), Bull Run Marsh (local references).

Bulls Point, point, Currituck County, Fruitville Township (F&WS 1984, map, 74). Protrudes into s central Barleys Bay just w of former Coreys, 2.5 mi. wnw of Knotts Island (village).

Bunch of Hair, island, 0.05 mi. long, Carteret County, Harkers Island Township (USGS 2013: Harkers Island). Just n of Shackleford Banks at entrance to Johnsons Bay, 2.5 mi. s of Harkers Island (village). Descriptive name refers to appearance.

Bunton Island, former islands, Dare County, Nags Head Township (C&GS 1923). Were in Croatan Sound, remnants of Roanoke Marshes just sw of Roanoke Island, 2.5 mi. sw of Wanchese. Several islands here known as Bunton Islands until 1930s, when only one island remained, accounting for last form used singular; last vestige disappeared in 1950s. *Other names:* Bunton Islands (historical local use), Bunton's Islands (C&GS 1883).

Buoy Shoal, mentioned by Weslager (1954). Probably does not apply to any specific shoal, likely a variant name applied to different shoals having buoys at some time. Interviews have yielded no specific information, confirmed by interviews with Ballance (2017, 2018) and Howard (2017, 2018).

Burden Channel, channel, 1.1. mi. long, Carteret County, White Oak Township (USGS 2013:

Swansboro). Trends ne-sw in Bogue Sound at w end Bogue Banks, 2.5 mi. se of Swansboro (mainland), connects Banks Channel and Intracoastal Waterway. Originally Burthen Channel on historical maps, evolved to Burden Channel just after mid-20th century. Legacy name 1700s when this part of Bogue Banks known as Bordens Banks. *Other names:* Burthen Channel (USGS: 1952 Swansboro; USGS: 1948 Swansboro 1:62,500 scale,), Burthon Channel (late 19th-century charts).

Burden Reef, island, Carteret County, White Oak Township (local use). Just s of mainland and just n of Burden Channel, 2 mi. w of Langston Bridge, 3.5 mi. se of Swansboro (mainland). Variant name Bordin Rif taken from report of wreck of steamer *Blanch #12267*, October 21, 1911; spelling was a challenge in these reports. "Reef" in Outer Banks geographic names usually refers to oyster colonies. *See* Burden Channel. *Other names:* Bordin Rif (Williamson 1992, 204).

Burnside Headquarters, historical site, Dare County, Nags Head Township (USGS 2013: Manteo). On w Roanoke Island, 1.5 mi. w of Manteo (center). Campsite from which Union General Ambrose Burnside directed defeat of Confederate forces, thereby establishing control of the Outer Banks and coastal area for Union. *Other names:* Camp Burnside, Fort Burnside (Civil War maps—camp, no real fort).

Burnside Wharf, former landing, Dare County, Nags Head Township (C&GS 1910c). Was just n of Pork Point at former Burnside Headquarters (Civil War) 1.5 mi. w of Manteo (center). No trace remains.

Burnt Island, marsh island, 0.5 mi. long, 0.3 mi. wide, Dare County, Atlantic Township (USGS 2013: Kitty Hawk). In Kitty Hawk Bay, in Kitty Hawk Bay Islands just n of Sloop Island (Frying Pan Island), 1.9 mi. s of original Kitty Hawk.

Burris Bay, bay, 0.6 mi. across, Currituck County, Poplar Branch Township (USGS 2013: Mossey Islands). Between Big Narrows and Beasley Bay, just e and n of Burris Islands complex, 1.9 mi. w of Currituck Banks, 6.5 mi. s of Corolla. *See* Burris Islands. *Other names:* Burris Channel (q.v.; based on perception, separates North Burris Island and South Burris Island).

Burris Break. *See* Jarvis Channel.

Burris Channel, water passage, Currituck County, Poplar Branch Township (local use). Separates North Burris Island from South Burris Island, 7 mi. s of Corolla. Actually two channels with remnants of Middle Burris Islands. Originally more usage for n-most channel, but recently shifted to s-most channel, more open now. Burris, surname here. *Other names:* Burrus Channel (some local spellings).

Burris Islands, marsh and shoal complex, Currituck County, Poplar Branch Township (USGS 2013: Mossey Islands). In Currituck Sound 2 mi. s of Mossey Islands complex; sometimes Burris Islands considered s portion Mossey Islands complex, 6.5 mi. s of Corolla. Burris Islands complex originally composed of North Burris Island (q.v.), West Burris Island (q.v.), East Burris Island (q.v.), South Burris Island (q.v.), and Middle Burris Islands (*sic*) (q.v.). Names South Burris Island and West Burris Island used interchangeably for same feature (today only South Burris Island is used). East Burris Island changed over the years, now w North Burris Island. Middle Burris Islands became three smaller islands between North Burris Island and South Burris Island. Burris, surname here.

Bush Island, island, Currituck County, Fruitville Township (Cox 1923). Is 2 mi. n of Currituck Bay, 3.5 mi. se of Knotts Island (village). Occasionally with Mary Island and North Bush Island referenced as Northern Islands in relation to Middle Marsh (now unknown).

Bush Island, island, less than 0.1 mi. across, Currituck County, Poplar Branch Township (USGS 2013: Mossey Islands). In Beasley Bay and Hog Islands complex, 6.7 mi. s of Corolla. Original name was Bull Island, fits naming scheme in Hog Islands (q.v.) complex, but corrupted over the years into Bush Island. *Other names:* Bull Island (C&GS 1852).

Bush Shoal, small shoal, Carteret County, Portsmouth Township (Williamson 1992, 120). In Pamlico Sound, 1 mi. nw of Casey Bay, 2.5 ml. w of former Portsmouth Life Saving Station in Portsmouth (village).

Buxton, village, Dare County, Hatteras Township (USGS 2013: Buxton). On n shore s Hatteras Island, 9.7 mi. ne of Hatteras (village). Post office est. 1873 as The Cape (original community name) until 1882, when it changed to Buxton to honor Judge Ralph P. Buxton. *Other names:* Cape (MacNeill 1958, 200), Cape Hatteras (Torres 1985, 116), Cape Hatteras Indian Town (NPS 2005b: NPS 1, 230), Indian Town (sometimes slang usage because original Hatteras Indian village was nearby), The Cape (Colton and Company 1887).

Buxton Beach, beach, Dare County, Hatteras Township (NPS 2016). At Cape Hatteras adjacent to old location of Cape Hatteras Lighthouse, 1.5 mi. se of Buxton. Variant name Buxton Lifeguard Beach used sometimes (NPS brochures) to indicate NPS provides lifeguard service here during the summer. *See* Buxton. *Other names:* Buxton Lifeguard Beach (NPS 2016).

Buxton Channel, channel, 1.3 mi. long, Dare County, Hatteras Township (Dare County Planning Department 2009, map 12 F, 72). Trends se-nw just n of e Buxton and Buxton Landing to Buxton Harbor Channel, 5.3 mi. ssw of original Avon. *See* Buxton.

Buxton Harbor, small harbor, Dare County, Hatteras Township (Dare County Planning Department 2009, map 12 F, 72). In w Buxton at s terminus Buxton Harbor Channel just n of Flowers Ridge, 8 mi. ssw of original Avon. *See* Buxton.

Buxton Harbor Channel, channel, 4.6 mi. long, Dare County, Hatteras Township (local use). Trends s from Cape Channel in Pamlico Sound, 1.3 mi. nw of Buxton. Inner portion originally referred to as Cape Channel, remnant of one of the inlet channels of Chacandepeco Inlet (q.v.). Made official by USBGN 1982 revising a previous decision (1976) to clarify relation to Cape Channel. *See* Buxton. *Other names:* Buxton Channel (USGS 1950: Buxton 1950; NOS field crew notes 1985), Cape Channel (historical local use), Muddy Slue (U.S. Navy 1918).

Buxton Inlet, former water passage, Dare County, Kinnakeet Township (Mallinson et al. 2008). Was 2.5 mi. nne of Buxton and 3 mi. s of original Avon near former Chacandepeco Inlet. Opened March 1962 and spanned by bridge; however, another "nor'easter" storm destroyed the bridge December of same year. Afterward, ACE concluded inlet should be filled, accomplished 1963. Canadian Hole remains from dredging fill for the inlet. Was between original Avon and Buxton known in scientific circles as an "overwash zone," today as breach zone, meaning even if no inlet opens, during storms often water covers the barrier beach for a time (named the Haulover [q.v.]). Breached a short time during a storm 1999. *See* Buxton. *Other names:* Cape Inlet (locational local use), New Buxton Inlet (Frankenberg 1995, loc. 920), New Inlet (practice then naming newly opened inlets "New" until remaining open—*see* Ophelia Inlet).

Buxton Landing, landing, Dare County, Hatteras Township (USGS 2013: Buxton). On Hatteras Island 0.2 mi. n of Buxton. *See* Buxton. *Other names:* Back Landing (historical use).

Buxton Woods, maritime forest, 1.2 mi. long, 0.5 mi. wide, 17 ft. high, Dare County, Hatteras Township (USGS 1950: Buxton). Is 1.3 mi. n of Cape Hatteras. Some reports, scientific studies, and local official documents apply Buxton Woods from s Buxton w to w Frisco. Spencers Woods (q.v.) is just s of Brigands Bay, and Frisco Woods (originally Trent Woods in part) is at Frisco. Subdivision named for feature. *See* Buxton. *Other names:* Buxton Wood (MacNeill 1958, 47), Cape Hatteras Woods (Stick 1958, 293), Cape Pines, Cape Woods (historical use, included Frisco Woods [q.v.]), Hatteras Pines (in part—recent use from subdivision name), and Hatteras Woods (Stick 1958, 293).

Buzzard Bay, bay, Currituck County, Fruitville Township (F&WS 1999, map 11). Just e of Buzzard Island in n Currituck Marshes 2 mi. e of Knotts Island (village). *Other names:* Crab Cove (some local use).

Buzzard Bay, bay, 1.1 mi. wide, Dare County, Atlantic Township (USGS 2013: Manteo). In Albemarle Sound just s of Colington Island, 4.2 mi. nw of Nags Head (center). Variant Jacoxe is a variation of Jacock, itself morphed into Jackey, and then to Jockey(s). Variations of Jacock found in deeds dating 18th century for land adjacent to Buzzard Bay and where Jockeys Ridge (q.v.) is located. *Other names:* Jacoxe Bay (Harris 2017, likely from deeds).

Buzzard Island, marsh island, 0.5 mi. across, Currituck County, Fruitville Township (Cox 1906). In maze of marsh islands just n of Walk Island, 2 mi. ne of Knotts Island (village).

Buzzard Lead, narrow water passage, 0.8 mi. long, Currituck County, Poplar Branch Township (USGS 2013: Mossey Islands). Passage through Mossey Islands complex connecting n extremity of Wells Creek and

Wells Bay at Currituck Sound, 5.2 mi. s of Corolla. Exact implication of "lead" here is unclear, probably reference to known passage through marsh since as nautical term "lead" refers both to following a direction and an opening through some impediment, marsh, or shoals. "Lead" appears several times on n Outer Banks where several large marsh complexes exist. Was also used early in process of taking sounding readings, where the line lowered for sounding termed "lead line," and might be applicable here. Only occurrences encountered in Pamlico Sound s-ward is Mail Lead at Rodanthe and Mailboat Lead in original Avon, where meaning is slightly different. "Lead" is also used as a nautical term referring to course or length of rope, and to an artificial watercourse. Known in local fishing by use with "lead net," but normally in open water and probably not applicable when used with names.

Buzzard Point, point, Currituck County, Poplar Branch Township (C&GS 1852). At sw entrance Buzzard Lead 1 mi. w of Three Dunes, 3 mi. ssw of Corolla.

Buzzard Point, point, Dare County, Atlantic Township (USGS 2013: Manteo). At e end of Buzzard Bay, 1.3 mi. s of Colington (community).

Buzzards Island, marsh island, Currituck County, Poplar Branch Township (C&GS 1852). Ne of and adjacent to Porpoise Marsh, 4 mi. ssw of Corolla. *Other names:* Sedge Island (Buzzard Island across Wells Creek from Sedge Island and features often confused).

Cabs Creek, water passage, 0.6 mi. long, Carteret County, Harkers Island Township (USGS 2013: Harkers Island). Trends sw-ne from Bald Hill Bay to Back Sound, 2.3 mi. ssw of Harkers Island (village).

Cactus Hill, sand dune, Hyde County, Ocracoke Township (local use). Soundside at Little Swash Opening, 1.3 mi. sw of The Knoll, 5 mi. ne of Ocracoke (village). Almost entire island can have prickly pear cacti (*Opuntia* sp.),

which grow well in sandy soil of the Outer
Banks. Area covered with plants.

Caffeys Inlet, former water passage, 0.1 mi.
long, Dare County, Atlantic Township
(historical maps). Formerly cut through
Currituck Banks, 4.3 mi. nnw of Duck
(center). Open from about 1770 to 1810
(closing process began about 1800) but
still shown on CS (1862a) marked "closed."
Named for George Caffey (sometimes Caffee
or Cafee), who owned considerable amount
of land around the inlet. Variant name
South Inlet still labeled here on J. Colton's
(1861) map, though closed for about 50
years (name used in relation to former New
Currituck Inlet). Most authorities place
location here, but some geomorphological
evidence (relict flood data) indicates location
possibly 1.5 mi. n near present Pine Island
Airport, or possibly this was another inlet
open for a short time and unrecorded. Stick
(1958) indicates families here but offers
no additional information nor a name.
One informant also corroborates this by
indicating a small scattered community
here historically named Sanderlin (*sic*) or
Sanderling (q.v.), but no documented (only
circumstantial) proof of this historical
community. Two subdivisions named for
feature. See Sanderling. *Other names:* Cafees
Inlet (Currituck DB 12, 1812, 177–78), Caffee
Inlet (Stick 1958), Caffees Inlet (Currituck
DB 7, 1794, 124–25), Caffess Inlet (Currituck
DB 7, September 17, 1796, 458), Caffey Inlet
(C&GS 1879), Caffreys Inlet (Stick 1958,
169), Carthey Inlet, Cartheys Inlet (Dunbar
1958), Carthys Inlet (Dunbar 1958; Price and
Strother 1798), Coffey Inlet (Currituck DB
1819, 434–35), Coffeys Inlet (Cobb 1906),
New Currituck Inlet (N.C. Division of Coastal
Management 1998, 14—misinterpretation),
Providance Inlet (Currituck DB 7, 1795, 183–
84), Providence Inlet (Stick 1958, 9), Smith
Inlet (Fisher 1962, 90), South Inlet (Meyer
and Tanner 1849), Trinety Harbor (confusion
with closed Trinety Harbor), Trinitie Harbor.

Caggs Creek, water passage, 0.4 mi. long,
Carteret County, Smyrna Township (USGS
2013: Horsepen Point). In Core Sound,
separates unnamed marsh island from Core
Banks, 4 mi. e of Harkers Island (village).
Name reportedly local surname, though an
alternate explanation for consideration is
"cagg," an early and corrupted form of "cag,"

itself evolved into "keg" used heavily on
ships of 16th–19th centuries.

Calf Island, former small island, Currituck
County, Poplar Branch Township (C&GS
1852). Was just se of and adjacent to North
Hog Island, 6.2 mi. s of Corolla. *See* Hog
Islands.

Calico Jacks Marina, harbor, Carteret County,
Harkers Island Township (former use). Was
at extreme se end of Harkers Island just w
of Cape Lookout National Seashore facilities,
reportedly no longer used.

California, former settlement (now
subdivision), Dare County, Nags Head
Township (USGS 2013: Manteo). On n-central
Roanoke Island in Manteo, 0.6 mi. wsw of
Manteo (center). Name origin unknown
specifically or not remembered but still used
today. Records indicate real estate venture
early 1900s originally named Manteo
Extended was here. However, California was
originally name of this area dating to Civil
War as a temporary place for freed slaves
supposedly yearning for California. Smith
(2001, 36) confirms many freed Negroes
settled here but does not mention name
origin. Two subdivisions named for feature.
Other names: Little California (local use),
Manteo Extended (subdivision name, local
documents).

Callis Drain, former waterway, Dare County,
Hatteras Township (1759 deed). Mentioned
1759 deed in conjunction with Cutting Sedge
Marsh (q.v.) likely between Buxton and Frisco
just w or n of Cutting Sedge Marsh.

Camp Bailey, former small temporary military
camp, Dare County, Hatteras Township
(Covey 2018, 60). Union camp (Civil War) in e
Frisco probably soundside halfway between
Buxton and Frisco.

Camp Burgwyn, former military camp, Carteret
County, Morehead Township (historical
documents). Confederate camp reportedly at
(now) Atlantic Beach.

Camp Cass Williams, camp, Hyde County,
Ocracoke Township (USGS 2013: Howard
Reef). Just s of Quokes Point, 5.1 mi. ne of
Ocracoke (village). Use of temporary "camps"
on the Outer Banks (mostly on Core Banks)
has been a practice of people who live
on mainland (and Outer Banks) used for
various purposes, mostly fishing and later
for sports hunting, though today former Ira
Morris Camp, now Long Point Camp, is for

fishermen and tourists. *Other names:* Cass Williams Camp (USGS 2002, 1950 Howard Reef).

Camp Dan Russell, former military camp, Carteret County, Morehead Township (historical documents). Temporary military camp 1898 just outside Fort Macon for African American troops during Spanish American War.

Camp Foster. *See* Fort Huger.

Camp Gary Braggs, camp, Hyde County, Ocracoke Township (USGS 2013: Green Island). On Ocracoke Island seaward of Knoll Creek, 7.6 mi. ne of Ocracoke (village). *See* Camp Cass Williams. *Other names:* Gary Braggs Camp (USGS: 2011, 1950 Green Island).

Camp Georgia, former military camp, Dare County, Nags Head Township (historical documents). Confederate camp on n Roanoke Island, exact location unknown. Not used by Union as were Camp Reno and Camp Foster.

Camp Jourdan, former military camp, Dare County, Nags Head Township (historical documents). Confederate camp on n Roanoke Island exact location unknown. Not used by Union as were Camp Reno and Camp Foster.

Camp Magellan, area, Carteret County, Morehead Township (PKS 2016). Specific location unknown, but was one of original lots in Aibonito, central Pine Knoll Shores. This named place was a rustic cabin where the owner, Captain Young, and family spent "several winters" according to PKS (2016). Many such seasonal places were given names by their owners. Entry included to illustrate usage of "camp" differing from traditional usage of temporary and seasonal fishing and hunting camps. Reason for choice of name not provided.

Camp Meeting Grounds, former area, Dare County, Atlantic Township (Wescott 1958, 5). Was at e end Kitty Hawk Bay and North Cove, 1 mi. s of original Kitty Hawk, 1.5 mi. se of Kitty Hawk Methodist Church. Late 19th-century churches held revivals and religious meetings known locally as camp meetings. One held here 1887, only such meeting known to be held by Kitty Hawk Methodist Church. Three other such meetings known to be held by other churches on Colington Island (Wescott 1958, 5).

Camp Point, point, Carteret County, Cedar Island Township (USGS 2013: Wainwright Island). On unnamed marsh (sometimes considered part of Hog Island), 2 mi. e of Cedar Island Ferry landing, 10.6 mi. sw of Ocracoke (village), used as temporary hunting and fishing campsite.

Camp Raleigh. *See* Fort Huger.

Camp Reno. *See* Fort Huger.

Camp Seatone, former recreational camp, Dare County, Nags Head Township (Downing 2013, 71). On ne Roanoke Island near Morrison Grove and Crab Claw Spit, 2 mi. n of Manteo (center). Founded 1935 by Mabel Evans who, after earning educational degrees, created camp to serve recreational needs of local children. Operated until beginning of WWII (Downing 2013, 71–74).

Camp Trent, former military camp, Dare County, Hatteras Township (Torres 1985, 103). Was located few miles n of Fort Wool at Trent (Frisco) 6 mi. n of Hatteras (village).

Camp Washington, former military camp, Carteret County, Portsmouth Township (historical documents). Was one of main encampments of Confederate army on the Outer Banks and was on Portsmouth Island at Portsmouth (village). Abandoned with capture of Fort Hatteras August 29, 1861. Reportedly, also a battery here of a few guns.

Camp Wilkes, former military camp, Carteret County, Morehead Township (historical documents). Confederate camp believed to be 2 mi. w of Fort Macon at Money Island Beach.

Camp Winfield, former encampment, Dare County, Hatteras Township (historical documents). Was near Fort Totten in e Hatteras (village), disembarking site for Union troops moving n to Roanoke Island during Civil War. *Other names:* Windmill Picket ("picket," soldiers forward for warning).

Canadas Hill, sand dune, Carteret County, Harkers Island Township (Stick 1958, 309). Considerably higher mid-20th century, as topography of Cape Lookout and environs has changed greatly over past 100 years. Precise location unknown nor remembered considering changing topography but somewhere within 1–2 sq. mi. on Cape Lookout just s of Cape Hills and former Cape Lookout (village), 1.5 mi. ssw of Cape Lookout Lighthouse. Name origin unknown, and no one there (and also at Harkers Island) has any information regarding location or meaning. Name reported by Stick (1958), known early 1800s so connection to Canada would be tenuous.

Canadian Hole, sound floor hole, Dare County, Hatteras Township (USGS 2013: Buxton). In Pamlico Sound, 1.8 mi. n of Buxton. Named for popularity with tourists from Canada and who reportedly discovered its qualities, with ideal conditions for windsurfing and kiteboarding and milder winter weather than Canada. Name origin related by all interviewed and also confirmed in Outer Banks Scenic Byway (2008, 14) and several brochures. Remnant of dredged area to fill Buxton Inlet accomplished by ACE in 1963. *Other names:* Buxton Canadian Hole (NCDOT website, projects), Canada Hole (occasional use).

Canadian Hole Beach, beach, Dare County, Kinnakeet Township (local use). Used for beach at Kite Point, differing applications but usually extending 0.5 mi. n-s of Kite Point, center 3 mi. s of Avon. Name is recently associated with windsurfing and kiteboarding activity here. Name also applied soundside.

Canal, The, canal, 0.9 mi. long, Carteret County, White Oak Township (local officials and informants). Enters Emerald Plantation subdivision from Bogue Sound on w side, continues s 0.3 mi. then 90 degree turn e and continues 0.6 mi. where it sort of joins Archer Creek (q.v.) 9 mi. w of Indian Beach (town, w part). Those interviewed indicated most consider the canal an extension of Archer Creek, but also reference the canalized part in Emerald Plantation subdivision as simply The Canal.

Canal, The, canal, Currituck County, Fruitville Township (local use and road sign). Man-enhanced small stream flowed s then w into a tidal creek, though s part now almost nondiscernable, at Swan Beach (village), 1.3 mi. n of Pennys Hill, 5 mi. n of Corolla. More pronounced and canal-like in its n-s part. Folk asked thought it must or ought to have another name, but everyone just uses The Canal.

Canal, The, canal, 1 mi. long, Dare County, Atlantic Township (local informants). E-w from just n of stabilized Kill Devil Hill at n Wright Brothers National Memorial Park in Kill Devil Hills (town) to Pastor Pond 3 mi. s of original Kitty Hawk. Barely discernable now other than a vegetated ditch for much of the length, but clearly filled with water soundside at lower end. Before being canalized, historically was Pastor Creek (sometimes Parkers Creek) and emptied into Pastor Pond at Lemors Bay. Today, known simply as The Canal; seven people who live in the neighborhood through which the canal passes (15–20 years) agree the canal (now) has no specific name and is known simply as The Canal, which has become its name. *Other names:* Pastor Creek (historical use).

Canal Ridge, sand ridge, 0.8 mi. long, Currituck County, Fruitville Township (local use). Trends s-n with several saddles or low points and distinctive e-w hook-like formation on n end, 1.5 mi. n of Pennys Hill, 5 mi. n of Corolla. Derived from lying just w of canal known locally as The Canal, though sometimes just The Ridge is used for this sand dune. *Other names:* The Ridge (occasional local use).

Canal Ridge, sand ridge, 1 mi. long, Dare County, Kinnakeet Township (local use). In e and ne original Avon (Kinnakeet) n-s from just s of Mill Creek, 7.5 mi. n of Buxton. Originally higher, altered by many years of use and development to less than 10 ft. Subdivision named for feature.

Canals at Atlantic Beach, canals, Carteret County, Morehead Township. W set of canals in Cedar Hammock at Atlantic Beach Isles subdivision, greatly modified by development. Nine canals here just w of Atlantic Beach Causeway (w set): Smith Canal, Shelor Canal, Barefoot Canal, Willis Canal, Gale Canal, Pond Canal, Stanton Canal, Ipock Canal, New Causeway Canal, with two entrance channels, Royal Channel and Chadwick Channel. Three canals (e set) just e of Atlantic Beach Causeway in Sound View Isles subdivision; East Canal, Center Canal, and West Canal with central harbor area, Cooper Bay. *See* individual entries for more information.

Canals at Avon. *See* South'ard Water.

Canals at Baumtown. *See* Baumtown Canals.

Canals at Brigands Bay, canals, Dare County, Hatteras Township (local informants). Six canals dredged when Brigands Bay subdivision created 1960s; in Brigands Bay, in Frisco, 3.2 mi. w of Buxton. Five canals trend e-w 0.3 mi. and one canal trends n-s 0.3 mi. Five local year-round residents interviewed and all agree the canals are unnamed. Road names and individual owners' names are used for specific references. One street named Snug Harbor, but not applied to canal system. Brigand Bay Canal (singular) provides access from Pamlico Sound.

Canals at Carova (Carova Beach), canals, Currituck County, Fruitville Township. Comprises 27 canals dredged in Carova to provide lot owners access to Knotts Island Bay, 3.5 mi. e of Knotts Island (village). Most canals trend e-w with short n-s connector canals (ranging 0.1–0.2 mi. long). One canal trends n-s 1.5 mi. providing access to Knotts Island Bay for n two-thirds of these canals. Interviews with officials at County GIS Office and at Carova Volunteer Fire Department confirm canals are unnamed. Reference is to street by the canal. Still, some homeowners and lot owners probably have assigned their own names to these canals, but none have yet been determined.

Canals at Cedar Island, canals, Dare County, Nags Head Township. Four canals (actually one continuous canal) and larger entrance basin 0.1 mi., with three canals (0.1 mi.) trending n-s connected by one e-w trending canal (0.5 mi.). At Cedar Island and service Lone Cedar Village subdivision. According to residents, canals are unnamed.

Canals at Colington Harbour, canals, Dare County, Atlantic Township. Eleven named canals at Colington Harbour trending e-w, each 0.3 mi.: Baggala Inlet, Barkentine Inlet, Boatswain Inlet, Corsair Inlet, Dandy Inlet, Felucca Inlet, Forecastle Inlet, Frigate Inlet, Ketch Inlet, Sloop Inlet, and Tartan Inlet. Refer to each entry for information. Tartan Canal at 1 mi. provides access to Albemarle Sound from other canals.

Canals at Harkers Island. *See* Harkers Island Canals.

Canals at Kitty Hawk Landing, canals, Dare County, Atlantic Township (local informant—HOA official). Four unnamed canals. W-most canal exits Avery Pond and 0.2 mi. to Albemarle Sound. N-central canal trends n-s 0.1 mi. then turns w into Avery Pond. S-central canal trends n-s 0.4 mi., and e-most canal just w of Dancing Ridge, trends n-s 0.7 mi. ending just w of Big Pond. Canals are unnamed; reference is by street name (HOA official).

Canals at Manteo, canals, Dare County, Nags Head Township. Eight canals (each 0.3 mi.

long) in e Manteo just e of Doughs Creek just n of Ice Plant Island (Festival Park Island). S-most canal is Mosquito Canal, the only named canal; partially surrounds Ice Plant Island n and ne. Of other seven canals (ranging 0.2–0.3 mi. long), three trend e-w parallel to and n of Mosquito Canal (q.v.), three trend n-s, and one trends nw-se. Repeated interviews with numerous local officials, including dock master at Manteo, and other folk have confirmed (to them, anyway) all of these canals are unnamed except Mosquito Canal (descriptive name), likely because it was dredged in 1980s in conjunction with improvements on Ice Plant Island for Festival Park.

Canals at Old Nags Head Cove, canals, Dare County, Nags Head Township. Canal system in Old Nags Head Cove subdivision in Nags Head, 2.5 mi. nnw of Whalebone Junction. Nine canals: four n-s (three 0.3 mi., one much shorter), and five e-w canals (all 0.1 mi.). Entrance canal named Blue Fin Canal (q.v.), while others unnamed according to residents, though in some interviews indication was all canals are Blue Fin Canal and indeed one continuous canal system. *See* Nags Head Cove.

Canals at Oyster Creek (Ocracoke Village), canals, Hyde County, Ocracoke Township. Four canals here including entrance canal from Pamlico Sound and three ancillary perpendicular canals. Numerous interviews locally determined canals are unnamed. Method of reference is to "three bridges area" and to closest named street, by inference attributes street names to canals.

Canals at Paradise Bay, canals, Carteret County, Morehead Township. Four s-n canals here at Rock Point 0.1 mi. long each. According to residents these canals are unnamed, referenced by row (access) identifier, a letter (except for w-most), at Tradewinds Access. No entry in gazetteer for Paradise Bay as no feature by that name: mobile home park where these canals are located.

Canals at Pirates Cove, canals, Dare County, Nags Head Township. Seven named canals at Pirates Cove subdivision in Manteo, named portions of one continuous canal reflecting names of subdivisions in Pirates Cove: Ballast Point Canal, Buccaneer Canal, Hammock Canal, Rudder Canal, Sailfish Canal, Sextant

Canal, and Spinnaker Canal. Reference each entry for information.

Canals at Pond Island, canals, Dare County, Nags Head Township. Canal (0.1 mi.) and basin (0.1 mi. wide). Canal trends n-s on w side of Pond Island in Pond Island Marina subdivision. Basin in e portion Pond Island in Pond Island subdivision. According to residents these features are unnamed.

Canals at Sound Shores (Ocracoke Village), canals, Hyde County, Ocracoke Township. Two canals here, one with access from Pamlico Sound and one tributary canal from main canal. Determined by local interviews, canals are unnamed but referenced by the one bridge carrying Terrapin Drive and by other street names.

Canals at Southern Shores, Dare County, Atlantic Township (Town of Southern Shores 2015). Nineteen named canals in Southern Shores: Canvas Back Canal, Cormorant Canal, Curlew Canal, Gallinule Canal, Gannet Canal, Gravey Pond Canal, Great Blue Heron Canal, Herring Gull Canal, Loon Canal, Merganser Canal, Oystercatcher Canal, Pelican Canal, Royal Tern Canal, Sand Hill Crane Canal, Sandpiper Canal, Snow Goose Canal, Snowy Egret Canal, Whistling Swan Canal, and White Ibis Canal. Reference each entry for information.

Canals at Wanchese. *See* Wanchese canals, ditches, guts, and water passages.

Cannon Point, point, Carteret County, Morehead Township (PKS 2016). North from Bogue Banks into Bogue Sound just e of Salter Path, 4 mi. w of Pine Knoll Shores. *Other names:* Sea Isle Point (road sign).

Canoe Island, small island, Currituck County, Poplar Branch Township (C&GS 1852). At s entrance to Buzzard Lead, 0.5 mi. w of Sedge Island, 4 mi. ssw of Corolla.

Canvas Back Canal, canal, Dare County, Atlantic Township (Town of Southern Shores 2015). E-w–trending connector between junction of Gallinule Canal (s) and Gravey Pond Canal (n) with Snowy Egret Canal (w), 3.3 mi. n of original Kitty Hawk. Names of Southern Shores canals are for shorebirds (except Gravey Pond Canal). The canvasback duck (*Aythya valisineria*) is here during winter. *See* Canvasback Point.

Canvasback Point, point, Currituck County, Poplar Branch Township (USGS 2013: Mossey Islands). Nw point Indian Gap Island just

s of Jarvis Channel, 2 mi. s of Three Dunes, 6.2 mi. s of Corolla. Named for presence of large quantities of canvasback duck (*Aythya valisineria*) in winter. Mossey Islands complex is frequent stop by migrating birds along Atlantic Flyway, as many of the place names indicate. *Other names:* Canvas Back Point (spelling variation some 19th-century maps).

Canvasback Pond, lake, 0.4 mi. long, 0.1 mi. wide, Currituck County, Poplar Branch Township (USGS 2013: Mossey Islands). In n portion Mossey Islands complex, 4.3 mi. ssw of Corolla. *See* Canvasback Point.

Canvass Back Point, point, Currituck County, Poplar Branch Township (Codman, Crowninshield, and Lawrence 1925). On ne shore Ships Bay, 2.3 mi. nnw of Corolla. Variant spelling and form of the word is used here since "canvasback" (one word, no second "s") is official spelling for name of the duck. *See* Canvasback Point.

Canyon, The, area, 3 mi. long, Dare County, Kinnakeet Township (limited local use). On Pea Island beginning (n) just e of Green Island Channel 2 mi. s of Oregon Inlet continuing s to just e of North Pond at Pea Island National Wildlife Refuge 6.5 mi. n of Rodanthe. Highly localized with limited usage based on perception caused by narrow (less than 0.5 mi.) width of the barrier island and very high dunes here.

Cape Amidas. *See* Cape Kenrick.

Cape Channel, channel, 3.8 mi. long, Dare County, Hatteras Township (USGS 2014: Buxton, Hatteras). Extends nw in Pamlico Sound along n side Clam Shoal from Buxton Harbor Channel, 2.5 mi. nnw of Buxton. Made official by USBGN (1982) to clarify association with Buxton Harbor Channel. *Other names:* Buxton Harbor Channel (some local use).

Cape Creek, stream, 1.5 mi. long, Dare County, Hatteras Township (USGS 1950: Buxton). Trends to Pamlico Sound 1 mi. w of Buxton. Remnant of Chacandepeco Inlet (q.v.) and during storms subject to overwash and sound surge. Now joined by small stream, and application of name extended 1.5 mi. w. Originally, entry into Pamlico Sound was just ne of wider area known historically as Back Landing Creek (q.v.) because configuration of marsh has changed over the years. Two variant names from Brooks 2010 are 18th-century and older name applications (no longer used) to what has become Cape Creek. Known by Cape Creek in different configurations since mid-1700s. *Other names:* Back Landing Creek (NPS 2005b: NPS 1, 280), Callises Creek (Brooks 2010), Callises Dreen (Currituck DB 1741, n.b., n.p.—*see* Loghouse Dreen), Wallis Drain (Brooks 2010).

Cape Emerald. *See* The Marsh.

Cape Hatteras, cape, Dare County, Hatteras Township (USGS 2013: Cape Hatteras). On Hatteras Island 4.4 mi. s of Buxton. Name is for Hatteras (or Hatoraske) Indians but meaning of Hatteras generally vague and unclear, reportedly refers to sparse vegetation. Use of Engano by Spanish (*engaño*, deception in Spanish) indicates difficulty negotiating shoals here, though this application might be an error on some maps, as it was more often applied to Cape Lookout.

Use of variant names (especially Cape Saint John) before early 18th century was to this broad area or more likely Cape Kenrick (q.v.); many authors subsequently have mistaken these name applications as referring to Cape Hatteras when they actually refer to Cape Kenrick, which was the cape depicted on White's (1585 map) because Cape Hatteras was not yet fully developed. Cape Kenrick began to disappear late 17th century, leaving only remnant Wimble Shoals (q.v.), and contributing further to development at Cape Hatteras, which by early 1700s was developed much as it remains today.

Painting the design of the lighthouse at Cape Hatteras and the lighthouse at Cape Lookout is an interesting story. Design of the lighthouse at Cape Hatteras is spiral, but reportedly was originally supposed to be diamond shapes to relate to Diamond Shoals just off Cape Hatteras; however, as the story goes, paperwork was apparently mishandled and opposite occurred: diamond shapes are at Cape Lookout Lighthouse and spiral shape (known worldwide) is at Cape Hatteras Lighthouse (for preservation 1999 moved inland 0.5 mi. by NPS). This "story" is apocryphal, as documented evidence indicates otherwise. The design on the Cape Lookout Lighthouse is not diamonds but squares (checkers), some think showing true points of the compass but possibly a nautical

danger symbol; verified by an official letter, but apparently not relevant when naming the former community across Barden Inlet on e end Shackleford Banks Diamond City for "design" on the lighthouse. Documentation indicates "Cape Hatteras tower will be painted in spiral bands, alternately black and white. Cape Lookout tower will be checkered, the checkers being painted alternately black and white. Body's [*sic*] Island tower is now painted black and white horizontal bands." Stanford for NPS reports "The Lighthouse Board ordered the three North Carolina red brick lighthouses (Lookout, Hatteras, and Bodie Island) painted exactly the way they are on April 17, 1873" (NPS 2012). Currituck Lighthouse was left as red brick.

The following quote (anonymous) suggests problems of shipping here until mid-20th century: "Hatteras has a blow in store for those who passing her howling door."

Other names: Annunciata (misapplication—*see* Cape Lookout), Cape Amadas (mistakenly applied—*see* Cape Kenrick), Cape de Engano (means deception—Blaeu 1640), Cape Hataras (Moll 1730), Cape Hateras (Wimble 1738), Cape Hatoras (Wimble 1733), Cape Hattaras (Gascoyne 1682), Cape Hattarass (Fisher et al. 1689, chart 11), Cape Hattera (typographical error), Cape Hatterass (Currituck DB 8, 1797, 28–29), Cape Hatterasse (Salley 1911, 45), Cape Hatoras (numerous historical maps), Cape Hatterasch (Blome 1672), Cape Hattoros (Portinaro and Knuisch 1987), Cape Lookout (Wingfield 1608, 15—mistaken application), Cape Hope (Keulen 1690), Cape on Currituck Banks (misapplication), Cape Saint John (Hill, from Quinn 1955, 26, based on Haklyut 1589 and Blaeu 1640—Cape Hatteras here not significant or developed fully, Cape Kenrick still existed 1640), Cape Trafalgar (Vespucci 1526; Blaeu 1640), Cap Hatteras (Frédéric 1807), Cap Hattoras (Bellin 1757), Capo Hatteras (Tardieu, ca. 1800), Capte Hatterass (Currituck DB 13, 1814, 188–89), Croatoan (White 1585 in part), Frisco Cape (in part, highly localized occasional use for undefined area w of Cape Point), Hatarask (historical), Hatorasck (historical), Hatorask (Haklyut 1589), Hatoraske (Haklyut 1589), Hattorask (Haklyut 1589), Hatrask (historical), Hotoros (historical), Otterasco (phonetic misinterpretation), Ottorasko (phonetic misinterpretation), The Cape (local use), The Hook (occasional whimsical local use), The Point (local use).

Cape Hatteras Battery, proposed fort (battery), Dare County, Hatteras Township (historical documents). WWII battery (gun emplacement) was to be at Cape Hatteras to protect Allied shipping but never built because a suitable location was not available. *Other names:* Battery Cape Hatteras (historical).

Cape Hatteras Lighthouse Beach, large beach, 3 mi. long Dare County, Hatteras Township (NPS 2016). At Cape Point, n-s 1.5 mi. around Cape Point and then e-w 1.5 mi., 3.5 mi. s of Buxton. Named because at Cape Hatteras Lighthouse, but 1999 NPS moved lighthouse inland 0.5 mi. for preservation because in danger of being surrounded and toppled by the encroaching sea. *See* Cape Hatteras. *Other names:* Cape Hatteras Beach (local use), Hatteras Lighthouse Beach (some use), Lighthouse Beach (Outer Banks Scenic Byway 2008, 62), Old Lighthouse Beach (some local use, Cape Hatteras Lighthouse moved inland 1999).

Cape Hatteras Ponds, lakes, Dare County, Hatteras Township (local use). Referenced numerous ponds at greater Cape Hatteras in what was termed Cape Woods. Covey (2018, 52) uses quote from mapping field crew indicating difficulty negotiating e portion terrain of these ponds. Configuration today different than 19th century.

Cape Hatteras Shoals. *See* Diamond Shoals.

Cape Hills, sand dunes, Carteret County, Harkers Island Township (local use). Today name is applied at Cape Lookout where former village (and remaining buildings) located 1.5 mi. n of Cape Point, 6.5 mi. s of Harkers Island (village). Originally, Cape Hills applied to oceanside dunes just e of Cape Lookout Lighthouse and in a broader sense applied to dunes continuing s also to include dunes around former Cape Lookout (village). Today, Cape Hills mostly used for dunes just at former Cape Lookout (village). Occasionally, name used historically on e Shackelford Banks before scattered community there named Diamond City (1885) when name Diamond City Hills applied to dunes on e Shackleford Banks.

Cape Kenrick, former cape, Dare County,

Kinnakeet Township (infrequent use historical documents). Formerly e projection of n Hatteras Island and s Pea Island 3 mi. sw of Rodanthe, 20 mi. nne of Cape Hatteras. Prominent cape existed until late 17th century, with remnants into early 18th century, when it disappeared (became inundated); today Wimble Shoals (q.v.) are remnants of Cape Kenrick. Appeared as the prominent cape without a name on White's (1585) map and DeBry's (1590) map. White mentions it as "the point that lyeth to the southwardes of Kenricks mounts." A few maps briefly displayed Cape Amidas, after one of two captains dispatched by Raleigh (Barlowe 1584) to find suitable colony location. Sometimes confused with Cape Hatteras, which developed after Cape Kenrick disappeared. The Lost Colony Research Center has on an annotated version of White-DeBry map labeled Cape Kenrick as False Cape but not normally used here as False Cape because feature used this name from early colonial times in Virginia just n of North Carolina–Virginia boundary. Probably descriptive attempt to indicate disappearance of this cape. There was some highly local use in 19th century when comparing to Cape Hatteras. A later version of the center's map does label the cape as "Kindrick's (False) Cape." While the process of inundating Cape Kenrick had probably begun by 1590, the cape was still prevalent when DeBry's (1590) map made and did not disappear completely for another 100 years or so. *See* Kenricks Mounts for meaning of Kenrick. *Other names:* Cabo (Spanish) or Capo (Italian) or Cap (French) Arenas (Lok 1582—arenas is depicted near Cape Kenrick [Cape Hatteras not yet developed]— unknown why "arenas" used, Spanish meaning sand, Verrazzano was Italian with financial backing by Italian merchants and French king with French bankers; *see* Cape Lookout for discussion of Verrazzano's visit to Outer Banks), Cabo de Arenas (Ortelius 1587—means sand cape), Cabo de Bôa Ventura (Portuguese means Cape of Good Fortune, unusual for this treacherous area, but recorded on Cantino 1502), Cape Amidas (Smith 1624, map—name did not survive because feature did not survive), Cape Canrick (Blaeu 1640), Cape Canrik (Keulen 1690), Cape Cenrick (variation on maps late

17th century), Cape Hataras (Moll 1730), Cape Hattaras (Moll 1708), Cape Hatteras (Keulen 1690), Cape Hatterask (early application based on use of Hatrask or Hatarask applied by White 1585), Cape Hattorasch (Schroeter 1859), Cape Kaneraick (spelling variation), Cape Kendrick (Haklyut 1589 — reference by inference citing Kenricks or Kenricks Mounts with reference to a cape), Cape Kendricks (Willard and Midgett 2007), Cape Saint John (Blaeu 1640), False Cape (added annotation to DeBry 1590 by Lost Colony Research Center), Kindricks Cape (Lost Colony Research Center), Wimble Shoals (Wimble 1738).

Cape Lookout, cape, 2 mi. long, 1 mi. wide, Carteret County, Harkers Island Township (USGS 2013: Cape Lookout). At s tip Core Banks just e of Onslow Bay, 6.3 mi. s of Harkers Island (village). Before European arrival, Cape Lookout was more than 3 mi. nne of present location (point) just e and n of Cape Lookout Lighthouse; the name Cape Shackleford used for this pre-European cape in scientific reports. The French were instrumental in building Fort Hancock here 17th century, referenced as The Colonies' Gibraltar for its strategic location 17th and 18th centuries. Use of Engano by Spanish (*engaño*, deception in Spanish) indicates difficulty of negotiating shoals here.

Giovanni da Verrazzano (1524) was first to record a visit to the Outer Banks, although reportedly John Cabot sailed along a portion (1497) but without landfall. He first stopped briefly at Cape Fear area (se North Carolina) and describes an encounter with indigenous peoples probably at Cape Lookout, though some researchers believe this to have been Cape Hatteras. The description by Verrazzano, "turning northward found there an isthmus one mile wide and about two hundred miles long," fits from Cape Lookout to Cape Henry in Virginia, where the isthmus ends. Some scholars analyzing the letter indicate "Verrazzano's hand-written letter in Italian . . . highlights the beginning of a marginal note referring to 'Annunciata,' identified as Cape Lookout in the Carolina Outer Banks" (Verrazzano Letter 1524). From Cape Hatteras, 200 miles crosses the opening of Chesapeake Bay (11 mi. wide) almost to Chincoteague Island, Virginia, near Maryland—difficult not to notice mouth of the Chesapeake Bay, but possible. One turns

n from Cape Hatteras also, and a fairly large indigenous presence was at Cape Hatteras (*see* Indian Town) known to be friendly. Still, a Coree Indian village existed on Harkers Island (*see* Coranine Town), and it is certain these Coree visited Cape Lookout constantly. So, most authors are noncommittal on the matter, and unresolved as to whether Verrazzano stopped at Cape Lookout or Cape Hatteras. Further, strange why Verrazzano would have used miles or, more specifically, English miles. The English mile was not standardized to 5,280 ft. until 1593, and if Verrazzano was using miles (possibly surfacing through translation errors), length of the mile used could vary considerably. So, distance of "200 miles" could be from Cape Lookout to Cape Henry or from Cape Hatteras to Cape Henry.

Regardless of which cape was his landfall, he named the area Annunciata. Verrazzano states, "We left this place [We called it 'Annunciata'] from the day of arrival, and found there an isthmus one mile wide and about two hundred miles long, in which we could see the east sea from the ship (Pamlico Sound), halfway between west and north." Verrazzano was at the Outer Banks in late March, and his quote referring to naming was probable reference to the Feast of Annunciata. Verrazzano continued on to New England before returning home to Italy. Later, Verrazzano's brother labeled the Outer Banks from Cape Lookout to Cape Henry (Virginia) Varazanio (*sic*) (supporting Cape Lookout landfall) and entire area Francesca in honor of Francis I, King of France, who financed the voyage. Other names were known to be applied, but none were ever used, and with 60 years until the Roanoke voyages, these names were forgotten.

Painting the design of the lighthouse at Cape Hatteras and the lighthouse at Cape Lookout is an interesting story. Design of the lighthouse at Cape Hatteras is spiral, but reportedly was originally supposed to be diamond shapes relating to Diamond Shoals just off Cape Hatteras; however, paperwork was reportedly mishandled and opposite occurred, diamond shapes are at Cape Lookout Lighthouse and spiral shape (known worldwide) is at lighthouse at Cape Hatteras (1999 moved inland 0.5 mi. by NPS for its preservation). This "story" is apocryphal as documented evidence indicates otherwise, as do residents. The design on the Cape Lookout Lighthouse is not diamonds but squares (checkers), some think showing true points of the compass, but probably as a nautical danger symbol; verified by an official letter, but apparently not relevant when naming the former community across Barden Inlet on e end Shackleford Banks Diamond City for "design" on the lighthouse. Some reports do note the design is squares decreasing in size upward and, the black "squares" point n-s, and the white "squares" point e-w. Though a black diamond now indicates navigational danger, it was not the case in 1873 when decision was made. Some believe shoals at Cape Lookout have also been known as Diamond Shoals; no known occurrence of a recorded instance of Diamond Shoals being applied to Cape Lookout Shoals. Documentation indicates "Cape Hatteras tower will be painted in spiral bands, alternately black and white. Cape Lookout tower will be checkered, the checkers being painted alternately black and white. Body's [sic] Island tower is now painted black and white horizontal bands." (NPS 2012). Stanford for NPS reports "The Lighthouse Board ordered the three North Carolina red brick lighthouses (Lookout, Hatteras, and Bodie Island) painted exactly the way they are on April 17, 1873" (NPS 2012). Currituck Lighthouse was left as red brick.

  Other names: Annunciata (Verrazzano 1524), Cabo dela Verazanas (Vespucci 1526), Cap de Lokout (Nolin 1783), Cape (Cabo) de Trafalgar (Blaeu 1640—probably named for Cape Trafalgar (before colonial references—Anglicized form from Arabic meaning West Cape, now off the sw coast of Iberian Peninsula or nw point of entrance to Strait of Gibraltar; Outer Banks name fell into disuse by early 18th century), Cape di Virginia Australe (Dudley 1647), Cape Fear (Henry 1860, from Raleigh expeditions 1584—"e" might have been dropped), Cape Feare (Hondius 1606; Smith 1624, map), Cape Hope (Schroeter 1859), Cape Lockout (DeLisle 1718), Cape Lookeout (Gascoyne 1682; Salley 1911, 84), Cape Look Out (Speed 1676), Cape-Look-Out (18th-century shipwreck reports), Cape-Lookout (18th-century shipwreck reports), Cape Look-out (18th century maps; Lawson 1709, 65), Cape Look-Out (18th-

century maps and shipwreck reports), Cape Lookout Beaches (occasionally used, mostly historically, entire cape mostly beach), Cape of Faire (Keulen 1690), Cape of Fear (18th-century maps copying earlier maps), Cape of Feare (Hondius 1606), Cape of Southern Virginia (early, rarely used application, Virginia and Carolina were separated 1663—see Carolina), Cape Trafalgar (Dudley 1647), Cap Lookout (Schroeter 1859), Capo Lookout (Tardieu, ca. 1800), Hook of Cape (some local use early 1900s—when viewed from above appearance is giant hook), Promontorium Tremendum (literally "dreadful promontory," White 1590), The Cape (local use), The Colonies' Gibraltar (Cottineau and Cambray comments in soliciting support for Fort Hancock, colonial period), The Hook (used early 1900s referencing protected area it creates), The Point (local use).

Cape Lookout, former village, Carteret County, Harkers Island Township (USGS 2013: Cape Lookout—still labeled though abandoned). On Cape Lookout at s tip of Core Banks, 6 mi. s of Harkers Island (village). Today Cape Lookout village is abandoned, but late as 1950 population was approx. 50; post office est. 1910 but discontinued 1915. Last residents left 1979 with assistance from NPS. Several houses and other buildings still standing, and visitors can walk through the former village or take the beach shuttle, all in Cape Lookout National Seashore. During WWII a temporary military installation established nearby to protect shipping and provide safe harbor for ships—known locally as The Rock, active only two years (1942–44). *Other names:* Cape Hills (Stick 1958, 193), Cape Lookout Village (local use), Cape Lookout Woods (historical local use), Cape Village (historical use and Outer Banks Scenic Byway 2008, 150), Coast Guard Village (some local use, Coast Guard station there, NPS 2012, 48), The Cape (local use).

Cape Lookout Banks, historical, generally mid-18th century and was s half of what is now Core Banks generally from Old Drum Inlet to Cape Lookout (Mouzon 1775), with Core Banks or Core Bank applied to n portion from Old Drum Inlet to Portsmouth Island and on some maps included Portsmouth Island. Today applications are for Portsmouth Island with the remainder of the barrier beaches to Cape Lookout as Core Banks. *Other names:*

Cape Lookout Bank (Pinkerton et al. 1809), Cape Look Out Banks (Wimble 1733), Core Banks (numerous maps and charts).

Cape Lookout Dock, landing, Carteret County, Harkers Island Township (brochures). Just nne of Cape Lookout Lighthouse 3 mi. n of Cape Point. Used by NPS for visitors' ferry (passengers only) from Shell Point e end Harkers Island, NPS Visitor Center.

Cape Lookout Grounds, historical reference, open sea e and s of Cape Lookout. Used extensively for whaling until late 19th century when most whales disappeared. Method of shore-based whaling on the Outer Banks was different from New Englanders' (who were present here). Local older men would watch for whales from high sand dunes, and when sighted the "Whalers" would put to sea in longboats to capture the whale. Men would harpoon the whale by hand (later by gun), tow the whale to shore, and beach it at high tide, yielding much less capture of whales. Two-week job processing or "trying" the whale, always considered a community project, and the profits shared accordingly. *See* Try Yard Creek. *Other names:* Cape Lookout Ground (early maps and Stick 1958), Lookout Grounds (some historical maps).

Cape Lookout Shoals, shoals, 9 mi. long, 2 mi. wide, Carteret County, Harkers Island Township (local use). In Atlantic Ocean just se of Cape Lookout. *Other names:* Cape Look-Out Shoals (18th-century shipwreck reports), Cape Look-out Shoals (18th-century shipwreck reports), Cape Look Out Sholes (18th-century spelling), Cape Look Out Shols (Wimble 1733), Cape Lookout Bank (perceptive observation), Cape Lookout Banks (Mouzon 1775—perceptive reference), Cape Lookout Shoal (USGS 1972: Beaufort 1:250,000 scale), Cape Shoal (some use), Cape Shoals (NPS 2004b, map, 402), Frying Pan Shoals (early maps probably confused with the Cape Fear, Southport, N.C.), Lookout Shoals (Williamson 1992), Seccagna (Dudley 1661—*seccagna* meaning shallows or shoals in Italian).

Cape Lookout Woods, woods, Carteret County, Harkers Island Township (local use). At Cape Lookout 1.5 mi. n of Cape Point; surrounds restored remains of some buildings making up former Cape Lookout (village). This maritime forest is mere remnant of previous size, as are all previous maritime forests that still exist. *Other names:* Cape Woods (local

use), Lookout Woods (Angley 1982, 30), The Woods (limited local use).

Cape Point, point, Carteret County, Harkers Island Township (USGS 2013: Cape Lookout). S-most tip of Core Banks at s tip of Cape Lookout 1.6 mi. s of former Cape Lookout (village). Originally more descriptive for referring to farthest projection of land of a prominent cape. Subdivision named for feature. *Other names:* Cape Lookout Point (Williamson 1992), South Spit (Blunt, 1857, 345—sometimes applied to the larger cape area).

Cape Point, point, Dare County, Hatteras Township (USGS 2013: Cape Hatteras). Extreme s tip of Cape Hatteras, 2.7 mi. s of Buxton. *See* Cape Point (Carteret County). Subdivision named for feature. *Other names:* Cape Hatteras Point (Sorrie 2014, 33; occasional local use), Cape Hatterass Point (Currituck DB 3, 1801, 277), Cape Nub (local fishermen), Cove Point (local use referring to adjacent Hatteras Bight), Hatteras Point (Godfrey 1976, 133), Point of Cape Hatteras (MacNeill 1958, 11), Point of the Cape (historical writing), The Point (MacNeill 1958, 119), The Point of Cape Hatteras (occasional historical writing).

Cape Pointe Marina, harbor, Carteret County, Harkers Island Township (signage). On Harkers Island, Back Sound side 1.5 mi. w of Cape Lookout National Seashore facility at e end Harkers Island. Use of spelling "Pointe" is modern and fanciful, not from historical name with original 17th-century English spelling. *Other names:* Barbours Harbour Marina (owner).

Cape Point Ponds, ponds, Dare County, Hatteras Township (NPS 2006a, 3). Reference to named and unnamed ponds at Cape Hatteras and environs (*see* Horseshoe Pond, Lighthouse Pond, Open Pond, Open Ponds).

Cape Woods, heavily wooded historically, Dare County, Hatteras Township (historical use mostly). S Hatteras Island at Cape Hatteras including Buxton and Frisco villages. Name is general application, including all of individually named woods, including Buxton Woods, Frisco Woods, and Spencers Woods. Used more historically, now used mostly in reports, scientific papers, and occasionally some brochures. *Other names:* The Great Woods (Cobb 1905—portion originally cleared early 1800s).

Capsies Creek, cove, 0.7 mi. wide, Currituck County, Fruitville Township (USGS 2013: Knotts Island). In Back Bay at ne end Knotts Island, 2.7 mi. n of Knotts Island (village). Usually applied upstream along course of small stream 0.5 mi. s from cove. *Other names:* Capps Creek (road sign), East Bay (Currituck DB 10, 1809, 99—applied historically to Capsies Creek or Porpoise Slough), Simpsons Creek (Currituck DB 6, 1716, 7–8—records not clear and name applied to Capsies Creek or Porpoise Slough).

Captains Landing. *See* Ocracoke Wharf.

Carolina, former region representing land granted to the eight Lords Proprietors 1663 by Charles II, King of England; the Proprietors named the grant in honor of Charles I (deposed and executed during brief Commonwealth period under Cromwell, 1649–60), father of Charles II, grantor. Some reports indicate Charles named it for himself. Carolina is from Carolus, early Latin form of Charles. Reportedly New Carolana appears in the original but was removed. A previous charter existed from Charles I of England (1629) granting essentially same area, between 31° N (s) and 36° N (n) to Sir Robert Heath. Nothing came of this grant, and charter ruled invalid (because Charles I was defeated and executed by Cromwell). Charles II was restored to the throne 1660 and issued the second charter three years after his restoration to the eight Lords Proprietors: Edward Hyde, Earl of Clarendon; George Monck, first Duke of Albemarle; William Lord Craven; John Lord Berkley; Anthony Lord Ashley-Cooper; Sir George Carteret; Sir William Berkley; and Sir John Colleton. The legitimate or second charter included all land from Virginia to Florida and from Atlantic Ocean to Pacific Ocean. Boundaries set at 36° N (n) and 31° N (s). Original boundaries just s of Albemarle Sound at Colington Island and Saint Matthias River, now Saint Johns River (Jacksonville, Florida). At request of the Lords Proprietors, n boundary extended slightly to 36°30′ N at Currituck Inlet (they thought, but actually 5 mi. s of former Currituck Inlet), later s another 100 miles or so. *Other names:* Carolana (Coxe 1722), New Carolana (Charles I 1629, original charter).

Carolina Cays, hummocks or islands, 2.5 mi. long, Dare County, Nags Head Township (local use, real estate offerings, newspaper articles). Unusual small equally spaced islands trending n-s e coast Roanoke Island from just s of Johns Creek (n) to tip Broad Creek Point (s). Spaced evenly because created from spoil from dredging n-s trending Roanoke Sound Channel in Roanoke Sound just offshore from e shore Roanoke Island. Origin is recent probably 1940s when additional money was appropriated for serious dredging of the channel (original dredging began around 1910). Name little known until last few years when advertised, by name, available for purchase. "Cay" is low-lying small island made of mostly sand, mud, gravel, etc. Originally from *cayo*, small island in Spanish, adopted into English where term transitioned to "cay" and pronounced (mostly by British) "key"; many Americans pronounce it "kay." Subdivision occupying same spatial footprint named for feature.

Carova (Corova Beach), village, 2.3 mi. long, Currituck County, Fruitville Township (signage). Center 2 mi. s of North Carolina–Virginia boundary, 3.2 mi. ene of Knotts Island (village). Small number of year-round residents who have been here since early 1970s (1967 the first). Access is by boat or 4-wheel-drive vehicles only (from s; no access allowed now from Virginia). Name origin a contraction of Carolina (Caro) and abbreviation for Virginia, "Va.," thus indicating its proximity to North Carolina–Virginia boundary. Original name was (and is) Carova but evolved (with signage) into Carova Beach, more used now than Carova, accounts for use in real estate brochures. Originally, NC 12 to be from Corolla as a hard-surface road to Carova, but opposition prevailed, though still occasional mention of doing so as far as Swan Beach. Ostensibly two wildlife refuges between would be impacted; hard-surfaced NC 12 ends just n of Corolla (Ocean Hill); from there NC 12 is marked as true beach road, literally driving on beach. Further, boundary between North Carolina and Virginia was closed here by F&WS (1987) to disallow heavy (or any) traffic from nearby, heavily populated Virginia Beach, to protect extensive Back Bay National Wildlife Refuge just n in Virginia. Often Midnight Pass mentioned in association with sw Carova. It is a small section of road (trail) just w of Wild Horse Estates subdivision named by the developer.

The county does not require reason for name, so reason is obscure. Subdivision named for feature. *Other names:* Carova Beach (signage and much local use), Corova (error in brochures, pronunciation), Corova Beach (error on numerous pamphlets and websites), South Shore (sometimes used referring to nearby Virginia).

Carova Beach, beach, 1 mi. long, Currituck County, Fruitville Township (local use). At Carova, 11 mi. n of Corolla. In local use since Carova settled in mid-1970s. *See* Carova. *Other names:* Cordova Beach.

Carrot Island, island, 2 mi. long, Carteret County, Harkers Island Township (USGS 2013: Beaufort, Harkers Island). In Back Sound, 2 mi. from Beaufort (mainland). Originally (confirmed by residents) was Cart Island. Local usage has become Carrot by perpetuated error on maps, and mapmakers (not local) might have heard "Carrot" from local accents when doing field investigation for mapping. Late as 19th century, Carrot Island (Cart Island) would occasionally be connected to mainland at low water, allowing "carts" to be taken to the island. Carrot Island became official by decision of USBGN 1949. Kell (1777) shows Carrot Island. *Other names:* Cart Island (NOS).

Carrot Island Channel, channel, 2.5 mi. long, Carteret County, Harkers Island Township (USGS 2013: Beaufort). Separates Carrot Island and Horse Island just se of Beaufort (mainland), 5.3 mi. w of Harkers Island (village). *See* Carrot Island. *Other names:* Carrot Island Slough (C&GS 1910a), Carrot Slough (C&GS 1905), Cart Island Slue (Williamson 1992, 171), Horse Island Slough (historical local use for adjacent Horse Island), Horse Island Creek (historical local use for adjacent Horse Island).

Carteret, intended settlement or town, Dare County, Nags Head Township. Charter granted 1723, lasted only until about 1733. Was on ne Roanoke Island, one of two attempts to establish a port town on Roanoke Island near Shallowbag Bay (Manteo just nw of Baum Point). Town never developed because Roanoke Inlet was "shoaling up" by changes in currents caused by natural closing of inlets through n portion Currituck Banks; by 1730s no direct or reliable inlet through barrier island near Roanoke Island (*see* Roanoke Island historical inlets). Oregon Inlet not open until 1846, and Roanoke Inlet was very shallow by this time. Proposed town was to be named for Sir John Carteret, one of the eight Lords Proprietors of Carolina (*see* Carolina). *Other names:* Roanoak Town (Sandbeck 2003, 19), Roanoke Town (casual references), Ronoak Town (Sanderson 1733), Town of Carteret (original statements for establishment).

Carteret County, civil division, 536 sq. mi. Atlantic, Beaufort, Cedar Island, Davis, Harkers Island, Harlowe, Marshallberg, Merrimon, Morehead, Newport, Portsmouth, Sea Level, Smyrna, Stacy, Straits, and White Oak Townships. Formed 1772 from Craven County. Bounded by Jones, Craven, Pamlico, and Hyde Counties. Named for Sir John Carteret, one of the original eight Lords Proprietors of Carolina (*see* Carolina). Before 1770 Ocracoke Island was independent and not in any county, but was then annexed by Carteret County. In 1845, most of what is now Ocracoke Island (from Green Island just w of Old Hatteras Inlet to Ocracoke Inlet) was moved from Carteret County into Hyde County by agreement. Remaining Ocracoke Island (Green Island to Hatteras Inlet) had been transferred from Currituck County to Hyde County 1823 with area s from New Inlet. From New Inlet to Hatteras Inlet became part of Dare County when created 1870.

Cart Island. *See* Carrot Island.

Casey Bay, cove, 0.3 mi. wide, Carteret County, Portsmouth Township (USGS 1950: Portsmouth). In Pamlico Sound, separates two marshes, just w of Portsmouth (village), 6.4 mi. sw of Ocracoke (village). *Other names:* Caseys Bay (C&GS 1900), Sheep Island Bay (George II 1753).

Casey Island, island, 0.3 mi. long, Carteret County, Portsmouth Township (USGS 1950: Portsmouth). In Pamlico Sound just n of Portsmouth (village), 6.5 mi. sw of Ocracoke (village). One building (observed) on island formerly used as small hunt club. *Other names:* Caseys Island (ACE 1893).

Caseys Point, point, Carteret County, Portsmouth Township (C&GS 1900). N point Casey Island 1 mi. n of Portsmouth (village), 6.5 mi. sw of Ocracoke (village). *Other names:* Casey Point (Williamson 1992, 115), Keys Point (NPS 2007, map, 27–28).

Cason Point, point, Currituck County, Fruitville Township (USGS 2013: Knotts Island). On Knotts Island, 1.3 mi. ne of Knotts Island (village). Early maps of Knotts Island indicate surname Cason or Casun here also appearing in early deeds, as does given name Cason. *Other names:* Casons Point (C&GS 1882), Caysons Point (C&GS 1913a), Cuson Point (CS 1852).

Catarines Swamp. *See* Mallard Marsh (NC 345).

Cateridges Point, former point, Currituck County, Fruitville Township (Currituck Deeds, miscellaneous, 1719). Was somewhere soundside near New Currituck Inlet or Broad Creek, probably 7 mi. n of Corolla. Name mentioned in Currituck Deeds (miscellaneous, 1719), only known occurrence. Location mentioned as "near Broad Creek and the inlett [*sic*]" and might have been soundside point of inlet (New Currituck Inlet).

Cates Creek. *See* Farrows Creek.

Catfish Point, point, Carteret County, Harkers Island Township (local use). At s end Core Banks on n shore Cape Lookout 1.5 mi. n of Cape Point, 4.8 mi. sse of Harkers Island (village). Made official by USBGN 1975. *Other names:* Golds Point (NPS 2005, 52).

Catfish Point. *See* Power Squadron Spit.

Catfish Pond, pond, Dare County, Atlantic Township (Burney, 1987, fig. 1, 157). In n Nags Head Woods just s of Run Hill 2 mi. n of Jockeys Ridge. One of numerous interdunal ponds (most unnamed).

Cat Hole, former hole or cove, Dare County, Atlantic Township (Currituck DB 12, 1811, 146–47). Possibly deeper area Jeanguite Creek, more likely vague reference to one of the small coves on e side of Jeanguite Creek historically in Great Marsh.

Cat Island, island, Carteret County, White Oak Township (USGS 2013: Salter Path). In Bogue Sound, 4.3 mi. w of Salter Path. *Other names:* Gull Island (C&GS 1888b).

Cat Island, former island, Carteret County, White Oak Township (C&GS 1905). Was in Bogue Sound 2.5 mi. w of Salter Path. Historically, two features named Cat Island in close proximity in Bogue Sound. This particular Cat Island disappeared 1960s, leaving smaller Cat Island, 4 mi. w, only feature now named Cat Island here.

Cat Island, island, 0.3 mi. long, 0.1 mi. wide, Currituck County, Poplar Branch Township (USGS 2013: Mossey Islands). In Currituck Sound just sw of Mossey Islands complex 8 mi. sw of Corolla.

Cat Island, island, 0.1 mi. wide, Dare County, Kinnakeet Township (USGS 2013: Pea Island). In Pamlico Sound just nw of Round Hammock Point, 3.1 mi. nw of Rodanthe. Represents remnants of primary shoal (Loggerhead Shoals) at Loggerhead Inlet but today is small, mostly attached to barrier island. *Other names:* Logerhead Shoal (Loggerhead misspelling from 1800s), Loggerhead Shoal (CS 1852).

Cat Ridge, area, Dare County, Kinnakeet Township (Garrity-Blake 2010, 169). Original Avon (Kinnakeet) on n side of Peters Ditch (The Creek), 6.3 mi. n of Buxton. Name derived reportedly from differentiating two clusters of families in original Avon, whom jokingly fought like cats and dogs (*see* Avon and Dog Ridge).

Cat Ridge, small sand dune, Dare County, Kinnakeet Township (local use). In original Avon just n and e of Avon Harbor, 6.5 mi. n of Buxton. Almost nonexistent now from development, originally small n-s ridge just e of Avon Harbor, application of name extended slightly w. Probably applied whimsically. *See* Cat Ridge (area), Dog Ridge (area), and Avon.

Cat Ridge, sand dune, Hyde County, Ocracoke Township (local use). On sw end Ocracoke Island just n of Springers Point in sw Ocracoke (village). Name of surrounding neighborhood and area reference (*see* Ocracoke Village areas).

Cattle Pen Point, point, Currituck County, Poplar Branch Township (USGS 2013: Mossey Islands). N-most point of Narrows Island, 6.6 mi. sw of Corolla.

Causeway, The, natural ridge-like hummock, Dare County, Nags Head Township (older local use). Natural higher ground ridge-like trending n-s from just s of US 64 and US 264 Bypass 1 mi. sse of Manteo (center) 5 mi. to a point 0.5 mi. e of Baumtown and 0.5 mi. n of Wanchese. NC 345 generally follows this natural causeway. Name not used as much because confusing with short version of the Manteo-Nags Head Causeway (originally itself just The Causeway).

Causeway Channel, small channel, 1 mi. long,

Carteret County, Morehead Township (local use). On e side Atlantic Beach Causeway as enters Bogue Banks, serves as entry channel from Bogue Sound to Sound View Isles subdivision just n of Atlantic Beach (town), 1 mi. s of Morehead City (mainland).

Causeway Marina, small harbor, Carteret County, Morehead Township (local use). Just w of Atlantic Beach Causeway at s edge of Moonlight Bay just n of Atlantic Beach (town), 1.5 mi. s of Morehead City (mainland).

Cedar Bush Bay, cove, 0.6 mi. wide, Dare County, Nags Head Township (USGS 2013: Wanchese). In Croatan Sound just sw of Roanoke Island, 1.9 mi. sw of Wanchese. *Other names:* Cedar Bay (USGS 1943: Roanoke Island, 1:125,000 scale).

Cedar Creek, water passage, 0.5 mi. long, Currituck County, Fruitville Township (USGS 2013: Knotts Island). Connects Deals Island Creek and Deals Island Pond, 2.2 mi. ene of Knotts Island (village). *Other names:* John Davis Creek (Currituck Deeds, miscellaneous, 1719).

Cedar Creek, small cove and tidal creek, Dare County, Kinnakeet Township (Garrity-Blake 2010, 136). Soundside in s Salvo just n of Clarks Bay and Cedar Hammock, 4 mi. s of Rodanthe.

Cedar Creek Point, point, Dare County, Kinnakeet Township (Garrity-Blake 2010, 492). N point at entrance to Cedar Creek just s of Opening Marshes in s Salvo, 4 mi. s of Rodanthe.

Cedar Hammock, marsh island, 0.3 mi. long, Carteret County, Harkers Island Township (USGS 2013: Harkers Island). In Back Sound at nw end Sheep Island Slue, 2.6 mi. sse of Harkers Island (village). *See* Black Hammock.

Cedar Hammock, marsh peninsula, 1.3 mi. wide, Carteret County, Morehead Township (USGS 2013: Beaufort, Mansfield). In Bogue Sound now connected to Bogue Banks by man-made land at Atlantic Beach (town), 1.7 mi. sw of Morehead City (mainland). Marsh with hummocks (hence name) altered considerably and man-enhanced 1960s and 1970s creating lots for sale, marina, and commercial enterprises. Sometimes, just e of The Atlantic Beach Causeway (Sound View Isles subdivision) included, but originally not included. *See* Black Hammock. *Other names:* Atlantic Beach Isles (subdivision name), Great Island (CS 1852).

Cedar Hammock, marsh, 0.2 mi. long, Carteret County, Stacy Township (USGS 2013: Styron Bay). Just w of Core Banks in Core Sound, 4.1 mi. s of Atlantic (mainland). *See* Black Hammock.

Cedar Hammock, hummock, Dare County, Atlantic Township (Currituck DB 2, 1770, 306). Somewhere along ne corner of Kitty Hawk Bay (North Cove) near Mingoes Ridge Gut as described in deed. *See* Black Hammock. *Other names:* Cedar Hamack (Currituck DB 2, 1770, 306).

Cedar Hammock, marsh, 0.5 mi. long, 0.2 mi. wide, Dare County, Kinnakeet Township (USGS 2013: Pea Island). Just n of Wreck Creek, 5 mi. nnw of Rodanthe. *See* Black Hammock. *Other names:* Cedar Hummock (Stick 1958, 173).

Cedar Hammock, small hummock, Dare County, Kinnakeet Township (USGS 2013: Rodanthe). Just n of No Ache in s Salvo at Clarks Bay. Use of double generic terms "hammock" and "isle" in variant name was to indicate, at time of naming, more island-like in Pamlico Sound rather than surrounded by marsh as are most hummocks. Use of "isle" rather than "island" was local in Chicamacomico (Rodanthe, Waves, Salvo). *See* Black Hammock. *Other names:* Cedar Hammock Island (CS 1852–82: 1854), Cedar Hammock Isle (Garrity-Blake 2010, 493), Cedar Hummock (Outer Banks Scenic Byway 2008 153—hammock, local use), Jenkins Hammock (Covey 2018, 13).

Cedar Hammock, hummock, Hyde County, Ocracoke Township (local use). At Hatteras Inlet, ne end Ocracoke Island just e of docking facility for Hatteras-Ocracoke Ferry, 13 mi. ene of Ocracoke (village). *See* Black Hammock and Cedar Hammock (former community).

Cedar Hammock, former small part-time community, Hyde County, Ocracoke Township (O'Neal et al. 1976, 18, 19). Was at ne end Ocracoke Island at Cedar Hammock just n of Styron Hills, 12.5 mi. ne of Ocracoke (village). Only five or six families near old Ocracoke (Hatteras Inlet) Life Saving Station at Cedar Hammock on Ocracoke Island (destroyed by storm 1955), of men stationed at lifesaving station; families here usually only in winter, being 12 mi. from Ocracoke (village). No trace of former place today. *See* Black Hammock and Cedar Hammock.

Cedar Hammock Channel, natural channel, 6 mi. long, Dare County, Kinnakeet Township (Garrity-Blake 2010, 493). Just s of Cedar Hammock and just s of No Ache to a point at ne point Gull Island, 3.5 mi. ssw of Salvo. *See* Black Hammock.

Cedar Hammock Creek, former water passage, Carteret County, Morehead Township (USGS 1951: Beaufort, Mansfield). Connected Hoop Pole Creek and Money Island Bay just n of Atlantic Beach, 1.2 mi. ssw of Morehead City (mainland). Remnants can be seen as coves in man-made areas of Cedar Hammock. *See* Black Hammock. *Other names:* Hammock Creek (G. Colton 1861).

Cedar Hammock Gut. *See* Mingoes Ridge Gut.

Cedar Hammock Island. *See* No Ache Island.

Cedar Inlet, former water passage, 0.5 mi. long, Carteret County, Stacy Township (USGS 2013: Styron Bay). Was in Core Sound, separated Outer Grass Lump from Big Marsh, connected Old Channel (inlet remnant) to Core Sound, 4 mi. s of Atlantic (mainland). Open approx. 1729–55 and 1770–1865, though Brazier's (1822) map indicates inlet "now filled up," so it must have been awash for some years. Reportedly named Cedar Inlet for a stand of cedars nearby. Remnants are in Old Channel nearby. Variant names associated with Cedar Inlet might be at exact location or within a few hundred yards since this inlet has moved about within a small area. *Other names:* Cedar Banks Inlet (N.C. Fisheries 1923, 27—small part of barrier island here known as Cedar Banks locally while Cedar Inlet was open), Cedar Island Inlet (listed separately, by Stick [1958] and Fisher [1962], but likely same inlet or migrating portion), Ceder Einfahrt (Lucas 1826—*einfahrt*, inlet in German), Hunting Quarter Inlet (Bowen 1747), New Inlet (Baldwin 1755), Normans Inlet (Wimble 1738), Old Cedar Inlet (USBGN staff), Passe Neuve (Bellin 1764—*neuve*, new or recent in French), Porters Inlet (Stick 1958, 9—from early grant including Shackleford Banks), Sand Inlet (Fisher 1962, 91).

Cedar Inlet Marshes, marsh, Carteret County, Stacy Township (local use). Composed of large named marsh islands (Inner Grass Lump, Outer Grass Lump, Big Marsh, Cedar Hammock) and smaller unnamed marsh islands, 4 mi. s of Atlantic (mainland).

Cedar Island, former island, Currituck County,

Fruitville Township (Currituck Deeds, miscellaneous, 1719). Was between Fresh Pond Island and Daugers Island (now just Currituck Banks), 4.5 mi. ese of Knotts Island (village). Location approximate as topography has changed.

Cedar Island, island, 0.4 mi. long, 0.3 mi. wide, Dare County, Nags Head Township (USGS 2013: Roanoke Island NE). In Roanoke Sound 0.6 mi. w of Whalebone Junction, supports causeway between Bodie Island and Washington Baum Bridge to Roanoke Island. Horse Islands used sometimes for two separate islands usually known as Horse Island and Cedar Island. By mid-20th century two islands had become one and today considerably altered by man. *See* Canals at Cedar Island. A hunt club was here 1920s. *Other names:* Horse Islands (used alternately with Cedar Island before human alteration).

Cedar Island, island, 0.1 mi. long, Dare County, Nags Head Township (USGS 2013: Oregon Inlet). In Roanoke Sound 0.2 mi. w of Cedar Point, 1.6 mi. ne of Duck Island. *Other names:* Folly Island (possibly: hand-annotated photograph 1944 aerial view Bodie Island Lighthouse [Oppermann 2005, 179, appendix H, and online] with arrow indicating direction pointing toward Cedar Island, possibly another smaller "unnamed" island though off direction—no other known reference to Folly Island).

Cedar Island. *See* North Burris Island and South Burris Island.

Cedar Island Bay, bay, 3.3 mi. long, 1.5 mi. wide, Carteret County, Cedar Island Township (USGS 2013: Atlantic). Indents ne portion Cedar Island 2 mi. e of Cedar Island Ferry landing, 10 mi. sw of Ocracoke (village). Made official by USBGN 1949. *Other names:* Cedar Bay (local use), Hog Island Bay (USBGN staff).

Cedar Point, small point, Carteret County, White Oak Township (local use). Just n of central Archer Creek, in w Emerald Isle (town), 1.3 mi. e of Langston Bridge.

Cedar Point, point, Currituck County, Fruitville Township (USGS 2013: Knotts Island). At e end Long Pond just w of Carova, 2.5 mi. ne of Knotts Island (village).

Cedar Point, point, Dare County, Kinnakeet Township (local use). On Cedar Hammock just n of Clarks Bay in s Salvo.

Cedar Point, peninsula, Dare County, Nags

Head Township (USGS 2013: Oregon Inlet). On sw Bodie Island just nw of Georges Creek, 0.4 mi. w of Bodie Island Lighthouse, 4.2 mi. wsw of Wanchese.

Cedar Snag Cove, cove, 0.4 mi. long, 0.2 mi. wide, Currituck County, Fruitville Township (USGS 2013: Knotts Island). In marsh islands just ne of Abes Island Cove, 2.5 mi. ne of Knotts Island (village).

Cemetery Ridge, small ridge, Dare County, Atlantic Township (Town of Kitty Hawk 2007). At s end of Kitty Hawk ridge-and-swale system (q.v.) just n of Poor Ridge Landing, 1 mi. sw of original Kitty Hawk.

Center Canal, canal, 0.3 mi. long, Carteret County, Morehead Township (Carteret County GIS 2019). Middle of three canals trending n-s in Sound View Isles subdivision (e-most part of Canals at Atlantic Beach [q.v.]).

Chacandepeco Inlet, former water passage, Dare County, Kinnakeet Township (17th-century maps). Connected Pamlico Sound to Atlantic Ocean through Hatteras Island, 1.1 mi. e of Buxton. Opened before 1585 and closed early 1670s. Name possibly Spanish corruption of Algonquian word referring to shallow. Inlet open during Roanoke voyages (1584–90), but known not to be used by any of the voyages, including the first colony (second Roanoke voyage) or the second, Lost Colony (fourth Roanoke voyage). Might be the "fret" (breach) to which John White refers, as where the ship anchored when searching for Lost Colonists (1590), but unclear whether White was describing Chacandepeco Inlet or Keneckid Inlet. White refers to anchoring at the extreme ne point of Croatoan, just about here on most map applications. White specifically states breach or water passage was at "35 degr. & a half," in No Ache area just s of Salvo at probable former Keneckid Inlet. However, if his calculations were off by about 15 minutes of latitude then he would have been anchored at the later cartographic limits of Croatoan, and the breach he was describing could be former Chacandepeco Inlet (near Buxton), open 1590 when White arrived (*see* Keneckid Inlet). Either instance is possible, and exact reference meant by White might never be known. *Other names:* Cape Channel (Hooker 1846), Cape Inlet (used sometimes locally; proximity to Cape Hatteras—Fisher 1962,

map, 79), Chancandepeco Inlet (alternate spelling rarely used), Chaneandepeco Inlet (used alternately with Chacandepeco on maps), Chewan de Poco (Blaeu 1640), Deep Creek (Covey 2018, 20), Grenvils Road (Smith 1624—*see* Nigh Inlet), Hatteras Inlett (Cheeseman 1982, 195, from Hack 1684—descriptive reference), The Haulover (local use for shallow inlets and occasional flooding, small boats could be "hauled over").

Chadwick Channel, channel, 1.5 mi. long, Carteret County, Morehead Township (Carteret County GIS 2019). Trends n-s and connects Moonlight Bay to Bogue Sound n part of Atlantic Beach Isles subdivision (w part of Canals at Atlantic Beach q.v.), 0.8 mi. s of Morehead City (mainland).

Chain Shot Island, island, 0.2 mi. long, Carteret County, Cedar Island Township (USGS 2013: Wainwright Island). In Core Sound 4.6 mi. w of Swash Inlet, 17.2 mi. sw of Ocracoke (village). Named early 18th century for cannon shot consisting of two balls or half balls joined by short chain, formerly used in naval warfare to cut ships' rigging or sails. Island's shape historically resembled a "chain shot" but changed shape over years. *Other names:* Chainshot Island (Holland 1794), Chain Shott Island (18th-century spelling).

Cheeseman Inlet, former water passage, Carteret County, Morehead Township (USGS 2013: Mansfield historical location). Connected Bogue Sound to Atlantic Ocean through Bogue Banks at Hoop Pole Bay, 1.6 mi. w of Atlantic Beach (town). Occasionally awash 1700-1750 and then open until 1816; occasionally awash until 1850s. Reported "nearly dry" by Blunt (1809), "near filled up" by Brazier (1833). Major hurricane in 1879 cut several temporary breaches in this area. Name origin unknown locally and elsewhere. *See* Stanford Islands. *Other names:* Cheesemans Inlet (USGS 2013: Mansfield, former site labeled).

Cherry Tree Ridge, small sand ridge, Dare County, Atlantic Township (Harris 2017). Ne of High Ridge, 1.7 mi. nw of original Kitty Hawk. Name origin, a surname (Currituck deeds, 1870); while cherries are known here, term is unusual in place names of the Outer Banks and not the case here.

Chicahauk Beach, beach, Dare County, Atlantic Township (local use). In Chicahauk section

Southern Shores, 5.5 mi. n of original Kitty Hawk. Chicahauk or Chickahauk is original indigenous name for Kitty Hawk, its name origin. *See* Chickehauk. Subdivision in Southern Shores named for feature.

Chicamacomico, historical area, Dare County, Kinnakeet Township (18th-century references). Indigenous reference applied historically late 18th, 19th, and early 20th centuries to scattered population of n portion Hatteras Island in vicinity of Rodanthe, Waves, and Salvo. Name still labeled on NOS 2014d. Reportedly means sinking sand, but as with most indigenous words, recording by early Europeans was inadequate, so actual meaning cannot be proved. Sometimes indicated in brochures, with Rodanthe, Waves, and Salvo referenced as Chicamacomico Banks, but historically, when named these three communities were referenced as simply Chicamacomico, *on* Chicamacomico Banks.

Rodanthe area of the Outer Banks is only known occurrence of this name except for a stream named Chicamacomico River in Dorchester County, Maryland. Limited interviews there confirm name has been used since late 1800s. All agree name is of indigenous origin, but meaning is unknown there. Could be a transfer name from Maryland to Outer Banks, but not likely as indigenous suffix "-comico" used for numerous place names in e shore Maryland and Virginia, as used here. This and numerous variations only known occurrence of suffix "-comico" on the Outer Banks.

Other names: Chicamicomico (CS 1862a), Chicamicomio (Bishop 1878), Chichinnacomoc (Stick 1958, 284), Chichinock-cominock (Stick 1970), Chick (Stick 1958, 284), Chickamacomack (Currituck DB 6, 1790, 81), Chickamacomick (Stick 1958, 284), Chickamacomico (Currituck DB 7, 1794, 80–81), Chickamacoomick (White et al. 2017), Chickamecomaco (Currituck DB 10, 1809, 105), Chickamicomack (Currituck DB 6, 1790, 81), Chickamicomico (historical form), Chickcomackco (Currituck DB 5, 1786, 257), Chickenemock (Currituck DB 8, 1798, 127–28), Chickinacommuck (Baldwin 1755), Chickinecomoack (Currituck DB 8, 1799, 161), Chickinnacomoc (Lawson 1859, labeled at Wimble Shoals; Moll 1729 at Wimble Shoals), Chickinocommock (Stick

1958, 284), Chickinocommuck (Stick 1958, 284), Chickmicomaco (Currituck DB 6, 1790, 78), Chickmiomachco (Currituck DB 7, 1794, 79–80), Chicknacomick (Currituck DB 11, 1810, 94–95), Chicknecomack (Currituck DB 7, 1796, 337–38), Chicknicomack (Currituck DB 7, 1796, 337–38), Chicknicomaco (Currituck DB 6, 1790, 78), Chicknicomackco (Currituck DB 7, 1794, 79–80), Chickony-Commock (Stick 1958, 284), Chicomocomico (quote, Charles F. Johnson, Union soldier, Ninth New York, from Downing 2008, 32), Chiconocomick (description, Thomas Paines Landing), Hatorask (applied occasionally on early maps; White 1585 used this name here).

Chicamacomico. *See* Rodanthe.

Chicamacomico Banks, former barrier island, 19 mi. long, Dare County, Kinnakeet Township (occasional 18th-century use). Included portion of present Hatteras Island n from Little Kinnakeet to former Chickinacommock Inlet or as far as New Inlet (reopened 2011) at s end Pea Island. Name Chewan de Poco applied on Blaeu's (1640) map might be misinterpretation of indigenous name here, Chicamacomico according to placement on map but is not because it is a peculiar spelling of Chacandepeco. Tempting to associate this name with Chowan, but Chowan was used inland in upper Albemarle region and not applicable here; no occurrences of Chowan used here. Lack of space on the map requires this misleading name placement: name is clearly a peculiar rendition of Chacandepeco Inlet (Chewan de Poco), open 1640. *See* Chicamacomico. *Other names:* Bald Buck (early deeds referring to beach between Chicamacomico [Rodanthe] and Kinnakeet [Avon] using archaic meaning of "buck" as stark—*see* Buck Ridge), Checkercomocomet (Wimble 1733), Checkercomoconet (historical), Chewan de Poco (Blaeu 1640), Chicamacomico Island (CS 1862a), Chicanocomack Banks (Currituck DB 3, 1800, 163–64), Chickamacomack Banks (Currituck DB 6, 1788, 39), Chickamacomico Banks (Currituck DB 6, 1788, 41), Chickamacomico Beach (Walton 1861), Chickamicomacko Banks (Currituck DB 6, 1788, 40), Chickamimacko Banks (Currituck DB 5, 1788, 325–26), Chickcomicomack Banks (Currituck DB 8, 1799, 225), Chickconacomo Banks (Tanner 1855), Chickconocomack Bank (Price et al. 1808), Chickemecomet Island (Baldwin 1755), Chickemeok Banks (Currituck DB 10, 1810, 105), Chickemmocomock (Brazier 1833), Chickenencommock Banks (Currituck DB 2, 1768, 56), Chickenenomock Banks (Currituck DB 11, 1810, 223–24), Chickenommack Bank (Price et al. 1808), Chickinacomack Banks (Currituck DB 2, 1768, 26–27), Chickinacommock Banks (NPS 2005b: NPS 1, 489), Chickineckcaminock Banks (Price and Strother 1798), Chickinnacomac (historical), Chickinnicomock Banks (Currituck DB 2, 1771, 291), Chickinockcominock Banks (Price and Strother 1798), Chicknacomack Banks (Currituck DB 3, 1802, 300–1), Chicknacomeeck Banks (Currituck DB 8, 1800, 206), Chicknacomico Banks (shipwreck records), Chickneacomack Banks (Currituck DB 7 date missing, 143), Chickneacomeeck Banks (Currituck DB 8, 1800, 206), Chicknecomack Banks (Currituck DB 7, date missing, 143), Chicknecomock Banks (Currituck DB 8, 1798, 100), Chicknicomack Banks (Currituck DB 6, 1788, 39–40), Chickoncomacke Banks (Currituck DB 6, 1788, 40–41), Chickonocomack Bank (Price et al. 1808), Chicmecomack Banks (Currituck DB 4, 1783, 227), Chicoicomac Banks (Currituck DB 15, 1761, 367), Chicomacomack Banks (Cobb 1905 — misrecorded from Tanner 1855), Chicomico (Blunt 1857, 341), Chicomorock Banks (Currituck DB 9, 1805, 195–96), Chicomycomemeck Banks (Currituck DB 12, 1813, 181–82), Chiconomack Bank (Gray 1872), Chihemecomet Banks (Russell and Lodge 1778), Chikemecomet Banks (Wimble 1733), Chikinacomet Island (Baldwin 1755), Chiknecomack Banks (Currituck DB 3, 1801, 127–28), Isle Chihemecomet (Nolin 1783).

Chicamacomico Beach, former beach, 17 mi. long, Dare County, Kinnakeet Township (historical use). Was at Chicamacomico Banks just n of Little Kinnakeet to former Chickinacommock Inlet. Some resurgence of use with historical awareness and tourism promotion, especially applied in Rodanthe. *See* Rodanthe Beach and Chicamacomico.

Chicamacomico Channel, channel, 2.5 mi. long, Dare County, Kinnakeet Township (local use). In Pamlico Sound just s of Rodanthe Channel, s approach to Blackmar Gut, harbor at Rodanthe. Only name still in current use using original Indian name. A remnant channel associated with former Chickinacommock Inlet. *See* Chicamacomico. *Other names:* Blackmar Gut (q.v. — 20th-century dredged Rodanthe approach), Chicamocomico Channel (Rodanthe Channel fig. 5, 11), North'ard Channel (Garrity-Blake 2010, 492 — *see* The North'ard), The Harbor (some local use).

Chick, apparent former barrier island, Dare County, Kinnakeet Township (Collet et al. 1770). Appears on numerous 18th-century maps, an apparent reference to a barrier island usually shown from historical Chickincommock Inlet (s) to historical Gunt Inlet (n). More likely an abbreviation of different forms of Chicamacomico but included as a separate entry here because it appears often with slightly different application.

Chickehauk, historical area (first appears Wimble 1738). Anglicized version of Indian name for Duck s to Whalebone Junction major tourist area of the Outer Banks today. Kitty Hawk is a further corruption of a variation of Chickehauk. Subdivision by this name (spelled Chicahauk) in Southern Shores. *Other names:* Chickehauk Island (Kitchen 1765), Isle Chickehauk (Bellin 1757), Isle Kikchauk (Nolin 1783).

Chickinacommock Inlet, former water passage, Dare County, Kinnakeet Township (Moseley 1737). Connected Pamlico Sound to Atlantic Ocean through Hatteras Island, 1.5 mi. n of Rodanthe. Opened in 1657 and closed 1683. Possibly open periodically in mid-1700s but did reopen 1862–65. Was in Chicamacomico (Rodanthe) but used this spelling. This land referenced by sailors (early 17th century) as Dugs (female breasts — *see* Dugs) because of prominent sand dunes, so variations of Dugs were applied in conjunction with this inlet name. Formerly in what is now known as S-Curves (q.v.; bypass bridge 3 mi. long under construction). *Other names:* Chicamacomico Inlet (Stick 1958, 279), Chick Inlet (Stick 1958, 279 — probable abbreviation), Chickinacommack Inlet (another spelling), Chickinock-Cominock Inlet (Romans 1776), Chickinockcominock Inlet (Mouzon 1775), Chickinock-comonock Inlet (historical), Chickinockcomonock Inlet (Collet et al. 1770), Chickinockcominock Inlet (Fry et al.

1775), Chickinocominock Inlet (Holland 1794), Chickinocommack Inlet (18th-century maps), Chickinoke Inlet (Fisher 1962, 93), Chickmacomack Inlet (Stick 1958, 33), Chickmockcommock Inlet (Collet et al. 1770), Chicomok Inlet (historical), Chickonockcominock Inlet (Cobb 1905 — misrecorded from Collet et al. 1770), Dugg Creek (variation of Dug or Dugs [q.v.]), Dugg Inlet (variation of Dug or Dugs—18th-century maps and Fisher 1962, 95 — Fisher unsure if this variant name applied to New Inlet or this inlet), Dug Inlet (*see* Dugs), Keneckid Inlet (used in references possibly to this inlet — Fisher 1962, 98).

Chinquapin Ridge, sand ridge, Dare County, Atlantic Township (Harris 2017). Just w of Chinquapin Swamp just n of Poor Ridge, 1.3 mi. wnw of original Kitty Hawk. *See* Chinquapin Swamp. *Other names:* Chincapin Ridge (Harris 2017), Chinkapin Ridge (Harris 2017; unknown, 1779), Chinquepin Ridge (Harris 2017; unknown, 1795), Chinquipen Ridge (Harris 2017; unknown, 1857), Chinquipin Ridge (Harris 2017; unknown, 1814).

Chinquapin Ridge Pond, lake, Dare County, Atlantic Township (local use). In Duck Pond Swamp, Sandy Run Swamp, Chinquapin Swamp just w of Chinquapin Ridge, 1 mi. nw of original Kitty Hawk. Associative name with Chinquapin Ridge. *See* Chinquapin Swamp. *Other names:* Chinquipin Ridge Pond (Harris 2017).

Chinquapin Swamp, linear swamp, Dare County, Atlantic Township (Town of Kitty Hawk 2007). In Kitty Hawk Woods just e of Chinquapin Ridge and Sandy Run Swamp, 1 mi. nw of original Kitty Hawk. In e Kitty Hawk Woods Swamps (q.v.). Chinquapin (also Chinkapin) refers to dwarf chestnut tree (*Castanea pumila*) native to e U.S., nuts used by indigenous peoples and early colonists. Name is used throughout the U.S. Southeast, but not so much on the Outer Banks. *See* Kitty Hawk ridge-and-swale system. *Other names:* Chinquipin Ridge Swamp (Harris 2017; unknown, 1829), Chinquopin Swamp (misinterpretation, local maps).

Chris Hole. *See* Cockrel Creek.

Christopher Ridge, sand ridge, Dare County, Hatteras Township (Covey 2018, 20). In s Brigands Bay subdivision in Frisco where Indian Town was reportedly located, 3 mi. w of Buxton; was extension of w end Indian Ridge obliterated by development of Brigands Bay.

Churches Swamp, swamp, Dare County, Nags Head Township (Currituck DB 6, 1788, 38–39). Included much of swampy marsh e of Broad Creek to Roanoke Sound, 2 mi. n of Wanchese. Used historically and unknown today.

Clam Rock, former rock, Carteret County, Morehead Township (former local use). Was in Bogue Sound between Money Island Bay and Tar Landing Bay, just nw of Clam Rock Slough and Triple S Marina (now), 1 mi. ne of Atlantic Beach. "Clam" used in place names is unusual on the Outer Banks, where oyster is much more prevalent. Clam is found in the name Clam Shoal in Pamlico Sound near Hatteras (village) considerable distance n of here.

Clam Rock Fish Camp, former camp, Carteret County, Morehead Township (Stephens 1989, 26). Was just e of Triple S Marina, 2.5 mi. e of Atlantic Beach. There were seven fishing clubs or camps used into 1970s for varying levels of fishing. Named for nearby Clam Rock (q.v.); Clam Rock Slough was just n here.

Clam Rock Slough, former channel, 0.1 mi. long and wide, Carteret County, Morehead Township (USGS 1951: Beaufort). Just w of Tar Landing Bay 1.7 mi. e of Atlantic Beach (town). Altered considerably since mid-20th century for Triple S Marina. *See* Clam Rock. *Other names:* McClamrock Slough (uncommon surname here and elsewhere on the Outer Banks, shown USGS 1951: Beaufort so possibly some credence).

Clam Shoal, shoal, 3 mi. long, Dare County, Hatteras Township (local use). In Pamlico Sound, 4 mi. ne of Hatteras (village). Exposed area named Bird Islands (q.v.).

Clara Crossroads, area, Carteret County, Harkers Island Township (signage). On e end Harkers Island, 0.5 mi. s of w end Eastmouth Bay, 0.8 mi. w of Cape Lookout National Park facility.

Clark Reef, shoal, 0.5 mi. long, Hyde County, Ocracoke Township (local use). In Pamlico Sound 0.9 mi. n of The Knoll, 3.7 mi. ne of Ocracoke (village). "Reef" in Outer Banks geographic names usually refers to oyster colonies. *Other names:* Clarks Reef (CS

1852), Darks Reef (misinterpretation found occasionally in papers of the Great Ocracoke Oyster War, 1890).

Clarks. *See* Salvo.

Clarks Bay, cove, Dare County, Kinnakeet Township (USGS 2013: Rodanthe). In Pamlico Sound just n of No Ache, 0.8 mi. ssw of Salvo. Retains its original associative name with nearby Clarks, now Salvo. *Other names:* Cedar Bay (occasional historical use, proximity to Cedar Hammock).

Clarks Island, former island, Dare County, Kinnakeet Township (historical charts). Was in n Clarks Bay just w of NPS Salvo Day Use Area. Late as 1948 shoals still visible at low water and into the 1980s some shoals would bare at extremely low water (NOS 2014b).

Clarks Landing, former landing, Dare County, Kinnakeet Township (historical use). Was in s Salvo (originally Clarks) at Cedar Hammock just ne of Clarks Bay at NPS day use area. *Other names:* Miss Kittys Landing (Covey 2018, 146).

Cliffs of Colington, distinctive sand ridge, 0.7 mi. long, Dare County, Atlantic Township (local use). On s end Colington Island just w of Colington Cut, 1.3 mi. se of Colington Harbour. Subdivision named for feature. *Other names:* Colington Cliffs (local use).

Clipper Lake, man-enhanced cove, Dare County, Atlantic Township (local use). At Eagleton Point, nw corner Colington Island just n of Colington Harbour, 3 mi. sw of original Kitty Hawk. Associated with Colington Harbour subdivision, where canal naming scheme is ships or nautical terms. "Clipper" is a fast sailing ship with large sail, in 19th century when sailing ships with cargo (especially tea from Asia) needed speed to "clip" along at rapid rate.

Clubhouse Creek, cove, Dare County, Hatteras Township (dwindling local use). Former creek in e Hatteras (village) now cove-like with creation of Hatteras–Ocracoke Ferry docks, 2.5 mi. ne of Hatteras Inlet. Austin Creek (q.v.) trended into this creek from ne; historically the two were separate features, though now Austin Creek is more used for entire complex at the ferry basin.

Clubhouse Creek. *See* Blossie Creek.

Coastal Plain, physiographic or landform region where the Outer Banks are situated; plain is flat sandy soil stretching 150 mi. inland in North Carolina to Piedmont region near Raleigh. Made up of two zones, submerged shelf and exposed plain, but generally only exposed portion is referenced as Coastal Plain.

Coast Guard Channel, short channel, Dare County, Nags Head Township (local use). Principal channel in Oregon Inlet, occupies much of Oregon Inlet Gorge, 11 mi. s of Whalebone Junction. Derived from channel's proximity to former Coast Guard facility, 1.5 mi. s of inlet; Coast Guard station was abandoned 1988, and new existing station opened 1990 on n side of inlet near Oregon Inlet Marina.

Coast Guard Creek, tidal creek, Carteret County, Portsmouth Township (USGS 1950: Portsmouth). At ne Portsmouth Island just e of Portsmouth (village), 6 mi. sw of Ocracoke (village). Named for and just ne of former Coast Guard station, no longer operational but preserved in Portsmouth Village section Cape Lookout National Seashore. *Other names:* South West Creek (NPS 2018, 90), Southwest Creek (relative direction from village; NPS 2006, 15—smaller and used before life-saving/Coast Guard station).

Coast Guard Dock, landing, Carteret County, Harkers Island Township (current maps). At Catfish Point, e side Cape Lookout Bight, 1 mi. sw of Cape Lookout Lighthouse. Former Army Dock site nearby.

Coast Guard Wharf, former landing, Carteret County, Portsmouth Township (former local use). Was at Portsmouth Coast Guard Station in Coast Guard Creek 0.2 mi. e of center Portsmouth (village).

Cockle Creek. *See* Silver Lake.

Cockle Marsh Island, island, 0.3 mi. long, Carteret County, Harkers Island Township (USGS 2013: Harkers Island). In Core Sound, 3.3 mi. ese of Harkers Island (village). "Cockle" has many meanings but on the Outer Banks generally refers to bivalve mollusks with ribbed shells common to the region.

Cockle Shoal, small shoal, Hyde County, Ocracoke Township (local use). Just offshore, just n of Springers Point, 1.5 mi. se of Ocracoke (village). A few place the shoal slightly farther n near The Ditch, entrance to Silver Lake. *See* Cockle Marsh Island. *Other names:* Cockel Shoal (Weslager 1954).

Cockle Shoal Swash, small breakers area, Hyde County, Ocracoke Township (local use). At

Cockle Shoal just n of Springers Point, 0.75 mi. sw of Ocracoke (village center).

Cockrel Creek, water passage, 0.4 mi. wide, Hyde County, Ocracoke Township (USGS 2013: Green Island). In Pamlico Sound just sw of Green Island, 12 mi. ne of Ocracoke (village). "Cockrel" is a corruption of the word "cockle" (*see* Cockle Marsh Island). Also, "cockerel" refers to a young cock or rooster and was in common use 17th and 18th centuries when many of these names were applied. Some of these names have been perpetuated for a long time, so source could be "cockrel," a misspelling of "cockerel." However, most believe misspelling of "cockle." *Other names:* Chris Hole (local use), Cockle Creek (confusion with Cockrel), The Creek (local use).

Cockrel Creek Island, island, 0.1 mi. long, Hyde County, Ocracoke Township (USGS 2013: Green Island). Just ne of Cockrel Creek, 3.8 mi. sw of Hatteras Inlet. *See* Cockle Marsh Island and Cockrel Creek. *Other names:* Cockeral Creek Island (transcribing error), Cockle Creek Island (Weslager 1954, 44), Cockrel Island (from NPS Director Conrad Wirth, letter in *Coastland Times*, October 27, 1952, in NPS 2005b: NPS 2, 493).

Codds Creek, water passage, 0.4 mi. long, Carteret County, Smyrna Township (USGS 2013: Horsepen Point). In Core Sound at entrance Try Yard Creek, 4.2 mi. e of Harkers Island (village). "Codd" is 16th-century English term for bag-like inner bay or marsh, used extensively in early Virginia records. Evidence for this meaning is supported by nearby Try Yard Creek (q.v.), also 18th-century English application. Additionally, used 17th century referring to mud, specifically containing shells, which might be applicable here. No relationship to cod fish (*Gadus morhua*), a cold-water fish prevalent off New England coast. Also, might have been a historical inlet at one time as area prone to constant and continuous overwash.

Cold Beach, former beach, Dare County, Kinnakeet Township (Currituck DB 3, 1784, 503). On Chicamacomico Banks referenced 1784 deed. No other locative information is provided other than surnames.

Colington, scattered community, Dare County, Atlantic Township (USGS 2013: Kitty Hawk). On Colington Island, 3.8 mi. s of original Kitty Hawk. Named for island, post office est. 1889 at Shingle Landing (q.v.), discontinued 1945. *See* Colington Island. Four subdivisions named for feature. *Other names:* Collington (common use until mid-20th century).

Colington Creek, water passage, 3.5 mi. long, Dare County, Atlantic Township (USGS 2013: Kitty Hawk, Manteo). Connects Kitty Hawk Bay and Buzzard Bay separates Colington Island from the barrier island, just e of Colington, 3 mi. s of original Kitty Hawk. *See* Colington Island. Two subdivisions named for feature. *Other names:* Colenton Creek (Currituck DB 5, 1784, 48–49), Colington Bay (early local use), Colinton Creek (Currituck DB 9, 1807, 323), Collenton Creek (Currituck DB 11, 1810, 33), Collington Creek (mostly early 20th century, but occasionally since mid-18th century), Collinton Creek (Currituck DB 5, 1781, 27–28), Collonton Creek (Currituck DB 11, 1810, 124–25), Colonton Creek (Currituck DB 11, 1810, 124–25).

Colington Cut, water passage, 0.8 mi. long, Dare County, Atlantic Township (USGS 1982: Kitty Hawk, Manteo). Canalized stream (s end) divides Colington Island into two sections (Big Colington and Little Colington) connects Blount Bay (n) and Buzzard Bay (s), 1.7 mi. ssw of Wright Brothers National Memorial. Canalized by extending stream s 18th century, originally and still often referenced as The Dividing Creek. *See* Colington Island. *Other names:* Colington Cut Ditch (limited use from dredging), Colington Ditch (limited use from dredging), Cross Ditch (Currituck DB 5, 1784, 4), Dividing Creek (Currituck DB 2, 1766, 270–71), The Dividing Creek (18th century mostly).

Colington Glen, small shallow swale, Dare County, Atlantic Township (local use). Trends n-s between n end Cliffs of Colington (e) and distinct vegetated dune at the s end of Colington Ridge (w). Recent usage from attractive marketing name of subdivision same name. Not really a glen in traditional sense of secluded, narrow valley.

Colington Harbour, harbor, 0.2 mi. long and wide, Dare County, Atlantic Township (signage). At nw Colington Island, 2.3 mi. ssw of original Kitty Hawk. Recent, commercial name, therefore spelling not from 16th- or 17th-century English. *See* Colington Island. *Other names:* Collington Harbor (N.C. Marine Fisheries 2013, map 9).

Colington Harbour, subdivision, Dare County, Atlantic Township (signage). On nw end

Colington Island, 4 mi. sw of original Kitty Hawk. Developed mid-20th century (1968) before major development period late 20th century. British spelling of Harbour was a marketing technique, not from long-established name from colonial period. *See* Colington Island. *Other names:* Colington Harbor (some local use; real estate listings; Binkley 2007, 7).

Colington Harbour Canal, small canal, Dare County, Atlantic Township (local use). Entrance from Albemarle Sound into canal system at Colington Harbour (*see* Canals at Colington Harbour). Colington Canal more used than official form. *See* Colington Harbour subdivision. *Other names:* Colington Canal (local use).

Colington Island, island, 2.1 mi. long, 2.5 mi. wide, Dare County, Atlantic Township (USGS 2013: Kitty Hawk, Manteo). In Roanoke Sound near mouth of Albemarle Sound just w of barrier island, 4.5 mi. s of original Kitty Hawk. Named for Sir John Colleton (one of the eight Lords Proprietors of Carolina—*see* Carolina) to whom island granted 1663 (hence one of the former names, Colleton Island).

Some buildings built, but no permanent plantation ever established by Colleton. Attempt to settle 1664, but storms and other misfortunes forced abandoning this attempt and scant evidence of settlement found. By 1700, settlers here. Name changed to Carlile Island for a short time reportedly for Christopher Carlile, stepson of Sir Francis Washington who accompanied Sir Francis Drake to the Outer Banks 1586, but Carlile Island dropped in favor of Colleton Island. Evident numerous spellings have existed and have evolved over centuries. These variant names have appeared on scores of historical maps and charts. Name originally Carlyle (or some form) for a short time on earliest maps, but by late 17th century had changed to Colleton Island (1666–1765) on most maps and continued until late 18th century when Collintons Island appeared (1768–94). From early 19th century through end of 19th century, Collington Island appeared (1839–1943), and present form, Colington Island (one "l"), came into usage around 1909. Both forms were used until Collington form fell into disuse by mid-20th century in favor of Colington. Made official by USBGN 1944 to establish newly evolved form with one "l."

Other names: Callitons Island (historical), Carelyle Island (one original form), Carlile Island (Speed 1676), Carlyle Island (original deed), Caryle Island (one original form), Colington Islands (O'Neal et al. 1976, 7—plural form occasionally, used especially 19th century, two islands created by dredging Colington Cut—*see* Big Colington and Little Colington), Colinton Island (Currituck DB 9, 1807, 328–29), Collenton Island (Currituck DB 9, 1802, 44), Colleton Ile (Schroeter 1859), Colleton Island (Currituck DB 2, 1766, 270–71; Cobb 1905), Colletons Island (early sources), Collington Island (mid-19th century through mid-20th century, including Binkley 2007, 34, referencing documents on national seashore creation 1937; and 1952 CHNS project map from Binkley 2007, 100), Collington Islands (early brochures for Big Colington and Little Colington), Collingtons Island (Russell and Lodge 1778), Collinton Island (Wimble 1738), Collintons Island (Collet et al. 1770), Collitan Island (early form), Collitons Island (historical), Ile Colleton (historical French maps), Isle de Colleton (Vaugondy 1753), Luck Island (Charles II 1663).

Colington Island Shoal, shoal, Dare County, Atlantic Township (local use). Junction of Croatan and Albemarle Sounds, 3.6 mi. ese of Colington Island. *See* Colington Island.

Colington Point. *See* Meter Point.

Colington Ridge, sand ridge, 3.5 mi. long, Dare County, Atlantic Township (local use). Trends nw-se n end Colington Island at Eagleton Point to just nw of Cliffs of Colington, 1 mi. nw of Bens Point. Series of about 10 distinct mostly vegetated dunes averaging 20–35 ft. high. *See* Colington Island. *Other names:* Bay Cliff (recent use from Bay Cliff Trail here from subdivision).

Colington Shoal, shoal, 2 mi. long, 6 ft. (1 fathom) deep, Dare County, Nags Head and Croatan Townships (local use). In Albemarle Sound, 2.5 mi. sw of Colington Island, 5.3 mi. nw of Manteo (center). *See* Colington Island. *Other names:* Colington Shoals (scientific reports).

Colington Woods, woods, Dare County, Atlantic Township (Dare County Planning Department 2009, 31, 61). Once covered much of Colington Island (Big Colington and Little Colington), with development is much smaller, now limited generally to Meter Point and central and s-central Colington Island.

Not used much now except in scientific reports and official documents. *See* Colington Island. Subdivision named for feature.

Collins Creek, small canal, 0.5 mi. long, Dare County, Nags Head Township (local use). In downtown Manteo from subdivision of same name ene into Scarboro Creek. Reportedly a landing here, and street name at entrance to subdivision is Landing Lane, but no documentation found and reports of a landing are sketchy (town official).

Colonel Browns Hill, small former sand dune, Dare County, Kinnakeet Township (Covey 2018, 28). Was in Waves at Waves Landing just s of Wenberg Ridge, 2 mi. s of Rodanthe. Covey indicates name from where Colonel Brown (Union) assembled troops during Civil War. Name unknown locally.

Colony Lake, lake, 0.1 mi. across, Dare County, Atlantic Township (local use). On nw Colington Island, 3 mi. s of original Kitty Hawk. Local residents indicate name honors Lost Colony on nearby Roanoke Island, and both attempts at colonization on Roanoke Island (1585—military; 1587—Lost Colony).

Community Square Docks, small harbor, Hyde County, Ocracoke Township (signage). On e side of Silver Lake in Ocracoke (village center), 3.5 mi. ne of Ocracoke Inlet. *Other names:* Jack Willis Dock (full name use occasionally), Willis Dock (Howard, August 21, 2013—no longer exists, destroyed during hurricane 1944, used as mail dock while Willis was mailboat captain).

Conch Shoal Marsh, marsh island, 0.05 mi. long, Carteret County, Harkers Island Township (USGS 1997: Harkers Island). Just n of Shackleford Banks just e of Johnsons Bay, 3 mi. s of Harkers Island (village). "Conch" refers to any large spiral-shelled marine gastropod mollusk (related to clams and oysters). Whelks are commonly found on entire length of the Outer Banks, but conchs only s of Cape Hatteras.

Cooper Bay, harbor, 0.3 mi. wide, Carteret County, Morehead Township (Carteret County GIS 2019). Part of the canal system centrally located in Sound View Isles subdivision (w part of Canals at Atlantic Beach, q.v.), 1.3 mi. s of Morehead City (mainland).

Coquina Beach, beach, Dare County, Nags Head Township (signage). On Bodie Island, 3.8 mi. nnw of Oregon Inlet, 9.5 mi. sse of Nags Head (center). Est. 1955 as swimming area and named by NPS. Originates from small shellfish (*Donax* spp.) of conch family found on the Outer Banks. A short debate followed regarding name. Park historian and chief ranger did not care for name "Coquina" and wanted a more descriptive term, Bodie Island Beach, but park superintendent "liked the euphonius sound" of Coquina, so Coquina Beach prevailed. *Other names:* Coquina Bench (error USGS 2013: Oregon Inlet, and prevalent on 2013 USGS maps of elsewhere on the Outer Banks—and misapplied 4 mi. s).

Cora June Island, island, Dare County, Hatteras Township (local use). Ne of Hatteras Inlet at ferry route 1.5 mi. w of Hatteras (village). Created by dredging ferry channel.

Coral Bay. *See* Hoop Pole Bay.

Coral Beach. *See* Whalehead Beach (subdivision).

Coral Ridge, barely discernable sand ridge, 0.5 mi. long, 10 ft. high, Carteret County, Morehead Township (local use). On Bogue Banks 2.5 mi. w of Pine Knoll Shores. No coral reefs anywhere along the Outer Banks; closest are in Florida and the Bahamas though a small one is in Bermuda because of the warmth of the Gulf Stream, 650 mi. e of Cape Hatteras. Also, cold-water (deep) coral (*Lophelia* spp.) reportedly discovered almost 100 mi. s of Cape lookout, but likely not relevant here. So, probable fanciful name applied during latter 20th century after major development here, an example of reversed usage, natural feature acquiring name of man-made feature. Three subdivisions named for feature.

Coranine Town, former Indian village, Carteret County, Harkers Island Township (Lawson 1709, 200). Primary Coree Indian's village (also Coranine and other spellings) somewhere on Harkers Island. Coree Indians were extinct by early 17th century as a result of introduced diseases and warlike nature with colonists and neighboring Indians.

Core Banks, barrier beaches, Carteret County; Portsmouth, Atlantic, Sea Level, Stacy, Davis, Smyrna, and Harkers Island Townships (USGS 2013). Now (and historically) breached in different places by inlets ne from Cape Lookout. Barden Inlet to Ocracoke Inlet, including Portsmouth Island to just n of Portsmouth (village), though some consider n limit to have been 3 mi. sw at Swash Inlet, some to former High Hills Inlet (Whalebone

Inlet) not including Portsmouth Island. Named for Coree or Coranine Indians known to have inhabited this area. *See* Coranine Town.

Historically divided into North Core Banks and South Core Banks, still used today; South Core Banks ne-ward from Cape Lookout to Drum Inlet (now closed), and North Core Banks n from Drum Inlet (now closed) to Ocracoke Inlet. Gradually, during late 19th century, Portsmouth Island (n-most of North Core Banks), itself islands and continuous sand dunes depending on tides and weather, from Ocracoke Inlet sw-ward to Swash Inlet considered separate. Portsmouth Island was differentiated from North Core Banks because it (with Sheep Island) was inhabited and location of Portsmouth (village). During 21st century, after September 2005 when Hurricane Ophelia swept through Core Banks, two additional names applied to small portion of uppermost South Core Banks. Ophelia Banks used for short time after Ophelia Inlet opened 2005 by Hurricane Ophelia and extended 1 mi. ne to New Drum Inlet, but expanding Ophelia Inlet has mostly captured shoaling New Drum Inlet. Additionally, Middle Core Banks came into use mostly in reports and on USGS topographic maps applied from New Drum Inlet (area) ne-ward 2 mi. to Drum Inlet (now closed). Core Banks made official by USBGN 1949. *See* North Core Banks for a note about Hurricane Dorian (2019).

Other names: Banc Core (Bellin 1764), Bare Inlet Banks (Wimble 1733), Cape Lookout Bank (misapplication), Cape Lookout Banks (misapplication), Cor Banck (Nolin 1783), Core Bank (Pinkerton et al. 1809), Coree Banks (historical maps), Cor Sound Banks (Wimble 1733), Croatoan (Schroeter 1859—misapplication), Endesoakes (indigenous term here and used on several early maps; Angley 1984, 80, from Quinn 1955, based on Haklyut 1589), Isle de Core (Bellin 1764), Ocracock Island (misapplication), Portsmouth Bank (misapplication), Portsmouth Banks (misapplication), Portsmouth Island (misapplication from hand-drawn map depicting CCC e Bogue Banks; Fred Hobson 1935 as presented in PKS 2016), Salvage Island (16th- and 17th-century spelling of "savage"—not salvaging from ships, as in present usage; Indians rarely frequented these narrow sand dunes so might have meant inhospitable nature instead of Indians), Savage Isle (Henry 1860—perhaps applied to Core Banks or Portsmouth Island, difficult to determine given general nature of map), Shoals Bank (map description used as name), The Banks (local use), Wococon Island (misapplication).

Core Beach, historical area vaguely applied to undefined portions of Core Banks s of Portsmouth Island and n of Cape Lookout though used on charts mostly defined by Merkle Hammock (Great Hammock Swash) (s) and former High Hills Inlet (Whalebone Inlet) (n) just s of Portsmouth Island. Still used by older residents for Portsmouth Beach but rapidly falling into disuse. *See* Core Banks.

Coree Cove, cove, Carteret County, White Oak Township (local use). Soundside at w end Bogue Banks in w Emerald Isle (town) 3 mi. sse of Swansboro (mainland), 8.5 mi. w of original Emerald Isle. Name is recent origin, named for Coree (or Coranine) Indians who inhabited this area and more heavily inhabited Harkers Island—*see* Core Banks. Street sign is Corree.

Core Sound, lagoon, 27 mi. long, 3 mi. wide, Carteret County, Cedar Island, Portsmouth, Atlantic, Sea Level, Stacy, Davis, Smyrna, and Harkers Island Townships (USGS 2013). S from Pamlico Sound at Ocracoke (village) and Portsmouth (village) to Back Sound at Cape Lookout and separates mainland from Core Banks. *See* Core Banks. *Other names:* Bogue Sound (Finley and Young 1827—misapplication), Cone Sound (Blunt 1857, 344—misinterpretation or misspelling), Coranine Sound (Lawson 1709, map), Corantung Sound (Cobb 1905, noted for peculiar name renditions), Corenines Sound (Stick 1958), Coresound (Wimble 1738), Core Sund (Lucas 1826), Corse Sound (Bachman 1861), Cor Sound (Wimble 1733), Cortaine Sound (Moll 1729), Crosond (Wimble 1733—notorious for wild orthography), Gore Sound (Leslie 1861—misrecording), Hunting Sound (Holland 1794—name used short time 18th century, mainland known as Hunting Quarter—q.v.), The Sound (some local use).

Core Sound Channel, former channel, 1.5 mi. long, Carteret County, Harkers Island Township (Kell 1777). Connected Beaufort Inlet through shoals to Back Sound, 2 mi. s of Beaufort (mainland). Hydrography has changed, but remnant channels here still used by smaller craft. Channel leads into and ends in Back Sound, unclear if name was to indicate passage toward Core Sound or if Back Sound was being considered as part of Core Sound on this map anyway. *See* Core Banks. *Other names:* Coresound Channel (Kell 1777)

Coreys, former settlement, Currituck County, Fruitville Township (USGS 2013: Knotts Island). Was on nw edge of Great Marsh, 2.9 mi. nw of Knotts Island (village). Built originally 1924 by William E. Corey, president U.S. Steel, as one of the many hunt clubs est. early 20th century. Small community grew 1930s from establishment of hunt club, destroyed by fire 1940. Today Coreys abandoned without a trace of buildings apart from some foundations, but late as 1950 reportedly a few families were living here. *Other names:* Corys (USGS 2010: Knotts Island et al.).

Coreys Ditch, canal, Currituck County, Fruitville Township (F&WS 1984, map, 74). Trends n-s from Barleys Bay (n), 1.3 mi. to mouth Back Creek (s) just n of Mackay Island, 3.5 mi. wnw of Knotts Island (village). Associative name with Coreys formerly just e of n terminus. Dug (dynamited) to control water level in Barleys Bay.

Cormorant Canal, canal, 1 mi. long, Dare County, Atlantic Township (Town of Southern Shores 2015). In Southern Shores, 4.5 mi. n of original Kitty Hawk. Names of Southern Shores canals are for shorebirds (except Gravey Pond Canal). Several kinds of cormorants, two found at the Outer Banks. The double-crested cormorant (*Phalacrocorax auritus*) here year-round and great cormorant (*Phalacrocorax carbo*) here in winter.

Corolla, village, Currituck County, Poplar Branch Township (signage). On Currituck Banks 17 mi. n of Duck. Post Office Department named its post office Corolla when est. 1895, gradually former village names Currituck Beach, Jones Hill, and Whales Head fell into disuse. Name origin formally unknown or lost; name refers to inner leaves or petals of a flower (*see* Rodanthe), local residents accept this as reason for naming. Explanation by some interviewed was field of wildflowers but is dismissed

by most residents, especially older folk, in favor of story that name was suggested by postmaster because overlapping petals (corolla) of a flower were reminiscent of how everyone was "into everyone's business." An interesting story accepted locally but no documented proof.

The name Currituck Beach was generally used to reference beach at Corolla, while name Whales Head used to reference village at Currituck Beach. Whales Head reported by some to be a reference to shape of local barchane, or crescent-shaped dunes (more prevalent historically—*see* Whale Head Hill). Village experienced significant growth and activity during last quarter 20th century and early 21st century mostly with enormous vacation houses with absentee owners. Five subdivisions named for feature. *See* Pony Pen for information regarding wild ponies.

Other names: Carolla (Binkley 2007, 26—probable typographical error), Corella (Fisher 1962, 109—transcribing error), Corolla Village (signage), Currituck Beach (historical local use), Jones Hill (historical local use and first name of village), Old Corolla Village (signage), The Village (used by some locals in spoken language), Whale Head (historical local use), Whalehead (historical local use), Whales Head (historical local use).

Corolla Bay. *See* Whale Head Bay.

Corolla Beach. *See* Currituck Beach.

Corolla Island, man-made island, Currituck County, Poplar Branch Township (Whalehead Club). In Corolla at Currituck Beach Lighthouse at n shore Whale Head Bay. Created 1925 when Edward Collings Knight Jr., avid waterfowl hunter and wealthy industrialist, built a lavish mansion here (Whalehead or Whalehead Club). Mrs. Knight (also liked to hunt) was disallowed admittance into all-male hunt clubs, so her husband responded by building a 21,000-sq.-ft. mansion between 1922 and 1925, first named Corolla Island (later became The Whalehead Club). Small harbor and canal dredged, creating the island, which became known as Corolla Island. *See* Corolla.

Corsair Inlet, canal, Dare County, Atlantic Township (local use). At Colington Harbour, 2.5 mi. wsw of Kill Devil Hills. "Inlet" not used in the traditional sense on the Outer Banks as barrier island breach. Indicative of dredging allowing water inward for access by boats to open water (Albemarle Sound). Canal naming scheme at Colington Harbour is ships or nautical terms. "Corsair" originally meant French privateers (pirates of sort with letters of marque or permission from a country to plunder enemy ships). Later referred to any privateer and eventually privateers' ships.

Cottage Cove, small cove, Currituck County, Poplar Branch Township (local use). E-most s Hicks Bay, 1.2 mi. n of Goose Island, 5.7 mi. n of Duck (village). Local disagreement, to which features Hicks Bay, Cottage Cove, and Longfellow Cove apply, each in close proximity. Applications presented most preferred.

Cottage Row. *See* Nags Head.

Cotton Hammock. *See* Salters Lumps.

Cove, The, small gentle-curving bight, 0.3 mi. long, Hyde County, Ocracoke Township (local use). At Teaches Hole Channel from Springers Point (s) to unnamed point at sw terminus of Lighthouse Road.

Cow Island, marsh island, 0.1 mi. long, Carteret County, Harkers Island Township (USGS 2013: Harkers Island). In Back Sound just n of Shackleford Banks, 2.2 mi. s of Harkers Island (village).

Cow Island, former island, Currituck County, Poplar Branch Township (C&GS 1852). Was just w of Currituck Banks at Piper Hill, 5.7 mi. s of Corolla. No longer exists because now joined to the barrier island.

Cow Island, former barrier island, Dare County, Nags Head Township (Lawson 1709, map). Was just e of Roanoke Island near Whalebone Junction between former Roanoke Inlet and former Gunt Inlet just n of Oregon Inlet. N-most of three small barrier islands (Dugs—descriptive, Body Island, and Cow Island—s-n) formed by historical inlets near Bodie Island and Oregon Inlet. Lawson (1709) shows three inlets here but without names, though "Ronoak" labeled without generic term slightly s of its eventual location, and provides additional evidence of inlet migration. Middle inlet is Port Lane or Port Ferdinando, likely latter as it was still open and Port Lane was closed or captured by Roanoke Inlet. S-most inlet creating these three islands near New Inlet, though map is small scale and placement could be general. *Other names:* Cowe Island, Cox Island (Cow misinterpretation), Lucks Island

(early applications between Gunt Inlet and Musketo Inlet, mostly n of now Kitty Hawk).

Cow Island Flats, flat, Dare County, Nags Head Township (Oppermann 2005, sketch, 135, and *Lydia Ann*, 1896 [White et al. 2017, 111]). Open marsh and sand in Bodie Island Marshes 0.7 mi. e of Tommy Hammock, 4 mi. s of Whalebone Junction. Legacy name used 1878 when from Cow Island (Dare County) early 18th century. Cow Island appeared as small barrier island here briefly with limited map usage. One of only few known applications of Cow Island Flats and on hand-drawn sketch of site selected 1878 for Tommy(s) Hammock (Bodie Island Station) Lifesaving Station in 2005 report. No additional information provided. *Other names:* Cow Island Marsh (Currituck DB 1818, 14, 476-77).

Cow Pasture, former marsh, Dare County, Kinnakeet Township (Garrity-Blake 2010, 112). Was between Waves (n) and Salvo (s) just s of Midgetts Island, 3.2 mi. s of Rodanthe. Drier area used for grazing cattle late 19th and early 20th centuries. Name has fallen into disuse.

Cowpen Creek. *See* Fort Macon Creek.

Cowpen Island, marsh island, 0.3 mi. wide, Carteret County, Smyrna Township (USGS 2013: Horsepen Point). In Core Sound just w of Core Banks, 4.8 mi. e of Harkers Island (village).

Cowpen Point, point, Carteret County, Cedar Island Township (USGS 2013: Wainwright Island). On unnamed marsh (sometimes considered part of Hog Island) just s of Camp Point, 2 mi. e of Cedar Island Ferry landing and 11 mi. sw of Ocracoke (village).

Cowpen Point, sandy point, Carteret County, Portsmouth Township (USGS 2013: Wainwright Island). Soundside of shoal between Pilontary Islands and Cricket Island, 15.2 mi. sw of Ocracoke (village). *Other names:* Cowpenpoint (early maps).

Cowpen Ridge, short sand ridge, 0.3 mi. long, Dare County, Atlantic Township (Currituck DB 7, 1794, 133). In w Kitty Hawk just e of Flat Ridge just s of Cherry Tree Ridge, 1.8 mi. w of original Kitty Hawk. *Other names:* Cowpen Rige (Currituck DB 5, 1785, 242).

Crab Claw Spit, peninsula, 1.1 mi. long, Dare County, Nags Head Township (USGS 2013: Manteo). Sand spit in Roanoke Sound at n end Roanoke Island, 2.4 mi. nw of Manteo (center). Descriptive of shape, name recent (20th century). In 21st century has become known as Banana Island (for shape though not an island from tourists and younger folk not familiar with name). Spits formed by material deposited by longshore drift, a process moving eroded material along shore by angular wave and current action. John Man (or Mann) was principal resident here early 1700s, hence variant Mans (or Manns) Point. *Other names:* Banana Island (local use), Manns Island (CS 1852), Mans Point (Maule 1718), Sand Spit (earlier local use).

Crab Cove. *See* Buzzard Bay (Currituck County).

Crab Hole, deep, 15 ft. deep, Dare County, Croatan Township (ACE 1948). In Pamlico Sound surrounded by shallow water, 3 mi. e of Stumpy Point (mainland), 7 mi. wsw of Oregon Inlet.

Crab Hole, area, Dare County, Hatteras Township (local informant). In Pamlico Sound n of Clam Shoal just e of Bird Islands, 5.5 mi. ne of Hatteras (village). Descriptive.

Crab Inlet. *See* High Hills Inlet.

Crab Slough. *See* Three Hats Channel.

Crane Hole, large cove, Currituck County, Poplar Branch Township (local use). At w shore Indian Gap Island, just se of Jarvis Channel, 7 mi. nnw of Duck (village). Unclear whether named for waterfowl or surname; most likely surname (prevalent here); though stop for migrating sandhill cranes (*Antigone canadensis*), they are not common. *Other names:* Crains Hole (local documents).

Crane Island, former large island, approx. 11 mi. long, Carteret County (Collet et al. 1770; Moseley 1737; Mouzon 1775). Was in Core Sound 2 mi. w of Core Banks, 10 mi. nne of Cape Lookout, 35 mi. sw of Ocracoke (village). Appeared as large island in central Core Sound on a few maps mid-18th century and could have been an exaggeration of numerous shoals (for lack of accurate information). Interestingly, even younger residents of mainland today s of Cedar Island have some recollection of stories of this island, which disappeared by end 18th century. Perhaps some were confusing this island with the same name originally applied to Harkers Island (q.v.), but most say "was in Core Sound in the Davis area."

Additionally, and adding to possible confusion on Moseley's (1733) map, Crane Island is "touching" Harkers Island on latter's ne end. Strangely, on Moseley's (1733) map sw portion is labeled simply Harker, without an "s" (signifying possession) and without generic "island" (usually in this time period, meant property owner or residence), but Crane Island (attached) does use generic term "island"; might mean (according to Mosley) Harker owned the se portion of a much larger island named Crane Island. So, perhaps Harkers Island (intriguingly, originally Crane Island) was larger, or an elongated island or extension of what is now Harkers Island farther ne in Core Sound labeled Crane Island, now no longer in existence; most agree on the latter. Maps mid-18th century (except Moseley) show Crane Island separate from Harkers Island (though often not showing a name for Harkers Island; Mouzon 1775). Crane Island disappeared from maps by first decade 19th century. *Other names:* Long Ile (Keulen 1690 — n of most applications, between Ocracoke and mainland).

Creeds Hill, hill, Dare County, Hatteras Township (USGS 2013: Cape Hatteras). Just n of Hatteras Bight, in Frisco, 3.1 mi. wnw of Cape Hatteras. Name origin lost as most interviewed do not recall for whom it was named. Mr. James Creed here mid-19th century, and could be name source. However, Covey (2018, 29) indicates with authority the name is for Solomon Creed. Largest of three hills of Stowes Hills (q.v.).

Creefs Ridge, sand ridge, Dare County, Nags Head Township (local informants). Remnant sand ridge, 1 mi. from Manteo (center). Known locally only because road along remnant ridge is Creefs Ridge Road. Creef, well-known local surname. Two subdivisions named for feature. *Other names:* Creef Ridge (real estate brochures).

Creek, The, tidal stream, Dare County, Hatteras Township (NPS 2005b: NPS 2, 294). One of two tidal streams (other The Slash) in Hatteras (village center) 4.5 mi. sw of Frisco.

Cricket Island, marsh island, 0.5 mi. wide, Carteret County, Portsmouth Township (USGS 2013: Wainright Island). Between Pilontary Islands and Sand Island, 15.9 mi. sw of Ocracoke (village).

Cricket Island Point, marsh point, Carteret County, Portsmouth Township (USGS 2013:

Wainwright Island). On Cricket Island, 15.2 mi. sw of Ocracoke (village).

Croatamung, former barrier island now part of Currituck Banks (White 1585). N from Kitty Hawk (or possibly Trinety Harbor) to just e of Knotts Island near present North Carolina–Virginia boundary. Hill (1983, 26) extends Croatamung from about Trinitie Harbro [sic—using Quinn 1975] (s) to just s of Corolla (s of Whale Head Bay), not quite far enough n. Some authors and investigators place s limit at Caffeys Inlet; however, not possible: Caffeys Inlet did not open until just after mid-1700s. These authors have confused Caffeys Inlet with Trinety Harbor, open here when White made his 1585 map (locations were just over 1 mi. apart). White labels this area Croatamung, obviously similar to Croatoan. So, initial part of each name was an indigenous general reference probably referring to place and the suffix reportedly generally means path. *See* Croatoan for information regarding an unsubstantiated and unwarranted claim regarding Croatia. *Other names:* Arundells Ile (Henry 1860—vague application; Arundel, officer in Grenvile expedition, second Roanoke voyage, first colony attempt), Croat (Blaeu 1640—shortened form of Croatamung), Croatamang, Croatamung Island (historical), Croatamonge (Wright 1599), Etacrewac (indigenous name just s—misapplication), Lucks Island (early applications between Gunt Inlet and Musketo Inlet, mostly n of now Kitty Hawk).

Croatan Shoal, small shoal, Dare County, Croatan Township (NPS 2012, 16). Junction of Albemarle Sound and Croatan Sound just e of Caroon Point (mainland), 7 mi. w of Manteo (center).

Croatan Shores, subdivision, Dare County, Atlantic Township (USGS 2013: Kitty Hawk). Is 3.3 mi. se of original Kitty Hawk. Kill Devil Hills (town) subdivision est. as real estate venture 1930s. Originally, just e of n Colington Creek, but after two annexations, now soundside to oceanside. Also, includes Hedricks Addition 0.5 mi. e. This form corruption (simplified version) of Croatoan.

Croatan Sound, strait, 11.3 mi. long, Dare County, Nags Head and Croatan Townships (USGS 2013: Manteo, Wanchese). Trends nw-se from Albemarle Sound to Pamlico Sound separates mainland and Roanoke Island. Created when

New Currituck Inlet closed (1828), more especially when Roanoke Inlet closed (1811), forcing water s and drowning Roanoke Marshes. Corruption (simplified version) of Croatoan, made official by USBGN 1891. Central part now double spanned by Virginia Dare Memorial Bridge, completed in August 2002 carrying US 64 and US 264 Bypass to alleviate severe traffic problem through Manteo. Virginia Dare, first English child born in Americas 1587 here on Roanoke Island and from now famous Lost Colony. N part spanned by William B. Umstead Bridge, single span built 1955 and modernized 1966. Umstead, member of the U.S. House of Representatives and the U.S. Senate and a North Carolina governor. Today, bridge used only for local traffic. *Other names:* Back Bay (Maule 1718—*see* Back Bay), Croatan Channel (historical use when narrow), Croatan Sound (early use, original spelling), Croaten Bay (Currituck DB 2, 1770, 294–95), Croaton Sound (Currituck DB 12, 1811, 144), Croetan Sound (typographical error), Crotan Sound (Sneden 1862; Currituck DB 13, 1814, 50–52), Croton Sound (Blunt 1857, 344), Occam (Haklyut 1589—Algonquian term reportedly meaning "opposite shore"), Roanoke Lake (Cram 1896), The Narrows (Comberford 1657—Roanoke Marshes prevalent and only small water passages here).

Croatan Woods. *See* Roanoke Woods.

Croatoan, former barrier island, Dare County and Hyde County (White 1585). S Hatteras Island and portion of Ocracoke Island. N and ne from The Great Swash or perhaps Little Swash Opening to just n of Cape Hatteras near former Chacandepeco Inlet, and Hatteras Inlet now bisects what used to be Croatoan Island. Reference Hatteras Indians used for Cape Hatteras, and could mean chief's residence or place of council. This application less extensive than used by White on his return voyage searching for Lost Colonists (1590). White placed n limit about 18 mi. farther n than later cartographic application (*see* Chacandepeco Inlet). Long viewed as one possible location to which colonists journeyed after leaving Roanoke Island. The word "Croatoan" was left on a fence post with "CRO" carved into a tree at the abandoned site on Roanoke Island.

Variant name Croutoon from Wingfield (1608), first president of Jamestown

Colony, Virginia; references indication Captain Christopher Newport, commander, Jamestown fleet, had gone to Croatoan (Croutoon). Used recently as so-called mounting proof there was indeed contact with colonists from Roanoke of 1587. Actual passage reads "They enquired after our shipping; w^{ch} [sic] the President said was gon [sic] to Croutoon" (superscripting was used in this period indicating some letters missing). Clear from text Indians worried about location of ships as they were fearful of them, and the president admittedly did not want Indians to think ships too far, so impossible to know if Captain Newport was indeed en route to Croatoan. Also, footnote in Wingfield (1608) provided by Deane indicates "Croaton" (sic) was an Indian town on s Cape Lookout (sic), where colonists or their remnants supposedly went upon leaving Roanoke. The reference to Cape Lookout is clearly an error. Cape Lookout is at s terminus of Core Banks and all references to Croatoan (and its variations) are as an island where Cape Hatteras is today, and which White clearly marks on his 1585 map. No known uses of Cape Lookout for Cape Hatteras.

White labels n Outer Banks Croatamung, obviously similar to Croatoan. Initial part of each name was an indigenous general reference in n Outer Banks. Of passing interest there has been an attempt to associate Croatoan and Croatamung with Croatians from what is now Croatia, late 1500s was not a country and was experiencing a tumultuous time under the Hapsburgs and the Ottomans. The claim is there were numerous Croatians associated with the Roanoke voyages and the two Roanoke colonies. Further claim is made initial sound in Croatoan and Croatamung is not found in the Algonquian language. None of this is substantiated, completely unfounded, and based on one source of undocumented information of questionable provenance; it is not true and very peculiar. The Pamlico Algonquian language is extinct, survived by only two lists of some words. See Croatamung. The Spanish in early references use Jacan for this area.

Other names: Abbots Ile (Smith 1624, map), Abbots Island (later maps using White's map), Chowanoke (misapplication of indigenous name originally applied along Albemarle Sound), Cortuan (Écija voyages references), Croacoan (Dudley 1661), Croatan (Blaeu 1640; Smith 1624, map), Croatoan Island (Quinn 1975), Croaton (Wingfield 1608, 15), Crooton (Smith 1624, map), Crotoan (Lane 1589), Croutoon (Wingfield 1608, 15), Iland of Croatoan (historical), Island of Croatoan (Haklyut 1589), Lord Admirals Iland (Haklyut 1589—applied short time and named probably by Lane for Lord Charles Howard of Effingham, from whom Raleigh was hoping to obtain funding), Raonack (early references), Roanack (early references).

Croatoan Ridge, sand ridge, 0.7 mi. long, Dare County, Hatteras Township (Brooks 2010). Trends e-w from just sw of Cape Creek (Back Landing Creek) between Back Landing Creek Marsh (se) and Muddy Marsh (n), 1 mi. ese of Buxton. Indigenous name for area (see Croatoan and Indian Town). Not used today except in scientific investigation and then applied in locations almost as descriptive term. **Other names:** Croatoan Dark Ridge (Brooks 2010—slightly s), Croatan Ridge, Dark Ridge (descriptive, used occasionally), Indian Ridge (Garrity-Blake 2010, 169—used locally and context allows differentiation from Indian Ridge at Frisco).

Crooked Creek, small water passage, Dare County, Kinnakeet Township (NPS 2005b: NPS 1, 154). Connects Brick Creek to Pamlico Sound just n of Midgett Cove just s of Horse Wading Creek 1 mi. from each Waves (n) and Salvo (s). Believed to be this stream as general location fits, as does descriptive name, but absolute verification not made.

Crooked Ridge, sand ridge, 3 mi. long, Dare County, Hatteras Township (signage). In e-w–trending ridges just n of Jennette Sedge, 0.8 mi. s of Buxton (also Flowers Ridge and Middle Ridge). Subdivision named for feature.

Cross Dike, dam, Currituck County, Fruitville Township (F&WS 1999, 10). On central Mackay Island in Mackay Island Wildlife Refuge, s from Mackay Island Road to just n of Little Bellows Bay, 2.5 wsw of Knotts Island (village). Constructed 1984 by F&WS with Long Dike and Parallel Dike to create East Pool and Middle Pool to enhance wildlife protection. "Dike" is a wall, embankment, or similar structure to function as a dam, preventing flooding or, as here, to contain and control water level.

Crossroads, The, former area, Carteret County, Portsmouth Township (historical local use). Main intersection of Portsmouth (village center)—formerly colonial commercial center but today deserted except for visiting tourists on day-trips.

Cross Rock, rock, Carteret County, Portsmouth Township (White 2012, 28—exact location not provided). A favorite "oystering" area of folk from Portsmouth (village), just n reportedly between Portsmouth (village) and Casey Island, 6 mi. se of Ocracoke (village).

Cross Rock, former rock, Currituck County, Poplar Branch Township (C&GS 1852). Formerly in Big Narrows 1 mi. sw of North Burris Island, 5 mi. ssw of Corolla.

Cross Run, stream, 1.5 mi. long, Dare County, Atlantic Township (Harris 2017; unknown, 1859). Begins just e of High Ridge flows s to Northern Gut (now labeled on maps as Jeanguite Creek [q.v.]) just e of Kitty Hawk Landing subdivision, 1.5 mi. w of original Kitty Hawk. *See* The Run.

Cross Shoal. *See* Austin Reef.

Cross Shoal Channel, channel, 0.6 mi. long, Carteret County, Atlantic Township (USGS 2013: Styron Bay). In Core Sound 2 mi. se of Atlantic (mainland).

Cross Shoals, shoal, 1.5 mi. long, Dare County, Kinnakeet Township (NPS 1987, appendix G, 133). Trends n-s adjacent to Hatteras Island, 1.3 mi. e of Gull Island separated from Gull Island and Gull Shoal by Gull Shoal Channel 4.5 mi. s of Salvo. Apparently named after a structure nearby on beach put there by Coast Guard as a "check station" for crew members of two adjacent life-saving stations, Gull Shoal Station and Little Kinnakeet Station, to check in while on patrol. *Other names:* Cross Shoal (Garrity-Blake 2010, 493).

Crow Inlet. *See* New Currituck Inlet.

Crow Island, island, 1 mi. across, Currituck County, Fruitville Township (USGS 2013: Barco). In Currituck Sound just s of South Channel (remnant New Currituck Inlet), 6 mi. se of Knotts Island (village), 5 mi. nne of Monkey Island. Named early 1700s (Currituck DB 2, 1771, 353). In 1833 began to become inundated and by 1861 had become merely tidal marshes, but late 20th and early 21st centuries again more well defined, now Shell Hall attached occasionally. Sometimes Swan Island, Johnson Island referenced as Swan Islands; occasionally Crow Island and Raymond Island might be included. *See* New Currituck Inlet and Swan Island (Fruitville Township). *Other names:* Big Raymond Island (Cox 1923), Crows Island (local use).

Crow Island. *See* Swan Island.

Cruz Bay. *See* Whale Head Bay.

Crystal Coast, area, approx. 50 mi. long (brochures). Applied to s Outer Banks generally from Harkers Island to Swansboro (mainland). Includes mainland communities of Beaufort, Morehead City, and Swansboro and communities on Bogue Banks. Applied 1980s solely for commercial and tourism purposes, occasionally uses the variant name Southern Outer Banks. *Other names:* North Carolina's Crystal Coast (visitor guides and commercial publications), Southern Outer Banks (commercial publications).

Crystal Lake, man-made lake, 0.5 mi. long, 0.2 mi. wide, Currituck County, Poplar Branch Township (local use). Just n of Corolla, confirmed name supplied by builder. Dredged and spoil used for fill in housing development (Ocean Hill). Story is water in the lake was very disturbed, murky, and brown but cleared quickly to a "crystal" clear look, an appropriate name. Variant name Lost Lake: reportedly lake is difficult to notice from main road. *Other names:* Lost Lake (used occasionally, road name, n shore is Lost Lake Drive).

Curiosity Corner, former area, Hyde County, Ocracoke Township (Howard, July 22, 2018). In Ocracoke (village) several local women (later joined by many more) would gather at the corner of British Cemetery Road (now) and Back Road to exchange local news and stories thereby acquiring the whimsical name.

Curlew Canal, small canal, Dare County, Atlantic Township (Town of Southern Shores 2015). In Southern Shores on e shore of Jeanguite Creek, 3.8 mi. n of original Kitty Hawk. Names of Southern Shores canals are for shorebirds (except Gravey Pond Canal). Long-billed curlew (*Numenius americanus*) are here in winter; the Outer Banks is a migratory route for the curlew sandpiper (*Calidris ferruginea*).

Currituck Banks, barrier spit, Currituck County, Fruitville and Poplar Branch Townships; and Dare County, Atlantic and Nags Head Townships (numerous sources). S from North Bay, Virginia to Bodie Island at former Roanoke Inlet. Over decades use has become associated only to part in Currituck County, while Dare County portion is known more as Dare Banks. Sometimes including Bodie Island, recent and completely political reference since former Roanoke Inlet was s terminus of Currituck Banks, though as a physical feature (a spit) many believe should now continue to Oregon Inlet, which would include what was Bodie Island, but would be confusing politically. Continuing n into Virginia there is a small breach at Rudee Inlet (sometimes Owl Creek) in s Virginia Beach, but does not create an island. Thought to be derived from Algonquian word *carotank* or *coretank* or *cortank*, referring to wild geese (indigenous languages were not written, and colonists recorded in English script of the time, itself not yet standardized orthographically). Suffix reportedly means "wealth" and most likely refers to profusion of wild geese here. Some authors believe the word might imitate the sound of the water fowl of the region, not likely. Use of Currituck Outer Banks as a name is late 20th- and early 21st-century application for commercial purposes to differentiate from Dare County beaches.

Use of Goade by John Smith on his 1624 map for upper Currituck Banks did not last in that form, but some older residents occasionally today use Gourd Island as a general application here. Unclear if Smith intended "gourd" or was using "goad" for some other reason.

Other names: Arundells Ile (Smith 1624, map—based on Arundel, officer in Grenville expedition, second Roanoke voyage and first colony attempt), Arundells Island (later applications from earlier use), Bald Beach (Bishop 1878—s portion, Pine Island to Nags Head mid-19th century; Currituck DB 7, 1795, 183–84—applied in part between New Currituck Inlet and Caffeys Inlet, sometimes to e of Kitty Hawk Bay), Bodie Island (Federal Writers Project 1940), Carahtuck (Stick 1958, 255), Caratock (Moll 1708), Caratuk (Stick 1958, 255), Caratut (Stick 1958, 255), Chickehauk Island (Anderson 1796), Chickhauk Island (form of Chicahauk), Corahtuck Banks (historical), Coratank (historical), Coratock Banks (historical), Coratuck (Schroeter 1859), Coratut Banks (historical), Corratuck Banks (deed, Malbone to Brooks, 1675), Corrituck

(Stick 1958, 255), Croatamung (indigenous name here), Corrotuck (deed, Keeling to Chicheley, 1680), Curahuk (Stick 1958, 255), Curatuck (deed, Picker to Newton, 1680), Curhuk Banks (historical), Curretucke (Stick 1958, 255), Currituc (Moll 1729), Currituck (local use), Currituck Bank (occasional local use), Currituck Banks Peninsula (scientific references), Currituck Liberty Plains (Samuel Jarvis, public comment, representative colonial period), Currituck Outer Banks (commercial applications; F&WS 1999, map, 8), Currituck Spit (various scientific papers, attached since Currituck Inlet and New Currituck Inlet closed), Currytuck (Stick 1958, 255), Etacrewac (Indian name for Nags Head area, but sometimes misapplied too far n), False Cape (confused misinterpretation with False Cape in Virginia), Goade Island (historical), Gourd Island (early local reference), Iland of Saint John (historical), Ile Goade (Smith 1624, map), Liberty Plains (colonial documents), Lucks Island (early applications between Gunt Inlet and Musketo Inlet, mostly n of now Kitty Hawk), Nags Head Banks (misapplication), North Bank (Wimble 1738; visitor guides), North Banks (CS 1852; used extensively in Currituck Deeds, different books, various pages), North Banks of Currituck (Stick 1958, 255), Northern Outer Banks (visitor guides), North Outer Banks (visitor guides), North Sand Banks (Currituck DB 3, 1739, 14–15), Point Bacon (q.v.; Smith 1624, map), Ronoak (Moll et al. 1731—misapplied), Sand Banck (Moll 1729), Sand Bank (Moll 1729), Sandy Banks (patent, Governor Howard to Mason, Jarvise [Jarves], and Willoughby miscellaneous deeds Currituck County 1688).

Currituck Bay, cove, 0.5 mi. wide, Currituck County, Fruitville Township (USGS 2013: Barco). In Currituck Sound, 0.9 mi. n of South Channel with Swan Island and Johnson Island at entrance, 6.8 mi. nnw of Corolla. Original name listed under Other names (USGS 1940: Kitty Hawk 1:62,500 scale) but changed officially 1963 because federal government adopted policy not using pejorative form of "Negro" on federal maps or in other federal publications, and substituted "Negro." Changed from Negro Bay to Currituck Bay 2006 by action of USBGN based on a request from N.C. State

Name Authority to change names containing "Negro." Authorities in Currituck County suggested honoring a living person, not legal for naming natural features in U.S. (since 1963), so county deferred to N.C. State Name Authority, which then named the bay for the county. *See* Currituck Banks. *Other names:* Negro Bay (N.C. Board on Geographic Names, 1969 introduction policy), Nigger Bay (USGS 1940: Barco, 1:62,500 scale).

Currituck Beach, beach, Currituck County, Poplar Branch Township (USGS 2013: Corolla, Mossey Islands). At Corolla on Currituck Banks, 16.8 mi. n of Duck. Originally and still often applied to beach at Corolla. Village sometimes known as Currituck Beach until post office named Corolla established, gradually using village name. Presence of large vacation rental houses and ever-increasing tourism has increased usage for Corolla Beach (relatively new name) instead of Currituck Beach, and use of name Corolla Beach has recently increased application n to Swan Beach. *See* Currituck Banks. *Other names:* Corolla Beach (local use or really modern visitor usage), Currituck Shore (early deeds), Whalehead Beach (local use, in part).

Currituck Beach. *See* Corolla Beach and Whalehead Beach.

Currituck Club Marsh, marsh, Currituck County, Poplar Branch Township (unknown, ca. 1900). On w South Burris Island just s of remnants of Middle Burris Islands in Burris Islands complex, 7.2 mi. s of Corolla. Referenced one of many hunting clubs (fowl) that existed in past on upper Currituck Banks. Many such clubs (almost 100 by 1900) with variations in their names, but present club named Currituck Club was originally known as the Currituck Shooting Club (Cox 1923) (not Moyock, on the mainland), but by 1900 shorter form Currituck Club used. The club was s of Corolla 2 mi. e of this marsh. Name has fallen into disuse over past 50 years and hardly known now except through real estate development known as The Currituck Club here. *See* Currituck Banks.

Currituck County, civil division. Ne-most county in North Carolina, bounded by Dare and Camden Counties in North Carolina and Virginia Beach and Chesapeake Cities in Virginia; includes Fruitville, Poplar Branch, Moyock, and Crawford Townships. *See* Currituck Banks. Formed 1670 as precinct of Albemarle County. Part of what is now Dare County (to New Inlet) was part of Currituck County until 1870. In 1823, s of New Inlet (Hatteras Island) to Green Island on what is now nw Ocracoke Island transferred to Hyde County; in 1870 from just n of Kitty Hawk Bay s-ward became part of Dare County. In 1920 Kitty Hawk to just n of Duck added to Dare County.

Currituck Inlet, former water passage, Currituck County, Fruitville Township (18th-century maps). Connected Currituck Sound and Atlantic Ocean through Currituck Banks just s of North Carolina–Virginia boundary. Open before 1585 but closed 1728–31 (listed closed 1713 meaning for ship passage), result of New Currituck Inlet opening. Selected as starting point for North Carolina–Virginia boundary, but when the boundary commission began surveying, North Carolina residents claimed the inlet had "shoaled up" n-ward and had migrated s, so boundary surveyed 200 yards n of inlet. Byrd (1728) indicated shoaling process began by late 1720s after a storm opened a new inlet "5 miles s of the old one" (Currituck Inlet), named New Currituck Inlet (q.v.), remnants are South Channel (q.v.). Now, name no longer used as Currituck Inlet, sometimes the site is referenced as Old Currituck Inlet. Original measurement of Currituck Inlet was 36° 31′, 3 mi. s of present boundary. Before 1728 measurement, boundary was thought to be at 36°30′ (at Fresh Pond Hill and former Deals or Wash Woods [village] reported by Lawson 1709), but after 1728 survey location was given as 36°31′ (s Carova at Sand Ridge). Both of these latitudes were in error, as present boundary is at 36°33′ (and a few seconds). Currituck Inlet was 200 yards s of the location when the discussion of the survey began, so measurement of the line was taken 200 yards n of rapidly closing inlet (Kerr 1875 reported by Van Zandt 1976). *See* Currituck Banks.

A "town" or possible settlement, Port Currituck, was to serve commerce in Currituck Sound, but by time an inspector was appointed and efforts were in process, Currituck Inlet had shoaled, so much nothing was ever established. Currituck Customs House eventually was on mainland at present-day Currituck Court House.

Other names: Carafuk Inlet (USBGN staff—probable mistaken long "s"—*see*

Bellows Bay variant Bellisses Bay), Carahtuk Gulet (Lawson 1709, map, 240—rendition of Second Carolina Charter, though this form does not appear in later facsimiles, and no other occurrence of "Gulet" has been discovered used on the Outer Banks—spelling of "gullet," throat passage, resembling action of an inlet, and not likely a reference to a "gullet," e Mediterranean sailing vessel, though the two words are related supposedly), Carahtuk River (Lawson 1709, 240—rendition of Second Carolina Charter, though this form does not appear in later facsimiles), Caratock Inlet (Sanson 1696), Caratuck Inlet (Seller 1682), Caratuk Inlet (Speed 1676), Caritock Inlet (historical), Carituck River (Homann 1714), Carotoke Inlet (Francis Yeardley voyage 1654), Carotuck Inlet (anonymous, 1684), Carotuck River (historical), Carotuck Rivier (Visscher and Anse 1717), Carratucks Inlet (historical), Choratuck Inlet (historical), Choretuck Inlet (historical), Conetto Inlett (historical), Coratauck Inlet (Byrd 1728), Coratuck Inlet (Byrd 1728), Coretuck Inlet (Fisher et al. 1689, chart 11; Wimble 1733), Coretucks Inlet (Wimble 1733), Coriuck Inlet (Fisher et al. 1689), Corotuck Inlett (Charles II 1663), Corotuck River (Stick 1958, 23), Corratuck Inlet (Currituck DB 1, 1713, 206), Corrattuck Inlett (early maps), Corrattuck River (early documents), Corretuck Inlet (historical), Corretucks Inlet (historical), Corrituck Inlet (historical), Curatock Inlet (historical), Curratuck Inlett (Fry et al. 1775), Curratuck Inlet (Stick 1958, 34), Curratucks Inlet (19th century), Currehuck Inlet (historical), Curretucke Inlet (historical), Curretuck Inlet (patent, Governor Howard to Mason, Jarvise [Jarves], and Willoughby miscellaneous deeds Currituck County 1688), Curritic Inlett (Lawson 1709, map—uses "Currituck Inlet" in text), Currituck Einfahrt (Lucas 1826—*einfahrt*, inlet in German), Currituck Inlett (historical), Currituck River (Charles II 1663 amended Carolina Charter 1665; Byrd 1728—used interchangeably with Inlet), Currituck Inlet (Bowen 1747), Currotuck Inlet (Anderson 1796), Detroit de Currituck (unknown, 1806—*detroit*, strait or water passage in French), Entrée d'Currituck (Frédéric 1807—*entrée*, entry in French), Entré de Curutuk (Nolin 1783), Hatteras Inlet (Dudley 1647—error), Inlet of Caretuck (Simpson and Simpson 1988, 6), Inlett of Currituck (Dunbar 1958, 49), Kuratuk Inlet (historical spelling), Old Coratuck Inlet (Byrd 1728), Old Corratuck Inlet (18th century), Old Currituck Inlet (Currituck DB 4, 1782, 61; Johnson 1863), Old Inlet (Byrd 1728), Port Currituc (colonial records), Port Currituck (colonial records), River de San Iago (Keulen 1682—*see* Barra San Ijago), Trinety Harbor (misapplication early maps).

Currituck Inlet. *See* Seagull.

Currituck Inlet Bar, former shoals and breakers, Currituck County, Fruitville Township (few 18th-century maps). Formerly at entrance to Currituck Inlet before it closed, 4 mi. ne of Knotts Island (village). Considered by some separately named part of Eastern Shoals. *See* Currituck Banks. *Other names:* Bar of Currituck (colonial text references; Lawson 1709, 64), Barra de Santiago (Aa 1729), Chorotuck Inlet Barr (Comberford 1657).

Currituck Marshes, marsh, 1.5 mi. long, 2 mi. wide, Currituck County, Fruitville Township (F&WS 1999, map, 5). Numerous marsh islands, including Walk Island, Runnels Marshes, Franks Island, and other named and unnamed smaller marsh islands. Used generically here and sparingly for larger application containing several other named marshes, but has become focused here since F&WS named a tract of Currituck National Wildlife Refuge (*see* South Marsh). *See* Currituck Banks. *Other names:* Currituck Marsh (F&WS 2006, map, 64). *See* Currituck Banks.

Currituck Sound, lagoon, 30 mi. long, 4 mi. wide, Dare County, Atlantic Township; and Currituck County, Fruitville and Poplar Branch Townships (numerous sources). Connects Back Bay, Virginia, to Albemarle Sound and separates mainland from Currituck Banks. S terminus at Albemarle Sound between Powells Point (w) (mainland) and Long Point (e) (w point Stone Island at sw terminus of Kitty Hawk ridge-and-swale system [q.v.]); lately many new residents and tourists have begun presuming Currituck Sound ends at Wright Memorial Bridge, incorrectly, based on a major man-made feature near terminus. The sound or mainland w of the sound was known locally by Indians as Tirepano, Algonquian word reportedly meaning swirling waters. Possibly name on White's map is Titepano, with a "t" not fully crossed, but probably not. Has become freshwater (except for occasional overwash during storms) since Currituck Inlet and New Currituck Inlet closed. *See* Currituck Banks and Albemarle Sound. S portion just n of junction with Albemarle Sound is spanned by double version of Wright Memorial Bridge honoring the Wright brothers, pioneers of flight (*see* Wright Brothers National Memorial). Private bridge constructed 1930 with toll and 1931 purchased by NCDOT, removing toll. In 1966, new concrete bridge (previous bridge wooden) was opened, then 1995 a parallel span was built, with older span improved 1997.

    Other names: Carrahtuck (historical), Carratuck (historical), Coretank (historical), Coratuck Bay (deed, Godfrey to Perry, 1685), Coratucke (historical), Coratuck Sound (deed, Conyers 1704), Corotuck Bay (early deeds), Corratuck Sound (Currituck DB 1, 1713, 206), Corrotuck Bay (Patent, Governor Howard to Mason, Jarvise (Jarves), and Willoughby miscellaneous deeds Currituck County 1688), Couratuck (historical), Couratucke (historical), Curetuck (historical), Currahtuck (historical), Curramck Sound (Morse 1794), Curratuck Sound (Faden and Cornwallis 1787), Currituck Creek (scientific publications—refers to preflooded stream occupying this stream valley before last major rise in sea level), Curotuck (historical), Curritcuk Sound (N.C. Division of Coastal Management 1998, map, 11—obvious error), Currituck Bay (Byrd 1728), Currituk Sound (Bowen 1747), Currotuck Sound (Russell 1799), Curutuck (historical), Northwest River (misapplication extending feature), Occam (early map application; later, Occam, indigenous name, applied to Albemarle Sound and perhaps wider application), Port Currituck (sometimes used on early maps signifying commercial aspect), River San Bartolome (limited historical), Teripano (Cobb 1905—misinterpretation of Tirepano on White's 1585 map), Tirepano (appears in Currituck Sound White's 1585 map, difficult to determine if intended water body name or something on mainland, latter more likely).

Cutoff, The, water passage, Dare County, Nags Head Township (USGS 2013: Oregon Inlet). At se end Roanoke Sound just s of Off Island (q.v.), 4.5 mi. se of Wanchese. *Other names:* Cutoff (C&GS 1923), The Cut Off (C&GS 1895a).

Cut Through, water passage, 2.5 mi. long, Dare County, Nags Head Township (USGS 2013: Oregon Inlet, Wanchese). Separates unnamed marsh islands just s of Roanoke Island and n of Hog Island, 2 mi. s of Wanchese. Descriptive and often applied to features providing passages for watercraft among marsh islands. Some more permanent such passages have retained descriptive term as proper name.

Cutting Sedge Marsh, extensive marsh, Dare County, Atlantic and Nags Head Townships (local use). Just sw and s of Fresh Pond, 1.3 mi. nw of Jockeys Ridge, 1.5 mi. nw of Nags Head. Much of this marsh contained smaller ponds historically associated with Fresh Pond. *See* Fresh Pond, Jennette Sedge, and Cuttin Sage Lake. *Other names:* Cutting Sege Marsh (Letter, Currituck DB 1, 1761, 35–37).

Cutting Sedge Marsh, large marsh, Dare County, Hatteras Township (Brooks 2010; 1759 deed). Just w and n of e-most e-w ridges at Cape Hatteras, including Crooked Ridge, Middle Ridge, and Flowers Ridge, 2.5 mi. e of Frisco. *See* Cuttin Sage Lake.

Cuttin Sage Lake, small cove, less than 0.1 mi. wide, Hyde County, Ocracoke Township (USGS 2013: Ocracoke). Very narrow opening to Pamlico Sound 0.3 mi. e of Northern Pond, 0.5 mi. ne of Ocracoke (village). The "g" in "Cutting" dropped, a common practice in spoken language throughout the U.S., but not usually written (road sign uses Cutting). While sage (*Salvia* spp.) are common plants of mint family, word is mispronunciation or more likely misrecording of "sedge," possibly by mapmaking crew. Sedges (*Carex* and *Juncus* spp.) common plants found in Outer Banks marshes, and "cuttin' sedge" is a common term used here. Local use confirms "sedge." *Other names:* Cutten Sage Lake (street sign, one section and Cutting Sage Lake another section), Cutting Sage (spoken usage), Cuttin Sedge (local use).

Cypress Swamp, small swamp, Dare County, Atlantic Township (Sorrie 2014, map, 168). In central Southern Shores, 4.5 mi. n of original Kitty Hawk. Descriptive of type of maritime forest here, has become rare on the Outer Banks. Used since 1790s (Currituck deeds before 1870). *Other names:* Cypress Pond (some local use when water higher) and Sipress Swamp (Currituck DB 7, 1795, 200, 1—

names often spelled as sounded or as people thought it ought to be spelled), Southern Shores Cypress Swamp (occasional use in documents).

D

Dacpa Shoal, former small shoal, Hyde County, Ocracoke Township (Coles and Price 1806). Was at se (larger then) Bulk Head Shoal 2 mi. n of entrance Ocracoke Inlet, 3.5 mi. wsw of Ocracoke (village). Meaning and name origin unknown (by anyone) and an unknown reference, but clearly spelled as such on Coles and Price's (1806) chart. Does not appear to be of indigenous origin, either, and only known occurrence. The name could be somehow related to the historical Dasamonquepeuc Indian Village but doubtful since that village was opposite Roanoke Island on the mainland 60 mi. n of Ocracoke Inlet. Apparently required separate name though attached to Bulk Head Shoal because often bare at half tide.

Dancing Ridge, sand ridge, 1 mi. long, Dare County, Atlantic Township (Harris 2017 and Angley 1995, 11). Trends n-s in Kitty Hawk Woods (*see* Kitty Hawk ridge-and-swale system) just wnw of original Kitty Hawk. Used more in colonial period and reportedly refers to sand movement. *Other names:* Danion Ridge (Currituck DB 7, 1797, 446), Dansing Ridge (Currituck DB 7, 1793, 172).

Dancing Ridge Pond, small lake, Dare County, Atlantic Township (Currituck DB 5, 1787, 271). In original Kitty Hawk just w of Dancing Ridge, 1.5 mi. n of Hay Point. Associative with Dancing Ridge. *Other names:* Dancing Pond (Harris 2017—occasionally used), Daning Ridge Pond (Currituck DB 7, 1794, 49).

Dancing Ridge Swamp, swamp, Dare County, Atlantic Township (Harris 2017; unknown, 1814). S-most in swamp complex containing Duck Pond Swamp, Sandy Run Swamp, and Chinquapin Swamp just w of Dancing Ridge surrounding Dancing Ridge Pond, 1 mi. nw of original Kitty Hawk. In e Kitty Hawk Woods Swamps (q.v.). Associative with Dancing

Ridge since early 1800s. *See* Kitty Hawk ridge-and-swale system.

Dandy Inlet, canal, Dare County, Atlantic Township (local use). At Colington Harbour, 2.5 mi. wsw of Kill Devil Hills (town). The term "inlet" was not used in traditional sense on the Outer Banks as barrier island breach, because indicative of dredging allowing water inward for access by boats to open water (Albemarle Sound). Canal naming scheme at Colington Harbour is ships or nautical terms. "Dandy" as a nautical term is a sailing ship with two masts: small mizzen mast aft (behind—though "mizzen" comes to English from Latin through Italian, meaning middle).

Daniels Creek. *See* Little Bridge Creek.

Daniels Marshes. *See* Roanoke Marshes.

Daniels Ridge, sand ridge, Dare County, Nags Head Township (Smith 2001, 121). North End (Roanoke Island) near Fort Raleigh National Historic Site, 2 mi. nw of Manteo (center). Penne Smith (2001) does not indicate precise location; only historical Etheridge Farm is nearby, near Fort Raleigh site.

Daniel Swash, water passage, 0.7 mi. long, Carteret County, Portsmouth Township (USGS 1950: Portsmouth). In Pamlico Sound, trends ese to wnw from Portsmouth Island to Pamlico Sound, 9.5 mi. sw of Ocracoke (village). "Swash" is normally advancement of water up beach after breaking of a wave (wave surge). On the Outer Banks "swash" (or "wash") often references overwash, and also in some cases breakers in shoals at inlets and low-lying areas of wash in the sound, with or without vegetation. Locally, "wash" can also be exposed hard sand on oceanside beach at low tide. *Other names:* Daniels Swash (C&GS 1900).

Dare Banks, area. Relatively recent term applied to Bodie Island and s Currituck Banks from Whalebone Junction to Southern Shores and now often Duck. Applied commercially and used as a reference in tourist industry. Though technically the barrier island portion from Currituck County boundary to former Roanoke Inlet is Currituck Banks, over the past years portion in Dare County has become known by this name. Dare County Banks was used rarely and mostly in reports, etc., by county government 1940s and 1950s, and applied to the barrier island(s) in Dare County or generally from Hatteras Inlet to former Caffeys Inlet. Also, Sir Walter Raleigh Coastland was term coined by Manteo newspaper *Coastland Times* to promote tourism and mostly was Oregon Inlet to Southern Shores, but often included the barrier island from Oregon Inlet to Hatteras Inlet. Has fallen into disuse and was never used much. *See* Dare County. *Other names:* Dare County Banks (visitor guides), Kitty Hawk Bars (Cobb 1905—only known reference, from source of peculiar name renditions), North Dare Banks (local use), North Banks (local use), North Dare Outer Banks (Sandbeck 2003, 2), Sir Walter Raleigh Coastland (*Coastland Times*), The Flats (occasional historical reference to area behind beach before intensive development).

Dare Beaches, reference, approx. 25 mi. long, Dare County, Atlantic and Nags Head Townships. Collective term for recreation beaches from Kitty Hawk, sometimes from Duck s to Oregon Inlet, sometimes as far as Cape Hatteras. Used primarily 1940s and 1950s, but resurgence 21st century. *See* Dare County. *Other names:* Central Beaches (sometimes used commercially for beaches Kitty Hawk to Oregon Inlet), Dare Coast (County Chamber of Commerce), Dare County Beaches (Deaton et al. 2012, 374—Kitty Hawk to Whalebone Junction), North Beaches (signage—Kitty Hawk to Duck, sometimes n to Corolla), South Beaches (road sign, Kitty Hawk—Kitty Hawk to Coquina Beach), Southern Beaches (rare, used occasionally commercially to differentiate beaches n of Kitty Hawk).

Dare County, civil division, 391 sq. mi. Formed 1870 from Currituck, Tyrrell, and Hyde Counties; bounded by Currituck, Camden, Tyrrell, and Hyde Counties and contains Atlantic, Nags Head, Kinnakeet (*see* Kennekeet), Hatteras, Croatan, and East Lake Townships. Named for Virginia Dare, first English child born in America on Roanoke Island during second attempt at colonization (1587), renowned as Lost Colony. Many names in the county are in Currituck County records since much of the Outer Banks of Dare County was part of Currituck County before 1870. In 1823, s of New Inlet (Hatteras Island) to Green Island on what is now nw Ocracoke Island was transferred to Hyde County from Currituck County, but became part of Dare County when created 1870 (to Hatteras Inlet). In 1920, Kitty Hawk to just n of Duck added to county.

Dark Ridge, elongated sand ridge, 1 mi. long, Dare County, Hatteras Township (Garrity-Blake 2010, 232). Trends e-w in se Buxton, just s of Croatoan Ridge, 3.2 mi. n of Cape Point at Cape Hatteras.

Dark Ridge. *See* Croatoan Ridge.

Darks Reef. *See* Clark Reef.

Daugers Island, former barrier island, Currituck County, Fruitville and Poplar Branch Townships (Currituck Deeds, miscellaneous, 1719). Now part of Currituck Banks but was bounded on n by former Currituck Inlet and on s by former New Currituck Inlet. Both inlets were open at the same time from about 1713 to 1731. Currituck Inlet began shoaling around 1728 and was closed by 1731, and New Currituck Inlet opened 1713. Dauge and Dauger surnames mentioned throughout 18th-century deeds. *Other names:* Dauges Island (Currituck DB 7, 1793, 14), Dauger Island (occasional reference), Denniss Island (occasional reference), John Daugers Island (Currituck Deeds, miscellaneous, 1719).

Davids Point, point, Dare County, Kinnakeet Township (USGS 2013: Rodanthe). Marsh point on n Hatteras Island, 0.1 mi. e of Great Island, 0.4 mi. sw of Waves.

Davis Channel, channel, 2.5 mi. long, Dare County, Kinnakeet Township (USGS 2013: Oregon Inlet). In Pamlico Sound just w of Pea Island, 7.6 mi. se of Wanchese. Davis Slough used originally, gradually usage changed to Davis Channel through use for navigation. Made official by USBGN 1975 to establish use of channel in the name. *Other names:* Davis Slough (ACE 1948 and local use—slough used more before 20th century, when channel came to be used from dredging).

Davis Island, marsh island, 0.6 mi. long, 0.2 mi. wide, Carteret County, Davis Township (USGS 2013: Davis). In Core Sound with a small higher center just se of mainland, 3 mi. se of Davis (mainland).

Davis Landing, landing, Carteret County, Morehead Township (PK Association 2016). At Pine Knoll Waterway (w section completed 1971) just w of bridge carrying Mimosa Boulevard in Pine Knoll Shores, 4 mi. w of Atlantic Beach. Named for A. C. Davis, a principal in building second section of Pine Knoll Waterway, researching and implementing eco-friendlier methods constructing canals, and provided some equipment.

Davis Landing, former landing, Dare County, Nags Head Township (historical use). Was on sw Roanoke Island, 1 mi. sw of Wanchese. Davis Landing Road still leads from Wanchese to the site.

Davis Salt Marsh. *See* Robbs Salt Marsh.

Dawsonville, former subdivision, Dare County, Nags Head Township (local informants). Early real estate venture by two brothers named Dawson from Elizabeth City; was just n of "Old Nags Head–oceanside" (probably Cottage Row). Exact location not remembered but was just s of boundary between Nags Head (town) and Kill Devil Hills (town). Not successful and short-lived.

Day Hill, sand dune, Dare County, Kinnakeet Township (probably) (Smith 2001). On (then) Bodie Island probably somewhere between present Oregon Inlet and New Inlet. Oregon Inlet was not yet open and Smith (2001, from Currituck DB 18, 1829, 310) indicates "along Bodie Island between the Day Hill and New Inlet" in sale of 50 acres from Markham to Adam Etheridge.

Deals, former village, Currituck County, Fruitville Township (Post Office Department). Formerly on Currituck Banks at North Swan Beach just s of Carova, 9 mi. nnw of Corolla. Originally known as Wash Woods from stumps on beach from former woods (maritime forest) flooded historically (even into Virginia historically). In 1907 post office established and named Deals because presumably Wash Woods was confusing. Though residents accepted post office name, still used Wash Woods as preferred name. Gradually, post office name adopted as village name. Surname here, but as with many late 19th- and early 20th-century post office names, no record exists as to origin. Post office was discontinued 1917; little evidence of former village because today newer community North Swan Beach is here. The Wash Woods Life Saving Station remains as a real estate office. *Other names:* Deals Island (Stick 1958, 258), Washwood (local use), Wash Woods (former local use).

Deals Island, marsh, Currituck County, Fruitville Township (historical deeds). Is 1 mi. w of Currituck Banks, 3.1 mi. ne of Knotts Island (village). Most published usage is Deal Island, but local use is for plural Deals Island and supported by nearby named features. Deals Island appears in deeds as early as 1795. *Other names:* Deal Island (USGS 2013: Knotts Island).

Deals Island Big Pond, elongated narrow pond, 0.5 mi. long, Currituck County, Fruitville Township (Cox 1923). On Deals Island just s of Deals Island Pond, 2.6 mi. ne of Knotts Island (village).

Deals Island Creek, tidal stream, 1.5 mi. long, Currituck County, Fruitville Township (local use). Begins near Carova and trends sw to Perch Island Bay, 2.5 mi. ne of Knotts Island (village). Not to be confused with Deals Creek (Deal Creek) just e of Simon Island in Virginia just n of North Carolina–Virginia boundary. *Other names:* Deal Island Creek (some local use), Grandies Island Creek (some local use), Millers Creek (Currituck Deeds, miscellaneous, 1719).

Deals Island Point, point, Currituck County, Fruitville Township (Cox 1923). S tip Deals Island (Deal Island) protruding into Buzzard Bay just e of Big Perch Island, 1.5 mi. ne of Knotts Island (village). Associative name of Deals Island.

Deals Island Pond, elongated pond, 0.5 mi. long, Currituck County, Fruitville Township (Cox 1923). E-w water on Deals Island, 2.7 mi. ne of Knotts Island (village). *Other names:* Deals Pond (some usage).

Deep Creek, narrow water passage, 1 mi. long, Currituck County, Fruitville Township (Cox 1906). Trends n-s dividing Walk Island into two portions, just e of Runnells Marshes, connects s Knotts Island Bay at mouth of Fresh Pond Bay to Perch Island Bay, 1.6 mi. ene of Knotts Island (village). *Other names:* Middle Creek (Currituck Deeds, miscellaneous, 1719).

Deep Creek, water passage, 0.1 mi. long, Currituck County, Poplar Branch Township (local use). Connects extreme n Dews Island Bay to Currituck Sound, just nw of Dews Island, 6 mi. nw of Duck. *Other names:* Deep Branch (Currituck DB 4, 1782, 127).

Deep Creek, short and narrow water passage, Currituck County, Poplar Branch Township (local use). Trends n-s and separates marsh containing Jones Point from barrier island, 1 mi. w of Corolla.

Deep Creek, tidal creek, Dare County, Kinnakeet Township (Currituck DB 3, 1736, 157). One of the tidal creeks in South'ard Water (q.v.) complex. S Askins Hill just e, and deed mentions running "northwardly" along Askins Hill; 2 mi. s of original Avon.

Deep Creek, former water passage (now cove), Dare County, Kinnakeet Township (Currituck DB 23, 1840, 48). Was on n tip Pea Island at site of first Bodie Island Lighthouse, now inundated by Oregon Inlet, 10 mi. s of Whalebone Junction. Described in 1840 deed as at site of a lighthouse on Body's (*sic*) Island. Oregon Inlet did not exist 1840, and Bodie Island extended to New Inlet. No trace today as a result of s-ward migration of Oregon Inlet. First two Bodie Island Lighthouses were on Pea Island s of future Oregon Inlet. First lighthouse was built 1847 (site was selected years earlier) and then abandoned because of structural problems. Second lighthouse at this location built 1859 and destroyed 1861 by Confederate troops. Third (present) lighthouse built 1872 at present location 3 mi. n of Oregon Inlet.

Deep Creek. *See* Askins Creek.

Deep Creek. *See* Drum Creek.

Deep Creek. *See* Indian Gap.

Deep Creek Island, marsh island, 0.3 mi. long, 0.2 mi. wide, Currituck County, Fruitville Township (Cox 1923). At nw entrance to Fresh Pond Bay at s end Deep Creek, 1.3 mi. e of Knotts Island (village). Associative from Deep Creek.

Deep Creek Point, point, Currituck County, Fruitville Township (local use). S tip Deep Creek Island at sw side of Deep Creek where it opens into Knotts Island Bay, between Oyster Cove and Deep Creek, 1.5 mi. e of Knotts Island (village). Associative from Deep Creek.

Deep Ditch, water passage, 0.8 mi. long, Dare County, Atlantic Township (local use). Separates Walker Island from Currituck Banks (barrier island), 4.3 mi. nw of Nags Head (center). *Other names:* Little Colington Creek (Currituck DB 12, 1812, 341–42—note use of one ell 1812, not normally the case until around 1900).

Deep Ditch Point, point, Dare County, Atlantic Township (USGS 2013: Manteo). S point of Walker Island, 4 mi. nw of Nags Head (center). *Other names:* Deep Point (Currituck DB 9, 1807, 323).

Deep Hole, deep, Currituck County, Fruitville Township (Cox 1923). In a maze of marsh islands, 2.1 mi. ne of Knotts Island (village).

Deep Hole, deep, Currituck County, Poplar Branch Township (Codman, Crowninshield, and Lawrence 1925). Abnormally deep in otherwise shallow s Raccoon Bay, 1 mi. w of Corolla.

Deep Hole, hole, Dare County, Nags Head Township (Currituck DB 9, 1808, 372). Somewhere in Croatan Sound near shore of nw Roanoke Island described in deed. Name is unknown now.

Deep Hole Creek, tidal stream, Dare County, Atlantic Township (Currituck DB 11, 1805, 33–34). Exact location unknown, not provided in the deed but does indicate somewhere near Jack Cabin Path (Jacks Cabin Hill). Could apply to any named streams in e Kitty Hawk ridge-and-swale system (q.v.) or could be a creek now thought to be unnamed. Implication is an associated feature named Deep Hole, but no known such reference here.

Deep Marsh Island, former marsh islands, Carteret County, Smyrna Township (C&GS 1896). At South Core Banks just s of Cowpen Island between Sheep Pen Creek and Codds Creek. Configuration changed during early 20th century and name has fallen into disuse, but reapplied in other forms to smaller islands sw.

Deep Neck, distinct water passage, 0.4 mi. long, Currituck County, Poplar Branch Township (USGS 2013: Mossey Islands). Just s of Tar Cove Marsh at sound-side Currituck Banks, 8 mi. nw of Duck. "Neck," as a generic term in geographic names, is usually used for large- to medium-sized protuberance of land (peninsula or interfluve—land between rivers), prevalent in nearby coastal or tidewater Virginia and Maryland, but here refers to a water passage, very unusual. *Other names:* Deep Neck Creek (some charts in more traditional manner).

Deep Slash, water passage, 0.5 mi. long, Currituck County, Fruitville Township (local use). Empties into Point of Sand Cove near se entrance Fresh Pond Bay, 2.5 mi. e of Knotts Island (village). Generic term usage indicates deeper water in restricted course.

Deep Slough, small channel, Dare County, Hatteras Township (local use). Trends se-nw near tip Inlet Peninsula, 1 mi. ne of Hatteras Inlet, 2.5 mi. sw of Hatteras (village). Enhanced by periodic overwash at nearby Little Inlet. *See* Allen Slough. *Other*

names: Peters Ditch (Dare County Planning Department 2009, map 5A, 46).

Deep Wear, canal, Dare County, Nags Head Township (local use). Tidal creek, now canal, at nw Roanoke Island at e shore Croatan Sound, 1 mi. sw of Manteo (center). Canalized for small boat access and has turn basin (*see* Deep Wear Turn Basin) at ne end. "Wear" likely misrepresentation of "weir" (*see* Weir Point) and surprisingly is not much used.

Deep Wear Point, point, Dare County, Nags Head Township (USGS 2013: Manteo). Is 1.5 mi. sw of Manteo (center). Appears on early maps, likely a corruption of "weir" (fishing apparatus); often names were recorded by early (and even later) mapmakers from oral interviews where lack of understanding of local accents led to misrecording names. Reference, however unlikely, could also be term used 17th and 18th centuries when "wear" meant bring a ship about or into the wind. Associative with Deep Wear.

Deep Wear Turn Basin, canal, Dare County, Nags Head Township (local use). At nw Roanoke Island at e shore of Croatan Sound 0.3 mi. inland at ne end of Deep Wear, 1 mi. sw of Manteo (center). Created for small boats reversing direction to exit canal. "Wear" probable misrepresentation of Weir (*see* Weir Point) and surprisingly is not much used; mostly clipped as The Turn Basin. *Other names:* The Turn Basin (usage).

Deerhorn Dunes. *See* Dolphin Ridge.

Deering Ridge, prominent sand ridge, 0.8 mi. long, Dare County, Hatteras Township (local use). Trends ne-sw in Hatteras (village), 4 mi. nw of Hatteras Inlet. Named for the *Carroll A. Deering*, five-masted schooner ran aground on Diamond Shoals (Outer Diamond Shoal) during a ferocious storm on January 31, 1921. Known to be some trouble among crew, first mate, and captain, so possibly mutiny. The ship was spotted passing Frying Pan Shoals at Cape Fear (Southport, N.C.) and then again at Cape Lookout Shoals (Cape Lookout), where a message was sent to the lightship at Cape Lookout Shoals (manned lightships were on these and other shoals before automation) indicating the *Deering* had lost her rudder or anchors (reports differ) and asked a tow be requested from Norfolk. The lightship's radio was not working, and attempt to hail a passing ship to send the message failed (under mysterious circumstances—passing ship noted to alter course and cover its name plate, leading to speculation it might have been involved). The storm was so fierce the *Deering* could not be approached far out on the shoals, so not until February 4 was she boarded. One of the famed stories of the so-called Bermuda Triangle (though 400 mi. nw): while much of the ship (including the captain's quarters) were in disarray, the galley was in perfect order, with a meal partially prepared and food on the table. Reportedly (undocumented websites) the word "Croatoan" was written as the last entry in the logbook inexplicably. Certainly apocryphal: legitimate, official reports confirm the logbook missing. However, both lifeboats were gone, as were the ship's navigation equipment, ship's log, and crew's personal items, indicating abandoning ship, but no trace was ever found. Supposition is lifeboats were drawn into Gulf Stream by the storm and disappeared. *Other names:* C Deering Ridge (street sign).

Deer Pond, cove, 0.3 mi. wide, Carteret County, Smyrna Township (USGS 2013: Horsepen Point). In Core Sound just e of Johnson Creek, 3.8 mi. s of Davis (mainland). Cove-like rather than tidal water passage for past 75 years or so, why local use is exclusively for the generic term "pond." *Other names:* Deer Creek (C&GS 1888b).

Deers Neck Island, island, Carteret County, White Oak Township (C&GS 1910a). Just e of Hunting Island, 1.5 mi. e of Langston Bridge, 2 mi. nw of Archer Point.

Demps Island, former small island, Dare County, Nags Head Township (ACE 1843). Was in Roanoke Sound just e of Penguin Islands 1 mi. nw of Whalebone Junction.

Devil Shoals, shoals, 1 mi. long, Dare County, Hatteras Township (local use). In Pamlico Sound, 2.5 mi. nw of Buxton. Made official by USBGN 1983.

Devil Shoals, shoal, Hyde County, Ocracoke Township (local use). In Pamlico Sound between Ocracoke Island and Six Mile Channel just nw of Island Creek, 2.5 mi. ne of Ocracoke (village). Used to cultivate oysters. *Other names:* Devil Shoal (less local use).

Dews Island, elongated island, 2.3 mi. long, Currituck County, Poplar Branch Township (USGS 2013: Jarvisburg). Trends n-s in Currituck Sound just s of Dowdy Bay, 5.2

mi. nw of Duck. Present-day local use is Dews Island, changed by USBGN decision. However, the variant name Jews Quarter Island was used more than 100 years, despite lack of a Jewish population here; as such, origin theory has always been suspect. The name Jews Quarter Island appeared late 18th century and persisted until 1982 on nautical charts. Deuce(s) also appeared on maps before use of Jews Quarter Island, but no one remembers that name. Du Island appears once 18th-century deeds but is also unknown today. Dues Quarter is another early (1735) reference to the island and surrounding area (*see* Hunting Quarter). In addition, Dews Quarter Island appeared in 1788 deed, so from deeds some form of Dews was the original name. Local residents still are aware of the name Jews Quarter Island, contrary to some reports.

The name changed officially by USBGN from Jews Quarter Island to Dews Island 1982. A proposal was submitted by USGS while revising maps citing four longtime native residents (including the postmaster at Jarvisburg on the mainland), each stated "Well known as Dews Island. Could not find anyone to call it Jews Quarter Island. One person said 'he thought the camp was once called Jews Quarter'" (reference documents available at geonames.usgs.gov: search for Dews Island under "Domestic Names"). However, scores of interviews conducted recently offered contradictory information. They acknowledged "recent" (1982) change to Dews Island, but without exception each confirmed earlier usage of Jews Island or Jews Quarter Island. None could offer reason for these names being used, though their application on numerous private and government maps and charts 19th century into mid-20th century likely explains their familiarity with the names. Many of those interviewed simply presumed change made because the former name Jews Quarter Island was not acceptable. Younger folk and newer arrivals know only Dews Island. No one was aware of use of Du, Dues, or Deuce.

Clear the original name was indeed Dews. Records indicate 1643 Governor Berkely of Virginia sent a military expedition to the region to deal with persistent Indian attacks. The expedition, led by Thomas Dew, entered Currituck Sound through (Old)

Currituck Inlet and continued to Albemarle Sound and passed by what is now Dews Island. So, original name was Dews Island for Thomas Dew, but somehow (cartographer's misinterpretation by speech) changed to Jews for over 100 years before original name restored.

Other names: Dences Quarters (some early maps), Deuces Quarters (early maps), Dews Quarter (Currituck DB 12, 1812, 362–63), Dews Quarter Island (C&GS 1876a; Currituck DB 6, 1788, 72), Duce Quarter Island (18th-century maps), Du Island (Currituck DB 7, 1794, 84), Dues Quarter (Currituck DB 3, 1735, 45–46), Duesquarter Island (Currituck DB 5, 1788, 369), Dues Quarter Island (Currituck DB 5, 1784, 62–63), Jewish Quarter Island (variation of Jews Quarter), Jew Quarter (Cram and Worret 1861), Jew Quarter Island (CS 1848), Jews Island (legacy local use), Jews Quarter Island (CS 1862a).

Dews Island Bay, bay, 2 mi. long, Currituck County, Poplar Branch Township (local use). Trends nw-se and separates Dews Island from mainland, 4.7 mi. nw of Duck. *See* Dews Island. *Other names:* Dews Quarter Creek (Currituck DB 11, 1810, 32–33), Duesquarter Creek (Currituck DB 5, 1784, 73), Jewish Island Bay (historical local use), Jewish Quarter Island Bay (historical local use), Jew Quarter Island Bay (historical local use), Jews Island Bay (historical local use), Jews Quarter Island Bay (historical local use).

Dews Island Point, point, Currituck County, Poplar Branch Township (local use). N-most point of Dews Island, 6 mi. wnw of Duck. *See* Dews Island. *Other names:* Dews Quarter Point (local use), Dew Quarter Point (local use), Jewish Quarter Island Point (historical local use), Jewish Quarter Point (historical local use), Jew Quarter Island Point (historical local use), Jews Quarter Island Point (historical local use), Jew Quarter Point (historical local use), Jews Quarter Point (historical local use).

Diamond City, former settlement, Carteret County, Harkers Island Township (historical use). Was spread over e end of Shackleford Banks 3 mi. nnw of Cape Lookout, 4 mi. sse of Harkers Island (village). Derived from the "diamond-shaped" pattern (though documentation indicates "checkered" design) of nearby lighthouse at Cape Lookout, and reportedly suggested by Joe Etheridge, former superintendent of lifesaving station at Diamond City (*see* Cape Hatteras or Cape Lookout for more information regarding lighthouse design). Major economy based on whaling and fishing industries. Village became deserted after several devastating storms in 1890s, especially hurricane of 1899, after which and by 1900 most residents moved to Harkers Island and Morehead City (mainland—known locally as the Promised Land); some moved "down the banks" to Salter Path (*see* Bogue Banks historical communities), Bogue Banks. *See* Cape Lookout Grounds for description of whaling Outer Banks style. *Other names:* Cape Banks (before change to Diamond City), Cape Hills (Stick 1958, 187), Diamond (local use, especially those who moved to Salter Path on Bogue Banks), Eastern End (local use), Lookout Hills (references before naming Diamond City for location), Lookout Woods (former local use—informal name before Diamond City was chosen 1885; historical sources; Mason 2000; NPS 1987, map, 38), The Eastern End (former local use).

Diamond City Hills, sand dunes, 15 ft. high, Carteret County, Harkers Island Township (USGS 2013: Harkers Island). On e Shackleford Banks 1.1 mi. wnw of Barden Inlet, 3.8 mi. sse of Harkers Island (village). Not used until community named Diamond City 1885. Prior, name Cape Hills and Lookout Hills sometimes used, though application of those names was most used with dunes on Cape Lookout. *See* Diamond City. *Other names:* Lookout Hills (before naming Diamond City).

Diamond Shoals, shoals, 25 mi. long, Dare County, Hatteras Township (USGS 2013: Cape Hatteras). Se from Cape Hatteras into Atlantic Ocean, 4.8 mi. se of Buxton composed of Hatteras Shoals (inner part), Inner Diamond Shoal (middle part), and Outer Diamond Shoal (outer part). Each of these names has been applied to the entire feature now known as Diamond Shoals. Hatteras Shoals separated from Inner Diamond Shoal by Hatteras Slough, and Diamond Slough separates Inner Diamond Shoal and Outer Diamond Shoal. The name originates from diamond shape created by the shoals. Might seem peculiar "inner" used for middle section but can be explained because 19th century Diamond Shoals

consisted of only inner part and outer part with, Hatteras Shoals considered separately as an extension off tip Cape Point. Today, by changing hydrography, Hatteras Shoals is considered as one of three sections of Diamond Shoals.

These shoals are where warm waters of Gulf Stream and cold waters of Labrador Current meet, causing constantly changing hypsography (shoals—nonhydrographic/water features) and hydrography. Collision destroys weaker Labrador Current and causes deflection ne of Gulf Stream, so all important to climate of Ireland and British Isles. These shoals were recognized as dangerous to shipping from early settlement of North America and reportedly termed "Graveyard of the Atlantic" by Alexander Hamilton 1773 after spending a most anxious night in passage during a storm; fire was aboard his ship. This is almost certainly apocryphal; no record of this reported act of naming in any of Hamilton's writings. However, Hamilton was well aware of the dangers here and was responsible for first attempt at establishing a lighthouse at Cape Hatteras to warn ships approaching dreaded Diamond Shoals (result of his tumultuous passage). Made official by USBGN 1949.

Other names: Cape Hatteras Shoal (Pinkerton et al. 1809), Cape Hatteras Shoals (18th century and Price 1795, 626), Carolina Reefs (O'Neal et al. 1976, 23), Diamond Shoal (MacNeill 1958, 2), Diamonds Shoal (C&GS 1916a), Graveyard of Ships (Olszewski 1970, 23), Graveyard of the Atlantic (Alexander Hamilton—attributed), Hatteras Sandy Shoals (ACE 2013, 33), Hattaras Sholls (Moll 1720), Hatteras Shoals (historical local use), Hatteras Sholes (Lawson 1709), Hell's Hole (Cobb 1905—name not found elsewhere), Inner Diamond Shoal (historical), Outer Diamond Shoal (historical), Point of the Diamonds (historical), Shoals of Cape Hatteras (Torres 1985, 3), Shoals of Hatteras (historical texts), Sholes of Hatteras (Moll 1729), The Diamond (Stick 1952, 209), The Diamond Graveyard of the Atlantic (Stick 1958, 209), The Diamonds (MacNeill 1958, 3), The Graveyard (MacNeill 1958, 185), The Graveyards (some writers), The Shoals (MacNeill 1958, 123), Torpedo Junction (originated in popular publications—high activity of German submarines during WWII).

Diamond Slough, natural channel, Dare County, Hatteras Township (numerous charts). Between Inner Diamond Shoal (middle Diamond Shoals) and Outer Diamond Shoal (outermost Diamond Shoals). Made official by USBGN 1949 to establish officially location. *See* Diamond Shoals. *Other names:* Hatteras Slough (historical), Outer Slue (CS 1883), Outer Slue Channel (historical).

Dicks Camp, camp, Hyde County, Ocracoke Township (USGS 2013: Howard Reef). On sw bank of Try Yard Creek 0.3 mi. ne of Parkers Hill, 7.7 mi. w of Hatteras Inlet, 6 mi. ne of Ocracoke (village). *See* Camp Cass Williams.

Dick Shoals, shoal, Dare County, Kinnakeet Township (Garrity-Blake 2010, 492). In Pamlico Sound just e of The Ridge (also a shoal), 1.5 mi. nw of Rodanthe.

Dippin' Vat, man-made lake, Dare County, Hatteras Township (local use and street sign). In Buxton, 2.5 mi. n of Cape Point at Cape Hatteras. Originally one of numerous small "vats" used for dipping livestock, ostensibly to rid cattle of disease-bearing insects, required by federal government mostly 1920s (no longer practiced). This one has become a sort of lake.

Ditch, The, water passage, 0.1 mi. long, Carteret County, Harkers Island Township (USGS 2013: Harkers Island). Trends e-w connecting Blinds Hammock Bay to Barden Inlet 4.3 mi. se of Harkers Island (village).

Ditch, The, small ditch, Carteret County, Morehead Township (Stephens 1989, 78). In Salter Path, 4.5 mi. w of Pine Knoll Shores. Divided Salter Path into two sections (e and w; *see* Salter Path).

Ditch, The, water passage, Hyde County, Ocracoke Township (local use). Entrance-way Pamlico Sound to Silver Lake, harbor at Ocracoke (village). *Other names:* Harbor Entrance (O'Neal et al. 1976, map back cover), The Gut (Garrity-Blake 2010, 355—only known occurrence of this use here).

Dividing Creek. *See* Colington Cut.

Divine Cove, small cove, Carteret County, Harkers Island Township (Wiss and Milner 2005, map, 52). Just s of Power Squadron Spit, 5.7 mi. sse of Harkers Island (village). Reportedly, given name of an older local resident of Harkers Island. *Other names:* Latham Hole (NPS, Cape Lookout, 2000, 52).

Dock of the Bay Marina, small harbor, Dare County, Atlantic Township (signage). At s terminus of Perry Ridge at beginning of canalized Roespock Run, 1 mi. sw of original Kitty Hawk.

Doctor Angle's Dock, former dock, Hyde County, Ocracoke Township (Howard, October 21, 2013). Was in Ocracoke (village) at se end Silver Lake. Used by mail skiff for transfer prior to dredging Silver Lake.

Doctors Creek, tidal creek, 0.2 mi. long, Carteret County, Portsmouth Township (USGS 1950: Portsmouth). Into former Portsmouth Harbor from Pamlico Sound at e edge Portsmouth (village), 6.2 mi. sw of Ocracoke (village). Terminates in two apparently unnamed branches. Named for Doctor Samuel Dudley (1830s), whose home was along the creek (NPS 2018, 63).

Doctors Folly, former area, Dare County, Nags Head Township (Currituck DB 3, 1784, 283–84). Tract of land was in nw Nags Head at originally Francis Creek (now Tillmans Creek) just n of and including Mann Point 1.3 mi. nw of Jockeys Ridge, 6.5 mi. s of original Kitty Hawk. Referenced in 1784 deeds and used as a named reference in deed transfers through 1805. Meaning of name seems obvious but actual origin is unknown. No one uses or knows name today. *Other names:* Docktors Folly (Currituck DB 3, 1784, 286–87), Doctors Folley (Currituck DB 9, 1805, 79–80).

Doctors Hole, artificial hole, Dare County, Hatteras Township (NPS 2005b: NPS 1, 233). Just offshore at Buxton Landing, 0.5 mi. e of Buxton; exact location unknown. Reportedly, created by engines from boats "kicking up" sand. Also reportedly originally for swimming and therefore after the hole a hazardous place. Name origin can be presumed but unknown (possibly for Doctor Falb, undocumented).

Doe Hammock, small hummock, Hyde County, Ocracoke Township (local use). In Ocracoke (village) 0.5 mi. se of Oyster Creek part of Ocracoke (village). *See* Black Hammock. *Other names:* Poe Hammock (indicated as recording error).

Doe Island, former island, Currituck County, Fruitville Township (Currituck DB 4, 1783, 174). Somewhere a short distance nnw of New Currituck Inlet, near Broad Creek, 7 mi. n of Corolla. Listed as "50 acres lying on Currituck Banks beginning North of the Inlett [*sic*] it being . . . lying about Doe Island" and "called Doe Island lying between Cateridges Point & Broad Creek". No way to know the specific island. Further, New Currituck Inlet closed, topography changed considerably with marsh islands disappearing, appearing, combining, etc.

Dog Islands, islands, Carteret County, Morehead Township (USGS 2013: Salter Path). Three or four islands (sometimes two, sometimes none, depending on tides and water level) in Bogue Sound, 1.2 mi. nw of Salter Path. Originally one island but has divided into three or four islands. *Other names:* Dog Island (sometimes used especially when referring to largest shoal, Moseley 1737, and Darden 2016).

Dog Point, point, Dare County, Atlantic Township (USGS 2013: Kitty Hawk). Just ne of Dog Point Creek at se tip Baum Point Island, 0.6 mi. ne of Blount Bay, 3 mi. s of original Kitty Hawk.

Dog Point Creek, water passage, 0.5 mi. long, Dare County, Atlantic Township (local use). Sw section of water passage trending ne from Blount Bay to Sloop Creek, 3.3 mi. s of original Kitty Hawk.

Dog Ridge, area, Dare County, Kinnakeet Township (NPS 2005b: NPS 1, 166). Original Avon (Kinnakeet) on s side Peters Ditch (The Creek), 6 mi. n of Buxton. Derived reportedly from differentiating the two clusters of families in original Avon, whom jokingly fought like cats and dogs (*see* Avon and Cat Ridge).

Dog Ridge, small sand ridge, Dare County, Kinnakeet Township (local use). Just s of Avon Harbor in original Avon, 6.3 mi. n of Buxton. Actually, extension of s Cat Ridge, and this part was named Dog Ridge for contrasting cultural reasons. *See* Cat Ridge (area), Dog Ridge (area), and Avon.

Dolbys Point. *See* Baum Point (Nags Head Township).

Dollys Point. *See* Baum Point (Nags Head Township).

Dolphin Ridge, sand ridge, 1 mi. long, Carteret County, White Oak Township (local use). Trends e-w on extreme w end Bogue Banks 1 mi. sw of Langston Bridge, 7 mi. wsw of original Emerald Isle. Road using name crosses the sand ridge. Subdivision named for feature. *Other names:* Deer Horn Dunes (from subdivision same name), Deerhorn Dunes (from subdivision transcribing error).

Dorcas Pond, lake, Dare County, Nags Head Township (local informant). Contains water in spots but is man-enhanced disturbed area in sw Wanchese, 1 mi. s of Baumtown. Female given name, albeit rare, originally Greek origin. Saint Dorcas (Tabitha) was an early Christian disciple who helped the poor.

Dorland Lump, small marsh island, less than 0.1 mi. across, Dare County, Kinnakeet Township (USGS 2013: Pea Island Overedge West). In Pamlico Sound 0.5 mi. s of Jack Shoal, 6.1 mi. nw of Rodanthe. Considerably smaller than in 19th century. "Lump" is a local descriptive term used throughout the Outer Banks, especially from Ocracoke s-ward; refers to small island, hummock, clump of grass, high portion of ground, sometimes shoal.

Dosiers Island, former small island, Currituck County, Fruitville Township (Byrd 1728, 14). Was soundside of Currituck Inlet just w of Carova, 12 mi. nnw of Corolla. Probable surname, as it occurs here. *Other names:* Dosiors Island (Byrd 1728), Doziers Island (18th century).

Dotty Pond, lake, 0.2 mi. long, less than 0.1 mi. wide, Currituck County, Poplar Branch Township (USGS 2013: Mossey Islands). On marshy soundside of Currituck Banks just w of n-most dune of Three Dunes, 4.5 mi. s of Corolla. Could have been Doudy (Dowdy) originally, surname known here historically—*see* Doudy Marsh. *Other names:* Dottie Pond (some local spelling), Dotties Pond (some local use), Potty Pond (probable typographical error; unknown locally).

Doudy Marsh, marsh, Currituck County, Poplar Branch Township (C&GS 1852). Just w of Three Dunes, 6 mi. s of Corolla. Dotty Pond is just n of Doudy Marsh and is possible mistranscription based on verbal exchange.

Doughs Bay, former cove, Dare County, Nags Head Township (early maps). In ne Manteo 3 mi. ese of site of Fort Raleigh (Lost Colony), where Doughs Creek (sometimes Gibsons Creek) empties into Shallowbag Bay. A few early maps labeled lower stream part (cove) Does Bay, but this variant spelling was a form of Dough, surname (not for deer), for a family whose farm was near present Fort Raleigh National Historic Site. Application of "Doe" was misinterpretation by early mapmakers. *Other names:* Does Bay (few early maps—misinterpretation).

Doughs Creek, stream, 1.3 mi. long, Dare

County, Nags Head Township (USGS 2013: Manteo). Begins 0.6 mi. w of Mother Vineyard on Roanoke Island, flows s to Shallowbag Bay at Manteo. Possibly named for original settler, James Dauge (*sic*). *See* Doughs Bay. *Other names:* Does Bay (early map misinterpretation), Does Kreek (Currituck Deeds, letter bk. 1—annex of bk. 1, 1765, 188–89—only encountered spelling of Kreek on the Outer Banks), Dough Creek (Sandbeck 2003, 18), Dowes Creek (Currituck Deeds, letter bk. 1, annex of bk. 1, 1766, 193), Gibson Creek (Currituck DB 2, 1770, 294–95), Gibsons Creek (Currituck DB 2, 1770, 294–95—Dough mentioned as owners of the land), Town Creek (Sandbeck, 18).

Doughs Grape Arbor, former area, Dare County, Nags Head Township (NPS 2010, map 4). Was at the Dough homesite now on grounds of Fort Raleigh National Historic Site, 2.5 mi. nw of Manteo (center). NPS reports the arbor was there from ca. 1850 until 1960. *See* Doughs Bay.

Doughs Point. *See* North Point and Sandy Point (Dare County).

Douglas Island, marsh and hummocks, 0.5 mi. long, 0.3 mi. wide, Dare County, Kinnakeet Township (USGS 2013: Pea Island, Pea Island Overedge West). Two areas of high ground surrounded by marsh just s of Terrapin Creek, 6.8 mi. nnw of Rodanthe. Still numerous hummocks (hammocks) here though altered naturally and by man (Pea Island National Wildlife Refuge) over past 400 years, where Dugs (q.v.) as a place name was persistently labeled on numerous 18th-century maps. Douglas (name not common here and no one knows who is Douglas) possibly substituted over the years by later mapmakers as similar in sound to Dugs, which had lost its familiarity and meaning by early 19th century and only still appears in slang.

Douglas Point, point, Carteret County, Davis Township (USGS 2013: Davis). On unnamed marsh island between Stone Point and Shingle Point, 2.9 mi. sse of Davis (mainland). Adjacent sw to former Duges Island (disappeared 1890s). *See* Douglas Island for possible similar name situation.

Dowdy Bay, bay, 2 mi. long, 0.5 mi. wide, Currituck County, Poplar Branch Township (USGS 2013: Jarvisburg, Mossey Islands). In Currituck Sound just nw of Dews Island, 7 mi. nw of Duck. *Other names:* Dowds Bay (Currituck DB 1921, 59, 315), Dowdys Bay (Currituck County 2015), Poplar Branch Bay (C&GS 1895a).

Dowdys Creek. *See* Neals Creek.

Down Creek Marina, small harbor, Hyde County, Ocracoke Township (signage). At se Silver Lake in Ocracoke (village), 3 mi. nw of Ocracoke Inlet. Reference used in Ocracoke (village) for e side of Silver Lake derived before Silver Lake was dredged. Also Down Creek subdivision. *See* Ocracoke Village areas.

Down East, area, Carteret County, Atlantic, Sea Level, Stacy, Davis, Smyrna, Harkers Island, Straits, and Beaufort Townships (signage). Reference to an area, which loosely includes Core Banks s of Portsmouth Island and Cedar Island and mainland area adjacent to Core Sound for a short distance inland, including Harkers Island, Shackleford Banks, and Beaufort (mainland). Used since mid-19th century and today promoted by signage. Some folk extend usage farther s in Carteret County, but not supported by signage.

Down Point, area, Hyde County, Ocracoke Township (local sources and Howard). One of three major sections in Ocracoke (village) defining certain historic parts within the village. Each generated a mild form of competition first half 20th century (and a bit beyond) as there were three major focal points of dwellings: w side of Silver Lake (Cockle Creek [q.v.]), Pointers (Springers Point reference) this entry; around s, n, and e sides Silver Lake, Creekers; and ne part of the village near Pamlico Sound, Trenters (*see* Up Trent).

Down the Road, former area, Dare County, Atlantic Township. Generally was e of original Kitty Hawk (not beach) n of North Cove (ne Kitty Hawk Bay) and s of e Kitty Hawk Woods. Unlike same reference used in Salvo, a n-s orientation on the narrow barrier island there, this reference was e-w reference differentiating w Kitty Hawk (Up The Road) from here.

Down the Road, former area, Dare County, Kinnakeet Township (Garrity-Blake 2010, 136). Reference to s Salvo differentiating from other parts. The "down" is common usage for s because s is bottom on most maps. Used in Buxton, Hatteras, and other communities between Oregon Inlet and Hatteras Inlet.

Doxee Dock, former landing, Hyde County,

Ocracoke Township (O'Neal et al. 1976, 2, 7). Was at s side of The Ditch, now entrance to Silver Lake in Ocracoke (village), 3.5 mi. ne of Ocracoke Inlet. A form of surname Doxey. The family built (moved from New York) a clam factory late 1800s, served by this landing.

Doxeys Salthouse, marsh, 1 mi. long, Currituck County, Poplar Branch Township (USGS 1982: Jarvisburg). Marsh with open water, soundside of Currituck Banks just e of Little Yankee Pond, 6.3 mi. nw of Duck. Likely reference to marsh itself, though could be reference to house being near salt marsh, and reference eventually was applied to marsh itself—local opinion is mixed. Also, Salt House Bay is just nw of here and could be related in the naming process. No evidence saltbox was used, a type of house with one floor less in back than front, subsequently with backward sloping roof (derives from the shape of box where salt was kept). This was a type of house used on the Outer Banks. Doxey, surname here. *Other names:* Doxeys Pond (more open water than marsh), Spit House (some historical local use—meaning unknown, not on a spit of land or peninsula).

Doziers Creek, small tidal stream, Dare County, Kinnakeet Township (Garrity-Blake 2010, 210). Believed just nw of Askins Creek, 1.8 mi. s of original Avon. Dozier surname here.

Drag Line Ditch, canal, 1.8 mi. long, Dare County, Atlantic Township (Town of Kitty Hawk 2007). Begins just ne of Kitty Hawk Landing subdivision, trends s to Tarkle Ridge Cove 2 mi. w of original Kitty Hawk. "Drag line" (or "dragline") usually refers to machine for digging ditches, uses sort of rotating buckets for scooping. Application descriptive of how ditch created and gradually (or soon) became a name.

Drain, The, cove, 0.3 mi. long, Dare County, Kinnakeet Township (USGS 2013: Little Kinnakeet). In Pamlico Sound just n of former Little Kinnakeet 4.9 mi. n of original Avon. Not to be confused with the tidal stream named The Drain, 12.5 mi. n in Waves, or The Drain, 8 mi. n near Cedar Creek in Salvo. Descriptor "The Drain" as a name is used liberally on Hatteras Island.

Drain, The, small tidal stream, Dare County, Kinnakeet Township (Garrity-Blake 2010, 492). Just s of Aunt Phoebes Marsh just n of Waves 1.3 mi. s of Rodanthe. Not to be

confused with cove named The Drain 12.5 mi. s in former Little Kinnakeet or The Drain 2.5 mi. s near Cedar Creek in Salvo. *Other names:* Rodanthe Drain (N.C. Marine Fisheries 2019, H5, map 7).

Drain, The, small tidal stream, Dare County, Kinnakeet Township (Garrity-Blake 2010, 492). Just s of Cedar Creek (Dare County) in s Salvo just s of Opening Marshes, 4 mi. s of Rodanthe. Not to be confused with The Drain 2.5 mi. n at Aunt Phoebes Marsh or The Drain 8 mi. s at former Little Kinnakeet.

Drain Ditch, former canal, Dare County, Kinnakeet Township (Garrity-Blake 2010, 169). Was in n Avon halfway between Gibbs Point and Peters Ditch (Avon Harbor), from Pamlico Sound almost to Mill Creek (Old Creek), 7.5 mi. n of Buxton. Not maintained and not discernable in some parts now.

Drain Islands, marsh islands, 0.1 mi. long, 0.05 mi. wide, Dare County, Kinnakeet Township (USGS 2013: Little Kinnakeet). At mouth of The Drain just n of Little Kinnakeet, 4.7 mi. n of original Avon. *Other names:* Drain Island (C&GS 1883).

Dredge Island, man-made shoal, Hyde County, Ocracoke Township (local use). Just e of n Big Foot Slough Channel, 2 mi. nnw of Ocracoke (village). Labeled as "disposal area" on NOS chart and formed from material from channel dredging and other activity. *Other names:* Big Foot Island (White et al. 2017, 24).

Drum Creek, former water passage, Carteret County, Morehead Township (USGS 1951 Beaufort). Connected Morehead City Channel and Bogue Sound just n of Goat Island 1.8 mi. s of Morehead City (mainland). *See* Drum Inlet. *Other names:* Deep Creek (historical).

Drum Inlet, former water passage, 0.3 mi. wide, Carteret County, Atlantic Township (USGS 1951 Atlantic). Connected Core Sound and Atlantic Ocean at what is now labeled Old Drum Inlet on USGS 2013: Atlantic, 3.5 mi. e of Atlantic (mainland), 4.5 mi. n of Ophelia Inlet. Most sources and local use generally apply Old Drum Inlet, but Drum Inlet used here because this was the original Drum Inlet and to avoid confusion as another, albeit historical, inlet named Old Drum Inlet at Hogpen Bay 13 mi. sw, never in Drum Inlet, New Drum Inlet, Ophelia Inlet complex.

Open periodically 1700s, because of shoaling open and closed during 19th century several times, closing by 1920s (dredged by ACE in early 1920s). Reopened 1933 from major hurricane but closed 1971. Inlet reopened 1999 from Hurricane Dennis (New Old Drum Inlet used) and with periodic overwash until shoaling up by 2008. Brief overwash here from Hurricane Irene 2011. Many locations of now closed inlets on narrow and low Core Banks tend to open briefly during storms or have some overwash during these storms.

True name origin might never be known but likely refers to drum fish (e.g., black drum [*Pogonias cromis*], red drum [*Sciaenops ocellatus*]; so-called for drumming noise made) common to Atlantic Coast. Accepted use by most. Other possibilities should be mentioned because drum has been applied to many inlets since early 18th century, and archaic references to the word "drum" might have relevance to its application and use on the Outer Banks. For example, early 18th century "drum" also was a sieve and might have been applied to inlets whose processes resembled action of a sieve. Another possibility is during 19th century "drum" was cylinder or canvas used as storm signal. Variant Drum Head Inlet might provide a clue because "drum head" (or "drumhead") refers to circular top of a device on a ship for raising and lowering. Drumhead (Court), though rare, refers to a court martial held at sea on a ship presided over by ranking officer. "Drum" also Gaelic meaning ridge, though used almost exclusively for glaciated features, so not likely, but 18th century could have been applied for the ridge-like dunes (far-fetched). Any number of meanings might have led to the name, but named for the fish is most accepted origin.

Use of Pillintary Inlet by Bishop (1878) is interesting because Bishop indicates clearly the name Pillintary Inlet was offered by and used by those with whom he spent "close time" sharing their houses and meals. Indication is the inlet opened around 1858 about 16.5 mi. s of Portsmouth (village) and was short-lived, yet no mention of an inlet by this name in any documents, on any maps, by any barrier island and inlet specialists (two possible exceptions below), and residents now have no recollection of such an inlet except for a few vague recollections that might or might not be relevant. "Pillintary" is a form of pilontary,

general local spelling for "pellitory" (*see* entry Pilontary Islands, about 8 mi. ne of this location). Based on Bishop's description as relayed by residents at the time, this inlet breached about 1858, could coincide with Drum Inlet, which opened and closed throughout the 1800s. Fisher (1962) is only expert to mention a possible inlet using a form of "pilontary," Pilentary Cubhouse Inlet, but only mentions it (if existed) was pre-1900s and existed only briefly. Fisher notes Pilentary (Pilontary) Clubhouse Inlet was mentioned in a congressional report from late 1800s but then indicates he could find no other reference. Pilontary Clubhouse Inlet is mentioned in N.C. Fisheries (1923, 27) but was really a reference to Swash Inlet since Pilontary Islands (reportedly the Pilentary [*sic*] Club) is just sw of Swash Inlet, 7.5 mi. ne of location reported by Bishop. Also, Sand Island Inlet, only 3 mi. ne of location reported by Bishop, was open and closed off and on during latter 19th century. So, this Pillintary Inlet "discovered" by Bishop could have been Drum Inlet or possibly Sand Island Inlet, but likely Swash Inlet for location at Pilentary Club. The name Pillintary Inlet was applied for a short time (locally) to Drum Inlet, Sand Island Inlet, and Swash Inlet (most likely Pillintary Inlet), or was a short-lived, small breach possibly between Drum Inlet and Sand Island Inlet opened so short a time it was not reported anywhere. Short-lived breaches were commonplace all along Core Banks because of narrowness of the barrier ridge here. Made official by USBGN 1978 to clarify Drum Inlet(s) situation. *Other names:* Drum Head Inlet (O'Neal, 6, 1976 reportedly from primary documents), New Drum Inlet (reopened 1999–2008, Hurricane Dennis), New Inlet (Wimble 1738), New Old Drum Inlet (Mallinson et al. 2008, 12), Old Drum Inlet (local use since closed 1971), Pillintary Inlet (Bishop 1878), Whalebone Inlet (Powell 1968—recording error).

Drum Inlet Shoals, shoals, Carteret County, Atlantic Township (local use). About 10 shoals soundside of New Drum Inlet (q.v.) 3 mi. s of Atlantic (mainland). *Other names:* New Drum Inlet Flats (Burkholder et al. 2017, 177).

Drum Island, former barrier beach, Carteret County (Wimble 1738). Applied on occasion to Core Banks between former Cedar Inlet (Normans Inlet) (n) and Old Drum Inlet (s—

not related to Drum Inlet complex farther north). *See* Drum Inlet (historical).

Drum Island, small marsh island, Currituck County, Fruitville Township (C&GS 1913a). In Currituck Sound just sw of Crow Island at s entrance Little Walkers Creek, 6.5 mi. nnw of Corolla. *See* Drum Inlet (historical).

Drum Island Shoal, shoal, Carteret County, Atlantic Township (Williamson 1992, 147). Near Core Banks 1 mi. ssw of Dump Island, 3 mi. w of Atlantic (mainland). *See* Drum Inlet (historical).

Drum Pond, cove, 0.5 mi. wide, Carteret County, Cedar Island Township (USGS 2013: Atlantic). On w side of unnamed marsh (sometimes considered part of Hog Island) 2 mi. e of Cedar Island Ferry landing, 10.5 mi. sw of Ocracoke (village). *See* Drum Inlet (historical). *Other names:* Oyster Bay (C&GS 1899b).

Drum Pond Point, point, Carteret County, Cedar Island Township (USGS 2013: Atlantic). Just w of Drum Pond at w side of unnamed marsh (sometimes considered part of Hog Island) 2 mi. e of Cedar Island Ferry landing, 10.5 mi. sw of Ocracoke (village). *See* Drum Inlet (historical).

Drum Shoal, shoal, Carteret County, Atlantic Township (Williamson 1992, 147). In Core Sound 3 mi. w of former Core Banks Life Saving Station, 10 mi. ne of Davis (mainland). *See* Drum Inlet (historical).

Drum Shoal, small shoal, Carteret County, Portsmouth Township (Williamson 1992, 126). Just ne of Wallace Channel, 2 mi. nne of former Portsmouth Life Saving Station in Portsmouth (village), 6.5 mi. w of Ocracoke (village). *See* Drum Inlet (historical).

Drum Shoals, shoal, 0.5 mi. long, Carteret County, Morehead Township (USGS 2013: Mansfield). In Bogue Sound 0.5 mi. n of Bogue Banks, 2.1 mi. w of Atlantic Beach, 3.5 mi. sw of Morehead City (mainland). *See* Drum Inlet (historical).

Dry Sand Shoal, former shoal, Carteret County, Portsmouth Township (19th-century maps). Was an extension of Portsmouth Island into Ocracoke Inlet 1.7 mi. e of Portsmouth (village), 4 mi. sw of Ocracoke (village). Originally, late 19th and early 20th centuries, much larger and usually connected to Portsmouth Island, so names Dry Sand Point, Dry Sand Shoal, and Dry Shoal Point were used. Much became inundated in late 20th century, remnants including Vera Cruz Shoal remained. Early 21st century all Dry Sand Shoal and Vera Cruz Shoal disappeared. Sometimes included in Oyster Rocks (q.v.) complex. *Other names:* Dry Sand (Price 1795, 627), Dry Sand Point (Blunt 1809), Drysand Point (historical use), Dry Shoal Point (Williamson 1992), Dry Shoals Point (shipwreck reports), Sandy Point (White 2012, 234).

Dry Sand Shoal. *See* Vera Cruz Shoal.

Dry Shoal, former shoal, Dare County, Nags Head Township (CS 1862b). Was just s of former location of Oregon Inlet (1862 inlet approx.. 2 mi. n of present location); Dry Shoal was 2.5 mi. ese of Duck Island, 10 mi. s of Nags Head. Remnants remain at low water; most has disappeared, becoming inundated since Oregon Inlet has migrated s.

Duck, town, Dare County, Atlantic Township (signage). On s Currituck Banks 16 mi. nnw of Nags Head (center), and 15 mi. sse of Corolla. Named for large numbers and varieties of ducks found here originally. Post office est. unofficially 1890, officially 1908, operating sporadically until 1920, discontinued 1941, with a substation reopening 1941. Some use for North Duck and South Duck from real estate agent usage. Incorporated 2002. *Other names:* Bank Woods (older local use), Duck Village (commercial publications).

Duck Beach, beach, Dare County, Atlantic Township. General reference since 1990s referring to beach between Southern Shores (s) and Sanderling (n), including developments during decades before 2010. Used in plural form interchangeably. *Other names:* Ducks Beach (some local use), Duck Beaches (rare use, probably reference to beaches at named separate subdivisions beachside in Duck).

Duck Blind Slue, channel, Hyde County, Ocracoke Township (NPS 2005b: NPS 2, 488). Exact location unknown but believed to be or have been in Pamlico Sound off ne shore of Ocracoke near Horsepen Point. *See* Allen Slough.

Duck Creek, water area, 0.5 mi. long, Currituck County, Fruitville Township (Cox 1923). In e Walk Island just w of Deep Creek, 1.4 mi. ene of Knotts Island (village).

Duck Hole, lake, 0.1 mi. across, Currituck County, Poplar Branch Township (USGS 2013: Mossey Islands). In Mossey Islands complex, 4.7 mi. s of Corolla. Indicative of feeding places for ducks in "hunting area" along Atlantic Flyway. *Other names:* Duck Creek Pond (C&GS 1852), Duck Pond (local use).

Duck Island, marsh island, 0.8 mi. long, 0.5 mi. wide, Dare County, Nags Head Township (USGS 2013: Oregon Inlet). In Roanoke Sound 2 mi. w of Herring Shoal, 4.4 mi. se of Wanchese. *Other names:* North Duck Island (Abbott 1866), South Duck Island (Sneden 1862).

Duck Island Flats, tidal flats, Dare County, Nags Head Township (local use). Shoals sometimes exposed, number of exposed fouls or muddy flats varies, 0.7 mi. e of Duck Island, 3.2 mi. nw of Oregon Inlet, 4 mi. se of Wanchese. *Other names:* North Duck Island (Sneden 1862).

Duck Landing, former landing, Dare County, Atlantic Township (historical use). Was soundside at Duck (center), 16.7 mi. nw of Nags Head (center). Subdivision named for feature.

Duckpond, cove, 0.2 mi. wide, Currituck County, Fruitville Township (USGS 2013: Knotts Island). In North Landing River 0.7 mi. nnw of Mackay Island, 2.7 mi. w of Knotts Island (village). Descriptive referring to one of many ponds and coves providing food and rest stop for migrating birds along Atlantic Flyway migration routes. Descriptor, applied many times in past on earlier maps as feature name; most have been replaced by other names. *See* Bay Tree and Adams Pond.

Duckpond, cove, 0.5 mi. long, 0.3 mi. wide, Currituck County, Fruitville Township (USGS 1940:). Is 3.8 mi. sw of Knotts Island (village). *See* Duckpond.

Duck Pond, man-enhanced lake, Dare County, Atlantic Township (Currituck DB 2, 1773, 377). Open water in Duck Pond Swamp where Duck Pond Creek begins, 1 mi. nw of original Kitty Hawk. Descriptive name dates from colonial period. *See* Duckpond. *Other names:* Duck Ponds (Currituck DB 6, 1789, 36).

Duck Pond Creek, waterway, Currituck County, Poplar Branch Township (CS 1852). Separates Mossy Pond, Duck Hole, and Old House Pond from Teals Island (s) 2 mi. s of Monteray Shores.

Duck Pond Creek, stream, 1.5 mi. long, Dare County, Atlantic Township (USGS 2013: Kitty Hawk). Begins 1 mi. w of original Kitty Hawk, flows s to Kitty Hawk Bay, 8.2 mi. nw of Nags Head (center). "Drean," as used in

the variant name, was a known dialectical variation of "drain" and used for a short time (albeit sparingly) here 1700s. *See* Duckpond. *Other names:* Duck Pond Ditch (Town of Kitty Hawk 2007), Duck Pond Drean (Currituck DB 6, 1789, 36), Duck Pond Gut (Harris 2017), Hickory Ridge Gutt (some 18th-century maps—misapplied).

Duck Pond Ridge, sand ridge, 1 mi. long, Dare County, Atlantic Township (Currituck DB 6, 1790, 126). Just e of Poor Ridge and the lower portion Duck Pond Creek, 1 mi. w of original Kitty Hawk. First usage 1790. *See* Kitty Hawk ridge-and-swale system.

Duck Ponds, lake, 0.4 mi. long, 0.02 mi. wide, Dare County, Hatteras Township (USGS 2013: Cape Hatteras). Just ne of Isaac Pond, 0.5 mi. s of Hatteras (village). Created 1930s by Gooseville Gun Club (near here). *See* Duckpond. *Other names:* Duck Pond (some newer usage, now mostly joined).

Duck Pond Swamp, linear swamp, Dare County, Atlantic Township (Town of Kitty Hawk 2007). Trends n-s just e of Ash Swamp, 1.8 mi. ene of Sound Landing, 1.5 mi. nnw of original Kitty Hawk. Ne-most swamp in Kitty Hawk Woods Swamps (q.v.). *See* Kitty Hawk ridge-and-swale system.

Duck Ridge. *See* Powder Ridge.

Duck Woods, woods, Dare County, Atlantic Township (local use). On Currituck Banks s from Duck to s boundary of Southern Shores, 16 mi. nnw of Nags Head (center). *Other names:* Southern Shore Woods (in part—used after town established).

Duck Woods Pond, elongated lake, 0.7 mi. long, less than 0.05 mi. wide, Dare County, Atlantic Township (local use). On Currituck Banks in Southern Shores, 3.3 mi. nw of original Kitty Hawk.

Dudleys Island. *See* Mon Island.

Duffys Point. *See* Baum Point (Nags Head Township).

Duges Island, former island, Carteret County, Davis Township (C&GS 1896). Was in Core Sound 1 mi. ne of Shingle Point, 3.5 mi. ese of Davis (mainland). *See* Dugs. Also, Douglas Point (q.v.) is just sw and might be derived from Duges (or Dugs), where usage declined over time and without recollection of original meaning (female breasts). No available information regarding name origin of Douglas Point, and residents do not know the name. Disappeared mid-20th century.

Duges Island. *See* Guthries Hammock.

Dugs, historical. Appeared as descriptor without generic term on maps 1600s, first appears as place name on Lawson's 1709 map as name of an island and recurs on several later maps. Applied in different places but most often to s-most of three islands in the Oregon Inlet area (Crisp 1711); Moseley (1733) applies name to an unbreached barrier island from Roanok (*sic*) Inlet to Gun Inlet (Gunt Inlet). Some authors and cartographers assumed this to be a place name and added the generic "creek" or "island" or "inlet" accordingly. Initially merely descriptive and appropriately appears in early references without a generic term, applied to places with distinctive and pronounced sand dunes. The word "dug" is 16th-century mildly derogatory term referring to female breasts, especially teat or nipple. "Dugs" and "paps" were used liberally by English seamen 16th and 17th centuries as descriptive terms for formations resembling female breast. Today, appears in some slang dictionaries. Variant name Euter or abbreviation appears only on Huber (1711), Swiss map completely in German. The map is based on Lawson (1709), who labels this small barrier island Dugs, so Huber's intent was to use German word *euter*, meaning udders, to correspond with Lawson's use of "dugs"; though Huber uses abbreviation "Ent I," little doubt Huber meant Eut and not Ent. Occasionally labeled Etacrewac, one of the original Indian names. *Other names:* Dogs (Wimble 1733), Euter (Huber 1711), The Dugs (Wimble 1733).

Dugs Creek, former tidal stream, Dare County, Nags Head or Kinnakeet Townships (vague references early 16th to early 17th centuries). Exact location unknown but generally just n of or just s of Gunt Inlet, which would also be just n of Oregon Inlet. *See* Dugs.

Dulls Point, marsh point, Dare County, Kinnakeet Township (USGS 2013: Pea Island). On Pea Island on center shore of Terrapin Creek Bay, 6.3 mi. s of Oregon Inlet.

Dump Island, elongated island, 0.5 mi. long, Carteret County, Atlantic Township (USGS 2013: Atlantic). In Core Sound 1.1 mi. n of Drum Inlet (Old Drum Inlet; *see* Drum Inlet, Portsmouth and Atlantic Townships), 3.1 mi. e of Atlantic (mainland). *Other names:* Old Drum Inlet Flats (Burkholder et al. 2017, 178).

Duncan Creek, cove, Dare County, Hatteras Township (local informants). In e Hatteras (village), just w of Duncan Point 4.5 mi. ene of Hatteras Inlet. The Slash and Little Ditch trend e and s, respectively.

Duncan Point, point, Dare County, Hatteras Township (USGS 2013: Cape Hatteras). At s entrance Sandy Bay, 1.2 mi. e of Hatteras (village). Covey indicates original name was Jackson Point for Francis Jackson, changed to Duncan when land was sold to Thomas Dunkin (*sic*). *Other names:* Duncans Point (Covey 2018, 13), Jackson Point (Covey 2018, 13), The Point (Garrity-Blake 2010, 292).

Dune Ridge, small distinct sand ridge, 1 mi. long, Carteret County, White Oak Township (local use). Formerly at Emerald Plantation subdivision, 6.2 mi. w of original Emerald Isle. Small but distinct before housing development, which has mostly obliterated the sand ridge.

Dunes of Dare, sand dunes, Dare County, Nags Head Township (historical local use). General and collective term referencing all sand dunes in and around Nags Head. Historical and not used today. *See* Dare County. *Other names:* Dare Dunes (limited local use), Nags Head Dunes (local use and subdivision name).

Dunns Point, point, Currituck County, Fruitville Township (diminished local use). W shore lower Capsies Creek, in Woodleigh 2 mi. n of Knotts Island (village center). Name rarely used though road still bears name.

Dunston Island, marsh island, less than 0.1 mi. across, Dare County, Atlantic Township (local use). In se Kitty Hawk Bay, 1.6 mi. sse of original Kitty Hawk. *Other names:* Dunstan Marsh (often islands are marsh and generic terms "island" and "marsh" used interchangeably, sometimes marsh a separately named feature).

Dunstan Marsh, marsh, Dare County, Atlantic Township (local use). In se Kitty Hawk Bay at Dunston Island (q.v.), 1.6 mi. sse of original Kitty Hawk.

Durant Point, point, Dare County, Hatteras Township (USGS 2013: Cape Hatteras). At n entrance to Sandy Bay, 1.1 mi. e of Hatteras (village). *Other names:* Durants Point (CS 1852).

Durants, former settlement, Dare County, Hatteras Township (Lathrop 1858). Was 0.5 mi. sse of Hatteras (village), 4 mi. ne of Hatteras Inlet. Local surname Durant dates from colonial period, named for family with commercial activity here.

Durants Bay. *See* Sandy Bay.

Durants Island, small hummock, Dare County, Hatteras Township (NPS 2005b: NPS 2, 294). Was just sw of Durant Point, 1 mi. nne of Hatteras (village). This "island" actually large hummock (hammock, but termed "hamlet" in Hatteras village), was factory location for processing porpoise in late 19th century.

Dykes Creek, canalized stream, 0.2 mi. long, Dare County, Nags Head Township (some local use). At e shore Roanoke Island just s of entrance to Roanoke Sound Bridge (Washington Baum Bridge), 2.2 mi. se of Manteo (center). Possibly descriptive name of embankment or dike ("dyke" is a form of "dike") created by dredging. McKnights Creek or McKnights Ditch just s of Dykes Creek; sometimes names are reversed. *Other names:* McKnights Creek (historical local use), McKnights Ditch (historical local use).

Dykstras Ditch, canal, 0.5 mi. long, Dare County, Nags Head Township (Brown 2015). Extends e-sw then nw separating Pond Island (n) from House Island and Grun Island (s) 1.5 mi. w of Whalebone Junction. Former location of fishing charter business 1950s. Dykes Creek (q.v.) opposite at Roanoke Island might have been confused with this feature. Dykstra is Dutch surname but unknown here.

E

Eagle Nest Bay, cove, 0.4 mi. wide, Dare County, Kinnakeet Township (USGS 2013: Pea Island Overedge West). In Pamlico Sound off Pea Island, trends ne-sw between Eagle Nest Point and Goat Island Point, 9.9 mi. nnw of Rodanthe. Made official by USBGN 1975. *Other names:* Eagle Nest (local usage), Eagles Nest Bay (NOS 2014b), Eaglenest Pond (Currituck DB 27, 1855, 300–1).

Eagle Nest Point, point, Dare County, Kinnakeet Township (USGS 2013: Pea Island Overedge West). N entrance point Eagle Nest Bay, 10.2 mi. nnw of Rodanthe. *Other names:* Eagle Nest (local version).

Eagle Shoal Island, island, 0.3 mi. long, 0.1 mi. wide, Currituck County, Fruitville Township (Cox 1923). In South Channel just s of Betseys Marsh, 5.5 mi. se of Knotts Island (village).

Eagleton, former settlement, Dare County, Atlantic Township (USGS 2013: Kitty Hawk). Was on Colington Island just n of Colington Harbour, 0.9 mi. nw of Colington (community), 2.5 mi. w of Wright Brothers National Memorial. Refers to scattered settlement nw Colington Island, no specific community. Locally, names Eagleton and Eagleton Point used interchangeably. Originates reportedly from local reference to large number of osprey nesting or formerly nested here. Osprey (*Pandion haliaetus*), large bird of prey often referenced as sea eagle, fishing eagle, or fish hawk. Alternatively, and according to Stick (1958), noted local author, name derives from need for a referent when surveying, and surveyor used name of company that made his equipment (not verified and unknown here). *Other names:* Eagleton Point (local use, also point name), Eagleston (occasional spoken use).

Eagleton Point, point, Dare County, Atlantic Township (USGS 2013: Kitty Hawk). At s entrance Kitty Hawk Bay and nw point Colington Island, 3.4 mi. sw of original Kitty Hawk. Use of McDototos Point probable here or maybe Rhodoms Point; the name McDototo is unknown, and no other known occurrence of this surname. *See* Eagleton. *Other names:* Eggleston Point (Powell 1968), McDototos Point (possibly, application unclear—Currituck DB 13, 1814, 52–55), North Point (C&GS 1969b; Binkley 2007, 100, referencing 1952 CHNS project map).

East Bay. *See* Capsies Creek.

East Bay. *See* Porpoise Slough.

East Bay Landing, former landing, Carteret County, Harkers Island Township (local references). Somewhere at ne end Harkers Island, 2.5 mi. e of Harkers Island (village). Subdivision named for feature.

East Bay Marina, harbor, Carteret County, Harkers Island Township (signage). N-central Harkers Island 6.3 mi. ese of Beaufort (mainland). Interestingly located at s Westmouth Bay 1 mi. west of Eastmouth Bay. *Other names:* Garners Marina (N.C. Marine Fisheries 2019, E7, map 27).

East Beach, beach, 2 mi. long, in Carteret

County, Harkers Island Township (NPS 2000). E side of Cape Lookout, 8.5 mi. s of Harkers Island (village). Only known occurrence of name, hand annotated on map, and used only by NPS.

East Burris Island, former island, Currituck County, Poplar Branch Township (C&GS 1852). In Burris Islands (q.v.) complex and was distinct 19th century, but now joined with w North Burris Island, 7 mi. s of Corolla. *Other names:* East Burows Island (C&GS 1852).

East Canal, canal, 0.25 mi. long, Carteret County, Morehead Township (Carteret County GIS 2019). Shortest and e-most of three canals trending n-s in Sound View Isles subdivision (e part of Canals at Atlantic Beach q.v.).

Eastern Channel, former channel, 10–15 ft. wide, Dare County, Nags Head Township (historical use). Was e-most passage through Roanoke Marshes, 2 mi. w of Wanchese. Descriptive, continued use led to being established as accepted proper name. Conflicting reports regarding width, 10 ft. is certain. Many residents of Roanoke Island reportedly have tales of great-great-great grandparents walking to mainland by carrying a large post or plank to assist in crossing the channel; no proof was possible or attempted other than stories. Smith (2001, 13) reports 1783 Adam Etheridge indicates his grandfather did indeed cross then emerging channel with a fence post. Today no trace of Eastern Channel because most of Roanoke Marshes was inundated from closing of Roanoke Inlet. *See* Roanoke Marshes, Ship Channel (Dare County), and Roan Oak Narrows. *Other names:* Croatan Channel (used 1783; Smith 2001, 14n31).

Eastern Marsh, small, narrow marsh, Currituck County, Fruitville Township (Cox 1923). Trends e-w in Currituck Bay, 4 mi. se of Knotts Island (village).

Eastern Pine Knoll Shores, area, Carteret County, Morehead Township (PKS 2016). Informal reference to e Pine Knoll Shores just e of e entrance to Pine Knoll Waterway, 3.2 mi. w of Atlantic Beach. Developed between 1955 and 1957 by Roosevelt heirs of Alice Hoffman, first lots sold 1957. Reference today is merely an unofficial section of Pine Knoll Shores, sometimes as Old Pine Knoll Shores. *Other names:* Old Pine Knoll Shores (PKS 2016).

Eastern Rocks, rocks, Carteret County, Portsmouth Township (Hooker 1850). E portion North Rock (q.v.) and Oyster Rocks (q.v.) complex, 1 mi. n of Shell Castle, 8.5 mi. w of Ocracoke (village). *Other names:* Little Shell Rock (historical use).

Eastern Shoals, former shoals, Currituck County, Fruitville Township (Byrd 1728). Were in Atlantic Ocean near entrance to former Currituck Inlet but today only remnants remain. *Other names:* Bar of Currituck (historical), Charotuck Inlett Bar (historical).

East Hog Island, marsh island, Carteret County, Cedar Island Township (local use). Part of Hog Island 2 mi. e of Cedar Island Ferry landing separated from West Hog Island by Hog Island Narrows. Actually sse of West Hog Island.

Eastmouth Bay, cove, Carteret County, Harkers Island Township (USGS 2013: Harkers Island). In Core Sound, separates Harkers Island from Browns Island, 1.5 mi. ene of Harkers Island (village). One-word and two-word forms used; one-word form more prevalent on official sources. *Other names:* East Mouth Bay (local maps).

East Point, point, Dare County, Kinnakeet Township (Goldstein 2000, loc. 2895). On s shore Oregon Inlet ne point of Pea Island, 11 mi. se of Whalebone Junction.

East Pond, pond, Carteret County, Morehead Township (signage). In Theodore Roosevelt Natural Area along Alice Hoffman Nature Trail just north of N.C. Aquarium, 1 mi. w of Pine Knoll Shores (center).

East Pool, man-enhanced, Currituck County, Fruitville Township (F&WS 1984, map, 74). Stages of marsh, dry, and open water is e-most of three in Mackay Island National Wildlife Refuge at e Mackay Island, 2 mi. w of Knotts Island (village). Created 1984 by establishing Cross Dike and Long Dike; status of its composition can be controlled. *Other names:* East Impoundment (F&WS 1984, 11), East Pools (sometimes used, F&WS 1984, 10), Large Impoundment (original name, F&WS 1984, 10).

East Portsmouth, former community, Carteret County, Portsmouth Township (CS 1856; Colton 1860). Just e of Portsmouth (village), 6 mi. se of Ocracoke (village). All named outlying communities part of Portsmouth (village) just clusters of houses separated by marsh and open area and referenced by separate names for convenience and clarity of location (*see* Middle Portsmouth, Portsmouth, South Portsmouth, and Sheep Island). *Other names:* Lower End (White 2012, 168—*see* Sheep Island, former community, for explanation of "reversed" usage of up banks, down banks, and lower), North End (White 2012, 168).

East Ridge, former sand ridge, Dare County, Atlantic Township (Currituck DB 1788, 6, 4). N-s in what is now Southern Shores (town) with various applications from just e of Cypress Swamp (1 mi. long) to entire s part of Southern Shores (3 mi. long). Considerably altered by development, name no longer used.

East Wicar Island, island, Carteret County, Davis Township (Piggott 1894a). In Great Island Bay just sw of Great Island, 4 mi. se of Davis (mainland). Meaning of name is not documented, but probably variation of surname Wicker, known here (Keziah Wicker married a son of John Shackleford). Numerous uses and variations of word "wic"; use of "wic" ("wich") relates to town or village used in England (also variations found in other Germanic languages), obviously has no meaning here. While "wic" ("wick") is an archaic reference to bay geographically from Scottish (originally Norse), no reason to believe relevant as no other known such use on the Outer Banks. "Wic" has referred to bay leaves from the bay tree of the Mediterranean (*Laurus nobilis*), and while sweetbay tree (*Magnolia virginiana*) is indigenous to se North America, no relationship here. There certainly is no evidence to suggest any relationship to Wicca related to paganism, since organized Wicca did not exist then. However, "wicca" also is an Old English reference to wizard or magician, and while many 16th- and 17th-century terms existed on the Outer Banks, no evidence suggests this is such a reference. "Wicker" also refers to twigs from the willow tree found on mainland (Carolina willow [*Salix caroliniana*] or swamp willow [*Salix nigra*]—not invasive weeping willow [*Salix babylonica*] from Asia) in swamps and used for making useful items and to chew usually for headache relief. Still, willow would not likely be found on the barrier island (Core Banks), which supports surname possibility; no one knows for sure. Likely variation of surname Wicker.

Also, name implies there ought to be a West Wicar Island, but none has been found. Location determined according to surrounding but unnamed features; plat used as source was inconclusive to which island in the group of several close islands name refers. Interviews with residents in Davis (mainland) area and Cedar Island yielded no knowledge of this feature, though a few individuals knew of a reference to "The Wickers" on the mainland (and might have just been a reference to where the Wicker family resided or possibly just to a stand of willow trees), but those interviewed were not sure exactly to what it refers. So, more likely this is a peculiar spelling of wicker, which might have some reasonable application here.

Eel Creek, tidal stream, 0.4 mi. long, Currituck County, Poplar Branch Township (local use). Just e of Great Gap, 5.4 mi. nnw of Duck. Local usage does not indicate whether named for its shape or for eels caught here. Eel catching was an economic activity at one time here, but all was shipped n, and "Bankers" never really liked to eat eel.

Egg Shoal, shoal, 0.1 mi. long, Dare County, Hatteras Township (local use). In Pamlico Sound, 2.3 mi. nnw of Hatteras (village). *Other names:* Egg Bank (CS 1856), Egg Island Shoal (Foster 1866b, Civil War era, double generic because mostly bare at this time), Egg Shoals (CS 1854), Shell Island (older local use).

Egret Lake, man-made lake, Carteret County, Morehead Township (local use). In Egret Lake section of Beacons Reach just ne of Coral Ridge, just w of Alligator Gut, 2.3 mi. w of Pine Knoll Shores. The great egret (*Ardea alba*) and snowy egret (*Egretta thula*) are here year-round, with the cattle egret (*Bubulcus ibis*) here in summer. Subdivision named for feature.

Egret Point, point, Carteret County, Morehead Township (signage). In Theodore Roosevelt Natural Area along Alice Hoffman Nature Trail just ne of N.C. Aquarium 1 mi. w of Pine Knoll Shores (center).

Eight & One-Half Marina, harbor, Carteret County, Morehead Township (signage). At Eight & Half Marina Village subdivision just n of Money Island Beach just e of Atlantic Beach, 2 mi. s of Morehead City (mainland). Assigned by builder, real reason probably lost. Numerous stories exist regarding name origin, but folk at the marina believe named because developers were principals in developing property at Figure Eight Island just n of Wrightsville Beach in extreme se North Carolina; perhaps name is but a whimsical association with that development. Subdivision named for feature.

Elijah Creek, former water passage, Carteret County, Morehead Township (USGS 1951: Beaufort). Connected Morehead City Channel and Back Sound just se of Elijah Lump, 2 mi. se of Morehead City (mainland).

Elijah Lump, former hummock, 20 ft. high, Carteret County, Morehead Township (USGS 1951: Beaufort). Was in Bogue Sound at Morehead City Channel, 1.5 mi. se of Morehead City (mainland). Formerly surrounded by water, but completely surrounded by tidal flat during past 20 years. Brant Island became incorporated into Elijah Lump. *See* Dorland Lump. *Other names:* Brant Island (historical).

Emerald Cove, small cove, Carteret County, White Oak Township (local use). Soundside at original Emerald Isle, 0.7 mi. s of Wood Island, 3.5 mi. w of Indian Beach (town), and recent vintage not used by many. Came into use after establishment of Emerald Isle 1950s and not used by original residents (an example of reversed usage, natural feature acquiring name of man-made feature).

Emerald Isle, town, Carteret County, White Oak Township (signage). On Bogue Banks, 4.5 mi. ssw of Salter Path. Incorporated 1957 after land was purchased 1954 for development. Numerous suppositions regarding name origin, obvious and not so obvious, but reportedly the developer when flying over remarked, "A solid green gem and should be known as Emerald Isle," commenting on dense maritime scrub forest. Generic term "isle" is used sparingly on the Outer Banks and usually for emphasis. Post office est. 1998.

Incorporated Emerald Isle from 0.5 mi. w of Indian Beach (town) along central and w Bogue Banks for 11.5 mi. to Bogue Inlet. Nickname Uptown Emerald Isle is applied (by signage) to original or e part of town generally numbered streets (1st–25th), 2.5 mi. long. Three subdivisions named for feature.

Hurricane Hazel (1954) created two breaches of the barrier island in e Emerald Isle: one just e of Yellow Hill Landing and the other near Rice(s) Path. Each was more overwash than breach, and neither lasted long enough to acquire a name or meaningful reference.

Other names: Bogue Inlet (early, short-lived reference based on location at w end Bogue Banks near Bogue Inlet and former reference to scattered families there), Emerald (21st-century media), Emerald Isle By-The-Sea (The State 1954), Uptown Emerald Isle (in part—signage).

Emerald Isle Woods, woods, Carteret County, White Oak Township (signage). Just sw of entrance to Langston Bridge, 7 mi. w of original Emerald Isle. Most preserved as a park. *Other names:* Emerald Woods (local usage).

Endesoeces, historical area (Blaeu 1640). Indigenous word appearing on early maps as reference to Portsmouth Island and n Core Banks. *Other names:* Endesockee (Cheeseman 1982, 195), Endesockes (Cheeseman 1982, 195), Endesokes (Quinn 1975).

End of Hills Bay. *See* Round Hammock Bay.

Engagement Hill, sand dune, 70 ft. high, Dare County, Nags Head Township (USGS 2013: Manteo). Just s of Jockeys Ridge, 0.7 mi. nw of Nags Head (center). Originated (according to story) because young couples visiting the sand dune found it easy to become engaged from the spectacular view of both ocean and sound (folk etymology, providing a reason when none is known, or maybe not).

Enoch Ridge, sand ridge, Dare County, Atlantic Township (Harris 2017). According to Harris (2017), somewhere in Kitty Hawk ridge-and-swale system (q.v.), w of original Kitty Hawk. Harris does not provide additional information, and the name, as a named feature, does not appear in early deeds, though Enoch is a popular given name in colonial period and occurs throughout early deeds.

Epstein Tract. *See* The Village at Nags Head.

Erb Creek. *See* Panters Creek.

Erb Point, point, Dare County, Atlantic Township (historical local use). N point at Panters Creek just s of Buzzard Point, 1.5 mi. nw of Jockeys Ridge, 1.7 mi. nw of Nags Head (center). Fallen into disuse being more prevalent historically. Meaning is reportedly lost, and many believe could have been recorded from pronunciation of "herb," but origin is a given name specifically that of Erb Tillett, whose homesite was here.

Esham Dock, former dock, Hyde County, Ocracoke Township (Howard, July 22, 2018). Was soundside in Oyster Creek subdivision e Ocracoke (village). No trace of dock today.

Essex Island. *See* Bodie Island.

Etacrewac, former barrier island, Dare County, Nags Head and Atlantic Townships (White 1585). From s tip of Bodie Island (original) at former Gunt Inlet (Port Ferdinando) n to s portion Currituck Banks near Kitty Hawk or maybe as far n as Trinety Harbor (inlet). Indigenous name applied generally in n parts of the Outer Banks by early European mapmakers, an Algonquian word reportedly meaning evergreen-type trees. Application of Etacrewac as place for some supports theories an inlet existed near Kitty Hawk Bay during historic times (rumors persist); however, proof is inconclusive at best, and no evidence of relict inlet features during post-European arrival. Early maps are confusing and unclear as to whether such an inlet ever existed; most indicate likely not (*see* Kill Devil Hills Inlet). *Other names:* Croat (Blaeu 1640—included as another name for Etacrewac by small-scale applications from 1640 map, but meant to be a short form of Croatamung, indigenous name n of Etacrewac), Essex Island (Smith 1624, map—probable gesture to Earl of Essex, England; most of Smith's names did not last), Rouoak (Crisp 1711).

Etheridges Hills, sand dunes (wooded), Dare County, Nags Head Township (historical local use). Distinct complex of sand dunes on n Roanoke Island 1 mi. e se of Griffins Hills, 1.5 mi. n of Manteo (center). Named for original landowner. *Other names:* Holly Hills (sometimes used, subdivision e end of feature), Sand Hills (Foster 1866a).

Etheridges Point, former point, Dare County, Nags Head Township (Brazier 1820). At Fort Raleigh National Historic Site (Lost Colony), 4.5 mi. nw of Manteo (center). Inundated indicative of erosion on n end Roanoke Island. Possibly point referenced by White when searching for Lost Colonists 1590 in his reference, "We returned by the water side, round about the Northpoint of the Iland, until we came to a place where I left our colony in the yeere 1586." White's use of 1586

is a transcribing error from his notes or just a mistake, because the year reference should be 1587. This reference could be to North Point but is more likely Etheridges Point. *Other names:* Etheridge Point (USGS 1986, 32), Ethridge Point (ACE 1843), Ethridges Point (Fulton 1820), North Point of Roanoke Island (Haklyut 1589), Northpoint of the Iland (Haklyut 1589).

Evergreen Island. *See* Sheep Island.

Evergreens, The, area, 1 mi. long, Carteret County, Portsmouth Township (historical local use). Higher e Sheep Island (q.v.) 1.5 mi. ssw of Portsmouth (village). Named Evergreen Island persistently on USGS Portsmouth (2013 and earlier versions). *Other names:* Evergreen Island (USGS 2013: Portsmouth).

Evergreen Slough. *See* Salters Creek.

Eves Pond, cove, Currituck County, Fruitville Township (Cox 1923). Is 1 mi. s of Bush Island, 4.5 mi. se of Knotts Island (village). *See* Adams Pond.

F

False Channel, former channel, Hyde and Dare Counties; Ocracoke and Hatteras Townships (Blunt 1857, 343). Was in e Hatteras Inlet, 3 mi. sw of Hatteras (village). Was not dependable even though marked with buoys in mid-19th century. No longer exists.

False Island, small occasional island, Dare County, Atlantic Township (Harris 2017). Surrounded by water completely on occasion and lies w of what has been labeled in recent years Jeanguite Creek (extension from original creek n of US 158, originally High Bridge Creek or High Ridge Creek), center just s of intersection of county 1208 (West Kitty Hawk Road) and county 1207 (Twifford Street), 1.3 mi. w of original Kitty Hawk.

False Island Ridge, sand ridge, Dare County, Atlantic Township (Harris 2017). Trends n-s 0.5 mi. from False Island, 1.5 mi. w of original Kitty Hawk. Associative with False Island. Suspicious this is named False Island Ridge only 0.3 mi. e of False Ridge, but enough evidence suggests the names are legitimate.

False Point, point, Dare County, Hatteras Township (local informants). Barely noticeable protrusion (hence name) from upper oceanside Inlet Peninsula into Atlantic Ocean, 1 mi. e of Hatteras Inlet, 3 mi. sw of Hatteras (village). Occasionally application expanded from just this point to slightly wider area when giving directions. Known mostly to local folk and fishermen. *Other names:* False Cape (occasionally on tourist maps).

False Ridge, sand ridge, Dare County, Atlantic Township (Harris 2017). Just w of n High Ridge, 0.3 mi. e of Sound Landing, 1.5 mi. w of original Kitty Hawk. Descriptive of appearance. Suspicious this feature named False Ridge is only 0.3 mi. w of False Island Ridge, but enough evidence suggests the names are legitimate.

Fanders Ridge, sand ridge, Dare County, Atlantic Township (Harris 2017; unknown, 1857). According to Harris (2017), somewhere in Kitty Hawk ridge-and-swale system (q.v.), w of original Kitty Hawk. Harris does not provide additional information, and the name, as a named feature, does not appear in early deeds. The name in this form not encountered elsewhere and could be transcription error.

Fannin Mill, former mill, Dare County, Nags Head Township (hearsay usage). Somewhere on central or n Roanoke Island, location is unsure. Smith (2001, 7) indicates "one of the two windmills on the island was located in this vicinity," meaning North End, Roanoke Island, but does not mention specific location. A short road named Fannin Mill Road is in central Manteo, and could be location for former mill. Most asked had never heard of a mill here, but a few thought maybe there had been one here. This could be mere suggestion by the road name.

Fanny Ridge, small sand ridge, Dare County, Atlantic Township (Harris 2017). In n Kitty Hawk Landing subdivision, 1.5 mi. w of original Kitty Hawk. *Other names:* Fanny Toler Ridge (Harris 2017).

Faraby Island, elongated marsh island, 0.7 mi. long, Currituck County, Fruitville Township (USGS 2016: Creeds). Trends ne-to-sw in North Landing River, 1 mi. sw of Sandy Point, 5.7 mi. w of Knotts Island (village). *Other names:* Sandy Point Island (some use—Sandy Point just ne).

Farrow Scarboroughs Landing, former landing, Dare County, Kinnakeet Township (Garrity-Blake 2010, 169). Was just s of Gibbs Point and North End in The North'ard new Avon, 7.2 mi. n of Buxton. *See* Farrows Creek.

Farrow Scarborough Windmill, former mill and windmill, Dare County, Kinnakeet Township (Garrity-Blake 2010, 169). Was at former Farrow Scarborough Landing just s of Gibbs Point and North End in The North'ard new Avon, 7.2 mi. n of Buxton. Windmills were often on or near shore of the sound at a landing to process corn brought by boat from mainland. Grain would be ground and distributed or purchased at mill, where sometimes a small community might develop. There were numerous transactions where windmills changed ownership and often between people with same surname; difficult to discern some of these transactions. Generally known and accepted there were two windmills in Avon. *See* Farrows Creek and Barnes Mill. *Other names:* Pharoah Farrows Mill (Covey 2018, 111, possibly), Bateman Mill (Covey 2018, 61), Ezekiel Hoopers Windmill (Covey 2015, 58), Scarborough Mill (occasional use).

Farrows Creek, small cove, Dare County, Kinnakeet Township (colonial deeds 1718). At Bald Point 2 mi. ne of Buxton. Farrow is an old and established name in Cape Hatteras and reportedly was originally Pharoe, with some stories originally the man, who married locally, was of Arabic origin and was shipwrecked. No proof, likely just folk etymology: the name recorded on deeds since the beginning of the 1700s is Farrow, with no mention of Pharoe (except one mention of Pharoah Farrow or with a given name as a version of Pharoe). Wahab Village Annex (Ocracoke village subdivision) has also similar renditions of (unproven) Arabic lineage. *Other names:* Cates Creek (historical use), Cates Drain (Currituck DB 3, 1803, 444–45), Through Fare (occasional use, mostly historical).

Felucca Inlet, canal, Dare County, Atlantic Township (local use). At Colington Harbour, 2.5 mi. wsw of Kill Devil Hills (town). "Inlet" not used in the traditional sense on the Outer Banks as barrier island breach, because indicative of dredging allowing water inward for access by boats to open water (Albemarle Sound). Canal naming scheme at Colington

Harbour is ships or nautical terms. "Felucca" is a traditional wooden sailing boat with one or two fore-and-aft (front and back) rigged sails (lateen sails) traditionally found in Red Sea and e Mediterranean Sea.

Fereares Cove, small cove, 0.2 mi. across, Currituck County, Fruitville Township (Cox 1923). Just ne of Spot Shoal Island at ne end of North Channel, 5 mi. se of Knotts Island (village).

Festival Park Island. *See* Ice Plant Island.

Fiddlers Ridge, small sand ridge, 0.3 mi. long, Carteret County, Morehead Township (local use). In Beacons Reach subdivision, 2.5 mi. w of Pine Knoll Shores. Subdivision named for feature.

Finger Point, small point, Currituck County, Fruitville Township (F&WS 1999, map). Just e of Deals Island 1 mi. w of Carova, 2.7 mi. ne of Knotts Island (village).

First Creek, tidal stream, Dare County, Kinnakeet Township (Garrity-Blake 2010, 169). In sw original Avon just s of entrance to Peters Ditch, 5.5 mi. n of Buxton. Almost joins mouth of Second Creek; remainder of stream is canalized and extends e then n 1.5 mi. almost to Mill Creek. Not many folk apply name to entire feature, especially historically, when applied mostly to mouth and 0.2 mi. inland as it was first major tidal stream s of center of original Avon (*see* Second Creek). Small (0.2 mi.) unnamed creek adjacent to n sometimes uses same name.

First Creeks, five tidal streams system, Dare County, Nags Head Township (USGS 2013: Manteo). At nw Roanoke Island in Croatan Sound, 1 mi. n of Ashbee Harbor, 1.5 mi. s of Manteo (center). Used since 18th century. *Other names:* First Creek (Fulton 1820).

First Flight Ridge, sand dune, 40 ft. high, Dare County, Atlantic Township (local use). In Bald Sand Hills (q.v.) just s of original Kitty Hawk. Remnant dune, second dune n-s in Bald Sand Hills connected to Jacks Cabin Hill (Keepers Hill) by Bay Ridge. Named for subdivision there, example of reversed usage.

First Grass, area, Hyde County, Ocracoke Township (USGS 2013: Ocracoke). On Ocracoke Island 1.7 mi. ssw of Ocracoke (village). Sparse vegetation on Ocracoke Island evident in this descriptive name; an early method of determining location: first vegetation encountered (grass or "scrag" trees—residents often referenced any vegetation collectively as "grass") after leaving Ocracoke (village) and traveling sw toward Ocracoke Inlet. *Other names:* Big Grass (Weslager 1954; confirmed by Ballance [2017, 2018] and Howard [2017, 2018]).

First Hammock Hills, sand dunes, 0.4 mi. long, Hyde County, Ocracoke Township (USGS 2011: Howard Reef, Ocracoke). Three hills on Ocracoke Island just s of Sand Hole Creek, 3.2 mi. ne of Ocracoke (village). Same principle can be applied to this feature as with First Grass (q.v.). "Hummock" is used as the generic term in variant name (First Hummock), correct term yet local version "hammock" is local form exclusively. *See* Black Hammock. *Other names:* First Hammock (Weslager 1954), First Hammock Hill (CS 1852), First Hummock (C&GS 1888c).

First Keel Landing, former landing, Dare County, Nags Head Township (former local use). Exact location is unknown but was likely somewhere in n bend (center) Great Gut, largest canal in Wanchese canals, ditches, guts, and water passages system (q.v.). Name preserved by subdivision here. "Keel," centerline of ship hull and can extend downward for greater stability. Nautical meaning of "first keel" unknown by anyone asked and no specific reference found. Slight chance originally name was "false keel," an old term for beam designed to protect the keel and other purposes, but no one has any idea.

First Pond, man-enhanced, Currituck County, Poplar Branch Township (local use). In central portion Dews Island, 4.7 mi. nw of Duck. Derived name since first of three large man-enhanced ponds from n to s on the island.

First Slough, natural channel, 10 mi. long, Dare County, Nags Head and Kinnakeet Townships (local use). Trends n-s just w of Platt Shoals, 2.5 mi. e of Oregon Inlet. Descriptive for first deep area e of Oregon Inlet used primarily by fishermen (not shown on official or local maps).

Fishermans Point, point, Carteret County, Harkers Island Township (NPS 2004a, 14). E point of extension of Catfish Point into Lookout Bight often inundated (w point is Wreck Point); 1 mi. n of former Cape Lookout (village), 5.2 mi. s of Harkers Island (village). Some families historically lived just s of here periodically (*see* Fish Wharf).

Fish House Creek, water passage, Dare

County, Atlantic Township (Town of Kitty Hawk 2007). Separates Stone Island from other marsh islands (n), 2 mi. sw of original Kitty Hawk. *Other names:* Hog Island Creek (misapplication).

Fishing Creek, water passage, 0.5 mi. long, Carteret County, Morehead Township (USGS 2013: Beaufort). Trends e-w, e end Bogue Banks between Goat Island and Tombstone Point, 2.5 mi. e of Atlantic Beach.

Fishing Point, point, Dare County, Kinnakeet Township (Currituck DB 8, 1800, 237). Soundside somewhere in n Avon probably historic Scarboro.

Fishing Shoal, former shoal, Hyde County, Ocracoke Township; and Dare County, Hatteras Township (CS 1861). At entrance to Hatteras Inlet, 3.8 mi. sw of Hatteras (village).

Fish Wharf, former landing, Carteret County, Harkers Island Township (C&GS 1915a). Former dock serving 20 or so fish houses (temporary fishing camps) around s shore Lookout Bight, just n of former Cape Lookout (village), 0.5 mi. s of Catfish Point and Wreck Point, 1 mi. se of Cape Lookout Lighthouse. Active 19th century.

Five Fathom Bank, shoals, Dare County, Kinnakeet Township (Pinkerton et al. 1809). S extension of Wimble Shoals (q.v.), 10 mi. s of Rodanthe. Changed considerably over last 100 years and continually changes. Name not used extensively and appears on only a few maps and charts. Some scientific papers have begun using Kinnakeet Banks and Kinnakeet Shoals for this feature. *See* Kinnakeet Shoals. *Other names:* Kinnakeet Banks (Mallinson et al. 2008), Kinnakeet Shoals (scientific papers).

Five Foot Slue, former shoal, Carteret County, Portsmouth Township (Ocracock [*sic*] Harbour [*sic*], 1807). Was in Pamlico Sound, separated massive shoals associated with Royal Shoal (n) and associated with Middle Ground (large shoal) (s) inside Ocracoke Inlet, 10 mi. w of Ocracoke (village). Hydrography has changed considerably, and this channel no longer exists. Name indicated depth. *See* Allen Slough. *Other names:* Five Feet Slue (Price 1795, 628—*see* Ten Feet Channel on use of "feet" not "foot"), Five Feet Sluice (Price 1795, 630—sluice used occasionally during this time, though not anywhere else on the Outer Banks; indicative of swift movement

of water through this channel restricted by massive shoals on either side).

Flag Cove, small bay, Dare County, Atlantic Township (Town of Kitty Hawk 2007). Just s of Tarkle Ridge Cove, 1 mi. se of Shellbank Point, 2 mi. sw of original Kitty Hawk.

Flag Creek, tidal stream, Dare County, Kinnakeet Township (Garrity-Blake 2010, 493). Just n of No Ache at South Dike e end of Clarks Bay, 4.5 mi. s of Rodanthe.

Flag Gut, former creek, Dare County, Atlantic Township (Currituck DB 1802, 3, 231). Was located e shore Jeanguite Creek in what is now Southern Shores (town).

Flag Hill, historical, Dare County, Kinnakeet Township (probably) (Covey 2018, 18). *See* Lookout Cedar.

Flag Island, small marsh island, 0.1 mi. across, Dare County, Atlantic Township (local use). In Currituck Sound, 4.4 mi. nw of Duck (center). More than 10 local people were interviewed, all of whom confirm Flag Island, while one did indicate "hearing" the name Doc's Island, but did not believe it to be so. No one knows name origin. *Other names:* Doc's Island (one local informant).

Flaglers Battery. *See* Fort Macon Siege Batteries.

Flag Marsh, marsh, Dare County, Kinnakeet Township (historical local use). Surrounds Flag Creek at e end Clarks Bay just n of No Ache 0.7 mi. s of Salvo. Used mostly historically (late 1700s–early 1800s), not now known.

Flag Point, point, Currituck County, Poplar Branch Township (Codman, Crowninshield, and Lawrence 1925). In Peters Quarter Marsh just s of Great Beach Pond, 2.5 mi. s of Corolla.

Flag Pond, cove, Dare County, Kinnakeet Township (Currituck DB 5, 1787, 167–68). Somewhere in South'ard Water, 2.5 mi. s of original Avon.

Flag Pond. *See* North Pond (Currituck County).

Flat Ridge, short sand ridge, 0.3 mi. long, Dare County, Atlantic Township (Harris 2017). In w Kitty Hawk just e of High Ridge, 2 mi. w of original Kitty Hawk. Descriptive of appearance. *Other names:* Flat Rige (Currituck DB 5, 1785, 242).

Flats, The, open water, Currituck County, Poplar Branch Township (mostly historical local use). In Currituck Sound, s end just ne of entrance to Neals Creek and n end just se of entrance to Little Narrows, 8 mi. sw of Corolla. "Flat" is usually for flat sandy areas of a barrier island or tidal mud flats, but also applied to open expanses of water (as here) throughout se U.S.

Flats, The, flat, 0.5 mi. across, Dare County, Atlantic Township (diminishing local use). Just n of Fresh Pond, 3.1 mi. n of Nags Head (center).

Flats, The, small flat, Dare County, Nags Head Township (local use). Descriptive feature in Manteo (center) just n of Vista Lake, just w of Scarboro Creek. Subdivision named for feature.

Flat Swamp, swamp, Dare County, Atlantic Township (former local use). In Kitty Hawk Woods Swamps (q.v.) in Kitty Hawk ridge-and-swale system (q.v.) just e of Flat Ridge, 1.5 mi. w of original Kitty Hawk.

Flint Island, former small marsh island, Currituck County, Fruitville Township (C&GS 1913a). In Currituck Sound just s of South Channel, just off nw Crow Island, 5 mi. nnw of Corolla.

Florida-Hatteras Shelf, area, general reference to Continental Shelf from Florida to Virginia (various scientific papers).

Flounder Rock, rock, Carteret County, Portsmouth Township (historical use). In Pamlico Sound just sw of North Rock, 7 mi. w of Ocracoke (village). Different rock from Flounder Slue Rock, but in close proximity. *Other names:* Flounder Rocks (Price 1795, 628, historically two rocks, one named Little Flounder Rock), Flounder Shoal Rock (ACE 1897), Flounder Slue Rock (C&GS 1945).

Flounder Slue, former channel, 1 mi. long, Carteret County, Portsmouth Township (historical use). Was in Pamlico Sound 6 mi. w of Ocracoke (village). Connected Wallace Channel to Ship Channel and open sound. Today, Flounder Slue is nw Wallace Channel. *See* Allen Slough. *Other names:* Flounder Slough (Angley 1984, 37), Flounder-Slue (Angley 1984, 35).

Flounder Slue Rock, rock, Carteret County, Portsmouth Township (NPS 2007, map, 27 and 28). In Pamlico Sound, just ne of former Flounder Slue, 1 mi. wsw of North Rock, 6.5 mi. w of Ocracoke (village). Different rock from Flounder Rock, but in close proximity. *Other names:* Flounder Slough Rock.

Flowers Ridge, sand ridge, 3 mi. long, Dare County, Hatteras Township (signage). In sand ridges just n of Jennette Sedge, 2 mi. s of Buxton (also Middle Ridge and Crooked Ridge). Subdivision named for feature. *Other names:* Flanner Ridge (Bratton and Davison 1985, map, 7—possibly mistake, no other known usage).

Folly Creek. *See* Mill Creek.

Folly Island. *See* Cedar Island (USGS Oregon Inlet).

Forecastle Inlet, canal, Dare County, Atlantic Township (local use). At Colington Harbour, 2.5 mi. wsw of Kill Devil Hills (town). "Inlet" not used in traditional sense on the Outer Banks as barrier island breach, because indicative of dredging allowing water inward for access by boats to open water (Albemarle Sound). Canal naming scheme at Colington Harbour is ships or nautical terms. "Forecastle" (pronounced "foke-sul") is a partial deck above upper deck and usually forward (front), served as living quarters for sailors (name from castle-like device in medieval period used to house soldiers when advancing on fortresses).

Fort Bartow, former fort, 2 acres in extent, Dare County, Nags Head Township (Foster 1866b). Was at Pork Point 1.5 mi. sw of Manteo near Burnside Headquarters (historical site), 2.5 mi. se of Fort Huger. One of several Confederate forts built on the Outer Banks during Civil War. Bombarded by Union forces on February 7, 1862. Each captured Confederate fort was renamed for one of three Union generals leading Union invasion of Roanoke Island, hence variant Fort Foster. However, most documents and today's signage use original names of forts. *Other names:* Fort Barlow (Andrews 1862—transcribing error), Fort Foster (Click 2001, map, 26).

Fort Blanchard, former fort, 2 acres, Dare County, Nags Head Township (Foster 1866b). Was just nw of Sunnyside, 0.6 mi. se of Umstead Bridge and Weir Point, 0.5 mi. s of Fort Huger. Smallest Confederate fort on Roanoke Island surrendered on February 8, 1862. Each captured Confederate fort was renamed for one of three Union generals leading Union invasion of Roanoke Island, hence variant Fort Parke. However, most documents and today's signage use original names of forts. *Other names:* Fort Parke (Click 2001, map, 26).

Fort Burnside, proposed fort, Dare County, Nags

Head Township (Stick 1958). Unclear whether this fort (to have been named for Union General Burnside) ever built because only few references using phrase "to be built" on n Roanoke Island, so likely never built—not needed. Was reportedly on n Roanoke Island near Fort Raleigh (q.v.) site 2 mi. n of Burnside Headquarters.

Fort Channel, small channel, Carteret County, Morehead Township (Williamson 1992, 173). Approach to Fort Macon Creek at Fort Macon, 4 mi. e of Atlantic Beach (town).

Fort Clark, former fort, 2 acres, Dare County, Hatteras Township (USGS 2002: Hatteras). Was just ne of Inlet Peninsula at sw tip Hatteras Island less than 1 mi. from Fort Hatteras, 2.6 mi. sw of Hatteras (village). Constructed 1861 on e side (soundside) of Hatteras Inlet to protect inlet from Union vessels but fell on August 29, 1861 after two-day siege. Some ruins still visible, but constant inundation is removing all traces. *Other names:* Battery Clark (some texts, for small size of the fort-battery, small placement of guns), Fort Clarke (Stick 1958, map, 123; some NPS brochures).

Fort Dobbs, former fort, Carteret County, Morehead Township (historical documents). Was at e end Bogue Banks. Building began 1756 but never completed and labeled as "in ruins" on a 1770 map (Sauthier); later (1809) replaced by Fort Hampton (q.v.), reportedly intended to guard against pirates, and then replaced by Fort Macon.

Fort Ellis. *See* Battery Monteil.

Fort Granville, former fort, Carteret County, Portsmouth Township (historical). Was at Portsmouth (village) near Ocracoke Inlet, though some sources indicate it was built on Ocracoke Island (not so), some Beacon Island. To protect coast from enemy raids; decision to build was result of King George's War (1744–48 and War of Austrian Succession). Begun 1749 and completed 1756 then enlarged 1757, though never totally completed (1777 last work); manned by about 50 men until 1764 at end of the French and Indian War (Seven Years War in Europe).

Fort Hampton, former fort, Carteret County, Morehead Township (Hooker 1850). Predecessor of Fort Macon (q.v.) built 1808–9, named for Andrew Hampton, Revolutionary War hero. Destroyed by erosion in hurricane 1825. First attempt to build a fort here to protect Beaufort Inlet and Beaufort (mainland) was 1756, when battery was attempted named Fort Dobbs (q.v.). Fort Hampton was 130 ft. ne of Fort Macon. Confusing use of Fort Dobb or Fort Dobbs sometimes for name of original fort or battery of guns here 1756. *Other names:* Fort Dobb (historical), Fort Dobbs (historical).

Fort Hancock, former fort, Carteret County, Harkers Island Township (colonial papers). Was on s end Core Banks at Cape Lookout just wnw of Cape Lookout Lighthouse, now mostly inundated by Barden Inlet, no trace today. Two French captains, De Cottineau and De Cambray, 18th century noted Cape Lookout Harbor or Lookout Bight only safe harbor between Cape Henry, Virginia, and Cape Fear in extreme se portion North Carolina; they referenced Cape Lookout Harbor or Lookout Bight as the Colonies' Gibraltar. For this reason, they approached North Carolina officials to allow French to build a fort at Cape Lookout (mostly to protect French ships), but found the idea already being considered by North Carolina and Continental Congress. No money had been appropriated for construction; De Cottineau convinced North Carolina officials to let him build the fort, which he and the French completed. However, named for Enock Hancock, who owned land where fort was built, instead of for the Frenchmen who completed the fort. Conflicting information, but apparently manned two years, 1778–1780, when reportedly dismantled. Ruins known to be visible until around 1900; some residents of Harkers Island (1950s) claim some faint ruins still visible nw of the lighthouse near The Drain (Barden Inlet). *Other names:* Old Ruins (Stick 1958, 62n).

Fort Hatteras, former fort, two acres, Dare County, Hatteras Township (USGS 2013: Cape Hatteras—historical site). Was on s tip Hatteras Island (soundside) just w of Fort Clark, 2 mi. sw of Hatteras Ferry landing, 3 mi. sw of Hatteras (village). Constructed 1861 on e side (soundside) of Hatteras Inlet, fell to Union forces August 29, 1861, after two-day siege. No trace of fort from constant inundation. Was actually 0.5 mi. n of where depicted on latest topographic map (USGS 2013: Cape Hatteras). *Other names:* Fort Cape Hatteras (historical), Fort Ellis (rarely used;

Ellis was N.C. governor, Confederate raiding boat named for him).

Fort Huger, former fort, two acres, Dare County, Nags Head Township (Foster 1866b). On Roanoke Island at Weir Point just nw of Sunny Side, just s of Umstead Bridge, 0.5 mi. from Fort Blanchard. Principal Confederate fort on Roanoke Island, surrendered February 8, 1862. Each captured Confederate fort renamed for one of three Union generals leading Union invasion of Roanoke Island, hence variant Fort Reno. However, most documents and today's signage use original names of forts. During initial occupation, an expanded camp was added nearby, known as Camp Reno (original Confederate camp known as Camp Raleigh). Barracks restored and built here served as quarters for first arriving Negroes (declared contraband so as to be freed, then known as freedmen). Reportedly, another camp was just s, named Camp Foster (not exactly at Fort Bartow renamed Fort Foster), and barracks were built here. Camp Reno was overwhelmed by Camp Foster, and both camps were known only as Camp Foster (Click 2001, 28). *Other names:* Fort Reno (Click 2001, map, 26).

Fortin Bay, cove, 0.3 mi. wide, Carteret County, Davis Township (USGS 2013: Davis). In Core Sound and separates Fortin Island and n Great Island, 3.3 mi. ese of Davis (mainland).

Fortin Island, island, 0.3 mi. long, 0.2 mi. wide, Carteret County, Davis Township (USGS 2013: Davis). In Core Sound 0.4 mi. w of Great Island, 3 mi. ese of Davis (mainland). Made official by USBGN 1948. *Other names:* Forten Island (C&GS 1876b), Forter Island (transcribing error).

Fort Macon, former fort, Carteret County, Morehead Township (USGS 2013: Beaufort). Preserved remains of fort are at e end Bogue Banks, 3.5 mi. e of Atlantic Beach (center). Built 1826–34 to protect Beaufort Inlet and still used as a coaling station late as WWI. Today maintained as a state park. Named for Nathanial Macon, speaker of U.S. House of Representatives and U.S. Senator from North Carolina. Mistaken use of Fort Dobb or Fort Dobbs and Fort Hampton because these two forts were built previously in succession at this site. *Other names:* Bogue Point Fort (casual references), Fort Dobb (historical), Fort Dobbs (historical), Fort Hampton (historical), Fort Makon (Colton 1870s).

Fort Macon Creek, cove, 0.1 mi. across, Carteret County, Morehead Township (USGS 2013: Beaufort). In Core Sound at e end Bogue Banks at Fort Macon, 3.1 mi. e of Atlantic Beach (center). Original name was Cowpen Creek (18th century), but stock grazing and influence of nearby Fort Macon declined, name was changed (evolved) to associative name (*see* Fort Macon). *Other names:* Cowpen Creek (historical use) and Cow Pen Creek (CS 1849b).

Fort Macon Marina, harbor, Carteret County, Morehead Township (signage). On e Bogue Banks just e of Atlantic Beach (center), 1.8 mi. s of Morehead City (mainland).

Fort Macon Siege Batteries, former forts, Carteret County, Morehead Township (Army Historical Register). Three Union siege batteries on w Bogue Banks near Fort Macon; Flaglers Battery, Morris Battery, and Proutys Battery. Fort fell to Union April 1862.

Fort Morgan. *See* Fort Ocracoke.

Fort Ocracoke, former fort, Carteret County, Portsmouth Township (historical documents, historical marker). Was on Beacon Island in Ocracoke Inlet 3.8 mi. w of Ocracoke (village), now submerged. Built on or near previous site of Beacon Island Fort (q.v.). No evidence remained until some remnants were discovered 1998, now underwater, but was constructed on Beacon Island 1861 in system of forts to protect the Outer Banks from Union forces. Abandoned when Fort Hatteras fell August 29, 1861; Union forces reestablished it as Fort Morgan. *See also* Beacon Island Fort and Granville Fort. *Other names:* Beacon Island Fort (historical use from island name), Fort Beacon (Olszewski 1970, 131), Fort Morgan (historical), Fort Morris (some initial use for Colonel Ellwood Morris engineer and designer of fort), Ockracoke Inlet Fort (occasional historical).

Fort Oregon, former fort, Dare County, Kinnakeet Township (historical documents). Was on Pea Island (then Bodie Island), 14 mi. sse of Nags Head. Built on s shore Oregon Inlet 1861 to protect inlet from Union forces. Completely obliterated from s migration of Oregon Inlet. Foster (1866b) shows fort misplaced n Oregon Inlet. *Other names:* Fort Oregon Inlet (Covey 2018, 73).

Fort Raleigh, former fort, 20 acres, Dare County, Nags Head Township (USGS 2013: Manteo). Was on ne Roanoke Island, 3 mi. nnw of

Manteo (center). Replica fort built here: earthen fort reconstructed 1950 by NPS in manner thought to be similar to original fort constructed by Roanoke Island colonists (first attempt at colonization in North America by English—military garrison 1585 and also used by Lost Colonists 1587). Actual site of fort reported by NPS near reconstructed fort, but settlement site not found and might be underwater just off n shore Roanoke Island because erosion has consumed almost 0.3 mi. over the past 450 years. Name applies to fort while Cittie of Ralegh (sic) applied to the small settlement, which uncharacteristically was outside the fort. Apparently, an outline of original fort was still visible late as 1888 (Joshua Judson Davis Papers, 1888, from Smith 2001, 99—diary reference).

Unclear (not explained) what variant Mayne Fort meant (Austin 1984). Could have been reference simply to Maine (now main), reference to mainland, but would be unusual since fort was on an island (Roanoke Island) and not on "the maine" or mainland. Historically, reference also means to sign or to enter into a contract but has no relevance here. Probable misrepresentation of Lane (Layne), who was in command of first attempted colony (not Lost Colony). Only occurrence or usage of Mayne encountered.

Some authors believe more than one location existed, especially because settlement was atypically for the time outside fort. Colonists perhaps would have wanted to protect the two inlets (Port Ferdinando and Port Lane), so it has been suggested also a fort was e of Shallowbag Bay, a well-protected harbor with better command of the two inlets, with reportedly more stable land than the marsh today. Known that colonists had small but well-fortified sconce (fort) to defend against Spanish near or at Port Ferdinando (Lane 1585, letter 2; see Gunt Inlet).

Regarding use of variant Pain Fort on a few historical maps, misinterpretation of Collet et al.'s 1770 map, where names of landowners are labeled throughout map, and Pain (form of surname here since settlement) labeled with a house symbol on nw point of Roanoke Island (Northwest Point) just left of where symbol for fort and word "Fort" are labeled (presumed original fort site) giving the casual appearance of

name Pain Fort. The error was repeated on several maps (1770s), as other cartographers often copied work of previous cartographers, thereby perpetuating errors.

Some question regarding first use of name, Fort Raleigh. Some just assume that was the original name, but that name is absent from maps of colonial era and from Lane's letters (he uses Newe Forte in Virginia); instead forms of Cittie of Raleigh can be found as reference, but this is to the settlement uncharacteristically outside fort and reported by some as possibly strung out for 0.5 mi. Not until after Civil War does Fort Raleigh begin to show on maps, so inference is name Fort Raleigh was a later application (incorrectly or by design) applied by researchers. Subdivision named for feature.

Other names: Citie of Ralegh (1590, different spellings used), Citie of Raleigh (Haklyut 1589), Cittie of Raleigh (Trebellas and Chapman 1999, 1), Cittie of Ralegh (White 1585), Cittie of Raleigh in Virginia (NPS 1952, 11), City of Ralegh (Quinn 1975), City of Raleigh (Willard 2008), Fort Lane (casual historical references), Fort Roanoke (casual historic references), Lanes Fort (NPS 1952, 17), Lane's Towne (Cheeseman 1982, 23—Lane, head of first, military colony attempt, 1585), Master Ralph Lane's Stronghold (Trebellas and Chapman 1999), Mayne Fort (Austin 1984), Newe Forte in Virginia (Lane 1585, letter 3), New Fort (historical maps), New Fort in Virginia (Lane 1585), Old Fort Raleigh (Downing 2013, 41), Pain Fort (see above), Pain Port (misinterpretation of surname and fort label—Romans 1776), Point Fort (Morse 1794—misinterpretation of Pain, believing Pain an error presuming point since the fort was at a "point"), Ralph Lanes Fort (Trebellas and Chapman 1999, 1), Ralph Lane's New Fort in Virginia (NPS 1952, 43), Roanoke Colony (NPS 2010, 22), Roanoke Island Fort (brochures), Sir Walter Raleigh's Fort (NPS 2010, 22).

Fort Raleigh National Historic Site, park, Dare County, Nags Head Township (USGS 2013: Manteo). On n Roanoke Island, 2.9 mi. nw of Manteo (center). Used to display information about history of attempts at colonization on n Roanoke Island, including Lost Colony (second attempt at colonization in North America by English 1587); contains reconstruction of type of fort constructed by colonists; however, actual site is reportedly nearby. *See* Etheridges Point.

Fort Sullivan, former small fort, Dare County, Nags Head Township (Army Historical Register). Somewhere on n or central Roanoke Island, probably near Ashbee Harbor, quickly captured by Union forces. Apparently of little significance as Union did not rename it as with three other forts and two batteries.

Fort Totten, former fort, Dare County, Hatteras Township (Civil War documents). Was on Hatteras Island, 1 mi. se of Hatteras (village). Temporary and erected during occupation by Union forces during Civil War.

Fort Wool, former encampment, Dare County, Hatteras Township (Civil War documents). Temporary encampment of Union troops just n of Hatteras (village) 2 mi. east of Hatteras Inlet. Named for Union officer. *Other names:* Camp Wool (Torres 1985, 103).

Fosters Channel, water passage, Currituck County, Poplar Branch Township (USGS 2013: Mossey Islands). In Currituck Sound joining Lone Oak Channel at s end Mossey Islands complex, 5.7 mi. ssw of Corolla. *Other names:* Foster Channel (local maps), Foster Creek (Currituck DB 16, 1822, 220), Fosters Creek (CS 1862b).

Fosters Quay, harbor, Dare County, Hatteras Township (signage). In Hatteras (village) just across from entrance to Hatteras Harbor from Pamlico Sound, 0.8 mi. ne of Austin Creek (Hatteras-Ocracoke Ferry docks). Use of "quay" not prevalent in Outer Banks names, here used as adoption of a term (for marketing purposes) meaning wharf, landing, or harbor related, and adopted by English from French term *quai* of that meaning (pronounced "key" in English and increasingly so in U.S., though "kay" is still heard).

Founders Ridge, small sand ridge, Dare County, Atlantic Township (local use). Trends e-w in s Duck, 3 mi. n of Southern Shores (center). Named for subdivision here.

Francis Creek. *See* Tillmanns Creek.

Franks Island, large marsh islands complex, Currituck County, Fruitville Township (Cox 1906; Currituck DB 25, 1848, 387). In maze of marsh islands just n of Runnells Marshes just ne of Walk Island, 2.5 mi. ne of Knotts Island (village). *Other names:* Pine Island (Currituck Deeds, miscellaneous, 1719).

Franks Reef, shoal, Dare County, Kinnakeet Township (Garrity-Blake 2010, 492). In Pamlico Sound just se of South'ard Channel, 2.5 mi. w of Waves. "Reef" in Outer Banks geographic names usually refers to oyster colonies. *Other names:* Franke Reef (schooner *R. C. Beaman*, 1910 [White et al. 2017, 57]), Frank Reef (White et al. 2017, 57), Franks Shoal (some local use).

Fraziers Creek, tidal stream, 1.5 mi. long, Carteret County, White Oak Township (Williamson 1992, 173). Trends n-s separating unnamed shoals and marshes from Bogue Banks, 2.5 mi. sw of Langston Bridge, 3.5 mi. sse of Swansboro (mainland). Variant name Phraziers Creek taken from report of wreck of motor boat Ruth January 6, 1915, and spelling was in some cases a challenge in these reports. *Other names:* Phraziers Creek (Williamson 1992, 206).

Freedmans Point, point, Dare County, Nags Head Township (NPS 2010, 4). At site of old ferry dock on nw Roanoke Island before Umstead Bridge across Croatan Sound was built just s of Heritage Point subdivision, 3 mi. nw of Manteo (center). Recent name in honor of Freedmens Colony (q.v.).

Freedmens Colony, former area, Dare County, Nags Head Township (NPS 2015). At nw Roanoke Island along Croatan Sound shore at a probable location between Pork Point (s) and Weir Point (n), though likely concentrated more toward n part. Once Union forces had secured coastal islands, slaves from nearby on mainland began to trickle into these areas (1862), including Roanoke Island; shortly hundreds began to arrive. This settlement was a sort of processing site and might have included some land given to freed Negroes who had come to Roanoke Island for homesteading. Temporary processing place was named Freedmens Colony but also known as James for Horace James, "superintendent of Blacks" for District of North Carolina. Almost all of these freed Negroes eventually left Roanoke Island (some remained, and their descendants are there today). No trace of former settlement. The "colony," while thriving with more than 1,000 residents at its height, was never permanent nor after a while was it intended to be more than a collection place for resettling freed Negroes. It was never formally named but for the record was referenced as Freedmens Colony or sometimes merely as James after its director (some evidence of later confusion with Elizabeth James sent by American Missionary Association, but Horace James correct reference). Eventually, after freedmen were dispersed, most of the land was returned to original owners. *Other names:* James (Outer Banks History Center), James Settlement (Outer Banks History Center).

Fresh Pond, lake, 125 acres, Dare County, Atlantic and Nags Head Townships (USGS 2013: Manteo). Originally more than one pond, 2 mi. s of Wright Brothers National Memorial, 5.8 mi. s of original Kitty Hawk straddling corporate boundaries of Kill Devil Hills and Nags Head. Some believe the ponds are possibly remnants of a former inlet, though no historical evidence or relict features of an inlet here, but stories persist (*see* Kill Devil Hills Inlet). The ponds more likely created first by swales and then by movement of sand. Ponds were historically connected to Roanoke Sound by The Run, but this by itself is not evidence of an inlet here. Over years these ponds have become one pond, hence general use today, Fresh Pond. Freshwater Lake appears on NCDOT (2005) bicycle route map more as a descriptor but presented as a name. It was useful to know if a pond was fresh or brackish, hence the descriptor name. Occasional use of Great Fish Pond 18th century is likely a misinterpretation. Subdivision Fresh Pond Beaches at central e shore, but name is not known to be used for shoreline. *Other names:* Fresh Ponds (previous local use—original name when more than one pond: originally seven), Freshwater Lake (Bicycle Map), Fresh Water Lake (tourist brochures, county map 1957), Fresh Water Pond (local government documents), Grate Fresh Pond (Currituck DB 4, 1783, 264–65), Great Fish Pond (Harris 2017; 1738, source unknown), Great Fresh Pond (Currituck DB 2, 1790, 218), The Fresh Pond (Town of Nags Head 2000, 99), The Great Fish Ponds (Currituck DB 3, 1737, 64), The Great Fresh Ponds (original deeds).

Fresh Pond Bay, bay, 1 mi. long and wide, Currituck County, Fruitville Township (Cox 1923). Ne arm of Knotts Island Bay, 2 mi. e of Knotts Island (village). *See* Beach Pond. *Other names:* Fresh Pond Island Bay (Currituck Deeds, miscellaneous, 1719).

Fresh Pond Hill, hill, Currituck County, Fruitville Township (local use). On Currituck Banks near Wash Woods at North Swan Beach 4 mi. s of North Carolina–Virginia boundary, 7.5 mi. nnw of Corolla. S portion of sand dune altered considerably for development. *See* Beach Pond. *Other names:* Fresh Point Hill (misrecording, U.S. War Department 1895), The Ridge (sometimes used, road name here).

Fresh Pond Island, marsh island, 1 mi. long, Currituck County, Fruitville Township (C&GS 1878). In se Knotts Island Bay just s of Fresh Pond Bay trends n-s 1.3 mi. w of Fresh Pond Hill, 3.5 mi. ese of Knotts Island (village). *See* Beach Pond. *Other names:* Freshpond Island, Great Fresh Pond Island (Currituck DB 5, 1743, 23).

Fresh Pond Receses [*sic*], area, 0.5 mi. wide, Dare County, Nags Head Township (Currituck DB 1820, 15, 105-106). Historical term no longer used for low area just s of Fresh Pond creating concavity in s part Round-About Hills (q.v.) 1.7 mi. n of Jockeys Ridge. *Other names:* The Glade (Currituck DB 1820, 15, 105–6).

Fresh Pond Run. *See* The Run.

Fresh Ponds, The, small freshwater lakes, Dare County, Kinnakeet Township (Fisher 1962, 99). Soundside n Hatteras Island just sse of Round Hammock Bay, 1.5 mi. n of Rodanthe. Not as prevalent today as latter 20th century; also in area of small tidal creeks and coves such as Pauls Ditch, remnants of former Chickinacommock Inlet (q.v.).

Freshwater Pond, small pond, Hyde County, Ocracoke Township (Mallin et al. 2006, 30). N Ocracoke Island just s of Hatteras-Ocracoke Ferry dock just n of Styron Hills. Used as descriptive name in various scientific papers and locally.

Freshwater Ponds, man-made lakes, Dare County, Kinnakeet Township (local use). In Pea Island National Wildlife Refuge, just n of New Inlet with center 10 mi. nnw of Rodanthe. An occasional collective reference to North Pond, New Field Pond, South Pond, and several unnamed ponds, most of which created as a project of CCC 1930s as stopover for migrating birds along Atlantic Flyway.

Friendly Ridge, small sand ridge, 0.1 mi. long, Hyde County, Ocracoke Township (local use). Higher ground (used in Ocracoke village) 0.7 mi. e of Silver Lake. Subdivision named for feature. Named 1960s by Lloyd Harkum (Howard July 22, 2018).

Frigate Inlet, canal, Dare County, Atlantic Township (local use). At Colington Harbour, 2.5 mi. wsw of Kill Devil Hills (town). "Inlet" not used in traditional sense on the Outer Banks as barrier island breach, because indicative of dredging allowing water inward for access by boats to open water (Albemarle Sound). Canal naming scheme at Colington Harbour is ships or nautical terms. "Frigate" originally referred to any warship 17th century onward, though over years acquired more specialized requirements.

Frisco, village, Dare County, Hatteras Township (USGS 2013: Buxton). On w shore Hatteras Island 2.8 mi. ne of Hatteras (village). Original name Trent but post office name (est. 1889) changed 1898 to avoid confusion with another village named Trent on mainland; eventually name became Frisco.

Frisco is said suggested by first postmaster, named Wallace, sailor who reportedly spent a considerable amount of time in San Francisco. Wallace had been shipwrecked on Hatteras Island, where he later married and settled. Believed Wallace suggested Frisco for post office because of his fondness for San Francisco. He probably suggested San Francisco (folk in San Francisco rarely use Frisco), but rejected by post office in favor of shorter form. *Other names:* Trent (numerous sources), Trent Woods (used occasionally, though Trent was prevalent).

Frisco Beach, beach, 2 mi. long, Dare County, Hatteras Township (local use). Trends e-w from South Beach, just s and se of Billy Mitchell Airport, 1 mi. sse of Frisco. Somewhat isolated with little access and rarely frequented. The name is used occasionally. *See* Frisco.

Frisco Dune, sand dune, 40 ft. high, Dare County, Hatteras Township (local use). On Hatteras Island just s of Frisco, 3.8 mi. ene of Hatteras (village). *See* Frisco. High Tor is sometimes used (through reversed usage) because subdivision (High Tor Sands) just s of feature. Use of generic term "tor" is slightly misused: "tor" (from Old English) is actually a rocky, craggy, and distinct elevation compared to local relief. This distinct dune has two separate "peaks": largest and most southerly 40 ft., smaller more northerly more than 30 ft. So, application of "tor" here is correct except applied to sand dunes

(partially covered in vegetation) but no rocky or craggy outcrops. *Other names:* High Tor (see above).

Frisco Mill. *See* Rollinson Mill.

Frisco Point, point, Dare County, Hatteras Township (recent local use). N shore Joe Saur Creek just sw of Frisco, 3 mi. ne of Hatteras (village). Occasionally referenced by local residents, more so in the past 25 years from small subdivision nearby named Frisco Point Cape Hatteras.

Frisco Woods, woods, Dare County, Hatteras Township (local use). In Frisco, 4 mi. ene of Hatteras (village). *See* Frisco. Subdivision named for feature. *Other names:* Cape Woods (some local use and historical use, then included Buxton Woods), Little Grove (highly localized use), Spencers Woods (sometimes considered in Frisco Woods), Trent Woods (original name before village name changed with post office).

Frog Marsh, marsh, Dare County, Kinnakeet Township (NPS 2005b: NPS 1, 171). Soundside somewhere in Avon, probably in n Avon or between Avon (The South'ard) and Mill Creek (The North'ard).

Frog Pond, lake, Dare County, Hatteras Township (local use). In Buxton, 10.3 mi. ene of Hatteras (village). In a man-enhanced canal, so itself man-enhanced.

Frosts Point, point, Carteret County, Morehead Township (Zaenker 2014). Soundside just e of Yaupon Point at Hoop Pole Bay, 2.5 mi. w of Atlantic Beach (town). Named for Frost family who lived here (referenced as at Hoop Hole [*sic*] Creek by Stephens 1984, 6).

Frying Pan Island. *See* Sloop Island.

Fuersteins Wharf, former landing, Dare County, Nags Head Township (C&GS 1910c). Was on sw Roanoke Island 1 mi. sw of Wanchese.

Fulfords Hill, former sand dune, Carteret County, Harkers Island Township (Stick 1958, 309). Was considerably higher mid-20th century; topography of Cape Lookout and environs has changed greatly over past 100 years. Precise location unknown, not remembered, considering changing topography, but somewhere within 1–2 sq. mi. on Cape Lookout just s of Cape Hills and former Cape Lookout (village), between Cape Hills and Cape Point at tip of Cape Lookout, 1.5 mi. ssw of Cape Lookout Lighthouse.

Fulker Islands, former island(s), Dare County, Nags Head Township (Brazier 1833; Cotton

1861). Formerly in Croatan Sound 2.5 mi. sw of Manteo (center). Disappeared but was formerly exposed portion Fulker Shoal; group of islands 17th and 18th centuries but by mid-19th century consolidated into one island as a result of flooding from Roanoke Inlet closing (1811). Remnants of former Roanoke Marshes (q.v.) and all trace of these islands disappeared early 20th century. Made official as Fulker Island (singular) by USBGN 1891, amended 1960 to indicate it (they) no longer exists. *Other names:* Falkners Island (U.S. Navy 1862), Fulker Island (C&GS 1895a), Fulkners Island (Hondius 1606; Mouzon 1775; CS 1865), Fulkers Island (CS 1862b), Fulkers Islands (Ogilby and Moxon 1676; Price et al. 1808; Brazier 1820).

Fulker Shoal, former shoal, Dare County, Nags Head Township (historical maps). Was formerly in Croatan Sound 2.5 mi. sw of Manteo (center). No longer exists but was in now submerged Roanoke Marshes (q.v.). *See* Fulker Islands. Made official as Fulker Shoal (singular) by USBGN 1899, amended 1960 to indicate it no longer exists. *Other names:* Fulkers Shoal, Fulkners Shoal (later transcribing error, but on early maps).

Full Moon Shoal. *See* Outer Diamond Shoal.

G

Gaffey Landing, landing, Currituck County, Poplar Branch Township (USGS 2013: Mossey Islands). At unnamed marsh island n end Dowdy Bay, 7.5 mi. sw of Corolla. Caffey might be original name because was surname prevalent here (*see* Caffeys Inlet), but Gaffey or Gaffys has been used for this landing for more than 100 years on most maps. *Other names:* Caffeys Landing (C&GS 1852), Gaffys Landing (C&GS 1895a).

Gale Canal, canal, 1 mi. long, Carteret County, Morehead Township (Carteret County GIS 2019). W-most and largest canal trending n-s in Atlantic Beach Isles subdivision (w part of Canals at Atlantic Beach q.v.); entrance canal from Bogue Sound to w part of Canals at Atlantic Beach, 1.5 mi. s of Morehead City (mainland).

Gales Island, former island, Hyde County, Ocracoke Township (Price 1795, 631). Was in Pamlico Sound, 1.8 mi. sw of Ocracoke (village). Highest part Gales Shoal, occasionally bare at low water but completely covered by water late 1800s. Named for an individual and not wind. *Other names:* Gates Island (typographical error).

Gales Island Point, former point, Hyde County, Ocracoke Township (Blunt 1857, 344). Was e point of Gales Island used for sighting in Ocracoke Inlet mid-1800s, 1.7 mi. sw of Ocracoke (village).

Gales Shoal, former shoal, Hyde County, Ocracoke Township (Price 1795). Was in Ocracoke Inlet just ese of Beacon Island, 3.2 mi. wsw of Ocracoke (village). Mid-19th-century portion Qualk Shoal was joined temporarily to Gales Shoal. *See* Gales Island.

Gallants Channel, channel, 2 mi. long, Carteret County, Beaufort Township (USGS 2013: Beaufort). From junction Taylor Creek and Beaufort Channel (formerly Bulkhead Channel) at Beaufort (mainland) n then nw to Newport River. Named for John Galland (sometimes Gallent), early settler here, stepson of Governor Charles Eden (colonial era). Originally Galland then Gallent, but through transcribing error and use name became Gallant. Made official by USBGN 1986 to clarify relation to Beaufort Channel. *Other names:* Beaufort Channel (USGS 1949: Beaufort), Gallance Channel (C&GS 1888a), Gallant Channel (USGS 1949: Beaufort), Gallent Channel (C&GS 1882).

Gallinule Canal, canal, 0.5 mi. long, Dare County, Atlantic Township (Town of Southern Shores 2015). In Southern Shores 3.5 mi. n of original Kitty Hawk. Names of Southern Shores canals are for shorebirds (except Gravey Pond Canal). The common gallinule (*Gallinula galeata*) is here year-round.

Gannet Canal, small canal, Dare County, Atlantic Township (Town of Southern Shores 2015). In Southern Shores on e shore of Jeanguite Creek 4.5 mi. n of original Kitty Hawk. Names of Southern Shores canals are for shorebirds (except Gravey Pond Canal). The northern gannet (*Morus bassanus*) here during winter.

Gannet Cove, small cove, Dare County, Atlantic Township (limited local use). In Sanderling just n of Head Slough 3.5 mi. n of Duck (center). Recent name by developer in past

20 years transferred by usage to this small cove. *See* Gannet Canal.

Gap, The, natural channel, Hyde County, Ocracoke Township (local use). Deeper water between Guesses Reef (sw portion Legged Lump) and Clark Reef, 2 mi. n of The Great Swash, 6 mi. ne of Ocracoke (village).

Gap Inlet, cove, less than 0.1 mi. long, Hyde County, Ocracoke Township (USGS 2013: Ocracoke). Just n of Ocracoke, 15 mi. sw of Hatteras (village). "Inlet" not used in traditional sense on the Outer Banks for breach in the barrier island. Unusual reference to a cove altered by man into marina. Only other known such use is Tar Hole Inlet also at Ocracoke Island.

Gap Point, point, Hyde County, Ocracoke Township (USGS 2013: Ocracoke). On Ocracoke Island 0.4 mi. n of Ocracoke (village).

Garden Hammock Cove, former cove, Currituck County, Fruitville Township (Currituck DB 1797, 8, 45). Described as s side Currituck Inlet (New Currituck Inlet—Currituck Inlet closed 1731) 4.5 mi. n of Corolla. Garden not normally used on the Outer Banks with names; reason not apparent.

Gar Point Cove, small cove, Currituck County, Fruitville Township (Cox 1923). Most of w side of Big Bird Island, 4.7 mi. se of Knotts Island (village). Gar (family Lepisosteidae) are primitive fish known to have been used by indigenous peoples of North America and European colonists for different uses for the hardness of scales.

Garr Island, former island, Dare County, Kinnakeet Township (19th-century charts). Was just w of Pea Island, 2 mi. s of Oregon Inlet, 12.4 mi. n of Rodanthe. Disappeared 1930s and 1940s. *See* Gar Point Cove. *Other names:* Gar Island (CS 1852).

Gaskins Creek. *See* Shallowbag Bay.

George Gilgos Creek, cove, 0.05 mi. long, Carteret County, Portsmouth Township (USGS 1950: Portsmouth). Joins Warren Gilgos Creek just e of Baymarsh Thorofare just wsw of Portsmouth (village), 6.7 mi. sw of Ocracoke (village). *Other names:* George Gilgos Slough (White 2012, 25).

George Hills, sand dunes, 15 ft. high, Carteret County, Portsmouth Township (USGS 2013: Wainwright Island). On Core Banks just ne of Cricket Island, 15.5 mi. sw of Ocracoke (village).

Georges Creek, cove, 0.2 mi. long, Dare County, Nags Head Township (USGS 2013: Oregon Inlet). Is 0.4 mi. e of Bodie Island Lighthouse, 4.3 mi. ese of Wanchese.

Gibbs Cove, small cove, Dare County, Kinnakeet Township (local use). Entrance to Mill Creek just e of Gibbs Point in n Avon 9 mi. n of Buxton. Associative from Gibbs Point.

Gibbs Creek, small tidal stream, Dare County, Hatteras Township (Brooks 2010). Trends s to n 0.2 mi. into Pamlico Sound just w of Buxton Harbor, 2.2 mi. e of Frisco. *Other names:* Robbs Creek (Brooks 2010).

Gibbs Point, marsh point, Dare County, Kinnakeet Township (USGS 2013: Buxton). On Hatteras Island just s of Big Island, 0.9 mi. nnw of original Avon. Reportedly named for Henry Gibbs with land grant for this area of Hatteras Island (1716) though name was likely for Henry Gibbs (nickname Gibsies) used locally. *Other names:* Gibsies Point (Garrity-Blake 2010, 169).

Gibbs Shoal, shoal, 1 mi. long, Hyde County, Lake Landing Township (NOS 2014b). In Pamlico Sound trends nw-se from mainland just w of Middletown Anchorage, 25 mi. nw of Hatteras (village).

Gibson Creek. *See* Doughs Creek.

Gillikin. *See* Salter Path.

Glovers Point, point, Carteret County, Morehead Township (PKS 2016). Soundside just w of McGinnis Point between Pine Knoll Shores and e section Indian Beach (town), 1.5 mi. w of Pine Knoll Shores.

Goat Hill, sand hill, Hyde County, Ocracoke Township (Weslager 1954). Just ne of Ocracoke Island Airport, 1.5 mi. se of Ocracoke (village). According to Weslager (1954, 47) named because hill is shaped like a goat, but local residents (now) do not verify this as the origin; reportedly goats grazed there. *Other names:* Billy Goat Hill (occasional local use and Garrity-Blake 2010, 367).

Goat Island, island, 0.3 mi. long, Carteret County, Morehead Township (USGS 2013: Beaufort). At e end Bogue Banks and w end Fishing Creek 2.2 mi. e of Atlantic Beach (town).

Goat Island, small irregular island, 0.2 mi. long, 0.1 mi. wide, Currituck County, Poplar Branch Township (USGS 2013: Mossey Islands). Separates Little Goat Island Bay and Goat Island Bay, 7.1 mi. nw of Duck. Sometimes applied to elongated island 1 mi. nw of this location.

Goat Island, marsh, 0.3 mi. long, 0.5 mi. wide, Dare County, Kinnakeet Township (USGS 2013: Pea Island Overedge West). Is 0.6 mi. n of Goose Island, 9.6 mi. nnw of Rodanthe.

Goat Island Bay, cove, 0.7 mi. wide, 0.4 mi. long, Currituck County, Poplar Branch Township (USGS 2013: Mossey Islands, Jarvisburg). In Currituck Sound 3.8 mi. s of Three Dunes, 6.8 mi. nw of Duck. *Other names:* Balance Point Bay (C&GS 1852).

Goat Island Bay, cove, 0.3 mi. across, Dare County, Kinnakeet Township (USGS 2013: Pea Island Overedge West). Between two marshes named Goat Island and Goose Island, 9.4 mi. nnw of Rodanthe.

Goat Island Point, point, Dare County, Kinnakeet Township (USGS 2013: Pea Island Overedge West). On w tip Goat Island at entrance of Eagle Nest Bay, 9.6 mi. nnw of Rodanthe.

Goat Pond, small pond, 0.2 mi. long, 0.1 mi. wide, Currituck County, Fruitville Township (local use). In marshy w Walk Island, 1.2 mi. ne of Knotts Island (village).

Golden Bluff, sand dune, Currituck County, Poplar Branch Township (local use). In Monteray Shores, just e of Sanders Bay, 3.8 mi. s of Corolla. Larger and more distinct before being altered by man when developing Monteray Shores (1988). Original name no longer remembered; Golden Bluff has been used since Monteray Shores was developed and the road altering this dune was built.

Gold Mine, The, area, Dare County, Kinnakeet Township (Garrity-Blake 2010, 493). In Pamlico Sound 6 mi. s of Gull Island, 3.5 mi. nw of original Avon. Exact meaning of reference and name unknown. On source map, "long-haul area" in parentheses after name or reference, latter in quotation marks, unlike all other names on the map. Feature not discussed in document text containing map, and no one (of all ages) interviewed had ever heard the reference. Garrity mentions (p. 550) "Gray trout (weakfish—*Cynoscion regalis*) was on its way to becoming a gold mine fishery here in the late 1970s"; perhaps name origin. Might be presumed it was prosperous for fishing but required extra time to achieve (purely speculative).

Golds Point. *See* Catfish Point.

Goodridge Island, former small isolated marsh island, Currituck County, Poplar Branch Township (CS 1862a). In Currituck Sound 2 mi. nw of Peters Quarter, 3 mi. ssw of Corolla. Disappeared by early 20th century. *Other names:* Gadridge Island (C&GS 1852), Goodrich Island (CS 1862a), Guttredge Island (Codman, Crowninshield, and Lawrence 1925).

Goose Bay, cove, 0.5 mi. across, Carteret County, Cedar Island Township (USGS 2013: Atlantic). Just e of Goose Bay Point on unnamed marsh (sometimes considered part of Hog Island) 2 mi. e of Cedar Island Ferry landing, 12 mi. sw of Ocracoke (village).

Goose Bay Point, point, Carteret County, Cedar Island Township (USGS 2013: Atlantic). Just w of Goose Bay on unnamed marsh (sometimes considered part of Hog Island) 2 mi. e of Cedar Island Ferry landing, 11.5 mi. sw of Ocracoke (village).

Goose Beach, former beach, Dare County, Atlantic Township (C&GS 1852). Applied to beach well before high development late 20th century 2 mi. n of Duck. Used 19th and early 20th centuries when used mostly for hunting fowl and before intense development here. Little use today.

Goose Beach Dunes, sand dunes, Dare County, Atlantic Township (historical local use). In n Duck just n of Sandy Ridge, 1.7 mi. s of Sanderling. Applied to five distinct dunes before dense subdivision development late 20th century. Used 19th and early 20th centuries when used mostly for hunting fowl and before intense development here. Apparently was name origin for two Snow Geese subdivisions (s part) and Wild Duck Dunes subdivision (n part).

Goose Creek, cove, 0.1 mi. wide, Dare County, Hatteras Township (USGS 2002: Hatteras). In Pamlico Sound 1.5 mi. sw of Hatteras (village).

Goose Creek Shoals, shoal, 0.7 mi. long, Carteret County, White Oak Township (USGS 2013: Swansboro), s of Goose Creek (mainland). Normally dry, in Bogue Sound, 6 mi. ese of Swansboro (mainland).

Goose Island, marsh island, 0.8 mi. long, 0.3 mi. wide, Carteret County, Davis Township (USGS 2013: Davis). In Core Sound 1 mi. e of Core Banks, 3.2 mi. se of Davis (mainland).

Goose Island, marsh island, 0.1 mi. wide, Dare

County, Atlantic Township (USGS 2013: Jarvisburg). Just w of Currituck Banks near former Caffeys Inlet, 4.6 mi. nnw of Duck. Water Bush Island not remembered by anyone and was apparently used sparingly only 19th century, but why this was used for this feature is unknown. Variant Water Bush can be specific reference or general reference to water-tolerant plants. Nothing is remarkable about flora on this island. *Other names:* Gose Island (C&GS 1852— recording error), Water Bush Island (deeds), Wester Bush Island (variation of Water Bush presumably).

Goose Island, marsh, 0.5 mi. across, Dare County, Kinnakeet Township (USGS 2013: Pea Island Overedge West). Is 0.6 mi. s of Goat Island Bay, 9.1 mi. nnw of Rodanthe.

Goose Island Point, marsh point, Dare County, Kinnakeet Township (USGS 2013: Pea Island Overedge West). On Goose Island and n point of The Trench, 8.1 mi. nnw of Rodanthe.

Goose Marsh. *See* Back Landing Creek Marsh.

Goose Pond, lake, Currituck County, Fruitville Township (Currituck DB 11, 1811, 163–65). Exact location not described but is one of numerous ponds in Great Marsh (Currituck County) 2–4 mi. nw of Knotts Island (village), depending on specific location. Spelling found in early deeds was most often as word with variations of same word in same sentence. *Other names:* Goos Pon (Currituck DB 11, 1811, 163–65), Goos Pond (Currituck DB 11, 1811, 163–65).

Goose Shoal, shoal, Dare County, Atlantic Township (Town of Kitty Hawk 2007). Just s of Stone Island in n entrance to Kitty Hawk Bay, 2.5 mi. sw of original Kitty Hawk. *Other names:* Goose Shoals (some local use).

Goose Shoal Point, point, Dare County, Atlantic Township (Harris 2017; unknown, 1878). At s tip of Stone Island just n of Goose Shoal, 2 mi. sw of original Kitty Hawk.

Goose Wing Club Dikes, former dams, Dare County, Nags Head Township (Hitchcock 2014). Was just n of Bodie Island Lighthouse Pond, 6.5 mi. s of Whalebone Junction. Small dams built 1930s to impound water, enhancing small ponds attracting waterfowl; remnants barely remain. *Other names:* Bodie Island Dikes (formerly occasional).

Goosing Point, point, Dare County, Atlantic Township (Town of Kitty Hawk 2007). Just n of Stone Island, 2 mi. sw of original Kitty Hawk. Name has nothing to do with current definition of poking or grabbing another's buttocks; historically local for goose hunting.

Gorvas Island, former island, Currituck County, Fruitville Township (Moll 1729). Was just inside Currituck Inlet (original Currituck Inlet), just s of North Carolina–Virginia boundary just e of Knotts Island (village). Could be related to Manns Islands or was in this general vicinity. Topography has changed considerably and is a maze of marsh islands, any of which could have been related to Gorvas Island. While depicted on Moll's 1729 map, the island was not shown or named on his 1708 map. *Gorvas* is Welsh term for shallow or flat, appropriately applied here but by whom and when is unknown (sometime between 1708 and 1729 based on Moll's application).

Goulds Lump, island, 0.2 mi. across, Dare County, Kinnakeet Township (USGS 2013: Pea Island). In Pamlico Sound just s of Wreck Creek, 4.8 mi. nnw of Rodanthe. *See* Dorland Lump.

Government Wharf, former landing, Currituck County, Poplar Branch Township (C&GS 1899b). Was just wsw of Currituck Beach Lighthouse on s edge of Corolla. Pier and landing were used for lighthouse.

Graben Island. *See* Indian Gap Island (Poplar Branch Township).

Grand Channel, former channel, Dare County, Hatteras Township (Mouzon 1775). Trended ne-sw through Inner Diamond Shoals, 30 mi. ene of Ocracoke Inlet. Useful only for ships of the 1700s and not dependable. Disappeared by 1800.

Grandies Island Creek. *See* Deals Island Creek.

Grand Pappys Island, marsh island, Dare County, Atlantic Township (local use). Largest of three just n of Tater Patch Cove separated from barrier island at Kill Devil Hills by Jones Creek, 3.2 mi. sse of original Kitty Hawk. Not as well known today but used mid-20th century.

Grandy Island, large marsh island, Currituck County, Poplar Branch Township (local use). At e side of The Narrows (Big Narrows and Little Narrows) just n of Grandy (mainland), 8 mi. nw of Duck. Grandy is surname here. *Other names:* Grandys Island (Currituck DB 5, 1787, 306).

Grants Cove, cove, 0.2 mi. wide, Dare County, Atlantic Township (Town of Kitty Hawk

2007). In Kitty Hawk Bay at its n shore, 1.6 mi. sw of original Kitty Hawk. *Other names:* Gants Cove (Harris 2017, source unknown), Grants Cove Bay (Harris 2017; unknown, 1798).

Granville District, former civil division, 60 mi. wide, Currituck and Dare Counties (historical documents). Was e-w portion of land including all of North Carolina approx. between Rodanthe and Virginia boundary. Lord Carteret was only one of eight original Lords Proprietors of Carolina Grant (1663; *see* Carolina) who wanted to retain ownership, which he and descendants did to 1777 or 1779, when the district reverted to state government with recognition of other legal land claims. Named because Carterets later acquired title Earl of Granville. *Other names:* Granville Grant (historical marker).

Grave Hill, sand dune, Dare County, Atlantic Township (Currituck DB 5, 1787, 247). In s Kitty Hawk Dunes one of the notable dunes just e of Kitty Hawk Bay. Used historically and no longer known.

Graven Island, marsh island, 0.3 mi. across, Currituck County, Fruitville Township (Cox 1923). Just sw of Walk Island, 1 mi. e of Knotts Island (village).

Graveyard Hill, small mostly stabilized sand dune, Dare County, Atlantic Township (Stick 1958, 264—general reference). In Round-About Hills near one of the old mostly now overgrown Baum Cemeteries, 2.5 mi. nw of Nags Head (center). *Other names:* Graveyard Ridge (Harris 2017; unknown, 1857).

Graveyard Landing, landing, Dare County, Atlantic Township (Stick 1958). One of numerous such landings in this area. Exact location is unknown but somewhere on Colington Island, possibly near Rhodoms Point.

Graveyard of the Atlantic. *See* Diamond Shoals.

Gravey Pond, lake, 0.2 mi. long, Dare County, Atlantic Township (Town of Southern Shores 2015 and street sign). In Southern Shores, n end Gravey Pond Canal (q.v.) just n of Gallinule Canal, 3.5 mi. n of original Kitty Hawk. Name origin unknown.

Gravey Pond Canal, canal, 0.5 mi. long, Dare County, Atlantic Township (Town of Southern Shores 2015). In Southern Sores 3.5 mi. n of original Kitty Hawk. Names of Southern Shores canals are for shorebirds (except this one); name's origin unknown (by those interviewed). *Other names:* Gravey Pond (street sign).

Graylyn Island, small marsh island, Currituck County, Fruitville Township (Cox 1923). In North Channel, 1 mi. e of Johnson Island, 5 mi. se of Knotts Island (village).

Grays Rock, rock, Currituck County, Poplar Branch Township (NOS 2014g). In Currituck Sound 4.3 mi. sw of Corolla. Throughout 19th century as many as five rocks here. *Other names:* Grays Rocks (C&GS 1852).

Great Beach, beach, Currituck County, Poplar Branch Township (Codman, Crowninshield, and Lawrence 1925). Encircles Great Beach Pond on protrusion of land into Currituck Sound, 2 mi. s of Corolla. Descriptive of expansive curve (1.3 mi. long) of Whale Head Bay, though sometimes the name is applied only to s portion of this shoreline. *Other names:* Grat Beach (Currituck DB 6, 1790, 290).

Great Beach Marsh, marsh, Currituck County, Poplar Branch Township (C&GS 1852). Small marsh islands and marsh ponds just w of Corolla just nw of Currituck Beach Lighthouse, 1 mi. n of Whale Head Bay. Applied because historically (19th century) name Great Beach; while usually applied to s shore of Whale Head Bay just n of Great Beach Pond, also had use throughout the entire length of shoreline of Whale Head Bay to this marsh.

Great Beach Pond, cove, 0.2 mi. across, Currituck County, Poplar Branch Township (USGS 1982: Mossey Islands). In Currituck Sound just s of Whale Head Bay (q.v.), formed by recent deposition in Currituck Sound, 2 mi. s of Corolla. Associative from Great Beach. Recorded use of Pateridges Inlet (see below) is only known occurrence, and clearly no known inlet (breach sound to sea) here at any time historically. Closest inlet was Musketo Inlet (pre-1585–1682) just n of Corolla 3 mi. n of Great Beach Pond. The deed indicates "Pateridges Inlet known by name of Great Beach." So, this must have been a reference to this distinct deeply incised cove. Though rare, there are occasional references to soundside coves as inlets (*see* Gap Inlet). Also, probably unrelated, Peters Quarter Creek is variant name for Great Beach Pond, and area known historically (still today by older folk) as Peters Quarter (*see* Hunting Quarter) is just s of here. While variant Pater is not a known form of Peter, it might be an unconventional spelling of Peter since unusual spellings are common in these early deeds—probable coincidence, and no known occurrence of Pater Ridge or Peter Ridge. One might also suspect "pateridge" might be another spelling of "partridge," but unlikely as partridges are not found on the Outer Banks or anywhere in e U.S. (only partridge found in U.S. is the gray partridge [*Perdix perdix*] of upper Great Plains). *Other names:* Pateridges Inlet (Currituck DB 10, 1809, 61–62), Peters Quarter Creek (more elongated early 20th century).

Great Blue Heron Canal, canal, 2 mi. long, Dare County, Atlantic Township (Town of Southern Shores 2015). In Southern Shores 5 mi. n of original Kitty Hawk. Formerly a stream canalized, former stream was Pine Creek (q.v.) 19th century but was originally Slippery Pine Branch 18th century. Names of Southern Shores canals are for shorebirds (except Gravey Pond Canal). Several varieties of heron are at the Outer Banks year-round and in summer, most notably great blue heron (*Ardea herodias*).

Great Bush Marsh, former marsh, Currituck County, Poplar Branch Township (C&GS 1852). Was just nw of Corolla 6 mi. s of South Channel (remnants of New Currituck Inlet). Mostly disappeared from development, though remnants remain.

Great Cypress Swamp, former swamp, Dare County, Atlantic Township (Currituck DB 5, 1784, 4). Was on mid-to-sse Big Colington just s of Colington (community). Historic reference 1700s and early 1800s, no longer used. *Other names:* Grate Cypress Swamp (Currituck DB 5, 1784, 41).

Great Ditch, water passage, 0.5 mi. long, Carteret County, Cedar Island Township (USGS 2013: Atlantic). Separates Hog Island from unnamed marsh (sometimes considered part of Hog Island) 2 mi. e of Cedar Island Ferry landing, 12.5 mi. sw of Ocracoke (village). *Other names:* Big Ditch (C&GS 1899b).

Great Gap, water passage, 1 mi. long, Currituck County, Poplar Branch Township; and Dare County, Atlantic Township (local use). From near Currituck Banks to Pine Island Bay and Shoe Hole Bay in Currituck Sound, 5.2 mi. nw of Duck. Feature trends generally nw from near former Caffeys Inlet, probably remnant of Caffeys Inlet's n channel. *See* New Currituck Inlet. *Other names:* The Lead (used sometimes mostly s part Great Gap).

Great Gap Island, island, 0.2 mi. long, Dare County, Atlantic Township; and Currituck County, Poplar Branch Township (local use). At Great Gap in Currituck Sound, 5 mi. nw of Duck.

Great Gap Point, point, Currituck County, Poplar Branch Township (signage). At Deep Neck just s of Tar Cove Marsh 0.7 mi. w of Pine Island subdivision, 6.5 mi. n of Duck. Interestingly, point is 2 mi. n of Great Gap.

Great Gut, water passage, Dare County, Nags Head Township (local use). Canalized water passage trending 2.5 mi. nw from Roanoke Sound then wsw, then sw-nw extension of Cut Through just e of Big Island through system of canals, ditches, water passages, and guts. Most folk agree with largest application presented here, though feature is wider at each extremity. Some apply name only to e section, from Roanoke Sound 1.5 mi. ne to where the passage turns wsw. Some apply name to a small water passage from Great Gut to Roanoke Sound near e terminus over which County Road 1141 (Thicket Lump Road) passes, though this small section is more often referenced as Great Gut Canal, just referring to an alternate route for this end, or is in relation to a sort of iconic restaurant there using Great Gut in its name. *See* Wanchese canals, ditches, guts, and water passages and Alligator Gut.

Great Gut Canal. *See* Great Gut.

Great Hammock, large hummock, Dare County, Nags Head Township (until early 20th century). Higher ground in extensive marsh on e Roanoke Island where much of Pirates Cove is today 2 mi. from Manteo (center). Reportedly two Confederate cannons were mounted here during Civil War but apparently never used. Considerably altered by development of Pirates Cove. *See* The Hammock (Dare County) and Black Hammock.

Great Hammock Swash. *See* Merkle Hammock.

Great Island, elongated marsh island, 1.5 mi. long, 0.3 mi. wide, Carteret County, Davis Township (USGS 2013: Davis). In Core Sound 0.4 mi. w of Core Banks just s of Horse Island, 3.5 mi. ese of Davis (mainland).

Great Island, elongated marsh island, 0.4 mi. long, 0.05 mi. wide, Dare County, Kinnakeet

Township (USGS 2013: Buxton). In Pamlico Sound 0.2 mi. ne of Bald Point, 1.5 mi. ne of Buxton.

Great Island, marsh island, 0.4 mi. long, 0.1 mi. wide, Dare County, Kinnakeet Township (USGS 2013: Rodanthe). In Pamlico Sound 0.5 mi. sw of Waves 0.1 mi. w of Davids Point. *Other names:* Grate Island (of schooner *Lonia Buren*, 1903 [White et al. 2017, 127]).

Great Island, island, 1.5 mi. long, 1 mi. wide, Hyde County, Swan Quarter Township (NOS 2014i). In Pamlico Sound just s of mainland 12 mi. e of mouth of Pamlico River, 21.5 mi. nw of Ocracoke (village). *Other names:* Swan Island (J. H. Colton 1856), Swan Quarter Island (Hooker 1846).

Great Island. *See* Cedar Hammock (Carteret County, Morehead Township).

Great Island Bay, cove, 0.7 mi. long, 0.3 mi. wide, Carteret County, Davis Township (USGS 2013: Davis). In Core Sound 1.3 mi. sw of Great Island, 3.5 mi. se of Davis (mainland).

Great Island Camp, camp, Carteret County, Davis Township (NPS 2018). On South Core Banks just s of Great Island, 3.5 mi. se of Davis (mainland). Tourist camp operated by NPS. *Other names:* Great Island Cabin Camp (NPS 2018), (Alger) Willis Fish Camp.

Great Island Creek, water passage, 0.8 mi. long, Carteret County, Davis Township (USGS 2013: Davis). In Core Sound, separates Horse Island and Great Island, 3.5 mi. e of Davis (mainland). "New Inlet" shown approximately here (maybe Great Island Bay) in few papers but no conclusive proof.

Great Island Landing, Carteret County, Davis Township (signage). Dock for ferry service 3.5 mi. se from Davis (mainland).

Great Island Marsh, marsh, Dare County, Kinnakeet Township (local use). On almost all of Great Island especially se end 1.5 mi. n of Buxton.

Great Island Narrows, water passage, 1 mi. long, Hyde County, Swan Quarter Township (NOS 2014i). Separates Great Island from mainland 12 mi. e of mouth of Pamlico River, 21.5 mi. nw of Ocracoke (village). *Other names:* Swan Quarter Narrows (NOS 2014i).

Great Island Point, point, Carteret County, Davis Township (USGS 2013: Davis). N point Great Island at entrance Great Island Creek, 3 mi. e of Davis (mainland). *Other names:* Great Point (CS 1855).

Great Marsh, marsh, 4.5 mi. long, 3.7 mi.

wide, Currituck County, Fruitville Township (USGS 2013: Knotts Island, Barco). Separates Knotts Island from mainland and Mackay Island from s Knotts Island, 2 mi. nw of Knotts Island (village). *Other names:* Grate Marsh (Currituck DB 11, 1811, 163–64), Greate Swamp (Currituck DB 14, 1817, 201), Great Swamp (Currituck DB 14, 1818, 348).

Great Marsh, former large marsh, 2 mi. long, 0.5 mi. wide, Dare County, Atlantic Township (Currituck DB 4, 1782, 49). Was at e boundary of Jeanguite Creek including portion of e Southern Shores, 2.5 mi. n of original Kitty Hawk. Was large in places, not as great in extent as Great Marsh nw of Knotts Island. Usage historical; name disappeared by early to mid-1800s when population increased. Today, little remains of this marsh as a result of development in Southern Shores. *Other names:* Grate Marsh (Currituck DB 4, 1782, 49).

Great Marsh Island, irregular island, 0.4 mi. long, Carteret County, Harkers Island Township (USGS 2013: Harkers Island). In Back Sound 3.8 mi. sse of Harkers Island (village).

Great Pasture Island, small marsh island, Dare County, Hatteras Township (Brooks 2010). Where Cape Creek enters cove formerly known as Back Landing Creek, now known mostly as Cape Creek, 1.5 mi. e of Buxton. Much larger historically but changed over years; originally separated historical route of Cape Creek from Back Landing Creek. Indicative of prevalent grazing activity (*see* Pasture Island). *Other names:* Pasture Island (usage on deeds and similar documents).

Great Ridge, sand ridge, 3 mi. long, Dare County, Hatteras Township (signage). Trends ne-sw, just nw of Creeds Hill to Flowers Ridge, 3.5 mi. se of Buxton. *Other names:* Great Grass Ridge (historical deeds), Grass Ridge (Brooks 2010), Second Ridge (MacNeill, 113).

Great River, tidal stream, Carteret County, Portsmouth Township (NPS 2007, 143). On n side of Portsmouth Island trending w-e between entrance to Doctors Creek and terminus of Coast Guard Creek at former Coast Guard Station, 5.5 mi. sw of Ocracoke (village). Embayment on s end of Ocracoke Inlet narrowing at Coast Guard Creek. Name is not well known or used much, especially considering feature size.

Great Shoal, narrow shoal, 1 mi. long, Carteret

County, Portsmouth Township (C&GS 1866). Is 1 mi. e of Portsmouth (village) (mid-19th century) 4 mi. sw of Ocracoke (village). No longer exists in original form, changed numerous times over past 150 years. Name not used much because part of other shoals through the years, most notably former Dry Sand Shoal.

Great Shoal, shoal, Carteret County, Smyrna Township (USGS 2013: Horsepen Point). In Core Sound just n of Horsepen Point 7.3 mi. ne of Harkers Island (village). Approximate location of historical Crane Island and Great Shoal likely remnants of Crane Island. *See* Crane Island for rendition of possible relationship between Crane Island and Harkers Island. *Other names:* Yellow Shoal (U.S. Congress 1876, 25)

Great Shoal Point, point, Carteret County, Portsmouth Township (C&GS 1866). N point Great Shoal (Portsmouth Township) 0.5 mi. e of Portsmouth (village) (mid-19th century) 4 mi. sw of Ocracoke (village). No longer exists in original form and has changed numerous times over past 150 years.

Great Swamp, large swamp, Dare County, Hatteras Township (Covey 2018, 51). Previously undeveloped at Cape Hatteras between Buxton and Frisco containing ridges interspersed with ponds and swamps with dense vegetation.

Great Swash, The, marsh, 2 mi. wide, Hyde County, Ocracoke Township (USGS Green Island: 1950). Just sw of Bitter Swash 10.5 mi. ne of Ocracoke (village). Site of Old Hatteras Inlet (q.v.). *See* Daniel Swash. Hurricane Helene (September 1958) temporarily breached the barrier island here; rapidly filled in. *Other names:* Great Swash (CS 1877), The Swash (local usage).

Great Wading Place. *See* More Shore.

Green Island, former marsh island, 0.5 mi. long, 0.05 mi. wide, Dare County, Kinnakeet Township (USGS 1943: Roanoke Island 1:125,000 scale). Was in Pamlico Sound 0.8 mi. w of Pea Island, s of Basnight Bridge (formerly Bonner) spanning Oregon Inlet, 8.1 mi. se of Wanchese. Ceased to exist during late 1940s, though occasionally exposed until 1970s. Green Island Channel still exists, named for this former island. *Other names:* Greens Island (Currituck DB 7, 1796, 273).

Green Island, marsh, 0.5 mi. long, Hyde County, Ocracoke Township (USGS 2013: Green Island). At Ocracoke Island, 3.1 mi. sw of Hatteras Inlet, 13 mi. ne of Ocracoke (village). Historically an island but today marsh attached to Ocracoke Island. Locally named from contrasting vegetation with surroundings. Documented use since 1812. Covey (2018, 14) suggests the name is much older and named for Roger Green in mid-1600s. Green Island's e end was boundary between Carteret County (before Ocracoke was ceded to Hyde County 1845) and Currituck County until 1823 when Currituck transferred everything s of New Inlet to Hyde County. *Other names:* Inner Green Island (some local use comparing Outer Green Island [q.v.]), Little Green Island (C&GS 1883), Outer Green Island (mistaken use).

Green Island Channel, channel, 2.2 mi. long, Dare County, Kinnakeet Township (USGS 2013: Oregon Inlet). In Pamlico Sound just w of Pea Island, s from Oregon Inlet, 8.4 mi. sse of Wanchese. Named for proximity to former Green Island, ceased to exist completely by 1975. Made official by USBGN 1975. *Other names:* Green Island Slough (Goldstein 2000, loc. 2895).

Green Island Club, former hunting and fishing club, Hyde County, Ocracoke Township (GNIS). Was on e end Ocracoke Island just s of Cockrel Creek, 3.5 mi. wsw of Hatteras Inlet.

Green Islands, former islands, Dare County, Nags Head Township (USGS 2013: Roanoke Island NE). Were at The Causeway, 1.4 mi. wsw of Whalebone Junction. Present islands of Grun Island (possibly a transcribing error of Green), Pond Island, House Island, and other small marsh islands were historically referenced as Green Islands. *Other names:* Green Island (in part—Martin 1829; *see* Grun Island).

Green Island Shoal, small shoal, Hyde County, Ocracoke Township (Weslager 1954). In Pamlico Sound just ne of Legged Lump, 2.5 mi. nw of Hatteras Inlet. Named for nearby Green Island and closer Outer Green Island. Though usually separate, at low water can be connected to Legged Lump, so considered by some as part of Legged Lump.

Green Lump, former small isolated island, Currituck County, Poplar Branch Township (CS 1862a). Was in Currituck Sound 1 mi. w of s portion Whale Head Bay, 1.5 mi. s of Corolla. Disappeared early 20th century. *See* Dorland Lump.

Green Point, marsh point, Dare County, Kinnakeet Township (USGS 2013: Rodanthe). At n entrance Blackmar Gut 0.4 mi. nw of Rodanthe. Note close proximity of two features named Green(s) Point, 1 mi. apart. Reportedly, a windmill (name suspected but unknown for sure) here mid-1800s (Bishop 1878). *See* Green Point Windmill. *Other names:* Greens Point (USGS 1983: Rodanthe), Windmill Point.

Green Point Shoal, shoal, 0.5 mi. wide, Dare County, Kinnakeet Township (local use). Soundside and refers to shallows (mostly 1–3 ft.) s from just n of Round Hammock Bay near former Loggerhead Inlet 5 mi. n of Green Point near Blackmar Gut in Rodanthe.

Green Point Windmill, former windmill, Dare County, Kinnakeet Township (White et al. 2017, 27). Was at Green Point in Rodanthe (also known locally sometimes as Greens Point). Original name probably not Green Point Windmill, but referenced as such in White et al. (2017) and based on several references, including Bishop (1878) and Covey (2018). Bishop indicates two windmills in Avon and one in Rodanthe. Also, several maps of windmills corroborate the location, but none provide names of these windmills. Numerous references (including Covey) are found to Midyetts (Midgetts) Windmill in Rodanthe and was likely this windmill. Ownership for windmills changed frequently, so names often changed 18th and 19th centuries. *Other names:* Banister's Mills (Covey 2018, 126, possibly), Greens Point Mill (Covey 2018, 107), Midyette Mill (possible name), Midyetts Mill (Covey 2018, 195), Midyetts Windmill (possible name), Rodanthe Mill (some alternate historical use).

Greens Point, point, Dare County, Kinnakeet Township (USGS 2013: Rodanthe). Just n of Rodanthe 3.5 mi. n of Salvo. Note close proximity of two features named Green(s) Point; 1 mi. apart.

Greys Island, small marsh island, 0.1 mi. across, Currituck County, Poplar Branch Township (USGS 2013: Mossey Islands, Jarvisburg). In Currituck Sound just w of Goat Island Bay, 6.9 mi. nw of Duck.

Griffin. *See* Nags Head.

Griffin Hills, sand dunes, 50 ft. high, Dare County, Nags Head Township (local informants). Distinct set of five connected sand dunes on n Roanoke Island 2 mi. n of Manteo (center). Name is from early landowner and, while similar, should not be confused with the Andy Griffith Estate just e. *Other names:* Roanoke Hills (occasional use, subdivision here Hills Over Roanoke).

Griggs Creek, small tidal stream, Currituck County, Poplar Branch Township (local use). At e end of Raccoon Bay 0.5 mi. nw of Corolla. Grigg established surname here.

Grun Island, marsh island, 0.2 mi. long, 0.3 mi. wide, Dare County, Nags Head Township (USGS 2013: Roanoke Island NE). In Roanoke Sound just s of The Causeway 1.7 mi. wsw of Whalebone Junction. Grun is probable transcribing error since this island originally one of Green Islands and Green probable original name. Another more colorful explanation also relies on clerical error. The name could have originally been Grunt, referring to grunter fish (found from Chesapeake Bay s-ward), named for sound they make when removed from water. The name is not short for grunion fish, found only off coasts of California in U.S. and Baja California in Mexico. *Other names:* Green Island (ACE 1843).

Guesses Shoal, shoal, Hyde County, Ocracoke Township (Weslager 1954). Sw of Legged Lump 2 mi. n of Terrapin Shoal, 10 mi. ne of Ocracoke (village). Guess is surname here but more used mid-20th century. Perhaps an oyster colony, given variant Guesses Reef, since in Outer Banks geographic names "reef" usually refers to oyster colonies. *Other names:* Guesses Reef (older local use and Weslager 1954).

Gulf Stream, ocean current originating in Gulf of Mexico and flowing through Straits of Florida to join Antilles Current, where it flows n along U.S. Atlantic coast to Cape Hatteras. Here veers ne after colliding with and destroying weaker cold Labrador Current, then flows ne toward Europe and becomes known as North Atlantic Drift. The collision of Gulf Stream and Labrador Current (destroyed) causes considerable turmoil and unpredictable hypsography (shoals—land features not hydrographic/water) and hydrography in Diamond Shoals. The boundary zone between the two (warm and cold) is Hatteras Front, moves between Cape Hatteras and Nags Head according to conditions. *Other names:* Florida Current (fishing guides), Gulfstream (visitor guides), Gulf Stream Current (brochures), Gulph Stream (misspelling), Ocean River (historical), The Great River (numerous historical sources).

Gull Island, former island, Carteret County, Harkers Island Township (C&GS 1896). Was centrally in Back Sound between Shackleford Banks and Harkers Island, 1.2 mi. s of Harkers Island (village). Prominent feature until mid-20th century; today no trace.

Gull Island, former small island, Carteret County, White Oak Township (C&GS 1915a). Was in Bogue Sound halfway between Wood Island (w) and former Cat Island (e) 1 mi. ne of original Emerald Isle. Disappeared early 20th century.

Gull Island, marsh island, 0.6 mi. long, 0.3 mi. wide, Dare County, Kinnakeet Township (USGS 2013: Gull Island). In Pamlico Sound 2.2 mi. w of Hatteras Island, 9.8 mi. sw of Rodanthe. Gull Island Hunting Club was at n end until 1933. *Other names:* Gull Shoal (some local use), Gull Shore (18th-century maps), Gull Shoal Island (Garrity-Blake 2010, 493).

Gull Island Bay, cove, 0.4 mi. long, Dare County, Kinnakeet Township (USGS 2013: Little Kinnakeet). In Pamlico Sound, 2.4 mi. nne of Gull Island, 7.8 mi. s of Rodanthe.

Gull Island Shoal, former small shoal, 1.5 mi. long, Hyde County, Lake Landing Township (CS 1862a). Sse from Gull Rocks (known historically as Gull Island Rock), 21 mi. n of Ocracoke (village). Shoal is shallow but no longer bare.

Gull Rocks, rock complex, 0.5 mi. wide, Hyde County, Lake Landing Township (NOS 2014i). Two distinct areas of rock in Pamlico Sound close to each other, each containing numerous rocks, 21.5 mi. n of Ocracoke (village). *Other names:* Gul Island (Collet et al. 1770), Gull Island (Moseley 1737), Gull Island Rock (C&GS 1865), Gull Shoal Rock (CS 1850s).

Gull Shoal, shoal, 1 mi. long, Dare County, Kinnakeet Township (local use). Sse from Gull Island (Dare County), 9 mi. ssw of Rodanthe. *Other names:* Gull Shoals (NPS 1987, appendix H, 141).

Gull Shoal, former settlement, Dare County, Kinnakeet Township (historic references). Was on Hatteras Island, 5.5 mi. s of Rodanthe (just s of Salvo). Small settlement named in association with Gull Island (also known as

Gull Shoal) just w in Pamlico Sound. No trace today.

Gull Shoal, shoal, 1 mi. long, Hyde County, Lake Landing Township (NOS 2014i). In Pamlico Sound 18.3 mi. n of Ocracoke (village). *Other names:* Gull Shore (historical maps).

Gull Shoal Channel, channel, Dare County, Kinnakeet Township (local use). N-s 3 mi. from Cedar Hammock Channel to Gull Shoal just s of Gull Island.

Gully, The, former area, 2 mi. long, Carteret County, Harkers Island Township (C&GS 1915b). Former valley-like, in semicircle around Cape Hills on w, s, and e, distinct swale-like between distinct high dunes of Cape Hills. Hypsography (landforms) here has changed over the years and only remnants remain.

Gum Swamp, swamp, Dare County, Nags Head Township (Currituck DB 1787, 6, 6). S part of Roanoke Island Marshes (not Roanoke Marshes) just n of beginning Broad Creek, 3 mi. s of Manteo (center). Descriptive for sweetgum trees at the time; name no longer used.

Gun Barrel Point, point, Hyde County, Ocracoke Township (historical local use). At n entrance Silver Lake in Ocracoke (village) just n of Windmill Point, 3.5 mi. ne of Ocracoke Inlet. *Other names:* Coast Guard Station Point (sometimes used as seasonal station).

Gun Cove, cove, Dare County, Atlantic Township (historical maps). In Southern Shores across Jeanguite Creek from tip of Martin Point, 4.5 mi. nnw of original Kitty Hawk. Name's origin categorically obvious, though specific reason unknown, used since early 19th century. There could be some relation to ever more embellished story involving Captain Gallop, who had a substantial plantation at Martins Point. As the story goes, he had acquired, by nefarious means, safes filled with valuables (from businesses in Baltimore) and threw them overboard in this cove to lighten his vessel (low tide), to be retrieved later because of approaching Union troops (during Civil War) or possibly other officials. However, unclear whether it was Captain Gallop or his son as the father was not alive during Civil War but the son was. Anyway, no proof of any of this.

Gunning Hammock Island, island, 0.5 mi. long, Carteret County, Harkers Island Township

(USGS 2013: Horsepen Point, Harkers Island). In Core Sound just s of Little Deep Marsh 3.8 mi. ese of Harkers Island (village). Reference to hunting.

Gunt Inlet, former water passage, Dare County, Nags Head Township (Bowen 1747 as Gun Inlet). Connected Pamlico Sound to Atlantic Ocean cutting through Bodie Island 2 mi. n of Oregon Inlet. Formed s limit of original extension of Bodie Island (q.v.), open before 1585, closed 1798 (known as Port Ferdinando originally). A few maps show open as late as 1812 (including Lewis). *See* Grun Island for a colorful explanation of possible name origin. The actual origin is likely a shortened form of "gunter," method using rings and hoops for sliding a top mast up and down on a lower mast; seamen often applied nautical terminology as place names.

From 1640 until early 1700s was a period of cartographic confusion regarding locations and names of inlets at and near Roanoke Island (*see* Roanoke Island historical inlets). Two inlets are shown as companion inlets here consistently 1585 to late 1600s. The name Port Ferdinando, importantly first English place name applied in what is now U.S., had long been forgotten by time Gunt Inlet came into use. A hiatus of about 100 years occurred between the Roanoke voyages and settlement of Roanoke Island area; the few original names had been forgotten. Topography had changed significantly during that period, so different names were applied. The inlet was usually unnamed on most maps, and while Port Ferdinando appeared sparingly, it was unnamed on most maps 1640 until early 18th century, when Gant Inlet and Gunt Inlet began to appear. Frankenberg (1995, loc. 152, 3) reverses locations of Gunt Inlet and Port Lane (adding Inlet) and places Hattorask Inlet between the two. Hattorask Inlet was actually Gunt Inlet (Port Ferdinando misapplied by some—*see* Roanoke Island historical inlets), so these three inlets were really Port Ferdinando (Gunt Inlet) and Port Lane in reverse locations.

Lane as governor of the first colony consistently referred in his letters to three "entries" Trinety (Trynytye Harboroughe), Ocracoke (Ococan), and Port Ferdinando (Porte Ferdynando): "Beste harborough of all the reste, ys the porte which is called Ferdynando, dyscoverdde by the master and pylotte maggiore of our fleete, you honor's servant, Symon Ferdynando." Named for Simon Fernándes, pilot on the first, second, and fourth Roanoke voyages. Compare Lane's other statement, "There bee only, in all, three entryes and portes: the one which wee have named Trynytye Harborough." Trinety Harbor is clearly named on this second Roanoke voyage; reference to Ferdynando only indicates named for him and possibly implies on this second Roanoke voyage but is not specific on the matter and perhaps indicates they named only one inlet on this voyage. So, regarding the question as to whether Port Ferdinando was named on the first Roanoke voyage (Amadas and Barlowe) or the second Roanoke voyage (Grenville), circumstantial evidence is still inconclusive. Torres (1985, 23) indicates Grenville's voyage or second Roanoke voyage. Further, this still leaves undetermined the particular inlet used by Amadas and Barlowe: Trinety Harbor or Port Ferdinando. Based on distances described, Trinety Harbor still fits better. Later versions of DeBry's 1590 map show English sailings from Trinety Harbor toward Roanoke Island, indicating Trinety Harbor the initial entry inlet.

It cannot be confirmed Amadas and Barlowe stopped at Ocracoke Island on their voyage of reconnoiter (1584), as Amadas's logs are not clear on the matter. However, reports exist that a member of the party named Richard Butler, in his deposition to the Spanish 12 years after the voyage, claimed, "We disembarked in central Florida at a place called Ococa. . . . Twenty Leagues further on, toward the north part we disembarked again in another place known to the English as Puerto Fernando and to the savages as Ataurras." This leads Quinn (1971) to suggest "Ococa" refers to Ocracoke and Puerto Fernando to Hatarask (with "Ataurras" likely being a phonetic rendition of Hatarask). Unclear why the generic "puerto" was used by Fernandes since he was Portuguese and would have used "porto," but perhaps it was in deference to his training in Spain or because Butler was giving his deposition to the Spanish. The English never used "puerto," only "port." His reference to central Florida is plausible because then the English applied the name Florida to anything Spanish in coastal North America. Twenty leagues would be approx. 60 mi., which would be almost to former Gunt Inlet (Port Ferdinando). If this is so, it implies the inlet was named Port Ferdinando (1584) during the first Roanoke voyage, and it, rather than Trinety Harbor, was the one used by Amadas and Barlowe. However, Butler's deposition wasn't given until 1596, also possible he was citing the place named later, possibly referring to being labeled on later version of DeBry's 1590 map. Indeed, this seems more likely, as it remains unclear if the English visited the inlet in 1584. Also, Cape Kenrick (q.v.) was a major feature impeding following close to the coast and could have been a factor for missing in 1584 the inlet named Port Ferdinando. So, still not clear whether Port Ferdinando was named during the first Roanoke voyage (Amadas and Barlowe, with Butler) or on the second Roanoke voyage (Grenville). Amadas's logs are less clear on the initial entry, while Butler's deposition is vague and often contradictory (Quinn 1975). Quinn (1975) believes from Amadas and Barlowe's logs they encountered the inlet at n tip of Hatarask, but comments are vague and could have been Trinety Harbor. Butler then indicates later from Hatarask they "moved 12 leagues to the n and found a port . . . which the savages call Ca-cho Peos . . . and these savages were enemies of those at Puerto Fernando [Hatarask]." Twelve leagues (about 35 miles) would be just beyond former Trinety Harbor from Port Ferdinando, further supporting that location being the initial entry. On the other hand, the reference to Ca-cho Peos strongly suggests mouth of the Chesapeake Bay, another 30 leagues (90 miles) from Hatarask. Amadas's log, then, is inconclusive regarding naming of Port Ferdinando, and neither his log nor Butler's later deposition provide the definitive location of the initial entry inlet. It could be further suggested from Butler's report that the inlet at Hatarask was named Port Ferdinando during the first Roanoke voyage, but evidence on this matter is also inconclusive.

No mention of the companion inlet (became Port Lane) probably because it was too small and not passable, though it clearly is depicted unnamed on White's 1585 map. Use of variant Port Scarborough has been a mystery to many researchers, as it appears in Sainsbury's (1860) rendition of Lane's second letter and nowhere else. But after examination it must be concluded in transcribing Sainsbury's rendition Lane's reference "beste harboroughe" was misinterpreted or it was transcribed incorrectly as "Scarborough" because its location in Lane's letter can be construed in this way. During this period of cartographic confusion, the name Port Ferdinando fell out of use and no permanent settlement here until after 1700. Blaeu's 1640 map was the last to use Port Ferdinando. Gascoyne (1682) locates the inlets correctly and uses Old Inlet for Port Ferdinando and New Inlet for what was becoming Roanoke Inlet (probably former Port Lane). Much of the confusion resulted from a reliance on the *English Pilot Fourth Book* (Fisher et al. 1689), based on Wildey and Thornton's 1685 map, which labels Old Inlet and New Inlet incorrectly farther n (corroborated Cumming 1969, 23). *See* Port Lane, Old Roanoke Inlet, Roanoke Inlet, and Roanoke Island historical inlets.

Many authorities on the geography of the Outer Banks believe this to be the inlet through which Amadas and Barlowe passed on their initial voyage of reconnaissance (1584). A historical marker at the site suggests no proof one way or the other and, indeed, indicates "Roanoke Voyages 1585–1590," thereby discounting Amadas and Barlowe's 1584 voyage. While Port Ferdinando (Gunt Inlet) was used for passage on all subsequent voyages, it might or might not be the one used by Amadas and Barlowe (first Roanoke voyage). Instead, Trinety Harbor (q.v.) is a strong candidate for that inlet, as demonstrated by distances described in the ship's log (unfortunately no directions are provided in these logs). Additionally, NPS's Fort Raleigh Brochure (NPS 1952, 4) referring to Amadas and Barlowe's 1584 voyage indicates "the party of explorers landed on July 13, 1584, on the North Carolina coast, about 7 leagues above ([meaning north]) Roanoke Island," suggesting Trinety Harbor as the inlet of entry, However, "above" does not appear in Amadas and Barlowe's logs and seems to have been inserted. Kitty Hawk Woods

Management Plan (1998, 6) indicates, "While scholars debate the precise location of this historic entry, considerable evidence favors Trinety Harbor," but no evidence provided.

Regarding variants Vieu Passage and View Passage, "view" results from an error transcribing the French word *vieu*, means old. Use of this word was a reference to Port Ferdinando as it had been open before 1585. Some authors believe Hatrask or Hatarask is the name of the inlet, and perhaps it was for a short time, but more likely this was the name used by local Indians for overall area or perhaps for the barrier island rather than the inlet. White's 1585 map places Hatrask a distance s of the inlet as if referring to the island; it was DeBry's 1590 map that moved the name Hatrask to a position opposite the inlet, causing some authors to presume an inlet name. "Port" was used on the Outer Banks referring to inlets for a brief time 16th and 17th centuries; indicated the passage was suitable for navigation and for riding at anchor by shallow draught of ocean-going vessels of that time. The name Port Ferdinando not well known, though it was the initial name applied to this inlet. However, it was used sparingly on maps through mid-17th century.

Apparently, the name Port Ferdinando was unknown or not used by the Lost Colonists (fourth Roanoke voyage), who used Hatarask: "The two and twentieth of July [1587] wee arrived safe at Hatoraske, where our ship and pinnesse ankered." (Pinnesse [pinnace] is small boat with shallow draught useful in Outer Banks waters.) This does seem strange since Port Ferdinando was named by 1585 *and* Simon Fernándes for whom the inlet was named and the ship's pilot on three of the voyages was actually pilot for this voyage, so was present. Not possible to determine if this reference is to the inlet or area (island), probably latter.

Other names: Bahia de Madelena (Blaeu 1640—*see* Bahia della MaDalena), Dugg Inlet (Angley 1985, 4), Ferdinando Inlet (Willard and Midgett 2007—authors stated contrived name, never existed on maps), Gant Inlet (Lewis et al. 1795), Gun Inlet (Bowen, 1747), Hataras (Stick 1958, 279), Hatarask (Haklyut 1589—probably not: island), Hatorasck (Cobb 1905; Stick 1958, 9), Hatorasck Inlet (historical), Hatoras Inlet (Stick 1958, 9),

Hatoraske (Haklyut 1589—probably not: island), Hatorask Inlet (Haklyut 1589), New Inlet (Byrd 1728—open before 1585; perhaps Byrd was referring to New Inlet 10 mi. s, which opened and closed periodically thereby always retaining the name New Inlet), New Inlett (Fisher et al. 1689, chart 2—unclear application), Old Inlet (some 18th-century maps; Gascoyne 1682), Old Inlett (Fisher et al. 1689, chart 15—shown just n of actual location; Visscher and Anse 1717), Passe Neuve (Bellin 1764—misapplication), Porte Ferdinando (Lane 1585, letter 3), Porte Ferdynando (Lane 1585, letter 1), Port Ferdinando (Quinn 1975), Port Ferdinando Inlet (Willard and Midgett 2007—not used on maps), Port Ferinando (GNIS, typographical error, not found elsewhere), Port Fernande (Cheeseman 1982, 193), Port Fernando (Blaeu 1640), Port Hatorack (Cheeseman, 1982, 193), Port of Hatarask (early reference to DeBry's 1590 reference), Port of Hatrask (early reference to DeBry's 1590 reference), Port Scarborough (Sainsbury 1860—see above), Puerto Fernando (Butler 1596), Roanoak Inlet (Speed 1676), Vieu Passage (Sanson 1696—see above), View Passage (misrecording of *vieu* from early French maps; Fisher 1962, 96).

Gut, The, former short tidal stream, 0.1 mi. long, Hyde County, Ocracoke Township (Weslager 1954; confirmed by interviews with Ballance [2017, 2018] and Howard [2017, 2018]). Was at se now Silver Lake (then Cockle Creek) in Ocracoke (village), formed where Big Gut and Little Gut joined. Big Gut and Little Gut filled in by ACE when Cockle Creek was dredged into Silver Lake. The Gut, Big Gut, and Little Gut comprised Old Guts (q.v.) complex. *See* Alligator Gut.

Guthries Hammock, hummock, 0.8 mi. long, 0.2 mi. wide, Carteret County, Smyrna Township (USGS 2013: Horsepen Point). At Core Banks 1.5 mi. ne of Great Shoal, 3.5 mi. s of Davis (mainland). Historically, semipermanent settlement here, today totally uninhabited. One of the few stands of vegetation on Core Banks. Variant name Duges Island is a variation and reference to Duggs or Dugs (q.v.), 16th-century English reference to teats or female breast and further identifies this feature as a landmark on this barrier beach. *See* Black Hammock. *Other names:* Duges Island (early historical maps), Guthrie Hammock (USGS 2011, 1950: Horsepen Point).

Guthries Hammock, former semipermanent settlement, Carteret County, Smyrna Township (Godfrey and Godfrey 1976, 104). Former semipermanent settlement at Guthries Hammock (today totally uninhabited) on Core Banks 1.5 mi. ne of Great Shoal, 3.5 mi. s of Davis (mainland). One of the few stands of vegetation on Core Banks, so provided some shelter for this small previous settlement (few families) late 19th and early 20th centuries. *See* Black Hammock and Guthries Hammock (hummock).

Guthries Hammock Woods, small woods, Carteret County, Smyrna Township (Godfrey and Godfrey 1976, 104). At Guthries Hammock on South Core Banks 1.5 mi. ne of Great Shoal, 3.5 mi. s of Davis (mainland). Historically was a semipermanent settlement here, but today totally uninhabited. One of the few stands of vegetation on Core Banks. *See* Guthries Hammock and Black Hammock.

Guthries Lump, former settlement, Carteret County, Harkers Island Township (historical records). A few families were in central Shackleford Banks near Bald Hill just w of Bald Hill Bay. Variety of interviewees had heard of the place, none (including older folk) knew exact location beyond somewhere on central Shackleford ("I think," they commented—*see* Winsors Lump). Other small settlements on Shackleford Banks, including Wades Shore (w end) and Diamond City (Lookout Woods—e end), with Winsors Lump (central), Whale Creek, and Whale Hill were settled for fishing and shore-based whaling (Outer Banks style—*see* Cape Lookout Grounds). Also, some families were around Wreck Point (*see* Fish Wharf) because a wharf there for processing and transferring fish catches. *See* Dorland Lump. *Other names:* Kib Guthries Lump (historical local use).

Guthries Lump, hummock, Carteret County, Harkers Island Township (historical records). Was in central Shackleford Banks just s of Bald Hill Bay, 1.8 mi. ssw of Harkers Island (village). *See* Guthries Lump (former settlement) and Dorland Lump. *Other names:* Kib Guthries Lump (historical local use).

Gutter Creek, water passage, 1 mi. long, Carteret County, Stacy Township (USGS 2013: Styron Bay). Separates Core Banks from Big Marsh and connects Old Channel to Core Sound 3.9 mi. s of Atlantic (mainland). Descriptive, shape and function.

Gutter Ridge, former sand ridge, Dare County, Hatteras Township (Covey 2018, 39). Was in Frisco near Brigands Bay subdivision mentioned in real estate transactions of Abraham Farrow.

Guys Hall, marsh island, Currituck County, Fruitville Township (Cox 1923). In ne North Channel just sw of Spot Shoal Island, 4.5 mi. se of Knotts Island (village). Unusual or probable whimsical use of generic term "hall," probably some sort of reference to temporary cabin or meager structure.

H

Halfway Point, point, Currituck County, Fruitville Township (USGS 2013: Barco). S point Mackay Island 3 mi. w of Knotts Island (village). Originally named Morses Point, changed to Halfway Point because approx. halfway along old steamship route between Norfolk and Nags Head; Morse was then applied to another point n-ward. *Other names:* Half Way Point (F&WS 1984, map, 74), Morses Point (ACE 1:62,500; sometimes applied to entire peninsula rather than small area 4 mi. n, until importance of using Halfway Point for steamship route).

Hall Haven Marina, harbor, Carteret County, Morehead Township (PKS 2016). In Pine Knoll Waterway (e section) in Pine Knoll Shores, 7 mi. w of Atlantic Beach. Named for A. C. Hall, instrumental with Don Brock in completing Pine Knoll Waterway. *Other names:* Hall Haven (local use).

Hamiltons Shoal, former shoal, Carteret County, Morehead Township (historical charts). Was at w approach Beaufort Inlet 3 mi. ssw of Beaufort (mainland).

Hammock, The, island, Currituck County, Poplar Branch Township (USGS 2013: Mossey Islands). N end of unnamed marsh just s of Little Narrows 8 mi. sw of Corolla. Labeled on USGS (2013: Mossey Islands) map in hydrographic type signifying water feature; however, an error since "hammock" (corruption of "hummock") is island or high ground in marsh or swamp, not water feature. *See* Black Hammock.

Hammock, The, man-enhanced, Dare County, Nags Head Township (local use). In Pirates Cove subdivision, 3 mi. w of Whalebone Junction. W high ground in marshes just e of downtown Manteo and w of Midgetts Hammock. Significantly altered in developing Pirates Cove part known as Hammock Village. *See* Black Hammock.

Hammock Canal, canal, 0.3 mi. long, Dare County, Nags Head Township (PC HOA 2016). Trends e-w then n-s 1 mi. se of Sandy Point at Roanoke Island Festival Park, 3 mi. w of Whalebone Junction. One of seven named canal segments interconnected throughout Pirates Cove, named portions corresponding with limits of adjacent named subdivisions. *See* Black Hammock and The Hammock (Dare County).

Hammock Cove, cove, Currituck County, Poplar Branch Township (unknown, ca. 1900). Just w of Narrows Cove 0.5 mi. sw of Little Narrows, 8.3 mi. sw of Corolla. *See* Black Hammock.

Hammock Creek, small tidal stream, Hyde County, Ocracoke Township (Weslager 1954). Is 1 mi. ne of First Hammock Hills, 4 mi. ne of Ocracoke (village). *See* Black Hammock.

Hammock Ditch. *See* Johns Creek.

Hammock Ditch. *See* Midgetts Ditch.

Hammock Hills, hummocks, Hyde County, Ocracoke Township (local use). Is 1 mi. ne of First Hammock Hills, 3 mi. ne of Ocracoke (village). Originally Second Hammock Hills in accordance with naming scheme at Ocracoke, as it followed First Hammock Hills heading ne toward Hatteras Inlet. Woods here known as Hammock Oaks and Hammock Woods. Local use has become simply Hammock Hills; First Hammock Hills still known and sometimes used, Second Hammock Hills has fallen into disuse. *See* Black Hammock. *Other names:* Hammock Oaks (historical local use), Hammock Woods (historical local use), Second Hammock (Weslager 1954), Second Hammock Hills (older local use, proximity to First Hammock Hills, and Weslager 1954).

Hammock Island, marsh island, 1 mi. long, less than 0.1 mi. wide, Currituck County, Fruitville Township (USGS 2013: Knotts Island). In marsh islands at n end of Knotts Island Channel, 2 mi. ne of Knotts Island (village). *See* Black

Hammock. *Other names:* The Hammock (local use), Websters Island (18th-century maps).

Hammock Oaks, former woods, Hyde County, Ocracoke Township (historical local use). Was just s of Island Creek 3.6 mi. ne of Ocracoke (village). Originally referred to stand of trees, though remnants as raised area remain (*see* Hammock Hills). Hammock Woods and Hammock Oaks were often used interchangeably. *See* Black Hammock. *Other names:* Hammock Woods (historical local use), Second Hammock Hills (former use).

Hammock Woods, woods, 1 mi. long, Hyde County, Ocracoke Township (historical local use). Was on Ocracoke Island just ne of Hammock Oaks 4.7 mi. ne of Ocracoke (village). Hammock Woods and Hammock Oaks were often used interchangeably. *See* Black Hammock. *Other names:* Hammock Oaks (former local use), Second Hammock Hills (used sometimes, just ne of First Hammock Hills), The Woods (local use).

Hammonds Island, small island, Currituck County, Poplar Branch Township (Codman, Crowninshield, and Lawrence 1925). In s part Raccoon Bay just nw of Log Blind Islands, 1 mi. wnw of Corolla.

Hammonds Landing, former landing, Dare County, Nags Head Township (Wise 2010, 308). Was on nw Roanoke Island 0.2 mi. n of Ashbee Harbor, 1 mi. se of First Creeks, 2 mi. s of Manteo. Where first 4,000 Union troops landed during Battle of Roanoke Island since a contingency of Confederate troops was waiting at Ashbee Harbor, where largest portion of Union troops later landed.

Hampton Street Pond, man-made lake, Currituck County, Poplar Branch Township (local use—Corolla Light HOA personnel). In Corolla Light subdivision just n of Great Beach Pond 1.7 mi. s of Corolla. Constructed for storm water drainage control, named for adjacent street.

Hanes Creek, water passage, Currituck County, Fruitville Township (Cox 1906). Trends e-w and separates Hanes Thicket from Wishes Hammock and Buzzard Island, 2.5 mi. ne of Knotts Island (village).

Hanes Thicket, marsh islands, 0.5 mi. wide, Currituck County, Fruitville Township (Cox 1906). In maze of marsh islands just e of Perch Island Bay, 2 mi. ene of Knotts Island (village).

Harbor Channel, channel, 0.7 mi. long, Carteret

County, Morehead Township (USGS 2013: Beaufort). At port facilities Morehead City (mainland) between Sugarloaf Island and port facilities 3 mi. nw of Beaufort Inlet.

Harbor Cove, cove, Hyde County, Ocracoke Township (local use). Man-enhanced cove in ne Ocracoke (village) n end of first (unnamed) canal from Pamlico Sound just se of Gap Inlet 1 mi. ne of Silver Lake.

Harbor Island, irregular island, 0.1 mi. wide, Carteret County, Cedar Island Township (USGS 2013: Wainwright Island). In Core Sound between Chain Shot Island and Wainwright Island 4 mi. w of Swash Inlet, 10.6 mi. sw of Portsmouth (village), 16.6 mi. sw of Ocracoke (village). Historically much larger, 2 mi. across; name originates from ideal "harbor" created by island's original irregular shape. Originally spelled Harbour from its early application but adopted American spelling. Hunt club here into 20th century. *Other names:* Barbage Island (transcribing error), Harbour Island (Holland 1794 and some 18th-century maps— legitimate spelling from 18th century).

Harbor Island Channel, channel, 3 mi. long, Carteret County, Cedar Island Township (N.C. Fisheries 1923, 26). Trends ne-sw in Core Sound from Harbor Island to entrance to Cedar Island Bay, 8.5 mi. (center) from Atlantic (mainland).

Harbor Island Shoal. *See* Kingfish Shoal.

Hard Working Lumps, shoal, Carteret County, Harkers Island Township (USGS 2013: Harkers Island). In Back Sound just off Shackleford Banks at nw point Johnson Bay 2.3 mi. s of Harkers Island (village). Descriptive. *See* Dorland Lump.

Hargraves Beach, beach, Dare County, Atlantic Township (local use). On Currituck Banks in s Duck just n of Southern Shores, 5.8 mi. nnw of original Kitty Hawk. *See* Station Landing and Bias Shores. Subdivision named for feature.

Hargraves Landing. *See* Station Landing.

Harkers Island, island, 4.2 mi. long, 1.1 mi. wide, 13 ft. high, Carteret County, Harkers Island Township (USGS 2013: Harkers Island). In Back Sound at sw end Core Sound separated from mainland by The Straits 3.2 mi. nne of Shackleford Banks, 5.6 mi. ese of Beaufort (mainland). Granted to Farnifold Green, then to Thomas Sparrow on March 21, 1714; sold to Ebenezer Harker

September 15, 1750. Crane Island (Craney Island) became known as Harkers Island 1783 when three brothers named Harker (Zachary, James, and Ebenezer) divided the island among themselves. *See* Crane Island for a possible ambiguation. Made official by USBGN 1948. *Other names:* Barbers Island (Colton 1870—misrecording), Crane Island (some 18th-century maps; Moseley 1733 inset), Craney Island (Stick 1958, 185), Crany Island (Angley 1982, 5—misrecording of Craney), Davers Ile (Smith 1624, map— Smith's names did not prevail), Davers Island (Henry 1860, from Raleigh expeditions 1584—possible misspelling of Danvers for Sir John Danvers, but no evidence to support), Davis Isle (Stanford 2015, 53— might be misinterpretation of Davers, though surname Davis common here), Harker Island (Moseley 1733), Markers Islands (misrecording, Prang 1863).

Harkers Island, village, Carteret County, Harkers Island Township (USGS 2013: Harkers Island). On s shore Harkers Island 2.4 mi. nne of Shackleford Banks, 5.6 mi. ese of Beaufort (mainland). Post office est. 1892 operated sporadically until becoming permanent 1904. Made official by USBGN 1948. Subdivision named for feature.

Harkers Island Canals, canals, Carteret County, Harkers Island Township (N.C. Marine Fisheries, 2019, E7, map 27). More than 20 n-s trending canals nw Harkers Island, w side Westmouth Bay 5.3 mi. ese of Beaufort (mainland).

Harkers Island Ferry Dock, former dock, Carteret County, Harkers Island Township (NCDOT 1933). Was at center s shore of Westmouth Bay just n of original Harkers Island (village). Served Harkers Island from the mainland from 1933 to 1941, when Davis Memorial Bridge opened.

Harkers Island Harbor, harbor, Carteret County, Harkers Island Township (USGS 2013: Harkers Island). Completed 1970, in Brooks Creek at w end Harkers Island, 1.8 mi. nw of Harkers Island (village). *See* Harkers Island (island).

Harkers Island Marina, harbor, Carteret County, Harkers Island Township (signage). Centrally on Back Sound shore of Harkers Island, 1.8 mi. w of Cape Lookout National Seashore facility. *See* Harkers Island (island).

Harkers Point, point, Carteret County, Harkers Island Township (USGS 2013: Harkers Island).

Nw point of Harkers Island 2 mi. nw of Harkers Island (village). *See* Harkers Island (island). Subdivision named for feature.

Hatarask, former region, Dare County, Kinnakeet Township (White 1585). Referenced by local Indians from former Cape Kenrick (q.v.) to probably Gunt Inlet (then Port Ferdinando; White 1585 and DeBry 1590). Reference used by Amadas and Barlowe (Barlowe 1584) and others on subsequent voyages; some confusion whether reference was to an inlet (if so, Port Ferdinando) or an island (area), which might have been a small island just n of Paquiac (q.v.; now mostly Pea Island) from Cape Kenrick. Original manuscripts are not completely clear on the reference, but likely to an island with possible later implication (DeBry 1590) of application to the inlet or fret (channel or inlet created by erosion—term used in original documents) by the same name. White (1585) places the name s of the inlet as if applying to the barrier island, but DeBry (1590) *moves* the name to opposite the inlet (Port Ferdinando). Bleau, late as 1640 uses Hantaraske (*sic*) s of Port Ferdinando (no longer an island) to Cape Kenrick (Canrick on Blaeu). Hatarask for the inlet was not used 1585 onward (except possible ambiguous statement of Lost Colonists— *see* below) because Lane, with Grenville on second Roanoke voyage, does not mention Hatarask as an inlet—he mentions only Trynytye Harborough (Trinety Harbor), Ococan (Ocracoke), and Ferdynando (Port Ferdinando, later Gunt Inlet—Hatarask). The inlet was Gunt Inlet, named Port Ferdinando possibly by Amadas and Barlowe (Barlowe 1584) or by Grenville (second Roanoke voyage 1585). *See* Gunt Inlet for more information on naming Port Ferdinando. Subdivision named for feature. *Other names:* Ataurras (Butler 1596), Hantorask (Blaeu 1640), Hatarask Island (Quinn 1975), Hatorasck (Cheeseman 1982, 194), Hatorask (Trebellas and Chapman 1999, 19), Hatoraske (Haklyut 1589), Hatoraske Island (NPS 1952, 5), Hatrask (early spelling, several documents—White used both Hatrask and Hatarask, though latter occurred more used later), Hatterask (synoptic renditions of history here, mostly websites, alteration of Hatrask made perhaps by misinterpretation or perhaps to seem more familiar; subdivision in Hatteras

village uses name), Hotoros (Cheeseman 1982, 194), Otterasco (Cheeseman 1982, 194), Ottorasko (Lane 1589).

Hatfield Timber, woods, Carteret County, Morehead Township (CS 1855). Exact location unknown but somewhere near Atlantic Beach. Referenced maritime forest here, used until mid-19th century. Generic term "timber" is unusual usage for the Outer Banks ("woods" was usual term) and might have been introduced by map or chart makers from outside or possibly by timber harvesters.

Hatorask Inlet. *See* Gunt Inlet.

Hatteras, village, Dare County, Hatteras Township (USGS 2013: Cape Hatteras). On sw Hatteras Island on marsh peninsula into Pamlico Sound, 2.3 mi. wsw of Frisco, 4 mi. ne of Hatteras Inlet. Possibly an English corruption of Algonquian word meaning sparse vegetation, but as with most indigenous words from early contact, meanings are obscure and difficult to prove.

During Civil War, Hatteras was capital of "the true and faithful (redeemed) State of North Carolina." The Outer Banks and some people on coastal mainland did not agree with secessionists who joined North Carolina with Confederacy. Antisecessionists elected a delegate to Washington, D.C., as did what became West Virginia, resulting from pressure from antisecessionists. However, delegate from the Outer Banks never seated in Congress, so government at Hatteras never recognized (*see* Outer Banks entry). Post office est. 1858, discontinued 1869, reestablished 1871, discontinued 1877, reestablished later 1877. Incorporated 1931.

Other names: Durants (sometimes misused with Hatteras by commercial activity associated with Durants), Hatteras Village (commercial sources), Hatterse (Garrity-Blake 2010, 372—mostly local pronunciation, spoken but occasionally written), Old Hatteras Village (current brochures referring to historical Hatteras village), Port of Hatteras (some nautical references, sometimes by post office clerk).

Hatteras Banks, former barrier island, Hyde County, Ocracoke Township; and Dare County, Hatteras Township (historical, Price and Strother 1798). From Cape Hatteras (Chacandepeco Inlet) sw to Old Hatteras Inlet (q.v.), including present s Hatteras Island from

Buxton (Chacandepeco Inlet) to Hatteras Inlet and then 5 mi. including ne portion Ocracoke Island to Old Hatteras Inlet. Application essentially same as Croatoan (q.v.), but later usage considerably after Croatoan fell into disuse (Croatoan occasionally slightly farther w). *See* Hatteras (village). *Other names:* Barrel Island (Russell 1795), Cape Hatteras Banks (Currituck DB 7, 1703, 50), Cape Hatterass Banks (Currituck DB 8, 1797, 72), Cape Hatterass Island (Currituck DB 1, 1714, 220), Hateras Bancks (Wimble 1738 — notorious for inaccurate orthography), Hateras Bank (Wimble 1733), Hatteras Bank (Bowen 1747), Hateras Banks (Currituck DB 4, 1780, 272–73), Hatterass Banks (Currituck DB 7, 1794, 140–41), Hattrass Banks (Currituck DB 2, 1771, 348), Hattress Banks (Currituck DB 2, 1771, 348), South Banks (early deeds).

Hatteras Bar, shoal, Dare County, Hatteras Township (local use). Entrance, Hatteras Inlet 5 mi. sw of Hatteras village; causes Hatteras Swash. *See* Hatteras (village).

Hatteras Beach, beach, Dare County, Hatteras Township (local use). At Cape Hatteras, 3.5 mi. s of Buxton. Immediately on both sides of Cape Point, more often applied to e-w portion at Hatteras Bight. However, name has been applied to varying extents of entire shore of Hatteras Island including Inlet Peninsula from end of paved road to Hatteras Inlet. *See* Hatteras (village). *Other names:* Hatteras Coast (general reference to beach from Cape Hatteras to Hatteras Inlet — White 2012, 140).

Hatteras Bight, bight, 6 mi. long, Dare County, Hatteras Township (USGS 2013: Cape Hatteras). In Atlantic Ocean on s shore Hatteras Island from Cape Hatteras (point) (e) to point 0.6 mi. s of Frisco (w). *See* Hatteras (village). *Other names:* Bight of Hatteras (MacNeill 1958, 2), Hatteras Cove (C&GS 1879), The Bight (MacNeill 1958, 117), The Cove (local use).

Hatteras Canyon, canyon (NOS 2014d). In Atlantic Ocean, 90 mi. se of Cape Hatteras leading from edge of continental shelf into deep ocean outside 3-mi. state limit and not considered to be in the state; also beyond 12-mi. national limit so outside U.S. *See* Hatteras (village).

Hatteras Channel Gorge, channel valley, Dare County, Hatteras Township; and Hyde County, Ocracoke Township (scientific papers). Submerged in Hatteras Inlet, containing much of Hatteras Inlet Channel 4 mi. se of Hatteras (village). More a scientific reference used in reports, but found occasionally. Use of "gorge" not from local usage but from those writing scientific reports; descriptive referencing deepest part of inlet and while somewhat stabilized by dredging is still changeable. *See* Hatteras (village). *Other names:* Hatteras Inlet Gorge (scientific papers).

Hatteras Dunes, sand ridges, 5 mi. long, Dare County, Hatteras Township (local use). Along beach from just sw of Frisco to periodic breach area sometimes referenced as Little Inlet 0.5 mi. s of Hatteras (village). *See* Hatteras (village).

Hatteras Flats, shallow tidal flat, Dare County, Kinnakeet and Hatteras Townships (scientific papers). Soundside, most of Hatteras Island and used in scientific papers as general reference when describing bathymetry (underwater landforms) of the sound adjacent to the barrier islands. *See* Hatteras (village).

Hatteras Ground, former reference to open sea, Dare County, Hatteras and Kinnakeet Townships. Whaling ground in Atlantic Ocean e and s of Cape Hatteras (Stick 1958). Former concentration of whales (mostly sperm whales), thus hunting and cruising ground for whaling. Discovered by whalers from New England (1830s), used extensively until whales depleted. Whalers of the Outer Banks did not hunt for whales in ships as did New England whalers but instead sighted whales from land and captured them by using boats similar to longboats, a method yielding less capture of whales. *See* Cape Lookout Grounds for a further description of whaling Outer Banks style. *See* Hatteras (village). *Other names:* Hatteras Grounds (historical).

Hatteras Harbor, harbor, 0.5 mi. long, Dare County, Hatteras Township (signage). Trends e-w in Hatteras (village), 5 mi. ne of Hatteras Inlet. Several individual harbors (marinas) here, dredged and widened 1936. *See* Hatteras (village). Subdivision named for feature. *Other names:* Rollinson Harbor (occasional casual reference, Rollinson Channel approach to Hatteras Harbor).

Hatteras Harbor Entrance, small water passage, Dare County, Hatteras Township (local use). Entrance to Hatteras Harbor from Pamlico Sound in Hatteras (village) 3 mi. ne of Hatteras Inlet. *See* Hatteras (village). *Other names:* Hatteras Harbor Inlet (limited usage because slightly confusing with nearby Hatteras Inlet).

Hatteras Harbor Marina, harbor, Dare County, Hatteras Township (signage). W end Hatteras Harbor in Hatteras (village), 0.5 mi. ne of Austin Creek (Hatteras-Ocracoke Ferry docks). *See* Hatteras (village).

Hatteras Inlet, water passage, Dare County, Hatteras Township; and Hyde County, Ocracoke Township (USGS 2013: Green Island, Hatteras). Connects Pamlico Sound to Atlantic Ocean and separates Hatteras Island and Ocracoke Island 4 mi. sw of Hatteras (village). Opened 1846 by same hurricane opening Oregon Inlet. Hatteras Inlet should not be confused with Old Hatteras Inlet (q.v.). Variant name East Inlet occasionally used for a short time while Wells Creek Inlet was open and when West Inlet was used for that inlet, both as descriptive names for distinguishing the two inlets. Some unsubstantiated rumors there might have been a British fort here of sorts 1750s, but no supporting documentation found. *See* Hatteras (village). *Other names:* Canal d'Hatteras (Blanchard 1856), Cape Hatteras Inlet (broad locational reference), East Inlet (CS 1852), Entré de Hatteras (Nolin 1783).

Hatteras Inlet. *See* Old Hatteras Inlet.

Hatteras Inlet Beach, beach, 2 mi. long, Dare County, Hatteras Township (Garrity-Blake, 2010, 19). On Inlet Peninsula oceanside at e side Hatteras Inlet, 3 mi. sw of Hatteras (village).

Hatteras Inlet Channel, channel, Dare County, Hatteras Township; and Hyde County, Ocracoke Township (local use). Main channel through Hatteras Inlet through which small craft navigate the inlet 4 mi. sw of Hatteras (village). *See* Hatteras (village).

Hatteras Island, island, 33 mi. long, Dare County, KInnakeet and Hatteras Townships (local, regional, and national use). Former island ne from Hatteras Inlet to Cape Hatteras, then n to former New Inlet (reopened 2011 at s end Pea Island, making Hatteras Island again an island) 5.6 mi. n of Rodanthe. Hatteras Island is made up of three historical segments, Hatteras Banks from Old Hatteras Inlet to Cape

Hatteras (partially now e Ocracoke Island); Kinnakeet Banks n from Cape Hatteras to Little Kinnakeet (former locality); and Chicamacomico Banks from Little Kinnakeet to former New Inlet (reopened 2011). Today the names Hatteras Island and Pea Island are still used, though these two former islands had been joined since 1945 when New Inlet closed, though reopened 2011 and are distinct islands again. In 2016 inexplicably a sign was erected at the s end of Basnight Bridge (Oregon Inlet) indicating former Pea Island is now n Hatteras Island, very curious since New Inlet reopened 2011. *See* Hatteras (village). Ten subdivisions named for feature.

Other names: Cape Hatteras Banks (Rollinson 1884), Cape Hatteras Island (Binkley 2007, 67—from Etheridge discussing area included in CHNS), Chicamacomico Banks (n part), Chicamacomico Island (Binkley 2007, 34, referring to 1937 documents concerning creation of a national seashore—use of Chicamacomico with island was unusual, especially in 1937 since name had fallen into disuse except as historical—*see* Rodanthe), Chickonocomack Bank (historical), Chiconomack Bank (Colton 1854), Croatoan (White 1585—historically applied to s part, Indian name, modern Cape Hatteras e Ocracoke Island), Croatan Island (modernized spelling of Croatoan), Currituck South Sand Banks (historical deed), Hartfords Ile (Henry 1860, from Raleigh expeditions 1584), Hatarask (White 1585), Hateras Banks (early deeds), Hatrask Island (historical), Hatteras Bank (Foster 1866b), Hatteras Banks (historical), Hatteras Bar (historical), Hatteras Reef (O'Neal et al. 1976, 24), Hattorask Island (historical), Hertfords Island (probable gesture to Earl of Hertford, England—most of these early names did not last), Island of Cape Hatteras (various 18th-century deeds), Island of Hatteras (Lord Carteret's grant, redrawn 1744), Kinakeet Banks (older extended local use), Kinnakeet Banks (older use), Raonack (misapplication Bodie Island s, DeLisle 1718), Sand Banks (historical deeds), Table Land (Wimble 1733—reference to flatness here).

Hatteras Island Beach, beach, Dare County, Kinnakeet and Hatteras Townships (tourist brochures). S from New Inlet, then w-s from Cape Point at Cape Hatteras to Hatteras Inlet. Occasionally used generally and in scientific studies and reports. *Other names:* North Hatteras Beach (in part—tourist use), South Hatteras Beach (in part—tourist use).

Hatteras Landing, landing, Dare County, Hatteras Township (local use). Developed area around Hatteras-Ocracoke Ferry terminal, 1.5 mi. se of Hatteras (village). Used more and more for adjacent Teachs Lair Marina area. *See* Hatteras (village). Subdivision named for feature.

Hatteras Landing Marina, harbor, Dare County, Hatteras Township (signage). Adjacent to Austin Creek (Hatteras-Ocracoke Ferry docks) 0.7 mi. sw of Hatteras (village). *See* Hatteras (village).

Hatteras Marlin Club Marina, harbor, Dare County, Hatteras Township (signage). In ne end Hatteras Harbor in Hatteras (village), 1.5 mi. ne of Austin Creek (Hatteras-Ocracoke Ferry docks). *See* Hatteras (village).

Hatteras–Ocracoke Island Ferry Dock, landing, Dare County, Hatteras Township (signage). Just wsw of Hatteras (village center), 2.5 mi. ne of Hatteras Inlet. Provides access to Ocracoke Island n side.

Hatteras Sand Banks, barrier beaches, Dare County, Kinnakeet and Hatteras Townships; and Hyde County, Ocracoke Township. Historically applied to Hatteras Island (from variously open New Inlet) and e Ocracoke Island (before Hatteras Inlet opened—1846). *See* Hatteras (village).

Hatteras Sand Flats, area, 3 mi. long, Dare County, Hatteras Township (Sorrie 2014, 116). Sand flats and sand dunes from just se of Austin Creek (Hatteras-Ocracoke Ferry docks) to Hatteras Inlet, center 3 mi. se of Hatteras (village). Result of couple of centuries sand deposition interspersed with linear dunes, including Ourdsleys Hammock and Round Hammock near w end Hatteras Island. *See* Hatteras (village). *Other names:* Hatteras Flats (local use).

Hatteras Shoals, shoals, 2 mi. long, Dare County, Hatteras Township (USGS 2013: Cape Hatteras). Inner section Diamond Shoals se from tip of Cape Point. *See* Hatteras (village) and Diamond Shoals. Made official by USBGN 1949 to establish location. *Other names:* Cape Hatteras Spit (Blunt 1857, 342), Diamond Shoal (NOS editions), The Diamond Shoal (Stick 1958, 291n), The Spit (C&GS 1910b).

Hatteras Shoals. *See* Diamond Shoals.

Hatteras Slough, natural channel, Dare County, Hatteras Township (USGS 2013: Cape Hatteras). Between Hatteras Shoals (innermost of Diamond Shoals) and Inner Diamond Shoal (middle Diamond Shoals) just off Cape Hatteras. *See* Hatteras (village) and Diamond Shoals.

Hatteras Slough. *See* Diamond Slough.

Hatteras Swash, swash, Dare County, Hatteras Township; and Hyde County, Ocracoke Township (limited boater use, some charts). Shoals where breakers occur (Hatteras Bar) at entrance Hatteras Inlet, including North Breakers and South Breakers, 6 mi. se of Hatteras (village). *See* Hatteras (village) and Daniel Swash. *Other names:* Hatteras Wash (occasional), The Swash (local use since inlet opened 1846).

Hatteras Woods. *See* Buxton Woods.

Hattie Creef Landing, former landing, Dare County, Kinnakeet Township (signage). Was soundside in Salvo, 0.5 mi. s of Midgett Cove, 4 mi. s of Rodanthe. Named for ship originally landed here supporting fishing trade, named *Hattie Creef*, built by George Washington Creef Jr., boat builder in Manteo, 28 mi. nnw of here, and named for his daughter Hattie Creef. Anchored a hundred yards or so offshore and was serviced by "shove skiffs" or small boats with little or no draught (reportedly could be shoved), no longer necessary when Coast Guard dredged a channel and harbor 1936 (*see* Blackmar Gut and Rodanthe Harbor). *Hattie Creef* was originally a sail-fitted shad boat (shallow-draft fishing boats invented by G. W. Creef for use on the Outer Banks' sounds and shad fishing) and later fitted with engine for passenger service between Manteo and Elizabeth City w on Albemarle Sound. Subdivision named for feature.

Haulover, The, area, Carteret County, Portsmouth Township (USGS 1950: Portsmouth). Just e of Piliauga Creek just sw of Sheep Island 1.5 mi. sw of Portsmouth (village). *See* Haulover Point. *Other names:* The Haul Over (White 2012, 23).

Haulover, The, flat, Dare County, Kinnakeet Township (older local use). Remnant of former Chacandepeco Inlet 1.1 mi. e of Buxton, 2.3 mi. n of Cape Hatteras. With Kite Point and Canadian Hole, apparently ideal for windsurfing and attracts such enthusiasts. NCDOT studying area for bridge (no decision as of 2019). *See* Haulover Point.

Haulover Point, point, Carteret County, Portsmouth Township (USGS 1950: Portsmouth). N point Portsmouth Island 0.3 mi. n of Portsmouth (village), 8.3 mi. sw of Ocracoke (village). "Haulover" a generic term referring to shallow place where boat must be "pulled over" from one place of deeper water to another, or to a narrow low isthmus where a boat can be pulled over, applied frequently on the Outer Banks; haulover frequently dry. *See* Haulover Point Dock. *Other names:* Haul Over Point (local written), Keys Point (Coles and Price 1806), Northwest Point (rarely used directional).

Haulover Point Dock, former landing, Carteret County, Portsmouth Township (NPS 2007, 172). At Haulover Point at Portsmouth (village) 0.5 mi. se of Casey Island, 5 mi. sw of Ocracoke (village). Served the village and also menhaden (*Brevoortia tyrannus*; small fish used mostly for fish meal, animal food, and fertilizer) processing factory 19th century nearby known as Grey's Factory. Today, dock used by small, local ferries for tourists from Ocracoke. *See* Haulover Point. *Other names:* Haulover Dock (shortened usage today),

Haulover Slew, water passage, 1.8 mi. long, Carteret County, Portsmouth Township (USGS 1950: Portsmouth). In Pamlico Sound, separates Casey Island and Portsmouth Island 5.4 mi. sw of Ocracoke (village). "Slew" (variants "slough" and "slue") can refer to various features; on the Outer Banks generally refers to a water passage, tidal stream, or channel. Variations of spelling are sometimes on same map or same feature on different maps; "slough" is more common usage on the Outer Banks. *See* Haulover Point and Allen Slough.

Hawthorne Point. *See* Mann Point.

Hayman Shore, beach, Dare County, Atlantic Township (local use and street sign). Soundside shore at e end Kitty Hawk Bay 1 mi. nw of Kill Devil Hills (town). Surname here since colonial period.

Hay Pond, small cove, Currituck County, Poplar Branch Township (F&WS 1999, map 16). Just n of Hay Point at s end Ships Bay 1 mi. n of Corolla.

Hay Point, point, Currituck County, Poplar Branch Township (Codman, Crowninshield, and Lawrence 1925). At se Ships Bay 1 mi. nnw of Corolla.

Hay Point, point, Dare County, Atlantic Township (USGS 2013: Kitty Hawk). At ne corner Kitty Hawk Bay, just s of original Kitty Hawk, 3.4 mi. nnw of Wright Brothers National Memorial.

Hay Point Ridge, sand ridge, 1 mi. long, Dare County, Atlantic Township (Harris 2017). In Kitty Hawk ridge-and-swale system (q.v.) w of Kitty Hawk, Herbert Perry Road terminating near Hay Point 0.5 mi. sw of original Kitty Hawk. Associative with Hay Point (Dare County).

Headens Landing, former landing, Carteret County, Morehead Township (Stephens 1984, 146). Reportedly was in Salter Path at or near present Homers Point Marina.

Head of the Hole, cove, 0.4 mi. long, Carteret County, Davis Township (USGS 2013: Davis). In Core Sound 0.9 mi. ne of The Swash, 4.5 mi. e of Davis (mainland). *Other names:* Head of the Hold (Carteret County GIS 2019).

Headquarters Island, marsh island, Dare County, Nags Head Township (USGS 2013: Roanoke Island NE). In Roanoke Sound 1 mi. s of The Causeway, 1.4 mi. sw of Whalebone Junction. Name origin unknown according to numerous local residents and historians. No structures on the island (now), not known to be headquarters of anything. Some locals speculate possibly related to former hunting camp. Bodie Island Lifesaving Station (Coast Guard) refurbished 1954 as Cape Hatteras National Seashore Headquarters (temporarily), but 4.3 mi. s with no known association. Well-known Lane (first Roanoke Colony) and probably Lost Colonists (second Roanoke Colony) wanted to establish small fortifications (sconces) between Port Ferdinando and colony site (*see* Fort Raleigh); evidence of at least one such sconce known to be at Port Ferdinando. Suggested name origin by some "researchers" since Headquarters Island is about halfway between the colony's site and Port Ferdinando; possible sconce was here, hence name. This is unfounded presumption based on fallible analysis, and almost surely inaccurate. The name does not appear until C&GS Chart 40 (1876). The name could be whimsical.

Head Slough, small tidal stream, Dare County, Atlantic Township (local informants). Just s of Sanderling 3 mi. n Duck. *See* Allen Slough.

Hearths Cove, man-made cove, Carteret County, Morehead Township (PKS 2016). At terminus of Kings Corner Arm (in Pine Knoll Waterway) in Pine Knoll Shores, 8 mi. w of Atlantic Beach. Named for Harry Hearth, Roosevelts' attorney developing Pine Knoll Shores.

Hegge Impoundment, area, 1 mi. wide, Currituck County, Fruitville Township (F&WS map 2018). In western Great Marsh 4 mi. wnw of Knotts Island (village). Area surrounded by canals and dikes to control water flow. *Other names:* Kitchin Impoundment (F&WS, map, 2001—original name).

Hells Gate, small channel, Dare County, Nags Head Township (local use). S end Oregon Inlet channel at entrance to soundside Oregon Inlet. Treacherous conditions created by changing migration of Oregon Inlet creating colorful application of name.

Henry Clarks Landing, former landing, Dare County, Hatteras Township (Covey 2018, 18). Was on Clark Plantation (colonial period) between former Indian Town (q.v.) and Buxton.

Henry Jones Creek, cove, 0.4 mi. wide, Carteret County, Harkers Island Township (USGS 2013: Harkers Island). In Westmouth Bay at n side of Harkers Island 0.7 mi. ne of Harkers Island (village).

Hen Turd Creek, small tidal stream, Dare County, Kinnakeet Township (Garrity-Blake 2010, 492). Soundside just s of Midgett Island halfway between Waves and Salvo. Interesting (and obvious) name with no documentation as to why name was applied, nor does anyone today know why this name was used, nor is it remembered; presumed whimsical.

Heritage Point Marina, small private harbor, Dare County, Nags Head Township (signage). In Heritage Point subdivision, extreme nw point Roanoke Island just s of Northwest Point, 3 mi. nw of Manteo (center). Selected (for related subdivision) presumably for its allure and attractiveness and possibly because adjacent to Fort Raleigh National Historic Site; no point here named Heritage historically.

Hermitage Island, former small island, Currituck County, Fruitville Township (Fry et al. 1775). Just s of former Currituck Inlet at n end Currituck Banks. Appeared on only a few early maps (including Comberford 1657) because it disappeared early 18th century. Meaning of the name's application is unknown, and limited colonial usage precludes anyone remembering. Probably (especially noting years used) referenced remoteness, one definition of the word. Additionally, Warxes (without generic) appears on five maps: Gascoyne 1682; Thornton & Fisher (1685), Thornton and Verner (1689); Moll 1708; and DeLisle 1718. Appears applied to this particular island (area) specifically. Term is unknown and not defined anywhere and is clearly Warxes on each map, though later maps might simply have copied from an earlier map. One might speculate a peculiar rendition of "marshes." Only similar spelling is *warze*, German for wart or nipple and might have been applied as was Dugs (q.v.), but no maps displaying the term used German, so use remains unknown. Old German *wangz*, which became *wang* in Old English, meaning field or meadow, does not fit here. Term appears as proto-Germanic for sort of cluttered and boils, might have applied to maze of large dunes here, but a stretch especially since not known to be used similarly elsewhere. Sporadic undocumented reference to *warxe* being dialectical Old English pronunciation of "wax," seemingly no relationship here unless possibly stand of wax myrtles (*Myrica* spp.). Some credence might be afforded to stand of wax myrtles since U.S. Coast Chart (C&GS 1852) "might" label this area as A. Baum's Waxer or Waxers (so it appears) Stand, Land, or Island—the annotation is handwritten and barely discernable. However, symbol refers to vegetation not hachures for sand dunes. No such label found on other maps. Old English *waroe* from original German *wareaz* meaning shore or beach seems plausible, still not used elsewhere in area on any historical maps. Balash (2008, 54) lists Warxes Island but provides no additional information and is the only known contemporary source to mention "warxes"; adding "island" to Warxes was apparently presumptive as no reason is given. *Other names:* Isle de l'Hermitage (Nolin 1783), Warxes (Island) (e.g., Gascoyne 1682).

Herring Beach. *See* Whalehead Beach (subdivision).

Herring Cove, cove, Currituck County, Fruitville Township (F&WS 1999, map). At s-central Runnels Marshes at n end Fresh Pond Bay

1.7 mi. e of Knotts Island (village). Herring (*Clupea harengus*) are found in large "schools" (shoals) off the Atlantic coast of North America. Of note, "school" used in this manner is not correct—"shoal" is correct term (fish congregate at shoals to feed), but through misuse, school of fish emerged.

Herring Gull Canal, small canal, Dare County, Atlantic Township (Town of Southern Shores 2015). In Southern Shores just e from Great Blue Heron Canal, 4.8 mi. n of original Kitty Hawk. Names of Southern Shores canals are for shorebirds (except Gravey Pond Canal). Herring gull (*Larus argentatus*) is at the Outer Banks year-round.

Herring Shoal Island, marsh island, 0.6 mi. long, Dare County, Nags Head Township (USGS 2013: Oregon Inlet). In Roanoke Sound 2 mi. e of Duck Island, 5 mi. se of Wanchese. Divided into lots known (presently) as Hale Division subdivision. *See* Herring Gull Island. *Other names:* Herring Shoal (from NPS Director Conrad Wirth, letter in *Coastland Times*, October 27, 1952, in NPS 2005b: NPS 1, 587).

Hickory Ridge, distinct sand ridge, 1.5 mi. long, Dare County, Atlantic Township (Harris 2017). In s Kitty Hawk just e of Duck Pond Ridge, 3.2 mi. s of Southern Shores. Hickory Ridge has been used sporadically since mid-18th century in deeds, but references are not specific. Some confusion surrounding application of the name Hickory Ridge (*see* next entries). Harris, noted Kitty Hawk historian, places the name at this location, as do many residents. However, the GIS system of Dare County government records subdivision Hickory Ridge along Ridge Road, which might imply Hickory Ridge at that location. Unclear if both of these ridges are known as Hickory Ridge or one is in error or feature at subdivision resulting from reversed usage, natural feature acquiring name of man-made feature, such as a subdivision (little restriction is placed on naming subdivisions). Harris has completed detailed field investigation here. Further, ridge at subdivision Hickory Ridge is locally known simply as The Ridge. So, both entries are included for informational purposes. Inclination, based on investigation, location, and application of Hickory Ridge Gut, is to recognize this location as Hickory Ridge, as presented by Harris, with the location at subdivision named Hickory Ridge to be at

what is often referenced locally as The Ridge. *See* Kitty Hawk ridge-and-swale system. *Other names:* Hickery Ridge (Currituck DB 2, 1773, 377).

Hickory Ridge, vegetated sand ridge, 1 mi. long, Dare County, Atlantic Township (local use). On nw Colington Island, extending e-w from s of Blount Bay almost to Rhodoms Point, at least five separate peaks, e-most largest and highest at 45 ft. Some alteration for subdivision development.

Hickory Ridge, sand ridge, 1 mi. long, Dare County, Atlantic Township (Dare County GIS 2017—implied). Trends n-s 1.2 mi. n of Kitty Hawk Landing subdivision, 2 mi. wnw of original Kitty Hawk. The name Hickory Ridge has been used sporadically since mid-18th century in deeds, but references are not specific. Harris (2017) labels this ridge Methodist Road Ridge but provides no further information. Dare County tax records record subdivision Hickory Ridge at n end of this ridge, which implies the name of the ridge as Hickory Ridge (little restriction is placed on naming subdivisions). Reference in Currituck DB 9 (1808, 368) is to Methedus (*sic*) Road, but exact location not provided. Also reference in Currituck DB 10 (1808, 101) to Methodist Road, but again no specific location. This could be the former name of Ridge Road. Road name now is Ridge Road and could have morphed from Methodist Road to Ridge Road, but name Methodist Road Ridge is unknown by anyone. First Methodist Church in Kitty Hawk was not est. until 1858 (Wescott 1958), but is only listed as "in the center of a 4-acre field owned by Elijah Sibborn, presently [1958] the 'B. F. Perry homesite.'" According to Dare County tax records numerous families with surname Perry here with land near Ridge Road, so this could have been what Harris indicated as Methodist Road. The present Methodist Church site was acquired 1887 nearer to the location in the entry above listed. So, both entries are included for informational purposes (*see* previous entries). Inclination, based on investigation, is to recognize this location more as The Ridge, with the location as presented by Harris to be Hickory Ridge. *See* Kitty Hawk ridge-and-swale system. *Other names:* Methodist Road Ridge (Harris 2017), The Ridge (some local use).

Hickory Ridge Gut, tidal stream, 1 mi. long,

Dare County, Atlantic Township (local use). In Kitty Hawk ridge-and-swale system (q.v.) just w of Hickory Ridge just w of original Kitty Hawk to n Kitty Hawk Bay 3 mi. n of Colington (community). Associative with Hickory Ridge and used since 18th century. *See* two separate entries for Hickory Ridge (ridge) and Alligator Gut. *Other names:* Hickery Ridge Gut (Currituck DB 4, 1783, 229–30), Hickley Ridge Gut (Currituck DB 5, 1787, 276), Hickory Ridge Gutt (early deeds, some maps reflecting early spelling "gutt"), Hickrey Ridge Gutt (Currituck DB 1819, 41, 43), Hickry Rige Gut (Currituck DB 5, 1783, 229).

Hicks Bay, small bay, Currituck County, Poplar Branch Township (local use). Soundside just ne of Pettys Pond just w of s Pine Island subdivision, 5.5 mi. n of Duck. Local disagreement to which features the names Hicks Bay, Cottage Cove, and Longfellow Cove apply, each in close proximity. The applications here presented are most preferred.

Hicks Bay. *See* Beasley Bay.

Hicks Creek, narrow tidal water passage, Currituck County, Poplar Branch Township (C&GS 1852). Trends nw-se, separates Hicks Island from Porpoise Marsh 4.2 mi. ssw of Corolla.

Hicks Island, island, Currituck County, Poplar Branch Township (C&GS 1852). Just sw of Porpoise Marsh separated from Porpoise Marsh by Hicks Creek 5.2 mi. ssw of Corolla. *Other names:* Loan Oak Island (Currituck DB 5, 1787, 298–99—name meant is Lone Oak Island, adjacent to Lone Oak Channel).

Hidden Dune, sand dune, 35 ft. high, Currituck County, Fruitville Township (local use and street sign). Descriptive term for highest and n of two dunes of Parkers Ridge (q.v.) just nnw of Pennys Hill, 11 mi. n of Corolla.

High Bridge Creek (High Ridge Creek), stream, Dare County, Atlantic Township (Town of Kitty Hawk 2007). Began just s of US 158, flowed s to Northern Gut 1.5 mi. wsw of original Kitty Hawk. Usage and application on the 2007 Kitty Hawk zoning map along the stream from US 158 s to a point just s of Midgetts Pond, where it becomes Northern Gut. N portion on same zoning map uses Ginguite Creek (*sic*) in parentheses on a portion of this stream just s of US 158. This application is in response to Jeanguite Creek being extended s on what is High Bridge

(Ridge) Creek. Additionally, following is found without explanation: "For regulatory purposes, High Bridge Creek is called Jean Guite Creek" (N.C. Division of Coastal Management 1998, 26). This might explain why new editions of USGS topographic map extend Jeanguite Creek from n of US 158 (original and historical application) s through Kitty Hawk ridge-and-swale system (q.v.) nw and w of original Kitty Hawk.

Some use has also been for High Ridge Creek. Easy to associate this stream with nearby High Ridge (just w of here) yielding High Ridge Creek, but the original name is High Bridge Creek (as displayed in Town of Kitty Hawk 2007; N.C. Division of Coastal Management 1998). According to Currituck Register of Deeds (DB 1795, 7, 200–201— area in Currituck County until 1870 when Dare County created), a "high bridge" here, mentioned in numerous other deeds. The bridge was a covered bridge, corroborated by a road originally named Covered Bridge Road here, though only remnants of this road remain. A repaired and enhanced version of the original bridge exists (no motorized traffic). Over years, especially after the bridge no longer existed, name gradually became (to some) High Ridge Creek because sand ridge w nearby named High Ridge and bridge no longer used because in disrepair. *Other names:* High Bridge Gut (Harris 2017; 1877, source unknown), High Ridge Creek (some local use).

High Dune, sand dune, 25 ft. high, Currituck County, Poplar Branch Township (local use). In n Ocean Hill subdivision just sw of ramp to beach route NC 12, 1 mi. n of Corolla. Former outlier n of Jones Hill before development of Ocean Hill subdivision, remnant of former high dunes just n of Corolla.

High Dune, distinct sand dune, 30 ft. high, Dare County, Atlantic Township (local use). In Southern Shores 3 mi. n of original Kitty Hawk. Used since establishment of Southern Shores (1947). Some consider this a single dune, but sometimes application extended 0.7 mi. s encompassing two additional sand peaks.

High Hill, sand dune, 10 ft. high, Carteret County, Harkers Island Township (USGS 2013: Harkers Island). On Shackleford Banks 3.7 mi. sw of Harkers Island (village).

High Hill Creek. *See* Long Point Creek.

High Hills, The, sand dunes, 25 ft. high, Carteret County, Portsmouth Township (local use). Is 4.2 mi. n of Drum Inlet (Old Drum Inlet) 4.6 mi. e of Atlantic (mainland). Descriptive, used especially on Core Banks to indicate dunes were never awash and used as landmarks.

High Hills, The, former sand dunes, 0.5 mi. wide, Carteret County, Portsmouth Township (USGS 1950: Portsmouth—still labeled). On Portsmouth Island just ne of High Hills Inlet (Whalebone Inlet), 4.4 mi. sw of Portsmouth (village). Much lower than historically, some hills indicated by the name are gone. Names The High Hills and Whalebone Hills used interchangeably; same with adjacent inlet, High Hills Inlet and Whalebone Inlet. *Other names:* High Hills (NPS 2018), Whalebone Hills (local use with The High Hills).

High Hills, hummocks, 0.2 mi. wide, Carteret County, Smyrna Township (USGS 2013: Harkers Island). Two hummocks, marsh islands in Core Sound just e of Great Shoal 4.6 mi. s of Davis (mainland). *See* Black Hammock.

High Hills Inlet, former water passage, 0.7 mi. long, Carteret County, Portsmouth Township (USGS 1950: Portsmouth). Was in Core Sound, separated The High Hills on Portsmouth Island from Whalebone Island, 10 mi. sw of Ocracoke (village). Opened 1865 and closed just after 1915; reopened 1942 and closed again early 1961. Secondary usage was for variant name Whalebone Inlet (also labeled USGS 1950: Portsmouth). Local use, meaning knowledgeable folk from Ocracoke (Portsmouth now abandoned), is for High Hills Inlet, though now closed. *Other names:* Crab Gut Inlet (Wimble 1733), Crab Inlet (Wimble 1738), Crab Slough (Wimble 1733, introduction), Drum Inlet (misapplication), High Hill Inlet (Powell 1968), Old Whale Bone Inlet (Whisnant and Whisnant 2010, map, 490), Onoconon Inlet (misapplied from Ocracoke Inlet), Three Hats Creek (vague 18th-century references and general reference Stick 1958—Three Hats Shoal 4 mi. n), Three Hat Creek (some usage, probably channel name approaching High Hills Inlet from Three Hats Shoal—C&GS 1866), Whalebone Inlet (limited use), Whale Bone Inlet (Rand McNally 1890), Wococon Inlet (Cobb 1905 and Austin 1984).

High Point of Hills, sand dune, 50 ft. high, Dare County, Hatteras Township (historical local use). Landmark on ne Great Ridge on Hatteras Island just nw of Creeds Hill, 4.5 mi. s of Buxton.

High Ridge, sand ridge, 2.5 mi. long, Dare County, Atlantic Township (Town of Kitty Hawk 2007; Currituck DB 6, 1792, 292). Trends n-s 1.5 mi. w of original Kitty Hawk. *See* Kitty Hawk ridge-and-swale system.

High Ridge Point, pronounced point, Dare County, Atlantic Township (diminished use since 20th century). S terminus High Ridge, 2 mi. wsw of original Kitty Hawk.

High Ridge Pond, lake, Dare County, Atlantic Township (local use). In marsh just n of Stone Island, 2.1 mi. sw of original Kitty Hawk.

High Sand Dune, sand dune, Currituck County, Poplar Branch Township (local use). N-most of Three Dunes (q.v.) in The Hammocks subdivision, 1 mi. sw of Ocean Lakes (subdivision—Ocean Sands part), 5.3 mi. s of Corolla. Recent descriptive application. This dune with other two dunes make up Three Dunes (used since 1700s), considerably altered by building golf course. *Other names:* High Dune (local use).

High Tor. *See* Frisco Dune.

Hillcrest Beach, beach, Dare County, Atlantic Township (signage). In Southern Shores 5 mi. n of original Kitty Hawk.

Hillcrest Overlook, hill, 40 ft. high, Dare County, Atlantic Township (local use). High point of a sand ridge in Southern Shores along which Hillcrest Drive travels 4 mi. n of original Kitty Hawk.

Hillcrest Ponds, ponds, each 0.1 mi. long, Dare County, Atlantic Township (local use). Two linear e-w trending ponds on n and s sides of Hillcrest Avenue in Southern Shores (town) between NC 12 and beach.

Hill of the Wreck, sand dune, Dare County, Atlantic Township (Letter, Orville Wright, 1900, from Stick 1958, 200). Represents third and fourth dunes (40 ft. and 35 ft. respectively) n-s in Bald Sand Hills (q.v.) 1 mi. sse of original Kitty Hawk. Wright brothers' first camp (1900) just n of this dune before establishing a more permanent camp just n of Kill Devil Hill (hill) where memorial is today. In a letter to his sister, Orville Wright mentions this hill was just s of their first camp and was originally known (locally) as Lookout Hill, but "is now known as Hill of the Wreck." Neither Hill of the Wreck nor

Lookout Hill appears on source materials historical or extant, so to which wreck the name refers is unknown (in the immediate vicinity before the Wright Brothers arrived were wrecks of Bladen McLaughlin 1853, Luola Murchison 1883, and Augustus Moore 1851—Charlet 2020, 214, 235, 235). Two dunes are connected by a saddle or low area, and not as prominent as historically, altered by development. They are third and fourth dunes s-ward in Bald Sand Hills (q.v.). *Other names:* Lookout Hill (Letter, Orville Wright, 1900, from Stick 1958, 200).

Hills, The, area, Dare County, Kinnakeet Township (NPS 2005b: NPS 1, 166). E part (not beachside) of original Avon 6.2 mi. n of Buxton.

Hills, **The**, sand dunes, Dare County, Kinnakeet Township (historical local use). Short unconnected sand dunes between marsh of original Avon and beach 6.2 mi. n of Buxton. Prominent until early 1970s, today almost nonexistent from development.

Hobbs Marsh, marsh, Currituck County, Poplar Branch Township (C&GS 1852). On Currituck Banks 1 mi. nw of Three Dunes, 5.5 mi. s of Corolla. Hobbs Marsh and Upper Hobbs Marsh named for local 19th-century landowner whose house was just e of Upper Hobbs Marsh.

Hodges Reef, shoal, 1 mi. long, Carteret County, Portsmouth Township (USGS 2013: Wainwright Island Overedge North, Wainwright Island). In Pamlico Sound 3.5 mi. ne of Chain Shot Island, 11.3 mi. sw of Ocracoke (village). "Reef" in Outer Banks geographic names usually refers to oyster colonies.

Hoffman Beach, beach, 0.5 mi. long, Carteret County, Morehead Township (local use). Between Pine Knoll Shores (e) and Salter path (w). Named for Alice Hoffman (*see* Pine Knoll Shores), who sued the residents of Salter Path because their livestock were roaming freely (practiced on the Outer Banks well into 20th century) onto her property, which led to a legal ruling. The "Bankers" argued that, while they held no deeds, they had occupied the land for centuries. The ruling allowed people of Salter Path to "live and fish in perpetuum" at this site provided they remove no trees and do not build oceanside. The ruling remained until 1979 when residents at Salter Path were given

title to the land they occupied. Sometimes the name Judgement Beach is used locally in a whimsical manner. Subdivision by this name here. *Other names:* Judgement Beach (historical local use).

Hoffman Canal, canal, Carteret County, Morehead Township (PKS 2016). W entrance to Pine Knoll Waterway in Pine Knoll Shores, 5 mi. w of Atlantic Beach. Named for Alice Hoffman (*see* Pine Knoll Shores), owner of all property that eventually became Pine Knoll Shores. E entrance was named for McNeill (Roosevelt heirs' attorney) and w entrance named for Alice Hoffman, but e entrance is closer to her original house.

Hog Creek, water passage, 0.4 mi. long, Currituck County, Poplar Branch Township (local use). Connects Baums Creek to Pine Island Bay, 6.3 mi. nw of Duck.

Hog Hill, small hill, Carteret County, Morehead Township (local use). At Hog Hill Creek between Pine Knoll Shores and Atlantic Beach 2.5 mi. from each. Originally large stand of hickory (*Carya* spp.) and live oak (*Quercus virginiana*) trees produced nuts attracting free-roaming animals, especially hogs (Zaenker 2014) *Other names:* Hogs Hill (spoken use).

Hog Hill Creek, small stream, Carteret County, Morehead Township (Stanford 2015, 35). Empties into Hoop Pole Creek, 2 mi. e of Pine Knoll Shores. *Other names:* Needlerush Bay (late local reference from nearby subdivision—needlerush or black rush [*Juncus roemerianus*, type of grass prevalent along se U.S. coast), Smiths Creek (CS 1855).

Hog Island, island, 2 mi. long, Carteret County, Cedar Island Township (NOS Charts). Separates Cedar Island Bay and Back Bay 2 mi. e of Cedar Island Ferry landing, 12.2 mi. sw of Ocracoke (village). Applied to two marsh islands known as East Hog Island and West Hog Island. O'Neal et al. (1976, 43) indicates former community Lupton was on Hog Island, but no additional locative information provided. All other sources indicate location se Cedar Island (not in gazetteer) just nw of Lola, and labeled there on USGS 2013: Atlantic, Lupton Cemetery also labeled. *Other names:* East Hog Island (in part—local use), West Hog Island (in part—local use).

Hog Island, former small isolated marsh island, Currituck County, Poplar Branch Township (CS 1862a). In Currituck Sound just w of Peters

Quarter just n of Mossey Islands complex, 4 mi. s of Corolla. Disappeared by early 20th century. *Other names:* Hogg Island (Codman, Crowninshield, and Lawrence 1925).

Hog Island, island, 0.1 mi. wide, Dare County, Atlantic Township (USGS 2013: Kitty Hawk). In nw portion Kitty Hawk Bay 1.7 mi. sw of original Kitty Hawk. *Other names:* Little Hog Island (sometimes used when Hog Island applied to Middle Island), Rush Island (probably for common rush [*Juncus effuses*], plant native to much of U.S. and the Outer Banks, though term is used sparingly mostly on s Outer Banks).

Hog Island, marsh island, 0.1 mi. long, 0.05 mi. wide, Dare County, Kinnakeet Township (USGS 2013: Pea Island). Is 0.3 mi. nnw of Cedar Hammock, 5.2 mi. nnw of Rodanthe.

Hog Island, island, 0.5 mi. wide, Dare County, Nags Head Township (USGS 2013: Wanchese, Oregon Inlet). Just s of Roanoke Island 2.2 mi. s of Wanchese.

Hog Island, island, 0.3 mi. long and wide, Hyde County, Lake Landing Township (NOS 2014i). In Pamlico Sound just se of mainland, 2 mi. sw of Gull Rocks, 18 mi. n of Ocracoke (village).

Hog Island Bay. *See* Cedar Island Bay.

Hog Island Creek, water passage, 0.7 mi. long, Dare County, Nags Head Township (USGS 2013: Wanchese). Trends n-s, separates unnamed marsh island from Hog Island, 2.2 mi. sse of Wanchese. *Other names:* Hog Island Bay.

Hog Island Narrows, water passage, 0.3 mi. long, Carteret County, Cedar Island Township (USGS 2013: Atlantic). Separates Hog Island from irregularly shaped ne portion Cedar Island 2 mi. e of Cedar Island Ferry landing, 12.8 mi. sw of Ocracoke (village).

Hog Island Point, point, Carteret County, Cedar Island Township (USGS 2013: Atlantic). Extreme s point of Hog Island 2 mi. e of Cedar Island Ferry landing, 12.1 mi. sw of Ocracoke (village).

Hog Island Reef, shoal, Carteret County, Cedar Island Township (USGS 2013: Wainwright Island Overedge North). In n Core Sound just sw of Kingfish Shoal, 20 mi. sw of Ocracoke (village). "Reef" in Outer Banks geographic names usually refers to oyster colonies.

Hog Islands, island complex, 1 mi. long, Currituck County, Poplar Branch Township (USGS 2013: Mossey Islands). N-s complex

of 8–10 marsh islands in Beasley Bay just w of Currituck Banks, 2 mi. s of Three Dunes, 6.8 mi. s of Corolla. Made up of the following named (and some unnamed) islands (*see* each individual entry): Long Hog Island, South Hog Island, North Hog Island, Pig Island (no longer exists), Calf Island (no longer exists), Steer Island, and Bush Island (Bull Island). Obvious theme naming these islands, and why Bush Island was originally Bull Island but changed over the years. *Other names:* Hog Island (occasional misapplication to entire complex by commercial maps).

Hog Island Shoal, small shoal, Hyde County, Lake Landing Township (C&GS 1985). Trends e then se from Hog Island 2 mi. sw of Gull Rocks, 17 mi. n of Ocracoke (village).

Hogpen Bay, cove, 0.7 mi. long, 0.5 mi. wide, Carteret County, Smyrna Township (USGS 2013: Horsepen Point). Shallows (remnants of Old Drum Inlet [q.v.]) at entrance Caggs Creek 4.2 mi. e of Harkers Island (village).

Hogpen Island, small island, Currituck County, Poplar Branch Township (unknown, ca. 1900). Just sw of South Burris Island in Burris Islands (q.v.) complex, 7.5 mi. s of Corolla.

Hog Pen Knole, former hummock, Currituck County, Fruitville Township (Currituck DB 13, 1814, 105–6). Was probably just as Indian Creek exits Indian Pond, only place today with a small hummock on w side of the creek 2 mi. sw of Knotts Island (village)—deed indicates "on the w part of the creek"—though topography could change considerably in almost 200 years and probably no longer exists. "Knole" is an earlier spelling of "knoll". *Other names:* Pig Pen Knole (Currituck DB 13, 1814, 105–6).

Hog Pen Point, point, Currituck County, Fruitville Township (local F&WS informants). Reportedly just se of Live Oak Point on sw Mackay Island 4 mi. wsw of Knotts Island (village). Confusion exists whether this is correct location from conflicting descriptions given; this is the most prevalent location, and Hog Pen Point Road generally follows Long Dike. Many consider the entire sw tip of Mackay Island to be Live Oak Point, though there are two distinct points.

Hog Pen Pond, small cove, Currituck County, Poplar Branch Township (local use). Just s of Narrows Island, just n of Neals Creek, 8 mi. sw of Corolla.

Hog Point, point, Dare County, Atlantic Township (local use). Just w of Grants Cove on n shore Kitty Hawk Bay, 1.6 mi. sw of original Kitty Hawk.

Hog Quarter Flats, large open water, Currituck County, Poplar Branch Township; and Dare County, Atlantic Township (local use). In Currituck Sound, shallow relatively even depth (3–6 ft.), 1.7 mi. e of mainland, 1.7 mi. w of the barrier island (Southern Shores). Associative with several names using Hog Quarter on mainland. "Flat" is used throughout se U.S. coastal areas to indicate open water of relatively even depth (usually shallow), and without much turbulence except in storms. *See* Hunting Quarter.

Hog Shoal, former small shoal, Carteret County, Portsmouth Township (Williamson 1992, 96). Reportedly just w of Wallace Channel, 2 mi. ene of former Portsmouth Lifesaving Station at Portsmouth (village). Weslager (1954, 45) indicates named because hogs found stranded here.

Hole, The, small deep, Dare County, Hatteras Township (local use). Oceanside near s end Hatteras Island, 2 mi. s of Hatteras (village), 3 mi. ne of Hatteras Inlet. Not well known, used sparingly by older local residents and fishermen.

Hole, The, open water, Hyde County, Ocracoke Township (Moseley 1737). Referenced open water between Ocracoke Island and shoals in Pamlico Sound just offshore from Ocracoke Island from Old Hatteras Inlet to Ocracoke (village). Found used on a few maps early 18th century, most notably Moseley's 1737 map.

Hole in the Wall, former small swash, Currituck County, Poplar Branch Township (C&GS 1852). Overwash at high water was on shoal connecting South Burris Island and Middle Burris Islands (one island then) 6.2 mi. s of Corolla. Descriptive middle to late 19th century and now small swash (overwash) on narrow isthmus connecting South Burris Island and Middle Burris Islands.

Holiday Marina, former harbor, Dare County, Atlantic Township (Downing 2013, 109). Was soundside in Kill Devil Hills (town) just s of More Shore 2 mi. s of original Kitty Hawk. Used for 30 years mid-1950s to mid-1980s, though during the later years more an entertainment venue.

Holly Hills. *See* Etheridges Hills.

Holly Point. *See* Archer Point.

Holly Ridge, former small sand ridge, Dare County, Nags Head Township (local use). On n Roanoke Island just s of Lost Colony Visitor Center, 2 mi. nw of Manteo (center). Rarely used, almost completely obliterated by housing development, which prompted application and limited use of this name.

Holy Island, island, Currituck County, Poplar Branch Township (Codman, Crowninshield, and Lawrence 1925). Trends e-sw just w of Currituck Banks, separates Jenkins Cove (n) from Ships Bay (s), 2 mi. nw of Corolla. Exact name origin unknown, though most agree a transcribing error of holly. *Other names:* Southeast Island (N.C. Wildlife Resources Commission 2016b).

Home Marsh, marsh, Currituck County, Poplar Branch Township (unknown, ca. 1900). Just w of Narrows Island separated from Narrows Island by Little Narrows, 6.8 mi. sw of Corolla.

Homers Point, point, Carteret County, Morehead Township (local use). Soundside in Salter Path just se of Sam Smiths Point, 4.5 mi. w of Pine Knoll Shores.

Homers Point Marina, harbor, Carteret County, Morehead Township (signage). At Homers Point in Salter Path, 4.4 mi. w of Pine Knoll Shores.

Homicky Land, historical reference. Rodanthe area (Chicamacomico) on n Hatteras Island and s Pea Island (Wimble 1733). Used earlier referring to hills or dunes and still sometimes used as a geological or geographical reference. "Homick" or "hommock" were variations of "hummock" and "hammock," terms still used widely referring to high places in sandy areas or in water; the name was applied and used accordingly on Wimble's 1733 map (notorious for unconventional orthography).

Hookers Field, former open area, Dare County, Nags Head Township (historical local use). Was on sw Roanoke Island, 0.8 mi. w of Wanchese.

Hookers Landing, former landing, Dare County, Nags Head Township (historical local use). Was at sw Roanoke Island, 1.1 mi. w of Wanchese. *Other names:* Old Wharf (road sign).

Hoop Pole Bay, bay, Carteret County, Morehead Township (Zaenker 2014). Just e of Bogue

View Shores subdivision just sw of Hoop Pole Creek, se portion contains remnants of Cheeseman Inlet, 1.5 mi. w of Atlantic Beach. Use of variant name Coral Bay is recent and mostly by tourists because some features here use Coral Bay (no coral here—not referring to *Lophelia* cold-water coral 100 mi. s); however, the name is Hoop Pole Bay (though some usage for extending Hoop Pole Creek into this bay). *See* Hoop Pole Creek and Coral Ridge (sand ridge). *Other names:* Coral Bay (some recent local use), Hoop Pole Creek (Town of Atlantic Beach 2016), Hoop Pole Creek Cove (Carteret County GIS 2019).

Hoop Pole Channel, channel, 0.3 mi. long, Carteret County, Morehead Township (Carteret County GIS 2019). Trends n-s connecting Hoop Pole Bay to Bogue Shores Channel (w end) and Hoop Pole Creek (sw end), 1.7 mi. w of Atlantic Beach (town).

Hoop Pole Creek, water passage, 1 mi. long, Carteret County, Morehead Township (USGS 2013: Mansfield). Into Bogue Sound from embayment w of Hog Hill Creek (some consider this embayment, Hoop Pole Basin, as separate feature) 1.3 mi. w of Atlantic Beach. Hoop pole, slender length of green sapling wood used for barrel hoops, was apparently relevant here. Site of a former prehistoric inlet (prehistoric inlet, meaning pre-European; these names are not included in this study) named Atlantic Beach Inlet (Fisher 1962, 33). *See* Coral Ridge (sand ridge). *Other names:* Coral Bay (some creeping usage by tourists, numerous features using Coral Bay here), Hoop Hole (presumed misinterpretation), Hoophole Creek (transcribing error), Hoop Hole Creek (misinterpretation created by historical sign marker, corrected 2015), Hoople Creek (misinterpretation), Hoopole Creek (original deed conveying area to Lowenberg brothers 1866, in Zaenker 2014), Hoop Pole (local use), Hoop Hole Basin (Zaenker 2014), Hoop Hole Creek (Stephens 1984, 6), Hoop-pole Creek (local written use).

Hoop Pole Creek (Hoop Hole Creek), community, Carteret County, Morehead Township (Stephens 1984, 6). Was located at Frosts Point at Hoop Pole Creek 1.5 mi. e of Atlantic Beach, 3 mi. w of Pine Knoll Shores. Stephens (1984) mentions former community only as Hoop Hole Creek,

presenting this as original name, though all other documentation records Hoop Pole for the creek. *Other names:* Bogue Banks (sporadic early 1900s use).

Hoop Pole Landing, landing, Carteret County, Morehead Township (USGS 2013: Mansfield). Soundside of Bogue Banks at Hoop Pole Woods 3.9 mi. w of Atlantic Beach. *See* Hoop Pole Creek.

Hoop Pole Lands (Hoop Hole Lands), area, Carteret County, Morehead Township (Stephens 1984, 141). Named large tract of land (almost 800 acres) around Hoop Pole Creek 2 mi. w of Pine Knoll Shores (Stephens consistently uses Hoop Hole).

Hoop Pole Point, point, Carteret County, Morehead Township (local use). On n shore Hoop Pole Bay 2.5 mi. e of Pine Knoll Shores. *See* Hoop Pole Creek.

Hoop Pole Tract, area, Carteret County, Morehead Township (PKS 2016). Was mostly what is now Bogue View Shores subdivision and Crystal Coast Country Club Golf Course. W boundary was at Yaupon Point (to ocean), e boundary was 1 mi. e at w end Hoop Pole Bay (PKS 2016). Was one of three parcels purchased by Alice Hoffman (*see* Pine Knoll Shores). Associative for features here, named Hoop Pole. *See* Hoop Pole Creek.

Hoop Pole Woods, woods, 10 mi. long, Carteret County, Morehead Township (USGS 1994: Mansfield). On Bogue Banks, 4 mi. w of Atlantic Beach. *See* Hoop Pole Creek. *Other names:* Hoop-pole Wood (locally written), Hoop-pole Woods (local written use), Piney Woods (nonlocal 19th century references).

Hopey Anns Hill, sand dune, 0.5 mi. long, 25 ft. high, Carteret County, Morehead Township (Zaenker 2014). Just w of Indian Beach (town), 3.2 mi. e of original Emerald Isle. *See* Hopey Anns Hill (former settlement). *Other names:* Aunt Hopey Ann Hill (Stephens 1984, map back cover).

Hopey Anns Hill, former settlement, Carteret County, Morehead Township (Stephens 1984, 5). Just n of large dune with same name 2 mi. w of Salter Path. Both dune and former community named for Hopey Ann Guthrie when she and her husband moved from Shackleford Banks in 1860s. As with small communities w of Salter Path, families eventually moved to Salter Path by early 20th century for various reasons. *See* Bogue

Banks historical communities. *Other names:* Hopey Ann Hill (Stephens 2007).

Hoppers Hideaway, cove, Carteret County, Morehead Township (PKS 2016). Centrally in w (completed 1971) Pine Knoll Waterway in Pine Knoll Shores, 4.7 mi. w of Atlantic Beach. Named for Harry Hopper, worked with the Roosevelt family developing the property.

Horsebone, small water passage, 0.4 mi. long, Currituck County, Poplar Branch Township (USGS 2013: Jarvisburg). Between two unnamed marsh islands just se of Goat Island Bay, 1.7 mi. w of Currituck Banks, 6.5 mi. nw of Duck. *See* Bay Tree.

Horse Island, island, 0.2 mi. long, Carteret County, Atlantic Township (USGS 2013: Atlantic). In Core Sound 0.2 mi. w of Core Banks, 3.6 mi. e of Atlantic (mainland). *See* Horsepen Creek (Hyde County).

Horse Island, island, 0.8 mi. long, Carteret County, Beaufort Township (USGS 2013: Beaufort). In Back Sound, 4.6 mi. e of Harkers Island (village). *See* Horsepen Creek (Hyde County).

Horse Island, marsh island, 1 mi. long, 0.6 mi. wide, Carteret County, Davis Township (USGS 2013: Davis). In Core Sound separated from Core Banks by Horse Island Creek, 3.6 mi. e of Davis (mainland). *See* Horsepen Creek (Hyde County). *Other names:* Johnsons Hammock (Williamson 1992, 165).

Horse Island, island, 0.05 mi. long, Carteret County, Harkers Island Township (USGS 2013: Harkers Island). In Core Sound 3.5 mi. se of Harkers Island. *See* Horsepen Creek (Hyde County).

Horse Island, irregular marsh island, 0.4 mi. long, Carteret County, Smyrna Township (USGS 2013: Horsepen Point). In Core Sound separated from Core Banks by Lewis Creek 5.3 mi. e of Harkers Island (village). *See* Horsepen Creek (Hyde County) and Horse Point (Smyrna Township).

Horse Island, small marsh island, Currituck County, Poplar Branch Township (local use). In Currituck Sound, on w edge Pine Islands complex, 0.6 mi. nw of Pine Island Bay, 5.3 mi. nnw of Duck.

Horse Island, former island, Dare County, Nags Head Township (C&GS 1877). Was in Roanoke Sound 1 mi. w of Whalebone Junction. Was just w of Cedar Island and over years joined Cedar Island.

Horse Island Bay. *See* The Swash.

Horse Island Channel, channel, 4 mi. long, Carteret County, Atlantic Township (N.C. Fisheries 1923, 25). Trends nw-se across Core Sound from Barry Bay (mainland) and Thorofare Bay (mainland), separates Dump Island from Horse Island just n of Drum Inlet (Old Drum Inlet).

Horse Island Channel, former channel, 2 mi. long, Carteret County, Portsmouth Township (USGS 1950: Portsmouth). Ocracoke Inlet just e of Portsmouth (village) to Haulover Point just se of Casey Island 4.2 mi. sw of Ocracoke (village). *Other names:* Brant Shoal Channel (*see* Brant Island, Pamlico County).

Horse Island Cove, cove, 0.1 mi. long, 0.05 mi. wide, Carteret County, Davis Township (USGS 2013: Davis). In Core Sound at nw portion Horse Island 3.4 mi. e of Davis (mainland). *See* Horsepen Creek (Hyde County).

Horse Island Creek, water passage, 0.5 mi. long, Carteret County, Davis Township (USGS 2013: Davis). In Core Sound, trends ne-sw separating Horse Island from Core Banks connecting The Swash and Great Island Creek, 4.7 mi. ese of Davis (mainland). *See* Horsepen Creek (Hyde County). *Other names:* Beach Creek (Piggott 1894b), Horse Island Slough (Williamson 1992, 150).

Horse Island Creek. *See* Carrot Island Channel.

Horse Island Point, point, Carteret County, Davis Township (USGS 2013: Davis). N point Horse Island 3.6 mi. e of Davis (mainland). *See* Horsepen Creek (Hyde County).

Horse Islands, former islands, Dare County, Nags Head Township (historical maps). Were in Roanoke Sound just w of Whalebone Junction, 4 mi. s of central Nags Head. Originally four or five islands here now joined into one island known as Cedar Island.

Horse Marsh, islands, 0.4 mi. wide, Carteret County, Harkers Island Township (USGS 1997: Harkers Island). Junction of North River and The Straits 2.3 mi. nw of Harkers Island (village).

Horse Pen Cove, cove, Dare County, Kinnakeet Township (Currituck DB 7, 1791, 157). In South'ard Water (q.v.) complex or just n of it since associated with Deep Creek (Dare County) just w of Askins Hill 2 mi. s of original Avon. *See* Horsepen Creek (Hyde County).

Horsepen Creek, cove, 0.2 mi. long, Carteret County, Atlantic Township (USGS 1951: Styron Bay). In Core Sound 2.9 mi. s of Atlantic (mainland). *See* Horsepen Creek (Hyde County) and Horse Point (Smyrna Township). *Other names:* Horse Pen Creek (local written use).

Horsepen Creek, water passage, 0.9 mi. long, Carteret County, Smyrna Township (USGS 2013: Horsepen Point). Separates Core Banks from unnamed marsh in Core Sound 4.8 mi. s of Davis (mainland). *See* Horsepen Creek (Hyde County) and Horse Point (Smyrna Township). *Other names:* Horse Pen Creek (local written use).

Horsepen Creek, small linear cove, Hyde County, Ocracoke Township (local use). At Horsepen Point in Ocracoke (village) just e of Sound Shores subdivision. Use of "horsepen" and other features using "horse" are in relation to previous semiannual events (until 1950s) of rounding up wild horses roaming freely on the banks and "penning" them with crude fences along specific points, where they would be branded and later sold or used. These events occurred throughout the Outer Banks but were prevalent on Ocracoke (where the Boy Scouts troop was mounted) and on Core Banks. In 1959, NPS wanted to remove ponies from Ocracoke because of mishaps with the horses after NC 12 was extended onto Ocracoke Island 1957. Residents protested removal, so the NPS established pens for the ponies midway on the island (*see* Pony Pen). Most names with "horse" are in some way related to these roundups or are places where banks ponies were known to congregate.

Horsepen Point, point, Carteret County, Smyrna Township (USGS 2013: Horsepen Point). In marsh opposite Great Shoal 5 mi. s of Davis (mainland). *See* Horsepen Creek (Hyde County) and Horse Point (Smyrna Township). *Other names:* Horse Pen Point (C&GS 1888b).

Horsepen Point, large point, Hyde County, Ocracoke Township (local informants). On central-e Ocracoke Island adjacent, e of Try Yard Creek, just nw of The Knoll, 10 mi. nne of Ocracoke (village). *See* Horsepen Creek (Hyde County).

Horsepen Point, point, Hyde County, Ocracoke Township (USGS 2013: Ocracoke). On Ocracoke Island 1.1 mi. w of The Plains, 0.8 mi. ne of Ocracoke (village). *See* Horsepen Creek (Hyde County). Reportedly named because Jim and Jennetta Henning kept a large horsepen at their property about 0.5

mi. ssw of here. *Other names:* Horse Pen Point (Weslager 1954, 47).

Horse Point, point, Carteret County, Harkers Island Township (USGS 2013: Harkers Island). On Shackleford Banks at n point of unnamed mud flat just nw of Johnsons Bay, 2.3 mi. s of Harkers Island (village). *See* Horsepen Creek (Hyde County).

Horse Point, point, Carteret County, Smyrna Township (C&GS 1888b). On South Core Banks just e of Great Shoal 6.5 mi. n of Cape Point at Cape Lookout. Several feature names nearby use "horse" because was a main area to round up wild Banks Ponies (diminutive horses) being driven to this place usually twice yearly. *See* Pony Pen and Horsepen Creek (Hyde County).

Horseshoe Pond, very small pond, Dare County, Hatteras Township (NPS 2006a 5), 1 mi. nw of Lighthouse Pond, 2 mi. s of Buxton. Man-enhanced, descriptive of shape.

Horse Wading Creek, small tidal stream, Dare County, Kinnakeet Township (Garrity-Blake 2010, 492). Soundside just s of Midgett Island 1.2 mi. s of Waves.

Hoskins Island. *See* Buck Island and Knotts Island (island).

Hotel De Afrique, former camp, Dare County, Hatteras Township (historical marker). Was on se Hatteras Island 3 mi. ne of Hatteras Inlet, and 2 mi. se of Hatteras (village). Was first place to house and process freed slaves coming to Hatteras on receiving news Union forces had arrived. First building 1 mi. ne of former Fort Hatteras. Later moved closer to former Fort Clark, ostensibly provided more shelter from insects and other problems of the former more open camp. Later, up to 12 buildings were constructed and the camp was descriptively labeled Negro Camp. Functioned late 1861 into 1864, though never reached size or functionality of Freedmans Colony (q.v.) on n Roanoke Island near General Burnside's headquarters. Reason for the name is obviously whimsical regarding its function; it showed on maps more often as simply Negro Camp. *Other names:* Hotel d'Afrique (*Harper's Weekly*, February 15, 1862), Negro Camp (ACE 1864).

Hotel Hill, sand dune, 65 ft. high, Dare County, Nags Head Township (historical local use). In Nags Head 3.7 mi. ne of Manteo. Named because 19th-century hotel nearby less than 1 mi. n of old Arlington Hotel site (possibly source of the name), which operated here early 1900s to 1974. However, earlier references to old Nags Head Hotel exist, second hotel built here just after Civil War. Nags Head Hotel had many owners, with John Z. Lowe fourth and apparently last owner. Destroyed by fire 1903, was hotel referenced by Lowe Hotel Lots subdivision and Old Hotel Lots subdivision. The road (Virginia Dare Trail, now NC 12) from Kitty Hawk to Nags Head was paved 1931 a year after the first bridge from mainland to Kitty Hawk opened. Another hotel (originally named Modlin's Hotel) was moved from soundside to near this location (near milepost 14) after paved road opened. In Seven Sisters complex and is of historical significance only. The name is rarely used today.

House Island, marsh island, 0.4 mi. long, 0.3 mi. wide, Dare County, Nags Head Township (USGS 2013: Roanoke Island NE). In Roanoke Sound 1.5 mi. wsw of Whalebone Junction. Original name was Horse Island but transcribing error perpetuated continually on maps until name has become changed to House Island. *Other names:* Horse Island (original name).

House Pond, lake, 0.5 mi. long, 0.2 mi. wide, Currituck County, Poplar Branch Township (USGS 2013: Mossey Islands). On Narrows Island 7 mi. sw of Corolla. *Other names:* Narrows Island Pond (C&GS 1852).

Howard Reef, shoal, 1.8 mi. long, 0.5 mi. wide, Hyde County, Ocracoke Township (USGS 2013: Howard Reef). In Pamlico Sound 2 mi. nne of Ocracoke (village). Sometimes e portion Howard Reef is referenced as Six Mile Hammock Reef because across from Six Mile Hammock and Howard Reef is quite long (5 mi.) with tapering e end. "Reef" in Outer Banks geographic names usually refers to oyster colonies. *Other names:* Howards Reef (C&GS 1910b), Our Reef (CS 1854), Six Mile Hammock Reef (local use).

Howards Cove, cove, Dare County, Hatteras Township (local use). At Duncan Point just s of Sandy Bay 1.2 mi. s of Durant Point, 1.2 mi. e of Hatteras (village). Named for William Howard, colonial landowner. *Other names:* Howards Creek (older usage).

Howards Point. *See* Springers Point.

Howard Street Oaks, woods, Hyde County, Ocracoke Township (Howard 2018). In Ocracoke (village) just e of s Silver Lake, 4.3 mi. ne of Ocracoke Inlet. Small but old stand of live oak (*Quercus virginiana*) trees used as a local reference.

Howards Windmill, former mill and windmill, Hyde County, Ocracoke Township (Howard, January 21, 2013). Was in Ocracoke (village) most likely at Springers Point 0.75 mi. sw from Ocracoke (village center) though Dunbar believes at Windmill Point (1956, 98). *See* The Ditch.

Hunting Island, island, 1 mi. long, 0.5 mi. wide, Carteret County, White Oak Township (USGS 2013: Swansboro). Between spoil banks (islands or shoals created by dredging channels) and mainland just e of Langston Bridge at entrance Deer Creek (mainland), 4 mi. sse of Swansboro (mainland). Descriptive of activity.

Hunting Quarter, historical area. General term referring to most of Core Banks and an extensive portion of mainland in and around present Cedar Island (mainland). An English translation of the Indian name for the area. In 15th through early 18th centuries common practice to name large undefined areas based on compass four quarters, and later "quarter" became a reference to a specific region or place. Swan Quarter n of this area is still used because it became the name of a town (Swan Quarter). Local people in Cedar Island explain they are aware of this historical use but have no reason to use it now so, while known, not used. *Other names:* Hunting Quarters (Stephens 2007—probable misprint or misinterpretation; originally "quarter" always used in singular).

Hunting Quarter Inlet. *See* Cedar Inlet.

Hunting Quarter Sound, historically named section Core Sound, Carteret County, Portsmouth, Cedar Island, and Atlantic Townships (Moseley 1737). Formerly ne portion Core Sound separated from Pamlico Sound by Chain Shot Island, Harbor Island, Wainwright Island, and Shell Island. S boundary of Hunting Quarter Sound was vicinity of Atlantic (mainland). *See* Hunting Quarter. *Other names:* Hunting Quarter Bay (some 18th-century maps).

Hyde County, civil division, 613 sq. mi., Ocracoke, Swan Quarter, Currituck, Fairfield, and Lake Landing townships. Bounded by Dare, Carteret, Tyrrell, Beaufort, and Pamlico Counties; Ocracoke Island is only part on the

Outer Banks. Originally formed as Wickham Precinct of Bath County 1705 and changed to Hyde 1712 when it was renamed for Governor Edward Hyde. Before 1770, Ocracoke Island was independent and not in any county, but then annexed by Carteret County. In 1823, s of New Inlet (Hatteras Island) to Green Island on what is now Ocracoke Island was transferred to Hyde County from Currituck County. In 1845, most of what is now Ocracoke Island (from just w of Old Hatteras Inlet at Green Island to Ocracoke Inlet) was moved into Hyde County from Carteret County by agreement. In 1870, when Dare County was formed the boundary was adjusted to Hatteras Inlet.

Hyters Island, small marsh island, Dare County, Nags Head Township (local informants). Just offshore in Croatan Sound just n of Cedar Bush Bay at n end Oyster Creek 2 mi. w of Wanchese. Hyter, surname common here.

Ice Plant Island, island, Dare County, Manteo Township (historical local use). In Manteo at nw Shallowbag Bay 4 mi. sw of Nags Head (center). Where Festival Park and Outer Banks Historical Center are located and replica of 16th-century sailing ship (*Elizabeth II*). Ice plant here operational 1913–1918. USGS 2013: Manteo has label placed incorrectly, s of waterfront in Manteo. The island was not renamed officially, though today only a few older folk actually remember Ice Plant Island; many use unofficial reference Festival Park Island. *Other names:* Festival Park Island (local use, and Town of Manteo 1987, table 8).

Indian Beach, beach, 1.5 mi. long, Carteret County, Morehead Township (USGS 2013: Salter Path, Mansfield). Soundside at and just e of Indian Beach (town) 9 mi. w of Atlantic Beach.

Indian Beach, town, Carteret County, Morehead Township (USGS 2013: Salter Path). Just w of Salter Path 9 mi. w of Atlantic Beach (town). Incorporated 1973. When Indian Beach incorporated, Salter Path was asked to join but declined, leaving Indian Beach in two noncontiguous portions on either side of Salter Path. Reportedly named when two Indian burial grounds were discovered.

Indian Creek, stream, 0.2 mi. long, Currituck County, Fruitville Township (USGS 1999: Barco). Source in se Great Marsh, flows s through Indian Pond to Currituck Sound, at Sandy Bay, 2 mi. sw of Knotts Island (village). Since 1794, appearing in Currituck DB 7 (1794, 48).

Indian Gap, water passage, Currituck County, Poplar Branch Township (USGS 2013: Mossey Islands). In Currituck Sound just s of Indian Gap Island, 7 mi. s of Corolla. *Other names:* Deep Creek (local use).

Indian Gap Island, marsh island, 0.1 mi. across, Currituck County, Fruitville Township (Cox 1923). At sw tip Rainbow Island, 5 mi. se of Knotts Island (village). Now mostly attached at sw tip Rainbow Island.

Indian Gap Island, elongated island, 0.8 mi. long, Currituck County, Poplar Branch Township (USGS 2013: Mossey Islands). Trends ne-sw in Currituck Sound just n of Indian Gap, 7 mi. s of Corolla. *Other names:* Graben Island (scattered early 18th-century use—no one knows this name; perhaps indicated adjacent water passage, Jarvis Channel, since *graben* is German for ditch, but no known German influence was here).

Indian Peak, former rock, Currituck County, Fruitville Township (Byrd 1728). Formerly large mound of shells near Currituck Inlet or midden, a pile of refuse; on the Outer Banks "midden" refers to mounds of shells discarded by indigenous peoples over decades and centuries of use. Prominent landmark early colonial period.

Indian Pond, lake, 0.3 mi. long, 0.1 mi. wide, Currituck County, Fruitville Township (USGS 2013: Barco). Wide swamp of Indian Creek in se Great Marsh, 2 mi. se of Knotts Island (village).

Indian Ridge, sand ridge, 1.5 mi. long, Dare County, Hatteras Township (local use). In Frisco (soundside) just s and se of Brigands Bay. Greatly worked and altered by man because NC 12 traverses more than one-half of what used to be this sand ridge. *See* Indian Town. *Other names:* Inden Ridge (uncatalogued deed 1764), Indian Hill (lesser local use).

Indian Ridge. *See* Croatoan Ridge.

Indian Shell Banks, former islands and marsh,

1 mi. long, Dare County, Nags Head Township (historical local use). Island complex was in Roanoke Sound at se end Roanoke Island, 2.5 mi. se of Wanchese.

Indian Town, former Indian village(s), Dare County, Hatteras Township (Lawson 1709, map). Formerly on Hatteras Island reportedly just s of Buxton near Creeds Hill but more probably just e of Brigands Bay subdivision. The population was probably never more than 100, and probable semipermanent fishing village cluster used by Indians from the mainland. MacNeill (1958, 2) locates the "town" about 4 mi. sw of Buxton near Creeds Hill and refers to it as "Hattorask Indian Capital." He also indicates there were reportedly two other smaller villages and sites one near the larger Indian Town (perhaps Buxton) but indicates the third village was "something of a mystery" on a point jutting n, at what is now Kings Point where Brigands Bay is today. The village at Kings Point (soundside) was more of a landing from the mainland villages according to MacNeill. However, recent archeological work (reported by Covey 2018) indicates the village was likely near Indian Ridge in Frisco near Brigands Bay 2.5 mi. w of Creeds Hill. The area of the village and 200 acres of the environs including several wooded and sandy e-w trending ridges was granted (1759) by N.C. Governor Dobbs to William Elks and the Hatteras Indians. The grant, known as the Indian Patent, was mentioned frequently through middle 19th century. Some authors propose there was also an Indian village in what is now Avon (probably temporary camp), though no documented proof and might be confused with a small village in the Buxton area. MacNeill claims this to be the site (near Creeds Hill) where Verrazzano likely stopped (1524) and sent a small party ashore for water, who had a friendly encounter with Indians. *See* Cape Lookout for discussion of Verrazzano's visit. Lawson (1709, 234) confirms the existence of this Indian Town (only one), indicating a town of the Hatteras Indians on the "Sand Banks." *Other names:* Cape Hatteras Indian Town (some text references for differentiation, and Torres 1985, 35), Croatan (later spelling of Croatoan sometimes used), Croatoan (Quinn 1975), Hattorask (historical), Hattorask Indian

Capital (MacNeill 1958, 2), Inder Hütte (Huber 1711—German for Indian village-huts), Indian Towne (Lawson 1709, map), Old Indian Town (Currituck DB 5, 1788, 326; Willard 2008, 15), Old Indian Towne (various documents), Village d'Indiens (early French maps).

Indiantown Pond, elongated lake, Dare County, Hatteras Township (local use). E-w-trending pond in Frisco just s of Brigands Bay subdivision at w end Indian Ridge. *See* Indian Town.

Ingles Creek, water passage, Currituck County, Fruitville Township (Cox 1923). Trends from North Rainbow Creek wnw then n 2 mi. to s entrance Knotts Island Bay. Separates Big Bird Island from Currituck Banks and North Marsh from Mary Island, 3 mi. se of Knotts Island (village).

Inlet Creek, tidal stream, Currituck County, Fruitville Township (Cox 1906). Trends ssw from Carova 1 mi. from junction of Hanes Creek and Bank Creek, 3.5 mi. ne of Knotts Island (village). Reference to former Currituck Inlet, which defined starting point for the survey to determine North Carolina–Virginia boundary. Remnant of former inlet. *Other names:* Inlet Channel (Currituck DB 1, 1719, 223).

Inlet Island, island and marsh, 1 mi. across, Carteret County, Beaufort Township (USGS 1951: Beaufort). Marsh islands and one large island just ne of Radio Island, 1.3 mi. nw of Beaufort (mainland). Ne portion of these marsh islands known historically as Reids Marsh (q.v.). Inlet Island fell into disuse in last half 20th century.

Inlet Peninsula, peninsula, 1.5 mi. long, Dare County, Hatteras Township (USGS 2013: Cape Hatteras). Sw tip Hatteras Island at ne shore Hatteras Inlet 3.4 mi. sw of Hatteras (village). Erosion has removed almost 1 mi. since 2000. *Other names:* Hatteras Inlet Spit (Garrity-Blake, 5, 2005), Hatteras Spit (Garrity-Blake 2010, 18), Point of Hatteras Island (local use), The Point (local use), The Point of Hatteras Island (local use).

Inlet Woods, former woods, Currituck County, Fruitville Township (Currituck DB 30, 1865, 401–2). Was just n of Currituck Inlet at North Carolina–Virginia boundary just n of Carova, 2.5 mi. ene of Knotts Island (village). Existing maritime vegetation known as woods, though process of creating larger Wash Woods (q.v.) had begun years earlier.

Inner Diamond Shoal, shoal, Dare County, Hatteras Township (NOS 2014b). Represents middle section of Diamond Shoals 3 mi. se of Cape Hatteras. Might seem peculiar "inner" is used for middle section, but can be explained because in 19th century Diamond Shoals consisted of only inner part and outer part, with Hatteras Shoals considered separately as an extension off tip of Cape Point. Today, by changing hydrography, Hatteras Shoals is considered as one of three sections of Diamond Shoals. Made official by USBGN 1949 to establish location. *See* Diamond Shoals. *Other names:* Diamond Shoal (Price 1795, 627), Inner Diamonds (Lawrence 2008), Inner Diamond Shoals (Cobb 1905), The Diamond Shoals (various documents), The Spit (declining local use).

Inner Grass Lump, island, 0.3 mi. wide, Carteret County, Stacy Township (USGS 2013: Styron Bay). In Core Sound 0.3 mi. s of Outer Grass Lump separated from Core Banks by Old Channel 3.4 mi. s of Sea Level (mainland). *See* Dorland Lump.

Inner Middle, shoal, 2.2 mi. long, Hyde County, Swan Quarter Township (local use). On central Middle Ground 17.8 mi. nw of Ocracoke (village).

Inshore Slew, former channel, Hyde County, Ocracoke Township (Hooker 1850). Was n approach to Ocracoke Inlet 3 mi. sw of Ocracoke (village). This approach was close to Ocracoke Island, hence name. No trace of this channel since Ocracoke Island extended into historic inlet at Ocracoke. *See* Allen Slough.

Inside, The, former area. Previously popular term, especially on Hatteras Island and Pea Island, used before building roadways. Any pathways or vehicle tracks behind beach dunes used for transportation. Fell into disuse 1940s and 1950s after extending NC 12.

Inside Channel, channel, 10 mi. long, Carteret County, Morehead and White Oak Townships (USGS 1948: Swansboro 1:62,500 scale). Was next to mainland and separated small marsh islands and spoils (dumping usually from dredging, building into shoals) from mainland trending from just sw of Morehead City (mainland) to just se of Swansboro (mainland).

Intracoastal Waterway, canal in Currituck, Dare, Hyde, and Carteret Counties. Network of inland waterways from New Jersey to Brownsville, Texas (by extension from Key West, Florida). As a system of inland waterways, little is related to the Outer Banks. From n to s the waterway crosses Currituck Sound 0.1 mi. sw of Mackay Island and crosses Albemarle Sound 12 mi. w of original Kitty Hawk. Does not appear near the Outer Banks again until it emerges from Adams Creek Canal into Bogue Sound at Morehead City (mainland), where it follows mainland coast 1.5 mi. from Bogue Banks until it leaves the Outer Banks at Swansboro (mainland). *Other names:* Atlantic Intracoastal Waterway (used along Atlantic coast), Inland Waterway (USGS 1948; Swansboro 1:62,500 scale), Main Channel Inland Waterway (early map usage).

Ipock Canal, canal, 0.25 mi. long, Carteret County, Morehead Township (Carteret County GIS 2019). N-most canal trending e-w in Atlantic Beach Isles subdivision (w part of Canals at Atlantic Beach q.v.), 0.8 mi. s of Morehead City (mainland). Ipock is a surname.

Ira Lump, marsh island, 0.1 mi. long, 0.05 mi. wide, Dare County, Kinnakeet Township (USGS 2013: Pea Island). In Pamlico Sound just s of Goulds Lump 4.5 mi. nnw of Rodanthe. *See* Dorland Lump.

Ira Morris Camp. *See* Long Point Camp.

Irene Breach. *See* Rodanthe Breach.

Irene Inlet. *See* New Inlet.

Iron Creek, cove, 0.4 mi. long, Carteret County, Harkers Island Township (USGS 1950: Horsepen Point). In Core Sound just se of Gunning Hammock Island 4.3 mi. se of Harkers Island (village).

Isaac Pond, lake, 0.2 mi. long, Dare County, Hatteras Township (USGS 2002: Hatteras). On Hatteras Island 0.7 mi. ssw of Hatteras (village). Name now extends to small adjacent ponds. *Other names:* Isaac Ponds (USGS 2013: Cape Hatteras).

Isabel Breach, former water passage, Dare County, Hatteras Township (limited temporary use). Was on sw Hatteras Island, 2 mi. ene of Hatteras Inlet, 2.2 mi. se of Hatteras (village). Result of Hurricane Isabel, made landfall at Cape Hatteras September 18, 2003. Unlike Isabel Inlet (q.v.), a potentially permanent inlet (but now filled by man-made project) 5 mi. ne of Isabel Breach, this feature awash only during very high tides and wave surges (historically often awash) but has now become mostly filled naturally, though previous episodes of overwash are clearly visible (*see* Little Inlet).

Isabel Inlet, former water passage, 0.3 mi. long, Dare County, Hatteras Township (local use while open). September 18, 2003, Hurricane Isabel, category 2 (formerly category 5) made landfall at Cape Hatteras, and within a matter of hours a new inlet was cut severing Hatteras Island 3 mi. ene of Hatteras (village), 1 mi. sw of Frisco, near Joe Saur Creek, itself breached and held water 1933. With width 1,700 ft., with two distinct channels (main channel and s channel used in reports) and a third lesser channel (middle), there was debate whether to bridge the inlet or fill it. Final decision was to fill the inlet, completed by ACE on November 22, 2003. The short-lived inlet was open for two months and four days. Named Isabel Inlet shortly after opening for the name of the hurricane that created it. Departure from historical naming practice for new inlets on the Outer Banks (hurricanes in the Atlantic Basin were not named formally until 1953). Such an inlet would acquire the name New Inlet for a period of time until determined whether it would remain open, then a suitable name would be applied. The two variant names were put into use quickly as referents were needed and with proximity to Hatteras Inlet. Mallinson et al. (2008) also reports an inlet or overwash for a short time near this location 1933. *Other names:* Isabelle Inlet (media error 2020), Isabels Inlet (Garrity-Blake 2010, 350), Lil Hatteras Inlet (local use), and Little Hatteras Inlet (local use).

Island Channel, natural channel, Currituck County, Fruitville Township (local use). Separates distinct n and s sections of Manns Islands just w of Deal Island 2 mi. ne of Knotts Island (village).

Island Creek, cove, 0.2 mi. wide, Hyde County, Ocracoke Township (USGS 2002: Howard Reef). In Pamlico Sound just n of Hammock Oaks, 3.5 mi. ne of Ocracoke (village). Has become a popular spot for windsurfing and kiteboarding.

Island Creek. *See* Spencer Creek.

Island Creek Hills, sand dunes, 25 ft. high, in Hyde County, Ocracoke Township (USGS 2013: Howard Reef). On Ocracoke Island 4.2 mi. ne of Ocracoke (village).

Island Harbor Marina, harbor, Carteret County, White Oak Township (signage). Soundside at w end Bogue Banks, 5.3 mi. w of original Emerald Isle. Subdivision named Emerald Landing adjacent, no evidence of a landing by that name; developer's contrivance.

J

Jack Brandys Creek, small tidal stream, Hyde County, Ocracoke Township (Weslager 1954). Se of Patch Fence Creek 14.5 mi. ne of Ocracoke (village). *Other names:* Brandys Creek (local use).

Jacks Cabin Creek, former small tidal stream, Dare County, Atlantic Township (Harris 2017). Was at extreme ne corner North Cove, ne Kitty Hawk Bay just s of original Kitty Hawk, just w of Mill Point Gut (colonial) 3 mi. n of Kill Devil Hills (sand dunes). Barely discernable today and name not used. Town of Kitty Hawk (2007) applies Penny Toler Ditch (q.v.) here, though signage applies Penny Toler Ditch to longer adjacent stream (e). Usage applies Penny Toler Ditch to both features (confusing). *See* Jacks Cabin Hill. *Other names:* Jack Cabin Creek (occasional use 18th century), Jacks Cabben Creek (Currituck DB 5, 1782, 95–96), Jacks Cabbin Creek (Currituck DB 5, 1782, 95).

Jacks Cabin Hill, sand dune, Dare County, Atlantic Township (Harris 2017). Was in e Kitty Hawk between village and beach and s Kitty Hawk Dunes 5 mi. n of Kill Devil Hills (sand dunes). Much lower today (40 ft.), unrecognizable from 18th-century appearance with development. Named for an original resident, exact person unknown as is exact location of Jack's Cabin; here probably middle to late 18th century. Jacks Cabin Creek was just w of here, as was Jacks Cabin Ridge, with Jacks Neck and Jacks Neck Island 2 mi. s. Name not remembered, used historically. Sometimes Keepers Hill is used from subdivision of that name here. N-most of five dune-remnants in Bald Sand Hills (q.v.). *Other names:* Army Camp Hill (World War II army radar installation), Keepers Hill.

Jacks Cabin Path, former path, Dare County, Atlantic Township (Currituck DB 7, 1796, 415). Trail or pathway through the dunes probably connecting soundside and oceanside. Precise location unknown but was near se original Kitty Hawk where Jack's Cabin is thought to have been and near Jacks Cabin Hill and Jacks Cabin Creek. Functionality of this path (when it existed) facilitated movement perhaps for a few individuals; however, no evidence it served a function for many, as did paths on sw Bogue Banks (*see* Lowenberg Path, Oglesby Path, Rice(s) Path, Roses Path, and Salter Path). At places labeled "path" on Bogue Banks, small communities developed, but no settlement known as Jacks Cabin Path existed. Path is found sporadically in descriptions of property deeds of 1700s in Kitty Hawk but are merely references to footpaths that later disappeared. This naming practice did not persist in Kitty Hawk or anywhere else on n Banks as it did on Bogue Banks. The name appears only in early records of deeds and is not found after late 1700s.

Jacks Cabin Ridge, former small sand ridge, Dare County, Atlantic Township (Harris 2017). Was just w of Jacks Cabin Hill just se of original Kitty Hawk on ne shore North Cove, ne Kitty Hawk Bay. *See* Jacks Cabin Hill.

Jacks Dock. *See* Ocracoke Wharf.

Jack Shoal, island, 0.4 mi. long, 0.3 mi. wide, Dare County, Kinnakeet Township (USGS 2013: Pea Island Overedge West). In Pamlico Sound 0.3 mi. sw of Jesse Shoal Point, 6.7 mi. nnw of Rodanthe. *Other names:* Jack Shoal Grass (NPS 2005B: 1, 90), Jacks Shoal (local use), Jack Shoals (historical).

Jacks Island, island, 0.2 mi. long, Carteret County, Harkers Island Township (USGS 2013: Harkers Island). In Back Sound at entrance Bald Hill Bay, 1.8 mi. ssw of Harkers Island (village). *Other names:* Bells Island (Mason 2000, NPS map, 1987, 38—*see* Bells Island), Jacks Place (Stick 1958, 308—reports Jacks Place on Core Banks near Cape Lookout), Jades Island (misinterpretation).

Jacks Island, small marsh island, Currituck County, Fruitville Township (C&GS 1878). In s Knotts Island Bay just ne of Bay Point 1.5 mi. se of Knotts Island (village). Label on C&GS (1878) chart is "Jack's House," informal designation.

Jacks Neck, small peninsula, Dare County, Atlantic Township (local use). On barrier island soundside in Kill Devil Hills (town) 2.7 mi. s of original Kitty Hawk. "Neck" only occasionally used on the Outer Banks and mostly historical (*see* Deep Neck, Simpson Neck, Whites Neck). Usually applied to larger protuberance of land and of colonial origin applied mostly to interfluves (land between tidal rivers or estuaries) in Virginia and Maryland. Found sparingly from here n-ward on the Outer Banks. *See* Jacks Cabin Hill.

Jacks Neck Island, small marsh island, Dare County, Atlantic Township (local use). Just e of Jacks Neck on barrier island at Kill Devil Hills (town), in n open water of Colington Creek 3 mi. s of original Kitty Hawk. *See* Jacks Neck and Jacks Cabin Hill. *Other names:* Jack Neck Island (original application).

Jackson Creek, cove, Dare County, Hatteras Township (local use). At Inlet Peninsula, 1.3 mi. ne of Hatteras Inlet. *Other names:* Jacksons Creek (some use).

Jackson Dunes, sand dunes, Hyde County, Ocracoke Township (local use). Is 1 mi. se of Silver Lake at Ocracoke (village center). Subdivision named for feature.

Jackson Point, point, Dare County, Hatteras Township (local use). Extreme e tip Southwest Spit, on n side of Inlet Peninsula 2.5 mi. se of Hatteras (village). *Other names:* Jacksons Point (some use).

Jackson Point. *See* Duncan Point.

Jacksons Island, former island, Dare County, Croatan Township (CS 1862b). Existed for some years as a remnant of Roanoke Marshes (q.v.), 2 mi. e of mainland, 6 mi. w of Wanchese. *Other names:* Jackson Island (Currituck DB 23, 1840, 39–40).

Jacks Ridge, small sand ridge, Dare County, Atlantic Township (Harris 2017). Just w of n Poor Ridge, 1.3 mi. w of original Kitty Hawk. *See* Jacks Cabin Hill.

Jacob Pond, lake, Dare County, Atlantic Township (Harris 2017; unknown, 1779). According to Harris (unpublished papers), somewhere in Kitty Hawk ridge-and-swale system (q.v.), w of original Kitty Hawk. Harris does not provide additional information, and as a named feature does not appear in early deeds.

Jacocks Beach. *See* Nags Head Beach.

Jacoxe Bay. *See* Buzzard Bay.

James. *See* Freedmens Colony.

James Howards Ditch, former ditch, Carteret County, Portsmouth Township (NPS 2004c, 10). Was in Portsmouth (village main part) just s of former Methodist Church location.

Janes Creek, cove, 0.4 mi. wide, Carteret County, Harkers Island Township (USGS 1997: Harkers Island). At nw end Harkers Island connected to The Straits by narrow water passage, 1.4 mi. nw of Harkers Island (village). *Other names:* James Creek (probable transcribing error), Jones Creek (probable transcribing error).

Jarvis Channel, water passage, 1.8 mi. long, Currituck County, Poplar Branch Township (USGS 2013: Mossey Islands). In Currituck Sound, 2 mi. w of Currituck Banks, separates South Burris Island, Long Island, and Indian Gap Island, 7.6 mi. s of Corolla. *Other names:* Burris Break (older local use—indicated significant separation by Jarvis Channel of Burris Islands complex and Pine Islands complex), Jarvis Creek (Currituck DB 1774, unnumbered, 499).

Jaybird Island. *See* North Rock.

Jay Crest, small sand ridge, Dare County, Atlantic Township (some local use). Applied by developer to small subdivision. Used sparingly for this small dune since development, not used before development.

Jeanguite Creek, bay and now stream, 5.5 mi. long, width varying 0.5 mi. wide (n) an embayment narrowing to minimal width for most of extension, Dare County, Atlantic Township (USGS 2013: Kitty Hawk, Martin Point). In Currituck Sound between main portion Currituck Banks and Martin Point just w of Southern Shores 3.7 mi. nw of original Kitty Hawk; stream portion (late 20th century) continues trending s just e of original Kitty Hawk into Albemarle Sound at Stone Island. Algonquian origin and originally was Chincoteague (used in peninsular Virginia), reportedly means large stream; Jeanguite is merely an Anglicized corruption of the Indian name. Current form of the name was first found 1782 and used off and on until early 20th century, when became preferred use. References abound to post-Revolutionary War deeds with the name Jeanguite and many of its forms, but no coalesced settlement here as some indicate, only scattered families. The name simply applied to the area around the bay.

No connection with Southern Shores, est. 1947 and to which the name Jeanguite is occasionally and whimsically applied. Some evidence variant Gingite might have been applied for a while to a broader area. Lawson (1709) makes vague reference to Chickehauk (q.v.) as Gingite, as does Moll on his 1729 map.

Large swale between two ridges flooded by Currituck Sound, and is not likely remnant of former inlet, as Stick (1958, 262), Dunbar (1958, 112), and Angley (1995, 30) hypothesized. As indicated by Fisher (1962) and Mallinson et al. (2008), no evidence of a relict inlet here and uninterrupted ridges w of Kitty Hawk confirms no inlet. *See also* Kill Devil Hills Inlet.

Official name is Jeanguite Creek, but in past Martins Point Creek was occasionally applied. Historically, name was applied only to flooded swale n of US 158 and just e of the Wright Memorial Bridge, but late 20th century name extended another 4 mi. s to Kitty Hawk Bay. Though not clear exactly when or why this happened, might result from influx of people in late 20th century who presumed a creek was linear and flowing, so the name was extended considerably. Portion (stream) s of US 158 was (still is) known as High Bridge Creek (High Ridge Creek [q.v.]). The s portion is shown as Northern Gut. Though local use still is more for High Bridge Creek (High Ridge Creek), extension of Jeanguite Creek along this stream is recognized and becoming more widely established. Ginguite often local use, especially newer arrivals because appears on Southern Shores maps and visitor's guides.

Other names: Gane Gite Creek (Currituck DB 8, 1798, 141), Gean Gite Creek (Currituck DB 8, 1798, 139), Gean Guite Creek (Currituck DB 9, 1807, 389), Geengite Creek (Currituck DB 5, 1786, 199–200), Gingite Creek (Lawson 1709, map), Ginguite Creek (various brochures), Ginguite Bay (Town of Southern Shores 2015), Guinguys Creek (Ruffin reported in Stick 1958, 262), Guiqak Creek (Currituck DB 1, 1714, 223), Gungueke Creek (Harris 2017; unknown, 1779), Gungues Creek (Harris 2017; unknown, 1779), High Bridge Creek (in part—Town of Kitty Hawk 2007), High Ridge Creek (in part—local use), Jaingete Creek (Currituck DB

1811, 12, 47), Jaingite Creek (Currituck DB 9, 1807, 317–18), Jain Gite Creake (Currituck DB 9, 1806, 218), Jane Gike Swamp (Harris 2017; unknown 1788), Jane Guika Creeks (Currituck DB 4, 1783, 131), Jane Guike Creek (Currituck DB 4, 1783, 138), Jane Gute Creek (Stick 1958, 262), Janigite Creek (Currituck DB 9, 1808, 371), Jean Creek (Vincent 2003, map, 3), Jeane Gite Creek (Currituck DB 8, 1798, 296), Jeangick Creek (misuses), Jean Gite Creek (Currituck DB 7, 1782, 4), Jeangite Creek (Currituck DB 6, 1789, 50–51), Jeangite Swamp (Currituck DB 6, 1790, 183), Jean Guike Creek (Currituck DB 4, 1782, 131), Jean Guite Bay (real estate brochures), Jean Guite Creek (USGS 2013: Kitty Hawk), Jean Guites Creek (C&GS 1879), Jean Gute Creek (historical), Jean Jite Creek (Currituck DB 7, 1795, 234–35), Jean Quite Creek (misrecording), Jeanquite Creek (misrecording—Angley 1995, 2; Currituck DB 9, 1804, 34), Jeen Gite Creek (Currituck DB 12, 1814, 342), Jeneguite Creek (Currituck DB 6, 1792, 254), Jene Gyte Creek (Currituck DB 5, 1783, 114), Jene Jaike Creek (Currituck DB 7, 1795, 246–47), Jengick Creek (Currituck DB 1, 1723, n.p.), Jennysey Cove (Harris 2017; unknown, 1740), Jennyseys Cove (Currituck DB 1740, 3, 28), Martin Point Creek (N.C. Marine Fisheries 2013, map 9), Martins Point Creek (Fink, n.d., 252), Northern Gut (Town of Kitty Hawk 2007).

Jeanguite Dock, former landing, Dare County, Atlantic Township (local informants). Was on ne Martin (*sic*) Point in Martins Point subdivision just w of Southern Shores 4 mi. s of Duck. Reportedly at the location where boat storage facility is now for Martins Point (gated subdivision). Reportedly used late 1800s and early 1900s for transferring fish and other material for shipment to n markets.

Jenkins Cove, cove, Currituck County, Fruitville and Poplar Branch Townships (USGS 2013: Corolla). In Currituck Sound just w of Currituck Banks, 2.1 mi. nw of Corolla.

Jenkins Cove, cove, Dare County, Kinnakeet Township (local use). In Pamlico Sound, 0.6 mi. n of Midgett Cove, 2.5 mi. s of Rodanthe. Used more historically; Jenkins, surname here since colonial period. *Other names:* Jenkins Bay (some use), Jenkins Creek (Currituck DB 8, 1800, 240).

Jenkins Hammock. *See* Cedar Hammock.

Jenkins Island, island, Dare County, Kinnakeet Township (local use and Garrity-Blake 2010, 493). In Pamlico Sound at No Ache Bay just n of No Ache Island, 1 mi. s of No Ache. *See* Jenkins Cove. *Other names:* Jenkins Isle (Garrity-Blake 2010, 493—use of "isle," not "island," was local in Chicamacomico—Rodanthe, Waves, Salvo).

Jennets Mill, former mill and windmill, Dare County, Hatteras Township (Dunbar 1956, 98). Was in Frisco/Buxton, though exact location unknown. Jennet or Jennette (*see* Jennette Sedge), well-established surname here. *Other names:* Jennettes Mill (spelling variation), and Trent Mill (location reference).

Jennette Sedge, marsh, 2.5 mi. long, Dare County, Hatteras Township (USBGN 1982). Sedge grass 1 mi. s of Buxton Woods, 1.1 mi. s of Buxton. Some applications (especially scientific study) inappropriately extend farther n through Buxton Woods to just s of Buxton. "Sedge" normally refers to any types of coarse grass found growing in marsh. Jennet or Jennette (*see* Jennets Mill), well-established surname here. Reportedly named for Unaka Jennette, Cape Hatteras Lighthouse Keeper (1919–37). Made official by USBGN 1982. *Other names:* Jeanette Sedge (NOS field notes, 1981), Jeanettes Sedge (Burney, 1987, 157), Jennets Marsh (CS 1852), Jennett Sedge (spelling variation).

Jesse Nole, former small hummock, Currituck County, Fruitville Township (Currituck DB 23, 1841, 156). Was on s Knotts Island at Indian Creek probably 2.5 mi. sw of Knotts Island (village). Abbeys Nole, Long Nole, and Whites Nole also here, according to deed, where named are "in Knotts Island . . . at an angle of Indian Creek." Only distinctive angle today is halfway between Indian Pond and Sandy Cove, no knolls or hummocks there. Topography could change considerably over 200 years and features might no longer exist or could be short distance ne on e side of Indian Pond where some hummocks exist. "Nole" is a variation of "knoll."

Jesses Ditch, canal, Dare County, Hatteras Township (local use). Short ditch in Buxton 3.5 mi. w of Frisco.

Jesse Shoal Point, marsh point, Dare County, Kinnakeet Township (USGS 2013: Pea Island Overedge West). Is 0.3 mi. ne of Jack Shoal, 6.8 mi. nnw of Rodanthe.

Jews Quarter Island. *See* Dews Island.

Jockeys Ridge, large sand dune, 1.1 mi. long, 150 ft. high, Dare County, Nags Head Township (USGS 2013: Manteo). In n Nags Head trends nnw to sse just e of Nags Head Woods 8 mi. sse of original Kitty Hawk. Local stories indicate sand dune acquired its name from the fact the top of the dune afforded an excellent view of a horse racetrack in the flats just sw (no evidence of a racetrack having ever existed at this location). This story is reproduced in local tourist guides and elsewhere, and recounted frequently by residents, both young and old; presumably it makes for an interesting story and perhaps promotes tourism and perhaps some horses were raced here. However, this explanation is pure folk etymology, as a result of the original meaning having been lost or obscure and no longer known. Subdivision named for feature. *See* Buzzard Bay (Dare County) and Nags Head Beach.

The true name origin, verified by representatives of Jockey's Ridge State Park and in historical deeds, is from an early landowner. Maps and deeds (1753) indicate surname Jaccock (Currituck DB 9, 1805, 127) or Jacock (shown late as 1854 on CS 1854), evolved into Jackey (CS 1882). Cartographic practice in 17th and 18th centuries was annotating surnames of land owners. Original name was Jacock Ridge (actually Nags Head originally—*see* Nags Head) and then later Jackey Ridge, labeled on USGS Manteo map until 1953. Some suggest perhaps mapmakers simply changed the name assuming it must be Jockey or Jockeys, given the proximity to Nags Head, but no evidence, unfounded, and not the case.

Other names: Jackey Ridge (USGS 1953: Manteo; USGS 1943; Roanoke Island 1:125,000 scale; early Currituck County deeds—before Dare County 1870), Jickeys Ridge (Powell 1968), Jockey Ridge (Stick 1958, 102), Jockeys Hill (Harris 2017), Nags Head (Dunbar 1958, 57—believes this to be original name 18th century as headland landmark when entering Roanoke Inlet; Price and Strother 1798, and other sources to mid-19th century), Nags Head Hill (Currituck DB 30, 1867, 13).

Jockeys Ridge Sand Dunes, sand dunes, Dare County, Nags Head Township. General term recently applied to Jockeys Ridge and other dunes in immediate vicinity with prominence of Jockeys Ridge and popularity of state park here. *See* Jockeys Ridge. *Other names:* Nags Head Hills (occasional general reference).

Joe Austins Creek, small tidal stream, Dare County, Kinnakeet Township (Garrity-Blake 2010, 210). Believed to be at Black Hammock 1 mi. n of Askins Creek, 1.5 mi. s of original Avon.

Joe Saur Creek, cove, 0.2 mi. wide, Dare County, Hatteras Township (USGS 2002: Hatteras). Just sw of Frisco 2.9 mi. ne of Hatteras (village).

Joes Creek, water passage, 0.6 mi. long, Currituck County, Poplar Branch Township (USGS 2013: Jarvisburg). Connects Doxeys Salthouse and Beach Creek, 5.9 mi. nnw of Duck.

Joes Hill, dune, Carteret County, Portsmouth Township (NPS 2018, 92). In s part Middle Portsmouth (Middle Community) s of "landing strip" just e of Big Hill.

John Gaskins Creek, small tidal stream, Hyde County, Ocracoke Township (Weslager 1954). Between Quork Hammock and Shingle Creek just s of Terrapin Island 11 mi. ne of Ocracoke (village). *Other names:* Gaskins Creek (local use), John Gaslins Creek (Weslager 1954—typographical error).

John Moss Ridge, sand ridge, Dare County, Atlantic Township (Harris 2017). Reportedly just ne of n terminus High Ridge 1.5 mi. wnw of original Kitty Hawk. Only known occurrence of this name and unknown locally.

Johns Creek, small tidal stream, Dare County, Kinnakeet Township (Garrity-Blake 2010, 494). Just s of Askins Creek just n of Long Point, 2 mi. s of original Avon.

Johns Creek, cove, 0.4 mi. long, 0.1 mi. wide, Dare County, Nags Head Township (USGS 2013: Wanchese). In Roanoke Sound 2.5 mi. se of Manteo (center). *Other names:* Hammock Ditch (Fulton 1820).

Johns Ditch, canal, 0.5 mi. long, Dare County, Nags Head Township (local informant). In sw Wanchese canals, ditches, guts, and water passages with a right-angle turn at mouth just ne of Big Island 1.3 mi. sw of Wanchese.

Johnson Creek, cove, 0.9 mi. long, Carteret County, Smyrna Township (USGS 2013: Davis, Horsepen Point). In Core Sound 0.4 mi. s of Goose Island 3.8 mi. se of Davis (mainland).

Some reports of a historical inlet here, but no specific evidence has been determined. There could have been inlets just about anywhere along Core Banks throughout the pre-European history of Core Banks because these barrier beaches are low and narrow. *Other names:* Johnsons Creek (C&GS 1888b).

Johnson Island, marsh island, 0.5 mi. wide, Currituck County, Fruitville Township (USGS 2013: Barco). In Currituck Sound just n of South Channel 0.4 mi. se of Swan Island, 6.5 mi. nnw of Corolla. Sometimes Swan Island, Johnson Island referenced as Swan Islands; occasionally Crow Island, Raymond Island might be included. *Other names:* Johnsons Island (USGS 1947: Barco 1:62,500 scale) and Johnson Joland (*sic*) (USBGN staff, no explanation in USBGN records, must be attributed to transcribing error).

Johnsons Bay, cove, 0.7 mi. wide, Carteret County, Harkers Island Township (USGS 2013: Harkers Island). In Back Sound just n of Shackleford Banks, 2.7 mi. s of Harkers Island (village). *Other names:* Johnson Bay (Carteret County GIS 2019).

Johnsons Hammock. *See* Horse Island (Carteret County, Davis Township).

Johnsons Marsh, large marsh, Carteret County, Smyrna Township (Williamson 1992, 156). Between Great Island Bay (ne) and Johnson Creek (sw), 4 mi. se of Davis (mainland).

Johns Ridge, sand ridge, Dare County, Nags Head Township (Currituck DB 1, 1767, 194–95). Somewhere on nw Roanoke Island from deed description, so anywhere from just nw of Manteo to 3.5 mi. nw of Manteo.

John Styrons Creek, cove, 0.05 mi. wide, Carteret County, Portsmouth Township (USGS 2013: Portsmouth). At Baymarsh Thorofare just wsw of Portsmouth (village) 7.3 mi. sw of Ocracoke (village).

Jollies Creek, former stream, Dare County, Hatteras Township (Covey 2018, 12). Was in former Lambards Marsh at Cape Hatteras 2 mi. s of Buxton. Today these streams are not identifiable, and Covey indicates exact location never known.

Jolly Roger Marina, dock, Hyde County, Ocracoke Township (signage). Small facility in Ocracoke (village) at se end Silver Lake. Jolly Roger referenced pirate flags in many displays; origin of name is unproved and has at least four different possibilities (check various origins).

Jonathans Creek, tidal stream, Currituck County, Poplar Branch Township (Currituck DB 1801, 3, 157). One of three n-s tidal creeks (1801) on e Pine Island just w of Baums Creek, 5.5 mi. n of Duck (center).

Jones Creek, small water passage, 0.5 mi. long, Dare County, Atlantic Township (USGS 2013: Kitty Hawk). Trends se-nw from Tater Patch Cove to n open water Colington Creek just s of Kitty Hawk Bay, 3.2 mi. s of original Kitty Hawk.

Jones Hill, sand dune, 35 ft. high, Currituck County, Poplar Branch Township (historical local use). On Currituck Banks just n of Corolla 10 mi. se of Knotts Island (village). Almost completely gone now as a result of natural processes and by man-made intervention to develop Ocean Hill subdivision; reference now is often Ocean Hill. Two subdivisions named for feature as Ocean Hill. *Other names:* North Whalehead (local informant, used only by older original residents—descriptive reference to Whale Head Hill 2.5 mi. s of Jones Hill), Ocean Hill (some new local use to remnants and subdivision name there now), Whalehead (former occasional local use mostly as descriptor).

Jones Hill. *See* Corolla.

Jones Island, former island, Currituck County, Fruitville Township (Currituck DB 9, 1805, 83–84). Was apparently in Back Creek between Mackay Island (s or se) and Great Marsh (n or ne) 2 mi. w of Knotts Island (village). Somewhere in Back Creek where rudimentary bridge reported late 18th century. No one really remembers this bridge or Jones Island, though there are some vague local references. *Other names:* Joneses Island (Currituck DB 2, 1761, 271–72).

Jones Marsh, marsh, Currituck County, Poplar Branch Township (Currituck DB 6, 1794, 89; C&GS 1852). Just nw of Porpoise Marsh 5.3 mi. ssw of Corolla. Here generic terms "pond," "marsh," and "island" are used for similar features and often local conflicting usage based on perception regarding amount of marsh versus open water or dry land. *See* Adams Pond. *Other names:* Jones Pond (often interchangeable), Jonses Marsh (C&GS 1852—peculiar attempt to show genitive case for Jones).

Jones Pond, cove, Currituck County, Poplar Branch Township (local use). In Jones Marsh,

5.3 mi. s of Corolla. *See* Adams Pond and Jones Marsh.

Jones Point, marsh point, Currituck County, Poplar Branch Township (USGS 2013: Corolla). On unnamed marsh island in Currituck Sound, 1.2 mi. w of Corolla.

Jones Thorofare, water passage, Currituck County, Poplar Branch Township (Codman, Crowninshield, and Lawrence 1925). Trends e-w, separates North Jones Island from South Jones Island, 1 mi. ese of Corolla. *Other names:* The Cut Through (local use).

Judgement Beach. *See* Hoffman Beach.

K

Kathryne Jane Islands, islands, Carteret County, Portsmouth Township (USGS 2013: Wainwright Island Overedge North). Four islands in Pamlico Sound 0.6 mi. w of Portsmouth Island, 11.2 mi. sw of Ocracoke (village). *Other names:* Kathryn-Jane Flats (Burkholder et al. 2017, 177).

Keepers Hill. *See* Jacks Cabin Hill.

Keneckid Inlet, former water passage, Dare County, Kinnakeet Township (occasional historical). Probably 3 mi. s of Salvo in No Ache Bay area. Only mentioned sporadically, and perhaps as a temporary inlet, in early references and a few early deeds, but location uncertain. Though specific open and close dates are unknown, it might be the "fret" (breach) to which John White refers as where the ship anchored when searching for Lost Colonists (1590). White refers to anchoring at extreme ne point of Croatoan, which must have extended farther n than the later cartographic application. White specifically states the breach or water passage was "35 degr. & a half," in No Ache area just s of Salvo. However, if his calculations were off by about 15 minutes of latitude he would have been anchored at later cartographic limits of Croatoan, and the breach he was describing would be former Chacandepeco Inlet (near Buxton) open 1590 when White arrived. Either instance described above is possible, and exact reference meant by White might

never be known—simply not clear whether White was describing Chacandepeco Inlet or more elusive Keneckid Inlet. *Other names:* Kendrick Creek (vague references to inlet or tidal stream somewhere near), Kenekit Inlet (Currituck DB 1, n.d., 188), Kenneket Inlet (Currituck DB 1, n.d., 188), Kennekid Inlet (occasional early reference), Kinnekid Inlet (occasional early reference).

Kennekeet Township, township, Dare County, n-s from Oregon Inlet to just n of Buxton at Cape Creek (cove, formerly Back Landing Creek) at former Chacandepeco Inlet. Throughout 20th century, an alternate spelling of Kinnakeet (best-known form), Kennekeet, was used exclusively for township name. Early 21st century, township name was changed on most sources (websites) to Kinnakeet. Unclear whether initiated by the county or was just done to be in accord with best-known spelling. Officials at the county government indicate there "seem to be no records on the matter." Townships are listed with each entry as a level of location within the county, but names of townships are not included as entries in their own right since use of townships for any purpose within a county in North Carolina has disappeared— they are legacy and no longer have any function. Townships functioned from their beginning (1868) when township structure was incorporated into the rewritten state constitution, and had elected officials whose duties were to administer aspects of government and services. However, by 1877 the system had failed, and the township's functions had been abolished. Townships should not be confused with incorporated towns, of which there are many on the Outer Banks; this is a separate process and completely unrelated. A legitimate spelling of the name as Kennekeet appears numerous times in late 18th-century deeds. *Other names:* Kinnakeet Township (numerous sources).

Kennigees Pond, cove, Dare County, Kinnakeet Township (Garrity-Blake 2010, 493). In Pamlico Sound 2 mi. e of Gull Island, 5 mi. s of Salvo. *Other names:* Kannigys Pond (NPS 2005b: NPS 1, 154).

Kenricks Mounts, historical applied to certain prominent sand dunes, Dare County, from just w of Cape Hatteras n to Nags Head, but originally and especially to just n of Cape Kenrick (q.v.). These dunes were on what are now Hatteras Island, Pea Island, Bodie Island, and Currituck Banks (Haklyut 1589). Use of this name is historical only and was originally descriptive, as were many early names applied by the English. Ken Rick was a reference to any large or prominent dunes or ridges first sighted (anywhere) and used as landmarks. The word is a combination of obsolete terms. "Ken" or "kenning" (kenning of land, as in journals of the original voyages to "Roanoak") referenced distance land is discernable from a ship, or about 20 mi. Use of "ken" as a generic place name term was applied in parts of England and Wales from Gaelic word *Ceann* meaning head or top. "Rick" is specifically a pile of something such as sand. The reference then was to the large dunes first visible from a ship. Some authors have suggested a surname as the origin, some indicate indigenous origin when compared to such terms as Chacandepeco and Kinnakeet. However, these attempts at explanation are groundless and are uniformed guesses because the references were used on the original voyages and appear in Haklyut (1589, 6:141, 220, 223). One such reference mentions the "Kenricks Mounts" just to sw of Hatorask, present Pea Island or n Hatteras Island. *Other names:* Costa Alta (upper coast—apparently Portuguese origin rather than Spanish, more description or possibly reference to entire coast n of Florida; Cantino 1502), Kendricker Mountain (MacNeill 1958, 9), Kendricker Mounts (Haklyut 1589), Kendricker Ridge (variation of Kendricker Mounts), Kendrickers Mounts (Haklyut 1589), Kendricks Mount (Covey 2018, 11), Kenrick Ridge (website mixing original term with perceived generic), Kindrikers Mountes (White 1590), Mount Kenrick (some historical documents).

Ketch Inlet, canal, 0.3 mi. long, Dare County, Atlantic Township (local use). At Colington Harbour, 2.5 mi. wsw of Kill Devil Hills (town). Only n-s-trending canal in Colington Harbour other than Tartan Canal. "Inlet" not used in traditional sense on the Outer Banks as barrier island breach, because indicative of dredging allowing water inward for access by boats to open water (Albemarle Sound). Canal naming scheme at Colington Harbour is ships or nautical terms. "Ketch" is a two-masted sailing ship with main mast forward and a mizzen (middle) mast. "Ketch" is centuries old and developed from "cache," meaning to catch.

Keys Point. *See* Haulover Point.

Kibbs Creek, water passage or cove, Dare County, Kinnakeet Township (Currituck DB 10, 1809, 79). Somewhere on Hatteras Banks (described in deed), probably South'ard Water (q.v.) area. *Other names:* Kebbs Creek (Currituck DB 1809, 11, 17).

Kill Devil Beach, area, Dare County, Atlantic Township (local use). General reference to housing developments just w of the beach just se of stabilized Kill Devil Hill 4 mi. se of original Kitty Hawk. Small section sometimes referred to as Ocean Acres Beach (subdivision). *See* Kill Devil Hill.

Kill Devil Hill, hill, 90 ft. high, Dare County, Atlantic and Nags Head Townships (USGS 2013: Kitty Hawk). On s Currituck Banks, 3.7 mi. se of original Kitty Hawk. In continuous use since beginning 19th century. From near n base of this sand dune (before stabilized by planting) Wright brothers made first heavier-than-air flight 1903. Dune successfully stabilized 1927 with different varieties of grass, today a national monument atop this stabilized dune commemorating that flight.

NPS still uses Big Kill Devil Hill (reportedly coined by Wright Brothers) and Little Kill Devil Hill for historical description and correctness (most rangers add "now Kill Devil Hill"), though what was Big Kill Devil Hill is now known as just Kill Devil Hill, Little Kill Devil Hill merely a remnant. Big Kill Devil Hill (Kill Devil Hill), Little Kill Devil Hill, West Hill, Run Hill (not used by Wright Brothers), and other small sand dunes known collectively as Kill Devil Hills.

Many legends, stories, and yarns exist concerning name origin. Sailors reportedly stated this portion of the sound was enough "to kill the devil to navigate." William Byrd of Virginia 1728 reportedly referred to rum here as being so bad it would kill the devil. By mid-17th century, in the West Indies (especially Barbados) rum was referenced as "rumbullion" or "killdevil." Also, a ship carrying a cargo of this "kill devil rum" reportedly wrecked on a nearby beach. While guarding the cargo of the wrecked ship, guards reported portions of the cargo would mysteriously disappear at night. A local resident (conveniently and reportedly) named "devil Ike" stated he would guard the cargo, and while standing guard he discovered another local person tying a rope around the cargo and pulling it away using a horse. Ike succeeded in frightening away the would-be culprit, and not wanting to implicate a neighbor, Ike stated the devil was stealing the cargo and he (Ike) had killed the devil.

Another legend indicates a local resident made a pact with the devil—the man's soul for a bag of gold—and the exchange was to be made atop what is now Kill Devil Hill. The day before the exchange was to take place, the local resident dug a hole from top to bottom of the sand dune. When the "Banker" and the devil met for the exchange, the devil was coaxed into the hole and was quickly covered with sand.

Also, *kill* is a Dutch generic term meaning stream or channel, and "devil" is used for sand spout or whirlwind. While the combination of these two terms utilizing their meanings is tantalizing and may be plausible, not likely because no Dutch influence here, and use of generic "kill" for stream is primarily in New York, New Jersey, and Pennsylvania. Some authors report the Dutch term *kill* was used for a short time as far s as the Outer Banks, but no evidence to support this assumption.

Many believe rum was distilled here, but no records indicate rum was ever actually made here (until 21st century). While many including some authors believe name is from one or more shipwrecks transporting "killdevil" rum, there are no records for verification. Some simply believe pirates stored rum here, but pirates rarely "stored" rum anywhere. Some have introduced a theory that the name stems from spiced rum prepared here since in cooking to "devil" something means to cook with spice, and distilling rum requires cooking on or in some apparatus like a kiln, so the kiln is deviled. This is simply another attempt at explanation through elaborate folk etymology. The actual name origin is from being home to numerous killdeer (*Charadrius vociferus*) or killdee (colonial references), common shore bird here year-round, and name evolved from Killdeer Hill to Kill Devil Hill. The bird's name reportedly mimics the sound that they make. *See* Roespock Run for explanation regarding variant "rowspock" and variations.

Other names: Big Hill (Wright Brothers, Patterson 2008, 34), Big Kill Devil Hill (NPS, Wright Memorial signage; Stick 1958, 267), Killdeer Hills (colonial use), Kildevel Hill (Harris 2017; unknown, 1809), Killdevil Hill (USGS 1940 Kitty Hawk 1:62,500 scale), Kill Devil Hills (q.v.; misnomer), Killdevil Hills (colonial use), Little Hill (some misapplications), Roesepock Hill (colonial use), Roespock Hill (colonial use), Rosepock Hill (colonial use), Rowspock Hill (colonial use), West Hill (misapplication from hill just nw).

Kill Devil Hills, sand dunes, 5 mi. long, Dare County, Atlantic Township (USGS 2013: Kitty Hawk, Manteo). Sand dunes from just ne of Kitty Hawk; largest is Kill Devil Hill. Big Kill Devil Hill (Kill Devil Hill), Little Kill Devil Hill, West Hill, Run Hill, and other small sand dunes are known collectively as Kill Devil Hills. Shown as Killdevil Hills first (Price and Strother 1798). *See* Kill Devil Hill. Refer to Roespock Run for explanation regarding variant Rowspock and variations. Made official by USBGN 1957 to reverse 1892 decision for Killdevil Hills. *Other names:* Killdeer Hills (Stick 1958, 267), Killdevil Hills (USBGN 1892), Kill Devils Hills (Foster 1866a misnomer), Roesepock (early deeds), Roespock (colonial use), Rosepock (Stick 1958, 269), Rousapock (Harris 2017, source unknown), Rowseypock (Harris 2017, source unknown), Rosypock (colonial use), Roucepock (Harris 2017, source unknown), Rowlypark (Currituck DB 3, 1738, 496—reference at North Bank; 18th century included Currituck Banks and later Bodie Island after Roanoke Inlet closed 1795–1811), Rowspock (Currituck DB 3, 1739, 33–34), Rowsypock (reported by some to be different spellings of Indian name here—not so; *see* Rowspock Point for correct explanation regarding Rowspock and variations), The Kill Devil Hills (Stick 1958, 267).

Kill Devil Hills, town, Dare County, Atlantic Township (USGS 2013: Kitty Hawk). On Currituck Banks 2.3 mi. se of original Kitty Hawk. Post office est. 1938, and incorporated as a town 1953. *See* Kill Devil Hill. *Other names:* Croatan Shores (real estate development 1950s and in Kill Devil Hills),

Kill Devil Hill (NCDOT 1953), Rowsypock (Stick 1958, 255—never used for the town).

Kill Devil Hills Inlet, former inlet—not likely, Dare County, Atlantic Township. Some sources report residents (and "old-timers") early to mid-18th century indicate inlet near Kill Devil Hills, most putting it at Kitty Hawk Bay, some at Fresh Pond, some at Jeanguite Creek. Little evidence to suggest inlet in either place historically, and most historical maps do not show an inlet in the area. Mallinson et al. (2008, 6, map fig. 6) does show three locations of relict inlets in the Kill Devil Hills area, two of which date from more than 1,000 years ago. The third is labeled Kill Devil Hills Inlet (Nags Head Inlet) and is listed as a relict inlet near Kitty Hawk Bay, but without specific dates only as "previously unrecorded relict data." Some early maps (Wildey and Thornton 1685; Moll 1708) depict the name "Old Inlet" at Colington Island n of where Roanoke Inlet was located and the name "New Inlet" in the Duck area, but these locations are in error (Cumming 1969, 23, 24). Crisp (1711) labels Gingite (*sic*) at an inlet he places at Jeanguite Creek. While these few maps suggest there might have been an inlet near Kitty Hawk Bay, they were maps produced during a time with known errors (*see* Roanoke Island historical inlets). Other maps in this period (Gascoyne 1682 and others) correctly label Old Inlet at Port Ferdinando (Gunt Inlet) and New Inlet near former Port Lane and/ or newly opening Roanoke Inlet. Cobb, in his 1905 analysis of historical maps (with some errors), vaguely refers to an "ancient" inlet "between Kill Devil Hills and the Fresh Pond" but does not elaborate and might have been referring to Roanoke Inlet (his reference is Nags Head Inlet—contrived name). Apparent some maps late 17th and early 18th centuries such as Fisher et al. (1689) misplaced what was later named Roanoke Inlet as being opposite Colington Island instead of correct location just n of Whalebone Junction, which might account for reports of an inlet in the Kitty Hawk Bay area. Stick (1958) favors an inlet location at Jeanguite Creek but does not elaborate or offer any additional information. Angley (1995, 1, 2) also indicates an inlet at or near Jeanguite Creek but offers no additional explanation. So, remains (to some) unanswered since there are stories of such an inlet, but no conclusive evidence; the conclusion is an inlet did not exist at Kitty Hawk Bay or at Jeanguite Creek since 1585.

Kingcrab Shoal, small shoal, Carteret County, Beaufort Township (Williamson 1992, 179). Separately named part of Bird Island on Bird Shoal sometimes covered with water, 1.5 mi. s of Beaufort (mainland).

Kingfish Shoal, shoal, 1.1 mi. long, Carteret County, Cedar Island Township (USGS 2013: Wainwright Island Overedge North). In Pamlico Sound 1.5 mi. nne of Chain Shot Island, 13.2 mi. sw of Ocracoke (village). Originally, was Harbor Island Shoal and most still use that name while acknowledging name has become Kingfish Shoal (maps and charts). When C&GS placed a beacon on the shoal for some reason (now forgotten), was labeled Kingfish Shoal Beacon, so name of the shoal gradually changed to agree with beacon name. "Kingfish" refers to any fish having a large size, but was in more frequent use 19th century. Original spelling of the name was the two-word form, but as with many place names and words in English, one-word form by process of concatenation is preferable today (consider "blue bird" vs. "bluebird"). *Other names:* Harbor Island Bar (C&GS 1915b), Harbor Island Shoal (Walton 1867), King Fish Shoal (C&GS charts).

Kings Channel, channel, 6 mi. long, Dare County, Hatteras Township (local use). In Pamlico Sound, ne from Old Rollinson Channel, trends e to join Buxton Harbor Channel 3.1 mi. nw of Buxton. From local surname here since colonial period (originally prevalent with Mattamuskeet Indians on mainland). Made official by USBGN 1982.

Kings Corner Arm, canal, Carteret County, Morehead Township (PKS 2016). "Arm" or offshoot of e (original) section of Pine Knoll Waterway in Pine Knoll Shores 4 mi. w of Atlantic Beach. Completed with first phase 1967. Use of generic term "arm" is unprecedented on the Outer Banks, not used in other names for canals. Used (in this book) in a few descriptions, but otherwise is not present in Outer Banks toponymy (geographic names). Reason for use here unknown by those asked. Generic term "arm" used with geographic names in other parts of the nation; usually with tributaries of streams inundated by creation of reservoirs. Named for Charles King, planner assisted developing Pine Knoll Shores. *Other names:* Kings Corner (PKS 2016).

Kings Creek, former tidal stream, Dare County, Hatteras Township (historical local use). Was at Kings Point at Brigands Bay 7 mi. ene of Hatteras (village). Altered beyond recognition when Brigands Bay subdivision established. Now, Brooks Creek entrance to unnamed waterways at Brigand Bay (*sic*) (*see* Canals at Briginds Bay). King, local surname since colonial period and prevalent with Matamuskeet Indians from mainland. Historically, Tom Kings Creek shown in several different but nearby locations, appropriate location s and e of present Brigands Bay. Kings Creek a misapplication of Tom Kings Creek historically, but Kings Creek used here so often became the name with Tom Kings Creek (q.v.) at its appropriate location. *Other names:* The Creek (Covey, 2018, 41),Tom Kings Creek (Brooks 2010).

Kings Island, marsh island, 0.1 mi. long, 0.05 mi. wide, Dare County, Hatteras Township (USGS 2013: Buxton). In Pamlico Sound 0.3 mi. nw of Kings Point, 7.3 mi. nne of Hatteras (village). King, local surname since colonial period and was prevalent with Matamuskeet Indians from mainland.

Kings Point, point, Dare County, Hatteras Township (USGS 2013: Buxton). On w Hatteras Island at s entrance Brooks Creek 7.1 mi. nne of Hatteras (village). Used since 1790 (Currituck DB 7, 1790, 82–83). King, surname prevalent with Mattamuskeet Indians on mainland; numerous deeds of sale to individuals from there named King. *Other names:* King Point (C&GS 1918).

Kings Pole, former area, Dare County, Hatteras Township (Covey 2018, 12). Referenced a marker and mentioned by Covey as descriptive name but provides no additional information or location. Presumably near Kings Point at Brigands Bay. Name is unknown today.

Kinnakeet, historical area, Dare County, Kinnakeet Township. Area of scattered population from Little Kinnakeet (n) to just s of Avon (s) centered n Avon. Residents by 1770s, mostly at Avon (n and s), but usually more general and included Little Kinnakeet and Scarboro. Indigenous (Algonquian) origin, and perhaps might mean "mixed," referring to several semipermanent Indian campsites or something else entirely. Note the difference from this spelling and original spelling for the township (division of Dare County), Kennekeet (q.v.; early spelling used in some 18th-century deeds). Some authors indicate an Indian village at this site; however, no real documentation to suggest more than temporary campsites (*see* Indian Town). Three subdivisions named for feature. *Other names:* Big Kinekeet (schooner *Lonia Buren*, 1903 [White et al. 2017, 129]), Big Kinnakeet (MacNeill 1958, 52), Chicomicomico (Foster 1862—misapplied), Cinnecett (Currituck DB 12, 1813, 198–99), Keneekut (J. Colton 1861), Kenekeet (Currituck DB 6, 1793, 269), Kinakeet (early records), Kinekeet (Currituck DB 8, 1798, 151), Kinnekeet (Currituck DB 6, 1792, 230–31), Kinneykeet (Currituck DB 8, 1799, 224–25), Kinnikeet (Rollinson 1884).

Kinnakeet Atlantic Anchorage Basin, sea, Dare County, Kinnakeet Township (Garrity-Blake 2010, 425). In open Atlantic Ocean 10 mi. offshore just n of Diamond Shoals. Used as stop for "resting" before or after navigating dreaded Diamond Shoals.

Kinnakeet Banks, former barrier island, Dare County, Kinnakeet and Hatteras Townships. Historical barrier island now part of Hatteras Island, n from former Chacandepeco Inlet at Cape Hatteras (historical limit now submerged) to historical s boundary of Chicamacomico Banks near Little Kinnakeet s of Rodanthe or occasionally as far as New Inlet (incorporating Chicamacomico Banks). *See* Kinnakeet. *Other names:* Bald Buck (found in early deeds referring to beach between Chicamacomico [Rodanthe] and Kinnakeet, now Avon, using archaic meaning of "buck" as stark—consider older term "buck-naked," meaning forgotten today, "butt-naked" is substituted), Kennekeet Banks (occasional early spelling—Currituck DB 10, 1809, 57–58), Kenneykeet Banks (Currituck DB 8, 1799, 227–28), Kineakeet Banks (Currituck DB 6, 1789, 38), Kineekeet Banks (Currituck DB 11, 1811, 122–23), Kinnekeet Banks (Currituck DB 7, 1793, 141), Kinnekett Banks (Currituck DB 13, 1815, 158–59), Kinneykeet Banks (Currituck DB 3, 1803,

444–45), Lower Banks (Garrity-Blake 2010, 93—s of Chicamacomico Banks).

Kinnakeet Dike, dam, Dare County, Kinnakeet Township (Garrity-Blake 2010, 169). Embankment along First Creek e from Pamlico Sound 0.5 mi. then n 1.2 mi. through all of Avon to Mill Creek (Old Creek); center is 7.5 mi. n of Buxton. Built 1933 when much of the work by ACE was done to control flooding in marsh. *See* Kinnakeet.

Kinnakeet Dunes, sand dunes, 10 mi. long, Dare County, Kinnakeet Township (local use). Historically 15 mi. from Great Island (s) (e of Canadian Hole) to just s of Little Kinnakeet sometimes as far n as Bay Point e of Cross Shoals. In historical Kinnakeet. *See* Kinnakeet Banks.

Kinnakeet Reef, shallow shoal, 1–3 ft. deep, 3 mi. long, Dare County, Kinnakeet Township (local use). Just offshore (soundside) from Hatteras Island from Gibbs Point (n) to Askins Creek (s), center at about Peters Ditch at original Avon, 6 mi. n of Buxton. Name from original area, Kinnakeet, before community adopted post office name (Avon) since Kinnakeet was deemed too cumbersome to use. *See* Kinnakeet. "Reef" in Outer Banks geographic names usually refers to oyster colonies.

Kinnakeet Shoals, shoals, 3 mi. long, Dare County, Kinnakeet Township (Deaton et al. 2012, 402). Oceanside just offshore 7.5 mi. s of Wimble Shoals, 12 mi. s of Rodanthe. Sometimes size perceived 5 mi. long and n portion then coincidental with the s portion Five Fathom Bank (q.v.), especially since name Five Fathom Bank is not used now as much as in 19th century. Five Fathom Bank is just s of Wimble Shoals (q.v.) and n portion Five Fathom Bank sometimes considered to be near or at the s portion Wimble Shoals. All of these shoals are remnants of massive Cape Kenrick (q.v.). *See* Kenricks Mounts and Kinnakeet.

Kinnakeet Shoals. *See* Five Fathom Bank.

Kinnakeet Woods, former woods, Dare County, Kinnakeet Township (historical documents). Was myrtles and other maritime vegetation in Avon n to former Scarboro. Historically, a few wooded areas along soundside between Cape Hatteras and Rodanthe, by 20th century these woods had been depleted for numerous uses. *See* Kinnakeet. *Other names:* Kinekeet Woods (some historical documents), Kinnket Woods (some historical documents).

Kitchin Impoundment. *See* Hegge Impoundment.

Kite Point, distinct point, Dare County, Kinnakeet Township (local use). On Hatteras Island 2 mi. e of Canadian Hole, 3 mi. ne of Buxton. New name applied during early 21st century because this is a gathering point for windsurfing and kiteboarding enthusiasts—conditions here are considered ideal for these sports. No known name here earlier.

Kitty Hawk, town, Dare County, Atlantic Township (USGS 2013: Kitty Hawk). On Currituck Banks (now often Dare Banks) 8 mi. nnw of original Nags Head. Used since late 18th century. Number of legends, theories, and stories exist to describe the name origin. Suggested the early settlers observed there were a large number of mosquito hawks (crane flies, family Tipulidae) here, referred to as "skeeter hawks," eventually evolved to Kitty Hawk. Crane flies are also known regionally as mosquito hawks, but mere presumption.

Reported name might have stemmed from earlier Indian reference to their conception of white man's year, from "kill a hauk to kill a hauk" or killing first goose of year to killing first goose the following year (mere storytelling). Also known *hauk* is an Indian reference to local wildfowl and might represent an imitation of sound made by wildfowl. Name bears resemblance to Kittiwake, name of gull-like bird (black-legged kittiwake, *Rissa tridactyla*) of Atlantic coast (in winter); however, little evidence to support any relationship since kittiwake less known s of Chesapeake Bay. An official at the now-defunct Life-Saving Service Office in a letter to USBGN suggested possibility of being named for a person with surname Hawk, but certainly not the case and based on no credible information.

A Delaware Indian reference exists translating *kitt* to big and *hakki* to land, which could be related to the name because this is one of the widest parts of the Outer Banks, but little Delaware influence here. Also barely possible corruption of Etacrewac, a broader Indian name for this area. However, the actual name origin is conclusively an Anglicized corruption of an Algonquian Indian name Chickehauk or Chicahauk, known to be used by indigenous peoples for this area.

Post office est. 1878. When a map of Kitty Hawk was published 1929, terms Down-the-Road (q.v.) and Up-the-Road (q.v.) were used for e and w parts of Kitty Hawk, ostensibly referring to two distinct clusters in 1929, used only short time. Incorporated 1981. Three subdivisions named for feature. Made official by the USBGN 1959 to clarify name is two words, thereby reversing 1892 decision where Kittyhawk is one word.

Other names: Chicahauk (indigenous reference), Chickahauk (Dunbar 1958, 56), Chickahawk (spelling variation), Chickehauk (e.g., Stick 1970), Chickhauk (real estate brochures), Citehawk (Harris 2017; unknown, 1792)—this form and variations used for Kitty Hawk Bay result from nonstandard spelling [until 1830s], but also could be peculiar form of Chickahauk), Down-the-Road Community (Angley 1995, 9), Keeterhook (early deeds), Ketterhock (Dunbar 1958, 56), Kettyhauk (Dunbar 1958, 46), Killy Hawk (misinterpretation), Kittehawk (Currituck DB 7, 1795, 169–70), Kittyhark (misinterpretation), Kitty Hark (Stick 1958, 262), Kitty Hauk (colonial deeds), Kitty-hawk (Stick 1958, 262), Kittyhawk (1948 War Department map, reported in Angley 1985, 46; Binkley 2007, 100, referencing 1952 CHNS project map), Kitty-hawk (early maps), Kitty Hawk Village (Stick 1958, 199), Kityhuk (visitors guides), Kittyhuk (Stick 1958, 262), Kittyhuke (colonial deeds), Old Kitty Hawk (Miller 1974), Skeeter Hawk (local whimsical reference), Up-the-Road Community (Angley 1995, 10).

Kitty Hawk Bay, shallow bay, 2.7 mi. long, 1.7 mi. wide, Dare County, Atlantic Township (USGS 2013: Kitty Hawk). At e end Albemarle Sound just n of Colington Island 1.6 mi. sw of original Kitty Hawk. Suggestions indicate Kitty Hawk Bay a remnant of former inlet Trinety Harbor or some other inlet. This is not so—Trinety Harbor was farther n (just n of Duck), and if an inlet at Kitty Hawk existed it had to be before 1585. Little evidence to indicate an inlet at Kitty Hawk Bay (*see* Kill Devil Hills Inlet). Scientific evidence suggests only two inlets here more than 1,000 years ago and a third at an undetermined time

(*see* Kill Devil Hills Inlet). *See* Kitty Hawk. The name was made official by USBGN 1959 to clarify Kitty Hawk is two words, thereby reversing 1892 decision where Kittyhawk is one word.

Other names: Bay of Kitty Hawk (Richard Etheridge will, reported in Stick 1958, 264; Angley 1995, 3), Chickehauk Bay (commercial brochures, attracting attention by using original form of Kitty Hawk), Citehawk Bay (Currituck DB 5, 1784, 92), Citty Hack Bay (Currituck DB 4, 1783, 172), Cittehawk Bay (Currituck DB 8, 1800, 254), Cittyhawk Bay (Currituck DB 5, 1787, 276), City Hock Bay (Currituck DB 8, 1800, 246), City Hawk Bay (Currituck DB 10, 1809, 106), Kille Hawk Bay (Harris 2017; unknown, 1763)—this form not encountered on any map), Kitehawk Bay (Currituck DB 6, 1793, 287–88), Kitihawk Bay (Currituck DB 7, 1794, 133), Kittihawk Bay (early deeds), Kittyhawke Bay (Currituck DB 2, 1770, 306), Kittyhawk Bay (CS 1862a; Binkley 2007, 100, referencing 1952 CHNS project map; USBGN 1892), Kitty Hoak Bay (Currituck DB 3, 1802, 231–32), Kitty Hock Bay (Currituck DB 4, 1783, 229–30), Kityhawk Bay (Currituck DB 8, 1801, 269), Kity Hawke Bay (Currituck DB 2, 1773, 377), Kity Hock Bay (Currituck DB 30, 1869, 175–76), Rousapock Bay (Harris 2017—*see* Rowspock Point for explanation), Rousypock Bay (Harris 2017).

Kitty Hawk Bay Islands, island complex, Dare County, Atlantic Township (Sorrie 2014, map, 124). In s Kitty Hawk Bay composed of Baum Point Island, Sloop Island, Burnt Island, Les Island, Sharp Island, numerous small unnamed marsh islands, just n of Colington Island, 2.5 mi. s of original Kitty Hawk. Southern Islands, was reportedly introduced middle to late 20th century as descriptive of location in Kitty Hawk Bay, so while known to some was never much used. *See* Kitty Hawk. *Other names:* Southern Islands (some local use).

Kitty Hawk Beach, beach, 3 mi. long, Dare County, Atlantic Township (local use). At Kitty Hawk (town), from just s of beach at Southern Shores to Avalon Beach 4 mi. n of Kill Devil Hills (town). Use of Carolina Beach was applied to a small part of Kitty Hawk Beach and used for short time from a club and recreation area here. The town of Carolina Beach near Wilmington, N.C., complained and filed a lawsuit; outcome favored Carolina Beach (town), so club and recreation area names changed to Kitty Hawk Beach (Downing 2008, 57–58). *See* Kitty Hawk. Two subdivisions named for feature. *Other names:* Carolina Beach (Downing 2008, 57).

Kitty Hawk Dunes, sand dune complex, 7 mi. long, Dare County, Atlantic Township (local use). Nnw to ssw from s Southern Shores to Kill Devil Hills (sand dunes) just w of beach. Numerous high locations within the complex, some named some not named. Some use for Sandy Ridge in n part Southern Shores (town). While some has been preserved, most has been altered considerably by man. *See* Kitty Hawk. *Other names:* Kitty Dunes (occasional use, four subdivisions use this form).

Kitty Hawk Landing, landing, Dare County, Atlantic Township (USGS 2013: Kitty Hawk). Protected landing for small watercraft soundside of Currituck Banks 2 mi. n of entrance Kitty Hawk Bay, 2.2 mi. w of original Kitty Hawk. *See* Kitty Hawk. Used for decades but is now within Kitty Hawk Landing subdivision and is only for use by residents. *Other names:* Shellbank Landing (some early use associated with nearby Shellbank Point), Shell Bank Point (NCDOT 1938).

Kitty Hawk Ridge, sand ridge, 3.5 mi. long, Dare County, Atlantic Township (local informants). Trends n-s from n Kitty Hawk to s Kitty Hawk near Old Landing Ridge, 4 mi. nnw of Kill Devil Hill (hill). While some of this ridge has been preserved by being on e edge Kitty Hawk Woods, several parts have been considerably altered by man. *See* Kitty Hawk. *Other names:* City Hawk Ridge (Currituck DB 11, 1810, 97–98), Kitte Hawk Ridge (Currituck DB 5, 1787, 271), Kittehawk Ridge (Currituck DB 7, 1794, 61), Kitty Hack Ridge (Currituck DB 4, 1783, 172), Kitty Ridge (Harris 2017; unknown, 1798), Kity Hoake Ridge (Currituck DB 9, 1806, 218–19).

Kitty Hawk ridge-and-swale system, sand ridges and depressions, Dare County, Atlantic Township (reports and papers). N-s mostly just w of original Kitty Hawk, but includes n to mouth of Jeanguite Creek and to Mill Point at tip of Martin Point (peninsula). Composed of n-s linear ridges and swales (depressions), where swales are filled with sluggish tidewater and marshes, locally referenced as swamps. Ridges covered with pine and other vegetation except where removed by development. A ridge-and-swale system is usually linear sand ridges (can be short or extensive) separated by lower linear, valley-type formations known as swales between the ridges. The topography here was created generally 3,000–4,000 years ago by alternating periods of erosion and accretion as the barrier islands were forming. This reference not a place name but is included because often referenced in scientific papers and useful for descriptive purposes. Scores of features; sand ridges, marshes, swamps, and similar features in this landscape contribute to the namescape. *See* Kitty Hawk.

Kitty Hawk Woods, woods, 3.5 mi. long, Dare County, Atlantic Township (numerous documents). On Currituck Banks from Kitty Hawk Bay n to Southern Shores 10 mi. nw of Nags Head (center). *See* Kitty Hawk. Subdivision named for feature. *Other names:* (Southern Woods—in part, from large subdivision here), The Woods (local use).

Kitty Hawk Woods Swamps, swamps, Dare County, Atlantic Township (some local use). Sort of semicircle from e to w from Pawpaw Ridge just w of original Kitty Hawk to just e of Sound Landing just n of Kitty Hawk Landing subdivision. Individually named swamps are from e to w: Pawpaw Swamp, Dancing Ridge Swamp, Chinquapin Swamp, Sandy Run Swamp, Duck Pond Swamp, Sage Swamp, Ash Swamp, Flat Swamp, Whidbee Swamp. Polly Ridge Swamp also in this system, but exact location unknown. *See* Kitty Hawk and each individual entry. *Other names:* Grate Swamp (Currituck DB 4, 1784, 227–28).

Kitty Midgetts Hammock, hummock, Dare County, Kinnakeet Township (Bishop 1878). Just n of Midgett Cove and just s of Midgett Island halfway between Waves and Salvo, 1 mi. from each. Midgett (originally Midyette) surname prevalent since original settlement. Kitty Midgett was from Salvo (Clarks) and probably lived there late 18th century. Also reference to Kitty Midgett's Hammock in letter (no location and no date on letter but likely 1940s) from now defunct Life-Saving Service (now U.S. Coast Guard) to C&GS (now NOAA), in which Kitty Midgetts Hammock is mentioned (actually Hummock, must have been inserted from within that office because, though correct term, "hammock" is form used exclusively at the Outer Banks). *Other names:* Kitty Midgetts Hummock (Life Saving Service letter 1940s).

Knight Point, peninsula, 1.3 mi. long, Currituck County, Fruitville Township; and Virginia Beach, Virginia (USGS 2013: Knotts Island). Often applied only to tip in Virginia, though applied to entire peninsula on USGS (1902, 1893 Norfolk 1:125,000 scale) maps. Peninsula is n point Knotts Island 3.3 mi. n of Knotts Island (village).

Knoll, The, sand dune, 25 ft. high, Hyde County, Ocracoke Township (USGS 2013: Howard Reef). On Ocracoke Island 7.8 mi. n of Ocracoke (village).

Knoll Cedars, former woods, 10 ft. high, Hyde County, Ocracoke Township (historical local use). Was on Ocracoke Island 0.4 mi. e of Parkers Hill, 7 mi. ne of Ocracoke (village). *Other names:* Knoll Woods (Weslager 1954).

Knoll Creek, cove, 0.1 mi. wide, Hyde County, Ocracoke Township (USGS 1950: Green Island). In Pamlico Sound just sw of Knoll Island 7.6 mi. ne of Ocracoke (village).

Knoll House Creek, cove, 0.1 mi. wide, Hyde County, Ocracoke Township (USGS 2002: Howard Reef). In Pamlico Sound 6.5 mi. ne of Ocracoke (village). *Other names:* Knollhouse Creek (Mallin, McIver, and Johnson 2006, fig. 3, 26).

Knoll Island, marsh peninsula, 0.3 mi. long, Hyde County, Ocracoke Township (USGS 2013: Green Island). Just sw of Great Swash 7.8 mi. ne of Ocracoke (village).

Knott Island Mill, former mill and windmill, Currituck County, Fruitville Township (CS 1877). At s end Knotts Island near former Bonnys Store and Knotts Landing 2 mi. s of Knotts Island (village). Use of "Knott" in singular nongenitive sense occasional 19th century. *See* Knotts Island (island).

Knotts Island, island, 5.8 mi. long, 1.7 mi. wide, 20 ft. high, Currituck County, Fruitville Township (USGS 2013: Knotts Island, Barco). Formerly an island but now separated from mainland by The Great Marsh and between Currituck Sound and Back Bay 2.4 mi. w of Currituck Banks, 9 mi. n of Waterlily (mainland). The peculiar notion the island was named for numerous pine trees and hence knots in these trees is utter nonsense, not worthy of folk etymology (creating reasons when none are known). Early deeds and other records indicate there were numerous individuals here with associated surname Knott. Named most likely for James Knott, who reportedly held land here as early as 1642. Variant Netsiland was a misrepresentation on earlier maps and records: should have been two words, and Nets is misspelling of Nots, form of Knotts; "iland" is 16th-century English spelling of island. Two subdivisions named for feature. *Other names:* Hoskins Island (Princess Anne County, Va., related to Currituck County before creation of Dare County; unknown, 1870, bk. 3, 411–12), Knobs Island (Byrd 1728 — recording error), Knot Ile (Comberford 1657), Knot Island (CS 1852), Knot Isle (historical maps), Knots Island (Price et al. 1808; Byrd 1728; Currituck DB 7, 1794, 41-42), Knots Islands (transcribing error), Knott Island (Fisher et al. 1689, chart 15; USGS 1940: Barco 1:62,500 scale), Mackeys Island (Stick 1958, 313), Mackys Island (Collet et al. 1770 — application error for Mackay Island just w of Knotts Island), Makys Island (Mouzon 1775), Netsiland (early deeds), Nots Island (Byrd 1728 — surveyors map 1727; Currituck DB 9, 1804, 75), Nott Island (early deeds), Notts Island (Collet et al. 1770), Notts Isle (Holland 1794).

Knotts Island, village, 15 ft. high, Currituck County, Fruitville Township (USGS 2013: Knotts Island). On Knotts Island 2.7 mi. w of Currituck Banks, 9 mi. nne of Waterlily (mainland). Knotts Island (village), settled 1642, considered oldest continuous settlement in North Carolina. Post office est. 1818. *See* Knotts Island (island). Short road named Moonrise Bay Landing extends from Woodleigh Road to s Knots Island Channel. Local residents indicate there was never a landing here by that name and was likely a marketing technique of a former winery here. County GIS office confirms road name did not exist before 1997, likely named by developer, no landing by that name although small dock present, privately used. *Other names:* Knott Island (USGS 1943: Back Bay 1:62,500 scale).

Knotts Island Bay, lagoon, 1.7 mi. wide, Currituck County, Fruitville Township (USGS 2013: Knotts Island, Barco). Separates Currituck Banks and Knotts Island 2 mi. ese of Knotts Island (village). *See* Knotts Island

(island). *Other names:* Broad Creek (early references), Knott Island Bay (USGS 1940: Barco 1:62,500 scale), Knotts Island Sound (recent mistake recording in some external internet websites—never used locally or on maps).

Knotts Island Causeway, man-enhanced hummock, 3.5 mi. long, Currituck County, Fruitville Township (USGS 1902: Norfolk 1:125,000 scale). Connects Morse Point on mainland to Knotts Island (former small settlement Coreys was halfway along The Causeway); 3 mi. nw of Knotts Island (village). Natural linear high ground worked over years into a man-enhanced causeway now containing NC 615. *See* Knotts Island (island). *Other names:* Marsh Causeway (County GIS), Old Road (C&GS 1882), The Causeway (some local use).

Knotts Island Channel, water passage, 2 mi. long, Currituck County, Fruitville Township (USGS 2013: Knotts Island). Connects Knotts Island Bay with Back Sound and separates Knotts Island from Currituck Banks 1.6 mi. ne of Knotts Island (village). *See* Knotts Island (island). *Other names:* Knott Island Channel (USGS 1943: Back Bay 1:62,500 scale), Manns Channel (misapplication but occasionally applied to n part).

Knotts Island Ferry Dock, landing, Currituck County, Fruitville Township (signage). Sw tip Knotts Island for Currituck–Knotts Island Ferry 2 mi. se of Knotts Island (village).

Knotts Landing, landing, Currituck County, Fruitville Township (USGS 2013: Barco). At ferry dock, s end Knotts Island 2.2 mi. s of Knotts Island (village). Late 18th century just anchorage in Currituck Sound until moved onto s tip Knotts Island near former Bonnys Store. *See* Knotts Island (island). Subdivision named for feature. *Other names:* Knott Landing (USGS 1943: Back Bay 1:62,500 scale), Knotts Island Landing (C&GS 1882), South End (local use).

Knotts Plain, historical area, from the present Knotts Island (village) n-ward to n tip Knotts Island in Virginia. Long since fallen into disuse. Referenced higher part of Knotts Island. *See* Knotts Island (island).

Kohler Landing, former landing, Dare County, Kinnakeet Township (historical local use). Was in Salvo, just s of Opening Marshes 3.7 mi. s of Rodanthe.

L

Labrador Current, ocean current formed by cold currents from Baffin Bay and around West Greenland. Flows s to Grand Banks off coast of Newfoundland, then continues s as Labrador Current and collides with Gulf Stream off Cape Hatteras, disintegrating but deflecting Gulf Stream ne-ward. Accounts for turbulent conditions in treacherous Diamond Shoals. The boundary zone between the two (warm and cold) is Hatteras Front, moves between Cape Hatteras and Nags Head according to conditions. *Other names:* Arctic Current (websites), Artic (*sic*) Cold Current (Torres 1985, 5), Virginia Coastal Drift (Torres 1985, 4).

Lake Burnside, elongated lake, 0.3 mi. long, 0.05 mi. wide, Dare County, Nags Head Township (local use). On n Roanoke Island, 0.4 mi. n of General Burnside's headquarters (former site), 1.3 mi. w of Manteo (center). Named for General Burnside, who commanded Union troops that occupied Roanoke Island and the Outer Banks during Civil War.

Lake Ridge, distinct sand ridge, 1 mi. long, Dare County, Atlantic Township (local use). In ne Round-About Hills (q.v.) just se of Run Hill 5 mi. s of original Kitty Hawk. Two distinct tops in n part, each 35 ft. high. Continues s across a saddle (lower part) to higher elevations at around 50 ft. to a point adjacent to n Fresh Pond. Several small lakes here but name is from adjacent Fresh Pond. Undeveloped but platted subdivision here using same name.

Lambards Marsh, large marsh, Dare County, Hatteras Township (Currituck DB 6, 1716, 7). Is 1.3 mi. nnw of Cape Point at Cape Hatteras 2 mi. s of Buxton. Name not used today, though was used on 17th- and into 18th-century maps. Unclear whether name is descriptive of some antiquated term (originally generic reference to land) or perhaps a surname. *Other names:* Grate Ditch Marsh (Currituck DB 10, 1808, 77), Lumberds Marsh (deed 1716).

Landing Creek, former tidal creek, Currituck

County, Poplar Branch Township (Currituck DB 1785, 5, 223-224). Was just w of Baums Creek 6 mi. n of Duck (center). Former Baums Mill use, no longer exists and name unknown.

Landing Ridge, low, short sand ridge, 0.5 mi. long, Dare County, Atlantic Township (Harris 2017). In Kitty Hawk ridge-and-swale system (q.v.) of w Kitty Hawk at Sound Landing 2 mi. w of original Kitty Hawk. Barely discernable, lowest s end and highest n end. Derived from proximity to Sound Landing.

Lands End, area, Dare County, Hatteras Township (local use). In Frisco, 4 mi. ene of Hatteras (village). *See* Lands End (historical area).

Lands End, historical area, Dare County, Nags Head Township (limited historical use). Sometimes used for n side of Oregon Inlet for a short time from 1940s, when permanent road was first built, and before Bonner Bridge built 1963 (replaced by Basnight Bridge 2019). Fallen into disuse since bridge was built 1963. Used as place name throughout coastal areas of the world to signify terminus of a particular island or place of use.

Lands End Beach, small beach, Carteret County, White Oak Township (mostly tourist use). At Lands End subdivision 1.2 mi. sw of Langston Bridge, 8 mi. w of original Emerald Isle. Informal name has come into use during past 20 years, mostly used by tourists and vacationers. *See* Lands End (clipped use). *Other names:* West End Beach (local use).

Large Shoal, shoal, Dare County, Hatteras Township (Holland 1794). In Pamlico Sound 0.8 mi. nnw of Buxton. Remnants of former massive shoal exist, but considerably more exposed historically, existed as barely covered reef almost uninterrupted soundside from historical Old Hatteras Inlet to Pea Island.

Latham Hole. *See* Divine Cove.

Latitude Hill, former sand dune, Carteret County, Harkers Island Township (Stick 1958, 309). Considerably higher mid-20th century, as topography of Cape Lookout and environs changed greatly over past 100 years. Precise location not known or remembered, considering changing topography, but was somewhere within 1–2 sq. mi. on Cape Lookout just s of Cape Hills and former Cape Lookout (village), between Cape Hills and Cape Point at tip of Cape Lookout, 1.5 mi. ssw of Cape Lookout Lighthouse.

Lawrences Creek, tidal stream, Carteret County, Portsmouth Township (NPS 2007, 139). On Portsmouth Island just s of Portsmouth (village) and 6.5 mi. sw of Ocracoke (village). Separated primary Portsmouth (village) from Middle Portsmouth (Middle Community).

Lazy Hill, former sand dune, Carteret County, Harkers Island Township (Stick 1958, 309). Considerably higher mid-20th century, as topography of Cape Lookout and environs changed greatly over past 100 years. Precise location not known or remembered, considering changing topography, but was somewhere within 1–2 sq. mi. on Cape Lookout just s of Cape Hills and former Cape Lookout (village), between Cape Hills and Cape Point at tip of Cape Lookout, 1.5 mi. ssw of Cape Lookout Lighthouse. Speculation suggests name from appearance, as meaning not remembered.

L B Morgan Island, possible former small island, Dare County, Nags Head Township. Was reportedly in Albemarle Sound 2 mi. nw of Roanoke Island just n of entrance Croatan Sound, 6.5 mi. nw of Manteo (center). Approximate location; not certain whether this island existed. Likely observation of an exposed part of Colington Shoal (just se) at low water.

Lead, The, small water passage, Dare County, Atlantic Township; and Currituck County, Poplar Branch Township (local use). Connects open water in Dare County to Great Gap, Currituck County, 1.5 mi. nw of Sanderling. "Lead" is reference to an approach. *See* Buzzard Lead.

Legged Lump, two shoals, 1 mi. long, Hyde County, Ocracoke Township (USGS 2013: Green Island). In Pamlico Sound 10 mi. ne of Ocracoke (village). Reportedly resembled two gigantic legs (Weslager 1954, 47). *See* Dorland Lump. *Other names:* Guesses Shoal (se part—Weslager 1954), Leggedy Lump (Weslager 1954, 47), Two Legged Lump (Weslager 1954, 47).

Lelands Harbor, former landing, Dare County, Kinnakeet Township (Garrity-Blake 2010, 492). Was soundside just n of Waves Landing 2.2 mi. s of Rodanthe. Use of harbor is unusual as landing was almost always used.

Lemors Bay, bay, Dare County, Atlantic Township (Currituck DB 7, 1797, 414–15; Harris 2017). According to 18th-century deeds somewhere at North Banks in association with Rowspock Point. Believed to be open water just e of Kill Devil Hill, just s of e Kitty Hawk Bay (n) and n entrance Colington Creek (s) between Kitty Hawk Bay Islands (w) and the barrier island, Currituck Banks (North Banks now Dare Banks) (e). Harris (2017) offers numerous variations from between 1800 and 1810 but has no additional information. While Lemor is known surname with some occurrences in North Carolina, Lemor (or variations) does not appear as surname here in any early deeds (1719–1870). The location name does not appear on any map examined and does not appear in deeds after 1823. Those interviewed had never heard the name, and occurrences almost always mentioned in association with Rowspock (or some variation—*see* Roespock Run). Further, use of variant Lemors Southern Creek suggests the more restricted "open water" se of Kitty Hawk Bay. Additionally, the island named Les Island (q.v.) is e-most marsh island in Kitty Hawk Bay Islands (q.v.) complex, adjacent to Lemors Bay, and that name has always been a bit of a mystery but could be a corrupted version of Lemors.

Other names: Lemar Bay (Harris 2017; unknown, 1809), Lemons Bay (Currituck DB 9, 1805, 61—only known mention, probable transcribing error), Lemores Bay (Currituck DB 12, 1813, 179), Lemors Southern Creek (Currituck DB 3, 1739, 33–34), Lemour Bay (Harris 2017; unknown, 1802), Lemours Bay (Harris 2017; unknown, 1802), Limars Bay (Harris 2017; 1797—misrecorded from deed), Moris Bay (Harris 2017; unknown, 1836), Simors Southern Creek (Harris 2017; unknown, 1739—typographical error of Limors).

Les Island, marsh island, Dare County, Atlantic Township (20th century). E-most island in Kitty Hawk Bay Islands (q.v.) complex, 2.5 mi. s of original Kitty Hawk. This name is not for personal given name so has always been a mystery. However, it might have originally been Lemors Island and Les might be a corrupted version of Lemors, after Lemors Bay (q.v.), believed to be name of open water

between this island and the barrier island (Currituck Banks or North Banks) in Kill Devil Hills. *Other names:* Las Island (some usage).

Lewis Creek, water passage, 0.5 mi. long, Carteret County, Smyrna Township (USGS 2013: Horsepen Point). Trends n-s, separates Horse Island from Core Banks 5.4 mi. e of Harkers Island (village).

Lewis Island, marsh island, 0.4 mi. long and wide, Carteret County, Smyrna Township (USGS 2013: Horsepen Point). In Core Sound, separated from Core Banks by Lewis Creek 5.5 mi. e of Harkers Island (village).

Lewis Thoroughfare, former water passage, Carteret County, Beaufort and Morehead Townships (C&GS 1888a). Trended se-nw through Reids Marsh from Bulkhead Channel to Newport River 1 mi. w of Beaufort (mainland). Name no longer used and a portion of what was Lewis Thoroughfare now reclaimed land for causeway supporting US 70 Business just w of Beaufort (mainland). Name for remaining water has fallen into disuse. *Other names:* Lewis Thorofare (G. Colton 1861), Thoroughfare (C&GS 1910a).

Licksville, former area, Dare County, Hatteras Township (NPS 2005b: NPS 2, 305). In Hatteras (village), used as local reference to gathering place centered around local store apparently named Lick. Exact location unknown. Most numerous small local stores everywhere on the Outer Banks were gathering points for activities; some had a telephone, some housed post office, and all were a place for obtaining news and gossip. Most were simply known by owner's name, and those are not included in this volume, but if a different, special name or reference was used an entry is warranted. The reason for this name was not provided in the source (except "after the store's owner"), and no one today remembers the name.

Lifeguard Beach, beach, Hyde County, Ocracoke Township (NPS 2016). Oceanside, se end Ocracoke Island 1.5 mi. se of Ocracoke (village). Recent origin and coined informally to differentiate this as only beach on Ocracoke Island with lifeguard service supplied by NPS during summer; Ocracoke Beach is now used almost as often. Judged to be best beach in U.S. in 2007. *See* Ocracoke Beach. *Other names:* Life Guard Beach (brochures), Ocracoke Beach (increasing local use).

Lighter Slew, former natural channel, Currituck County, Poplar Branch (C&GS 1852). Was in Currituck Sound, s from Shell Rock just e of Dowdy Bay, 9.5 mi. ssw of Corolla. Descriptive of activity of lightering practiced 18th and 19th centuries along the Outer Banks where there were open inlets used by ships with cargo. Ships with large draughts were too large to navigate shallow sounds, so for delivering from deep water or a channel the cargo would be transferred to shallow-draft skiffs for retransporting. Caffeys Inlet (open until 1810) was 3 mi. e of this channel. Caffeys Inlet not noted for commerce, but by virtue of this name there must have been some. *See* Allen Slough.

Lighthouse Bay, water passage, 0.8 mi. long, 0.5 mi. wide, Carteret County, Harkers Island Township (USGS 2013: Harkers Island). Junction Core Sound and Back Sound. Ne extension of Barden Inlet connects Barden Inlet to Core Sound near Cape Lookout Lighthouse 4 mi. sse of Harkers Island (village).

Lighthouse Bay, cove, 0.4 mi. long, 0.1 mi. wide, Dare County, Nags Head Township (USGS 2013: Oregon Inlet). In Roanoke Sound 0.3 mi. wsw of Bodie Island Lighthouse, 4.5 mi. ese of Wanchese. *Other names:* Light House Bay (various sources).

Lighthouse Channel, channel, 1.3 mi. long, Carteret County, Harkers Island Township (USGS 2013: Harkers Island). Trends n-s, junction Core Sound and Back Sound n from Lighthouse Bay near Cape Lookout Lighthouse between Whitehurst Island and Morgan Island to Shell Point at se point Harkers Island, 3 mi. se of Harkers Island (village). *Other names:* Cape Lookout Channel (Godfrey, 1976, 141).

Lighthouse Pond, lake, 0.2 mi. across, Currituck County, Poplar Branch Township (USGS 2013: Corolla). Just w of Currituck Beach Lighthouse, 0.5 mi. w of Corolla. *Other names:* Goose Pond (Codman, Crowninshield, and Lawrence 1925), Lighthouse Cove (some local use), Light House Pond (realty maps).

Lighthouse Pond, lake, Dare County, Hatteras Township (local use). On Cape Hatteras just nw of Cape Point 3 mi. s of Buxton. Named because it was at Cape Hatteras Lighthouse, but lighthouse moved inland just over

0.5 mi. in 1999 for its preservation by NPS because in danger of being surrounded and toppled by encroaching sea. *Other names:* Cape Hatteras Lighthouse Pond (Sorrie 2014, 85—scientific reports), Fish Cleaning Station Pond (NPS, Water Quality Report 2006a, 11), Freshwater Pond (Vincent 2003, 22), Salt Pond (trail maps).

Lighthouse Wharf, former landing, Hyde County, Ocracoke Township (ACE 1939). Was in Silver Lake just ne of Ocracoke Lighthouse, 0.3 mi. se of Ocracoke (village center).

Lindseys Marsh, marsh, Currituck County, Poplar Branch Township (C&GS 1852). At s entrance Neals Creek separated from Rattlesnake Island by Strait Creek, 9 mi. sw of Corolla.

Little Bay Tree, small island, Currituck County, Poplar Branch Township (unknown, ca. 1900). Was in Currituck Sound halfway between Bay Tree and North Burris Island 0.5 mi. from each, 7.6 mi. ssw of Corolla. Name mostly forgotten. *See* Bay Tree.

Little Bellows Bay, bay, 0.7 mi. long, 0.4 mi. wide, Currituck County, Fruitville Township (USGS 2013: Barco). N arm of Bellows Bay between Mackay Island and Great Marsh 3.3 mi. wsw of Knotts Island (village). *Other names:* Duckpond (USGS 1943: 1:62,500 scale).

Little Bird Island, small marsh island, 0.1 mi. wide, 0.2 mi. long, Currituck County, Fruitville Township (Cox 1923). Extreme ne end Currituck Bay just s of Big Bird Island, 4 mi. se of Knotts Island (village). Now mostly connected on se side to Rainbow Island.

Little Bridge Creek, small water passage, Dare County, Nags Head Township (local use). E anabranch or arm of Roanoke Sound between Pond Island (e) and Cedar Island (w) 1 mi. w of Whalebone Junction. Trends n-s under Daniels Bridge (known locally as Little Bridge and named for Melvin R. Daniels of Wanchese later Elizabeth City, who served as state senator and was involved heavily in civic matters of the Outer Banks and in Elizabeth City). Two informants indicated "it must be Daniels Creek since that's the name of the bridge." *Other names:* Daniels Creek (occasional use).

Little Channel, water passage, 0.5 mi. long, Carteret County, Portsmouth Township (USGS 1950: Portsmouth). In Pamlico Sound just sw of Casey Island, just wnw of

Portsmouth (village), 6.6 mi. sw of Ocracoke (village).

Little Colington, historical island reference, Dare County, Atlantic Township. E portion Colington Island. *See* Big Colington, Colington, and Bay Tree. *Other names:* Little Colenton (Stick 1958, 266), Little Colington Island (some local use; according to Harris 2017 recorded early as 1785—document unknown), Little Colenton Island (Currituck DB 5, 1784, 48–49), Little Collenton (Currituck DB 9, 1802, 44), Little Collington (Currituck DB 28, 1859, 428).

Little Deep Marsh Island, island, 0.2 mi. long, Carteret County, Harkers Island Township (USGS 2013: Harkers Island, Horsepen Point). In Core Sound just n of Gunning Hammock Island 3.5 mi. e of Harkers Island (village).

Little Ditch, tidal stream, 0.3 mi. wide, Dare County, Hatteras Township (local informants). Just s of The Slash 0.8 mi. e of Hatteras (village). *Other names:* The Ditch (some local use).

Little Flounder Rock, former rock, Carteret County, Portsmouth Township (Price 1795, 631). Was in Pamlico Sound at Flounder Rock just sw of North Rock, 7.3 mi. w of Ocracoke (village). Submerged, historically was one of two rocks of Flounder Rocks.

Little Fresh Pond Island, small marsh island, Currituck County, Fruitville Township (Currituck DB 5, 1787, 211). In e Knotts Island Bay 1 mi. n of Fresh Pond Island, 2 mi. se of Knotts Island (village). Variant Freh (*sic*) could be a recording error, perhaps not considering no standard spelling in U.S. until around 1830. Use of variant Pon (*sic*) is also not likely an error since this form appears countless times throughout deeds from early 1700s through early 1800s. These two variant names appeared in *same* sentence, same deed. *Other names:* Little Freh Pond Island (Currituck DB 4, 1782, 117), Little Fresh Pon Island (Currituck DB 4, 1782, 117).

Little Goat Island Bay, cove, 0.6 mi. wide, 0.3 mi. long, Currituck County, Poplar Branch Township (USGS 2013: Mossey Islands). Enclosed by marsh islands just n of Goat Island Bay 8.2 mi. nw of Duck. *Other names:* Goat Island Bay (C&GS 1852).

Little Gut, former tidal stream, 0.2 mi. long, Hyde County, Ocracoke Township (Weslager 1954—confirmed by interviews with Ballance [2017, 2018] and Howard [2017, 2018]). Was at se of what is now Silver Lake (then Cockle Creek) in Ocracoke (village) and joined with Big Gut to form The Gut. Was e creek in Old Guts (q.v.) complex and filled in by ACE when Silver Lake dredged. The Gut, Big Gut, and Little Gut comprised Old Guts complex. *See* Alligator Gut.

Little Hatteras Island, former island, 7 mi. long, Dare County, Hatteras Township (temporary local use). Formerly from Isabel Inlet (historical) sw to Hatteras Inlet with Hatteras (village) the center. Short-lived name used for reference just over two months from September 18, 2003, through November 2003. During this period, Isabel Inlet (historical) existed 3 mi. ene of Hatteras (village) just sw of Frisco, created by Hurricane Isabel September 18, 2003, existed until November 22, 2003, when filling completed by ACE. While in existence severed Hatteras Island necessitating, use of Little Hatteras Island for isolated part sw of Isabel Inlet (historical). *Other names:* Little Hatteras (local spoken use and temporary sign).

Little Hills, sand dunes, Dare County, Kinnakeet Township (local use). Comprises 7–10 dunes, each 10–15 ft., on central Hatteras Island at Bald Beach near former Little Kinnakeet center 5 mi. n of original Avon. Sometimes only most central dune is indicated as Little Hill.

Little Hog Island, small marsh island, 0.1 mi. across, Currituck County, Poplar Branch Township (USGS 2013: Mossey Islands). In Currituck Sound at n end Jarvis Channel 6.4 mi. s of Corolla.

Little Inlet, occasional water passage, Dare County, Hatteras Township (newspaper articles and local use). Ephemeral inlet more than mere overwash in October 2016 on Inlet Peninsula (Hatteras Spit) 2 mi. sw of Hatteras (village). Often overwash and temporary small inlets present (hence oft-applied name) during hurricanes, nor'easters, and other severe storms. Isabel Breach (not Isabel Inlet) here September 18, 2003, referenced as Isabel Breach rather than Little Inlet. However, most overwashes and temporary inlets here are termed "Little Inlet" in comparison to nearby Hatteras Inlet, including from Hurricane Matthew on October 9, 2016. *Other names:* Little Hatteras Inlet (local use).

Little Island, small marsh island, Carteret County, Portsmouth Township (C&GS 1866). At n entrance Casey Bay, just wsw of Portsmouth (village), 6 mi. sw of Ocracoke (village).

Little Island, small marsh island, Currituck County, Fruitville Township (C&GS 1878). In Knotts Island Channel just ne of Cason Point, 2 mi. ne of Knotts Island (village).

Little Island, island, Dare County, Atlantic Township (Currituck DB 2, 1766, 270–71). S entrance Colington Cut (The Dividing Creek 1700s) at n end Buzzard Bay (Dare County) 5 mi. s of original Kitty Hawk.

Little Island Shoal, former shoal, Carteret County, Portsmouth Township (Williamson 1992, 89). Probably near Little Island at entrance Casey Bay 0.5 mi. wsw of former Portsmouth Lifesaving Station.

Little Kill Devil Hill, former sand dune, Dare County, Atlantic Township (historical local use and NPS). Was just sw of Kill Devil Hill (Big Kill Devil Hill) and Wright Brothers National Memorial just n of Nags Head (center), mere remnant of former size. NPS still uses Big Kill Devil Hill and Little Kill Devil Hill for historical description and correctness, though what was Big Kill Devil Hill is now just Kill Devil Hill. Big Kill Devil Hill (Kill Devil Hill), Little Kill Devil Hill, West Hill, Run Hill, and other small sand dunes are known collectively as Kill Devil Hills. *Other names:* Little Hill (Wright brothers' correspondence).

Little Kinnakeet, former settlement, Dare County, Kinnakeet Township (USGS 2013: Little Kinnakeet—no trace, location still labeled). Scattered population was on Hatteras Island 4 mi. n of original Avon. *Kinnakeet* reportedly means mixed, but as with all words from indigenous languages of early European contact, meanings are vague and unclear and are difficult to prove because recording by early Europeans was haphazard. Post office est. 1873 at Kinnakeet (changed to Avon) served this area. By 1870s, harbor here was shoaling, so residents put their houses on barges and floated them to Avon (formerly Kinnakeet or Big Kinnakeet). No trace today, though still labeled on USGS (2013: Little Kinnakeet). *See* Kinnakeet. *Other names:* Keneekut (Foster 1866b), Kennekut (historical), Little Avon (Dunbar 1958, 202), North Kinnakeet (Bishop 1878).

Little Kinnakeet, area, Dare County, Nags Head Township (limited local use late 19th and early 20th centuries). On Roanoke Island 0.5 mi. nw of Manteo (center). Settled by some former residents of Little Kinnakeet on Hatteras Island when village was abandoned. Name moved with them but is generally known only as local reference and now rarely used. *See* Little Kinnakeet (former settlement).

Little Kinnakeet Beach, beach, 1 mi. long, Dare County, Kinnakeet Township (signage). At Ramp 32 Cape Hatteras National Seashore, 4.2 mi. n of original Avon. NPS has parking and beach access ramps variously placed, and a few have acquired names. *Other names:* Kinnakeet Beach (shortened in spoken use but Kinnakeet was Avon).

Little Morgan Island, island, Currituck County, Poplar Branch Township (C&GS 1913a). Smaller of two islands (sw most) in group known as Morgan Islands (q.v.) in Currituck Sound at nw tip of Mossey Islands complex 4.5 mi. sw of Corolla. *See* Morgan Islands.

Little Narrows, water passage, Currituck County, Poplar Branch Township (USGS 2013: Mossey Islands). Trends n-s separating unnamed marsh (w) from Narrows Island (e); Narrows Island separates Big Narrows and Little Narrows 7 mi. sw of Corolla. Used since 1801 (Currituck deeds). *Other names:* Narrows (C&GS 1852).

Little Otter Foot Point, point, Dare County, Kinnakeet Township (Garrity-Blake 2010, 210). Soundside just s of Otter Pond Point (Big Otter Foot Point) just n of Black Hammock in former original Avon known as The South'ard, 1 mi. s of original Avon (center), 6 mi. n of Buxton. *See* Big Otter Cove.

Little Oyster Creek, small tidal stream, Hyde County, Ocracoke Township (local use and Weslager 1954). In Oyster Creek subdivision in e Ocracoke (village) near Oyster Creek (Hyde County) just e of Silver Lake 3.2 mi. ne of Ocracoke Inlet. Tidal stream, as with Oyster Creek has been altered by development.

Little Pea Island, marsh island, 0.2 mi. long, 0.5 mi. wide, Dare County, Kinnakeet Township (CS 1852). 2 mi. s of Eagle Nest Bay, 8.6 mi. nnw of Rodanthe. Originally named Pea Island from wild peas once growing in abundance. Name Pea Island later transferred to adjacent barrier island

and applied from New Inlet to Oregon Inlet, so this island acquired the qualifier "little." *Other names:* Pea Island (Foster 1866b).

Little Penguin Island, marsh island, 0.1 mi. long, 0.05 mi. wide, Dare County, Nags Head Township (USGS 2013: Roanoke Island NE). In Roanoke Sound 3.1 mi. s of central Nags Head, 0.8 mi. n of The Causeway, 0.8 mi. nw of Whalebone Junction. *See* Penguin Islands. *Other names:* Demps Island (ACE 1843), Penguin Isle (some recent local use associatively because former nearby restaurant used this name, but never used as an actual name).

Little Perch Island, marsh island, less than 0.1 mi. across, Currituck County, Fruitville Township (USGS 2013: Knotts Island). In marsh islands at n end Knotts Island Channel 1.8 mi. ne of Knotts Island (village). *See* Big Perch Island and Perch Islands. *Other names:* Perch Island Number 1 (Cox 1923), Perch Island Number 3 (Cox 1906).

Little Raccoon Island, island, Currituck County, Poplar Branch Township (Currituck DB 24, 1842, 104). In Raccoon Islands (q.v.) complex in Raccoon Bay 0.3 mi. s of Big Raccoon Island, 0.5 mi. nnw of Corolla.

Little Raccoon Island Slew, small water passage, Currituck County, Poplar Branch Township (Currituck DB 24, 1842, 104). Just e of Little Raccoon Island separating Little Raccoon Island from the barrier island (Currituck Banks) 0.5 mi. nnw of Corolla. *See* Allen Slough.

Little Ridge, small sand ridge, Dare County, Kinnakeet Township (local use). Oceanside just e of Clarks Bay just e of n No Ache, 1 mi. s of Salvo.

Little Rock, small shoal, Dare County, Atlantic Township (local use). More shoal than rock in Currituck Sound in nw corner of Dare County, 2.5 mi. wnw of Sanderling.

Little Sheep Marsh, shoal, Currituck County, Fruitville Township (some local use). N Sheep Marsh on e approach to entrance Knotts Island Bay just e of Bush Island and North Bush Island 2.5 mi. se of Knotts Island (village). More shoal than marsh though more marsh mid-19th century. *See* Sheep Marsh.

Little Skinner Island, marsh island, 1 mi. long, 0.5 mi. wide, Currituck County, Fruitville Township (Cox 1923). Just se of Big Skinner Island, 8.5 mi. se of Knotts Island (village).

Other names: Hickory Island (occasional 18th century references).

Little Swash Opening, cove, 0.2 mi. wide, Hyde County, Ocracoke Township (USGS 2013: Howard Reef). In Pamlico Sound 5 mi. ne of Ocracoke (village). Possible location of Nigh Inlet. *See* Daniel Swash. *Other names:* Little Swash (Weslager 1954).

Little Tim Island, marsh island, 0.05 mi. long and wide, Dare County, Nags Head Township (USGS 2013: Oregon Inlet). In Roanoke Sound 0.3 mi. n of Walter Slough, 0.2 mi. sw of Big Tim Island, 4.5 mi. se of Wanchese. Entire island is subdivision named for feature.

Little Wade Island, small linear island, Carteret County, Smyrna Township (Leffers 1896). Trends se-nw in Johnson Creek 1 mi. s of Shingle Point, 5 mi. se of Davis (mainland).

Little Walkers Creek, water passage, Currituck County, Fruitville Township (Cox 1923). N-s trending, separates Walkers Island (e) from Crow Island (Big Raymond Island) (w) 7.5 mi. se of Knotts Island (village).

Little Yankee Pond, cove, 0.1 mi. long, Currituck County, Poplar Branch Township (local use). Just s of Big Yankee Pond, 6.2 mi. nw of Duck. *See* Yankee Ponds. *Other names:* Yankee Pond (USGS 2013, 2010, 1982: Jarvisburg).

Little Yopan Hill, sand dune, Dare County, Atlantic Township or Nags Head Township (Currituck DB 5, 1787, 247). Exact location or present condition unknown and not remembered now. Deed book provides only a textual entry with no locative information. Stick provides only general reference to Yopon Hill (q.v.) being one of the sand dunes somewhere in Kill Devil Hills complex, Round-About Hills complex, Scraggly Hills complex, or Jockeys Ridge complex; believed smaller dune related to Yopon Hill (slight spelling difference, these sand dunes extend n-s from n Kill Devil Hills to n Nags Head). Spelling unusual and only known occurrence in this form; accepted spelling is "yaupon." *See* Black Hammock and Yopon (*sic*) Hill.

Live Oak Camp, temporary military camp, Dare County, Kinnakeet Township (Stick 1958, 131; numerous Civil War sources). Union facility reported by many to have been established at Chicamacomico or what is now Rodanthe. Was temporary as there were back-and-forth advances and retreats by both Union and Confederates (known humorously as Chicamacomico Races). Not relevant since

Union forces captured Roanoke Island a short time later and Confederate presence was removed. Covey (2018) suspects from detailed excavation and research there might have been some Union earthworks here, but not yet proven. He also believes, and has written extensively, the camp was in Waves not Rodanthe (Covey 2018, 15). *Other names:* Camp Live Oak (Union maps).

Live Oak Hammock, former hill, Dare County, Kinnakeet Township (Henry Black survey, 1760, from Covey 2018, fig. 5, 20). Only remnants remain just ne of Askins Hill just n of Deep Creek 3 mi. s or original Avon.

Live Oak Hammock, hummock, Dare County, Nags Head Township (Currituck DB 1a, 1766, 194–95). Somewhere on nw Roanoke Island near Johns Ridge according to description in deed. Was anywhere from just nw of Manteo to 3.5 mi. nw of Manteo. Intended as descriptor but used as place name. Live oak (*Quercus virginiana*) ranges from extreme se Virginia in narrow coastal band to Georgia, then expanding throughout Florida and continuing along Gulf Coast to Texas, iconic symbol of the "Old South." *See* Black Hammock.

Live Oak Point, point, Currituck County, Fruitville Township (USGS 2013: Barco). Sw point Mackay Island 1 mi. nw of Halfway Point, 11.6 mi. nw of Corolla. *See* Live Oak Hammock. *Other names:* Oak Point (clipped usage, including local media).

Liza Lumps, islands, 0.3 mi. long, 0.1 mi. wide, Dare County, Kinnakeet Township (USGS 2013: Pea Island). Four islands in Pamlico Sound 1.1 mi. se of Jack Shoal, 5.6 mi. nw of Rodanthe. *See* Dorland Lump.

Log Blind Islands, marsh islands, Currituck County, Poplar Branch Township (Codman, Crowninshield, and Lawrence 1925). At se end Raccoon Bay 1 mi. w of Corolla. Reference to numerous duck blinds used for duck hunting here still today, though more extensively late 19th and early 20th centuries.

Log Channel, former small channel, Carteret County, Portsmouth Township (historical usage). Was through e end Sheep Island Shoal between Log Channel Rock (w) and Bush Shoal (e), 7.5 mi. w of Ocracoke (village).

Log Channel Rock, former rock, Carteret County, Portsmouth Township (C&GS 1900). Was in Pamlico Sound 1.8 mi. w of Portsmouth (village), 8 mi. w of Ocracoke (village).

Logerhead Shoal. *See* Cat Island (Dare County).

Loggerhead Hills, sand dunes, 0.3 mi. long, Dare County, Kinnakeet Township (USGS 2013: Pea Island). On Hatteras Island 3.5 mi. nnw of Rodanthe. Refers to loggerhead turtles (*Caretta caretta*) at one time abundant here; not reference to loggerhead shrike (*Lanius ludovicianus*), bird sometimes found here but only during migration. Loggerhead turtles named for their large, heavy heads; "loggerhead," heavy piece of wood to check movement of animals. "Loggerhead" also nautical term referring to piece of wood on whaling ships for assisting with harpoon line (but this style of whaling did not exist on the Outer Banks—*see* Cape Lookout Grounds). Also metal orb attached to a long handle used for melting, especially tar used in sailing ships 16th to 18th centuries. However, presence of loggerhead turtles is name source. Variants Lagerhead and Laggerhead are transcribing errors by mapping crews using only verbal exchange, perpetuated on many state and local maps based on USGS (2013: Pea Island) topographic map. *Other names:* Lagerhead Hills (USGS 2013: Pea Island), Laggerhead Hills (misspelling).

Loggerhead Inlet, former water passage, Dare County, Kinnakeet Township (mid-19th century charts). Connected Pamlico Sound to Atlantic Ocean through present Hatteras Island just n of Rodanthe. Open 1657–1683, reopened 1843–1870. Periodically opened for brief intervals since last closing and was just s of New Inlet in zone of opening and closing (*see* S Curves). During 1800s two distinct breaches about 0.25 mi. apart separated by Cat Island (q.v. now mostly attached to barrier island) to which inlet name was applied. Loggerhead Inlet was only 4 mi. s of New Inlet. *See* Loggerhead Hills. *Other names:* Logger Head Inlet (Colton 1863).

Loggerhead Shoals, former shoals, Dare County, Kinnakeet Township (shad boat *Anna Laura*, 1896 [White et al. 2017, 50]). Formerly soundside of Loggerhead Inlet between Round Hammock Bay and Loggerhead Hills 3 mi. n of Rodanthe. Disappeared mostly by early 1900s about 25 years after Loggerhead Inlet last closed. Cat Island (Dare County) here today is a remnant. *See* Loggerhead Hills.

Loghouse Dreen (Drain), cove or water passage,

Dare County, Kinnakeet Township (Currituck DB 8, 1800, 243–44). Was in Kinnakeet area, most likely one of Avon's sections or possibly n to Little Kinnakeet. "Dreen" was known dialectical variation of "drain" used for short time (albeit sparingly) 1700s. Names were spelled as sounded or as folk (many without organized education) thought the name ought to be spelled.

Log Landing, former landing, Dare County, Atlantic Township (local informant). Was soundside immediately s of US 158 in nw Kitty Hawk just sw of Southern Shores. Used for about 20 years early 20th century to service lumber mills (hence name) harvesting lumber from Kitty Hawk Woods (q.v.—now preserved). On then upper Jeanguite Creek (name application extends s now); however, most likely at one of the lumber mills. There is no trace of a landing today.

Log Shoal, shoal, 0.6 mi. long, Dare County, Hatteras Township (USGS 2013: Hatteras Overedge North). In Pamlico Sound just e of Clam Shoal 3.7 mi. n of Hatteras (village).

Logtown, former area, Dare County, Nags Head Township (Smith 2001, 7). Was near intersection of old US 64 and Dare County Regional Airport Road 2 mi. nw of Manteo (center). Was part of Adam Etheridge farm, included over 125 acres, reportedly contained a windmill. General reference to clusters of log corncribs in North End; n Roanoke Island, remembered only by older local residents.

Lone Creek, tidal stream, Carteret County, Portsmouth Township (C&GS 1866). On se Sheep Island (Portsmouth Township) tributary of and n of Piliauga Creek, 1.2 mi. se of Portsmouth (village), 7.2 mi. sw of Ocracoke (village).

Lone Oak Channel, water passage, 1.3 mi. long, Currituck County, Poplar Branch Township (USGS 2013: Mossey Islands). In Currituck Sound just n of Big Narrows separating Mossey Islands complex from North Burris Island 6 mi. s of Corolla.

Long Cove, elongated cove, 0.5 mi. long, Currituck County, Fruitville Township (USGS 2013: Knotts Island). Trends n-s in Runnells Marshes as arm of Fresh Pond Bay, 2 mi. e of Knotts Island (village).

Long Dike, dam, Currituck County, Fruitville Township (F&WS 1984, 1). On e and s Mackay Island in Mackay Island Wildlife Refuge from where Mackay Island Road enters Mackay Island from e, s-ward, then sw-ward, then w-ward to Live Oak Point; center 2.3 mi. wsw of Knotts Island (village). Constructed 1984 by F&WS with Cross Dike, Parallel Dike, and West Dike to create East Pool, Middle Pool, and West Pool to enhance wildlife protection. "Dike" is wall, embankment, or similar structure to function as a dam to prevent flooding or as here to contain and control water level.

Longfellow Cove, small cove, Currituck County, Poplar Branch Township (local use). Just e of Baum Creek just e of s Pine Island subdivision 6 mi. n of Duck. Local disagreement to which features names Hicks Bay, Cottage Cove, and Longfellow Cove apply, each in close proximity. Applications presented here are most preferred. Name is recent application and use.

Long Hog Island, linear island, Currituck County, Poplar Branch Township (C&GS 1852). Trends n-s in Hog Islands (q.v.) complex in Beasley Bay, 6.7 mi. s of Corolla. *See* Hog Islands.

Long Island, elongated island, 0.75 mi. long, Carteret County, White Oak Township (USGS 2013: Salter Path). In Bogue Sound, 1 mi. ne of Bell Cove, 6.2 mi. w of Salter Path. Stephens (1984, 25) reports according to Alice Guthrie Smith (memoirs) Long Island named by Alfred Bavis for Long Island, New York, since he was from there originally. He was lone resident of Long Island, reportedly attending church at former community of Bell Cove and preached there on occasion (Stephens 1984, 25–26). *Other names:* Snake Island (C&GS 1937, unknown whether for shape or presence of snakes, probably the latter).

Long Island, elongated island, 0.3 mi. long, less than 0.1 mi. wide, Currituck County, Poplar Branch Township (USGS 2013: Mossey Islands). In Jarvis Channel at Currituck Sound between South Burris Island and Indian Gap Island 7.7 mi. s of Corolla. Referenced in deed from Malbone to Brooks 1675.

Long Lake, linear lake, 0.3 mi. long, Dare County, Atlantic Township (local use). Trends n-s in Kill Devil Hills 1.3 mi. n of stabilized Kill Devil Hill, 3 mi. sse of original Kitty Hawk. Subdivision named for feature.

Long Marsh, island, 0.5 mi. long, Carteret County, White Oak Township (USGS 1994: Swansboro). In Bogue Sound, 7 mi. ese of

Swansboro (mainland). *Other names:* Long Island (USGS 1952, 1948: Swansboro 1:62,500 scale).

Long Marsh, elongated marsh, 0.5 mi. long, Currituck County, Poplar Branch Township (local use). On Straight Creek Island trends nw-se in Mossey Islands (q.v.) complex 1.5 mi. e of Three Dunes, 5.5 mi. s of Corolla.

Long Nole, former small hummock, Currituck County, Fruitville Township (Currituck DB 23, 1841, 156). Was on s Knotts Island at Indian Creek probably 2.5 mi. sw of Knotts Island (village). Abbeys Nole, Jesse Nole, and Whites Nole also here, according to deed, where named are "in Knotts Island . . . at an angle of Indian Creek." Only distinctive angle today is halfway between Indian Pond and Sandy Cove, no knolls or hummocks there. Topography could change considerably over 200 years, and features might no longer exist or could be short distance ne on e side Indian Pond where hummocks exist. "Nole" is a variation of knoll. *Other names:* Round Nole (various deeds early 1800s).

Long Point, marsh point, Carteret County, Atlantic Township (USGS 2013: Atlantic). On Core Banks 0.5 mi. w of Long Point Camp, 4.5 mi. e of Atlantic (mainland).

Long Point, point, Currituck County, Poplar Branch Township (USGS 2013: Mossey Islands). Se point of Marsh Island, 8 mi. nw of Duck.

Long Point, point, Currituck County, Poplar Branch Township (USGS 2013: Mossey Islands). On Woodhouses Island just nw of Long Point Pond 12 mi. nw of Duck. *Other names:* Long Pond Point (some local use), West Point (Currituck DB 16, 1822, 220).

Long Point, point, Dare County, Atlantic Township (USGS 2013: Kitty Hawk). At n entrance to Kitty Hawk Bay on sw point Stone Island 2.6 mi. sw of original Kitty Hawk. *Other names:* Long Marsh Point (C&GS 1865), Long Point of Marsh (early use locally).

Long Point, marsh point, Dare County, Kinnakeet Township (USGS 2013: Buxton). On unnamed island in Pamlico Sound just w of Hatteras Island 2.4 mi. s of original Avon.

Long Point. *See* Brooks Point.

Long Point Camp, camp, Carteret County, Atlantic Township (USGS 2013: Atlantic). On North Core Banks, 5 mi. e of Atlantic (mainland). Now managed by NPS. The most

significant breach from Hurricane Dorian (2019) was here. *See* North Core Banks and Camp Cass Williams. *Other names:* Ira Morris Camp (original name, fish camp originally, now accepts tourists), Long Point Cabin Camp (NPS 2018), Morris Fish Camp (Mallinson et al. 2008, 12).

Long Point Creek, cove, 0.1 mi. wide, Dare County, Kinnakeet Township (USGS 2013: Buxton). In Pamlico Sound 4.5 mi. n of Buxton, 2.3 mi. s of original Avon. *See* South'ard Water. *Other names:* High Hill Creek (historical use referencing Askins Hill, high sand dune just n), Hill Creek (Currituck DB 7, 1794, 57–58).

Long Point Dock, dock, Carteret County, Atlantic Township (local use). At Long Point Camp, 4.5 mi. e of Atlantic (mainland). Arrival docks for ferry from Morris Marina in Atlantic.

Long Point Inlet, former water passage, Carteret County, Atlantic Township (Fisher 1962, 100). Was on n Middle Core Banks 1.3 mi. ne of historical Drum Inlet, 5 mi. e of Atlantic (mainland). Fisher (1962) only one to mention this former inlet (from 1846 congressional document); indicates it was likely open for only a short time early 1800s but indicates he does not know its location and could find no feature named Long Point on Core Banks. However, a feature named Long Point is on n Middle Core Banks (n South Core Banks) 1 mi. n of Horse Island (Atlantic Township), and clear inlet relicts are here, so this is location of this short-lived inlet. Normans Inlet mentioned this area (U.S. Congress 1876)

Long Point Marsh, marsh, Dare County, Atlantic Township (CS 1862a). On Stone Island at Long Point at n entrance Kitty Hawk Bay, 2.7 mi. sw of original Kitty Hawk.

Long Point Pond, lake, 0.2 mi. across, Currituck County, Poplar Branch Township (USGS 2013: Mossey Islands). On nw Woodhouse Island just s of Wells Bay, 1.2 mi. n of Big Narrows, 2.4 mi. w of Three Dunes, 3.2 mi. ssw of Corolla. *Other names:* Long Pond (has become name by use).

Long Pond, former freshwater lake, Carteret County, Morehead Township (Stephens 1984, 127). Was just w of Salter Path in an area of small ponds. Now filled in.

Long Pond, elongated tidal stream, 0.3 mi. long,

Currituck County, Fruitville Township (Cox 1906). Just w of Carova, 3 mi. ne of Knotts Island (village).

Long Pond, lake, 0.3 mi. long, 0.1 mi. wide, Currituck County, Poplar Branch Township (USGS 2013: Mossey Islands). In unnamed marsh, 1 mi. sw of Big Narrows, 7 mi. sw of Corolla.

Long Pond, lake, 0.2 mi. long, Currituck County, Poplar Branch Township (USGS 1982: Mossey Islands). In unnamed marsh at Brant Island, 4 mi. ssw of Corolla.

Long Rock, rock, Carteret County, Portsmouth Township (Williamson 1992, 126). In Pamlico Sound between Beacon Island and North Rock, 3 mi. n of former Portsmouth Life Saving Station in Portsmouth (village), 5 mi. w of Ocracoke (village). Also known as Long Dry Rock part of Oyster Rocks (originally), with Remus Rock and Shell Castle (Old Rock). Smaller application today than 20th century. *Other names:* Long Dry Rock (Stick 1958, 77).

Long Shoal, shoal, 5 mi. long, Dare County, Croatan Township (NOS 2014b). In Pamlico Sound trending nw to se from mainland at Parched Corn Bay 16 mi. w of Rodanthe. *Other names:* Long Shoals (Wimble 1738), Long Shole (Wimble 1733).

Long Shoal Point, shoal, Dare County, Croatan Township (local use). At center of Long Shoal (5 mi. long) where water is shallowest (1–3 ft.), often exposed at low water, 2.5 mi. e of mainland, 17 mi. w of Rodanthe. *Other names:* Long Shole Point (Collet et al. 1770).

Lookout Bight, bight, 2.3 mi. wide, Carteret County, Harkers Island Township (USGS 2013: Cape Lookout; USGS 1997: Harkers Island). In Atlantic Ocean formed by Cape Lookout s end of Core Banks and e end of Shackleford Banks at Onslow Bay. Bight (embayment creating protected water, gentle coastline curve) was popular place 19th century for ships with small enough draft to "ride out" a storm safely, but never developed as commercial harbor. Use of variant Cape Harbour is further evidence of feature's historical use as "harbor" and is authentic name reflecting original English spelling. Similarly, variant Harbor of Refuge originally historically descriptive term referencing protected water created by Cape Lookout. Regarded as safe haven for shallow-draft ships (most of those in early period on the Outer Banks) from its earliest discovery. ACE authorized maintenance of harbor 1912, but improved shipping and warning devices caused decline in use, and abandoned 1918.

Other names: Baia di Trafalgar (Dudley 1647, 1661—Cape Lookout appeared on some early maps as Cape Trafalgar), Bay of Cape Lookout (early maps), Cape Bay (Brazier 1833), Cape Harbour (Holland 1794—spelling legitimate from 18th century), Cape Lookout Bay (Stick 1958, 41), Cape Lookout Bight (Williamson 1992), Cape Lookout Harbor (Williamson 1992; CS 1865), Cape Lookout Harbor of Refuge (ACE 1895), Cape Lookout Harbour (Stick 1958, 59), Harbor of Refuge (several colonial documents' references regarding protective nature), Lookout Harbor (NPS 2005, 355), Point Lookout Bay (Stick 1958, 185; Simpson and Simpson 1988, 20), Point Look Out Bay (Angley 1982, 6), The Bay (Mackay 1756), The Bight (Williamson 1992).

Lookout Breakers, breakers, Carteret County, Harkers Island Township (19th- and 20th-century charts). Just s of Cape Point at Cape Lookout; evidence of shoals at Cape Lookout. *Other names:* Cape Lookout Breakers (early maps).

Lookout Cedar, historical, Dare County, Kinnakeet Township (probably) (Covey 2018, 18). Described by Covey as named landmark "in Chicamacomico" found in deeds. He attributes the name to need for navigation aids, possible but historical inlets in the Chicamacomico area were never really used for shipping as they were short-lived and shallow, but as general landmark applies. Covey does not indicate specific location.

Lookout Cypress, historical area, Dare County, Kinnakeet Township (probably) (Covey 2018, 18). *See* Lookout Cedar.

Lookout Dune, sand dune, 1 mi. long, Carteret County, Harkers Island Township (Mason 2000; NPS 1987, map, 38). Highest in dunes known as Diamond City Hills (after community changed its name from Lookout Hills) today is 20 ft. but was higher and more prominent and distinct last half 19th century. On e Shackleford Banks just wnw of Barden Inlet just s of former Diamond City. Named from use as lookout for whales when shore-based whaling was prevalent 19th century (*see* Cape Lookout Grounds). *Other names:* Lookout Hill (Stick 1958, 190).

Lookout Hill, large linear sand dune, 1.5 mi. long, Dare County, Hatteras Township (local use). E-w with several sand peaks, highest in center at 30 ft., 1 mi. sw of Buxton.

Lookout Hill. *See* Hill of the Wreck.

Lookout Woods, former woods, Carteret County, Harkers Island Township (19th and early 20th centuries). Was on e Shackleford Banks at former Diamond City.

Loon Canal, small canal, Dare County, Atlantic Township (Town of Southern Shores 2015). Trending n-s in Southern Shores on e shore of Jeanguite Creek, 4 mi. n of original Kitty Hawk. Names of Southern Shores canals are for shorebirds (except Gravey Pond Canal). The common loon (*Gavia immer*) and red-throated loon (*Gavia stellata*) here in winter.

Loop Shack Hill, sand dune, 15 ft. high, Hyde County, Ocracoke Township (USGS 2013: Ocracoke). On Ocracoke Island 1 mi. se of Ocracoke (village). Reportedly named for the Loop Road from a former U.S. government facility to a shack near the hill, and presumed name origin is road made a "loop." Eventually included nine buildings to monitor submarine activity. However, older residents and documentation indicate otherwise, corroborated by Phillip Howard (local historian) and NPS. During WWII, a magnetic "loop" wire was run into the ocean offshore and underwater for 16 mi., looping to Portsmouth Island, which served as a detector for enemy submarine activity at Ocracoke Inlet. *Other names:* Bald Beach (use before WWII), Look Shack Hill (transcribing error or misinterpretation, though reported as local use by Weslager 1954, 47).

Loran Station Slough, canalized stream, Dare County, Hatteras Township (Goldstein 2000, loc. 2889). At Cape Hatteras, 1.7 mi. n of Cape Point, 1.7 mi. sse of Buxton. Sometimes applied to smaller perpendicular canal extended 0.2 mi. from Loran Station to this larger canal. Name is from proximity (just n) to old Loran Station (almost completely gone). LORAN, acronym for Long Range Navigation (such acronyms often become words, e.g., radar, sonar), with advanced technology fell into disuse here by 1980s. Station abandoned early 1981.

Lost Colony. *See* Fort Raleigh.

Lost Lake. *See* Crystal Lake.

Lost Tree Ridge, sand ridge, 0.7 mi. long, Dare County, Hatteras Township (local use). One of the e-w ridges along Cape Hatteras just n of Flowers Ridge just s of Middle Ridge, 1 mi. s of Buxton.

Lou's Shoal, former shoal, Carteret County, Portsmouth Township (Williamson 1992, 100). Was reportedly just n of former Portsmouth Life Saving Station at Portsmouth (village).

Lovers Hill, hill, Hyde County, Ocracoke Township (Howard, March 21, 2013). In Ocracoke (village) area, exact location unknown. Howard presents local islander's conversation from 1861 about wreck of "The Black Squall," a circus ship wrecked here in April 1861 (Chalet 2020, 246). One account indicates a couple found "drowned and embraced" were buried on Blackbeards Hill, known since as Lovers Hill. Local folk interviewed were unaware of the feature or the story. *Other names:* Blackbeards Hill (Howard, October 29, 2007).

Lovett Island, island, 0.2 mi. long, Carteret County, White Oak Township (USGS 2013: Salter Path). In Bogue Sound 6.9 mi. w of Salter Path. Named for family who lived near here. *Other names:* Lovetts Island (C&GS 1888b).

Loving Canal, canal, Dare County, Atlantic Township (Town of Kitty Hawk 2007). At s end of Kitty Hawk ridge-and-swale system (q.v.), 0.8 mi. w of Poor Ridge Landing, 2 mi. sw of original Kitty Hawk.

Lowenberg Path, area, Carteret County, Morehead Township (Zaenker 2014). On Bogue Banks at e edge Pine Knoll Shores from Yaupon Point (soundside) to beach (oceanside) 3 mi. w of Atlantic Beach. *See* Bogue Banks historical paths.

Lower Channel, former channel, Dare County, Hatteras Township (CS 1850b). Was in Pamlico Sound just n and nw of Durant Point 2 mi. w of Rollinson Channel (Old Rollinson Channel) just n of Hatteras (village). Labeled on only a few charts.

Lower Middle, large shoal, 2.2 mi. long, Hyde County, Swan Quarter Township (NOS 2014i). On sw Middle Ground, in Pamlico Sound, 14.3 mi. nw of Ocracoke (village).

Luark Hill. *See* Pennys Hill.

Lucke Island, former island in Currituck County and Dare County. Was part of Currituck Banks and might have included a portion of Bodie Island. N from near former Roanoke Inlet to former Musketo Inlet, perhaps to

Currituck Inlet (Charles II 1663). Lucke Island (Lucks Island) was first n limit of Carolina as stated in charter granting Carolina to the eight Lords Proprietors (*see* Carolina), later to Currituck Inlet. Some maps restrict the island to that formed between Currituck Inlet and New Currituck Inlet. Land grant from King Charles II to Earl of Clarendon 1663 indicates Luck Island is same as Colleton Island, though most maps give it a larger application. *Other names:* Croatamung (indigenous), Currituck Banks (numerous maps), Luckar Island (Saunders 1882, 32), Luckes Island (Saunders 1886, 21–23), Luck Island (various sources), Lucks Iland (Comberford 1657—common spelling in colonial period), Lucks Island (various sources), Luke Island (Lawson 1709, map, 240—rendition from Second Carolina Charter though this form does not appear in later facsimiles).

Lupton. *See* Hog Island (Carteret County).

Lyle Bays, bay area, Dare County, Kinnakeet Township (Currituck DB 27, 1855, 300–301). Were in, at, or near Eagle Nest Bay (Eaglenest Pond) as described in deed probably 3 mi. s of Oregon Inlet and probably 12 mi. n of Rodanthe. Exact location unknown because area has changed and been changed dramatically since mid-19th century, especially 1930s when Pea Island National Wildlife Refuge established, creating North Pond and South Pond and later New Field Pond. Use of "s" with bay also indicates name applied to sort of open but naturally impounded water including ponds (term used on the Outer Banks for open water within marsh). An 1855 deed still indicated Lyle Bays "on Body's Island Beach" though Oregon Inlet had opened 1846. Illustrates it takes time (sometimes) for usage and application of a place name to change following a topographical change. Before Oregon Inlet opened 1846, and came to be recognized as s limit of Bodie Island (Roanoke Inlet had closed 1811, fusing n end Bodie Island to Currituck Banks or North Banks), Bodie Island and Bodie Island Beach considered to extend to New Inlet. *See* Pea Island.

Machapunga Shoal, former linear shoal, Hyde County, Ocracoke Township (Moseley 1733). Shown as extension of e side Royal Shoal (Ryals Shoal) just n of Ocracoke (village) to what is now known as Bluff Shoal (q.v.). Arrangement of features on Moseley's 1733 map are, as with many early 18th-century maps, not as they are today because information was not as good and this area changed dramatically over the years. Machapunga was name of indigenous tribe on mainland in Hyde County, Lake Mattamuskeet area. Also appeared on Collet et al.'s 1770 map as Machapunga Bluff, referring to n-most shoal attached to mainland. *Other names:* Machapunga Bluff (Collet et al. 1770).

Mackay Creek, small stream, Currituck County, Fruitville Township (local use). On nw Mackay Island, flows n from small lake to Duckpond, cove at Mingers Point, 5 mi. w of Knotts Island (village). *See* Mackay Island.

Mackay Island, island, 1.7 mi. long, Currituck County, Fruitville Township (USGS 2013: Knotts Island, Barco). Separated from Knotts Island by portion of The Great Marsh 2.6 mi. w of Knotts Island (village). Local use was divided between Mackay Island and Mackys Island but was settled by USBGN 1891 in favor of Mackay Island. Named for John Mackie (*sic*), original landowner. *Other names:* Jones Island (F&WS 2001 indicates John Jones original owner), Mackays Island (various sources), Mackees Island (Price-Strother 1808), Mackey Island (Currituck DB 24, 1842, 104), Mackeys Island (Currituck DB 5, 1785, 56; C&GS 1878), Mackie Island (original owner), Mackies Island (Currituck DB 8, 1799, 156—original owner), Mackys Island (Collet et al. 1770), Notts Island (early map misapplication), Orphans Island (F&WS website 2016 posting—contradicts 2001 brochure, see above—Orphans Island encountered no other source).

Mackerel Beach. *See* Whalehead Beach (subdivision).

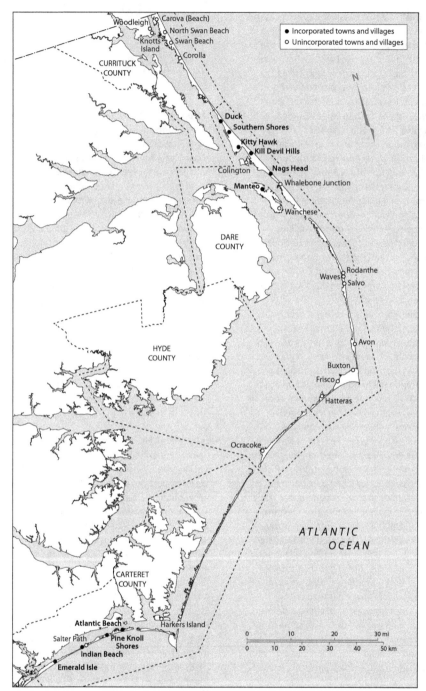

Map 1. Existing towns and communities. The towns and villages shown here are in existence in 2020 and represent incorporated and unincorporated places. "Incorporated" means there is a legal government with a legal boundary recognized as such by the state government. "Unincorporated" means the village is the responsibility of the county government, and there is no legal boundary. Mapworthy subdivisions included in the gazetteer are not included on this map. Historic communities are on a separate map. (Virginia Geographic Information Network [2016] and North Carolina Department of Transportation/Geodetic Survey [2016])

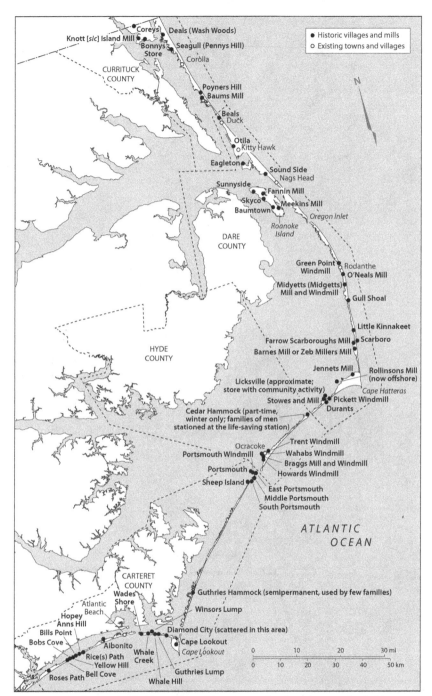

Map 2. Historic villages and mills. These villages did not necessarily exist at the same time in history; see each entry in the gazetteer for specific and particular information. There were more than 100 windmills and possibly associated mills historically on the Outer Banks (not necessarily at the same time). Those shown on this map, while economic ventures, often also served as gathering places with other functions. Most mill and windmill names were for the owner and often changed with sale; many are unknown. (Virginia Geographic Information Network [2016] and North Carolina Department of Transportation/Geodetic Survey [2016])

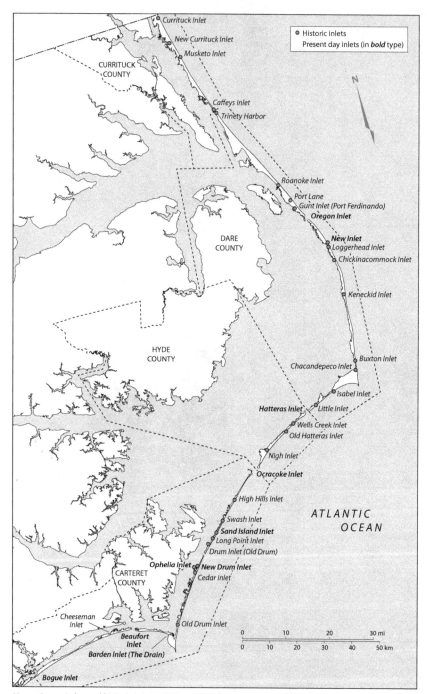

Map 3. Present-day and historic inlets. Old Roanoke Inlet was reported on a couple of maps between Gunt Inlet (Port Ferdinando) and Roanoke Inlet, but this, no doubt, was misinformation and was really Port Lane migration and named or renamed Roanoke Inlet. Kill Devil Hills Inlet was reported to be in the Kitty Hawk Bay area, but there is no evidence of an inlet there during the historical period (1584–present). Wokokon Inlet believed by some to be just south of Ocracoke Inlet, 16th century (see entry), and New Inlet reported by some to be south on Core Banks (see Great Island Creek entry). Refer to individual gazetteer entries and the "Current and Historic Inlets" table in this volume for more information. (Virginia Geographic Information Network [2016] and North Carolina Department of Transportation/Geodetic Survey [2016])

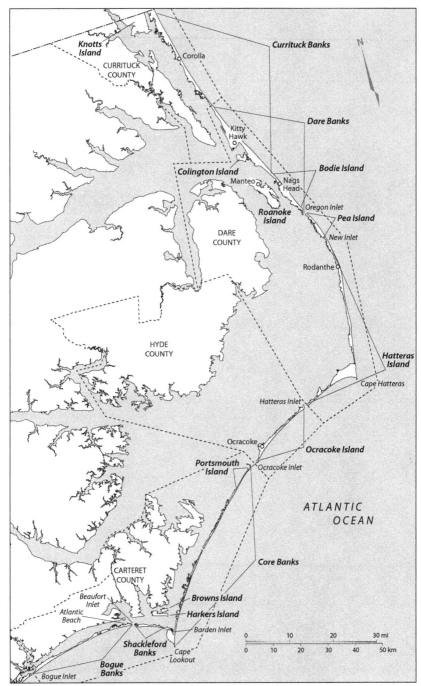

Map 4. Present-day barrier islands. (Virginia Geographic Information Network [2016] and North Carolina Department of Transportation/Geodetic Survey [2016])

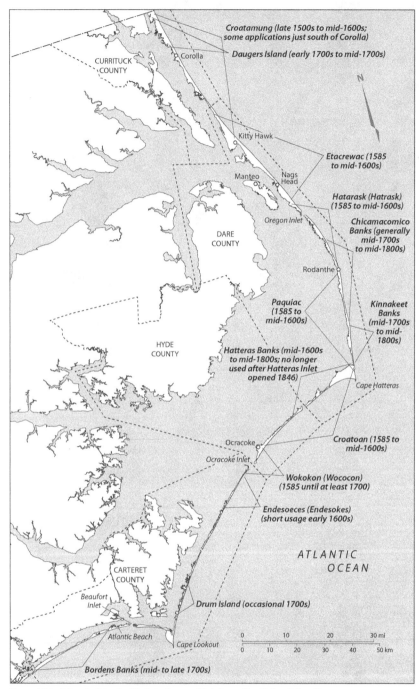

Croatamung (late 1500s to mid-1600s; some applications just south of Corolla)

Daugers Island (early 1700s to mid-1700s)

CURRITUCK COUNTY

Corolla

N

Kitty Hawk

Etacrewac (1585 to mid-1600s)

Nags Head

Manteo

Hatarask (Hatrask) (1585 to mid-1600s)

Oregon Inlet

Chicamacomico Banks (generally mid-1700s to mid-1800s)

DARE COUNTY

Rodanthe

Paquiac (1585 to mid-1600s)

Kinnakeet Banks (mid-1700s to mid-1800s)

HYDE COUNTY

Hatteras Banks (mid-1600s to mid-1800s; no longer used after Hatteras Inlet opened 1846)

Cape Hatteras

Ocracoke

Croatoan (1585 to mid-1600s)

Ocracoke Inlet

Wokokon (Wococon) (1585 until at least 1700)

Endesoeces (Endesokes) (short usage early 1600s)

ATLANTIC OCEAN

CARTERET COUNTY

Beaufort Inlet

Drum Island (occasional 1700s)

Atlantic Beach

Cape Lookout

0   10   20   30 mi
0 10 20 30 40 50 km

Bordens Banks (mid- to late 1700s)

Map 5. Historic barrier islands. (Virginia Geographic Information Network [2016] and North Carolina Department of Transportation/Geodetic Survey [2016])

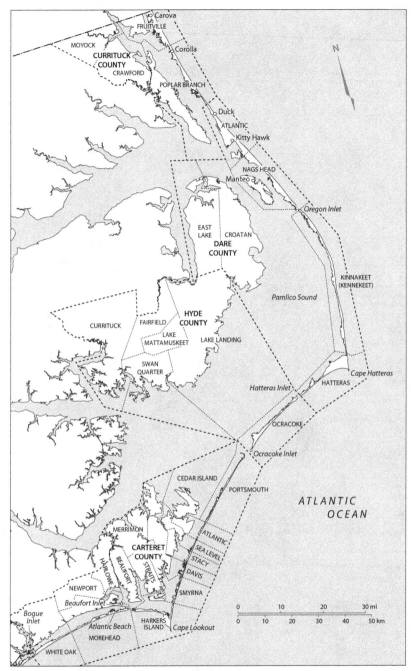

Map 6. County townships. Townships are listed with each entry in the gazetteer as a level of location within the county, but names of townships are *not* included as entries in their own right since use of townships for any purpose within a county in North Carolina has disappeared. They are a legacy and no longer have any function. Townships functioned from their beginning (1868) when township structure was incorporated into the rewritten State Constitution and had elected officials whose duties were to administer aspects of government and services. However, by 1877, the system had failed, and the townships' functions were abolished. Townships should not be confused with incorporated towns, of which there are many on the Outer Banks; this is a separate process and completely unrelated. (Virginia Geographic Information Network [2016] and North Carolina Department of Transportation/Geodetic Survey [2016])

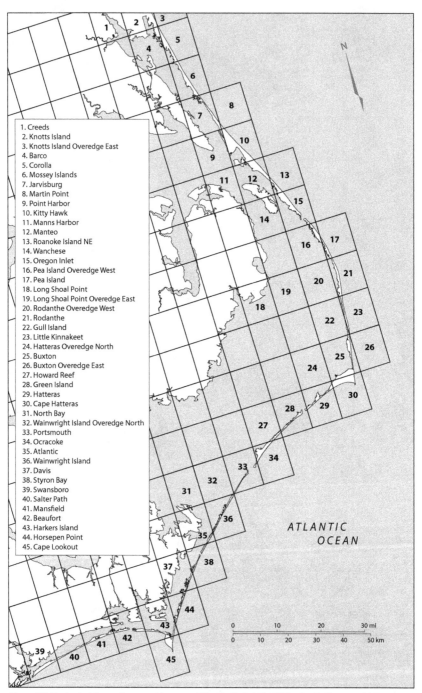

1. Creeds
2. Knotts Island
3. Knotts Island Overedge East
4. Barco
5. Corolla
6. Mossey Islands
7. Jarvisburg
8. Martin Point
9. Point Harbor
10. Kitty Hawk
11. Manns Harbor
12. Manteo
13. Roanoke Island NE
14. Wanchese
15. Oregon Inlet
16. Pea Island Overedge West
17. Pea Island
18. Long Shoal Point
19. Long Shoal Point Overedge East
20. Rodanthe Overedge West
21. Rodanthe
22. Gull Island
23. Little Kinnakeet
24. Hatteras Overedge North
25. Buxton
26. Buxton Overedge East
27. Howard Reef
28. Green Island
29. Hatteras
30. Cape Hatteras
31. North Bay
32. Wainwright Island Overedge North
33. Portsmouth
34. Ocracoke
35. Atlantic
36. Wainwright Island
37. Davis
38. Styron Bay
39. Swansboro
40. Salter Path
41. Mansfield
42. Beaufort
43. Harkers Island
44. Horsepen Point
45. Cape Lookout

Map 7. U.S. Geological Survey topographic maps of the North Carolina Outer Banks. Topographic maps are published by the U.S. Geological Survey and portray horizontal and vertical positions on the earth's surface determined by geographic coordinates; they specifically portray altitude or elevation by isohypse or lines connecting points of equal elevation, which are termed "contour lines." These maps are large-scale or depict considerable detail. The scale of each map is 1:24,000 (one inch on the map equals about 2,000 feet on the earth's surface). (Virginia Geographic Information Network [2016] and North Carolina Department of Transportation/Geodetic Survey [2016])

MacWilliams Dock, former landing, Hyde County, Ocracoke Township (Howard, May 4, 2001). Was at s end of Silver Lake (Cockle Creek before dredging). Served economic concerns of MacWilliams (no longer exists).

Mad Mags Hill, hill, Hyde County, Ocracoke Township (story known locally). Reportedly "in" Paddys Hollow, just e of Silver Lake in Ocracoke (village), several references, especially as lyrics in song ("Paddy's Holler" by Walter Howard): "So everybody ponied up a dollar to build a little home for Maggie all alone livin' on a hill in Paddy's Holler." Accordingly, from *Ocracoke Island Journal* (January 8, 2009), Maggie (Mad Mag) was "Mad Mag Howard," wife of John Simon Howard, sea captain who took Margaret Eaton from Rockland, Maine, when she was only fifteen years old, married her, and brought her to Ocracoke. She became legendary for her quirky, odd, and peculiar habits, hence her local name, "Mad Mag." Most know the story from the song lyrics, but difficult to document. Ballance (2017), noted Ocracoke historian, has verified the story in correspondence. Further, as corroborated by Ballance, use of hill in Ocracoke can mean any high(er) ground not marshland. So, "Mad Mag" lived on higher ground "up" Paddy's Holler. *See* Paddys Hollow.

Maes Pond, cove, Currituck County, Fruitville Township (Cox 1923). Cove-like open water just e of Mary Island 0.5 mi. ne of Middle Marsh, 4 mi. se of Knotts Island (village). *See* Adams Pond.

Maiden Paps, historical islands, Dare County, Kinnakeet Township (Collet et al. 1770). Were in Pamlico Sound just nw of Chickinacommock Inlet 10 mi. se of Roanoke Island (Mouzon 1775). "Pap" (with "dugs" [q.v.]) used frequently by seamen late 16th and 17th centuries for hills or islands protruding upwards out of water or marsh. "Pap" is an archaic English word referring to teats or nipples of a woman's breast. "Barn" as used in a variant is most likely a clipped form of barnacle and can also be slang term for a large rudder, but no evidence suggesting this usage here. *Other names:* The Barn (Holland 1794), The Maiden Paps (Holland 1794), The Paps (early 1800s maps), Two Round Black Hills (Holland 1794).

Mailboat Lead, former anchorage, Dare County, Kinnakeet Township (Garrity-Blake 2010, 169). Was in Pamlico Sound 0.5 mi. w of former Bennies Landing, 1 mi. sw of Avon Harbor. The mail boat would anchor offshore because closer to shore too shallow even for shallow-draft boats. Shove skiff or flat-bottom boat would pole out to mail boat to collect mail, thereby serving as a "lead" to shore. "Lead" as used on the Outer Banks (mostly n Outer Banks) referenced a known passage through marsh complex since as a nautical term "lead" means both follow a direction and an opening through some impediment, marsh, or shoals. The generic appears several times on n Outer Banks, where there are several large marsh complexes (*see* Buzzard Lead). However, here and at Rodanthe names reference directional use for shove skiffs (flat-bottom boats, which reportedly could be shoved) to pole out to mail boats as almost no marsh here.

Mail Landing, landing, Dare County, Hatteras Township (Garrity-Blake 2010, 232). Was in Buxton, 9 mi. ene of Hatteras (village). Recent origin and applied to dredged landing with close proximity to Buxton Post Office (0.1 mi.).

Mail Lead, former small anchorage, Dare County, Kinnakeet Township (NPS 2005b: NPS 1, 88). Was just offshore in Pamlico Sound created specifically as anchorage for mail boat (near former post office) late 19th and early 20th centuries because water in Pamlico Sound here is shallow several hundred yards offshore. *See* Mailboat Lead. *Other names:* Mail Boat Lead (Garrity-Blake 2010, 78), Mailboat Lead (Garrity-Blake 2010, 492).

Main Channel, channel, Carteret County, White Oak Township; and Onslow County, Swansboro Township (USGS 2013: Swansboro). In Bogue Sound trending n-s connecting Bogue Inlet and Intracoastal Waterway, 1.9 mi. se of Swansboro (mainland).

Mallard Cove, small cove, Dare County, Atlantic Township (local use). In Southern Shores in e Jeanguite Creek just across from peninsula, Martins Point, 3.5 mi. nnw of original Kitty Hawk. Indicates large amount of ducks at Currituck Banks along Atlantic Flyway. Subdivision named for feature.

Mallard Creek, small man-enhanced canal, Currituck County, Poplar Branch Township (local use). Flows generally s from Mallard

Pond to Dews Island Bay, 5.6 mi. nw of Duck. *See* Mallard Cove.

Mallard Marsh, small marsh, Dare County, Nags Head Township (local use). In n Nags Head, just e of Jockeys Ridge. Subdivision named for feature. *See* Mallard Cove.

Mallard Marsh, small marsh, Dare County, Nags Head Township (local use). Just e of NC 345 (The Causeway) 2 mi. n of Wanchese. *See* Mallard Cove. *Other names:* Catarines Swamp (Currituck DB 1796, 8, 35—historically larger than marsh area today; probably was Catherines).

Mallard Pond, cove, 0.2 mi. across, Currituck County, Poplar Branch Township (USGS 2013: Mossey Islands). At unnamed marsh in far ne corner Goat Island Bay, 7.9 mi. nw of Duck. *See* Mallard Cove and Adams Pond.

Mallard Pond, water area, Currituck County, Poplar Branch Township (CS 1852). Cove-like but enclosed by marsh in Mossey Islands complex just n of Duck Hole, 1.5 mi. e of Wells Bay, 4.5 mi. s of Corolla. *See* Mallard Cove and Adams Pond.

Mallard Pond, small man-enhanced water, Currituck County, Poplar Branch Township (local use). Near central Dews Island connected to Dews Island Bay by Mallard Creek, 5.5 mi. nw of Duck. *See* Mallard Cove and Adams Pond.

Mann Point, marsh point, Dare County, Nags Head Township (USGS 2013: Manteo). Is 0.6 mi. n of Nags Head Woods, junction Albemarle Sound and Roanoke Sound, 2.6 mi. wnw of central Nags Head. *See* Manns Island. *Other names:* Hawthorne Point (early references—different species of hawthorn [*Crataegus* spp.] indigenous to e North Carolina), Haw Tree Point (colonial references—haw refers to fruit [berries] of hawthorn tree—mentioned in passing in Currituck DB 4, 1783, 134–35), Hawtree Point (Currituck DB 3, 1739, 14–15), Manns Point (CS 1852).

Manns Channel, water passage, 0.5 mi. long, Currituck County, Fruitville Township (USGS 2013: Knotts Island). Separates Manns Island from Deals Island 2.4 mi. ne of Knotts Island (village). *See* Manns Island. *Other names:* Manns Island Creek (local references), Mons Channel (Currituck DB 30, 1842, 401–2), Mounds Channel (though occurring in some early deeds, misinterpretation—associated with Mon Island [q.v.]).

Manns Cove, cove, 0.4 mi. long, Currituck County, Fruitville Township (Cox 1906). On e side between two parts of Manns Island 2.3 mi. ne of Knotts Island (village). *See* Manns Island. *Other names:* Mounds Cove (occurs in couple of early deeds, misinterpretation—associated with Mon Island [q.v.]).

Manns Harbor–Roanoke Island Ferry Dock, former dock, Dare County, Nags Head Township (historical signage). Was at Freedman Point just n of Weir Point, 3 mi. nw of Manteo (center). Connected mainland to nw Roanoke Island operating from about 1935 to 1955, when Umstead Bridge was opened. Still labeled on USGS 2013: Manteo.

Manns Island, islands, 1.5 mi. wide, Currituck County, Fruitville Township (USGS 2013: Knotts Island). Applied to two marsh islands separated by sand flats in n Knotts Island Bay between Currituck Banks and Knotts Island, 1.6 mi. s of North Carolina–Virginia boundary, 2 mi. ne of Knotts Island (village). Man or Mann, longtime surname here. Name was settled by USBGN 2004 concerning a problem with the name Buckle Island (q.v.— now South Buckle Island). Use of "mounds" (piles of shells) scattered throughout deeds of 1700s here for features now named Mon and Mann, so there could be some basis for "mound" as original use. However, without exception those interviewed indicate Mann, local surname as origin. *Other names:* Manns Islands (historically more than one), Mauns Islands (early documents).

Manns Thoroughfare, water passage, 0.3 mi. long, Currituck County, Fruitville Township (USGS 2013: Knotts Island). Separates Manns Island and South Buckle Island 2.3 mi. ne of Knotts Island (village). *See* Manns Island.

Man's Grave Point, point, Dare County, Kinnakeet Township (Garrity-Blake 2010, 493). Soundside at central No Ache 1.5 mi. s of Salvo. Named after discovery of an unmarked grave—apparently male was presumed (NPS 2005b: NPS 1, 154).

Mans Point. *See* Crab Claw Spit.

Manteo, town, Dare County, Nags Head Township (USGS 2013: Manteo). On n Roanoke Island just e of Shallowbag Bay 4.3 mi. sw of central Nags Head. Originally, name sometimes used was Shallowbag Bay. When post office est. 1870 operated as Roanoke Island, but changed 1873 to Manteo. Name is one of the Indians from Hatrask or Hatarask

(Hatteras or Croatoan) taken to England (1584) by explorers Amadas and Barlowe. Unlike Wanchese, Manteo remained friendly to the colonists and was granted title "Lord of Roanoke" by Queen Elizabeth I for his assistance to the colonists (not second, Lost Colony but first, military colony), first English title to be granted in the "New World." For a time, Upper End used and Wanchese referenced as Lower End from their relative locations on Roanoke Island, but was not popular and over the years gradually fell into disuse. Manteo incorporated 1899. *Other names:* North End (Wise 2010, 37), Roanoak (historical associative use), Shallow Bag Bay (associative use), Shallowbag Bay (at Manteo), Upper End (*see* Wanchese).

Manteo–Shallowbag Bay Interior Channel, small channel, Dare County, Nags Head Township (local use and local media). From entrance of Shallowbag Bay to Manteo Waterfront Marina for small boat usage.

Manteo Waterfront Marina, harbor, Dare County, Nags Head Township (local use). In downtown Manteo at mouth of Doughs Creek (historically—Doughs Bay) just s of Ananias Dare Street Bridge at nw Shallowbag Bay. *See* Manteo. *Other names:* Doughs Creek Marina (occasionally used informally, mouth Doughs Creek), Shallowbag Bay Harbor (Town of Manteo, 1987, 55), Town Docks (local use), Waterfront Marina (Town of Manteo, 1987, 55).

Mariners Cove, small harbor, Dare County, Kinnakeet Township (local use and incidental use in Dare County GIS). In Avon (n part) 0.3 mi. se of Big Island 7 mi. n of Buxton. Upper Mill Creek man-enhanced to become harbor (marina), near former Scarboro (settlement).

Mariners Point, point, Carteret County, Morehead Township (local use). Between Salter Path (w) and Indian Beach (town, separated e part) (e), 4.5 mi. w of Pine Knoll Shores. Considerably altered when Mariners Point Marina constructed.

Mariners Point Marina, harbor, Carteret County, Morehead Township (signage). At Mariners Point (condominiums) between Salter Path (w) and Indian Beach (town, separated e part) 4.5 mi. w of Pine Knoll Shores.

Marlin Cove, small cove, Dare County, Hatteras Township (local use). In Hatteras (village) 1 mi. s of Durant Point, 4.5 mi. wsw of Frisco.

Considerably enhanced by man on sw shore. Subdivision named for feature.

Marlin Harbor, man-made harbor, Carteret County, Morehead Township (limited local use). In Atlantic Beach (town) in Sound View Isles subdivision just e of Atlantic Beach Causeway 1.5 mi. s of Morehead City (mainland). Not well known or used, and recent (and unofficial). Unclear if harbor was named before or after adjacent (w) subdivision Marlin Harbour (note spelling for marketing) docking facilities developed in Cooper Bay (q.v.).

Marsh, The, marsh, Carteret County, White Oak Township (Subdivision Plat, Carteret County GIS Office 2019). Low-lying, often flooded peninsula in w Emerald Isle protruding from w end of Bogue Banks into Bogue Sound at n end of Royall (*sic*) Oaks subdivision, 1 mi. w of entrance Langston Bridge, 3.5 mi. se of Swansboro (mainland). Marked as simply "Marsh" on plat of Royall Oaks subdivision, and repeated interviews indicate no known name other than The Marsh. Of note, subdivision name adjacent (e) is Cape Emerald, and apparently solely for marketing, with no basis in name of a feature.

Marsh Cove, small cove, Carteret County, White Oak Township (local use). Soundside in Bogue Sound 1 mi. se of Archer Point, 3.2 mi. w of original Emerald Isle. Subdivision named for feature. *Other names:* Baypole Cove (CS 1852), Bodines Cove (CS 1853), Old Cove (local use, road sign), Shell Cove (occasional reference likely from nearby subdivision name).

Marsh Cove, small cove, Dare County, Nags Head Township (local use). Soundside in Nags Head (Nags Head Village), 1.3 mi. nnw of Whalebone Junction. Recent origin with development at first merely descriptive, as marsh here preserved during development.

Marshes Light Marina, harbor, Dare County, Nags Head Township (signage). At Shallowbag Bay shore in Manteo (center) 1.8 mi. w of Washington Baum Bridge; spans Roanoke Sound from The Causeway at Whalebone Junction to Roanoke Island. Named for Roanoke Marshes Light (replica) here; original was in s Croatan Sound off sw Roanoke Island. *See* Powells Island.

Marsh Island, elongated island, 0.8 mi. long, Currituck County, Poplar Branch Township

(USGS 2013: Mossey Islands). N-s–trending defined marsh (hence name) in Currituck Sound just sw of Mossey Islands complex 8.5 mi. nw of Duck. Over years, usage gradually shortened to Marsh Island from Long Point Marsh Island, with Long Point applied as separate name to s-most point on island. *Other names:* Long Point Marsh Island (C&GS 1852).

Marsh Island, island, Dare County, Nags Head Township (N.C. Marine Fisheries 2019, H2, map 5). Just se of Back Marsh se tip Roanoke Island 2 mi. se of Wanchese.

Marsh Landing, former landing, Dare County, Nags Head Township (historical use). Was just s of Nags Head Woods 2 mi. nw of central Nags Head.

Marshy Ridge, short sand ridge, Dare County, Atlantic Township (local use). On Colington Island, 1.7 mi. sw of Kill Devil Hills. Descriptive of low ridge.

Martin Point, point, Dare County, Atlantic Township (USGS 2013: Jarvisburg, Martin Point, Point Harbor, Kitty Hawk). Peninsula just w of Southern Shores 5 mi. wnw of original Kitty Hawk. In different forms as early as 1760s. Variant Martins Pint is misspelling in transcribing the name, though "pint" is also a little-known antiquated British reference referring to the laughing gull (*Leucophaeus atricilla*), which frequents the Outer Banks during the summer (but not relevant here). Points of land referenced in 18th-century deeds occasionally use the spelling "pint." Though Martin Point (singular) is the official name, Martins Point now used more often (Martins Point subdivision). Certain the name is for former owner of peninsula, though some have proposed name is from bird purple martin (*Progne subis*)—not so, based on wishful thinking and forced presumption, not even an example of folk etymology. Former Martin's Point Club, one of numerous hunt clubs 19th and early 20th centuries, was here. *Other names:* Martains Point (Currituck DB 9, 1806, 218), Martens Point (misspelling), Martins Pint (periodically in early deeds), Martins Point (Foster 1866a), Martyns Point (Currituck DB 1a, 1765, 110–11), Mill Point (a few maps, extreme n tip of Martin Point where probably was a windmill), Williams Point (vague references to what

might be Martin Point in colonial documents and wills).

Martins Point, point, Currituck County, Fruitville Township (Cox 1923). Near se entrance Fresh Pond Bay, 2.2 mi. e of Knotts Island (village), 9.4 mi. nw of Corolla.

Mary Anns Pond, former cove, 0.1 mi. wide, Hyde County, Ocracoke Township (USGS 2002: Ocracoke). In Pamlico Sound just w of Northern Pond 0.3 mi. nnw of Ocracoke (village). Named for Mary Ann Styron Williams (born 1790s—Howard, July 22, 2018). Now, mostly dry, filled in. *Other names:* Mary Annes Pond (Goerch 1956).

Mary Ann Swamp, swamp, Dare County, Atlantic Township (Harris 2017; unknown, 1898). According to Harris (2017), somewhere in Kitty Hawk ridge-and-swale system (q.v.), w of original Kitty Hawk, likely somewhere in the Kitty Hawk Woods Swamps (q.v.). Harris does not provide additional information, and as a named feature does not appear in early deeds.

Mary Island, marsh island, Currituck County, Fruitville Township (Cox 1923). Just ne of Middle Marsh, 4 mi. se of Knotts Island (village). Occasionally with Bush Island and North Bush Island referenced as Northern Islands in relation to Middle Marsh (now unknown). *Other names:* Pine Island (Currituck Deeds, miscellaneous, 1719).

Mary Island, elongated marsh island, Currituck County, Poplar Branch Township (USGS 2013: Corolla). In Currituck Sound 1.7 mi. wnw of Corolla, 3.3 mi. e of Waterlily (mainland). Only occurrence known of variant Merrys Island, suggests misinterpretation in spoken language by chart maker and unusual occurrence of "merry" as plural. *Other names:* Marys Island (CS 1862a), Merrys Island (C&GS 1852).

Mary Sanders Creek. *See* Neals Creek.

Mary Tillett Place, area, Dare County, Atlantic Township (early 20th century). On e shore of Currituck Sound 2.5 mi. nw of original Kitty Hawk. Historical significance primarily, lingers today basically as reference point. Name origin seems obvious but is obscure today.

Mayos Creek, cove, Carteret County, Portsmouth Township (C&GS 1866). In Pamlico Sound at w end of Sheep Island just w of Sheep Island (former community), 1.3

mi. sw of Portsmouth (village), 7.2 mi. sw of Ocracoke (village). Believed named for John Mayo or his family. Mayo was close friend of John Wallace, one of the principals in economic concerns of Shell Castle late 1700s and early 1800s.

Mayos Hill, former dune (now inundated), Hyde County, Ocracoke Township (Garrity-Blake 2010, map, 356). Was in n Ocracoke (village) just e of Northern Pond, 4 mi. ne of Ocracoke Inlet. *See* Mayos Creek.

McGinnis Point, point, Carteret County, Morehead Township (CS 1855). At w Pine Knoll Shores just w of w entrance to Pine Knoll Waterway 5 mi. w of Atlantic Beach (town). Reportedly named for early residents (squatters) on Bogue Banks 19th century; their stay apparently was only for a decade or so. Subdivision named for feature.

McKnights Ditch, canal, 0.5 mi. long, Dare County, Nags Head Township (Brazier 1820). In ditches trending toward Johns Creek 2.5 mi. se of Manteo (center). Just s of Dykes Creek, using alternatively McKnights Creek or McKnights Ditch. *Other names:* McKnights Creek (local use).

McNeill Inlet, canal, Carteret County, Morehead Township (Zaenker 2014). E entrance Pine Knoll Waterway in Pine Knoll Shores 3.8 mi. w of Atlantic Beach (town). "Inlet" not used in traditional sense on the Outer Banks of barrier island breach, because indicative of dredging allowing water inward for access by boats to open water (Bogue Sound). Named for George H. McNeill, attorney representing Roosevelt heirs of Alice Hoffman Estate (*see* Pine Knoll Shores). Interesting that e entrance named for McNeill and w entrance named for Alice Hoffman, since e entrance is closer to her original house.

Meekins Anchorage, former landing, Dare County, Nags Head Township (Sandbeck 2003). Was at Blackhall Bay just s of Dare County Regional Airport, 2 mi. w of Manteo (center). Named for landowner, Meekins long-established name on Roanoke Island.

Meekins Hill, hummock, Dare County, Nags Head Township (CS 1870). In central Roanoke Island 2 mi. nnw of Wanchese. Not as prominent today as 19th century and name rarely used. *See* Meekins Anchorage. *Other names:* Meekims Hill (Foster 1866a—recording error).

Meekins Mill, former mill and windmill, Dare County, Nags Head Township (CS 1854). Was in Wanchese 5.3 mi. s of Manteo (center). Historically, settlement at s Roanoke Island was scattered, with several focal points of activity. *See* Meekins Anchorage.

Mekins Hill, former sand dune, Dare County, Nags Head Township (CS 1870). In Nags Head (center) just nne of Jockeys Ridge 1 mi. nnw of Nags Head Pier. No longer exists with constant change of dunescape and also local development. Name recorded with only one "e," an error since Meekins is surname here.

Merganser Canal, canal, 0.5 mi. long, Dare County, Atlantic Township (Town of Southern Shores 2015). In Southern Shores 4.5 mi. n of original Kitty Hawk. Names of Southern Shores canals are for shorebirds (except Gravey Pond Canal). The hooded merganser duck (*Lophodytes cucullatus*) here during winter.

Merkle Hammock, tidal flat, 1.5 mi. long, 0.3 mi. wide, Carteret County, Portsmouth Township (USGS 2013: Wainwright Island). Frequently inundated mud flat between Portsmouth Island and unnamed marsh islands 12.3 mi. sw of Ocracoke (village). "Merkle" is local pronunciation of myrtle, referring to small shrub-like wax myrtles (*Myrica* spp.) native to the Outer Banks and se U.S. *See* Black Hammock. *Other names:* Great Hammock Swash (C&GS 1900).

Merkle Hammock, hummock, Dare County, Kinnakeet Township (historical deeds). In South'ard Water and contained Merkle Ridge just s of Long Point 3 mi. s of original Avon. *See* Merkle Hammock above. *Other names:* Myrtle Hammock (attempts to correct name in historical documents).

Merkle Ridge, sand ridge, 0.5 mi. long, Dare County, Kinnakeet Township (local use). Trends n-s at tidal streams formerly known as South'ard Water (q.v.) just se of Long Point 3 mi. s of original Avon. Separates tidal streams from beach; tidal streams are oriented n-s (mostly—*see* South'ard Water) instead of usual short, e-w tidal streams. *See* Merkle Hammock. *Other names:* Mirkles Ridge (Garrity-Blake 2010, map, 211—form of Myrtle—Merkle here usually).

Meter Point, point, Dare County, Atlantic Township (USGS 2013: Kitty Hawk). On n Colington Island into Colington Creek just n of Colington (community) 3 mi. s of original Kitty Hawk. *Other names:* Colington Point (subdivision name here).

Meter Point, point, Dare County, Hatteras Township (local use). Protrudes into Sandy Bay 0.3 mi. s of Durant Point, 1 mi. nw of Hatteras (village). Recent application becoming better known.

Methodist Road Ridge. *See* Hickory Ridge.

Middle Burris Islands, small islands, Currituck County, Poplar Branch Township (local use). In Burris Islands (q.v.) complex between North Burris Island and South Burris Island, 6.2 mi. s of Corolla. In 19th century one larger island (not as large as North Burris Island or South Burris Island) now three or more small islands. *See* Burris Islands. *Other names:* Middle Burows Island (C&GS 1852).

Middle Burris Point, point, Currituck County, Poplar Branch Township (C&GS 1852). E-most point of the remains of Middle Burris Islands, 6 mi. s of Corolla.

Middle Core Banks, barrier beach, 3 mi. long, Carteret County, Atlantic, Sea Level, and Stacy Townships (some new local tourism use). On South Core Banks with ne end at Drum Inlet (now closed) and sw-ward to New Drum Inlet (now merging with Ophelia Inlet). Name evolved 21st century from descriptive term to place-name usage on maps. North Core Banks and South Core Banks are used more often by local residents, while Middle Core Banks rarely used except in some reports and on USGS topographic maps. *See* Core Banks. Made official by USBGN 2006.

Middle Core Beach, beach, 3 mi. long, Carteret County, Atlantic, Sea Level, and Stacy Townships (some new local tourism use). Corresponds with Middle Core Banks on South Core Banks from Drum Inlet (now closed) to new Drum Inlet just ne of Ophelia Inlet. Came into use with increased tourism and opening of Ophelia Inlet (q.v.). No usage before 21st century. *See* Core Banks.

Middle Core Island. *See* Ophelia Banks.

Middle Creek, small tidal creek, Hyde County, Ocracoke Township (Weslager 1954 — confirmed by interviews with Ballance [2017, 2018] and Howard [2017, 2018]). Soundside Ocracoke Island at ne edge First Hammock Hills 2.5 mi. ene of Ocracoke (village). Reason for use of "middle" is unknown, though

halfway between Ocracoke (village) and The Knoll (prominent feature) and also Dicks Camp.

Middle Ground, former shoal, Carteret County, Beaufort and Morehead Townships (CS 1850a). Was in Beaufort Inlet 1.3 mi. s of Beaufort (mainland). *See* Middle Ground (Hyde County, Swan Quarter Township).

Middle Ground, open water, Dare County, Atlantic Township (local use). Relatively even depth, in Albemarle Sound halfway between Powells Point (mainland) and ridge-and-swale system just e of original Kitty Hawk. Descriptive and often applied to shoals between channels. However, here application is open water and references its location. *Other names:* Middle Grounds (occasional use).

Middle Ground, extensive shoal, 2.5 mi. across, Hyde County, Ocracoke Township (CS 1852). Was in Pamlico Sound between Wallace Channel and Teaches Hole Channel, smaller now between Teaches Hole Channel and Blair Channel, 1.4 mi. w of Ocracoke (village). *See* Middle Ground (Hyde County, Swan Quarter Township). *Other names:* The Middle Ground (Price 1795).

Middle Ground, former small shoal, Hyde County, Ocracoke Township (Moseley 1733). Was separating North Breakers and South Breakers (18th century) at then (shifted over years) n entrance Ocracoke Inlet 2.8 mi. s of Ocracoke (village). *See* Middle Ground (Hyde County, Swan Quarter Township). *Other names:* Middle Bar (McGuinn 2000, 22).

Middle Ground, former shoal, Hyde County, Ocracoke Township (Blunt 1857, 343). Was in center of Hatteras Inlet, 4.5 mi. wsw of Hatteras (village). Remnants exist in various forms but name not used after 19th century.

Middle Ground, shoal, 6.6 mi. long, Hyde County, Swan Quarter Township (NOS 2014i). In Pamlico Sound 17.8 mi. nw of Ocracoke (village). Three sections are Upper Middle, Inner Middle, and Lower Middle. Descriptive and often applied to shoals between channels. Upper Middle, Inner Middle, and Lower Middle are each separate features on this larger shoal and are sometimes used for the larger shoal. *Other names:* Inner Middle (directional perception), Lower Middle (directional perception), Middle Ground Shoal (CS 1862b), Middle Ground

Shoals (Lathrop 1858), Midel Ground (Wimble 1733-notorious spelling), Upper Middle (directional perception).

Middle Island, linear island, 1.3 mi. long, Carteret County, Beaufort Township (local use). E-w trending just s of Beaufort (mainland) just w of Carrot Island, 1.3 mi. n of Shackleford Point, w tip Shackleford Banks.

Middle Island, island, Dare County, Atlantic Township (local use). At sw edge Kitty Hawk ridge-and-swale system (q.v.), created by Fish House Creek (s) and Tarkle Creek (n), 1.6 mi. sw of original Kitty Hawk. *Other names:* Hog Island (occasional map application).

Middle Marsh, large marsh, Currituck County, Fruitville Township (Cox 1923). Is 1 mi. n of Currituck Bay, 4 mi. se of Knotts Island (village).

Middle Marsh Channel, channel, Carteret County, Harkers Island Township (Williamson 1992, 184). In Back Sound, separates Middle Marshes (n) and Big Shoal Marsh (s), 4.5 mi. sw of Harkers Island (village).

Middle Marshes, islands, 1.7 mi. long, 0.7 mi. wide, Carteret County, Harkers Island Township (USGS 1997: Harkers Island). Tidal marsh in nw Back Sound 1.4 mi. n of Shackleford Banks, 2.6 mi. wsw of Harkers Island (village). *Other names:* Middle Marsh (CS 1852–82).

Middle Marsh Pond, marsh cove, Currituck County, Fruitville Township (local use). In s Middle Marsh 0.7 mi. ne of Swan Island, 2.7 mi. se of Knotts Island (village). *See* Adams Pond.

Middle Morgan Island, former island, Currituck County, Poplar Branch Township (Currituck DB 1839, 22, 296). Was in Currituck Sound between Big Morgan Island and Little Morgan Island, 1.5 mi. nw of Brant Island, 3.5 mi. ssw of Corolla. *See* Morgan Islands.

Middle Point, point, Dare County, Kinnakeet Township (Garrity-Blake 2010, 168). Halfway (hence name) between Southwest Point (Dare County) and Southeast Point (Dare County) on Big Island (Dare County, Kinnakeet Township) 1 mi. n of original Avon.

Middle Pond, irregular water, 0.3 mi. long, Currituck County, Fruitville Township (USGS 2013: Knotts Island). In marsh n central Walk Island, 2 mi. ne of Knotts Island (village).

Middle Pool, man-enhanced area, Currituck County, Fruitville Township (F&WS 1984,

map, 74). Stages of marsh, dry area, and open water is middlemost of three such areas Mackay Island National Wildlife Refuge at central Mackay Island 2.3 mi. w of Knotts Island (village). Created 1984 establishing Cross Dike, Long Dike, and Parallel Dike; composition can be controlled in accordance with the situation. *Other names:* Middle Impoundment (original name, F&WS 1984, 11), Middle Marsh (F&WS 1984, 10).

Middle Portsmouth, former community, Carteret County, Portsmouth Township (local informants from Ocracoke familiar with Portsmouth). Was central community of "upper" Portsmouth Island just s of main former Portsmouth (village) 5.7 mi. sw of Ocracoke (village). Was between East Portsmouth and South Portsmouth separated by marsh and open area. All named outlying communities part of Portsmouth (village) just clusters of houses separated by marsh and open area and referenced by separate names for convenience and clarity of location (*see* East Portsmouth, Portsmouth, South Portsmouth, and Sheep Island). Variant Middle Community used more than Middle Portsmouth. *Other names:* Middle Community (White 2012, 93—spoken language reference to location regarding East Portsmouth and South Portsmouth), Midway (White 2012, 268).

Middle Ridge, sand ridge, 1 mi. long, Dare County, Hatteras Township (signage). In e-w–trending sand ridges just n of Jennette Sedge 1 mi. s of Buxton (also Flowers Ridge and Crooked Ridge).

Middle Rock, shoal, Currituck County, Poplar Branch Township (local use). More shoal than rock-like in Currituck Sound just off mainland 3.5 mi. w of Duck. *Other names:* Middle Sound Rock (descriptor).

Middle Slew, former channel, Carteret County, Portsmouth Township; and Hyde County, Ocracoke Township (historical local use). Was center approach to Ocracoke Inlet 3.5 mi. sw of Ocracoke (village). *See* Allen Slough.

Middletown, former settlement, Carteret County, exact location unknown (Angley 1984). Small collection of people, early settlement on Bogue Banks in what is now original Emerald Isle. The name is not shown on any maps and is likely more of a local reference to its probable location on the island where a few families lived (indicated as squatters). Very little information available.

Middletown Anchorage, anchorage, 1 mi. across, Hyde County, Lake Landing Township (NOS 2014b). In Pamlico Sound 2 mi. s of Engelhard (mainland) 24 mi. nw of Hatteras (village). "Anchorage" where boats can anchor relatively close to land with some protection, here deeper water (10–15 ft.) just off mainland with deep-water approach from s, surrounded by shoal water or shallower water. *Other names:* Middleton Anchorage (C&GS 1883).

Midgett Cove, cove, 0.4 mi. long, Dare County, Kinnakeet Township (USGS 2013: Rodanthe). In Pamlico Sound 0.6 mi. n of Salvo. Midgett (Midyette), old, established Outer Banks family name, especially in Rodanthe (Chicamacomico). *Other names:* Grande Harbor (recent very limited use from small subdivision at s part), The Harbor (Garrity-Blake 2010, 136—historical usage).

Midgett Field, former open area, Dare County, Nags Head Township (Gray 2009, 31). Was just n of Sandy Ridge just e of Skyco 2 mi. s se of Manteo (center). Gray indicates probably site of first Methodist church on Roanoke Island built 1799 or 1800.

Midgett Impoundment, area, Dare County, Nags Head Township (N.C. Wildlife Resources 2016a, map). Project completed 2005 to control waterflow in 40 acres of northwestern Roanoke Island Marshes 2.5 mi. s of Manteo (center).

Midgett Island, marsh island, 0.05 mi. long, 0.02 mi. wide, Dare County, Kinnakeet Township (USGS 2013: Rodanthe). In Pamlico Sound near Midgett Cove, 1.1 mi. nnw of Salvo. *See* Midgett Cove.

Midgett Point, former point, Dare County, Nags Head Township (appeared sporadically on maps, colonial era). Was n point former Cow Island near s side former Roanoke Inlet just sse of Whalebone Junction 4 mi. sse of central Nags Head. *See* Midgett Cove. *Other names:* Midgetts Point (local use).

Midgetts Camp, former camp, Dare County, Kinnakeet Township (NPS 2005b: NPS 1, 150). Was soundside at Clarks Bay just s of Salvo 4.5 mi. s of Rodanthe. Unlike most camps on middle and s "banks," mostly fishing camps, this camp was for hunting (entertaining sports hunters). *See* Midgett Cove. *Other names:* G. Midgett Hunt Club (Garrity-Blake 2010, map, 136).

Midgetts Ditch, canal, 0.4 mi. long, Dare County, Nags Head Township (USGS 2013: Manteo). Canalized tidal stream on e shore of n Roanoke Island at Midgetts Hammock 1.7 mi. ese of Manteo (center). *See* Midgett Cove. *Other names:* Hammock Ditch (numerous historical maps, including Brazier 1820), Hammocks Ditch (early maps).

Midgetts Hammock, hummock, Dare County, Nags Head Township (local use). On Roanoke Island in Pirates Cove subdivision 0.9 mi. s of Ballast Point 1.6 mi. se of central Manteo. Confederate forces placed a few guns here during Civil War, but not used (*see* Battery Monteil). *See* Midgett Cove and Black Hammock. Much of high area in these marshes was developed into Pirates Cove.

Midgetts Pond, lake, Dare County, Atlantic Township (Town of Kitty Hawk 2007). Just e of Jeanguite Creek (recent extended application) 1.3 mi. nw of Poor Ridge Landing 1.5 mi. sw of original Kitty Hawk. *See* Midgett Cove.

Midnight Pass. *See* Carova.

Midway Hammocks, small hummocks, Dare County, Atlantic Township (Harris 2017). Five notable hummocks, just e of Sound Landing 2 mi. w of original Kitty Hawk. Reportedly derived from location halfway between Roberson Creek and Sound Landing. *See* Black Hammock.

Midway Intersection, area, Dare County, Nags Head Township (local use—mostly historical). Highway intersection in Manteo of US 64, 264, 64 Business, 264 Business, and NC 345 (to Wanchese). More historic originally (middle to late 20th century) referencing present intersection and just s of present intersection before US 64 and 264 Bypass were built with Virginia Dare Bridge (2002). Descriptive of location, not used much today.

Midyetts (Midgetts) Mill and Windmill, former mill, Dare County, Kinnakeet Township (Covey 2018, 44). Was somewhere in Midyetts vast holdings in Chicamacomico, s Rodanthe or possibly s Salvo. Actually, might have been two windmills, s Rodanthe and s Salvo. Bishop (1878) does not mention this windmill, but shown unnamed on Dunbar's (1958) map.

Midyetts Windmill. *See* Green Point Windmill.

Mill Cove, cove, 0.2 mi. wide, Currituck County, Fruitville Township (USGS 2013: Knotts Island). At Knotts Island 0.9 mi. e of Knotts Island (village).

Mill Creek, cove, Dare County, Kinnakeet Township (USGS 2013: Buxton). In Pamlico Sound just s of Big Island 1.1 mi. n of original Avon in newer Avon. Topography here has changed dramatically, affecting several tidal streams, altered by man; topography and name applications are different from 50–100 years ago and earlier. Deeds indicate formerly a mill here, though name is forgotten; might have been Farrow Scarboroughs Mill (q.v.). *Other names:* Follies Creek (Currituck DB 8, 1745, 29–30), Folly Creek (Currituck DB 9, 1804, 104–5), Mariners Cove (est. late 20th century—limited usage usually applying to upper portion), Old Creek (originally two separate features until development; Garrity-Blake 2010, 494), Robbs Creek (historical use, 1793 and 1797 deeds).

Millers Creek. *See* Deals Island Creek.

Mill Landing, former landing, Dare County, Kinnakeet Township (Garrity-Blake 2010, 169). Was at sw entrance Mill Creek (Old Creek) in The North'ard section of Avon, just se of Big Island 7.5 mi. n of Buxton. Altered considerably by development; no longer exists as originally.

Mill Landing, landing, Dare County, Nags Head Township (USGS 2013: Oregon Inlet). On small marsh island 1.3 mi. e of Wanchese at mouth Mill Landing Creek. Major fish-processing facility here, with larger facilities near lower portion of the Outer Banks at Morehead City (mainland). Occasional references of Pughs Landing near Mill Landing are misapplied, as Pughs Landing was sw of Wanchese near Hookers Landing (Pugh Road still leads there). *Other names:* Pughs Landing (misapplied), Wanchese Mill Landing (Sandbeck 2003, 18).

Mill Landing Creek, man-enhanced water passage, 0.5 mi. long, Dare County, Nags Head Township (USGS 1983: Oregon Inlet). At Roanoke Sound 1.3 mi. e of Wanchese. Became Wanchese Harbor, important harbor for fishing industry of Wanchese and Roanoke Island, began 1930s and expanded through 1990s to more easily accessible Norfolk area. Catch unloaded and processed here. Turning basin completed 1979, now much local usage for Mill Landing Creek or Mill Creek (subdivision named for this form) as entrance Wanchese Harbor. Made official by USBGN 1983 to clarify name is not Mill Creek. *Other names:* Mill Creek (C&GS 1883), Wanchese Harbor (ACE 1879; local media, 2016).

Mill Landing Hill, dune, 5 ft. high, Dare County, Kinnakeet Township (Garrity-Blake 2010, 207). At former Mill Landing in North'ard area of Avon, just s of Mill Creek (Old Creek). Observation point early 20th century; highest point soundside (bit higher early 1900s).

Mill Point, point, Dare County, Atlantic Township (Currituck DB 5, 1787, 216). Extreme se Kitty Hawk ridge-and-swale system (q.v.) just s of original Kitty Hawk 7.8 mi. nnw of central Nags Head. Sporadic use since 18th century. Mill here late 1700s and reportedly until late 1800s; no trace now. Mill Point Gut (Mill Pond Ditch) and former Mill Pond nearby. Some implication today is Thickety Point (*see* Thickety Ridge).

Mill Point, point, Dare County, Atlantic Township (historical maps and documents). Extreme n point of peninsula, Martin Point, just w of Jeanguite Creek and Southern Shores, 5 mi. n of original Kitty Hawk. Only incidental usage today where probably was a windmill because road here is Mill Point Road (interesting application since name almost unknown). Referenced on a few colonial-era maps and old legal papers.

Mill Point Gut, stream, 0.5 mi. long, Dare County, Atlantic Township (Currituck DB 5, 1787, 276). At Mill Point in extreme se Kitty Hawk ridge-and-swale system (q.v.) just s of original Kitty Hawk. Powls (Pawls) Creek might have been another adjacent stream as topographic configuration 1700s and before development was considerably different. Named for mill here in late 1700s. Local use now applies Penny Toler Ditch to a considerable portion of the stream. *Other names:* Mill Gut (Harris 2017; unknown, 1823), Mill Pond Ditch (Town of Kitty Hawk 2007), Millpoint Gut (Harris 2017; unknown, 1804), Mill Point Gutt (18th-century maps; Currituck DB 4, 1783, 187), Pawls Creek (Harris 2017; unknown, 1879), Pole Creek (Currituck DB 1819, 15, 43–44), Pools Creek (Currituck

DB 1805, 9), Powls Creek (Currituck DB 7, 1784, 133).

Mill Pond, former pond, Dare County, Atlantic Township (historical deeds). Used for operation of a mill (name unknown) here late 1700s at mouth of Mill Point Gut (q.v.) just s of original Kitty Hawk.

Mimosa Beach, small beach, Carteret County, Morehead Township (local use). At Ocean Park across from primary entrance to original Pine Knoll Shores at Mimosa Boulevard 4 mi. w of Atlantic Beach. Ocean Park where beach is located was earlier Mimosa Park. Beach name and park reference are from being directly across from Mimosa Boulevard. Mimosa refers to an invasive tree (*Albizia julibrissin*) originally from Southeast Asia but prevalent in much of se U.S. Different color flowers with different species, mostly pink here, though believed the drink by that name was from species with yellow flowers.

Mingers Point, point, Currituck County, Fruitville Township (F&WS 1984, map, 74). At s entrance Duckpond on n Mackay Island 3.5 mi. w of Knotts Island (village). Might be surname, though not prevalent here. *See* Mingoes Ridge Gut.

Mingoes Ridge, sand ridge, Dare County, Atlantic Township (local use). Just e of Mingoes Ridge Gut just n of Hay Point in s original Kitty Hawk. *See* Mingoes Ridge Gut. *Other names:* Minger Ridge (local reference), Mingers Ridge (Harris 2017), Mingle Ridge (Harris 2017—only known reference using this form).

Mingoes Ridge Gut, tidal stream, 0.6 mi. long, Dare County, Atlantic Township (early deeds). In Kitty Hawk entering nw North Cove 8.5 mi. nw of central Nags Head. Could be surname Minger. Alternatively, "mingo" or "mingoe" roughly translates as treacherous, originally reference to Indians of the Mengwe group (note variant Mingues) more commonly known as Iroquois. Predominately a confederation of five tribes in upper New York State, but for a time included a sixth tribe, the Tuscarora (joining around 1722), which had migrated to central and e North Carolina. Tuscarora left the confederation during American Revolution to fight with colonists, while most Iroquois in New York fought with British. Eventually many "Mingo" left New York and settled in Ohio Valley. Even so, used loosely for all Indians who were members of Iroquois Confederation, so there could be some relation to the origin of this name (Mingoes Ridge Gut), but connection yet to be documented. So, this name must have been introduced if not from Minger. Considerable local use now for Mingers Ridge Creek or Mingers Ridge Gut, probably from labeling on maps or just local pronunciation; however, application Mingoes has been used for over 200 years (in deeds). Associative with Mingoes Ridge.

> *Other names:* Cedar Hammock Gut (Currituck DB 1a, 1763, 147–48—slight possibility applied to neighboring creek or separately named creek, but evidence [deeds] suggests Mingoes Ridge Gut), Mangos Gutt (Currituck DB 5, 1787, 216—transcribing error, no mangos here), Mingers Gut (Harris 2017; unknown, 1791), Mingers Ridge Gut (census block maps), Mingers Ridge Creek (Town of Kitty Hawk 2007), Mingoes Gut (Currituck DB 6, 1788, 142), Mingoes Gutt (Currituck DB 5, 1787, 216), Mingoes Ridge Swamp (Harris 2017; unknown, 1898), Mingos Gut (Currituck DB 2, 1763, 306), Mingues Ridge Gut (Harris 2017; unknown, 1855).

Mirlo Beach, beach, Dare County, Kinnakeet Township (signage). On Hatteras Island n edge of Rodanthe 15 mi. s of Oregon Inlet. From a tanker ship attacked and sunk August 16, 1918, by German U-boat just off this beach, where there was a heroic struggle by men of Chicamacomico (original name of Rodanthe) Life Saving Station in foulest weather to reach the sinking ship; the crew had already abandoned ship, and 6 of 15 crew members were rescued. Evidence of periodic overwash here and just n of Mirlo Beach connecting to Pamlico Sound just s of Pauls Ditch (*see* S-Curves). Subdivision named for feature.

Mirlo Breach. *See* Rodanthe Breach.

Mirtle Hamocks, hummocks, Dare County, Kinnakeet Township (Currituck DB 8, 1800, 240). Was somewhere on Hatteras Island, historical part Chicamacomico Banks, between Little Kinnakeet (s) and Rodanthe (n). Descriptive noting higher land and more vegetation in otherwise stark environment (use of "buck" in variant name uses an archaic definition of "buck" for stark, as in "buck-naked"). Original spelling encountered presented, but is really "myrtle" and here is and was pronounced "merkle" (*see* Merkle Hammock). "Hamock" is likely misrecorded since spelling normally used is hammock. *See also* Black Hammock. *Other names:* Mirtle Buck Hammocks (Currituck DB 7, 1796, 337–38).

Misty Pond, small man-enhanced lake, Currituck County, Poplar Branch Township (local use). Recent feature and name in Monteray (*sic*) Shores, 2.5 mi. s of Corolla; descriptive, by whom applied unknown.

Moccasin Creek, water passage, 1 mi. long, Currituck County, Fruitville Township (Cox 1923). Trends n-s separating Big Skinner Island from Little Skinner Island and Currituck Banks, 5 mi. se of Knotts Island (village). Reference to water moccasin snakes (*Agkistrodon piscivorus*; poisonous and dangerous) plentiful here because Currituck Sound mostly freshwater since Caffeys Inlet and New Currituck Inlet closed early 1800s.

Molasses Creek, small stream, Hyde County, Ocracoke Township (signage and Weslager 1954). On Ocracoke Island, flows into Little Swash Opening just ne of Quokes Point 5 mi. ne of Ocracoke (village). Weslager indicates (1954, 45) from cargo of wrecked ship, but many local folk indicate name origin because slow-moving.

Money Island, island, 0.2 mi. long, Carteret County, Morehead Township (USGS 2013: Beaufort). At s end Money Island Bay separated from Bogue Banks at Atlantic Beach by Money Slough; 1.5 mi. s of Morehead City (mainland). Reportedly named because according to legend was a favorite place where pirates would bury treasure (as they likely did all along the Outer Banks). *Other names:* Money Isle (Holland Consulting Planners 2006, 3).

Money Island Bay, cove, 0.6 mi. wide, Carteret County, Morehead Township (USGS 1951: Beaufort). In Bogue Sound at Atlantic Beach 1.3 mi. s of Morehead City (mainland). *See* Money Island. *Other names:* Money Bay (NOS 2014a).

Money Island Beach, beach, Carteret County, Morehead Township (USGS 2013: Beaufort). On e part Bogue Banks 0.9 mi. e of Atlantic Beach (town). *See* Money Island. Subdivision named for feature. *Other names:* Atlantic View Beach (Willis, n.d.), Money Beach (early

advertisements), Money Isle Beach (Willis, n.d.), Ocean Beach (Willis, n.d.).

Money Slough, water passage, 0.3 mi. long, Carteret County, Morehead Township (USGS 2013: Beaufort). In Money Island Bay at Atlantic Beach (town) 1.5 mi. ssw of Morehead City (mainland). "Island" in variants was dropped in usage by end of 20th century. *See* Money Island. *Other names:* Money Island Channel (Carteret County GIS 2019), Money Island Slough (USGS 1951: Beaufort).

Mon Island, marsh island, 0.3 mi. long, 0.2 mi. wide, Currituck County, Fruitville Township (USGS 2013: Knotts Island—still labeled). At n end Knotts Island Channel 2.4 mi. nne of Knotts Island (village). Origin unknown in this form, but (as most indicate) "Mon" is likely a dialectical derivation of Man or Mann, local surname and prevalent in local place names. Originally applied to Buckle Island (now changed to South Buckle Island [q.v.]), so Mon Island not used on maps and other publications since 2006, but still known locally so included as an entry. Variant Dudleys Island sometimes used because Dudley brothers operated a hunt club here early 20th century known as Dudley's Island Club, leading to the misnomer. *See* Manns Island. *Other names:* Buckle Island (local use), Buckle Islands (local use), Dudleys Island (some unintentional use), Man Island (GNIS), Mounds Island (Currituck DB 12, 1812, 119–21—though occurring here, misinterpretation of Mon or Mann—"Mounds" rejected locally and reported to USBGN), South Buckle Island (official 2006).

Mon Island. *See* South Buckle Island.

Monkey Island, island, 0.2 mi. long, Currituck County, Poplar Branch Township (USGS 2013: Corolla). In Currituck Sound 2.7 mi. nw of Corolla. Corruption of Pumonkey, name of Indians who inhabited area and frequented the island; no monkeys here. One of many hunt clubs of early 20th century operated here 1869–1978. *Other names:* Monkey Isle (Cary 1783), Monkeys Island (18th century), Munkey Island (Currituck DB 1802, 3, 244–45), Munkeys Island (Currituck DB 3, 1801, 47).

Monteray Shores, subdivision, Currituck County, Poplar Branch Township (signage). Soundside at Sanders Bay, 3.5 mi. s of Corolla. Unusual spelling of Monterey, with an ending "a" instead of "e," because is surname of a developer. *Other names:* Monterey Shores (Currituck County 2013, 9—mistake assuming conventional spelling).

Montgomery Point, point, Carteret County, White Oak Township (CS 1855). Soundside just s of Long Island 1.5 mi. w of original Emerald Isle.

Moon Island, island, 1 mi. long, Dare County, Nags Head Township (local informant). In se Croatan Sound 2.5 mi. sw of Wanchese. Named for crescent-shape of island; recent name.

Moonlight Bay, cove, Carteret County, Morehead Township (local use). Just e of Atlantic Beach Causeway in Atlantic Beach (town), 1.5 mi. s of Morehead City (mainland). In former Cedar Hammock (q.v. unrecognizable from original topography), considerably altered and man-enhanced 1960s and 1970s. Ne Cedar Hammock Creek just w of Atlantic Beach Causeway enhanced by development and alteration of Cedar Hammock. Name recently applied as attractive for commercial purposes. *Other names:* Moonlite Bay (brochures using incorrect, increasingly accepted spelling).

Moonrise Bay Landing. *See* Knotts Island (village) for information.

Moore Dock, former landing, Carteret County, Harkers Island Township (Wiss and Milner, 2005). Was just s of Cape Lookout Lighthouse, center shore Lookout Bight 2 mi. n of Cape Point. Several ruins of historical docks exist in area but names are lost.

Morehead City Channel, channel, 2.2 mi. long, Carteret County, Beaufort and Morehead Townships (USGS 2013: Beaufort). Trends ne-sw connecting Beaufort Inlet and Newport River at Morehead City Port facility, 2.1 mi. ese of Morehead City (mainland). Approach channel to port and docking facilities at Morehead City for transporting phosphate and in support of (former) menhaden (*Brevoortia tyrannus*) fishing industry. *Other names:* Banks Channel (Kell, 1777), Main Ship Channel (Tompson and Albert 1854), Ship Road (unknown, 1777—*see* Beacon Island Roads).

More Shore (Moor Shore) (Moore Shore), shore section, 0.7 mi. long, Dare County, Atlantic Township (well-known local use). At e end Kitty Hawk Bay just s of original Kitty Hawk 7.4 mi. nnw of original Nags Head. Early name Great Wading Place reported by some older residents and confirmed by several occurrences in early deeds. Descriptive because here Kitty Hawk Bay is extremely shallow, 1–3 ft. deep, for a considerable distance from shore. This theory corroborated in deed to William Etheridge referring to transfer of 50 acres "beginning at a swamp at Kittehawk Ridge [*sic*] and ending at the Great Wading Place." Kitty Hawk Ridge is a large ridge with its s terminus a short distance nnw of More Shore (Great Wading Place). The other names entered the vocabulary and namescape over the years. Some maps (including Town of Kitty Hawk 2007 zoning map) use spelling Moore. A road sign shows Moore, but it originally indicated Moor. Stick (1958) indicates "Avalon Beach, was originally Moore's Shore." Harris (2017) uses both Moore Shore and Moore Shores (plural) on his hand-annotated maps, without further explanation. Other local informants suggest Moor is correct because used to moor boats despite being quite shallow. Older folk favor More and younger folk favor Moore or Moor. Nearby subdivision named Moor Shores. Name is originally More Shore, from the shallowness a considerable distance into Kitty Hawk Bay, and other forms are folk etymology (substituting name for forgotten meaning). *Other names:* Great Wading Place (Currituck DB 7, 1795, 169–70), Moore Shore (conflicting road signage), Moores Shore (Stick 1958), Moor Shore (local informants), Moore Shores (Harris 2017).

Morgan Creek, tidal creek, Carteret County, Harkers Island Township (local use). Small cove-like tidal creek at s end Morgan Island in Lighthouse Channel 3 mi. se of Harkers Island (village).

Morgan Island, irregular marsh island, 0.5 mi. long, Carteret County, Harkers Island Township (USGS 2013: Harkers Island). Junction Core Sound and Back Sound 3.1 mi. sse of Harkers Island (village). *Other names:* Morgans Island (C&GS 1931).

Morgan Islands, islands, Currituck County, Poplar Branch Township (CS 1862a). Two islands, Big Morgan Island and Little Morgan Island, in Currituck Sound at nw tip Mossey Islands complex, 3 mi. w of Peters Quarter, 3 mi. sw of Corolla. Must have been three islands initially as Currituck DB 22 (1839,

296) indicates Middle Island (q.v.) of Morgan Islands.

Moris Bay. *See* Lemors Bay.

Morris Battery. *See* Fort Macon Siege Batteries.

Morris Cove, cove, Currituck County, Poplar Branch Township (C&GS 1852). Junction Joes Creek and Beach Creek, 5.2 mi. nnw of Duck.

Morrison Grove, area, Dare County, Nags Head Township (signage). On n Roanoke Island just e of Fort Raleigh National Historic site, 2.3 mi. nw of Manteo (center). Housing site for cast of outdoor drama *The Lost Colony*.

Morse Point, peninsula, 2 mi. long, Currituck County, Fruitville Township; and City of Virginia Beach, Virginia (USGS 2016 Knotts Island). S from Virginia into North Carolina 4 mi. w of Knotts Island separated from Knotts Island by Great Marsh 11 mi. nw of Corolla. Variants Mossy Point (Byrd 1728), Mosses Point (Collet et al. 1770), and Mossess Point (Mouzon 1775) might create some doubt on what was original name; however, Morse was used as early as 1782 in deeds. *Other names:* Morses Point (Currituck DB 4, 1782, 15), Morses Point Neck (Currituck DB 5, 1787, 270—*see* Deep Neck), Mosses Point (Collet et al. 1770), Mossess Point (Mouzon 1775), Mossy Point (Byrd 1728).

Morses Point. *See* Halfway Point.

Morses Slue, former small channel, Carteret County, Beaufort Township (C&GS 1876b). Trended n-s from Carrot Island Channel at Carrot Island to Shackleford Slue, 2.2 mi. se of Beaufort (mainland). Almost disappeared and of little practical use. *See* Allen Slough.

Mosquito Canal, man-enhanced, 0.3 mi. long, Dare County, Nags Head Township (local informants). In area of other minor man-enhanced creeks, n and ne boundary of Ice Plant Island (q.v.—Festival Park location) in ene Manteo, 2 mi. nw of Pirates Cove subdivision. Created Ice Plant Island (often Festival Park Island now used) but considerably enhanced by dredging 1980s (when name was applied) when Festival Park was created (celebrates Lost Colony and a venue for education, performances, and Outer Banks History Center, a research center dedicated to Outer Banks research). *See* Canals at Manteo and Ice Plant Island. *Other names:* Mosquito Ditch (local descriptive name—Ditch and Canal used interchangeably).

Mossey Islands, island complex, 3 mi. long, 1 mi. wide, Currituck County, Poplar Branch Township (USGS 2013: Mossey Islands). Marsh islands complex and shoals in Currituck Sound, 1.2 mi. w of Currituck Banks, 4.7 mi. s of Corolla. Major stopover and feeding area for migrating birds along Atlantic Flyway and one of few still open to hunters. On some historical maps labeled with descriptor "pilentery" or "pilontary," both corruptions of "pellitory" (*see* Pilontary Islands). Also, Burris Islands (q.v.) complex is sometimes included as s portion Mossey Islands complex. *Other names:* Duck Marsh (C&GS 1852), Mawsey Island (spelled as pronounced—Currituck DB 5, 1788, 342—apparently only one of more prominent islands here), Mossey Island (historical local use), Mossy Island (Codman, Crowninshield, and Lawrence 1925).

Mossey Pond, lake, 0.1 mi. across, Currituck County, Poplar Branch Township (USGS 2013: Mossey Islands). At center Mossey Islands complex, 4.8 mi. ssw of Corolla. *Other names:* Mossy Pond (USGS 2013: Mossey Islands).

Moss Island, former island, Currituck County, Poplar Branch Township (Currituck DB 24, 1825, 406-7; C&GS 1852). Was adjacent to and just ese of Brant Island 3.7 mi. ssw of Corolla. Now attached to Brant Island (Currituck County). *Other names:* Mossy Island (limited local use).

Mother Vineyard, area, 15 ft. high, Dare County, Nags Head Township (USGS 2013: Manteo). On ne shore Roanoke Island 1 mi. n of Manteo (center). Named for ancient and large scuppernong grape vines, first discovered by Amadas and Barlowe while exploring here for Sir Walter Raleigh (Barlowe 1584). Exact age of vines unknown but at least 500 years old. Reportedly reference to great age and stamina of the vine. Existence is somewhat of a mystery because these vines show evidence of some cultivation, but while Indians had some advanced agricultural practices, their knowledge of viticulture was rudimentary. Subdivision named for feature. *Other names:* Old Vineyard (occasional reference).

Motts Creek, cove, 0.3 mi. long, 0.4 mi. wide, Dare County, Nags Head Township (USGS 2013: Oregon Inlet). In Roanoke Sound 1.2 mi. nnw of Oregon Inlet 6.1 mi. se of Wanchese.

Mount Truxtun, apparent sand dune, Carteret County, Portsmouth Township (Blunt 1809;

Meyer and Tanner 1849; Tanner, 1855). Appears applied to a sand dune just s of East Portsmouth (community) 1 mi. se of Portsmouth (village). Not now or historically any high or distinct dunes here, so reason for this name, and especially use of the generic term "Mount," is unclear. Several publications indicate used as sighting point, but historically no more than 5 ft. Name was short-lived, appearing on only a few maps, and no published information or local recognition of this appellation. Name appeared at beginning of 19th century and lasted sporadically until mid-19th century. Speculation is it must have been (for some unknown reason except for popularity in the navy) applied in honor of Admiral Thomas Truxtun, who arose from privateer (during American Revolution) to U.S. Navy admiral and has had numerous ships named for him. Truxtun was active as high-ranking and successful naval officer from early 1790s through 1812, so time frame of his popularity and appearance of this name coincide. However, no direct connection to the Outer Banks or Portsmouth on the Outer Banks, though among things named for him is a neighborhood in Portsmouth, Virginia (just n of Currituck County), 125 mi. n of *this* Portsmouth (village). First ship named for Truxtun was a brig (short for "brigantine," two-mast sailing ship) and launched coincidentally in Portsmouth, Virginia, and while in and out of Portsmouth, Virginia, no record of any activity at this Portsmouth or anywhere along the Outer Banks—most of ship's action along Africa and Mediterranean and in Mexican-American War, when the ship ran aground in Mexico and was later destroyed. All other ships named for Truxtun were 20th century. Additionally, there was also Commodore William Talbot Truxtun, who served in U.S. Navy during mid-19th century and was involved in action along the Outer Banks. However, this particular naval officer named Truxtun was active considerably after name appears on maps, so it must be named for Thomas Truxtun (if named for anyone). Also a street is named Truxton Street in Kill Devil Hills 1.3 mi. s of original Kitty Hawk.

Alternatively, name origin possibility could be for house or land owned by someone who was particularly fond of Commodore Truxtun, or perhaps someone who had served under him and who had come to Portsmouth (village) (conversation with owner of Mount Truxton Publishing, his preference of name origin). Even if this is the actual name origin, use of "Mount" in the name is intriguing. Interestingly, on Coles and Price (1806) chart, Mount Truxtun is clearly labeled beside a hachured-lined (crude lines drawn on a map or chart, method used initially for depicting topography) sand dune and also several houses depicted just n of the dune, some with owners' names. Further, NPS (2007, map, 27, 28) indicates (sort of) Mount Truxtun "might" be a sand dune by circling a (hachured) image of a sand dune and labeling it "Mount Truxston [*sic*]: high point of island." Curiously, several NPS reports persist in referring to this feature as the highest point on the island (19th century, anyway) and persist using Truxston with an "s" and an "o." Impossible to determine if this is individual and confirmed research or perpetuation of an error. As with other names on this map, no additional information is provided, and "s" in "Truxston" (and "o" for "u") must be errors, whether named for Admiral Truxtun or not, since all map occurrences except this one use Truxtun. So, whether this name is for a sand dune or a house named for Admiral Truxtun or a house named for someone else, or both reasons, still not completely known why the name was chosen. Additionally, elevation at this spot today is less than 5 ft., as is most of the surrounding area. Personal observation confirms the site is barely discernable. The highest spots on the island are between 5 ft. and 10 ft. at s end Portsmouth Island and on Sheep Island, considered on Portsmouth Island in general, extending 3 mi. s to High Hills Inlet (Whalebone Inlet). Former residents referenced former Portsmouth village as "down banks" though n-most, and referred to Sheep Island as "up banks" though s, because perceptibly s is slightly higher (**see** Sheep Island— former settlement). So, after numerous conversations, especially people with direct ties to Portsmouth, it seems name likely applied to a house as surname or in honor of Admiral Truxtun (for unknown reason), and the few references to a sand dune and this highest point reference are predicated on hearsay and error. *Other names:* High Hill (White 2012, 162—vague reference possibly to former Mount Truxtun, ceased to be used after mid-19th century), The Hill (White 2012, 169—same comment as High Hill).

Mount Vernon Rock, former rock, Carteret County, Portsmouth Township (*Wilmington Gazette*, n.d.). Was in Pamlico Sound 1.5 mi. wnw of Portsmouth (village), 6 mi. sw of Ocracoke (village). On maps and charts since early 19th century, named for schooner *Mount Vernon*, perished nearby in October 1806 storm (*Wilmington Gazette*, n.d.). *Other names:* Mount Vernon (spoken reference).

Mud Cove, small cove, Currituck County, Fruitville Township (local use). At se tip Knotts Island, s beginning of Bay Point 2 mi. s of Knotts Island (village).

Muddy Creek, water passage, 0.5 mi. long, Dare County, Hatteras Township (local use). Ne-sw–trending creek in n Hatteras (village) from Sandy Bay to Pamlico Sound 4.3 mi. ne of Hatteras Inlet.

Muddy Creek. *See* Abes Creek.

Muddy Marsh, marsh, Dare County, Hatteras Township (U.S. Navy 1918). Just w of cove at terminus of Cape Creek (Back Landing Creek) just n of Croatoan Ridge and extension of Cape Creek just e of Buxton 4 mi. e of Frisco (Currituck DB 4, 1784, 251–52). Muddy Marsh Ditch passes through this marsh, known historically as Muddy Creek before being altered. *Other names:* Muddy Creek Marsh (Brooks 2010).

Muddy Marsh Ditch, canal, Dare County, Hatteras Township (U.S. Navy 1918). Near former radio station operated by Navy Department 1918, 2 mi. n of original Cape Hatteras Lighthouse location (next to ocean) before being moved inland by NPS 0.5 mi. 1999 for preservation. Not well known and name no longer in much use. *See* Muddy Marsh. *Other names:* Muddy Creek (original historical use).

Mud Island, island, 0.2 mi. wide, Carteret County, Portsmouth Township (USGS 2013: Wainwright Island). In Core Sound 0.3 mi. sw of Cowpen Point, 15.5 mi. sw of Ocracoke (village).

Mud Island, small island, 0.1 mi. across,

Currituck County, Fruitville Township (Cox 1923). In s terminus Ingles Creek at North Rainbow Creek, 5 mi. se of Knotts Island (village).

Mud Point, point, Carteret County, White Oak Township (USGS 2013: Swansboro). On Bogue Banks s of Langston Bridge 3.5 mi. se of Swansboro (mainland).

Mulberry Bay, bay, Carteret County, White Oak Township (Powell 2010). Powell indicates between Banks Channel and Bogue Inlet; probably references water between Trout Creek and Frazier Creek and Banks Channel. Name unknown locally.

Mullet Cove, cove, 0.3 mi. long, 0.1 mi. wide, Carteret County, Smyrna Township (USGS 2013: Horsepen Point). In Core Sound 1.6 mi. s of Horsepen Point, 5.1 mi. e of Harkers Island (village). Named for mullet (family Mugilidae), small fish found at the Outer Banks.

Mullet Creek, water passage, 0.7 mi. long, Currituck County, Poplar Branch Township (USGS 2013: Jarvisburg). On nw Pine Island, 6.2 mi. nw of Duck. *See* Mullet Cove.

Mullet Pond, lake, 0.1 mi. wide, Carteret County, Harkers Island Township (USGS 2013: Beaufort). Freshwater pond on sw tip Shackleford Banks, 1.5 mi. e of Beaufort Inlet. Formed by enclosure with w migration of sand spit or hook at w end Shackleford Banks. Spit or hook forms by process of longshore drift, or movement of sand and materials by oblique or angular wave action. Depositional activity is apparent on USGS (2013: Beaufort) map. *See* Mullet Cove.

Mullet Shoal, shoal, Carteret County, Harkers Island Township (USGS 2013: Horsepen Point). In Core Sound 2 mi. e of Horsepen Point, 5.6 mi. nne of Harkers Island (village). *See* Mullet Cove. *Other names:* Bells Shoal (U.S. Congress 1876, 14—2 mi. se of Bells Point on Bells Island; often part of mainland), Bells Point Shoal (U.S. Congress 1876, 25).

Mullet Shoal, shoal, 2 mi. long, Carteret County, Portsmouth Township (USGS 2013: Wainwright Island). In Core Sound near junction with Pamlico Sound just w of Merkle Hammock 10.5 mi. sw of Ocracoke (village). *See* Mullet Cove. *Other names:* Mullett Shoal (Weslager 1954), Mullett Shoals (Goldstein 2000, map, location 3104).

Mullet Shoal, shoal, 1 mi. long, Dare County,

Kinnakeet Township (Garrity-Blake 2010, 492). In Pamlico Sound 5.5 mi. nw of Rodanthe. *See* Mullet Cove.

Mullet Shore. *See* Wades Shore.

Murkel Branch, tidal stream, Dare County, Nags Head Township (Currituck DB 6, 1789, 80). On e Roanoke Island "at Broad Creek" as described in 1789 deed. Probably just e of where Broad Creek begins, 2 mi. se of Manteo (center). Description in deed could be anywhere along e side Broad Creek, but today lack of defined creeks in marsh along wide, flooded section Broad Creek also applied in 1789. Likely near beginning of Broad Creek and probable tributary of Sand Beach Creek. Reference probably not to Sand Beach Creek because name was referenced in other early deeds (as Sandy Beach Creek) and use of generic term "branch" normally indicates a tributary of larger creek such as Sand Beach Creek. "Murkel" is one of many spelling variations based on local pronunciation of myrtle, referencing small shrub-like wax myrtles (*Myrica* spp.) native to the Outer Banks and se U.S. Merkle is usual form. *See* Alder Branch.

Musketo Inlet, former water passage, Currituck County, Poplar Branch Township (historical maps). Connected Currituck Sound through Currituck Banks to Atlantic Ocean at a point just n of Corolla between Ocean Hill subdivision and ramp for NC 12 onto beach. Open before 1585 until 1680s. "Musketo" can be a variation in spelling of "mosquito," but this name is actually a reference to *moskity*, reportedly Algonquian for grassland. Frankenburg (1995, location 152, 3) indicates between Currituck Inlet and New Currituck Inlet, vaguely citing Fisher 1962, but incorrect location. Shown on numerous early maps n of and in Corolla area, but former location is accurately labeled (Fisher 1962 and Mallinson et al. 2008 agree) on USGS (2013: Corolla) map. *Other names:* Bay of Musketo (historical), Miesquetaugh Inlet (Fisher 1962, 100), Moskito Inlet (Mouzon 1775), Motoskite Inlet (unknown, Accurate Map 1779), Musqueto Inlet (Morden 1688), Musquito Inlet (occasional misinterpreting references), New Inlet (misapplied on some historical maps).

Muskrat Bend, small cove, Currituck County, Fruitville Township (Cox 1923). Gradually curving at n side of North Marsh, 1 mi. n

of Swan Island, 3 mi. se of Knotts Island (village). Muskrats (*Ondatra zibethicus*) are medium-sized semiaquatic rodents native to marsh and wetlands of North America.

Muskrat Pond, marsh pond, Currituck County, Fruitville Township (local use). In Middle Marsh just e of Muskrat Bend 2.5 mi. se of Knotts Island (village). Those interviewed confirm Muskrat Pond while a couple of folk indicate they have "seen Webster Pond on a map." *See* Muskrat Bend. *Other names:* Webster Pond (local informants).

Myrtle Bay, small cove, 0.3 mi. across, Currituck County, Poplar Branch Township (USGS 2013: Mossey Islands). In unnamed marsh just n of Little Goat Island Bay, 8.3 mi. s of Corolla. "Myrtle" refers to small shrub-like wax myrtles (*Myrica* spp.) native to the Outer Banks and se U.S. Usually, especially Rodanthe s-ward, "myrtle" is pronounced "merkle." *See* Merkle Hammock.

Myrtle Hammock, hummock, Currituck County, Poplar Branch Township (local use). Higher marsh of Pine Island just e of Baums Creek, 5.5 mi. nnw of Duck. *See* Myrtle Bay.

Myrtle Island, island, 0.5 mi. across, Carteret County, White Oak Township (USGS 2013: Swansboro). Just barely separated from mainland just w of Langston Bridge 2.7 mi. se of Swansboro (mainland). *See* Myrtle Bay.

Myrtle Pond, man-enhanced lake, Currituck County, Poplar Branch Township (local use). In Pine Island subdivision, 8 mi. n of Duck. *See* Myrtle Bay.

Myrtle Pond Island, small island, Currituck County, Poplar Branch Township (some local use). In Myrtle Pond (man-enhanced), Pine Island subdivision, 8 mi. n of Duck. Several interviewed did not believe named, but two indicated "we just call it Myrtle Pond Island."

Nags Head, town, Dare County, Nags Head Township (signage). Is 4.4 mi. ene of Manteo. Name appears as early as Wimble's 1738 map, not as a village but as a sand dune (Jockeys Ridge [q.v.]). An easy leap to associate Jockeys Ridge with early naming of

Nags Head, but would be purely coincidental as Jockeys Ridge is named for an original landowner. According to Dunbar (1958, 57) reference was to a "headland" as a landmark when negotiating former Roanoke Inlet labeled by Wimble 1738. Jockeys Ridge then was a high bluff overlooking n shore of Roanoke Inlet and given name Nags Head, transfer name (probably) from many such occurrences in England. Used liberally in England as "nag" derives from an Old English term of similar form meaning simply small horse, evolved over years into applications related to horses, especially an old or worthless horse. Same word meaning to annoy is from a different source (Norse word entering the language much later and not relevant here). Naming here was by Wimble because Jockeys Ridge resembled a horse's head or was reminiscent of one of the many such named places in England; Wimble was born in Sussex, s England, where he lived until his early 20s.

Number of legends, stories, and yarns concerning Nags Head name origin. Reported by sailors when the beach was viewed from a ship it resembled a horse's head or neck. Looking s from atop Currituck Beach Lighthouse, a slight e protuberance here, but nothing pronounced.

One story indicates certain unscrupulous "Bankers" would hang a lantern around a horse's neck and walk the horse along the beach, thereby giving impression of lights of a ship. This illusion would then sometimes lure ships dangerously close to shoals and beach, where they would wreck or run aground, and the ship could then be plundered. No historical evidence to support this story, and hanging a smoking lantern around a horse's neck is not a task easily accomplished.

There is the story of a tavern existing here, very early, named Nag's Head, and while the name was used for taverns in England, absolutely no documented proof such a tavern ever existed here. Other stories declare a racetrack here (also so-called Jockeys Ridge name origin, but not so), but no racetrack known to exist here. Another recount describes a horse discovered with his head lodged among gnarled branches of a tree (an invented-origin folk etymology). Commercial enterprises mid-20th century

depicted this image on advertisements for tourism. Also suggested named because horses grazed there—again, not name origin.

"Head" is a generic for piece of land protruding into sea, but protuberance here slight, not pronounced. Another fabricated explanation is an Englishman who had moved to Albemarle of North Carolina purchased a sizable tract of land here 1832 and named it for a place in England named Nags Head because it reminded him of that place. However, a made-up story as name was already present on maps 1738 onward. Nags Head commonly used in England as a place name, and is the name of one of the highest points on Sainte Agnes Island in Scilly Islands off coast of Devon, one of the last features seen when leaving England by ship. So, as Dunbar suggests, the name was applied (initially by Wimble) to this distinctive landmark (now Jockeys Ridge and clearly marked on Wimble 1738) when approaching former Roanoke Inlet; marked labeling Jockeys Ridge as Nags Head as late as 1829 (Graham 1843).

Post office est. 1884 (operated with spelling Naghead 1893–1909). Second post office est. 1909 named (for some reason) Griffin. Nags Head Post Office was discontinued 1915, Griffin was creating confusion so was quickly (same year) changed to Naghead (name of original post office) then to Nags Head 1916. Incorporated 1923, disincorporated 1949, reincorporated 1961.

Original Nags Head oceanside referenced as "Old Nags Head" (not to be confused with Sound Side, formerly referenced as Old Nags Head). Original oceanside part known locally as "Cottage Row," directly e of Jockeys Ridge, built beginning 19th century, continuing through 1940s and 1950s. Remains much as it was, with original architecture, today with building restrictions.

Made official by USBGN 1892. Local stories abound to explain why the apostrophe in the name disappeared, all untrue and are simply fabricated or folk etymology (attempting to explain when the real reason is unknown or forgotten). The genitive apostrophe was not used by direction of USBGN. Specifically, intent of genitive apostrophe is to show possession, does not normally apply in application of most place names, especially a generation after naming. Three subdivisions named for feature.

    Other names: Cottage Row (in part; Town of Nags Head 2000, 60—local use), Etacrewac (White 1585—indigenous), Griffin (U.S. Post Office Department), Naghead (NCDOT map, 1930s), Nag Head (misnomer), Nags head (*sic*) (Wimble 1738), Nagshead (Norfolk and Southern Railway 1881), Nagshed (NPS 2007, bibl., item 8—transcribing error), Old Nags Head (in part; local use), The Nags Head (Pinkerton et al. 1809).

Nags Head. *See* Jockeys Ridge.

Nags Head Beach, beach, Dare County, Nags Head Township (local use). Ocean shore at Nags Head, 4.3 mi. e of Manteo. Use of Sea Beach mostly late 19th century, where the only "tourist" facilities were located. Jacock Beach used sparingly for undefined beach historically opposite Jockeys Ridge in late 18th and early 19th centuries; original landowner here was Jacock (*see* Jockeys Ridge). *See* Nags Head. Subdivision named for feature. *Other names:* Jacocks Beach (Harris 2017—further support for Jockeys Ridge [q.v.] name origin), Sea Beach (historical local use).

Nags Head Cove, former cove, Dare County, Nags Head Township (historical local use). Was soundside at Nags Head in Old Nags Head Cove subdivision 2.5 mi. nnw of Whalebone Junction. Shown but not named on USGS 1943: Roanoke Island, 1:125,000 scale. Landing for vacationers at Nags Head (*see* Sound Side). Today, cove no longer recognizable, developed into canals for Old Nags Head Cove subdivision. *See* Canals at Old Nags Head Cove and Nags Head. *Other names:* Old Cove (local form), Old Nags Head Cove (reference used less and less, prompted by subdivision name).

Nags Head Inlet. *See* Roanoke Inlet.

Nags Head Island, marsh island, 0.3 mi. long, 0.1 mi. wide, Dare County, Nags Head Township (USGS 2013: Roanoke Island NE). In Roanoke Sound 1.1 mi. n of The Causeway, 1.1 mi. nw of Whalebone Junction. *See* Nags Head. *Other names:* Duck Island (one local resident—no other known occurrences).

Nags Head–Manteo Causeway, The, man-enhanced hummock, 1.3 mi. long, Dare County, Nags Head Township (local use). Carries US 64 and US 264, beginning (or ending) at Whalebone Junction. From just w of Whalebone Junction to Washington Baum Bridge, crossing Roanoke Sound to Roanoke Island. Utilizes now man-enhanced islands, Cedar Island and Pond Island. *Other names:* Manteo Causeway (some local use), Manteo-Nags Head Causeway (point of view), The Causeway (local use).

Nags Head Pond, lake, Dare County, Nags Head Township (local use). In Nags Head 1.5 mi. se of Jockeys Ridge 10 mi. se of original Kitty Hawk. *See* Nags Head. Subdivision named for feature.

Nags Head Ponds, ponds, Dare County, Atlantic (mostly) and Nags Head Townships (Burney, 1987, 156). About 30–50 interdunal ponds in Nags Head Woods (mostly n part) between Run Hill and Jockeys Ridge. All except Reflection Pond and Catfish Pond are unnamed but this and other papers use this term as referent.

Nags Head Woods, woods, 15 ft. high, 0.9 mi. wide, 2.5 mi. long, Dare County, Nags Head and Atlantic Townships (USGS 2013: Manteo). On s Currituck Banks, trends nw-se from Run Hill to just s of Hotel Hill 2.5 mi. nw of central Nags Head. About 30–50 interdunal small ponds n part, only Reflection Pond and Catfish Pond seem to be named. *See* Nags Head and Nags Head Ponds. Subdivision named for feature. *Other names:* The Woods (Town of Nags Head 2000, 15).

Nannies Creek, small cove, Dare County, Nags Head Township (local informants). At sw end Roanoke Island 1 mi. n of Cedar Bush Bay, 2 mi. w of Wanchese.

Narrows Cove, cove, Currituck County, Poplar Branch Township (C&GS 1852). Just s of Little Narrows just w of Narrows Island, 7 mi. sw of Corolla.

Narrows Island, large marsh island, 1 mi. across, Currituck County, Poplar Branch Township (USGS 2013: Mossey Islands). In Currituck Sound separating Big Narrows from Little Narrows 7 mi. sw of Corolla. Used since 1801 (early deeds). A hunt club was here. *Other names:* Johnsons Island (C&GS 1852).

Narrows Island Pond. *See* House Pond.

Narrows Shore, shoreline, Currituck County, Poplar Branch Township (Currituck DB 1839, 22, 296). Reference to ne shore Narrows Island (q.v.—sometimes including nw shore and e shore indicating Duck perspective) 3.5 mi. s of Morgan Islands, 10 mi. nw of Duck (center). Mostly colonial usage, occasional use today.

Nausegoc, former Indian camp, Dare County, Kinnakeet Township. Was applied on a number of early maps at Pea Island and n Hatteras Island. Might be a misinterpretation of White's 1585 vague reference since he labels name in middle of Pamlico Sound; could have referred to sound, mainland, or something else. Meaning unclear, but could have indicated temporary place used by Indians for camping while on fishing and foraging trips. The "s" is also the long "ʃ" (*see* Bellows Bay variant Bellisses Bay).

Neals Creek, water passage, 2.5 mi. long, Currituck County, Poplar Branch Township (USGS 2013: Mossey Islands). N portion from Currituck Sound in n-s arc through unnamed marsh islands back to Currituck Sound between Narrows Island and Dowdy Bay 8.3 mi. sw of Corolla. Used throughout 19th and early 20th centuries, as some form of Mary Sanders, but changed mid-20th century to Neals. Made official by USBGN 1982 instead of Nells Creek (also used). *Other names:* Dowdeys Creek (Currituck DB 8, 1800, 248–49—vague reference), Dowdys Creek (Currituck DB 8, 1800, 248–49—vague reference), Grandies Island Creek (Currituck DB 8, 180, 248–49—vague reference), Mary Sander Creek (C&GS 1913a), Mary Sanders Creek (C&GS 1860), Mory Sanders Creek (C&GS 1852), Nells Creek (NOS 2014e), Nelson Creek (N.C. Marine Fisheries 2013, map 9).

Ned Baum Ridge, small sand ridge, Dare County, Atlantic Township (Harris 2017). Just w of original Kitty Hawk 1 mi. n of Poor Ridge Landing. *See* Baum Bay.

Needlerush Bay. *See* Hog Hill Creek.

Negro Bay. *See* Currituck Bay.

Negro Creek, former cove, 0.05 mi. wide, Carteret County, Atlantic Township (USGS 1951: Styron Bay, as variant). Was in Core Sound 2.3 mi. sse of Atlantic (mainland). Name associated with New Drum Inlet and came into local use when feature changed from soundside cove to occasional sound-to-ocean water passage; New Drum Inlet made official by USBGN 2006 at request of N.C. Name Authority to change names containing the word "Negro." *See* Drum Inlet. *Other names:* Negro Creek Bay (GNIS), Nigger Creek

(USGS 1951: Styron Bay), Nigger Creek Bay (USBGN staff).

Negro Creek, water passage, Currituck County, Poplar Branch Township (local use). Trends n-s through e side Narrows Island 2 mi. w of South Burris Island, 7.5 mi. sw of Corolla. In nonpejorative form as early as 1801 (Currituck DB 3, 1801, 1). *Other names:* Niger Creek (recording error, also found in Currituck DB 3, 1802, 228), Nigger Creek (C&GS 1852).

Negro Creek Island. *See* Sheep Island (Currituck County, Poplar Branch Township).

Negro Hammock, hummock, Hyde County, Ocracoke Township (early 20th century). On Ocracoke Island, 0.8 mi. e of Ocracoke (village). *See* Black Hammock and Negro Hammocks.

Negro Hammocks, former islands, Hyde County, Ocracoke Township (Price 1795). Two islands formerly in Pamlico Sound just ne of s Ocracoke Island 1 mi. ne of Ocracoke (village). After one island disappeared, other became known as Negro Hammock. *See* Black Hammock. *Other names:* Negro Island (C&GS 1918).

Negro Island, former island, Hyde County, Ocracoke Township (Weslager 1954). Was in Pamlico Sound 1 mi. w of Ocracoke (village). Higher shoal on Middle Ground, occasionally bares at low water. Loosely associated with Negro Hammocks before disappearing. *Other names:* Nigger Island (occasional early map usage).

Nelsons Swamp, small swamp, Dare County, Hatteras Township (Brooks 2010). Just beyond ne terminus of Great Ridge just w of e terminus Flowers Ridge 1.3 mi. sw of Buxton.

Neunsiook, historical. Indian word generally applied to s Core Banks just n of Cape Lookout (Keulen 1690).

New Causeway Canal, canal, 0.25 mi. long, Carteret County, Morehead Township (Carteret County GIS 2019). Trends n-s and ne most canal in Atlantic Beach Isles subdivision (w part of Canals at Atlantic Beach q.v.), 0.8 mi. s of Morehead City (mainland). Named after enhancement of Atlantic Beach Causeway (1987).

New Currituck Inlet, former water passage, Currituck County, Fruitville Township (early 19th-century maps). Connected Currituck Sound to Atlantic Ocean through Currituck

Banks at e end South Channel (q.v.), 5.8 mi. n of Corolla, 6 mi. s of North Carolina–Virginia boundary. Began opening early 1700s and opened by 1713; closed 1828, ending any thoughts of economic development using Currituck Sound as shipping lane. Reopening was considered, but no work done.

Remnants still present and during storms and periods of high water can contain water for short periods. Remnants 2 mi. long and named Old Currituck Inlet on USGS 1982: Corolla). These maps are supposed to reflect local preference and usage; application of Old Currituck Inlet to feature originally known as New Currituck Inlet indicates an evolution of usage from adjective "new" to adjective "old" because inlet has been closed for more than 150 years. When original Currituck Inlet at North Carolina–Virginia boundary closed and this inlet opened, New Inlet was applied. Later, New Currituck Inlet was applied while former Currituck Inlet retained its original name. New inlets are often created during storms but quickly close again. So, use of "New Inlet" was a naming practice on the Outer Banks until 21st century (now name of hurricane creating the inlet is used). New inlets acquire appropriate names if indication is they will remain open. Original Currituck Inlet at North Carolina–Virginia boundary had closed, and this new inlet remained opened; Currituck was applied to newly opened inlet because of its close proximity (6 mi. s) to original Currituck Inlet and adjective "new" was retained to indicate subsequent opening and to avoid confusion with original Currituck Inlet. While evidence exists New Currituck Inlet has at times been referenced as simply Currituck Inlet, the application of Old Currituck Inlet here is recent; USGS still used New Currituck Inlet in publications other than maps late as 2000, but subsequently changed to using Old Currituck Inlet. When used locally, used as if old is all lowercase, indicating merely a former location. Old Currituck Inlet usually is a secondary name for original Currituck Inlet at North Carolina–Virginia boundary.

For clarity and historical correctness, former inlet at North Carolina–Virginia boundary will be Currituck Inlet, and remnants of this inlet, 6 mi. s of North Carolina–Virginia boundary will be New Currituck Inlet.

Stick (1958) suggests an inlet named Crow Inlet a few miles s of New Currituck Inlet "at Crow Island." Frankenberg (1995, 3) lists Crow Inlet at about Corolla, which was actually Musketo Inlet location. However, Crow Island (*see* Swan Island, Fruitville Township) was, in mid-18th century, just inside New Currituck Inlet and still named at w end South Channel, remnants of New Currituck Inlet. So, Crow Inlet was listed as secondary name for New Currituck Inlet (Fisher [1962, 94] agrees), presumably never existing as a separate inlet. Fisher does not cite any historical maps showing an inlet named Crow. Mallinson et al. (2008, fig. 6, map, 6) also lists no evidence of an inlet here (other than long-closed Musketo Inlet). However, Crow Inlet does show on Price and Strother (1798) halfway between New Currituck Inlet (labeled Currituck Inlet) and Caffeys Inlet (labeled Carthys Inlet); this small-scale map places the inlet just n of Corolla near Ships Bay. Musketo Inlet (q.v.) was near here but closed 1680s; however, no inlet is known to have existed here since 1585, other than Musketo Inlet (already closed well before 1798). So, depiction of Crow Inlet on Price and Strother (1798) is bit of a mystery and must be a misinterpretation.

Other names: Caratauk Inlet (historical), Coretucks Inlet (Wimble 1733), Crow Inlet (Stick 1958), Currchuck Inlet (Wimble 1738—notorious for wild spelling), Currituc [*sic*] Inlet (N.C. Fisheries 1923, 65), Currituck Inlet (deed use middle to late 1700s—original Currituck Inlet closed 1731, only inlet open n of Caffeys Inlet), Currituck Inlett (18th-century deeds, Currituck DB 14, 1818, 298), Curritucks Inlet (historical), New Corratuck Inlet (18th century), New Inlet (Baldwin 1755; Byrd 1728; Currituck DB 4, 1782, 61), North Currituck Inlet (some local use—peculiar but confirmed by interviews; is inexplicable as it was s of two inlets named Currituck—perhaps referring to n-most inlet open or remembered), Old Currituck Inlet (USGS maps), Passe de Curratuk (Bellin 1757), S. Nouveau Passage (Sanson 1696), South Inlet (Burr 1834—used for short time based on direction from Currituck Inlet near North Carolina–Virginia boundary).

New Drum Inlet, water passage, Carteret County, Atlantic Township (USGS 2013:

Styron Bay—still labeled). Occasional sound-to-ocean passage just northeast of Ophelia Inlet, near former Negro Creek before topographic changes (Hurricane Ophelia, 2005) created present structure. Was forcibly opened 1971 by ACE when Drum Inlet 3 mi. ne closed, so Core Sound fisherman could have ocean access. However, inlet quickly shoaled up and was not used. Open periodically and occasionally had water. Reopened by Hurricane Irene 2011 but generally merged with expanding Ophelia Inlet just s. *See* Drum Inlet and Negro Creek (Carteret County). Made official by USBGN 2006 to clarify Drum Inlet(s) situation. *Other names:* Negro Creek (USGS files), Nigger Creek (USGS 1951: Styron Bay).

New Field Pond, man-made lake, Dare County, Kinnakeet Township (F&WS 2015). In Pea Island Wildlife Refuge 4.5 mi. sse of Oregon Inlet. Constructed well after North Pond and South Pond, both constructed by CCC to enhance and preserve stopover feeding areas for migrating birds along Atlantic Flyway. Indicates this middle lake was added after North Pond and South Pond created. *Other names:* New Field (spoken usage).

New Found Creek, tidal stream, Currituck County, Fruitville Township (F&WS 1999, map). Trends n-s 0.7 mi. nw of Pennys Hill (Luark Hill) 4 mi. nnw of Corolla.

New Inlet, water passage (former inlet reopened 2011), 1.3 mi. long, Dare County, Kinnakeet Township (USGS 2013: Pea Island). Connects Pamlico Sound to Atlantic Ocean and separates Pea Island from Hatteras Island 6 mi. n of Rodanthe. Opened and closed periodically (moving locations slightly) since 1650s. Bellin's maps of 1757 and 1764 show Neuve (New) Passe generally at Gunt Inlet, but that inlet had been open before 1585 (under several different names), so Bellin mislabeled the location since New Inlet location is not labeled. Closed 1922 with attempts at artificial opening 1925; reopened 1933 (storm) and closed 1945. During this opening was five distinct channels (spanned by two wooden bridges—remnants still visible), each channel being depicted on a few maps 1930s, but all collectively known as New Inlet. By 1935 only one distinct channel remained. NCDOT (1933–35) indicates ferry here but no supporting documentation.

The inlet last opened (not exactly in same place—slightly farther s hence NCDOT's use of Pea Island Inlet) in August 2011 from Hurricane Irene. Has been moving slightly s but attempts have been made to stabilize movement. Attempt to reopen and maintain the inlet 1922–25 by N.C. Fisheries Commission to stimulate Outer Banks fishing industry failed. Many Outer Banks inlets have been referenced at one time or another as "New Inlet" by an established practice referring to any newly opened inlet as New Inlet for a period of time, until the inlet indicates it will remain open or until a newer inlet opens. Practice apparently has changed 21st century, influenced by external forces. Now, inlets seem named for the (named) storms creating them, beginning with Hurricane Isabel 2003.

Apparently, this inlet opened and closed so frequently the name New Inlet was always applicable and still so as of 2019. Secondary name Pea Island Inlet was applied (mostly by NCDOT) when New Inlet reopened 2011 defining s boundary of Pea Island separating it from Hatteras Island (though the Hatteras Island sign is inexplicably now at n end Pea Island), used sporadically, but New Inlet is still preferred. Began to close in May 2013, but still (2019) is distinct and clearly an inlet, though mostly dry and now filled with sand except under adverse conditions. Still, NCDOT decided to bridge the inlet because it opens and closes so frequently; now spanned by Richard Etheridge Bridge (begun 2011, completed 2018). When Hurricane Irene reopened New Inlet 2011 a temporary iron bridge was put into place while permanent bridge was constructed. The bridge is low and designed to be short-term solution as will be bypassed by now Rodanthe Bridge (Jug Handle Bridge), a bridge over sound bypassing the breach-prone S-Curves (q.v.). This bridge appropriately honors Richard Etheridge, who was crew captain from the early 1880s to early 1890s at nearby Pea Island Life Saving Station, with the only all-African-American life saving station crew.

Other names: Chickinacommack Inlet (spelling and application confusion with Chickinacommock Inlet), Chickinacommock Inlet (Stick 1958, 9—confusion with Chickinacommock Inlet), Chick Inlet (Stick 1958, 9), Chickinockcominok Inlet (confusion with Chickinacommock Inlet), Chickinocom-inock Inlet (confusion with Chickinacommock Inlet), Dugg Inlet (Fisher 1962, 95—Fisher unsure if this name applied to Chickinacommock Inlet or New Inlet), Dug Inlet (*see* Dugs), Gunt Inlet (confused application), Irene Inlet (NCDOT 2013, map, B-91—informal report reference, breach created by Hurricane Irene), Irenes Inlet (surfing websites), Neue Einfahrt (Lucas 1826—*einfahrt*, inlet in German), New Inlet at Pea Island (limited local use since 2011), Nouvelle Entré (Nolin 1783), Passe Neuve (Bellin 1757), Pea Island Breach (Montoya 2018, 57, fig. 4.1—New Inlet complex), Pea Island Inlet (NCDOT 2013, 1–3, fig. 1—limited use since opening 2011).

New Inlet Shoal, former shoal, Dare County, Kinnakeet Township (Price and Strother 1798). Was at ne entrance New Inlet in late 18th century 6.5 mi. n of Rodanthe. Though location recorded by Price and Strother (1798), existence and locations vary with whether New Inlet is or is not open and its particular location when open. *Other names:* New Inlet Shoals (shipwreck reports).

New Inlet South Point, former point, Dare County, Kinnakeet Township (CS 1854). Was s side New Inlet 7 mi. n of Rodanthe. Both points of inlets often acquired names needed as referents for charting; names were often directional and/or descriptive. Name was used mostly through mid-19th century.

New Ocracoke Ditch, former channel, Carteret County, Portsmouth Township (Williamson 1992, 117). Was in w Ocracoke Inlet 2 mi. e of former Portsmouth Life Saving Station in Portsmouth (village). New beginning of 20th century, but no mention made today.

Newtons Point, point, Carteret County, Portsmouth Township (USGS 1950: Portsmouth). On nw Portsmouth Island, just w of Portsmouth (village) 6.8 mi. sw of Ocracoke (village).

New Water Hold, tidal area, 0.1 mi. across, Currituck County, Fruitville Township (Cox 1923). Just e of Wishes Hammock Creek, 2.4 mi. ene of Knotts Island (village). Use of "hold" is rare on the Outer Banks, refers to restricted water formation, almost pond-like ("pond" used on n Outer Banks—*see* Adams Pond).

Nigh Inlet, former inlet (possibly), Hyde County, Ocracoke Township (local discussion and Cheeseman, 1982, 195). Was somewhere just s or se of Ocracoke (village). Illusive inlet might or might not have existed, as few references exist. Little or no evidence of relict inlets exists where the inlet is thought to have been located, but a location where Croatoan Island ended near Little Swash Opening is a distinct possibility. Possible reference was to Ocracoke Inlet since it has migrated over several centuries, and after all, "nigh" means near or close, so it could have been a reference to some sort of branch or companion inlet in relationship to Ocracoke Inlet, or could have been a reference to a small ephemeral inlet close to Ocracoke Inlet (which was open continuously since 1585). Some older folk in Ocracoke (village) recall stories of an inlet just n of present airstrip, just before The Plains (present location), also a possibility. A likely location for this inlet might have been Little Swash Opening, which is about 5 mi. ne of where Ocracoke Inlet would have been in the late 1500s, which coincides with the sw terminus of Croatoan. A few references to Nye, a surname, but more likely a phonetic rendering of Nigh. *Other names:* Note: the few maps of the period are small scale and portray little information but indicate an inlet se of present Ocracoke (village) different from Ocracoke Inlet and apply the Grenville names to this inlet. Grenvills Rode (this was a reference to Sir Richard Greenvil or Greenevill, who commanded second Roanoke voyage establishing first military colony Roanoke Island lasting about a year before returning to England with Drake—application did not last; "rode," version of "road," meant where ships ride at anchor for protection or commercial activity; term preserved today at Hampton Roads, Virginia), Nye Inlet (less used), Old Nigh Inlet, Old Nye Inlet (Garrity-Blake 2010, map 356), Port Greneuile (Cheeseman 1982, 195—"u" and "v" used interchangeably in 1500s, split into two letters early after 1600), Port Grenvil (Hill 1983, 26), Port Grinuil (Cheeseman 1982, 195), Port Grinvil (Quinn 1977 map).

Nine Foot Shoal, former shoal, Hyde County, Ocracoke Township (C&GS 1918). Was in Pamlico Sound at Nine Foot Shoal Channel, 3 mi. nw of Ocracoke (village). Mostly covered by water, occasionally bare. *Other names:*

Eight Foot Shoal (ACE 1893), Nine Feet Shoal (Walton 1867; *see* Ten Feet Channel), Nine Foot Shoals (White 2012, 133).

Nine Foot Shoal Channel, channel, Hyde County, Ocracoke Township (NOS 2014i). In Pamlico Sound trending nw-se just w of Big Foot Slough Channel 1.8 mi. nw of Ocracoke (village). *See* Nine Foot Shoal. *Other names:* Nine Foot Slough (clipped version), South Channel (Blunt 1857, 344).

No Ache, marsh, 1.2 mi. long, 0.5 mi. wide, Dare County, Kinnakeet Township (USGS 1983: Rodanthe). Juts w protruding into Pamlico Sound from Hatteras Island between Clarks Bay and No Ache Bay 1.5 mi. s of Salvo. Legend indicates name origin is whimsical response to a place name on mainland. A family near Stumpy Point across Pamlico Sound on mainland named Payne or Paine or Pain (surname common there) referred to a small bay at mouth of Long Shoal River by family name: Paynes Bay. Over years, spelling changed to Pains Bay. Some "Bankers" near Salvo decided to name a feature No Ache, revealing typical Outer Banks humor. Today this explanation is only known by some (older) folk; one explanation for the name includes lack of generic in the name (*see* Bay Tree).

The actual reason or name origin is less dramatic. Early maps and charts (into mid-19th century) label this marsh as "No Eggs," a descriptive reference that, through pronunciation and transcribing errors, became No Ache labeled on later maps. No Eggs was important as descriptive place name because egg gathering from wild birds' nests was an important activity supplementing diet of early Bankers. Covey (2018, 78) does not subscribe to lack of eggs here as name origin. He indicates, without additional information, "ache" refers to grazing cattle, hence the flooded and floating vegetation of this complex rendering the area unsuitable for grazing. No evidence supporting the grazing presumption, but a long-forgotten meaning of "ache" is reference to umbelliferous plants (hollow stemmed, found in salt marsh), might indirectly have some relevance to grazing theory. Covey also suggests a possible relation to surname Noake reportedly present in colonial se Virginia. He also alludes to lack of a possible wake from passing vessels because of tangled vegetation, but no evidence (presented) to support either origin, nor does he indicate the explanation preferred. So, no eggs or not good for grazing: one may take one's pick—I go with no eggs. Name also applied to nearby bay, island, shoal, and slough. Often when name origins are lost, forgotten, or unclear, definitions emerge through a process known as folk etymology whereby explanations are "developed" to explain a particular name. Also, *No Egg* is the benchmark (specific surveyed point) labeled on USGS: 1943 Roanoke Island 1:125,000 scale). CS 1852 also refers to this feature as No Egg Point.

Other names: Noache Island (from NPS Director Conrad Wirth, letter in *Coastland Times*, October 27, 1952, in NPS 2005b: NPS 1, 587), No Ache Marsh (local use), No Ache Point (local use), No Egg Point (CS 1852).

No Ache Bay, cove, 0.4 mi. long, 0.3 mi. wide, Dare County, Kinnakeet Township (USGS 2013: Rodanthe). In Pamlico Sound bordered by marsh with No Ache Island at entrance 1.9 mi. s of Salvo. *See* No Ache. *Other names:* No Ache Creek (Garrity-Blake 2010, 493).

No Ache Island, island, 0.3 mi. long, 0.2 mi. wide, Dare County, Kinnakeet Township (USGS 2013: Rodanthe). In Pamlico Sound at entrance No Ache Bay 2.2 mi. s of Salvo. *See* No Ache. *Other names:* Cedar Hammock Island (misapplied just n), Noache (colonial deeds), Noache Island (plat to Pugh, 1897, from Covey 2018, 14), No Ache Isle (Garrity-Blake 2010, 493—use of "isle" rather than "island" local in Chicamacomico—Rodanthe, Waves, Salvo).

No Ache Shoal, shoal, 1 mi. long, Dare County, Kinnakeet Township (diminishing local use). Into Pamlico Sound from marsh just s of No Ache Bay 2.5 mi. s of Salvo. *See* No Ache. *Other names:* No Ache Shoals (Covey 2018, 78).

No Ache Slough, canalized tidal stream, 1.4 mi. long, Dare County, Kinnakeet Township (diminishing local use). In marsh named No Ache just s of Clarks Bay 1 mi. s of Salvo. *See* No Ache.

Nob Island, narrow island, 0.3 mi. long, 0.1 mi. wide, Dare County, Atlantic Township (local use). One of the islands in se Kitty Hawk Bay Islands complex in Dog Point Creek between Baum Point Island (Angel Island) and Meter

Point on Colington Island 3.7 mi. s of original Kitty Hawk.

No Egg Point. *See* No Ache.

No Name Ridge, small altered sand ridge, 0.5 mi. long, Dare County, Hatteras Township (signage). N-s offshoot-ridge from Crooked Ridge in Buxton 3 mi. n of Cape Point. Used sometimes locally in whimsical manner because street name is same.

Normans Inlet. *See* Cedar Inlet and Sand Island Inlet.

North'ard, The, area, Dare County, Kinnakeet Township (Garrity-Blake 2010, 169). Local name used to distinguish extreme n Avon (near former Scarboro), 1 mi. n of original Avon (Kinnakeet), 7.5 mi. n of Buxton. Directional term contracting "northward" used in conjunction with The South'ard (q.v.). The North'ard was at newer Avon just s of historical Scarboro (settlement). Often Scarboro and The North'ard considered together or adjacent. *Other names:* Spain (Garrity-Blake 2010, map, 169—reason lost), The Northard (occasional modern interpretation).

North'ard Reef, shoal, Dare County, Kinnakeet Township (Garrity-Blake 2010, 493). In Pamlico Sound 1 mi. nnw of Gull Island (Dare County) 3 mi. w of Gull Island Bay, 4 mi. sw of Salvo. Is 3 mi. n of South'ard Reef, each a directional name. *See* The North'ard. "Reef" in Outer Banks geographic names usually refers to oyster colonies.

North Bar, shoal, Dare County, Hatteras Township (CS 1853). N side primary channel Hatteras Inlet 4 mi. wsw of Hatteras (village). *See* North Breakers.

North Bar, former shoal, Hyde County, Ocracoke Township (Price et al. 1808). Was 2.7 mi. s of Ocracoke (village) at then n entrance Ocracoke Inlet. *Other names:* North Breaker Head (Coles and Price 1806).

North Beach, small beach, Dare County, Hatteras Township (Goldstein 2000, location 2889). Just n of Cape Hatteras Lighthouse Beach, 1 mi. n of Cape Point, 3.7 mi. s of Buxton. Used more by fishermen; sometimes application extends to Cape Point overlapping e portion application of Cape Hatteras Lighthouse Beach.

North Beach, exposed beach, Dare County, Nags Head Township (Goldstein 2000, loc. 2869). On n shore oceanside of Oregon Inlet just n of South Beach, 1.5 mi. n of Oregon Inlet, 9.5 mi. s of Whalebone Junction. Relatively new name associated with s-ward migration of Oregon Inlet used mostly by local folk, fishermen, and off-road enthusiasts.

North Beaches, beaches, 11.5 mi. long, Currituck County, Poplar Branch and Fruitville Townships (local use). Application from ramp at n end of Ocean Hill subdivision n to North Carolina–Virginia boundary, including subdivisions and communities of Pennys Hill, Seagull, Swan Beach, North Swan Beach, Carova (Beach), and a few other smaller named subdivisions. Used mostly locally to indicate communities and beaches beyond NC 12 ramp (end hard-surface road) onto beach 1 mi. n of Corolla; entire length requires 4-wheel-drive vehicles.

North Bitterswash Creek, cove, 0.05 mi. wide, Hyde County, Ocracoke Township (USGS 1950: Green Island). In Pamlico Sound, 0.4 mi. ne of South Bitterswash Creek, 11.2 mi. ne of Ocracoke (village). Today collective name Bitterswash Creeks used more than individual names North Bitterswash Creek and South Bitterswash Creek.

North Breakers, breakers, Carteret County, White Oak Township (Williamson 1992, 197). Near Bogue Inlet Bar 4.5 mi. sw of Langston Bridge, 5.5 mi. s of Swansboro (mainland).

North Breakers, breakers, Dare County, Hatteras Township (CS 1850b). At n approach to Hatteras Inlet, 2.8 mi. sw of Hatteras (village).

North Breakers, former breakers, Hyde County, Ocracoke Township (Moseley 1733). Was at North Bar on n side Ocracoke Inlet (18th century before deposition filled it) 2.7 mi. s of Ocracoke (village). *Other names:* North Breaker (Price 1795, 627), North Breaker Head (Coles and Price 1806—shallows causing breakers).

North Burris Island, island, 0.8 mi. long, 0.3 mi. wide, Currituck County, Poplar Branch Township (USGS 2013: Mossey Islands). In Currituck Sound at Big Narrows separated from South Burris Island by Burris Bay, 7.1 mi. s of Corolla. Now joined on w with East Burris Island. *See* Burris Islands. *Other names:* Burrouses Island (Currituck DB 5, 1787, 298–99—at Loan [Lone] Oak Channel), Cedar Island (occasional early use, also used for South Burris Island), North Burows Marsh (C&GS 1852), North Pine Island (Currituck DB 7, 1782, 132).

North Bush Island, island, Currituck County, Fruitville Township (Cox 1923). Directly n of Bush Island at extreme se end Knotts Island Bay, 2.7 mi. se of Knotts Island (village). Occasionally with Mary Island and Bush Island referenced as Northern Islands in relation to Middle Marsh (now unknown). *Other names:* North Island (shortened generic use).

North Carolina, **State of**, civil division. One of original thirteen states and twelfth to ratify the U.S. Constitution after agreeing to give up claims to its w lands. Bounded on e by Atlantic Ocean (and the Outer Banks), s by South Carolina and Georgia, w by Tennessee, and n by Virginia. Contains 57,712 sq. mi., 3,645 are water.

North Carolina Sound, lagoons, Currituck, Dare, Hyde, Carteret Counties. Historical term referencing sound or lagoon system of coastal North Carolina, now composed of Currituck Sound, Albemarle Sound, Croatan Sound, Roanoke Sound, Pamlico Sound, Core Sound, Back Sound, and Bogue Sound. Used collectively for all major lagoons in coastal system, and primarily used only as a written reference in scientific studies. Sometimes referenced as Virginia Sounds before Carolina formed (1663).

North Channel, channel, Currituck County, Fruitville Township (Cox 1923). Just n of South Channel and Crow Island, 4 mi. se of Knotts Island (village). One of two large remnant channels (other is South Channel) of New Currituck Inlet, closed 1828.

North Core Banks, barrier beach, 17 mi. long, Carteret County, Portsmouth and Atlantic Townships (local use). Part of Core Banks, ne end at Ocracoke Inlet just ne of Portsmouth (village) sw-ward to Drum Inlet (now closed). Usage varies, with most original residents still using North Core Banks and South Core Banks. Ophelia Banks and Middle Core Banks are recent terms also applied to n South Core Banks (q.v.) since Ophelia Inlet opened from Hurricane Ophelia 2005. However, Portsmouth Island, itself islands and dunes, depending on weather and tides, from Ocracoke Inlet to Swash Inlet has generally been referenced separately, though technically included with North Core Banks. The name North Core Banks has evolved 21st century from a more descriptive term to place name usage on maps. NPS applies

name on its brochures from Ocracoke Inlet (ne) to Ophelia Inlet (USBGN). *See* Core Banks.

On September 6, 2019, Hurricane Dorian passed very close to the s Outer Banks, making brief landfall at Cape Hatteras. There was particularly heavy storm surge oceanside and soundside impacting Ocracoke (village) and Core Banks from Drum Inlet (Old Drum Inlet—sw) to former High Hills Inlet (ne) at the sw end of Portsmouth Island. Media reported (unsubstantiated) more than 50 new "inlets." However, there were only about 20 surge remnants, with a few significantly (but probably temporarily) breaching the island completely (NOS imagery, September 7, 2019). The most significant breach was at Long Point, where NPS operates rental cabins. None were known to have acquired names. NPS indicated natural processes will mostly restore or fill in the breaches, though change will be apparent. This narrow part of the Outer Banks is prone to such activity and reshaping. *Other names:* Drum Island (some occasional local use).

North Core Beach, beach, 15 mi. long, Carteret County, Portsmouth and Atlantic Townships (local use). Corresponds generally to North Core Banks from near Swash Inlet to New Drum Inlet. Used usually when North Core Banks is used but never extended onto Portsmouth Island as North Core Banks occasionally was applied historically because Portsmouth Beach was well-established name. *See* Core Banks and North Core Banks.

North Cove, cove, Currituck County, Poplar Branch Township (local use). In s Beasley Bay just e of s islands in Hog Islands complex (Long Hog Island and Calf Island), 7.5 mi. n of Duck.

North Cove, cove, 0.6 mi. wide, Dare County, Atlantic Township (diminishing local use). In ne Kitty Hawk Bay just s of original Kitty Hawk 8.2 mi. nw of Nags Head (center). Some usage recently for Harbour (Harbor) Bay since North Cove has fallen into disuse and there is a road and subdivision named Harbour Bay along n More Shore (q.v.) at se entrance to North Cove. *Other names:* Harbour (Harbor) Bay.

North Dike, embankment, Dare County, Kinnakeet Township (Garrity-Blake 2010, 492). Created man-enhanced tidal stream-canal just n of No Ache at e end Clarks Bay 0.7 mi. s of Salvo. "Dike" refers specifically to man-made or man-enhanced embankment for water-control functions. However, here on Hatteras Island generic term "dike" can also mean canal created or its embankment and even just the canal itself.

North Dock, former landing, Hyde County, Ocracoke Township (local informants). Was in Ocracoke (village) just n of The Ditch (Silver Lake entrance). Sometimes used by mailboat prior to dredging Silver Lake. Probably not official but descriptor relating to The Ditch. No trace remains.

North Drain, canalized stream, 2 mi. long, Dare County, Kinnakeet Township (USGS 2013: Rodanthe). Flows s to become a tidal cove in Pamlico Sound 0.2 mi. n of Aunt Phoebes Marsh 1.1 mi. s of Rodanthe. Originally Sand Drain, but became Paines Drain when Thomas Paine (*see* Thomas Paines Landing) received a land grant (1730s) where this drain defined s boundary. Later known as The Drain and now North Drain (Covey 2018, 13) as there is a South Drain. *Other names:* Paine Drain (Covey 2018, 52), Paines Drain (historical), Sand Drain (older use), The Drain (local use).

North Dune, sand dune, 0.5 mi. long, Dare County, Atlantic Township (local use). In n Southern Shores (town) 1.25 mi. s of Duck (center). Newer name (1980s) used by Southern Shores (town) developing area altering original dune formation.

Northeast Channel, former channel, Hyde County, Ocracoke Township (ACE 1893). Was n approach to Inshore Slew and Ocracoke Inlet, 4 mi. s of Ocracoke (village). Only remnants remain and no longer used.

Northeast Point Franks Reef, shoal point, Dare County, Kinnakeet Township (schooner *R. C. Beaman*, 1910 [White et al. 2017, 57]). N-most point of Franks Reef 2.5 mi. sw of Rodanthe. Directional names were necessary referents for functional actions—here for describing shoal-bound vessel location.

Northeast Pond, lake, 0.1 mi. across, Currituck County, Poplar Branch Township (USGS 1982: Mossey Islands). On ne Brant Island just nw of Mossey Islands complex, 3.3 mi. ssw of Corolla.

North End, area, Dare County, Kinnakeet Township (local use). Casual reference just s of Mill Creek at Gibbs Point 1 mi. n of original

Avon, reference to its location relative to Avon.

North End, sort of collection of communities, Dare County, Nags Head Township (restricted local use). General reference to scattered housing subdivisions along with Mother Vineyard and Sunnyside on n end Roanoke Island n and nw of Manteo. Used as collective reference mostly for research and scientific investigations. Not used much today. Subdivision named for feature.

Northern Beach, beach, 2 mi. long, Hyde County, Ocracoke Township (websites). Ne end Ocracoke Island 0.75 mi. s of Ocracoke Dock North (Ocracoke-Hatteras Ferry Landing), 12 mi. ene of Ocracoke (village).

Northern Beaches, beaches, Dare County, Nags Head and Atlantic Townships; and Currituck County, Poplar Branch and Fruitville Townships (local use). Originally general reference to all named beaches from Kitty Hawk or Duck to Carova, but reference in some cases (depending on point of view) has come to include s to Nags Head Beach. Often overlapping usage now (2015) from Nags Head to Duck, and usage now often includes Northern Currituck Beaches from Duck (at Dare–Currituck County boundary). Use in Dare County applies from Kill Devil Hills to just n of Duck. Use is application dependent, changes with need and function of topic. *Other names:* Northern Currituck Beaches (Duck to Carova, commercial use), Northern Dare Beaches (only Dare County–Nags Head to Duck–Currituck County boundary— commercial use).

Northern Gut, small tidal stream, 1 mi. long, Dare County, Atlantic Township (Town of Kitty Hawk 2007; Currituck DB 7, 1795, 246). Trends from Midgetts Pond to cove at High Ridge Point 1.3 mi. sw of original Kitty Hawk. Appears on Town of Kitty Hawk (2007) zoning map now an extended (s portion) application of Jeanguite Creek, occurring late 20th century. High Bridge Creek (High Ridge Creek) used for section n of Northern Gut, but Jeanguite Creek is recognized (in parentheses) from map usage. Based on forms of this name during 1700s, not known or able to determine original form of name before it morphed into "northern," probably for clarity. Evidence from early deeds indicates man named Nathan (with spelling variations) owned this property, but over time name presumably morphed into "northern." "Dreen," used in variant name, was a known dialectical variation of "drain" used for a short time (albeit sparingly) here 1700s. Names were spelled as sounded or as folk (many without organized education) thought the name ought to be spelled. *See* Alligator Gut.

Other names: Dreen of Northerns Gut (Currituck DB 5, 1787, 216), Great Northern Creek (Currituck DB 8, 1798, 53), High Ridge Creek (local use), Jeanguite Creek (USGS 2013: Kitty Hawk), Nathans Gut (Harris 2017; unknown, 1838), Nathens Gut (Harris 2017; unknown, 1783), Noathans Gut (Currituck DB 6, 1792, 292), Northan Gut (Harris 2017; unknown, 1809), Northans Gut (Harris 2017; unknown, 1836), Northen Gut (Harris 2017; unknown, 1819), Northens Gut (Currituck DB 4, 1783, 134–35), Northerns Gut (Currituck DB 8, 1798, 53), Northers Gut (Harris 2017; unknown, 1779 — "norther" (former) local pronunciation of "northern"), Northons Gut (Currituck DB 7, 1794, 133), Nothans Gut (Currituck DB 7, 1794, 133).

Northern Islands, islands, Currituck County, Fruitville Township (historical use). Just n of Middle Marsh 2.5 mi. se of Knotts Island (village). Composed of Mary Island, Bush Island, North Bush Island (q.v.). Historical, in relation to Middle Marsh; name no longer known.

Northern Pond, cove, Hyde County, Ocracoke Township (USGS 2013: Ocracoke). In Pamlico Sound at Gap Point 0.3 mi. n of Ocracoke (village). Subdivision named for feature. *Other names:* North Pond (local use, subdivision name).

Northern Woods, former woods, Dare County, Kinnakeet Township (historical documents). Was a maritime wooded area near Rodanthe, including much of Waves. Historically, a few woods were soundside between Cape Hatteras and Rodanthe; by the 20th century, these wooded areas had been mostly depleted for numerous uses. *See* Southern Woods.

North Graven Creek, small water passage, Currituck County, Fruitville Township (Cox 1923). At n end Graven Island, separates Graven Island (s) from Walk Island (n) 0.3 mi. n of South Graven Creek, 1.5 mi. e of Knotts Island (village).

North Hatteras Beach, reference, Dare County, Kinnakeet Township (brochures). S from New Inlet to Cape Point. Some local use, but mostly in scientific reports.

North Hatteras Island, reference, Dare County, Kinnakeet Township (brochures). Hatteras Island s from New Inlet to Cape Point. The term has had some local use but mostly appears in scientific reports.

North Hog Island, island, Currituck County, Poplar Branch Township (C&GS 1852). In Beasley Bay, n-most in Hog Islands (q.v.) complex, 6.2 mi. s of Corolla. Pig Island now joined to North Hog Island.

North Jones Island, marsh island, Currituck County, Poplar Branch Township (Codman, Crowninshield, and Lawrence 1925). Just n of South Jones Island at s end Raccoon Bay, 1.3 mi. w of Corolla. *Other names:* Northwest Jones Island (some historical local use), Jones Island (Currituck DB 9, 1805, 83–84).

North Landing River, stream, 23 mi. long, Currituck County, Fruitville Township; and City of Norfolk, Virginia. Begins in Norfolk, flows s becoming an estuary (drowned river valley) at halfway point (10 mi.) and continuing to Currituck Sound.

North Marsh, marsh, 1.5 mi. long, 1 mi. wide, Currituck County, Fruitville Township (F&WS 1984, 10). Mostly natural with minor enhancements on n Mackay Island between North Landing River and Back Creek and Mackay Island Road; separates marsh from East Pool and Middle Pool 2.5 mi. w of Knotts Island (village).

North Marsh, small marsh, Currituck County, Fruitville Township (Cox 1923). Just nw of Middle Marsh, 1 mi. n of Swan Island, 3 mi. se of Knotts Island (village).

North Piney Island, island, Currituck County, Poplar Branch Township (C&GS 1852). Just s of Sedge Island 1 mi. w of Three Dunes, 5 mi. ssw of Corolla. Was part of Pine Island 1800s; changed over years, now joined in n with Sedge Island. *Other names:* North Poiney Island (Currituck DB 17, 1827, 44), Piney Island (Currituck DB 14, 1818, 496).

North Point, small point, Dare County, Atlantic Township (local use). In n Duck (village), just s of historical Trinety Harbor (inlet), 1.3 mi. s of Sanderling.

North Point, small man-enhanced point, Dare County, Hatteras Township (local use). On n shore of small peninsula separating Austin Creek (Hatteras-Ocracoke Ferry docks) and marina near Hatteras Fire Department in se Hatteras (village), 2.8 mi. nw of Hatteras Inlet.

North Point, former point, Dare County, Hatteras Township (historical use). Was at n shore Clam Shoal, 5.2 mi. nne of Hatteras (village). Prominent 19th century but often covered at high tide, today completely inundated.

North Point, former point, Dare County, Kinnakeet Township (CS 1854). Was n point Pea Island (q.v.) on s shore Oregon Inlet 13 mi. nnw of Rodanthe. Prevalent middle to late 19th century, descriptive of n point Pea Island, last joined with Hatteras Island 1945, island again when New Inlet reopened 2011. Name fell into disuse when South Point came into use for same point, indicating a change in perception in naming process, focusing on inlet (Oregon Inlet) reference rather than land reference.

North Point, point, Dare County, Nags Head Township (CS 1862a). On nw end Roanoke Island adjacent to site presumed to be Lost Colony (second attempt at colonization in North America by English, 1587), 5 mi. wnw of Manteo (center). While site of original fort (first colony) reportedly found, the settlement (uncharacteristically outside the fort) not located and likely inundated off n shore, eroded more than 0.3 mi. since 1585. A point was mentioned by White when searching for Lost Colonists 1590 in his reference, "We returned by the water side, round about the Northpoint of the Iland, until we came to a place where I left our colony in the yeere 1586 [sic]" (reference should be 1587). Could be this feature named North Point but more likely Etheridges Point. *Other names:* Doughs Point (land owner late 19th century), Northpoint of the Iland (possible reference White 1585).

North Point, point, Dare County, Nags Head Township (USGS 2013: Oregon Inlet). S-most point of (now) Bodie Island at Oregon Inlet 6.5 mi. se of Wanchese. Named North Point because on n side of Oregon Inlet (more nw point from inlet migration). Shifted considerably over years, especially since 1953 from shoaling on n side Oregon Inlet. Application indicates change in perception for applying names, based on inlet rather than land. *See* North Point New Inlet, North Point (Dare County, Kinnakeet Township),

and South Point. Made official by USBGN 1975.

Northpoint, man-enhanced point, Hyde County, Ocracoke Township (local use). In Ocracoke (village) at Northern Pond just w of Gap Point. Road sign uses one-word form. *Other names:* North Point.

North Point Cape Hatteras Inlet, former point, Hyde County, Ocracoke Township (Lawson 1709, 64). Was somewhere soundside 3 mi. beyond historical Old Hatteras Inlet toward Cape Hatteras.

North Point Great Island, point, Dare County, Kinnakeet Township (local use). N extremity of elongated Great Island 1.5 mi. n of Buxton.

North Point New Inlet, former point, Dare County, Kinnakeet Township (vendue records). Was n point former New Inlet (reopened 2011) at s terminus Pea Island 7.2 miles n of Rodanthe. Both points of inlets often acquired names needed as referents for a particular reason, and were often directional and/or descriptive. Reference needed for wrecked vessel 1794; variant name was for charting. Used mostly through mid-19th century. *Other names:* New Inlet North Point (CS 1854).

North Point Roanoke Inlet, former point, Dare County, Nags Head Township (Currituck DB 9, 1805, 193–94). Interestingly, deed's date is 1805. Shoaling began 1795 and closed completely 1811; shoaling process was about half complete 1805 but was still a reference point. *Other names:* North Point Roan Oak Inlet (Currituck DB 9, 1805, 193–94).

North Point South Jones Island, marsh point, Currituck County, Poplar Branch Township (Codman, Crowninshield, and Lawrence 1925). N point of South Jones Island nw tip, 1 mi. wsw of Corolla.

North Pond, lake, Currituck County, Poplar Branch Township (local use). At n Dews Island, 5.8 mi. nw of Duck. *Other names:* Flag Pond (Currituck DB 5, 1784, 73).

North Pond, man-made lake, Dare County, Kinnakeet Township (F&WS 2015). In Pea Island Wildlife Refuge 8.5 mi. nnw of Rodanthe. With South Pond, constructed by CCC to enhance and preserve stopover feeding for migrating birds along Atlantic Flyway. *Other names:* North Pool (occasional references).

North Rainbow Creek, water passage, 1 mi. long, Currituck County, Fruitville Township

(Cox 1923). Trends e-w separating Rainbow Island (s) from Big Bird Island (n), 3.5 mi. se of Knotts Island (village). Directional likely because n of Rainbow Island. Remnants of New Currituck Inlet. *Other names:* Rainbow Creek (local use).

North Ridge, small sand ridge, Dare County, Nags Head Township (local use). N-most tip Jockeys Ridge, noticeably distinct by dense vegetation separating it from main Jockeys Ridge; in n Nags Head 6.5 mi. s of original Kitty Hawk. Subdivision named for feature.

North River, stream, 10.5 mi. long, Carteret County, Harkers Island, Straits, and Beaufort Townships. Flows 2 mi. until becomes an estuary for remainder of length. Begins in marsh on mainland and flows then trends s to Back Sound 3.7 mi. e of Beaufort (mainland). *Other names:* North Rever (Wimble 1733).

North River Channel, channel, 1.5 mi. long, Carteret County, Beaufort Township (USGS 2013: Harkers Island). Separates Middle Marshes from Carrot Island 2.8 mi. se of Beaufort (mainland).

North River Marsh, marsh 1.4 mi. wide, 1.2 mi. long, Carteret County, Beaufort Township (USGS 1997: Harkers Island). In North River separated from Sheephead Marsh by North River Thorofare 3.6 mi. e of Beaufort (mainland). *Other names:* North River Marshes (N.C. Marine Fisheries 2019, E6, map 29).

North River Thorofare, water passage, 1.4 mi. long, Carteret County, Beaufort Township (USGS 2013: Harkers Island). Connects North River and North River Channel separating Sheephead Marsh and North River Marsh 3.8 mi. e of Beaufort (mainland).

North Rock, rocks, 0.3 mi. long, Carteret County, Portsmouth Township (USGS 1950: Portsmouth). In Pamlico Sound at w end Ocracoke Inlet, 2.5 mi. n of Portsmouth (village), 5.1 mi. wsw of Ocracoke (village). Late 18th century middle section submerged and w end was Western Rocks or Great Shell Rock, e end was Eastern Rocks or Little Shell Rock. Middle section periodically becomes submerged, but today this middle section usually above water. Directional name refers to position relative to Portsmouth (village). Historically, numerous named rocks here. Oyster Rocks (q.v.) was a historical broader application including North Rock complex. *Other names:* Big Rock (some historical use),

Eastern Rocks (Hooker 1850), Great Shell Rock (Price 1795, 628), Jaybird Island (White 2012, 165—vague reference to rocks for camping, Portsmouth area, but only rocks where camping while tending to fish nets at this rock complex), Little Shell Rock (Price 1795, 628), North Rocks (local use), Oister Rocks (Stick 1958, 79), Shell Island (CS 1856), The Rocks (local use), Western Rocks (Hooker 1850).

North Shoar, former point, Hyde County, Ocracoke Township (Lawson 1709, 64). Was at historical Old Hatteras Inlet 5.7 mi. sw of Hatteras Inlet, 9.5 mi. sw of Hatteras (village). Name used as navigational aid to follow North Shoar (*sic*) approaching Old Hatteras Inlet because was best and safest channel, so marked on maps and charts. "Shoar" is older spelling of "shore."

North Swan Beach, beach, Currituck County, Fruitville Township (Currituck County Tax Records). At community of North Swan Beach 2.5 mi. s of Carova. *See* North Swan Beach (community).

North Swan Beach, community, Currituck County, Fruitville Township (local maps). On n Currituck Banks just n of Swan Beach, 2.5 mi. s of Carova. Originally subdivision, at site of older place named Wash Woods, changed to Deals when post office est. 1907. Original name Wash Woods referred to numerous stumps from previous maritime forest here inundated historically. This name is recent origin.

North Swash, former large swash, Carteret County, Portsmouth Township (Price 1795). Was in Core Sound n of massive Sheep Island Shoal sw of shoals w and s of Shell Castle.

Northwest Island, island, Currituck County, Poplar Branch Township (C&GS 1852). Just s of Woodhouses Island in w Mossey Islands (q.v.) complex 5.7 mi. ssw of Corolla.

Northwest Places, fishing areas, Carteret County (local use). About 5–10 mi. offshore in Onslow Bay (Atlantic Ocean) near beginning of approach channel to Beaufort Inlet. There are numerous fishing areas inside and outside this area many with cryptic alphanumeric references.

Northwest Point, point, Currituck County, Poplar Branch Township (Codman, Crowninshield, and Lawrence 1925). Nw point of marsh island (formerly connected to Currituck Banks) 0.8 mi. nw of Corolla. *Other*

names: N. W. Point (Codman, Crowninshield, and Lawrence 1925).

Northwest Point, point, Dare County, Kinnakeet Township (Garrity-Blake 2010, 168). Nw point Big Island 1.2 mi. n of original Avon. Only three points on Big Island named with ordinal (interdirectional as opposed to cardinal or prime directional) directions; "northeast point" not used.

Northwest Point, point, Dare County, Nags Head Township (USGS 2013: Manteo). Nw point Roanoke Island 3.6 mi. nw of Manteo (center). John Man (or Mann) was principal resident here early 18th century, hence variant names. Back Bay Point used early 1700s since Croatan Sound originally named Back Bay because historically blocked at s end by Roanoke Marshes. *Other names:* Back Bay Point (Maule 1718), J. Manns Point (ACE 1843), John Mann Point (Fulton 1820), John Manns Point (Brazier 1820), North West Point (Click 2001, map, 26), NW Point (USGS 1943: Roanoke Island 1:125,000 scale), West End (NPS 2010, map 33), West Point of Roanoke Island (rare reference).

Northwest Point, former point, Hyde County, Ocracoke Township (Blunt 1857, 343). Was tip of Ocracoke Island at Hatteras Inlet, 5 mi. sw of Hatteras (village). Inlet topography has changed considerably since the point was used for sighting in mid-1800s; no longer exists. *Other names:* North West Point (Blunt, 1857, 343), Northwest Point Reef (Blunt 1857, 343).

Northwest Point Loggerhead Shoals, former shoal point, Dare County, Kinnakeet Township (shad boat *Anna Laura*, 1896 [White et al. 2017, 118]). Was nw-most point at Loggerhead Shoals 3 mi. n of Rodanthe. Directional names were necessary referents used for functional actions—here for describing shoal-bound vessel location. *See* Loggerhead Shoals.

Northwest Point Shoal, shoal, Carteret County, Cedar Island Township (Williamson 1992, 123–24). Extreme nw point Royal Shoal at Northwest Straddle (also named Northwest Point), 5.5 mi. w of Ocracoke (village). Associative with Northwest Point of larger better-known shoal, Northwest Straddle. *Other names:* North West Point (White 2012, 262), Northwest Point (some use), North West Point Royal Shoal (19th-century maps),

Northwest Point Royal Shoal (historical use), NW Point Shoal (Williamson 1992, 123–24).

Northwest Pond, pond, 0.5 mi. long, 0.1 mi. wide, Currituck County, Fruitville Township (USGS 2013: Knotts Island). Within marshy central n portion Walk Island, 1.8 mi. ne of Knotts Island (village). *Other names:* NW Pond (abbreviated map-use version).

Northwest Pond, cove, 0.1 mi. across, Currituck County, Poplar Branch Township (USGS 2013: Mossey Islands). Just e of Brant Island just sw of Northeast Pond. In Brant Island Pond 3.3 mi. s of Corolla.

Northwest Spit, peninsula, Currituck County, Poplar Branch Township (Codman, Crowninshield, and Lawrence 1925). Trends se-nw on a marsh island (formerly connected to Currituck Banks) between Raccoon Bay and Parkers Bay 1 mi. nw of Corolla. Spits form by sand moving along shore by oblique wave action, known as longshore or littoral (meaning shore) drift. Feature created is usually curved. *Other names:* Northwest Point Little Raccoon Island (Currituck DB 24, 1842, 104), N. W. Spit (Codman, Crowninshield, and Lawrence 1925).

Northwest Straddle, submerged point, Carteret County, Cedar Island Township (Hooker 1850). At nw point Royal Shoal in Pamlico Sound, 9 mi. wnw of Ocracoke (village). "Straddle," generic used to indicate extreme points of measurement and space between these points. Indicates nw extremity of w part Royal Shoal; used more extensively historically. *Other names:* North Swash Straddle (Price 1795, 631), Northwest Point (Williamson 1992, 124), Northwest Point Royal Shoal (NPS 2012, 17), North West Royal Shoal (Walton 1867), NW Straddle (unknown, 1807).

Nubbins Ridge, small sand ridge, Hyde County, Ocracoke Township (local use). Higher ground in Ocracoke (village) just ne of Silver Lake 0.2 mi. e of Ocracoke–Cedar Island–Swan Quarter Ferry docks. Named by residents Carrie, Elnora, and Delphin Williams for an area where they had connections in Richmond, Virginia (Howard, July 22, 2018). Also, neighborhood or area name (*see* Ocracoke Village areas).

Oak Hammock, hummock, 1 mi. long, 5 ft. high, Carteret County, Harkers Island Township (USGS 2013: Harkers Island). On nw Harkers Island just w of Westmouth Bay 1.3 mi. nw of Harkers Island (village). *See* Black Hammock.

Oak Hill, small hill, Carteret County, Morehead Township (local use). In Indian Beach (town, w section) just nw of Salter Path, 3.5 mi. ene of original Emerald Isle.

Oak Island, elongated island, 0.2 mi. long, less than 0.1 mi. wide, Dare County, Atlantic Township (local use). In Currituck Sound, 4.6 mi. nw of Duck.

Oak Island Shoal, small shoal, Dare County, Atlantic Township (local use). In Currituck Sound 1 mi. sse of Oak Island, 2.2 mi. nw of Duck. Currituck Sound is shallow almost everywhere, but here rarely covered by more than 1–3 ft. of water.

Oak Knoll, small rounded hill, Dare County, Nags Head Township (local use). Stabilized by natural vegetation; isolated outlier between e edge of central Round-About Hills and sand dunes oceanside, 1 mi. n of Jockeys Ridge, 4 mi. s of Kill Devil Hills (town).

Oakland Hills, small sand dunes, Carteret County, White Oak Township (local use). In w Emerald Isle 1 mi. s of Oak Point, 4.3 mi. from original Emerald Isle. In several housing subdivisions, with center in Oakland Hills subdivision, named for sand dunes.

Oak Point, point, Carteret County, White Oak Township (local use). Just w of Archer Point, 1 mi. n of Oakland Hills, 5.8 mi. e of Swansboro (mainland).

Oak Point, point, Currituck County, Fruitville Township (local use). On e side Fresh Pond Bay, 2.4 mi. e of Knotts Island (village).

Oak Pond, lake, 0.3 mi. long, 0.1 mi. wide, Currituck County, Fruitville Township (USGS 2013: Corolla). In marsh just w of Currituck Banks, 0.4 mi. s of remnants New Currituck Inlet, 5 mi. nnw of Corolla.

Oak Run, small stream, Dare County, Atlantic Township (local use). Flows into extreme ne Kitty Hawk Bay just s of original Kitty Hawk,

2 mi. nnw of Kill Devil Hills (town). *See* The Run. Subdivision named for feature.

Ocean Acres Beach. *See* Kill Devil Beach.

Ocean Hill. *See* Jones Hill.

Ocean Lake, man-made lake, Currituck County, Poplar Branch Township (signage). In n Ocean Sands subdivision, 5 mi. s of Corolla. Named for subdivision here.

Ocean Ridge, sand dune, 1 mi. long, Carteret County, Morehead Township (local use). Oceanside, protective berm here at w edge of Atlantic Beach (town), 3 mi. e of Pine Knoll Shores. Originally descriptive but morphed into geographic name after development 1980s and naming road Ocean Ridge Drive. Subdivision named for feature.

Ocracock (sic) Woods, former woods, Hyde County, Ocracoke Township (Cole and Price 1806). S from Springers Point to just n of former Ocracoke Point (South Point), now built to more than 1 mi. to sw over past 100 years. Was 1.3 mi. s of Ocracoke (village). Only remnants remain at and around Springers Point known now as Springers Point Oaks. Presented in original since only form known.

Ocracoke, village, Hyde County, Ocracoke Township (signage). On sw end Ocracoke Island 18 mi. sw of Hatteras (village). *See* Ocracoke Island for name origin.

In 1715 North Carolina Assembly passed "An Act for Settling and Maintaining Pillotts [*sic*] at Roanoke and Ocaacock Inletts [*sic*]," leading to Pilot Town as early name of Ocracoke since most pilotmen who steered ships over shoals through Ocracoke Inlet to Portsmouth (historical village) just s of Ocracoke lived at this new village on Ocracoke Island. However, not so much settling here until after 1718, when Blackbeard the pirate was killed off Springers Point (*see* Ocracoke Island). Port Bath was a secondary name for a while because most ships stopping at Ocracoke were bound for Bath on the mainland. Post office est. 1840; mail delivery was usually daily by boat from Atlantic (mainland). Name of post office was Ocracoke. Curiously, Post Office Department did not consider Ocracoke too difficult to spell.

There were three major parts of Ocracoke (village) defining historic parts within the village. Each generated a mild form of competition first half 20th century (and a bit beyond) as there were three major focal points of dwellings: w side of Silver Lake (Cockle Creek [q.v.]), Pointers (Springers Point reference); around s, n, and e sides Silver Lake, Creekers; and ne part of village near Pamlico Sound, Trenters (*see* Up Trent). Refer to each entry individually. Also, there were other neighborhoods of reference in the village, but not quite as large. Others were Cat Ridge, Windmill Point, Paddys Holler (Hollow), and Nubbins Ridge (refer to Ocracoke Village areas and to the entry for each as a natural feature). Also, entire remaining Ocracoke Island e of village referenced as "Down Below," sometimes "down the banks," as there was no other settlement permanent or temporary anywhere else on the island (except for Cedar Hammock [q.v.], a temporary settlement for a while at opposite end of the island near the Coast Guard Station [O'Neal et al. 1976, 48; and local informants for verification]).

Other names: Cockle Creek (Stick 1958, 300), Oacock (Torres 1985, 51), Oakerecok (historical), Ocacock (Lawson 1709, map), Occacock (Angley 1984, 35), Occraook (colonial records), O'cock (Garrity-Blake 2010, 371—mostly spoken, occasionally written as shorthand), Ocracock (Lewis and Shallus 1807), Ocracock Town (J. Colton 1861), Ocracoke Village (commercial websites), Okcrecock (historical), Okerecock (colonial documents), Okok (historical), Okracoke (historical), Oracoke (Cram 1889), Pilot Town (Price et al. 1808—probably near Springers Point se of Silver Lake), Port Bath (colonial references), Port Town (Garrity-Blake 2010, 457), West End (casual local use indicating island section), Woccock (historical), Wococan (historical), Wococon (Cumming 1998, 118), Wocokon (historical).

Ocracoke Bar, shoal, Carteret County, Portsmouth Township; Hyde County, Ocracoke Township (Williamson 1992, 122). Entrance, Ocracoke Inlet, includes Ocracoke Swash, 4 mi. sw of Ocracoke (village). *See* Ocracoke. *Other names:* Oacock Bar (Stick 1958, 43), Oakerecock Barr (Wimble 1733), Ocacoc Bar (Angley 1984, 11), Ocacock Bar (Angley 1984, 13), Occacock Bar (Price 1795, 626), Occracock Bar (Hooker 1850), Ocracock Bar (Coles and Price 1806), Ocracoke Inlet Bar (shipwreck reports), Ocricock Bar (Torres 1985,

43), Outer Reef (White 2012, 140), The Bar (Angley 1984), The Swash (Angley 1984, 34).

Ocracoke Beach, beach, Hyde County, Ocracoke Township (brochures and websites). Applications at different times to all or parts oceanside beach Ocracoke Island. Increasingly prevalent early 21st century and especially since Ocracoke (Lifeguard Beach) was judged best beach U.S. in 2007. Today often applied only to Lifeguard Beach because NPS provides lifeguard service here during summer. *See* Ocracoke.

Ocracoke Dock North, landing, Hyde County, Ocracoke Township (signage). State ferry landing for Hatteras-Ocracoke Ferry, ne end Ocracoke Island, just n of Styron Hills at Hatteras Inlet, 13 mi. ene of Ocracoke (village). Ocracoke Dock South sometimes wrongly used because s side of Hatteras Inlet.

Ocracoke Dock South, landing, Hyde County, Ocracoke Township (signage). State ferry landing in Ocracoke (village) for Ocracoke-Cedar Island and Ocracoke-Swan Quarter Ferries 4.5 mi. nne of Ocracoke Inlet. *Other names:* Old Navy Docks (former local use for several docks removed 1955–1957 by NPS).

Ocracoke Inlet, water passage, 2 mi. long, Hyde County, Ocracoke Township; and Carteret County, Portsmouth Township (USGS 1950: Portsmouth). Connects Pamlico Sound to Atlantic Ocean separates Ocracoke Island from Portsmouth Island 3.6 mi. sw of Ocracoke (village). One of three Outer Banks inlets continuously open since before 1585; Beaufort Inlet and Bogue Inlet other two continuously open inlets. Ocracoke Inlet served as major commercial artery serving former port of Portsmouth 18th and early 19th centuries, later responsible for economic support of Ocracoke (village). *See* Ocracoke Island for name origin.

Ocracoke Inlet and surroundings mentioned as Wococon by Grenville's second Roanoke voyage (1585). Here one of their ships, the *Tygre*, ran aground, destroying most food stores for the first colony (not the Lost Colony). Reported loss was miscalculation by pilot, Simon Fernándes, for whom the inlet near s end Roanoke Island was named Port Ferdinando (then later Gunt Inlet [q.v.]). Grenville explored parts of mainland before leaving Wococon (Ocracoke) more than two weeks later to land Lane and his men for the first colony on Roanoke

Island. Variant Port of Saynt Maris (Saint Marys) indicates spelling inconsistencies of 16th century and probably refers to Ocracoke Inlet. A hand annotation is on an early map written just se of Ocracoke Island labeled Wococon and probably refers to Ocracoke Inlet, open in 1585. Some authors believe the name might refer to a smaller inlet just s named Wokokon Inlet (q.v.) at the s terminus of Wokokon in the High Hills area, but evidence is sketchy at best. The annotation has been interpreted as "the port of saynt maris wher we arivid first," and this second voyage is known to have landed at Wococon (Ocracoke Island) before proceeding to Roanoke Island. This is the only known use of this name for Ocracoke Inlet.

Ocracoke Inlet has been highly complex in many respects, especially toponymically (application and use of names). Specifically, Ocracoke Inlet has been one of three inlets open continuously since English discovery and settlement of North America; with its changeable nature, many names have been applied to numerous features in and around the inlet, historical, changed, and extant.

Portsmouth was highly utilized port, and Ocracoke (village) historically provided services. Further, during 18th and early 19th centuries a bustling business at Shell Castle (q.v.; island in Ocracoke Inlet) created much activity through the inlet providing commercial services and especially lightering service (transfer of cargo to smaller boats with less draught to navigate shallow sounds and rivers [estuaries] to inland ports). Additionally, nature of this and all inlets is one of constant change and geographic adjustment. So, names and applications were constantly changing as features (especially shoals) altered shape, disappearing and appearing, some gradually, and some instantly resulting from storms. Therefore, names (and entries here) might appear in many cases to occupy the same site, or different names might appear to be applied in same area, all possible from changeable nature of this inlet and its commercial activity through the years, decades, and centuries. This activity is often reflected in the naming process and is explained in entries and with their interrelationships. *See* Ocracoke, Nigh, and Wokokon Inlets.

Other names: Beacon Island Roads (historical local use when commercial venture on Beacon Island—18th and early 19th centuries), Entrata di Occacoke (Tardieu, ca. 1800), Entré de Ocacok (Nolin 1783), Entrée d'Occacoke (Frédéric 1807), Inlett at Wococock (Angley 1984, 29, from T. Woodward), Inlett at Wococon (historical), Oakerecock Inlet (Wimble 1733), Oakerocock Inlet (Wimble 1733), Ocacock Inlet (Moseley 1737), Ocacock Inlett (N.C. General Assembly 1716), Ocacok Channel (historical), Ocacok Inlet (historical), Ocakok Inlet (Purcell 1788), Occacock Inlet (Collet et al. 1770), Occacock Inlett (historical), Occacoe Inlet (O'Neal et al. 1976, 5), Occacoke Inlet (Russell 1799), Occeh Inlet (O'Neal et al. 1976, 5—1716 letter, Virginia Governor Spotswood), Occek Inlet (O'Neal et al. 1976, 5), Occocock Inlet (shipwreck records), Occracock Inlet (historical), Occracoke Inlet (Russell and Lodge 1778), Ococan Entry (Sainsbury 1860; Lane 1585, second letter, August 12, 1585, mentions ship named *Tyger* ran aground here—Grenville second Roanoke voyage), Ococock Inlet (Currituck DB 1, n.d., 295—seller from Ocracoke), Ococoke Inlet (Pinkerton et al. 1809), Ococon (historical), Ocracocke Inlet (historical), Ocracock Einfahrt (Lucas 1826—*einfahrt*, inlet in German), Ocracock Inlet (Burgess and Smith 1841), Ocracoke Harbor (limited general reference), Ocracook Inlet (colonial use), Ocrecock Inlet (Denison et al. 1796), Okeracock Inlet (U.S. Congress 1876), Okerecock Inlet (Wimble 1733), Okerecok Inlet (Wimble 1738), Okok Inlet (Speed 1676), Okracoke Inlet (shipwreck reports), Onoaconan (Cobb 1905—indicates shown on White's map, but not shown), Onoconon Inlet (Cobb 1905, 5—misreading White's 1585 map interpreting an island as an "O" and "W" in Wokokon as "n"), Oracoke Inlet (Cram 1889), Passe d'Ocacock (Bellin 1757), Port of Ocracock (Angley 1984, 23—18th-century reference to commercial activity here), Port of Ocracoke (reference to commercial activity used 18th century), Port Saynt Maris (hand annotation early map—only known use from Lane to Walsingham), Portsmouth Inlet (NPS 2006, 125—Life-Saving Station diagram, labeled at extreme se entrance, a mistake), Rio del Principe (often used by Spanish and Portuguese as labels while exploring, means

Prince River or Prince Passage), Roanok Inlet (presumably an application error by careless mapping; Fisher et al. 1689, chart 11—also applied at Roanoke Inlet area), Roanok Inlett (application error, careless mapping), South Point Inlet (localized notes, etc.), Wococon Inlet (Cheeseman 1982, 195), Wakokon Inlet (historical), Wekekon Inlet (N.C. Fisheries 1923, 61), Woccock Inlet (Stick 1958, 9), Woccocock Inlet (O'Neal et al. 1976, 4), Woccocon Inlet (O'Neal et al. 1976, 4), Woccon Inlet (O'Neal et al. 1976, 4), Wococock Inlett (historical), Wococon Inlet (Quinn 1975), Wococon Inlett (historical), Wokokon Inlet (Haklyut 1589), Wokoken Inlet (N.C. Fisheries 1923, page 62), Wokokon Inlet (Stick 1958, 9), Wosoton Inlet (Fisher et al. 1689, chart 15), Woston Inlet (Fisher 1962, 103).

Ocracoke Inlet Channel, channel, Hyde County, Ocracoke Township; and Carteret County, Portsmouth Township (NOS 2014h). In Ocracoke Inlet through which small craft pass 4 mi. sw of Ocracoke (village). Constantly changing and shifting, though generally maintaining similar course for past century. *See* Ocracoke. *Other names:* Main Channel (local use), Ocacock Channel (Torres 1985, 52), Ocracoke Bar Channel (local use), Ocracoke Channel (Howard 2016, 38), Ocracoke Swash Channel (in part, more historical—House of Representatives 1895), Southeast Channel (ACE 1893).

Ocracoke Island, barrier island, 17 mi. long, Hyde County, Ocracoke Township (USGS 2013: Green Island, Howard Reef, Ocracoke; Portsmouth: 1950). Sw from Hatteras Island at Hatteras Inlet to Ocracoke Inlet at Portsmouth Island. Original owner John Lovick by grant 1719. Later owner Richard Sanderson sold island to William Howard 1759 (first to live on island).

One legend attributes the name to Blackbeard the pirate, who made Ocracoke and Bath (mainland) semipermanent homes. He was killed here at Springers Point by Lieutenant Robert Maynard of Virginia, dispatched by Governor Spotswood of Virginia to subdue Blackbeard and his pirates because of their threat to commerce and shipping. Blackbeard was reportedly in league with Governor Eden of North Carolina, and Virginians were frustrated with lack of any action. Legend indicates Blackbeard, eager to do battle, waiting for

sunrise repeatedly cursed "O cry cock," hence name Ocracoke. Of course, this is merely a fanciful story, and variations of the name were used long before Blackbeard arrived here or was even born.

Name origin could be Anglicized corruption of Algonquian word *Waxihikami*, *Wakauan*, or other varieties, reportedly meaning enclosed place, fort, or stockade, or maybe curve or bend, supported by many including Weslager (1954), and would indicate distinct shape at sw end of the island. Some suggest name variation of Indians originally frequenting the island, perhaps. Ocracoke evolved through pronunciation and misspelling of Wococon or Wokokon, indigenous name for the island and Portsmouth Island, common terms used on early maps of the island and over years evolved into Ocracoke. Wokokon might be from a subgroup of Hatteras or Hatrask Indians reported by several authors, including Brickell (1743). As with most indigenous names from this period, meaning is lost or difficult to prove.

It cannot be confirmed Amadas and Barlowe stopped at Ocracoke Island on their voyage of reconnoiter in 1584 (first Roanoke voyage), as Amadas's logs are not clear on the matter. Grenville's logs (second Roanoke voyage) clearly indicate stopping and spending about two weeks at Ocracoke (Wococon)—*see* Ocracoke Inlet. However, reports from a member of Amadas and Barlowe's party (1584) named Richard Butler, in his deposition to the Spanish 12 years after the voyage, claimed "We disembarked in central Florida at a place called Ococa, so named by the nature of the country. Twenty Leagues further on, toward the north part we disembarked again in another place known to the English as Puerto Fernando and to the savages as Ataurras." This leads Quinn (1971) to suggest Ococa refers to Ocracoke and Puerto Fernando to Hatarask (with Ataurras likely being a phonetic rendition of Hattrask or Hatteras). Unclear why the generic Puerto was used because Fernandes was Portuguese and would have used Porto, but perhaps it was in deference to Fernandes's training in Spain or because Butler was giving his deposition to the Spanish. The English never used Puerto, only Port. Butler's reference to central Florida is plausible as the English then applied the name Florida to anything Spanish in coastal North America. However, since Butler's deposition was not given until 12 years later, his recollection might be confused and based on publications subsequent to 1590. *See* Gunt Inlet for more information.

Before 1770, Ocracoke Island was independent and not in any county but was then annexed by Carteret County. In 1823, s of New Inlet (Hatteras Island) to Green Island on what is now nw Ocracoke Island was transferred to Hyde County from Currituck County. In 1845, most of what is now Ocracoke Island (from Green Island near Old Hatteras Inlet [q.v.] to Ocracoke Inlet) was moved into Hyde County by agreement. Today all of what is now Ocracoke Island is in Hyde County by adjustment when Dare County was formed 1870.

Variant Pearl of the Outer Banks for Ocracoke Island is of recent origin, late 20th and early 21st centuries. Name is marketing technique and popularized by a book about Ocracoke. Today the promotion continues with signage.

Other names: Gordens Ile (Smith 1624, map—Smith's names did not last), Island of Ocacock (Angley 1984, 13), Island of Ocreecock (Angley 1984, 6), Isle Ocacock (Bellin 1757), Isle of Ocracoke (promotion gimmick by Stanley Wahab 1950s), Isle of Ocreecock (Sanderson 1733—owned all Ocracoke Island albeit slightly smaller since Hatteras Inlet not opened, measured from Old Hatteras Inlet [q.v.]), Oacock (historical), Oa Cock Bar (historical), Oakacock (Ocracoke Island History 2016), Oacrecock Island (Currituck DB 2, 1771, 347—seller from Ocracoke), Oakerccock (Wimble 1733), Oakerecock Bancks (Wimble 1733), Oakerecok (Wimble 1738), Oakocock (historical), Oarcock Island (Currituck DB 2, 1771, 350—seller from Ocracoke), Oatcok (Moll et al. 1731), Ocacoc (Weslager 1954, 46), Ocacock (Lawson 1709, map), Ocacock Island (Baldwin 1755), Ocacoe (historical), Ocacok (Huber 1711; Crisp 1711), Ocarock Island (Moseley 1733), Occacock (Price et al. 1808), Occacock Bar (N.C. provincial records), Occacock Island (Collet et al. 1770), Occacoe (O'Neal et al. 1976, 5), Occacode Island (historical), Occacoke Island (Pinkerton et al. 1809), Occacok Island (*South Carolina and American General Gazette* 1775), Occeh (O'Neal

et al. 1976, 5, Spotswood letter 1715), Occek (O'Neal et al. 1976, 5), Occocock (shipwreck records; Weslager 1954, 46), Occracoke Island (Russell and Lodge 1778), Ococa (Butler 1584, cited by Runyon et al. 2005), Ocock (Schroeter 1859), Ococock Island (Angley 1984, 13), Ocraacocke (variation), Ocracoak (Currituck DB 12, 1812, 17–18—seller from Ocracoke), Ocracock (Stick 1958, 49), Ocracock Bar (N.C. provincial records), Ocracocke (Pub. L. 1844-45, Corbitt 1950, 58), Ocracok (Ocracoke Island History 2016), Ocracoke Bar (Stick 1958, 30), Ocrcok (Ocracoke Island History 2016), Ocrecock (Currituck DB 7, 1794, 174—purchaser from Ocracoke Island), Ocrecok Island (historical), Ocreecock (NPS 2005b: NPS 2, 9), Ocrucoke (Rand McNally 1888), Okerccock (Wimble 1738), Oecceh, Okercock (Ocracoke Island History 2016), Okerecock Island (Wimble 1733), Okok (Speed 1676), Okrakoke (occasional brochures, reason unknown), Ononanpke (Comberford 1657), Port of Saynt Maris (McMullan and Willard 2015, showing anonymous map, 1585), Pearl of the Outer Banks (signage), Sequotan (indigenous for mainland village misunderstood by early mapmakers), Vokokon (historical), Woccacon (historical), Woccock (historical), Woccocock (Ocracoke Island History 2016), Woccocon (Weslager 1954, 46), Woccon (O'Neal et al. 1976, 4), Wococock (Comberford 1657), Wococon (Blaeu 1640), Wocoken (Torres 1985, 21—from Bancroft 1879 within Torres), Wocokon (Hakluyt 1589), Wocotan (Keulen 1690), Wocoton (Lawson 1709), Wokokon (Ocracoke Island History 2016), Wosotan (Sanson 1696), Wosoton (Wildey and Thornton 1685), Wossoton (McGuinn 2000, 8—indicated 1689, no other information), Wosston (Cobb 1905), Wukokon (historical).

Ocracoke Landing, former landing, Hyde County, Ocracoke Township (C&GS 1900). Was in Pamlico Sound, 2 mi. n of Ocracoke (village). Was hulk of a sunken ship where boats anchored to transfer goods for Ocracoke (village). Used only a short time. Today Big Foot Slough Channel extends s from here. *See* Ocracoke.

Ocracoke Point, point, Hyde County, Ocracoke Township (ACE 1893). Sw-most point Ocracoke Island, 4 mi. sw of Ocracoke (village). Location changed and extended by 1 mi. over past 100 years and over 2 mi.

since late 1500s. Ocracoke Point and South Point used interchangeably. Variant South Point more widely used, but Ocracoke Point is official name. *See* Ocracoke. *Other names:* Ocracoke Point of Beach (ACE 1950), South Point (local use, road name), South Point Ocracoke (Garrity-Blake 2010, 2), South Point of Ocracoke Island (atypical actual spoken use), South Point Spit (NPS brochures).

Ocracoke Swash, breakers, Hyde County, Ocracoke Township; and Carteret County, Portsmouth Township (local use). At entrance Ocracoke Inlet, 4 mi. sw of Ocracoke (village). *See* Ocracoke. "Swash" is usually used in overwash, but sometimes as here where waves break on shoals in inlets. *Other names:* Oakercock Barr (historical), Oakerecock Barr (Wimble 1733), Occacock Swash (O'Neal et al. 1976, 8), Ocracock Bar (historical), Ocracoke Bar (local use), Ocracoke Shoals (Bishop 1878), The Swash (Angley 1984, 34).

Ocracoke Village areas, neighborhoods, Hyde County, Ocracoke Township, within Ocracoke village (local interviews and Howard 2016). Minor competition and continuous banter among these well into 20th century. Three major areas and four smaller ones. The three larger ones were w side of Cockle Creek (Silver Lake), Pointers (reference to Springers Point); e, n, and s sides of Cockle Creek (*see* Silver Lake), Creekers; and soundside e, Trenters (*see* Up Trent). Refer to each entry individually. Additionally, with no less competition, were smaller Cat Ridge, Windmill Point, Paddys Holler (Hollow), and Nubbins Ridge. Refer to entries for natural features by same name. *See* Ocracoke.

Ocracoke Wharf, historical landing originally, but now reactivated, Hyde County, Ocracoke Township (signage). Former docking facility in Silver Lake at Ocracoke. Name used originally late 19th century but experiencing some reuse with name Jacks Dock. *See* Ocracoke and Community Square Docks. *Other names:* Captains Landing (historical use—approximate location, possibly adjacent), Jacks Dock (Outer Banks Scenic Byway Report 2008, 67), Ocracoke Station (Williamson 1992, 116).

Odens Dock, harbor, Dare County, Hatteras Township (signage). Across from entrance Pamlico Sound into Hatteras Harbor, 1 mi. ne of Austin Creek (Hatteras-Ocracoke Ferry docks).

Off Island, marsh island, 0.4 mi. long and wide, Dare County, Nags Head Township (USGS 2013: Oregon Inlet). In Roanoke Sound separated from Bodie Island by Blossie Creek 0.9 mi. n of Herring Shoal Island, 4.8 mi. se of Wanchese. Reference to island's proximity to The Cutoff, just s of the island. "Off," spoken version of Cutoff signifying a sort of shortcut, which evolved over years. Name origin could be any of several references (though reference to The Cutoff is most accepted) because "off" has many nautical meanings, usually referring to lying seaward or a ship riding a distance from shore. Can also mean away from the wind. *Other names:* Cutoff (C&GS 1913b), Cutoff Island (USGS 1943: Roanoke Island 1:125,000 scale, 1943b), Off Islands (USBGN staff).

Off Island Dock, landing, Dare County, Nags Head Township (Hitchcock 2014, 59). On ne Off Island 0.5 mi. s of Bodie Island Lighthouse across Blossie Creek, 7 mi. s of Whalebone Junction. Complex present, mostly inactive.

Oglesby Path, area, Carteret County, Morehead Township (Zaenker 2014). Was on Bogue Banks halfway between Pine Knoll Shores and Indian Beach (town), 6 mi. w of Atlantic Beach (town). *See* Bogue Banks historical paths. *Other names:* Ogilbys Path (PKS 2016).

Old Birding Grounds, former area, Dare County, Kinnakeet Township (Garrity-Blake 2010, 168). Was in The North'ard, former Scarboro, and n Avon, 0.5 mi. e of Big Island (Dare County, Kinnakeet Township), 8 mi. n of Buxton. Was for hunting fowl and collecting eggs important to supplementing residents' diets.

Old Channel, water passage, 0.6 mi. long, Carteret County, Stacy Township (USGS 2013: Styron Bay). In Core Sound, separates Inner Grass Lump from Core Banks 4.4 mi. s of Atlantic (mainland).

Old Channel Point, point, Carteret County, Davis Township (USGS 2013: Styron Bay). On Outer Grass Lump 1 mi. nw of Core Banks, 5.5 mi. e of Davis (mainland). Was sw point former Cedar Inlet.

Old Creek, linear cove, Hyde County, Ocracoke Township (local use). In Ocracoke (village) on e side of Horsepen Point just e of Sound Shores subdivision.

Old Cypress Point, point, Dare County, Atlantic Township (local informant). E point at mouth Jeanguite Creek in Southern Shores 0.5 mi.

n of Southern Shores Marina, 0.5 mi. ene of Mill Point (n tip Martins Point), 4.5 mi. n of original Kitty Hawk. Named for an old and gigantic cypress tree here. Name not used much today but remembered by longtime residents. *Other names:* Old Cypress (local usage).

Old Dike, former dike, Dare County, Nags Head Township (Hitchcock 2014, 59). Was 0.2 mi. se of Bodie Island Lighthouse just n of Blossie Creek. Used 1920s by Bodie Island Gun Club to enhance Bodie Island Lighthouse Pond.

Olde Towne Marina, harbor, Carteret County, Beaufort Township (signage). E-central Radio Island, 1.3 mi. west of Beaufort (mainland).

Old Dominion Docks. *See* Ashbee Harbor.

Old Drum Inlet, former water passage, Carteret County, Smyrna Township (Fisher 1962, 105). Connected Core Sound and Atlantic Ocean at what is now Hogpen Bay (inlet remnants), 7.8 mi. s of Davis (mainland), 15 mi. sw of complex of features using variations of Drum Inlet. Open throughout much of 18th century, 1722–70. Reportedly open early 1920s for a couple of years, but no documentation and probably just awash at high tides (Fisher 1962, 105). Some question as to actual name of this inlet. While the inlet existed, reason referenced as Old Drum Inlet unknown since supposedly opened during same general (early) period as what was then known as Drum Inlet and today is also known as Old Drum Inlet. *See* Drum Inlet. *Other names:* Drum Einfahrt (Huber 1711—*einfahrt*, inlet in German), Drum Inlet (Moll 1729), Drum Inlett (Barnwell-Hammerton 1721), Drum Passage (Graffenried 1710), Entré de Tambour (means drum—Nolin 1783), Passe Drum (Bellin 1757), Salt Creek (colonial maps—another name for Old Drum Inlet or applied to nearby water passage in marsh).

Old Field, former area, Carteret County, Portsmouth Township (White 2012, 31). Reportedly adjacent to Little Channel, just se of Casey Island 0.5 mi. nw of Portsmouth (village). "Fish houses," used for storing the catch in fish boxes with layers of ice to preserve fish, were here.

Old Green Island Club, former hunting and fishing club, Hyde County, Ocracoke Township (GNIS). Was on e end Ocracoke Island just s of Green Island 3 mi. wsw of Hatteras Inlet. Original camp location— *see* Green Island Club.

Old Guts, former tidal streams, Hyde County, Ocracoke Township (Garrity-Blake 2010, 356). Three small tidal creeks were at se corner of what is now Silver Lake in Ocracoke (village) 2.5 mi. ne of Ocracoke Inlet. Eventually filled in by ACE by 1940s though dredging began in earnest 1931 for Silver Lake. For a short distance one creek named The Gut bifurcated into two longer creeks (still quite short), named Big Gut (w creek) and Little Gut (e creek) and known collectively as Old Guts. *See* Alligator Gut. *Other names:* The Guts (historical local use, Howard 2017 and 2018).

Old Hammock, hummock, Hyde County, Ocracoke Township (local use). Soundside in sand hills and live oaks (*Quercus virginiana*) just sw of Quokes Point, 1 mi. ne of Hammock Oaks, 5 mi. ne of Ocracoke (village). *See* Black Hammock. *Other names:* The Hammock (O'Neal et al. 1976, 17).

Old Hammock Creek, cove, 0.05 mi. wide, Hyde County, Ocracoke Township (USGS 2002 Howard Reef). In Pamlico Sound 4.5 mi. ne of Ocracoke (village).

Old Hatteras Inlet, former water passage, Hyde County, Ocracoke Township (Moseley 1737). Connected Pamlico Sound to Atlantic Ocean near ne end Ocracoke Island at The Great Swash (q.v.) 7 mi. sw of *present* Hatteras Inlet, 8.3 mi. ne of Ocracoke (village). Several authors have provided different locations in this general area, including Shingle Creek (Stick 1958, 296), Bitter Swash (Dunbar 1958, 129), and this general area (Price and Strother 1798), but Fisher (1962, 106) agrees that The Great Swash is the location. Opened 1650s (possibly earlier, but no supporting evidence) and closed 1764. The few older maps showing the inlet are small scale so location is generalized and the original name, Hatteras Inlet (not the present one), is shown. *Other names:* Hateras Inlet (Wimble 1733), Hattaras Inlet (Gascoyne 1682), Hattares Inlett (Barnwell-Hammerton 1721), Hattars Inlett (Visscher and Anse 1717), Hatteras Inlet (Vaugondy 1755; Pinkerton et al. 1809—location shown), Hatteras Einfahrt (Huber 1711—*einfahrt*, inlet in German), Hatterask Inlet (O'Neal et al. 1976, 1719 deed, 6), Hatorasch Inlett (historical), Passage de Hattarxis (Stick 1958, 9), Passage de Hattaxis (Fisher 1962, 106), Passage de Hatteras (Cobb 1905), Passe d'Hatteras (Bellin

1757), Port Grenvil (Angley 1984, 80—from Quinn 1955, "based on maps in Haklyut," but in error, this inlet opened over 75 years after Grenville's voyage), West Inlet (directional).

Old House Beach, beach, 1.6 mi. long, Carteret County, Portsmouth Township (USGS 2013: Wainwright Island). On Core Banks just sw of Sand Inlet 13 mi. sw of Portsmouth (village), 18.8 mi. sw of Ocracoke (village). Name origin not remembered but probably refers to a structure used at temporary campsites.

Old House Channel, channel, 5.5 mi. long, Dare County, Nags Head and Kinnakeet Townships (USGS 2013: Oregon Inlet). Trends ne-sw in Pamlico Sound from Oregon Inlet Channel 5.4 mi. se of Wanchese. Known as "slough" early 20th century, but local usage changed to channel once dredged and marked for navigation. *See* Old House Beach and Old House Creek. Made official by the USBGN 1975 to reflect evolution from slough to channel. *Other names:* Old-house Channel (Oregon Inlet Survey 1882, reported by Angley 1985, 11), Old House Slough ("slough" or "slue" often used 19th century before channel became popular from use by traffic).

Old House Creek, small tidal water passage, Currituck County, Poplar Branch Township (C&GS 1852). Connects Old House Pond and junction of Sanders Creek and Buzzard Lead 4 mi. ssw of Corolla. Usually reference to nearby old structure used as landmark.

Old House Pond, lake, Currituck County, Poplar Branch Township (USGS 2013: Mossey Islands). In Mossey Islands complex, 4.6 mi. s of Corolla. *See* Old House Creek. *Other names:* Old House Cove (C&GS 1852,), Mallard Pond (C&GS 1852).

Old Landing, former landing, Dare County, Atlantic Township (local informants). Was at central shore North Cove, in s original Kitty Hawk, 3.5 mi. s of Southern Shores. No trace today.

Old Landing, landing, Dare County, Hatteras Township (local use). In Frisco, 1 mi. sw of Brigands Bay.

Old Landing Canal, canal, Dare County, Hatteras Township (local use). Provided access from Pamlico Sound to Old Landing 1 mi. sw of Brigands Bay. Dredged and widened for location of Island Boat Works.

Old Landing Ridge, small sand ridge, Dare County, Atlantic Township (Harris 2017). In s original Kitty Hawk just e of Mingoes Ridge n from Old Landing for 0.3 mi. Associative from former Old Landing.

Old Overhaul. *See* Phipps Overhaul.

Old Roanoke Inlet, possible former inlet, Dare County, Nags Head Township (CS 1862a). If existed, open just a short time, and apparently 2 mi. sse Whalebone Junction, 3 mi. s former Roanoke Inlet. Often confused with Gunt Inlet 3.5 mi. farther sse. From 1640 until early 1700s was a period of cartographic confusion regarding locations and names of inlets at and near Roanoke Island (*see* Roanoke Island historical inlets). Some question as to whether this inlet ever existed as only a few maps display the name. It likely did not exist by this name, but confusion was created by transition of inlet names here in late 17th and early 18th centuries. Old Roanoke Inlet is name assigned by some cartographers to what was formerly Port Lane, but the site was already long closed and name lost or not remembered, so Old Roanoke was used to distinguish from former Roanoke Inlet location.

Lindenkohl, in U.S. Coast Survey chart (CS 1862a), applied Old Roanoke Inlet to a location 8 mi. n of Oregon Inlet, 3 mi. s of former Roanoke Inlet (he labeled Old Inlet), but Old Roanoke Inlet location is clearly former Port Lane in later years, depicted as closed. Bishop (1878) indicated Old Roanoke Inlet (now closed) to be 4 mi. n of Oregon Inlet, placing it near former Gunt Inlet (Port Ferdinando). Bishop was off slightly and merely repeating incorrectly a map or chart of the time, probably Lindenkohl. This name and feature were no more than a toponymic (name) contrivance, or at best a misconstruance of historical maps to account for location and migration of Port Lane or a newer inlet nearby eventually being renamed Roanoke Inlet. The name Port Lane had simply been forgotten and a label (name) was needed to describe this former inlet location. *Other names:* Old Inlet (Gascoyne 1682).

Old Rollinson Channel, channel, 3.6 mi. long, Dare County, Hatteras Township (local use). In Pamlico Sound se from Kings Channel, 2.5 mi. n of Hatteras (village), 3 mi. sw of Bird Islands. Made official by USBGN 1982 to correct Rollenson and add Channel. *See* Rollinson Channel. *Other names:* Old

Rollenson Channel (NOS field notes 1981, acknowledged this to be typographical error), Old Rollenson Sound (*sic*) (USBGN 1982—misconception), Rollinson Channel (local use).

Old Slough, cove, 0.2 mi. long, 0.05 mi. wide, Hyde County, Ocracoke Township (USGS 2013: Ocracoke). In Pamlico Sound just s of Springers Point 1 mi. ssw of Ocracoke (village). *See* Allen Slough. *Other names:* Old Slew Drain (Weslager 1954).

Old Station Area, former area, Dare County, Atlantic Township (former local use). Referenced beach at small Kitty Hawk Beach section, 1 mi. e of North Cove (ne part Kitty Hawk Bay), 4 mi. s of Southern Shores. Rarely used today, but previously a convenient reference to this Kitty Hawk Beach section. Basis for name is site of Kitty Hawk Life Saving Station (Number 7 and one of a chain of 29 such stations). By 1905 about every 7 mi. along the coast of the Outer Banks had such a station except remote parts of Core Sound and a break between Bogue Inlet and Cape Fear (near Wilmington). There were two structures at this station, the first built 1874 and second structure added 1911. Today, 1874 structure moved short distance n and incorporated into a restaurant; second structure purchased and moved short distance s as private residence.

Old Swash Channel, former small channel, 1 mi. long, Carteret County, Portsmouth Township (historical local use). Was in Pamlico Sound from Wallace Channel to Flounder Slue in an arc between Shell Castle and North Rock, 4 mi. w of Ocracoke (village). *See* Daniel Swash. *Other names:* Swash Channel (Angley 1984, 35).

Old Swimming Hole, former area, Dare County, Nags Head Township (local use). Used as place for swimming (in past) near N.C. Aquarium adjacent to Dare County Regional Airport 2 mi. w of Manteo. Many indicate reportedly not safe for swimming; supposedly submerged pilings from an old abandoned ferry dock exist, and several very serious accidents have reportedly taken place. Today a Dare County Park here.

Old Tower Hill, sand dune, Dare County, Hatteras Township (NPS 2005b: NPS 1, 253). Near original Cape Hatteras Lighthouse site 2 mi. n of Cape Point, 1.5 mi. se of Buxton. Temporary steel tower reference used for Cape Hatteras Light 1935–42 while CCC and WPA worked to reclaim land encroached on by the sea (accomplished for a while). Eventually, 1999 Cape Hatteras Lighthouse was moved 0.5 mi. w and inland to save it from the sea.

Old Wading Place, former area, Currituck County, Fruitville Township (Currituck DB 1791, 6, 155–56). Was in n Knotts Island (village) on w shore middle part Capsies Creek (where cove begins) along property of principals in deed (depth now and historically 1–2 ft.), 3 mi. w of Carova.

Old Well Hill, sand dune, Carteret County, Harkers Island Township (Stick 1958, 309). Considerably higher in mid-20th century, as topography of Cape Lookout and environs has changed greatly over past 100 years. Precise location not known or remembered considering changing topography but was somewhere within 1–2 sq. mi. on Cape Lookout just s of Cape Hills and former Cape Lookout (village), between Cape Hills and Cape Point tip Cape Lookout, 1.5 mi. ssw of Cape Lookout Lighthouse, 7 mi. sse of Harkers Island (village).

Oliver Channel, former channel, less than 1 mi. long, Dare County, Hatteras Township (historical local use). In Pamlico Sound just sw of Oliver Reef, 3.3 mi. nw of Hatteras (village). Prominent in 19th century. Some of Oliver Channel is now Rollinson Channel. *Other names:* Olivers Channel (CS 1861).

Oliver Point, former shoal point, Dare County, Hatteras Township (CS 1861). Ne point Oliver Reef just w of Egg Shoal 5 mi. nw of Hatteras (village). Inundated, no longer exists.

Oliver Reef, shoal, 1 mi. long, Dare County, Hatteras Township, Hyde County, Ocracoke Township (USGS 2013: Cape Hatteras). In Pamlico Sound 3.4 mi. n of Hatteras Inlet. Given to U.S. government 1874 for use in naval target practice; returned to North Carolina 1965. "Reef" in Outer Banks geographic names usually refers to oyster colonies. Made official by USBGN 1891. *Other names:* Olivers Reef (Downing 2008, 22).

O'neals Mill, former mill, Dare County, Kinnakeet Township (Covey 2018, 44). Was in Chicamacomico in n Waves. Bishop does not mention this windmill, but shown unnamed on Dunbar's (1958) map.

Onslow Bay, bight, 100 mi. long, Carteret, Onslow, New Hanover, and Brunswick

Counties. In Atlantic Ocean trending ne-sw from Cape Lookout to Cape Fear (extreme s North Carolina).

Opening Creek, tidal stream, Dare County, Kinnakeet Township (local use). Exact location unknown but somewhere in Opening Marshes soundside at Salvo near Hattie Creef Landing. Descriptive name.

Opening Marshes, marsh, Dare County, Kinnakeet Township (local use). On n Hatteras Island w of Salvo 1.8 mi. s of Waves. Descriptive name. *Other names:* Opening Marsh (CS 1852).

Open Pond, lake, Dare County, Hatteras Township (Mallin NPS 2006, 21). At Cape Hatteras 1.7 mi. nw of Cape Point, 1.7 mi. sw of Buxton. Used descriptively, locally becoming a name (*see* Open Ponds).

Open Ponds, lakes, Dare County, Hatteras Township (local use). Seven ponds originally between Buxton Woods and Jennette Sedge, 1 mi. s of Buxton. In 18th and early 19th centuries joined into one continuous e-w pond known as Great Ditch (q.v.), now only remnants known as Open Ponds (descriptive term). *Other names:* Fresh Lakes (occasional local use), Fresh Water Lakes (occasional local use), Great Ditch (Brooks 2010), Open Pond (some local use—*see* Open Pond).

Ophelia Banks, barrier beach, 1.5 mi. long, Carteret County, Atlantic Township (USGS 2013: Styron Bay). Extreme n South Core Banks between former New Drum Inlet (ne end) and Ophelia Inlet (sw end) 3 mi. s of Atlantic (mainland). Applied and came into use when Ophelia Inlet opened 2005, named for hurricane that created it. Name no longer used except as previous short-lived reference since Ophelia Inlet expanding, capturing what remains of New Drum Inlet. Made official by USBGN 2006. *Other names:* Middle Core Island (Wikipedia—no other known usage), New Core Banks (Mallinson et al. 2008, 12), New Core Island (Wikipedia, misrecorded from Mallinson et al. 2008, 12), Ophelia Island (NPS 2006).

Ophelia Beach, small beach, 1 mi. long, Carteret County, Atlantic Township (some local tourism use). Corresponds to Ophelia Banks on South Core Banks from New Drum Inlet to Ophelia Inlet. Name no longer used except as previous reference since Ophelia Inlet expanded, capturing what remains of New Drum Inlet. *See* Ophelia Banks.

Ophelia Inlet, water passage, 0.5 mi. long, expanding width, now over 1 mi., Carteret County, Atlantic Township (USGS 2013: Styron Bay). At remnants of Horsepen Creek former soundside cove before Ophelia Inlet opened 2005, 3.5 mi. s of Atlantic (village). Originally a cove named Horsepen Creek here, but when Ophelia Inlet opened in September 2005 by Hurricane Ophelia, cove was transformed into part of inlet, but name Horsepen Point is used still in conjunction with name Ophelia Inlet. Has been expanding merging with New Drum Inlet just n. Made official by USBGN 2006. Originally, naming practice for new inlets was to apply name New Inlet. If the inlet showed indication of remaining open, a more appropriate name would be applied. With the opening (temporary) of Isabel Inlet 2003, this process apparently changed to using storm name opening the inlet. New Inlet (reopened 2011 by Hurricane Irene) was not renamed because it opened and closed periodically over past 300 years, so New Inlet was always appropriate, and apparently it was not considered appropriate to rename the inlet Irene Inlet.

Orange Hill, small dune, Dare County, Nags Head Township (possible historical use). In South Nags Head area 1.5 mi. s of Whalebone Junction. Name not remembered nor used; for a small subdivision no longer recorded in Dare County GIS. Unknown if the feature was referenced for the subdivision or earlier.

Oregon Inlet, water passage, 1.5 mi. long, Dare County, Nags Head Township (USGS 2013: Oregon Inlet). Trends nne to ssw, connects Pamlico Sound to Atlantic Ocean, separates Bodie Island from Pea Island, and is spanned by Basnight Bridge 15 mi. n of Rodanthe. Opened during a hurricane 1846, named for first vessel to pass through it, side-wheeler Oregon. Today, channel through inlet constantly dredged and maintained to provide necessary outlet to sea, supporting fishing industry of the Outer Banks (what remains of it) centered at Wanchese. North Point migrating s from deposition shifting orientation more n-s. Since opening 1846, migrated just over 2 mi. Use of variant name Inlet of 1849 was cartographic method (rarely used) indicating new inlets not yet named. Practice only lasted a short time and was used primarily by mapmakers; use of "1849" a transcribing error (for 1846). *See* New Inlet and Ophelia Inlet for an explanation of new inlet naming. Spanned by Marc Basnight Bridge, opened 2019, replacing Herbert C. Bonner Bridge (opened 1963). Marc Basnight from Manteo was N.C. Senator for more than 17 years and was Senate president. Herbert Bonner was from e North Carolina and represented his local district in the U.S. Congress 1940–1965. The old bridge was deemed past its intended period of use; construction was begun March 2016 for more modern bridge, which opened February 25, 2019. Parts of old bridge are scheduled to be retained as a pedestrian and fishing pier, keeping name Bonner Bridge. *Other names:* Inlet of 1846 (CS 1849a), Inlet of 1849 (transcribing error), New Inlet (Throop 1850—presumably because just opened when Throop recorded observations, not aware of name).

Oregon Inlet Bar, shoal, 0.3 mi., long, 5 ft. deep, Dare County, Nags Head and Kinnakeet Townships (local use). At Oregon Inlet entrance 10 mi. s of Whalebone Junction. *See* Oregon Inlet.

Oregon Inlet Beach, beach, 2 mi. long, Dare County, Nags Head Township (local use). Just n of Oregon Inlet, straight stretch of beach trending nne to ssw 15 mi. se of Nags Head. Relatively new name (new deposition from migrating Oregon Inlet), limited usage mostly by recreationists and fishermen referring to this distinctive beach. *See* Oregon Inlet.

Oregon Inlet Channel, channel, 3 mi. long, Dare County, Nags Head Township (USGS 2013: Oregon Inlet). Trends nw in Pamlico Sound from Oregon Inlet to Roanoke Sound Channel 4.5 mi. se of Wanchese. *See* Oregon Inlet. Made official by USBGN 1975. *Other names:* The Crack, Main Channel (Montoya 2018, 6, fig. 2.1), Oregon Inlet Cut (local media).

Oregon Inlet Ferry Docks, former landings, Dare County, Nags Head and Kinnakeet Townships (historical signage). Connected Bodie Island to Pea Island and villages on Hatteras Island. Begun 1920s by Toby Tillet (*see* Tillets Landing Areas) with no dock facilities. Sold to state government 1950 and dock facilities established both sides (Bodie Island Dock near present Oregon Inlet Fishing Center), 8 mi. s of Whalebone Junction. Service ended with opening of

Bonner Bridge 1963 (now new Basnight Bridge, 2019).

Oregon Inlet Gorge, channel valley, Dare County, Nags Head and Kinnakeet Townships (NCDOT 2013, 4–5). Hypsographic (land feature) in Oregon Inlet containing much of Coast Guard Channel, 6 mi. se of Wanchese. More a scientific reference used in reports, but as a result can be found occasionally. "Gorge" is not from local usage but from those writing scientific reports. Descriptive referring to deepest inlet part and, while somewhat stabilized by dredging, still changeable. *See* Oregon Inlet.

Oregon Inlet Marina, harbor, Dare County, Nags Head Township (signage). At Motts Creek 1.5 mi. nnw of Oregon Inlet 5.5 mi. e of Wanchese. *See* Oregon Inlet.

Orlando Jones Settlement, attempted settlement, Dare County, Nags Head Township (Maule 1718). Was to be 2 mi. se of Wanchese but never developed and apparently to be named for short-time landowner from Williamsburg, Va.

Osprey Bluff, distinct sand dune, 35 ft. high, Carteret County, White Oak Township (local use). Adjacent to Osprey Ridge in Emerald Isle Woods 3 mi. ne of Bogue Inlet. Reversed usage, natural feature acquiring name of man-made feature (subdivision).

Osprey Pond, pond, 0.2 mi. long including narrow drain, Dare County, Atlantic Township (HOA official). In s Sanderling, drains from just e of NC 12 to Currituck Sound, 3 mi. n of Duck (village center). Enhanced and named by developer.

Osprey Ridge, small sand ridge, 0.3 mi. long, Carteret County, White Oak Township (local use). At w end Bogue Banks just sw of Langston Bridge, 7 mi. w of original Emerald Isle. Unclear whether name was used before subdivision established or if name came into use after subdivision est. last quarter 20th century (probably latter, so an example of reversed usage, natural feature acquiring name of man-made feature).

Osprey Ridge, small sand ridge, 0.3 mi. long, Dare County, Atlantic Township (local use). In s Duck at Osprey Ridge subdivision, 7 mi. nnw of original Kitty Hawk. Unclear whether the name was used before subdivision established or name came into use after subdivision established in last quarter of 20th century. If latter, example of reversed usage, natural feature acquiring name of man-made feature. Part of Powder Ridge (q.v.).

Otila, former community, Dare County, Atlantic Township (postal service). Was on Currituck Banks just nw of original Kitty Hawk near Sound Landing 8.3 mi. nnw of central Nags Head. Post office established in community surrounding Sound Landing 1905, but discontinued 1918, though was only sporadically operational after 1914. Postmaster requested Sound or Atlantic as name, both rejected by Post Office Department. Today name remembered by many local residents but not used for any application. Name origin not remembered, and post office records are lost. *Other names:* Botella (C&GS 1932), Botilla (C&GS 1913a), Ottilla (historical local use).

Otis Cove, marsh cove, 0.6 mi. long, 0.1 mi. wide, Dare County, Nags Head Township (USGS 1986, 32). At n end Roanoke Island separated from Roanoke Sound by Crab Claw Spit 1.5 mi. nnw of Manteo (center). No one recalls who is Otis; some speculation (whimsically) from a character of *Andy Griffith Show* since adjacent to Andy Griffith estate; no documentation found regarding naming.

Otis Point, point, Dare County, Nags Head Township (local use). E tip Crab Claw Spit just ne of Otis Cove 2 mi. n of Manteo. *See* Otis Cove.

Otter Island, former island, Currituck County, Poplar Branch Township (C&GS 1852). Was at s Sanders Bay at n entrance Sanders Creek 4.5 mi. ssw of Corolla. *See* Big Otter Cove.

Otter Pond, former lake, Dare County, Kinnakeet Township (former local use). Was just s of Otter Pond Point (Big Otter Foot Point) just n of Little Otter Foot Point in The South'ard, 1 mi. s of original Avon. Almost nonexistent today by altering from development; several man-made ponds to support development here. *See* Otter Island.

Otter Pond Point, marsh point, Dare County, Kinnakeet Township (USGS 2013: Buxton). Just n of Black Hammock, in The South'ard, 1 mi. s of original Avon. Originally Otter Point or Big Otter Foot Point (*see* Little Otter Foot Point), changed over the years on map usage; both names used now. Locally originally pronounced "auta." *See* Big Otter Cove. *Other names:* Big Otter Foot Point (Garrity-Blake

2010, 210), Otter Point (Currituck DB 11, 1809, 191, 193a–b).

Ourdsleys Hammock, sand dune, Dare County, Hatteras Township (CS 1857c). Is 2.3 mi. sw of Hatteras (village). Round Hammock and Ourdsleys Hammock were used interchangeably 19th century when more prominent, but names have fallen into disuse. Ourdsleys Hammock was originally applied to a much larger sand dune than more distinctive dune using name Round Hammock, applied to smaller more round part of Ourdsleys Hammock. *Other names:* Baileys Hammick (CS), Ourdleys Hammock (CS 1857b), Round Hammock (historical expanding application—*see* Round Hammock), and Round Hommock (unusual spelling—*see* Round Hammock).

Outer Banks, barrier complex in Currituck, Dare, Hyde, Carteret Counties. Narrow chain of barrier islands, barrier beaches, and barrier spits s from North Carolina–Virginia boundary to Cape Hatteras, then sw to Bogue Inlet. From n to s (today) barriers are named Currituck Banks and recently Dare Banks, then Bodie Island, Pea Island, Hatteras Island, Ocracoke Island, Portsmouth Island, Core Banks, Shackleford Banks, and Bogue Banks. Currituck Banks and Bodie Island are now joined just n of Whalebone Junction at former Roanoke Inlet; Pea Island and Hatteras Island joined 1945 at former New Inlet just n of Rodanthe, but since 2011 have again been separated. Many divisions of the Outer Banks exist for various reasons. No official names or boundaries for regions in any government or elsewhere exist, as regions are determined according to need and functionality. So, delineation of the Outer Banks is subjective and differs according to perception and application. As with most regions, a core usually can be identified and agreed on. According to this study, the Outer Banks is based on what is considered to be logical physical and cultural delimitation, from Virginia–North Carolina boundary s to Cape Lookout, then w to Bogue Inlet.

"Bank" as a geographic term has been used for centuries and originally was merely a pile of something (from Old English and Norse as elevation), usually linear, evolving to contain slopes. Applied to shoals and constantly exposed areas, hence barrier islands. Use of "banks" on maps and deeds of the Outer Banks dates from early 1700s onward sporadically, generally beginning with Lawson 1709 as first major map to use "banks," but then only descriptively (Sand Banks). Used sparingly and only descriptively until mid-1800s, when place names using generic term "banks" appeared, generally beginning with CS charts. Prior, maps labeled then existing barrier islands with indigenous terms without a generic reference. Names using "banks" did not appear consistently on maps or charts until mid-1800s onward. While sporadic use occurred from late 1800s, specific term "Outer Banks" not used consistently until 1930s and is an external application associated with tourism from building bridge 1930 from Powells Point (mainland) to Kitty Hawk (Wright Memorial Bridge spans today).

First recorded European visit to the Outer Banks made by Verrazzano 1524 searching for a route w; for very short time named Verazania. Refer to Roanoke voyages at website (OBXplacenames.com) for full account of this and Roanoke voyages with a focus on toponymic aspects. *See* Cape Lookout for an explanation of Verrazzano's visit.

When the English increased their activity and visits, entire region in this part of New World known briefly as New Brittaine because 1651 Edward Bland attempted to establish colonies w and s of Jamestown (settled 1607), which he named New Brittaine (Bland 1651). He received an agreement from Virginia Assembly to proceed with settlements, but no attempts were made, especially since Bland died 1653.

Eventually, entire area was named Virginia for Queen Elizabeth I of England, the "virgin queen." In 1663 part now known as two Carolinas was granted to eight Lords Proprietors by Charles II, King of England, and Lords Proprietors named grant in honor of Charles I (who was deposed and executed, creating the brief Commonwealth period under Cromwell), father of Charles II, the grantor (*see* Carolina).

During Civil War, residents of the Outer Banks had little sympathy for Southern cause or Northern cause. Dissatisfied with North Carolina joining the Confederacy, some individuals on the Outer Banks and some other N.C. counties attempted to form the "true and faithful" government of North Carolina (also termed the Redeemed State). A convention was held at Hatteras proclaiming Hatteras the capital, and President Lincoln designated provisional capital of the "retrieved State of North Carolina" at Hatteras. A representative was elected and sent to Washington, D.C., but unlike the West Virginia situation, the Outer Banks representative was not seated in Congress because of concern over legitimacy of the entire situation. Shortly afterward, Union forces easily captured hastily fortified Confederate posts on the Outer Banks with only minimum fighting, with major battle occurring on Roanoke Island. During entire occupation, "Bankers" were quite indifferent to the affair.

During mid-19th century, many people in North Carolina referred to the Outer Banks as "Arabia," alluding to its inaccessibility, but this name was not used on the Banks. History here is filled with reports of hundreds of shipwrecks because of dreaded Diamond Shoals off Cape Hatteras, which earned the infamous name "the Graveyard of the Atlantic" (attributed to Alexander Hamilton, but no record of this appellation in any of his papers); today shipwrecks are not prevalent because of sophisticated warning equipment. Shipwrecks were at one time easily visible at many places along the Outer Banks, but only remnants of a few are visible today.

Other names: Annunciata (Verrazzano 1524), Arabia (late 19th and early 20th centuries), Arcadia (applied by Verrazzano, only slight possibility applied along the Outer Banks; applied to now New Jersey or New York; in Greece, secluded and reportedly beautiful [reason for name], eventually reference to such areas), Carolanean Islands (in original charter, later removed), Carolina Banks (Stick 1958, 7—used more 18th century), Carolina Outer Banks (Angley 1982, 2), Dare Coast (commercial), Francesca (Verrazzano 1524; referred to the Outer Banks and all other lands discovered by Verrazzano on this voyage, named for Francis I, King of France, sponsor of voyage), Hatteras Sand Banks (historical), New Brittaine (Bland 1651), North Carolina at Hatteras (use during Civil War by antisecessionists), North Carolina Banks (generic reference), Sand Banks

(Lawson 1709, map), Sand-Banks (Lawson 1709, map), Sandy Banks (numerous deeds), Sea Banks (colonial deeds), Sir Walter Raleigh Coastland (mid-20th century in tourist brochures, coined by *Coastland Times* [Manteo] to promote tourism), The Banks (Stick 1958, 115), Verazania (Verrazzano's voyage), Verazzano Isthmus (simplified application used very short time from name applied in account of Verrazzano's voyage), Varazanio (Verrazzano 1524), Virginia (all settlement by English in area known as Virginia until King Charles II granted huge amount of land 1663, Carolina (q.v.), to eight noblemen [Lords Proprietors] who helped restore British monarchy from brief Commonwealth).

Outer Banks Marina, harbor, Dare County, Nags Head Township (signage). In central e side of Wanchese Harbor, 1.5 mi. e of Wanchese. *Other names:* Broad Creek Marina (former name, changed 2015).

Outer Diamond Shoal, shoal, 4 mi. long, Dare County, Hatteras Township (NOS 2014b). Se-most extension of Diamond Shoals in Atlantic Ocean 6.5 mi. se of Cape Hatteras. Made official by USBGN 1949 to establish location. *See* Diamond Shoals. *Other names:* Diamond Shoals (full feature), Full Moon Shoal (much larger late 18th century), Outer Diamond (O'Neal et al. 1976, 22), Outer Diamonds (MacNeill 1958, 3), Outer Diamond Shoals (Rollinson 1884), Outer Shoal (Binkley 2007, 100, referencing 1952 CHNS project map), Outer Shoals (Blunt 1857, 342), Outward Shoal of Cape Hatteras (Rollinson 1884), Point of the Outer Diamonds (Rollinson 1884).

Outer Grass Lump, marsh island, 0.3 mi. wide, Carteret County, Smyrna Township (USGS 2013: Styron Bay, Davis). In Core Sound 0.3 mi. n of Inner Grass Lump, 3.1 mi. s of Sea Level (mainland). *See* Dorland Lump.

Outer Green Island, marsh island, 0.1 mi. across, Hyde County, Ocracoke Township (USGS 2013: Green Island). In Pamlico Sound just n of Green Island, 13 mi. ne of Ocracoke (village). *Other names:* Little Green Island (C&GS 1883).

Outer Point, point, Hyde County, Lake Landing Township (NOS 2014i). S-most point (hence name) of Great Island 21 mi. nw of Ocracoke (village).

Overhaul Pond, lake, 0.1 mi. across, Currituck County, Poplar Branch Township (USGS 2013: Mossey Islands). W Mossey Islands complex just e of Wells Bay, 4.6 mi. ssw of Corolla. Name origin unknown for sure. Mossey Islands complex is not normally a place where "haulover" (normal usage) is used; "haulover" ("overhaul" is rarely used) usually applied on low beaches or shoals with shallow water where boats are literally hauled over sand or shoal. So, name likely has an entirely different meaning here.

Oystercatcher Canal, small canal, Dare County, Atlantic Township (Town of Southern Shores 2015). In Southern Shores on e shore Jeanguite Creek 4.5 mi. n of original Kitty Hawk. Names of Southern Shores canals are for shorebirds (except Gravey Pond Canal). The American oystercatcher (*Haematopus palliatus*) frequents the area.

Oyster Cove, cove, 0.8 mi. long, 0.3 mi. wide, Currituck County, Fruitville Township (USGS 2013: Knotts Island). Sw Walk Island, entrance between Deep Creek Island and Graven Island, 2 mi. e of Knotts Island (village).

Oyster Creek, water passage, 0.3 mi. long, Carteret County, Cedar Island Township (USGS 2013: Wainwright Island, Atlantic). Separates unnamed marsh islands (sometimes considered part of Hog Island) 1.2 mi. e of Cedar Island Ferry landing, 11.2 mi. sw of Ocracoke (village).

Oyster Creek, water passage, Currituck County, Poplar Branch Township (C&GS 1852). Separates Brant Island (n) and Oyster Creek Island (s) 4 mi. ssw of Corolla. Used since 1788 (Currituck DB 5, 1788, 342).

Oyster Creek, water passage, Dare County, Kinnakeet Township (Garrity-Blake 2010, 492). Separates Great Island from Davids Point soundside on Hatteras Island in s Waves, 2.5 mi. s of Rodanthe.

Oyster Creek, water passage, 1 mi. long, Dare County, Nags Head Township (USGS 2013: Wanchese). In Croatan Sound trending n-s, 0.7 mi. s of Baum Creek, 1.4 mi. w of Wanchese.

Oyster Creek, water passage, 0.5 mi. long, Dare County, Nags Head Township (USGS 2013: Oregon Inlet). Trends n-s in Roanoke Sound, just ne of Hog Island, 3.2 mi. s of Wanchese. *Other names:* Oyster Creek Cutthrough (sometimes used, close proximity to Cut Through).

Oyster Creek, cove, Hyde County, Ocracoke

Township (O'Neal et al. 1976, map, 65). In Oyster Creek subdivision in Ocracoke (village) 1 mi. ne of Silver Lake. Four canals (*see* Canals at Oyster Creek) created here and cove is no longer discernable or recognizable. *Other names:* Big Oyster Creek (Weslager 1954).

Oyster Creek Harbor, natural harbor, Dare County, Nags Head Township (ACE 1948). Just e of Oyster Creek near Davis Landing, 1.5 mi. w of Wanchese.

Oyster Creek Island, island, Currituck County, Poplar Branch Township (Currituck DB 24, 1845, 406–7; C&GS 1852). Just s of Brant Island separated from Brant Island by Oyster Creek, 4.5 mi. ssw of Corolla.

Oyster Creek Point, point, Carteret County, Cedar Island Township (USGS 2013: Wainwright Island). Just s of Oyster Creek on e unnamed marsh (sometimes considered part of Hog Island) 2 mi. e of Cedar Island Ferry landing, 12.5 mi. sw of Ocracoke (village). Variant Oyster Creek *Pit* transcribing error from abbreviation "Pt" (USGS 2010: Wainright Island; labeled correctly 2002). *Other names:* Oyster Creek Pit (USGS 2013: Wainwright Island).

Oyster Landing, possible former landing, Carteret County, White Oak Township (general references). Reportedly formerly near mouth of Archer Creek, w Emerald Isle (town). Now dredged and modernized into N.C. Wildlife Public Boat Ramp. Subdivision nearby using this name.

Oyster Point, point, Dare County, Atlantic Township (local use). S point at Pastor Pond, 1.7 mi. nw of stabilized Kill Devil Hill, 5 mi. s of original Kitty Hawk. Oyster Point subdivision here and was named for the point.

Oyster Point, point, Dare County, Kinnakeet Township (local use). N point Great Island, separated from Davids Point by Oyster Creek just s of Waves.

Oyster Rocks, shoals and rocks, Carteret County, Portsmouth Township (historical local use). Numerous applications and several named rocks over past several centuries. From North Rock se-ward to Wallace Channel just sw of Beacon Island in Pamlico Sound, 4 mi. w of Ocracoke (village). E end sometimes known as Eastern Rocks and w end sometimes known as Western Rocks in broader application. Most of the "rocks" were huge piles of oyster shells (middens—piles of refuse of anything), discarded by indigenous peoples accumulated over centuries. Oister Rocks originally applied as descriptor, became a name. At least five named rocks, including Long Rock (Long Dry Rock—40 acres 1790), Shell Castle (Old Rock, though not included by some—20 acres 1790), and Remus Rock (15 acres 1790). Beacon Island (20 acres 1790—marsh not oyster shell) and Dry Sand Shoal (50 acres 1790—sand not oyster shell) were often included in the complex for discussion purposes. Today, application is to smaller mostly North Rock complex and other smaller rocks. *Other names:* Eastern Rocks (historical local use), Long Rocks (Weslager 1954), Oister Rocks (Stick 1958, 77), Western Rocks (historical local use).

Oyster Shell Banks, shoal, Dare County, Hatteras Township (local use). Three or four exposed at low tide at shore and just offshore created from oyster shells, 0.6 mi. n of Buxton.

P

Pacoles Creek, stream, Dare County, Atlantic Township (Harris 2017, source unknown). According to Harris (2017), somewhere in Kitty Hawk ridge-and-swale system (q.v.), w of original Kitty Hawk. Harris does not provide additional information, and as named feature it does not appear in early deeds. Name is peculiar and not encountered on any source as given name or surname. Possible this form could be transcribing error or variant name for named stream in Kitty Hawk ridge-and-swale system or variant name for Panters Creek. There is a river in what is now w Turkey (in Asia, historically Lydia) named Pactolus (possibly Pacoles) often quoted formerly having gold-bearing sands. Mentioned here because a small town in Pitt County (e North Carolina) named Pactolus, named by a local teacher of Greek, named Lincoln, because the soil along Grindle Creek was fertile, reminding Lincoln of that area in Asia Minor. Harris implies name 18th century; Pactolus (100 miles w) was named in 1770. Still, no known connection.

Paddocks Creek, former tidal stream, Dare County, Kinnakeet Township (C&GS 1883). Was just s of Oregon Inlet on Pea Island near former Coast Guard Station, 17 mi. n of Rodanthe.

Paddys Hollow, flat, Hyde County, Ocracoke Township (USGS 2013: Ocracoke). In Ocracoke (village) 0.3 mi. e of Silver Lake. Use of "hollow" is unprecedented on the Outer Banks; "hollow" usually associated with mountainous environments. Certainly nothing hollow-like geographically here. Reason is unclear and unknown, but might have been introduced by someone originally not from here. Reported locally, name is from a bar (tavern) in Philadelphia—maybe so. A restaurant is in Philadelphia named Paddys Hollow Restaurant & Pub. Name popularized in a tune (Paddy's Holler by Walter Howard) but does not reveal specifics about name origin. Ballance (2017), noted Ocracoke historian, suggests name might mean "Hollow in an area of Oak Trees" meaning a simile comparing the road to a hollow used at e Howard Street. Also, this was a neighborhood name (using Holler; *see* Ocracoke Village areas). *Other names:* Paddys Holler (some brochures, reflect local pronunciation), Pattys Holler (local variation).

Palmer Island. *See* Pine Island.

Palmetto Swamp, former swamp, Dare County, Hatteras Township (William Elks warrant, 1759, from Covey 2018, 22 and CS 1857c). Was reportedly in Frisco near former Indian Town (q.v.) 2 mi. w of Buxton. Spelling and pronunciation of "palmetto" was apparently "permetoe." Dwarf palmettos are sometimes found here. *Other names:* Old Indian Town Bog (Covey 2018, 22).

Pamlico Canyon, canyon. Underwater canyon se of Cape Hatteras leading from continental shelf edge into deep ocean and outside 3-mi. state limit, so not considered to be in state; also beyond 12-mi. national limit so outside U.S. *See* Pamlico Sound.

Pamlico Inn Dock, former landing, Hyde County, Ocracoke Township (local informants). Was used by historical Pamlico Inn s of Silver Lake just n of the Ocracoke Lighthouse 3 mi. ne of Ocracoke Inlet. Destroyed by storm August 1933; inn was destroyed by storm 1944. Formerly Taylor House. *See* Pamlico Sound.

Pamlico Point. *See* Sandy Point (Dare County, Hatteras Township).

Pamlico Ridge. *See* Peach Tree Ridge.

Pamlico Sound, lagoon, 80 mi. long and 30 mi. wide, Carteret County, Cedar Island and Portsmouth Townships; Dare County, Croatan, Nags Head, Kinnakeet, and Hatteras Townships; and Hyde County, Ocracoke Township. From Oregon Inlet and s ends of Croatan Sound and Roanoke Sound s to s end Portsmouth Island separating Pea Island, Hatteras Island, Ocracoke Island, and Portsmouth Island from mainland. Combination of fresh to brackish waters from Roanoke River (through Albemarle Sound, Croatan Sound, and Roanoke Sound), Pamlico River, and Neuse River then drains to Atlantic Ocean through Oregon Inlet, New Inlet (periodically), Hatteras Inlet, and Ocracoke Inlet. Named for Pamlico (Pamticough) or Paquiac Indians who inhabited its (mainland) shores; it is the largest inland water body on U.S. East Coast. European mapmakers applied Verrazzanos Sea for short time since Verrazzano passed by on his explorations (*see* Cape Lookout). One-word variant name applications are spelling variations of name of Indians or their villages on mainland near shore of the sound, but these names were haphazardly applied to the sound by early mapmakers because exact locations were unknown. Made official by USBGN 1891.

Other names: Albemarle Sound (misapplication, Lodge and Adair 1775), Bahia Santa Maria (Cumming 1998, 115), Baye de Pamticoe (Bellin 1764), Der Sund (Huber 1711), Detroit de Pamlico (Frédéric 1807—*detroit*, French meaning strait or water passage; unusual application for such a wide, open water body), Detroit de Pamticoe (unknown, 1806), Lago Luncoz (Quinn 1975), Le Sound (Graffenried 1710), Mare de Verrazana (*sic*) (Lok 1582—name followed on map by year 1524 and labeled on greatly exaggerated depiction of Pamlico Sound stretching nw to open ocean revealing hope it was illusive Northwest Passage to Asia), Mentso (White 1585—might have meant sound or mainland—uses "ʃ" [long "s"]—*see* Bellows Bay variant Bellisses Bay; reportedly refers to cooking, perhaps stopping place), Occam (Haklyut 1589—vague reference to far n part, more often limited to Albemarle Sound, and ostensibly could apply to entire sound system or at least Pamlico Sound n-ward), Occam River (Haklyut 1589), Pameyok (historical), Pamplickoe Sound (Sauthier 1769b), Pamlicoe Sound (Purcell 1797), Pamlico Sund (Lucas 1826), Pamplico Sound (Maule 1718), Pamptico Sound (USBGN 1891), Pamticoe Sound (Moseley 1737), Pamtico Sound (Lewis and Shallus 1807), Pamtico Sounde (Vincent 2003, map, 8), Pamticough River (historical), Pamticough Sound (d'Anville 1756), Pamtigough Sound (Kilian 1764), Pemtico Sound (Torres 1985, 68, reported from Johann David Schoepe, "Travels in the Confederation—1783–1784" [1968], 111–12), Pomeiok (historical), Pomouik (historical), River Sea of Verrazzano (Stick 1998), Stretto di Palmico (Tardieu, ca. 1800—*stretto*, Italian for passage), The Sound (casual, usually verbal references since largest inland water here; Ogilby 1671; Fisher et al. 1689, chart 15; Lea 1690), Verrazana Sea (Verrazzano 1529—believing part of Pacific Ocean, no mainland or land w shown, as Verrazzano did not enter any inlets on his voyage), Verrazzanos Sea (Stick 1998, 13).

Panters Creek, cove, 0.3 mi. across, Dare County, Nags Head Township (Currituck DB 6, 1790, 126; 18th-century maps). Just e of s end Colington Island, 2.3 mi. nw of Jockeys Ridge, 4.5 mi. nw of central Nags Head (some previous local use). Today name is unknown, and presumed by many when asked to be surname. However, name has been displayed (sparingly) since early 18th century. Known throughout se U.S. (and w U.S.); rural folk pronounced name of North American great cat, cougar or panther (earlier name), as "painter" or "pänter." Cougars (panthers) were known to be here in colonial times, and known to be in similar such areas in se U.S. This origin is supported by previous islands named, Panthers Islands (q.v.) in nearby former Roanoke Marshes, and confirmed by variations found in old deeds. Further extant evidence is Panthers Landing, Northwest River 45 mi. nw at Moyock (mainland). *Other names:* Erb Creek (historical use—meaning forgotten; speculation is application of pronunciation of "herb," but actually given name of land owner [*see* Erb Point]), Panter Branch (Currituck DB 8, 1794, 149–50), Panter Creek (Harris 2017; unknown, 1779), Panters Branch (Currituck DB 4, 1784, 226), Pantery Creek (Currituck DB 6, 1792, 292), Panther Creek (Currituck DB 7, 1796, 338–39), Planters Creek (Currituck DB 8, 1800, 254), Poire Creek (early deeds—*poire*, French for pear; while pears grow here they are not prevalent, so meaning unknown).

Panther Islands, former small islands, Dare County, Nags Head Township (Click 2001, map, 26). Were in Croatan Sound 2.5 mi. nw of Wanchese, and remnants of ne Roanoke Marshes (q.v.). Only known occurrence of this name. *See* Panters Creek.

Paquiac, former region, Dare County, Hatteras and Kinnakeet Townships (White 1585). Applied by White and early mapmakers to what are now portions of Hatteras Island and Pea Island from Cape Hatteras to former now submerged Cape Kenrick at Wimble Shoals near Rodanthe. Reportedly, Algonquian word for shallow and probably was Pamlico Sound but misapplied by early mapmakers. Torres (1985, 15) lists the name as Paquimock Island from Hondius (from Cumming 1998), but this is a misinterpretation of Paquiwock. *Other names:* Pacuiac (early maps), Paqueack (Cheeseman 1982, 194), Paquiak (early spelling variation), Paquimock Island (misinterpretation), Paquipe (Blaeu 1640), Paquiwac (Dudley 1647), Paquiwack (Visscher 1680), Paquiwoc (DeBry 1590), Paquiwock (Hondius 1606).

Paradise Bay, small cove, Dare County, Hatteras Township (local use). Just e of Brigands Bay subdivision 2.7 mi. w of Buxton. Name acquired only when subdivision established as result of naming subdivision (reversed usage, natural feature acquiring name of man-made feature); no prior usage.

Parallel Dike, dam, Currituck County, Fruitville Township (F&WS 1984, 1). On e-central Mackay Island in Mackay Island Wildlife Refuge s from just s of Bay Tree Point to 0.7 mi. n of Halfway Point, 3.2 mi. wsw of Knotts Island (village). Constructed 1984 by F&WS with Cross Dike, West Dike, and Long Dike to create Middle Pool and West Pool, enhancing wildlife protection. "Dike" is a wall, embankment, or similar structure to function as a dam to prevent flooding or, as here, to contain and control water level.

Parkers Bay, bay, Currituck County, Poplar Branch Township (Codman, Crowninshield, and Lawrence 1925). At ne Raccoon Bay just s of Raccoon Islands 1 mi. nnw of Corolla. N.C. Wildlife Resources Commission's map of Currituck Banks Game Land (2016) indicates Parkers Bay is a small embayment at s end of Jenkins Cove 1 mi. n of here. Most interviewed were not aware of the name, and the few who were aware, 50/50 split on which location is correct.

Parkers Creek, former short stream, 0.7 mi. long, Dare County, Atlantic Township (Currituck DB 5, 1787, 255–56). Tributary of Pastor Creek; flowed s-n beginning near Kill Devil Hill.

Parkers Creek, former tidal stream, 0.3 mi. long, Hyde County, Ocracoke Township (USGS 1950: Howard Reef). Begins in Parker Hills trended nw to Little Swash Opening in Pamlico Sound, 5.4 mi. ne of Ocracoke (village). Became nondiscernable as channel through marsh late 20th century. *Other names:* Parker Creek (Mallin et al. 2006, fig. 3, 26).

Parkers Hill, sand dune, 15 ft. high, Hyde County, Ocracoke Township (USGS 2013: Howard Reef). On Ocracoke Island between Try Yard Creek and Little Swash Opening 5.8 mi. ne of Ocracoke (village). Variant name indicates originally multiple hills or sand dunes here. *Other names:* Parker Hills (occasional use).

Parkers Ridge, sand ridge, 0.5 mi. long, 30 ft. high, Currituck County, Fruitville Township (local informants). N-s-trending sand ridge (sand dunes here are changing size, height, and location constantly) on n Currituck Banks 1 mi. sw of Swan Beach, 3.7 mi. n of Corolla. Subdivision named for feature. *Other names:* Hidden Dune (q.v.; in part, local use, street sign—largest and n dune of Parkers Ridge).

Parkers Slough. *See* Porpoise Slough.

Parnell Island, island, Dare County, Nags Head Township (ACE 2013). Center of seven exposed sandy spoil or disposal islands of Bird Islands exposed Bulkhead Shoal at w end Oregon Inlet 10 mi. s of Whalebone Junction. *See* Bird Islands.

Passage, The, water passage, 1 mi. long, Carteret County, Cedar Island Township (USGS 2013: Wainwright Island). Separates unnamed marsh islands and Hog Island Reef from large unnamed marsh (sometimes considered part of Hog Island) 2 mi. e of Cedar Island Ferry landing, 10.5 mi. sw of Ocracoke (village).

Pastor Creek, former stream (now canal), Dare County, Atlantic Township (Currituck DB 5, 1787, 255–56). Flows into Pastor Pond (cove) at n end Colington Creek. Name is historical and no longer known here. Today, former stream canalized and known simply as The Canal (Dare County—numerous residents). *Other names:* Parkers Creek (Currituck DB 5, 1787, 255–56).

Pastor Point, point, Dare County, Atlantic Township (historical deeds). In w Kill Devil Hills (town); n point at Pastor Pond at n end Colington Creek. Used historically, unknown today.

Pastor Pond, small cove, Dare County, Atlantic Township (local use). Soundside in Kill Devil Hills (town) in n end Colington Creek in Lemors Bay 3 mi. s of original Kitty Hawk at soundside terminus of The Canal—historically, Pastor Creek or Parkers Creek. *Other names:* Pastor Creek (Currituck DB 5, 1787, 255–56).

Pasture Island, small marsh island, Dare County, Hatteras Township (local use). Just w of Long Point Creek, 1.8 mi. s of original Avon. Used more historically when use was for grazing livestock.

Patch Fence Creek, cove, 0.2 mi. wide, Hyde County, Ocracoke Township (USGS 2013: Green Island). In Pamlico Sound at Cockrel Creek, 8.3 mi. sw of Hatteras (village).

Pateridges Inlet. *See* Great Beach Pond.

Pathemos Creek, small cove, Hyde County, Ocracoke Township (Ballance 2017, 2018). Just ne of Bitterswash Creeks, 2 mi. ne of The Great Swash (Old Hatteras Inlet site), 13 mi. ne of Ocracoke (village). By local interview with Howard, and with an older resident of Ocracoke, reportedly named for Greek ship that ran afoul, itself named for Greek Island of Patmos. Records of this wreck or of the ship have not been located.

Patricks Creek. *See* Tillmans Creek.

Patricks Hammock, former hammock, Dare County, Nags Head Township (Currituck DB 25, 1850, 393–94). Was somewhere on Bodies Island; exact location unknown, and no hint provided in several deeds where name is mentioned. Suspected, but cannot (yet) prove feature was near Tillmans Creek near Panters Creek because Padricks (*sic*)

Creek is listed 1794 deed as most likely referring to what is now Tillmans Creek, but reference too is vague. Without exception, three deeds referring to Patricks Hammock (fourth to Patricks Creek) indicate feature(s) being on Bodies (sic) Island. Tillmans Creek is just n of historical n terminus of Bodie Island, Roanoke Inlet s to historical Chickinacommock Inlet, sometimes New Inlet, but later s terminus revised to Oregon Inlet (opened 1849) as other inlets nearby were closed. Deeds referring to Patricks Hammock are 1789–1869. Roanoke Inlet was clearly open 1789 but was beginning to shoal and close by 1795 closing by 1811. Next mention of Patricks Hammock on Bodie Island is 1814. So, Patricks Hammock (and Creek) was unknown location on Bodie Island or mentions in the deeds simply are in error, (slightly) extending Bodie Island a few miles n. *Other names:* Patricks Hamock (Currituck DB 6, 1789, 79).

Paul Gamiels Hill, sand dune, Dare County, Atlantic Township (historical local use—only older folk remember). On s Currituck Banks, 5.8 mi. nnw of original Kitty Hawk. *Other names:* Paul Gamiel Hill (some older use), Paulgamiel Hill (CS 1848).

Pauls Ditch, cove, 0.3 mi. long, 0.1 mi. wide, Dare County, Kinnakeet Township (USGS 1983: Rodanthe). In Pamlico Sound 0.9 mi. n of Rodanthe.

Pawls Creek. *See* Mill Point Gut.

Pawpaw Ridge, low regular ridge, 5 ft. high, 1.3 mi. long, Dare County, Atlantic Township (Harris 2017; unknown, 1816). In Kitty Hawk ridge-and-swale system (q.v.) n Kitty Hawk through e Kitty Hawk Woods 1.5 mi. e of Kitty Hawk Landing subdivision. N-s from a complex of sand ridges in Kitty Hawk Estates subdivision to Pawpaw Ridge subdivision. Everyone interviewed unaware of this name, citing Poor Ridge 0.5 mi. e as only known similar name. Complicated by Poor Ridge Landing being known originally as Paw Ridge Landing, ostensibly for a different reason and evolving through pronunciation to Poor Ridge Landing and then "Poor" becoming applied to ridge terminating at landing. Further complicated because paw paw (usual spelling) fruit, while indigenous to almost all North Carolina, is not indigenous to the Outer Banks or a portion of central e North Carolina on Pamlico Peninsula, though the fruit was known here. *Other names:* Popo Ridge (Harris 2017—recorded from mispronunciation).

Pawpaw Swamp, swamp, Dare County, Atlantic Township (Harris 2017; unknown, 1898). E-most swamp in Kitty Hawk Woods Swamps (q.v.) just e of Dancing Ridge Swamp and just w of Pawpaw Ridge, just nw of original Kitty Hawk 1.5 mi. n of Hay Point. *See* Pawpaw Ridge (ridge) and Kitty Hawk ridge-and-swale system.

Paxon Island, peninsula (often island), Carteret County, White Oak Township (Carteret County Tax Records). In original Emerald Isle protruding from Bogue Banks n into Bogue Sound just w of Yellow Hill Landing 3.5 mi. w of Indian Beach (town). Alternately a peninsula and island, latter used more. Interviews indicate no known name for this well-defined peninsula, confirmed by county GIS Office. So, owner's surname used as unofficial name.

Peach Tree Ridge, small sand ridge, 0.3 mi. long, Dare County, Hatteras Township (Brooks 2010). Soundside, trends e-w just ne of Indian Ridge halfway between Buxton (e) and Frisco (w) 1.5 mi. from each. Not remembered by folk today so exact origin unknown., though peaches will grow at the Outer Banks, not known to be cultivated there. *Other names:* Pamlico Ridge and Pamlico Ridges (increasing use, subdivision with name here).

Pea Island, former island, 8.2 mi. long, 10 ft. high, Dare County, Kinnakeet Township (USGS 2013: Oregon Inlet, Pea Island, Pea Island Overedge West). Was just n of Hatteras Island and n from New Inlet to Oregon Inlet (now an island again). Originally applied to small island nearby in Pamlico Sound and name originated from wild peas once growing in abundance on this smaller island (*see* Little Pea Island). Later, name transferred to larger barrier island (mid-1800s) from former New Inlet to Oregon Inlet. Latest closure of New Inlet was 1945, but name Pea Island prevailed since New Inlet opens and closes periodically (2011 latest opening by Hurricane Irene); mostly still open 2020 and now bridged. On occasion, Pea Island also applied on some maps as s portion Bodie Island. Major stopover for many varieties of birds migrating along Atlantic Flyway. Birds are protected and area designated Pea Island National Wildlife Refuge.

There is a newly erected sign just after crossing Basnight Bridge (spans Oregon Inlet) entering Pea Island indicating "Welcome to Hatteras Island." Seems to indicate after more than 100 years of use Pea Island no longer considered (by someone) separate use for this former and reestablished (2011) island. Specifically, New Inlet last closed 1945 connecting Pea Island to Hatteras Island, but New Inlet reopened 2011 once again, making Pea Island separate from Hatteras Island. So, strange this sign appears 2017. Pea Island National Wildlife Refuge is still named as such. The name appears on NCDOT highway maps until 1953 as Pea Island C.G.S. (Coast Guard Station), then 1954–61 without C.G.S. indicating a community; never a community here.

Other names: Bodie Island (originally s portion), Bodies Island (Kerr 1882), Body Island (Lathrop 1868), Chicamacomico Banks (historical in part), Chickannaccomac Banks (historical in part), Chihemecomet Island (D'Anville 1756), Currituck South Sand Banks (historical deeds), Dugs Island (Moll 1729 — *see* Dugs), Hartfords Ile (Henry 1860, from Raleigh expeditions 1584 — misrecording of Hertford), Hataras (historical in part), Hataras Banks (historical in part), Hatarask (White 1585), Hatteras Island (in part — much misinformed use today enhanced by sign at Basnight Bridge), Hertford Island, Hertfords Ile (1585 reference, Smith 1624, map — probable gesture to Earl of Hertford, England; most of Smith's names did not last), Hertfords Island, North Banks (historical in part), Pen Island (shipwreck records 1918), Peo (*sic*) Island (ACE 1862 — transcribing error), South Bank (Maule 1718).

Pea Island Bay, cove, 0.3 mi. wide, Dare County, Kinnakeet Township (USGS 2013: Pea Island Overedge West). In Pamlico Sound 0.2 mi. s of Pea Island Creek between Pea Island Point and Terrapin Creek Point, 8.4 mi. nnw of Rodanthe. *See* Pea Island.

Pea Island Beach, beach, Dare County, Kinnakeet Township (local use). Between New Inlet (s) and Oregon Inlet (n). Used sporadically as reference to this specific

beach when New Inlet is open (reopened 2011). Some local residents, including fishing and surfing enthusiasts, know portion of this beach as "The Boiler" (Ramp 6) since for a time wreck of *The Oriental* 1862 was visible from the beach. It was not a boiler, though resembled look of a boiler. *See* Pea Island.

Pea Island Breach. *See* New Inlet.

Pea Island Creek, cove, 0.3 mi. long, 0.05 mi. wide, Dare County, Kinnakeet Township (USGS 2013: Pea Island Overedge West). In Pamlico Sound, 7.5 mi. nnw of Rodanthe. *See* Pea Island.

Pea Island Point, point, Dare County, Kinnakeet Township (USGS 2013: Pea Island Overedge West). N point at Pea Island Bay 8.6 mi. nnw of Rodanthe. *See* Pea Island.

Pear Pad, area, Dare County, Nags Head Township (signage). Undefined and amorphous area generally n of Fort Raleigh on n Roanoke Island where prickly pear cactus (*Opuntia* sp.) grows, which has pear-shaped fruit.

Pebble Beach, beach, Carteret County, White Oak Township (local use). At Pebble Beach subdivision, 6.5 mi. w of original Emerald Isle. Reversed usage, natural feature acquiring name of man-made feature.

Pebble Shoals, shoals, Currituck County, Fruitville Township (NOS charts). In Atlantic Ocean just e of Currituck Banks near North Carolina–Virginia boundary.

Peeles Landing, former area, Dare County, Hatteras Township (Howard, April 21, 2014). On Hatteras Island just beyond Hatteras (village) near ferry landing today. Ferry (3 or 4 cars) operated 1950s; landing was makeshift and none existed on Ocracoke side forcing vehicles occasionally to land in inches of water. Also, ferry service to and from Engelhard (mainland) from 1940 to 1952.

Pelican Canal, small canal, Dare County, Atlantic Township (Town of Southern Shores 2015). In Southern Shores leading into Jeanguite Creek 4.7 mi. n of original Kitty Hawk. Names of Southern Shores canals are for shorebirds (except Gravey Pond Canal). The brown pelican (*Pelecanus occidentalis*) here year-round.

Pelican Point, point, Carteret County, Morehead Township (local use). Ne Beacons Reach 0.5 mi. ene of Westport Marina, 2 mi. w of Pine Knoll Shores. *See* Pelican Canal. Subdivision named for feature.

Pelican Shoal, shoal, 0.2 mi. long, 0.5 mi. wide, Hyde County, Ocracoke Township; and Dare County, Hatteras Township (USGS 2013: Green Island). In Hatteras Inlet, 3.9 mi. wsw of Hatteras (village). *See* Pelican Canal. *Other names:* Pelican Island (O'Neal et al. 1976, 64).

Penguin Islands, islands, Dare County, Nags Head Township (Fulton 1820). Two islands (sometimes three) in Roanoke Sound just n of The Causeway, 1 mi. nw of Whalebone Junction. Big Penguin Island, Little Penguin Island, sometimes Nags Head Island, and other small marsh islands (when exposed) were historically referred to as Penguin Islands. Name used on several early maps but origin is apparently lost or more likely never was known (locally). Appears first on Fulton (1820) as Penguins Islands, suggesting perhaps surname by making it possessive. Penguin does exist as a surname but very rare. No known individuals here with surname but could have been from a seaman visiting—pure speculation. A former restaurant nearby (the islands) was named Penguin Isle (so name was apparently known), but no use of name using "isle" found in any documentation or on any map, so a marketing technique.

Possible the islands (Big Penguin and Little Penguin) were named because the shape(s) resembled a penguin. Viewed from above and obliquely, one might be able to force such a resemblance, especially Big Penguin. No documentation regarding this possible reason for naming.

Scores of people, including local officials, fisherman, old-time residents, etc., have been interviewed, and without exception no one has any idea of name origin, nor are younger folk aware of the name. Labeled on maps since 1820 (Fulton 1820), and islands shown on earlier maps, but since these earlier maps were small scale (showed little detail), islands were not labeled.

A possible explanation, completely speculative because no documentation nor local knowledge found: The now extinct great auk (*Pinguinus impennis*) was as large as many penguins today and existed until mid-18th century. The great auk not related to penguins of s hemisphere, but those penguins were named "penguin" for their resemblance to the great auk. Not likely any great auks encountered here by seamen since these islands were apparently not named until early 1800s, and former range of the great auk was no farther s than approx. Maine. Still, one might speculate or presume the islands were named because seamen must have seen birds on these islands appearing to be penguins or perhaps reminded seamen of great auks, though penguins are found no farther n than the s limits of Africa and Australia, and w coast of South America. The only penguin n of s regions is the Galapagos penguin on those islands (at the equator). However, seamen known in 18th and early 19th centuries to consider penguins to be in the auk family by similar appearance, though they are not. One species of auk, the Atlantic puffin (*Fratercula arctica*), is prevalent in winter as far s as the Chesapeake Bay, sometimes n Outer Banks (Currituck County), possibly occasionally as far s as Oregon Inlet. So, entirely possible (especially early 19th century), seamen noticed Atlantic puffins here and referred to them as penguins—purely speculative.

Other names: Peguin Island (CS 1862b—probable typographical error), Pengun Island (C&GS 1895a), Penguins Islands (Fulton 1820).

Peninsula, The, man-enhanced, Dare County, Nags Head Township (local use). In Manteo 3.5 mi. w of Whalebone Junction. Stabilized and enhanced for development of subdivision (named The Peninsula).

Pennys Hill, distinct sand dune, 70 ft. high, Currituck County, Fruitville Township (USGS 2013: Corolla—labeled Luark Hill). On Currituck Banks 3.7 mi. nnw of Corolla, 2 mi. sse of remnants New Currituck Inlet (USGS 2013: Corolla—labeled Old Currituck Inlet). Pennys Hill, originally just n of Luark Hill, latter (in different forms) surname prevalent here, but changeable nature of these dunes often causes dune movement and name application sometimes moves with the sand dune. While the location varies, Pennys Hill was originally 1–1.5 mi. n of its present location (also known as Luark Hill); only remnants remain at that location. Over the past 35 years the dune has moved s about 1–1.5 mi., merging with and overtaking Luark Hill, and name Pennys Hill moved with the feature. Today, if one asks, both Luark Hill and Pennys Hill are given as names for this large dune. Luark Hill is given from older residents, though hikers from outside often use Luark Hill since still shown as Luark Hill on USGS 2013: Corolla, but most today use Pennys Hill. Surrounding land is still known as the Lewark Tract (note spelling—disputed property). Also, while still substantial, is less than half of its original size. The name is from the daughter of original land owner. S migration of Pennys Hill has covered completely any evidence of former Seagull village (q.v.). Used since 1786 (Currituck DB 5, 1786, 139) at local locations. Subdivision named for feature. *Other names:* Dunton Hill (Cram and Worret 1861), Lewark Hill (local surname), Lewarks Hill (Sandbeck, 6), Luark Hill (USGS 2013: Corolla), Penney Hill (occasional scientific reports), Penneys Hill, Penny Hill (CS 1852, occasional current and historical local use), Sand Hill (Mouzon 1775).

Pennys Hill. *See* Seagull.

Penny Toler Ditch, canal, Dare County, Atlantic Township (Census Block Maps and signage). Canalized stream trends s 3.7 mi. into North Cove just s of original Kitty Hawk. The Kitty Hawk zoning map (Town of Kitty Hawk 2007) applies name to a much smaller stream just w of this application, and local use apparently is for *both* applications. S portion coincides, in part, with colonial application of Mill Point Gut.

Perch Beach. *See* Whalehead Beach (subdivision).

Perch Creek, tidal stream, 1 mi. long, Currituck County, Fruitville Township (Cox 1923). Large and tidal for w half portion, with e half being small and more stream-like. E portion begins less than 0.5 mi. from oceanside, and w portion is at e head of North Channel remnant of New Currituck Inlet 4.5 mi. se of Knotts Island (village). *See* Big Perch Island.

Perch Creek, small water passage, Dare County, Atlantic Township (Town of Kitty Hawk 2007). On ne end Stone Island, occasionally passes through to sw end at Kitty Hawk Bay, 2 mi. sw of original Kitty Hawk. *See* Big Perch Island.

Perch Island Bay, cove, 0.5 mi. across, Currituck County, Fruitville Township (Cox 1906). Open water within maze of marsh islands 2.5 mi. ne of Knotts Island (village). Usage is singular, though feature is just e of Big Perch Island one of three islands together named Perch Islands. *See* Big Perch Island.

Perch Island Number 1, small island, Currituck County, Fruitville Township (Cox 1906). Smallest of three islands in Perch Islands, most s just nw of n entrance Deep Creek, 2.5 mi. ne of Knotts Island (village). *See* Big Perch Island and Perch Islands.

Perch Islands, three islands, Currituck County, Fruitville Township (Cox 1906). In maze of marsh islands: Big Perch Island, Little Perch Island, and Perch Island Number 1, 1 mi. ne of Knotts Island (village). Each island has been referenced as Perch Island Number 1, Perch Island Number 2, and Perch Island Number 3. The largest (Perch Island Number 2) became known locally as Big Perch Island, and Perch Island Number 3 by comparison became Little Perch Island, but Perch Island Number 1, smallest, did not acquire any comparative name, perhaps because reference would be cumbersome or perhaps usage was not as widespread. *See* Big Perch Island.

Perch Pond, lake, 0.1 mi. across, Currituck County, Poplar Branch Township (USGS 2013: Mossey Islands). On unnamed marsh island just n of Gaffey (*sic*) Landing, 8.2 mi. sw of Corolla. *See* Big Perch Island.

Percys Landing, former landing, Dare County, Kinnakeet Township (Garrity-Blake 2010, 493). Soundside just n of Phipps Cove, 7.5 mi. s of Salvo. Individual for whom named fished mainly at Gull Shoal and processed fish here, hence variant Percys Net Rack. Local reports indicated there were so many snakes in summer it acquired name Snake Pit Landing. *Other names:* Percys Net Hang (Covey 2018, 13), Percys Net Rack (NPS 2005b: NPS 1, 154), Snake Pit Landing (NPS 2005b: NPS 1, 154).

Perry Ridge, sand ridge, Dare County, Atlantic Township (local use). In Kitty Hawk ridge-and-swale system (q.v.) just e of Jeanguite Creek, 1 mi. n of Perry Ridge Landing, 1 mi. wsw of original Kitty Hawk.

Perry Ridge Landing, landing, Dare County, Atlantic Township (local use). Terminus Bob Perry Road, 1.2 mi. sw of original Kitty Hawk. Occasionally confused with Poor Ridge Landing (1.1 mi. e) from similar sound, but are two distinctly named landings and ridges.

Perrys Island, former island, Carteret County, Beaufort and Morehead Townships (C&GS 1889b). Was in Beaufort Inlet, 1.8 mi. s of Beaufort (mainland). Disappeared early 20th century.

Persimmon Hole, small cove, Currituck County,

Poplar Branch Township (C&GS 1852). Is 1.5 mi. s of Three Dunes, 5.3 mi. s of Corolla.

Persimmon Branch, stream, Dare County, Nags Head Township (local use). Just se of Weir Point and Alder Branch, 3.2 mi. wnw of Manteo (center). *Other names:* Posimon Tree Branch (Currituck DB 1763, Miscellaneous, 39–40).

Peters Ditch, canal, 4.5 mi. long, Dare County, Hatteras Township (Mallin, NPS 2006, 21). Drainage ditch e-w across broad part Cape Hatteras from 0.3 mi. e of oceanside shoreline just s of mouth Cape Creek to Pamlico Sound 0.7 mi. se of Brigands Bay. Peters Ditch drains n Buxton Woods into Pamlico Sound at Frisco (Mallin et al. 2006, 21). Name not well known locally. Also, should not be confused with Peters Ditch, entrance Avon Harbor at original Avon 6 mi. n of e terminus of this feature, also named Peters Ditch. *Other names:* Saint Peters Ditch (NPS 2006a 5).

Peters Ditch, tidal stream, originally 0.5 mi. long, Dare County, Kinnakeet Township (USGS 2013: Buxton). In Pamlico Sound 0.3 mi. w of original Avon 7.3 mi. n of Cape Hatteras. Now entrance Avon Harbor extending a bit inland. Originally, known locally as simply The Creek and divided Cat Ridge (n) from Dog Ridge (s) (*see* Avon). Not to be confused with Peters Ditch at Cape Hatteras. *Other names:* Avon Harbor (some local use, "appears better than ditch"), Scarboro Harbor (historical), Scarborough Harbor (both variant spellings used historically referring to Peters Ditch or occasionally Avon Harbor, though historical Scarboro or Scarborough settlement was 1 mi. n of here), The Creek (historical local use).

Peters Marsh, marsh island, Currituck County, Poplar Branch Township (C&GS 1852). Is 1 mi. se of Poyners Hill, 8.3 mi. s of Corolla. *See* Peters Quarter Marsh and Peters Quarter.

Peters Quarter, historical area, Currituck County, Poplar Branch Township. Soundside Currituck Banks, 2.6 mi. s of Corolla. Variant name Brocks in some local use early 20th century applying to older area using name Peters Quarter. In 15th through early 18th centuries, common practice to name large undefined areas based on four quarters of the compass, and later "quarter" became reference to a specific region or place. This early usage for "quarter" here uncharacteristic because "quarter" is usually a reference to large undefined area; probably indicated portion of larger tract mostly on mainland. *See also* Hunting Quarter and Hog Quarter Flats. *Other names:* Brocks (Codman, Crowninshield, and Lawrence 1925), Peter Quarter (CS 1852; Currituck DB 6, 1789, 94), Peters Guater (misinterpretation or misrecording), Peters Quarters (misnomer).

Peters Quarter Creek. *See* Great Beach Pond.

Peters Quarter Marsh, marsh, Currituck County, Poplar Branch Township (Currituck DB 22, 1840, 369–70; Codman, Crowninshield, and Lawrence 1925). Just se of Great Beach Pond at n end soundside in Peters Quarter (q.v.), 2 mi. s of Corolla. Now contains large man-made, apparently unnamed lake. Not to be confused with Peters Marsh, 10 mi. s of here. Possibly originally name was one reference to one feature but became confused application late 19th century, and now these are two differently named features. *See* Hunting Quarter.

Pettartory Hill, sand hill, Carteret County, Portsmouth Township (Stick 1958, 308). Was three sand dunes covered with vegetation (today dunes merged into two dunes) on back-of-the-beach side of Pilontary Islands at n limit North Core Banks just s of Swash Inlet, 10 mi. sw of Portsmouth (village). One of the many spellings of Pilontary (most common spelling on the Outer Banks) or specifically plants of pellitory family (*Parietaria* spp.). *See* Pilontary Islands.

Pettys Creek. *See* Straight Creek.

Pettys Point, distinct point, Currituck County, Poplar Branch Township (local use). N point on elongated marsh 1 mi. n of Pettys Pond, 5.2 mi. nw of Duck. Evidence suggests original name was Poteets Point, reported surname of local resident was Poteet, and name changed through recording or pronunciation error to Petty. *Other names:* Potteets Point (C&GS 1852).

Pettys Pond, lake, 0.3 mi. long, 0.05 mi. wide, Currituck County, Poplar Branch Township (USGS 2013: Jarvisburg). In marsh between Pine Island Bay and Currituck Banks, 5.7 mi. n of Duck. *See* Pettys Point. *Other names:* Prettys Pond (recording error), Potteets Pond (C&GS 1852).

Pettys Pond Cove, cove, 0.2 mi. wide, Currituck

County, Poplar Branch Township (USGS 2013: Jarvisburg). At Great Gap, 5.5 mi. nnw of Duck. *See* Pettys Point. *Other names:* Potteets Pond Cove (C&GS 1852).

Pettys Pond Point, point, Currituck County, Poplar Branch Township (local use). Sw point of small marsh island in marsh islands from Pettys Pond, 2.5 mi. sw of Pine Island subdivision, 5 mi. nnw of Duck. *See* Pettys Point. *Other names:* Sprig Point (previous local map usage).

Phipps Cove, cove, 0.2 mi. long and wide, Dare County, Kinnakeet Township (USGS 2013: Little Kinnakeet). In Pamlico Sound 5.9 mi. n of original Avon.

Phipps Haulover, low flat, Dare County, Kinnakeet Township (Garrity-Blake 2010, 494). Beach just n of Kite Point, 2.5 mi. n of Buxton. Active overwash, swash, and former inlets. Historically, an active place for hauling boats from oceanside to soundside because of its vulnerability to overwash. Now, this activity is no longer done, hence variant Old Overhaul. Former Phipps Hunt Club here. *See* Haulover Point. *Other names:* Old Haulover (original name), The Haulover (recent).

Phoebe Ann Ridge, former small sand ridge, Dare County, Kinnakeet Township (local informants). Was just e of Aunt Phoebes Marsh (probably) 1.7 mi. s of Rodanthe. According to some older residents, name known or recalled but exact location unknown or not remembered. Some say sand ridge was near Aunt Phoebes Marsh (q.v.), but might be by presumed association; unknown if these two features using the specific name Phoebe indicate same person. Name Aunt Phoebes Marsh disappeared from maps by mid-1980s and Phoebe Ann Ridge never appeared on maps. An extremely small and short sand ridge was just e of Aunt Phoebes Marsh until mid-1980s, when it disappeared from development. Ridge only 0.2 mi. long and no more than 10 ft. high. Obvious spoken similarity between "Ann" and "aunt," which could have been misheard by field crews from mapmaking teams— pure speculation.

Picket Windmill, former windmill, Dare County, Hatteras Township (Johnson sketch from Howard, January 21, 2013). Implied location near former Camp Winfield (Civil War picket area), which is in Hatteras village just north of Durants (historical and clustered area), which might have had a windmill, but no evidence has been found. *Other names:* Hatteras Windmill (Howard, January 21, 2013).

Piggott Dock, former small landing, Carteret County, Portsmouth Township (NPS 2018, 135). Was at Henry Piggott house in n-central Portsmouth (main village) on n shore Doctors Creek 0.1 mi. from Ocracoke Inlet. In disrepair but still visible as late as 1976.

Pig Island, former small island, Currituck County, Poplar Branch Township (C&GS 1852). Was in Beasley Bay just w of North Hog Island, 6.2 mi. s of Corolla. Was between North Hog Island and Bush Island (Bull Island), now joined with North Hog Island though occasionally awash. *See* Hog Islands complex.

Pilentary Clubhouse Inlet. *See* Drum Inlet and Swash Inlet.

Piliauga Creek, tidal stream, Carteret County, Portsmouth Township (C&GS 1866 and NPS, map, 27 and 28, 2007). Just sw of Sheep Island, just w of The Haulover, 1.5 mi. sw of former Portsmouth (village). Name and meaning are unknown by anyone interviewed (even its existence). Appears on chart C&GS (1866) and site history map in NPS (2007). No additional information provided regarding this name from NPS (2007). "Auga" could, of course, be local corruption of *agua*, Spanish meaning water, but why Spanish here unknown. Also, *auga* is old German or old Scandinavian meaning eye, but this is far-fetched for this application and not relevant. The prefix "pili" could, of course, refer to pellitory (*Parietaria* spp.; many spelling variations used on the Outer Banks), a plant plentiful on the Outer Banks here (Pilontary Islands [q.v.] 6 mi. sw), used locally for medicinal purposes.

Orthography and actual meaning is dialectical form of "periagua" or "periauger" (correct term, Dunbar 1958, 140), flat-bottomed boat that worked well here (sometimes term "swampboat" used in swamps of the se). The "auga" suffix might be plausible based on a phonetic rendering of "periauger." French version still used today in Louisiana as "pirogue," clearly a misrecording of "piliagua" a corruption of "periauger," and Spanish corruption of *pirau* (transcribed) from Carib, an indigenous Caribbean language, meaning dugout canoe-like boat. Used on the Outer Banks in colonial period, but this is only known occurrence on the namescape. Probably other features named using a version of "periauger," but used very early and just not recorded, thereby falling into disuse. Preliminary to "periagua" or "periauger" was "kunner or cooner (probably a corruption of canoe)," a later version of a split-log canoe evolving into the shad boat. Term is not usually encountered past colonial period on the Outer Banks (except Bogue Banks—see Bogue Banks historical communities) or especially after Civil War because shad boat is later local invention (Roanoke Island) for fishing and navigating shallow waters of sounds (occasionally encountered in Wanchese into late 1800s—Gray 2009, 24, mentions sailing across Roanoke Sound in a "kunner" in this time period). Shad boat developed by George Washington Creef 1870s and based on design of periaugers, but vastly improved and popular from Roanoke Island to Ocracoke. Byrd (1728, 11–15, 17) does refer to their boats as "periaguas," when they were first traveling w through sounds and marshes. Periauga (spelling) used on page 13. So, "piriagua" was known and had some use, and known to be used throughout sounds and creeks of the Outer Banks. However, this is only known occurrence in the namescape, and "cooner" and "kunner" are not found in any names. Explanation for lack of names using "piriagua" is probably early use not recorded, and use in remote areas. *Other names:* The Haulover (USGS 2013: Portsmouth—mislabeling on tidal creek instead of actual "haulover"—*see* Haulover Point), Three Hats Creek (19th century—most usage was for channel in Core Sound approaching High Hills Inlet from Three Hats Shoal q.v.).

Pilontary Creek, cove, 0.1 mi. wide, Hyde County, Ocracoke Township (USGS 2013: Green Island). In Pamlico Sound just e of Cockrel Creek Island, 13 mi. ne of Ocracoke (village). *See* Pilontary Islands. *Other names:* Pilinterry Creek (Weslager 1954, 48).

Pilontary Islands, marsh islands, 0.6 mi. wide, Carteret County, Portsmouth Township (USGS 2013: Wainwright Island). In Core Sound 8.4 mi. sw of Portsmouth (village). Corruption of "pellitory," an irritant and salivant from plants in the nettle family (*Parietaria* spp.). From Latin term *parietaria*, meaning wall plant, native worldwide, with a variation applied on the Outer Banks. "Pellitory" or "pilontary" (Outer Banks pronunciation) commonly found on the Outer Banks and was used as herb medicine 17th, 18th, and 19th centuries, primarily as a sedative and to induce vomiting. These islands were named for large numbers of plants found here. Interestingly, variant Aromas Keck Marshes was most likely not an applied name but merely a descriptor labeled on Ogilby's map (Ogilby and Moxon 1671) since "aromas keck" was a reference of the time to disgusting and noxious odor (originally from vomiting); labeled just sw of Portsmouth Island, it presumably referenced Pilontary Islands, which historically contained many of these plants. Hunt club here into early 20th century. *Other names:* Aromas Keck Marshes (Ogilby 1671), Peltatory Hill, Pettartory Hill (Stick 1958, 308), Pilentary (Williamson 1992, 155), Pilontary Hills (local use), The Pilentaries (White 2012, 55), Pilontary Island (Whisnant and Whisnant 2010, map, 490), The Pilintaries (Williamson 1992, 155).

Pilontary Marsh, marsh, Currituck County, Poplar Branch Township (unknown, ca. 1900). Nw North Burris Island in Burris Islands complex, 6.8 mi. s of Corolla. Though used throughout the Outer Banks, term and the plant are more prevalent s of Oregon Inlet. *See* Pilontary Islands.

Pilot Town. *See* Ocracoke.

Pine Creek, former stream, Dare County, Atlantic Township (deeds 1719). In Southern Shores along e shore Jeanguite Creek beginning in small pond flowing s to Jeanguite Creek 1 mi. n of Mallard Cove, 4 mi. s of Duck. No longer used as the stream has been canalized and named Great Blue Heron Canal (q.v.) in Southern Shores canal system, where canal names theme is for shorebirds (except Gravey Pond Canal). *Other names:* Slipery Pine Branch (Currituck DB 4, 1782, 131), Slipperepine Branch (Currituck DB 7, 1795, 237—spelling not standardized until 1830s), Slipper Pine Branch (Currituck DB 7, 1792, 238), Slippery Pine Branch (Currituck DB 4, 1783, 131).

Pine Hill, small hill, Dare County, Atlantic Township (local use). In Kitty Hawk just s of Martin Point, 1.5 mi. sw of Southern Shores. Subdivision named for feature.

Pine Hills, sand dunes, Currituck County, Fruitville Township (local use). Eight dunes 2 mi. n of former New Currituck Inlet (South Channel), 3 mi. n of Swan Beach. Sometimes largest known singularly as Pine Hill.

Pine Island, island, Currituck County, Poplar Branch Township (local use). Largest island in Pine Islands (q.v.) complex 1 mi. w of Pine Island Airport, 6.5 mi. nw of Duck. Pine Island known as Palmer Island (on a few maps for short time), and Pine Island Club (hunting club) here known as The Palmer Club until around 1910, when the club name was changed to Pine Island Club to agree with usage for name of island where located. Short usage for Palmer Island is source for name of Palmers (*sic*) Island subdivision 2 mi. s. Two subdivisions named for feature. *Other names:* Palmer Island (sketchy records), Palmers Island (sketchy records, subdivision using name), Piney Island (Currituck DB 21, 1836, 224), Poiney Island (Currituck DB 3, 1803, 437), Poyne Island (Currituck DB 12, 1814, 333–34), Poyney Island (Currituck DB 12, 1814, 333–34), South Pine Island (historical use), South Piney Island (C&GS 1852).

Pine Island Bay, bay, 0.5 mi. across, Currituck County, Poplar Branch Township (USGS 2013: Jarvisburg). In Currituck Sound, 1.4 mi. e of Currituck Banks, 5.9 mi. nw of Duck.

Pine Island Lead, narrow water passage, 0.5 mi. long, Currituck County, Poplar Branch Township (USGS 2013: Mossey Islands; USGS 1982: Jarvisburg). In Currituck Sound through thick marsh just e of Goat Island Bay at Currituck Banks, 7 mi. nw of Duck. *See* Buzzard Lead. *Other names:* Island Lead (local usage), Thoroughfare (C&GS 1852).

Pine Island Marshes, marsh, Currituck County, Poplar Branch Township (local use). Amorphous marsh area in Pine Island area just w and nw of Pine Island Airport and Pine Island Audubon Sanctuary surrounded by Baums Creek and Pine Island Lead, 6.5 mi. n of Duck (village center).

Pine Islands, marsh island complex, 4 mi. long, 2 mi. wide, Currituck County, Poplar Branch Township (local use). Marsh islands in Currituck Sound, 6.4 mi. nw of Duck. Complex of numerous (nearly 100) named and unnamed islands and marshes. *Other names:* Pine Island (Sorrie 2014, 34; local use), South Piney Island (C&GS 1852).

Pine Island Sanctuary Dock, dock, Currituck County, Poplar Branch Township (Audubon website). Boat facility at Pine Island Audubon Sanctuary 7 mi. n of Duck (center).

Pine Island Swamps, swamp, Currituck County, Poplar Branch Township (local use). Within Pine Island Marshes, dense boggy area especially in summer, 6.5 mi. n of Duck (village center).

Pine Knoll Shores, town, Carteret County, Morehead Township (signage). On Bogue Banks just e of Hoop Pole Woods 3.4 mi. w of Atlantic Beach (town). Part was originally platted and marketed as Aibonito (q.v.; central and w parts). Alice Hoffman purchased large tract here after visiting 1918 and moved here full-time early 1940s. She was successful in having post office est. (at her house) 1919 (closed 1926) named Bogue Banks Post Office. She was married to Theodore Roosevelt's eldest son, Theodore Roosevelt Jr., so on her death land was left to her Roosevelt heirs, who were involved with development of Pine Knoll Shores originally as subdivision (name first announced 1954 regarding disposition of the Roosevelt property). Most of Pine Knoll Shores was developed from Alice Hoffman's estate in mid-1950s (wealth of information presented on this topic online and conventionally). Original plat of Pine Knoll Shores is e portion. Name reportedly invented (devised) by Pete Rempe when meeting with the Roosevelts (heirs of Alice Hoffman) to begin development (PKS 2016). No evidence exists there was ever a specific feature known as Pine Knoll, further corroborated by indication name was put forth by Rempe. A maritime forest was here before extensive development with numerous sand hillocks and stands of pines. Chartered by state legislature 1973, incorporated 1973. *Other names:* Bogue Banks (used sparingly early 20th century here before Pine Knoll Shores established because post office est. 1919 in Alice Hoffman's house; she listed Bogue Banks as one of her two places of residence—other was Paris, France), Isle of Pines (historical and originally used by John A. Royall (*sic*), who early 20th century bought property on Bogue Banks now part of Pine Knoll Shores; also name of Alice Hoffman's estate), Isle of the Pines (Stanford 2015, 74), Old Pine Knoll Shores (PKS 2016—e part, e of Pine Knoll Waterway),

Pine Bluff Knoll (PKS—local Chamber of Commerce Announcement, 1950s), Pine Bluff Knolls (PKS—local Chamber of Commerce Announcement, 1950s), Pine Grove Farm (in part—Alice Hoffman's dairy farm; PKS 2016), Pine Knoll Shore (Deaton et al. 2012, 410, map—typographical error), Pinewood Knoll (PKS—1950s unidentified "tourist map"), Pine Wood Shores (reported in PKS 2016 as appearing on a 1940 army map, not verified).

Pine Knoll Shores Beach, beach, 1.5 mi. long, Carteret County, Morehead Township (local use). Oceanside directly opposite Pine Knoll Shores 4.5 mi. w of Atlantic Beach (town). Came into some usage when Pine Knoll Shores est. 1950s; not used much today. *See* Pine Knoll Shores.

Pine Knoll Waterway, canal, Carteret County, Morehead Township (PKS 2016). From e entrance in semicircle through central and w portion Pine Knoll Shores to w entrance; center 3.7 mi. w of Atlantic Beach (town). Built to complement development of Pine Knoll Shores. Project was two phases; first completed 1968 and extended from McNeill Inlet, e entrance to bridge (built 1972) carrying Mimosa Boulevard. W section completed 1971 from Hoffman Inlet, w entrance, to Mimosa Boulevard, still a roadway then. The bridge carrying Mimosa Boulevard completed 1972 allowing water in two canal sections to connect and circulate. *Other names:* Pine Knoll Waterways (some use because e and w sections built at different times), The Big Canal (local use), The Canal (occasional use).

Pine Ridge, vegetated sand ridge, Currituck County, Poplar Branch Township (local use). Just w of Pine Island Airport just e of South Pine Island, 5.5 mi. n of Duck (center). For profusion of pines (originally) and related to numerous names here containing term "pine." Altered by building Pine Island Airport. *Other names:* Bee Ridge (origin unknown, couple of those interviewed "recollect" hearing the name).

Pines, The, area, Carteret County, Harkers Island Township (NPS, 2004b, map 1907, 55). Pine trees just ne of Cape Lookout Lighthouse, 1.5 mi. e of Power Squadron Spit, 6 mi. se of Harkers Island (village). Referent in contrast to general lack of vegetation here. *Other names:* Ring of Pines (NPS 2006a).

Piney Bank, small marsh island, Currituck County, Poplar Branch Township (C&GS 1852). Just s of North Piney Island 0.5 mi. sw of Piney Cove, 7 mi. s of Corolla. Unusual use of generic term "bank" but might signify position in relation to North Piney Island, specifically a barrier. Geographic names on this poorly aged chart (C&GS 1852) are handwritten; some including this name are slightly blurred.

Piney Cove, cove, 0.3 mi. long, 0.2 mi. wide, Currituck County, Poplar Branch Township. In marsh soundside Currituck Banks, 0.8 mi. ssw of Three Dunes, 5.8 mi. s of Corolla.

Piney Creek, former cove, Carteret County, White Oak Township. Was in Bogue Sound at Piney Island 15.7 mi. w of Atlantic Beach (town). Name Piney Creek often confused with Archer Creek (q.v.) short distance away at Bogue Banks.

Piney Island, island, 0.2 mi. long, Carteret County, White Oak Township (local use). In Bogue Sound 6.7 mi. ese of Swansboro (mainland). Name appears in deeds as early as 1836. *Other names:* Pine Island (USGS 1948: Swansboro 1:62,500 scale).

Piney Island. *See* Bean Island.

Piney Island Creek. *See* Archer Creek.

Piney Point, point, Carteret County, Morehead Township (Rivers and Ball 1955). Soundside in e section Indian Beach (town) just e of Salter Path, 4.5 mi. w of Pine Knoll Shores. Powell (2010) infers small settlement here, not mentioned other sources; probably Hopey Anns Hill (q.v.).

Piney Point, point, Carteret County, White Oak Township (local use). On Piney Island, 15.6 mi. w of Atlantic Beach (town).

Piney Point, point, Currituck County, Poplar Branch Township (signage). Between Baum Creek and Longfellow Cove 0.3 mi. e of Pine Island, 5.7 mi. n of Duck (center). *Other names:* Pine Island Point (local use), Pine Point (some use).

Piney Point. *See* Archer Point.

Piney Point Shoal, former shoal, Carteret County, Davis Township (U.S. Congress 1876, 25). Was in central Core Sound just off Piney Point (mainland) 3 mi. s of Stacy (mainland). Remnants are Big Island and Salters Lump (q.v.).

Piney Ridge, remnant larger sand ridge, Dare County, Hatteras Township (signage). Is 1.5 mi. nw of Creeds Hill, 2 mi. w of Frisco. *Other names:* Pine Ridge (sometimes used).

Piney Swamp, swamp, Dare County, Atlantic Township (local use). In ne corner Kitty Hawk Woods just s of s entrance Southern Shores 2 mi. n of original Kitty Hawk. Still large but reduced by development. *Other names:* Viney Swamp (Angley 1995, 11—Angley prefers this name but acknowledges Piney Swamp).

Piney Woods Landing, former landing, Dare County, Kinnakeet Township (Currituck DB 9, 1805, 101–2). Was somewhere on Hatteras Island apparently at Cape Hatteras (by description), likely somewhere in Buxton. Name not encountered elsewhere. *Other names:* Poiney Woods Landing (Currituck DB 9, 1805, 101–2).

Pingleton Shoal, shoal, 1 mi. long, Hyde County, Lake Landing Township (NOS 2014b). In Pamlico Sound trending nw-se from mainland just s of mouth Long Shoal River, 23.5 mi. w of Rodanthe. *Other names:* Pilkinsons Shoal (CS 1862a).

Pin Hill, small sand dune, Dare County, Nags Head Township (Stick 1958, 264). In Jockeys Ridge complex just n of Engagement Hill just sw of main part Jockeys Ridge, 1.5 mi. w of Nags Head (center). Some have placed the hill as the larger dune just sw of Hotel Hill; small road named Pin Hill Court is 0.3 mi. nw. Reportedly named for thousands of straight pins found there, but no documentation supports this story.

Piper Hill, sand dune, Currituck County, Poplar Branch Township (USGS 2013: Mossey Islands). On s Currituck Banks 7 mi. s of Corolla. Not nearly as prominent or stable as during 19th century. *Other names:* Pipers Hill (C&GS 1879).

Pirates Cove, man-enhanced, Dare County, Nags Head Township (signage). At Pirates Cove Marina 1 mi. se of Shallowbag Bay, 2 mi. ese of Manteo (center).

Pirates Cove, subdivision, Dare County, Nags Head Township (signage). In Manteo just n of where Washington Baum Bridge (Roanoke Sound Bridge) enters Roanoke Island 2 mi. wsw of Manteo (center—now part of Town of Manteo). Pirates Cove (originally subdivision since 1987) composed of numerous sections with signage: Ballast Point (q.v.; point); Ballast Point Villas; Buccaneer Village; Gulf Stream Village; Hammock Village (*see* The Hammock and Black Hammock); Harbour Place (note spelling); Rudder Village; Sailfish Point

(q.v.); Sailfish Point Villas; Sextant Village; Spinnaker Village; and Village Landing(s) (PC HOA 2016). Each canal named, though sections of one continuous canal named for subdivisions within Pirates Cove. Each has a separate entry in this volume: Ballast Point Canal, Buccaneer Canal, Hammock Canal, Rudder Canal, Sailfish Canal, Sextant Canal, and Spinnaker Canal. *See also* Canals at Pirates Cove.

Pirates Cove Marina, harbor, Dare County, Nags Head Township (signage). In Pirates Cove 2 mi. ese of Manteo (center).

Pivers Island, island, 0.3 mi. long, 0.1 mi. wide, in Carteret County, Beaufort Township (USGS 2013: Beaufort). Just w of Beaufort (mainland) 3 mi. e of Morehead City (mainland). Piver, surname here. *Other names:* Piver Island (C&GS 1938).

Plains, The, flat sandy area, 2 mi. long, Hyde County, Ocracoke Township (USGS 2013: Ocracoke). S end Ocracoke (village) e to NPS campground. Derived from extreme flatness and pure white sand found there (often inundated with standing water). Historically applied to sw tip Ocracoke Island just ne of Ocracoke Inlet on some charts mid-19th century. Perhaps misapplication of current position, or name was applied historically to much larger area (ne of Ocracoke village to Ocracoke Inlet), or name moved application. Likely applied historically to larger area with similar topography (CS 1857b) until intervention by NPS. Devoid of plants and dunes—flat as were barrier islands from Oregon Inlet to Ocracoke Inlet. Were periods of large moving dunes naturally, and also many dunes were built or enhanced by WPA and CCC during period of recovery after the Great Depression (1930s). Current application locally and on USGS 2013: Ocracoke is between s side Ocracoke (village) and NPS campground.

Platt Shoals, shoals 5.5 mi. long, Dare County, Kinnakeet Township (NOS charts). In Atlantic Ocean 3.7 mi. e of Oregon Inlet.

Plover Pond, cove, Currituck County, Fruitville Township (Cox 1923). Surrounded e and s by Middle Marsh n by North Marsh open water w, 3 mi. se of Knotts Island (village). Named for plovers (birds in order Charadriiformes) frequenting here in winter. Only two species of plover visit in winter stopovers, but since historically a fowl hunting area, name seems to fit. *See* Adams Pond. *Other names:* Blubber Pond (some references, but Plover is preferred—*see* Blubber Islands).

Plum Orchard, woods, Carteret County, White Oak Township (CS 1852). Was on Bogue Banks, 1.5 mi. w of Archer Point 4.8 mi. ese of Swansboro (mainland). Became a reference from plum tree grove here.

Point, The, point, Carteret County, White Oak Township (local use). Extreme sw point Bogue Banks with broad beach from deposition by littoral drift (sand traveling parallel to shore), 9 mi. wsw of original Emerald Isle. Subdivision named for feature. *Other names:* Bogue Inlet Point (PKS 2016), Point Emerald (recent use from subdivision), The Pointe (F&WS 2002, 59—unusual use, might be misprint because federal agencies rarely use fanciful spellings from 17th century unless official).

Point, The, point, Dare County, Nags Head Township (local use). In Shallowbag Bay subdivision in Manteo, 1 mi. sw of Ballast Point, 4 mi. w of Whalebone Junction.

Point Bacon, former barrier spit, Currituck County, Fruitville Township (Smith 1624). S from Cape Henry, Virginia, to former Currituck Inlet included a portion of n Currituck Banks. Appeared only on Smith's 1624 map, and probably named for Sir Francis Bacon, whom Smith was trying to impress (though Bacon died two years later). Common practice 17th- and 18th-century Age of Exploration was to name features for prospective sponsors to gain favor and backing. Name lasted only short while and was never really applied on any other maps. Barely possible it could be surname here, but not likely this early (1624) and assuredly has no relationship to Bacon's Castle plantation in nearby Surry, Virginia, which acquired its name when owner (Allen) was evicted by Nathaniel Bacon and his men during Bacon's Rebellion (1676), all of which occurred over 50 years after the name appeared on Smith's map. *Other names:* La Punta (Dudley 1647).

Point Box, former point, Hyde County. Middle of three points protruding into Pamlico Sound on Ocracoke Island partly referenced as Gordens Ile on Smith's 1624 map. As with many names on Smith's map, duration of use was short. "Box," 17th-century nautical term used as reference for continually sailing back and forth. Name might have been

descriptive representing a landmark along course of "boxing about" or sailing routinely along the coast. Name was never used other than Smith's map.

Point Comfort, point, Dare County, Atlantic Township (signage). N point Mallard Cove in Southern Shores, 3.7 mi. nnw of original Kitty Hawk.

Point Emerald, point, Carteret County, White Oak Township (limited later local use). Extreme w end Bogue Banks sw of Langston Bridge, spanning Bogue Sound. Recent application (end 20th century) based on location relative to w Emerald Isle (town). Fanciful name meant to be alluring and never used locally. Reversed usage, natural feature acquiring name of man-made feature. Subdivision named for point.

Point O'Beach, point, Hyde County, Ocracoke Township (Goerch 1956). Reference in Ocracoke to point at terminus of Ocracoke Island, changed considerably over past 100 years. Can indicate any place representing a point on the beach jutting into Ocracoke Inlet. Not used much today.

Point of Beach, point, Carteret County, Atlantic Township (USGS 2013: Atlantic). Formerly sw point n portion Core Banks at n shore Drum Inlet (Old Drum Inlet soundside) 3.4 mi. e of Atlantic (mainland).

Point of Beach, point, Hyde County, Ocracoke Township (USGS 2013: Green Island). At s shore Hatteras Inlet, 5.1 mi. sw of Hatteras (village). *Other names:* Point Beach (Soil Conservation Service 1978).

Point of Currituck, former point, peninsula, barrier spit Dare County, Nags Head Township (Brazier 1833). Was s-most tip or point Currituck Banks from Virginia to n shore Roanoke Inlet before closing 1811, just n Whalebone Junction. S limit historically of Currituck Banks was Roanoke Inlet. Name rarely shown on maps.

Point of Grass, point, Carteret County, Atlantic Township (USGS 2013: Atlantic). Formerly n point on Core Banks at s shore Drum Inlet (Old Drum Inlet oceanside) 3.1 mi. e of Atlantic (mainland). *Other names:* Grass Point (CS 1877).

Point of Grass Creek, cove, 0.1 mi. wide, Carteret County, Atlantic Township (USGS 2013: Atlantic). In Core Sound 0.7 mi. s of Old Drum Inlet, 2.7 mi. e of Atlantic (mainland).

Point of Marsh, point, Carteret County, White

Oak Township (Stephens 1984, 127). Distinct point just w of Bell Cove, 2 mi. e of Yellow Hill. Descriptive of vegetation.

Point of Marsh, former point, Hyde County, Ocracoke Township (Lawson 1709, 64). Was 5.6 mi. sw of Hatteras Inlet. Formerly at ne complex Old Hatteras Inlet; today remnants are barely discernable.

Point of Marsh Island, island, 0.3 mi. long, 0.1 mi. wide, Currituck County, Fruitville Township (USGS 2013: Knotts Island). In Knotts Island Bay near entrance Fresh Pond Bay just nw of Point of Marsh Shoal, 1 mi. e of Knotts Island (village). *Other names:* Point of Marsh (clipped use).

Point of Marsh Shoal, small shoal, Currituck County, Fruitville Township (USGS 2013: Knotts Island). In Knotts Island Bay near entrance Fresh Pond Bay just se of Point of Marsh Island, 1.2 mi. e of Knotts Island (village).

Point of Sand, point, Currituck County, Fruitville Township (Cox 1923). Ne point, Point of Sand Cove on e side Fresh Pond Bay 2.5 mi. e of Knotts Island (village). *Other names:* Sand Point (some local use).

Point of Sand Cove, cove, 0.2 mi. across, Currituck County, Fruitville Township (USGS 2013: Knotts Island). Near se entrance Fresh Pond Bay, 2.4 mi. e of Knotts Island (village). *Other names:* Sand Cove (some local use).

Poire Creek. *See* Panters Creek.

Polly Ridge, sand ridge, Dare County, Atlantic Township (Currituck DB 30, 1869, 175–76). Exact location unknown, but one of numerous ridges in Kitty Hawk ridge-and-swale system (q.v.) just w and up to 3 mi. w of original Kitty Hawk.

Polly Ridge Swamp, swamp, Dare County, Atlantic Township (Currituck DB 30, 1869, 175–76). Exact location unknown, near Polly Ridge somewhere in Kitty Hawk Woods Swamp (q.v.) complex, from just w and up to 3 mi. w of original Kitty Hawk.

Pond, The, man-enhanced harbor, Carteret County, Morehead Township (original plat Atlantic Beach Isles Subdivision). At Cedar Hammock Creek, n end Atlantic Beach (town), 1.3 mi. s of Morehead City (mainland). In former Cedar Hammock (unrecognizable from original form), considerably altered and man-enhanced 1960s and 1970s. Cedar Hammock Creek (ne) just w of Atlantic Beach Causeway and Moonlight Bay, enhanced by development and alteration of Cedar Hammock. *Other names:* Fishin' Lake (recent highly localized use), Pond Canal (in part—Carteret County GIS 2019 database extends Pond Canal [q.v.] into this area).

Pond, The, small man-made lake, Dare County, Atlantic Township (local use). At waterfront shops and boardwalk in Duck (center), 3.2 mi. s of Sanderling.

Pond, The, man-made lake, Dare County, Nags Head Township (local informants). In Wanchese at Baumtown 5 mi. s of Manteo. Reportedly created by forced labor (variant name Convict Hole) 1930s. According to local folk, some dark tales accompany the creation regarding fate of those who constructed the feature. *Other names:* Convict Hole (local use).

Pond Canal, short canal, Carteret County, Morehead Township (Carteret County GIS 2019). Connects Gale Canal and The Pond (q.v.) center of Atlantic Beach Isles subdivision (w part of Canals at Atlantic Beach q.v.), 1 mi. south of Morehead City (mainland).

Pond Island, marsh island, 0.5 mi. long, 0.4 mi. wide, Dare County, Nags Head Township (USGS 2013: Roanoke Island NE). In Roanoke Sound, supports The Causeway 1.4 mi. wsw of Whalebone Junction. N part now reclaimed marsh for two subdivisions using name. *See* Canals at Pond Island. *Other names:* Walter Island (Holland 1794—Walter Slough 7 mi. s of this island and name might be related; Walter surname of early 18th-century homesteader here, or might be from Walter Raleigh since it appears on maps as early as 1770, but doubtful).

Pond Island Marina, small private harbor, Dare County, Nags Head Township (local use). In subdivision of same name n (reclaimed marsh) Pond Island (n of The Causeway) between Whalebone Junction and Pirates Cove (1.3 mi. from each), 3.2 mi. e of Manteo (center). *See* Pond Island (island) and Canals at Pond Island.

Pond Run, stream, Dare County, Hatteras Township (local use). Begins in large linear pond just s of Brigands Bay, 3.5 mi. wsw of Buxton. Use of "run" this far s on the Outer Banks is rare and not normally encountered; used in Nags Head n-ward and likely transferred usage from there. *See* The Run.

Ponds, The, lakes, Carteret County, White Oak Township (local official and informant). Six ponds complex trending e-w, each 0.3 mi. long (one considerably shorter), constructed for Lands End subdivision 1.5 mi. se of entrance Langston Bridge 10 mi. w of Salter Path. Ponds are unnamed, confirmed with officials, and just referenced as The Ponds (by some) through usage has become the name.

Ponds, The, lakes, Currituck County, Poplar Branch Township (local informants). Five large ponds and seven smaller ponds in The Currituck Club subdivision at Three Dunes 6 mi. s of Corolla. Created when subdivision's golf course built, and subdivision officials insist they are unnamed.

Ponds, The, two small lakes, Dare County, Atlantic Township (local use). In n-central Martins Point subdivision on peninsula, Martin (*sic*) Point, just w of Southern Shores 3.7 mi. nnw of original Kitty Hawk. No specific name for either pond individually or both collectively, by design of developer (confirmed by developer), and repeated interviews locally confirm collectively two ponds are still known simply as The Ponds (so is the name).

Pony Pen, corral, Hyde County, Ocracoke Township (NPS 2015). For protecting island's wild ponies just sw of Knoll Creek and Knoll Island 6.5 mi. ne of Ocracoke (village). Originally these horses (termed "ponies" because of diminutive size from sparseness of vegetation) roamed freely almost entire length of the Outer Banks, but today are found in only four specific places: n Currituck Banks (about 20 miles n to s, roam freely), Ocracoke Island (fenced), Shackleford Banks (roam freely), and on certain islands (Town Marsh, Carrot Island, Bird Shoal, and Horse Island) in Rachel Carson Reserve (though horses here are of a different lineage) just off mainland at Beaufort. Before late 1950s horses roamed freely on Ocracoke, but with extension of NC 12 (1957) onto Ocracoke Island, and 1987 from Duck to just beyond Corolla, interactions between cars and horses occurred. NPS attempted to remove horses from Ocracoke, but protests from residents caused NPS to relent; since 1959 horses on Ocracoke Island have been fenced. Corolla horses moved to several wildlife refuges and privately owned land beginning 1.5 mi. n of Corolla n to North Carolina–Virginia boundary; prevented from wandering s or n by fences and cattle

grates in the road. Corolla horses do wander unmolested among houses in communities of Swan Beach, North Swan Beach, and Carova (accessible only by 4-wheel-drive vehicles); several companies offer tours to see horses roaming freely and experience remoteness (serious and major crime to approach or attempt to feed horses in any of four places, considerable hazard to do so for both humans and horses). Shackleford Banks horses can be viewed (from appropriate distance) by visiting e end Shackleford Banks by passenger-only ferry service operated from Harkers Island by NPS. Rachel Carson Reserve can be accessed only by small, shallow-draft boats, and approaches are treacherous, usually requiring services of experienced, local guides. Horses in Rachel Carson Reserve, unlike other three areas, are not descended from Spanish mustang lineage (though there has been some cross-breeding) but are feral from mainland residents using these off-mainland islands for grazing purposes. Occasionally, stock is exchanged among three areas of Spanish mustangs to prevent in-breeding. Originally suggested these horses are descendants of shipwrecked Arabian horses, but DNA tests reveal descendants of Spanish breed of mustangs. Horses on Shackleford Banks, Ocracoke Island, and n Currituck Banks are from shipwrecks and escaped from Spanish known to have landed along the Outer Banks 1500s before arrival of English 1584.

Other names: NPS Pony Pen (Ocracoke Civic and Business Association 2015), Ocracoke Island Wild Pony Pasture (Google Maps), Ocracoke Pony Pasture (local use), Ocracoke Pony Pen (Ocracoke Island History 2016), Ocracoke Pony Pens (Outer Banks Scenic Byway 2008, 145), Ocracoke Wild Pony Pens (some usage), Pony Pen Pasture (signage), Pony Pens (local use).

Pony Pen Beach, beach, 1 mi. long, Hyde County, Ocracoke Township (websites). Just e of Pony Pen area 8 mi. ene of Ocracoke (village). Applied associatively but couple of decades after Pony Pen (q.v.). *Other names:* Pony Pasture Beach (tourist's misconception).

Ponzer Hotel Dock, former landing, Hyde County, Ocracoke Township (ACE 1893). Was at former Ponzer Hotel in Ocracoke (village) just n of Silver Lake (then Cockle Creek). *Other names:* Hotel Wharf (generic use).

Poor Ridge, sand ridge, Dare County, Atlantic Township (Town of Kitty Hawk 2007). Trends n-s 2 mi. w of Duck Pond Ridge 1 mi. w of original Kitty Hawk. Used since mid-19th century. *See* Kitty Hawk ridge-and-swale system and Poor Ridge Landing. Subdivision named for feature. *Other names:* Duck Pond Ridge (Harris 2017).

Poor Ridge Landing, landing, Dare County, Atlantic Township (local use). On n shore Kitty Hawk Bay, 1.1 mi. sw of original Kitty Hawk. Some indicate name was originally Paw Ridge Landing because around landing reportedly resembles cat's paw when viewed from the air. Protuberance vaguely resembling a cat's paw, but could resemble other formations, so not possible to know validity of this indication, as many interviewed have not heard this story. Name known as Poor Ridge Landing through interpretation from pronunciation and association with Poor Ridge. Used since mid-19th century. *See* Poor Ridge and Pawpaw Ridge. *Other names:* Paw Ridge Landing (likely local pronunciation misinterpretation, *but see* Pawpaw Ridge).

Poplar Branch Bay. *See* Dowdy Bay.

Pork Point, point, Dare County, Nags Head Township (USGS 2013: Manteo). On w Roanoke Island 1.6 mi. w of Manteo (center). Was to be e terminus for embankment across Croatan Sound to be designed to divert waters of Albemarle Sound and Currituck Sound through proposed Raleigh Canal, project to "restore" Roanoke Inlet so commerce could develop. Project never materialized. Some reports of Confederate battery of three guns here during Civil War, but reports are sketchy. Named because used exclusively as a hog farm from late 18th until early 20th centuries. Subdivision named for feature.

Porpoise Island. *See* South Buckle Island.

Porpoise Marsh, large marsh, Currituck County, Poplar Branch Township (C&GS 1852). W of and separated from Sedge Island by Wells Creek 5 mi. ssw of Corolla.

Porpoise Marsh Point, point, Currituck County, Poplar Branch Township (C&GS 1852). Se point of Porpoise Marsh 1.5 mi. wsw of Three Dunes 4.5 mi. ssw of Corolla.

Porpoise Pond, lake, 0.1 mi. across, Currituck County, Poplar Branch Township (USGS 2013: Mossey Islands). In s-central Mossey Islands

complex, 1.3 mi. wsw of Three Dunes, 5.8 mi. s of Corolla.

Porpoise Slough, water passage, 0.8 mi. long, Currituck County, Fruitville Township (USGS 2013: Knotts Island). Separates Simpson Neck and former Mon Island connecting Knotts Island Channel to Back Bay in Virginia 2.5 mi. nne of Knotts Island (village). *Other names:* East Bay (Currituck DB 10, 1809, 99—applied historically to Porpoise Slough or Capsies Creek), Parkers Slough (Currituck Register of Deeds), Simpsons Creek (Currituck DB 6, 1716, 7–8—records unclear, applied to Porpoise Slough or Capsies Creek).

Porters Inlet. *See* Cedar Inlet.

Port Ferdinando. *See* Gunt Inlet.

Port Lane, former small inlet, Dare County, Nags Head Township (Blaeu 1640). Was described as companion inlet to Gunt Inlet (Port Ferdinando), 3 mi. n of Gunt Inlet (Port Ferdinando), 6 mi. n of Oregon Inlet. From 1640 until early 1700s was a period of cartographic confusion regarding locations and names of inlets at and near Roanoke Island (*see* Roanoke Island historical inlets). Two inlets are shown as companion inlets here consistently 1585 until late 1660s. Named for Ralph Lane, leader of first, military Roanoke colony, 1585, which returned to England 1586 with Sir Francis Drake, who had stopped by Roanoke on his return to England. Likely same inlet as eventually named Roanoke Inlet, or closed nearby just before what became Roanoke Inlet opened. Included as separate entry since farther s historically in late 1500s to around middle to late 1600s and because perceived by some as a separate inlet. So, it might have existed separately from Roanoke Inlet a short time and former location misnamed Old Roanoke Inlet by a few cartographers to explain what was former inlet, but eventually closed or was absorbed by what became Roanoke Inlet. No activity here by colonists or settlers for over 100 years, 1587 to around 1700, and any names had been lost or forgotten. Possibly a new inlet opened and absorbed this smaller inlet (companion to Port Ferdinando, later Gunt), or it simply migrated and became larger. The inlet was later named Roanoke Inlet because Port Lane had been forgotten, and this inlet was in a slightly different location anyway. Alternatively, Port Lane might have closed and shortly thereafter what would become Roanoke Inlet opened farther n. Regardless, it is certain Roanoke Inlet (by that name) was not open before 1585, as mentioned by many authors. Can be concluded Port Lane was same inlet as Roanoke Inlet and agreed to by Fisher (1962, 108, migrated just n and received name Roanoke Inlet), existed separately a short time before being captured by Roanoke Inlet, or closed shortly before Roanoke Inlet opened nearby. The actual letter (Lane 1585, August) identifies three "entries" "Trynytye Harborough," "Ococan," and "Porte Ferdynande." There is no mention of another inlet, which would later be Port Lane because it was a close companion to Port Ferdinando or simply too small and unimportant to mention, but labeled clearly (unnamed) on White's map of 1585. Use of Port Scarborough has been a mystery to many researchers, as it appears in Sainsbury's (1860) rendition of Lane's second letter and nowhere else. However, examination concludes that in transcribing Sainsbury's rendition, Lane's reference "beste harboroughe" was misinterpreted or transcribed incorrectly as "Scarborough" because its location in Lane's letter can be construed in this way.

Other names: Old Roanoke Inlet (used for short time on a few sources and probable cartographic contrivance to compensate for this inlet's former site), Port Ferdinando (Lost Colony Research Center website), Port Lane Inlet (some secondary papers, abbreviated historical presentations part fact and part presumption, Frankenberg 1995, loc. 152, 3), Port Scarborough (Sainsbury 1860: letter from Lane to Walsingham, 1585, before being named Lane for himself).

Port Lane. *See* Roanoke Inlet.

Portsmouth, former village, Carteret County, Portsmouth Township (signage). On Portsmouth Island 6 mi. sw of Ocracoke (village). Named for Portsmouth, England (presumably and reportedly—*see* Portsmouth Island), and est. (officially) by N.C. legislative act April 12, 1753 (*see* Portsmouth Island). First map depicting Portsmouth (village) is Collet et al. (1770). During 18th century, Portsmouth was a thriving commercial port and stimulated trade between coastal North Carolina and outside and helped establish Ocracoke

(village) on neighboring Ocracoke Island, where many pilots for Ocracoke Inlet dwelled (Ocracoke village known awhile as Pilot Town). Development of larger ships and more sophisticated shipping forced establishment of other ports and caused decline in importance of Portsmouth as a port because of complex shoals in Ocracoke Inlet and shallow waters of Pamlico Sound. At its height late 18th and early 19th centuries more than 500 residents, but by 1950 only 18 residents and by 1960 only three people living at Portsmouth; post office est. 1840 was discontinued 1959. The last two residents (women) moved (reluctantly) to mainland 1971. Today former colonial port is abandoned. NPS has maintained the village since 1974, in Cape Lookout National Seashore, but much of the property was held privately until recently. Now a passenger ferry service operates from Ocracoke to Portsmouth. Mouzon (1775) uses "ʃ" (long "s") in Portsmouth (*see* Bellows Bay variant Bellisses Bay).

Four other named communities in Portsmouth area, though all were really in "greater" Portsmouth, with some marsh and open space between each community (see entries for each): East Portsmouth, South Portsmouth, Middle Portsmouth, and Sheep Island (former community). All outlying communities were clusters of houses separated by marsh and open area and given separate names for convenience and clarity of location.

Other names: Lower End (n island was "down banks and lower end," referring to higher ground being s—White 2012, 268), North End (White 2012, 268), Port of Portsmouth (Williamson 1992), Portsmouth Village (USGS 1950: Portsmouth and Portsmouth Village labeled at site).

Portsmouth Battery. *See* Camp Washington.

Portsmouth Beach, former beach reference, Carteret County, Portsmouth Township (Williamson 1992, 122). Was on ne end Portsmouth Island at Ocracoke Inlet 1 mi. e of former Portsmouth Life Saving Station Portsmouth (village). Today name is rarely used because no one lives here. Local folk, when island was populated, used "east beach" and "west beach" when referring to oceanside and backside of beach adjacent to Portsmouth Flats (White 2012, 240). *See*

Portsmouth. Sometimes name was extended length of Portsmouth Island to Swash Inlet.

Portsmouth Flats, large tidal flat, 6 mi. long, Carteret County, Portsmouth Township (NPS brochures). Separates islands on sound side from barrier beach on Portsmouth Island just s and sw of Portsmouth (village) 6 mi. sw of Ocracoke (village). Susceptible to unpredictable flooding rapidly at high tide, depending on conditions. *See* Portsmouth. *Other names:* Great Pond (Olszewski 1970, 33), The Flats (White 2012, 154).

Portsmouth Harbor, former harbor, Carteret County, Portsmouth Township (historical local use). Was small creek that served as harbor for Portsmouth (village) 6 mi. sw of Ocracoke (village). Approached through what is now Doctors Creek. Active about 1685 until late 18th century, when ships became too large and with too deep a draught to use the harbor, and Portsmouth began its decline. No longer useful port by early 19th century. *See* Portsmouth.

Portsmouth Island, barrier island, Carteret County, Portsmouth Township (USGS 2013: Portsmouth, Wainwright Island). From Ocracoke Inlet to Swash Inlet (today some consider Long Point s limit mostly from promotion of Long Point Camp). Though considered part of North Core Banks, historically often referred to as Portsmouth Banks.

Original grant to Richard Lovat 1738, but eventually transferred to to John Kersey 1753. Original land grant for most of Portsmouth Island was examined and is from *Acts of Colonial North Carolina*, book 2, 46, file 144. "George the Second, etc., To all, etc., Know ye that we have given and granted unto John Kersey a Tract of Land Containing Six Hundred and Forty Acres Lying and being in the County Carteret. Beginning on the W side of Ocacock Inlet at a Small Creek. Running up the Creek S. S. 41 W/// 320 poles to a poynt of Marsh on Sheep Island Bay, the E side thence s. 49-thence 320 poles to a Hamock or Island in Great Pond. Then N° 41 E 320 Poles to a Small Gutt that Comes Out of the Harbour, called Beacon Island Harbour."

A pole is a surveyor's measure equaling about 16.5 ft., so 320 poles is about 1 mi. Interestingly, date of land grant is April 11, 1753, and act creating "a town on Core Banks" is dated April 12, 1753, from N.C.

General Assembly (1753, 23:382–91). Note, the name Portsmouth for this town is not mentioned in the act; the name came later, and name Portsmouth is not mentioned in the grant from King George II, either. Three years later, 1756, Portsmouth was mentioned in first deed recorded for sale of a lot in new town named "Portsmouth."

Also, some place name differences apparent interpreting wording of the grant: 640 acres is just about the size of n portion of now Portsmouth Island, meaning parts with former settlements except not including Sheep Island (formerly some families). If one calculates n portion Portsmouth Island including Portsmouth Flats, but not Sheep Island, amount is almost exactly 640 acres (stated amount granted), generally 1 sq. mi. The topography and names have changed considerably since 1753, the year of the grant. For example, "W side of Ocacock Inlet (now Ocracoke Inlet) at a Small Creek": the presumption here is the reference to Small Creek is Baymarsh Thorofare. "Running up the Creek S 320 poles . . . (meaning south) . . . to a poynt of Marsh on Sheep Island Bay" is a point actually on Sheep Island Creek, but probably meant to be what is now Casey Bay. Description then reads, "thence 320 poles to a Hamock or Island in Great Pond." Here Great Pond can only refer to what is today Portsmouth Flats, which must have been more inundated 1753, and almost to where largest of three hummocks (hammocks or vegetated dunes) is today and was probably slightly farther n 1753. Then the description reads "320 Poles to a Small Gutt that Comes Out of the Harbour, called Beacon Island Harbour." Of course, this is confused with Doctors Creek, Coast Guard Creek, or Great River (known sparingly mostly 19th century) and nothing to do with Beacon Island or its harbor, about 2 mi. nne, both now and then (as early as 1770 on maps and in documents as early as 1755). Presumption might be the grant writers (1753) simply were unaware of the exact topography and namescape.

Use of variant Salvage Ile is not from "salvage," meaning to acquire from abandoned material, though was certainly an Outer Banks practice, but from time period of use and application is reference to a form of "savage," 18th century. Was often applied to indigenous peoples 18th century, but there were not many here; reference might have applied to the land itself. Peculiar reference since no permanent Indian settlements here, only occasional visits. *See* Portsmouth.

Made official by USBGN 1949. *Other names:* Core Bank (Price 1795, 627), Core Banks (Price 1795, 625), Core Beach (mistaken extension term "Core" n-ward onto Portsmouth), Crab Inlet Bancks (Wimble 1733), Croatan Island (early misinterpretations), Crotan (misspelling of Croatoan or Croatan as application error considerably s of appropriate application), Island of Portsmouth (Williamson 1992), North Core Banks (generalized extension of descriptive term by many sources), Northern Core Bank (Goldstein 2000, loc. 3084), Portsmouth Bank (CS 1865), Portsmouth Banks (Price and Strother 1798), Salvage Ile (Smith 1624, map, some early 18th-century maps), Savage Isle (Henry 1860, from Raleigh expeditions 1584—might have been applied to Core Banks or Portsmouth Island, difficult to determine given general nature of map), The Island (local use when people lived there until 1971), Wococock Ile (Comberford 1657), Wococon (misinterpreted application).

Portsmouth Point, point, Carteret County, Portsmouth Township (ACE 1893). Ne-most extension of Portsmouth Island 1 mi. from Portsmouth (village), 6 mi. se of Ocracoke (village). *See* Portsmouth.

Portsmouth Windmill, former windmill, Carteret County, Portsmouth Township (Price et al. 1808). Was in central Portsmouth (main village). Probably originally Nelson Windmill, later Piggott Windmill mentioned in sales record 1774 (NPS 2018, 62). There were reportedly three other windmills in Portsmouth, but names and locations unknown.

Pot Head, former area, Dare County, Kinnakeet Township (Garrity-Blake 2010, 169). References se section of original Avon e of Uncle Bates Ditch 5.5 mi. n of Buxton. From early 20th century, but meaning and origin unknown and not remembered. Garrity (2010, 167) indicates informant states "eventually all moved away or moved up to the village here in Avon, and their houses just went to pot" (meaning abandoned and deteriorated suggesting name origin). Use

of Head unexplained; no marked "headland" here although soundside bulges from n of Avon s for about 3 mi. Pothead, nickname applied to Pilot Whales because their black rounded heads reminded whalers of cooking pots, but no known association here (also pothead oil). Pothead refers to electrical wiring in connecting housings, but modern and not related. Name assuredly has nothing to do with smoking marijuana. *Other names:* The Pothead (Garrity-Blake 2010, 169).

Potteets Creek. *See* Straight Creek.

Potters Dock, former landing, Carteret County, Portsmouth Township (NPS 2018, 94). Exact location unknown, on small creek near Bragg Dock, n-central Portsmouth (main village).

Powder Ridge, high, distinct sand ridge, 0.5 mi. long, Dare County, Atlantic Township (historical plaque). Trends n-s in Duck (center), 3.2 mi. s of Sanderling, 9 mi. n of original Kitty Hawk. Was higher before development here. Sometimes applied to larger dune structure 2 mi. long where other reversed-usage names (natural feature acquiring name of man-made feature) for later housing developments are located, such as Schooner Ridge and Osprey Ridge. Controversy whether this was original name or result of reversed usage because Powder Ridge Gun Club (est. 1921) was soundside here. More believe gun (hunt) club was named for the ridge, and most assure the ridge name was first (possibly for composition of the sand). Also, some hearsay information a feature named Powder Ridge 15 miles n in Corolla, but no documentation or even firm verbal information to substantiate the name in Corolla. *Other names:* Duck Ridge (local use by tourists and late-comers, association with village name and also subdivision name).

Powells Island, former large island, Dare County, Croatan Township (historical records). Was largest island in Roanoke Marshes (q.v.) complex, 1.5 mi. e of mainland, 4 mi. sw of Wanchese. Began to disappear 1680s and completely inundated by early 18th century, but shallow shoal remained, contained original Roanoke Marshes Lighthouse, illuminated 1877, operated (U.S. Coast Guard) until decommissioned 1955. During an attempt to move old Roanoke Marshes Lighthouse to private property, the building was destroyed. An exterior replica of this lighthouse is now in downtown Manteo at Shallowbag Bay.

Power Squadron Spit, point, Carteret County, Harkers Island Township (USGS 2013: Cape Lookout). At Cape Lookout 2.5 mi. nnw of Cape Point, 4 mi. s of Harkers Island (village). Named (or changed) for U.S. Power Squadron, which meets there weekly. U.S. Power Squadrons are national nonprofit educational organizations founded 1914, striving to promote maritime safety, and offer classes in maritime navigation and related topics. Variant Breadwater Point is mistaken recording of Breakwater Point, original name from a jetty built here by ACE to stabilize shore. Construction began 1913 but was only about two-thirds complete when abandoned 1918 and determined usage would not be warranted. Name change originally proposed to USBGN 1971 as Power Squadron Point, but the generic term was changed to spit (1971), unusual as USBGN rarely changes generics and no longer makes such changes unless generic term proposed could be confusing or misleading. A spit is a curled, hook-like formation caused by longshore or littoral (means shore) drift, movement of sand along the shore by action of oblique waves. *Other names:* Albacore Point (local use), Breadwater Point (USBGN staff—recording error), Breakwater Point (local use—breakwater built here), Catfish Point (NPS 2004b, 52), Golds Point (NPS 2004b, 52).

Poyner Bar, shoal, Currituck County, Poplar Branch Township (USGS 2013: Mossey Islands). In Lone Oak Channel 1.5 mi. w of Beasley Bay, 5.8 mi. s of Corolla.

Poyners Hill, sand dune, Currituck County, Poplar Branch Township (USGS 2013: Mossey Islands). Just e of Beasley Bay on Currituck Banks, 4.6 mi. s of Corolla. Currently four sand ridge remnants of former size because most eroded away. *Other names:* Poyner Hill (C&GS 1969), Wilets Hill (CS 1852), Willets Hill (J. Colton 1861).

Poyners Hill, former settlement, Currituck County, Poplar Branch Township (historical local use). Was just s of Poyners Hill at now Pine Island subdivision 15 mi. nnw of original Kitty Hawk. Only a few families here, 3 mi. n of former Caffeys Inlet and might be scattered settlement mentioned by Stick (1958: 260) (*see* Sanderling). *See* Poyners

Hill (sand dune). *Other names:* Poyner Hill (some use), Wilets Hill (CS 1852), Wilnets Hill (GNIS—transcribing error).

Priscilla Curve, area, Dare County, Hatteras Township (signage). Created by an extreme curve in road 0.3 mi. s of Durant Point, 1 mi. from nnw of Hatteras village (center), named as referent to curve.

Proutys Battery. *See* Fort Macon Siege Batteries.

Providence Inlet. *See* Caffeys Inlet.

Pughs Channel, small channel, 0.5 mi. long, Dare County, Kinnakeet Township (White et al. 2017, 20). Natural cut through shallow shoal 2 mi. w of Hatteras Island allowing access to open water of Pamlico Sound from Rodanthe Channel. *Other names:* Pugh Channel (some use).

Pughs Landing, former landing, Dare County, Nags Head Township (Stick 1958, 145). Was 1 mi. sw of Wanchese. Mentioned in records Confederates placed some guns here, so small (possibly a diversion) number of federal troops were landed here; or Confederates thought this might be a landing place, though the primary landing was at Ashbee Harbor 3 mi. n. A road from Wanchese named Pugh Road still leads to near the site. *Other names:* Pugh Landing (some use).

Pughs Reef, shoal, Dare County, Kinnakeet Township (schooner *Two Sisters*, 1914 [White et al. 2017, 126]). Just n of Pughs Channel just nw of Rodanthe Channel, 5 mi. w nw of Rodanthe. "Reef" in Outer Banks geographic names usually refers to oyster colonies. *Other names:* Pugh Reaf (shipwreck reports), Pugh Reef (sail shad boat *Lula Tillett*, 1898 [White et al. 2017, 120]).

Quack Shoal, shoal, Carteret County, Harkers Island Township (Williamson 1992, 173). In wreck report (1906) schooner *Alson Miller* listed as "seven miles e of the station," meaning Fort Macon Life Saving Station. Exact location unknown but somewhere in Middle Marshes. Use of forms of "quake" are found concentrated on Ocracoke Island;

unknown if this is named for sound made by a duck or meant to be quake. *See* Quokes Point.

Quail Ridge, small sand ridge, Carteret County, White Oak Township (local use). On w Bogue Banks just w of entrance Langston Bridge, 7 mi. w of original Emerald Isle. Quail Ridge subdivision here, not clear whether name existed before subdivision, probably not, so would be reversed usage, natural feature acquiring name of man-made feature (subdivision). Virginia quail or bobwhite (*Colinus virginianus*) indigenous to entire se US.

Qualk Shoal, shoal, 1 mi. long, Hyde County, Ocracoke Township (local use). In Pamlico Sound on Middle Ground just n of Teaches Hole 1.7 mi. sw of Ocracoke (village). Mid-19th century Qualk Shoal joined temporarily to Gales Island. "Qualk" is a variation of "quoke," variation of "quake." *See* Quokes Point.

Quokes Point, marsh point, Hyde County, Ocracoke Township (USGS 2013: Howard Reef). On Ocracoke Island 5.1 mi. ne of Ocracoke (village). Pronounced by some "cock" originally. One story of name origin indicates an irreverent castaway named Old Quork (so-called from sounds he made) disappeared near the point while trying to put to sea during a storm, but not actually supported by local evidence and is purely apocryphal.

Another reference believed by some indicates is breeding grounds of black-crowned night heron (*Nycticorax nycticorax*; here year-round) and "kwak" and other similar spellings are sound made by the birds. Both of these represent folk etymology or developing name origins when actual meaning is unknown or forgotten. Some evidence indicates a suffix from an indigenous language possibly used here was "quecoc" or "quaquin" and could have had some influence, though doubtful and no evidence.

Actually, name origin is derived from quaking or, more specifically "quake-mire," which became "quagmire" (Skeat, *Etymological Dictionary*, 1888). A low wet marsh or hummock (hammock) was a quaking hammock or quake hammock from sometimes almost gel-like movement from plough (pronounced "pluff") mud. Also,

some sources indicate if marsh contains certain species of grass whose spikelets make a rattling or quaking noise in wind, known as a quaking hammock—perhaps. But, "quaking hammock" is the name origin. "Quaking" or "quake" hammock is from Middle English "quaghe," evolving to "quag" (quagmire) or "quake," referring to wet low marshes. Quaking bog is common reference 14th and 15th centuries in England and was applied here because these early terms were known to have been used for place names (*see* Try Yard Creek [Carteret County]).

Other names: Kwak Point (Weslager 1954), Kwawk Point (Weslager 1954, 47), Old Quork Point (older local use), Old Quorks Point (older local use), Qualk Hommock Point (C&GS 1883—unusual spelling of "hammock," local spelling for "hummock"), Quawks Point (*Ocracoke Island Journal*, March 16, 2017), Quolk Hommock Point (C&GS 1883, unusual spelling of "hammock"), Quoke Point (some older local use), Quorks Point (*Ocracoke Island Journal*, March 16, 2017).

Quorkes Creek, cove, Hyde County, Ocracoke Township (USGS 2013: Howard Reef). In Pamlico Sound just ne of Hammock Woods 5.4 mi. ne of Ocracoke (village). Quorke variation of "quoke" variation of "quake." *See* Quokes Point. *Other names:* Old Quawks Creek (former), Old Quokes Creek (former road sign), Old Quorks Creek, Quawks Creek (*Ocracoke Island Journal*, March 16,), Quawks Point Creek (older local use), Quokes Point Creek (older local use), Quorks Point Creek (older local use).

Quork Hammock, marsh, 0.3 mi. wide, Hyde County, Ocracoke Township (USGS 2013: Green Island). On Ocracoke Island between North Bitterswash Creek and Shingle Creek 12 mi. ne of Ocracoke (village). "Quork" variation of "quoke," variation of "quake." *See* Quokes Point. *Other names:* Kwawk Hammock (reportedly, sound of black-crowned night heron here year-round; Weslager 1954, 47—*see* Quokes Point for actual origin), Quake Hammock (reflects original meaning Quark Hammock), Quarks Hammock (Fisher 1962, 106), Quawk Hammock (*Ocracoke Island Journal*, March 16, 2017), Quoke Hammock (older local use).

Quorks Hill, sand dune, 20 ft. high, Hyde County, Ocracoke Township (USGS 2013:

Howard Reef). On Ocracoke Island, just ne of Hammock Woods 5.2 mi. ne of Ocracoke (village). "Quork" variation of "quoke," variation of "quake." *See* Quokes Point.

R

Rabbit Alley, historical area, Dare County, Nags Head Township (local informants). Was just n of The Causeway near sw Cedar Island 4 mi. e of Manteo. Informal reference for approach to hunting camp on Cedar Island named for abundance of rabbits. Name remembered but no longer used.

Rabbit Hollow, area, Dare County, Atlantic Township (local use). In s Kitty Hawk (town) just e of Kitty Hawk Bay. Small valley-like feature here (barely discernable now) trending n-s. Limited usage earlier, but has now become a reference in local town documents and by local media.

Raccoon Bay, cove, 0.7 mi. wide, Currituck County, Poplar Branch Township (USGS 2013: Corolla). In Currituck Sound 0.7 mi. nw of Corolla, 0.8 mi. s of Ships Bay.

Raccoon Islands, islands, Currituck County, Poplar Branch Township (Codman, Crowninshield, and Lawrence 1925). Trend e-w from Currituck Banks, four large islands at n shore of Raccoon Bay, including other small islands 1 mi. nnw of Corolla.

Race Flat, former flat, Dare County, Kinnakeet Township (Garrity-Blake 2010, 169). Was in se original Avon (just se of former Pot Head), 1 mi. se of Avon Harbor 7 mi. n of Buxton. Natural flat used for activities descriptive of name. Today developed.

Rack Creek, tidal stream, Currituck County, Fruitville Township (F&WS 1999, map). Trends ne-sw 0.6 mi. e of Pennys Hill (Luark Hill), 3.5 mi. nnw of Corolla.

Radio Island, island, 1.4 mi. long, 0.7 mi. wide, Carteret County, Beaufort Township (USGS 2013: Beaufort). Just e of Morehead City Channel, 1.3 mi. w of Beaufort (mainland). Former marsh, but substantial island created from dredge material creating and improving port at Morehead City (mainland) between 1930s and 1950s. From radio station WMBL operating here late 1940s, mostly 1950s and 1960s. *Other names:* Inlet Island (occasional historical use, proximity to Beaufort Inlet confirmed by PKS 2016), Island of Marsh (Kell, 1777).

Radio Island Marina, harbor, Carteret County, Beaufort Township (signage). At n end Radio Island between Morehead City (mainland) and Beaufort (mainland) 1.2 mi. w of Beaufort (mainland). *See* Radio Island.

Ragged Island, irregular island, Dare County, Atlantic Township (local use). In se Kitty Hawk Bay Islands complex at nw Colington Creek 3 mi. s of original Kitty Hawk. Descriptive name.

Ragged Island Cove, small distinctly incised cove, Dare County, Atlantic Township (local use). At s end Ragged Island 3 mi. s of original Kitty Hawk. *See* Ragged Island.

Rainbow Island, marsh island, 1 mi. long, 0.5 mi. wide, Currituck County, Fruitville Township (Cox 1923). E of Currituck Bay, North Bay (s) North Rainbow Creek (n), 3.5 mi. se of Knotts Island (village). Indian Gap Island (Fruitville Township) attached now to Rainbow Island at sw tip. Little Bird Island now attached on se side.

Raleigh Bay, bight, 75 mi. long, Carteret County, Portsmouth, Atlantic, Sea Level, Stacy, Davis, Smyrna, Harkers Island Townships; Dare County, Hatteras Township; and Hyde County, Ocracoke Township. In Atlantic Ocean from Cape Hatteras sw to Cape Lookout. Named for Englishman Sir Walter Raleigh, who was organizer of a number of ventures in New World, including first attempted English colony in New World (other than short failed semiattempt at Newfoundland by Sir Gilbert Humphrey 1583, Raleigh's half-brother) at Roanoke Island and second attempted colony there (Lost Colony). Subdivision named for feature. *Other names:* Ocracoke Bight (McGuinn 2000, 5—only known use), Raleighs Bay (occasional).

Raleigh Canal, formerly proposed canal, Dare County, Nags Head Township (Brazier 1820). N.C. General Assembly incorporated "Raleigh Canal Company" for improving navigation and commerce in Albemarle Sound area and to construct an inlet to be known as Raleigh Canal. Some mild interest as early as 1787, when it became clear Roanoke Inlet was closing (closed 1811); project never really materialized. Brazier's (1820) map showed proposed embankments and proposed new "inlet" near former Roanoke Inlet just n of Nags Head Island 1 mi. n of Whalebone Junction (Whalebone). Dredging began 1856, but futility and high cost were realized, and reopening the inlet (canal) was abandoned. Raleigh refers to Englishman Sir Walter Raleigh, who was organizer of a number of ventures in New World. *See* Raleigh Bay.

Raptor Point. *See* Bens Point.

Rattlesnake Island, island, 0.5 mi. long, 0.3 mi. wide, Currituck County, Poplar Branch Township (USGS 2013: Mossey Islands). In Currituck Sound just sw of Mossey Islands complex 8.5 mi. sw of Corolla. *Other names:* Ratle Snake Island (*sic*) (Currituck DB 7, 1794, 124–25), Rattle Snake Island (C&GS 1895a).

Rattlesnake Island, marsh island, Currituck County, Poplar Branch Township (Currituck DB 7, 1796, 338–39). Se of Pettys Pond 1 mi. nw of former Caffees Inlet, 5 mi. nnw of Duck (center). Topographic configuration changed considerably over past 200 years when name first used. *Other names:* Ratle (*sic*) Snake Island (Currituck DB 7, 1796, 338–39).

Rawson Creek, cove, 0.5 mi. long, Carteret County, Smyrna Township (USGS 2013: Horsepen Point). In Core Sound just e of Core Banks 0.6 mi. s of Rush Island, 4.3 mi. ese of Harkers Island (village).

Raymond Island, marsh island, 0.3 mi. long, Currituck County, Fruitville Township (USGS 2013: Barco). In Currituck Sound just s of South Channel, 0.7 mi. s of Johnsons Island, 5.5 mi. nnw of Corolla. Sometimes Swan Island, Johnson Island referenced as Swan Islands; occasionally Crow Island, Raymond Island might be included.

Raymonds Creek, water passage, Currituck County, Fruitville Township (Cox 1923). E-w trending near center of Runnells Marshes separating Long Cove (e) from Set Net Creek (w) 2 mi. e of Knotts Island (village). Associated with Raymond Island 5.5 mi. s.

Rebecker Shoal, small shoal, Carteret County, Portsmouth Township (USGS 1950: Portsmouth). Near entrance former Portsmouth Harbor 0.5 mi. nnw of former Portsmouth Life Saving Station at Portsmouth (village). *Other names:* Rebecker High (signifies higher ground).

Redbirds Creek, small tidal stream, Dare County, Kinnakeet Township (Garrity-Blake 2010, 168). In The North'ard, Avon, and former Scarboro, just e of Big Island, 7.8 mi. n of Buxton. Canalized, with docking facility altered beyond recognition by development.

Reeds Point, former point, Dare County, Kinnakeet Township (Currituck DB 1716 unnumbered, n.p.). Was s Salvo in No Ache Bay area; probably n or s point Keneckid Inlet (q.v.).

Reflection Pond, small lake, Dare County, Nags Head Township (local informants). In n Nags Head Woods 0.5 mi. w of Fresh Pond, 1.5 mi. nw of Jockeys Ridge, 2.5 mi. nw of original Nags Head. Descriptive of stillness of water usually. One of many interdunal ponds, most unnamed.

Reids Creek, tidal stream, Carteret County, Beaufort Township (C&GS 1888a). In ne Radio Island sw former Reids Marsh 1 mi. w of Beaufort (mainland).

Reids Marsh, former marsh, Carteret County, Beaufort Township (historical local use). Was at junction of Bogue Sound and Beaufort Inlet, 1.1 mi. w of Beaufort (mainland). Most now is ne Radio Island.

Remus Rock, former rock, Carteret County, Portsmouth Township (Stick 1958, 77). Was in Pamlico Sound just e of North Rock, 4 mi. n of Portsmouth (village). Location approximate, only general references available; name now unknown. Records indicate named by 1790, part of Oyster Rocks (q.v.). Additionally, reference to another feature, named Rimus Shoal (q.v.) 2 mi. se found only on Price (1795) and might (or likely) could be same as Remus Rock because many of these shoals were rock-like or middens (piles of oyster shells). However, many authors including Stick (1958), while vague on location of Remus Rock, generally place it in present North Rock complex. "Rimus" might be a phonetic spelling of original Latin pronunciation of what came to be spelled "Remus," an unusual name here. One might suspect such an unusual name was a ship that ran afoul in or near the inlet (such names occasionally were used—*see* Vera Cruz Shoal and Mount Vernon Rock), but none has been found in numerous lists of shipwrecks with spelling "Remus" or "Rimus," though there are and have been many ships named *Remus*. Not conclusive whether Remus Rock and Rimus Shoal are same feature or two different features. Both are included as entries for the widest interpretation of vague references

in their perceived locations. *Other names:*
Remus's Rock (Stick 1958, 77), Rimeses Rock
(McGuinn 2000, 33), Rymeses Rock (McGuinn
2000, 33).

Rhodoms Point, point, Dare County, Atlantic
Township (USGS 2013: Kitty Hawk). At w end
Colington Island, 4.4 mi. ssw of original Kitty
Hawk. Used since 1768 (Currituck DB 2, 1768,
336). Use of variant McDototos Point might
have been here but more likely at Eagleton
Point, especially since Rhodoms Point known
to have been used since 1760s. *Other names:*
Bodens Point (C&GS 1865), Rhodums Point
(Currituck County 2015), McDototos Point
(possibly—Currituck DB 13, 1814, 52–55),
Roden Point (CS 1852), Rodens Point (CS
1862a).

R Hooper Goose Pound, former area, Dare
County, Kinnakeet Township (Garrity-Blake
2010, 169). Was at former R Hooper Landing
at Mill Creek (Old Creek) in The North'ard
section new Avon, 7.3 mi. n of Buxton.
"Goose pounds" existed along the Outer
Banks from Rodanthe to Portsmouth, as
many folk kept geese to supplement their
diet. Unclear why this particular goose
pound is considered mapworthy but provides
opportunity to highlight this feature type
and important activity on much of the Outer
Banks well into 20th century.

R Hooper Landing, former landing, Dare
County, Kinnakeet Township (Garrity-Blake
2010, 169). Was in The North'ard section new
Avon just s of former Mill Landing at Mill
Creek (Old Creek), just se of Big Island, 7.3 mi.
n of Buxton.

Rice(s) Path, former settlement, Carteret
County, Morehead Township (USGS 2013:
Salter Path—still labeled). On Bogue
Banks 1.5 mi. w of Salter Path, 11 mi. w of
Atlantic Beach (town). Origin of Rice(s)
Path reportedly from wrecked ship
(1870s) containing cargo of rice people
retrieved from the wreck, with permission
apparently. By late 18th century there were
rules regarding wrecked ships and their
cargo; many "Bankers" until middle 20th
century subsidized income by salvaging
ships and cargo (usually not commercially
salvageable). From late 18th century,
cargo from wrecked ships was supposed
to be held and guarded, then returned to
owner or become a vendue, essentially an
auction of what remained of the cargo. As

early as beginning of 1800s, state of North
Carolina established "wreck districts" with
commissioners to take charge of wreckage
and hold vendues if warranted. There was
give-and-take on all sides. While the story
of name origin for "Rice" here is well known,
difficult to verify with lack of documents. As
with small communities w of Salter Path,
families eventually moved to Salter Path by
early 20th century for various reasons. *See*
Bogue Banks historical communities. *See also*
Bogue Banks historical paths. *Other names:*
Rices Path (USGS 2013: Salter Path), Rick Path
(typographical error, Stephens 2007).

Ridge, The, small shoal, Dare County, Kinnakeet
Township (Garrity-Blake 2010, 492). In
Pamlico Sound 2 mi. sw of Round Hammock
Bay, 2 mi. nw of Rodanthe.

Ridge, The, small sand dune, Dare County,
Nags Head Township (local use). Soundside
in Nags Head, 2 mi. nnw of Whalebone
Junction. Not named until development and
acquired descriptive reference, example of
reversed usage, natural feature acquiring
name of man-made feature. Dune altered
with development.

Rimus Shoal, former small shoal, Carteret
County, Portsmouth Township (Price 1795,
630). Was maybe somewhere just inside
Ocracoke Inlet between Ocracoke Inlet and
former Dry Sand Shoal (now former Vera
Cruz Shoal), near Wallace Channel 1 mi.
n or ne of Portsmouth (village). The only
reference to Rimus Shoal is Price (Occacock
Inlet [sic], Price 1795) and probably same as
Remus Rock (q.v.); many of these shoals were
rock-like or middens (piles of oyster shells).
However, many authors including Stick
(1958, 77), while vague on location of Remus
Rock, generally place it in present North
Rock complex. Price's location might not
be specific. *See* Remus Rock for additional
information.

Rise, The, small sand dune, Hyde County,
Ocracoke Township (local use). On e
Ocracoke Island 12 mi. e of Ocracoke (village).
Descriptive, elevation 11 ft. in contrast to
surroundings 1–3 ft.

Roanoak, former Indian village, Dare County,
Nags Head Township. Formerly site of Indian
village most likely now submerged off n
coast of Roanoke Island (Haklyut 1589, 127).
Possibly permanent or semipermanent but
smaller than those on mainland. Where a

party of soldiers (first Roanoke voyage, 1584) was entertained overnight. White and a few other mapmakers referred to entire island as Roanoak. *See* Roanoke Island. *Other names:* Roanoac (DeBry 1590), Roanok (Accurate Map 1779).

Roan Oak Narrows, former narrow water passage, Dare County, Croatan Township (Maule 1718). Was historically way through Roanoke Marshes from Croatan Sound (originally Back Bay) into Pamlico Sound between sw point Roanoke Island and mainland, 8 mi. sw of Wanchese, but accessible only by small craft. This "channel" began to disappear as Roanoke Marshes flooded after Roanoke Inlet closed 1811. *See* Ship Channel, since much of this feature became Ship Channel; descriptive term became name after use of Roan Oak Narrows fell into disuse. Variant Narrow of Rone Oake Marshes and Ship Channel used as descriptors in same deed 1810. So, names were used together for a short while until Roan Oak Narrows (and variations) disappeared. *See* Roanoke Island, Eastern Channel, Roanoke Marshes, and Ship Channel. *Other names:* Narrow of Rone Oake Marshes (Currituck DB 11, 1810, 56–57), Narrows of Roan Oake Marshes (Currituck DB 11, 1811, 58; Maule 1718), Roanoak Narrows (Cheeseman 1982, 55), Through Fare (Collet et al. 1770).

Roanoke Bar, former shoal, Dare County, Nags Head Township (Maule 1718). Was at entrance Roanoke Inlet. *See* Roanoke Island.

Roanoke Hills. *See* Griffin Hills.

Roanoke Inlet, former water passage, Dare County, Nags Head Township (Bowen 1747). Connected Roanoke Sound to Atlantic Ocean through barrier island and formed boundary between Currituck Banks and Bodie Island 1 mi. n of The Causeway and Whalebone Junction. From 1640 until early 1700s was a period of cartographic confusion regarding locations and names of inlets at and near Roanoke Island (*see* Roanoke Island historical inlets). Reportedly opened before 1585, though contrary to some published reports did not use this name and has been misreported and confused with Port Lane or a newer inlet nearby. Roanoke Inlet began to close 1795 and by 1811 had completely shoaled up. Lucas's (1826) map indicated "filled up." Port Lane is

associated and was likely original name for this inlet for a short time, named for Ralph Lane, leader of first, military colony (not Lost Colony). Port Lane had been forgotten in the 100 plus-year hiatus since naming and attempted settlement. The inlet as Port Lane had expanded and/or migrated or closed and a newer inlet opened nearby. The inlet was reportedly farther s initially but according to Fisher (1962) had migrated to just s of Whalebone Junction by 1730s; he believes Port Lane (inlet) was original name of migrating inlet renamed Roanoke Inlet (Fisher 1962, 108), so cartographers for few maps using a form of Roanoke for this inlet in late 1600s were not aware of former use or Port Lane and applied associative name from nearby Roanoke Island such as Ogilby (1672). Whatever the exact situation, Roanoke Inlet has been confused by some authors with what was Port Lane or a newly opened inlet. *See* Gunt Inlet, Old Roanoke Inlet, and Port Lane.

Roanoke Inlet was always shallow but utilized as much as possible especially by smaller craft for its ideal commercial location to the Albemarle region. After closing, people of Albemarle region wanted to reopen the inlet, and studies made over 30 years (1820–50) on how best to reopen the inlet. Each study and proposal suggested necessity of damming Croatan Sound and/or Roanoke Sound to force water from Albemarle Sound to seek a new outlet through the barrier island and water could be funneled through the old site at Roanoke Inlet. Fulton 1820 map shows locations of proposed embankments and proposed new inlet, at former Roanoke Inlet 1 mi. n of Whalebone Junction (Whalebone). Some maps through the 1820s still showed Roanoke Inlet open, though the inlet had closed by 1811, illustrating how later maps often display erroneous information. Lucas's (1826) map labels the inlet but marks it as "filled up." Actual dredging begun 1856, but futility and high cost realized and reopening abandoned.

While open, Roanoke Inlet provided outlet for much of the water from Roanoke River through Albemarle Sound. When closing started, water from Albemarle Sound was naturally diverted through Croatan Sound, and over period of years Roanoke

Marshes became inundated; today only few shoals are remaining remnants of the marshes. *See* Roanoke Marshes, Roanoke Island, and Old Roanoke Inlet.

Other names: Bodie Inlet (casual historic references n terminus Bodie Island), Entré de Roanok (Nolin 1783), Entrée de Roanoc (Bellin 1764), Inlet of Roanoak (Simpson and Simpson 1988, 6), Inlet of Roanoke (some text references 19th century), Inlett of Roanoke (Dunbar 1958, 49), Nags Head Inlet (Lawson 1709, map), New Inlet (Gascoyne 1682—could also refer to former or migrating Port Lane on this small-scale map since Port Lane was open before 1585, and now positioned across from n Roanoke Island with Old Inlet labeled just s-ward, referring to Gunt Inlet, shoaling by 1682), Northwest Passage (occasional reference to most direct inlet to Albemarle Sound and nw Carolina), Nouveau Passage (Sanson 1696), Old Inlet (Moll 1708—curious, at this time inlet open and other references are New Inlet; still labeled Old Inlet on U.S. Navy 1862, closed 1811; CS 1862a; Foster 1866a—more than 50 years after closure, perhaps awash at times), Old Roanoke Inlet (Stick 1958, 85), Port Lane (Blaeu 1640), Port Lane Inlet (Fisher 1962, 108), Port of Currituck (not meant as a name for the inlet but to signify use for commercial activity in Currituck), Port Roanoke (deeds, "Port" used in names of inlets in 17th and 18th centuries to signify economic activity), Port Scarborough (Sainsbury 1860, second letter from Lane, governor first colony, to Secretary Walsingham, August 12, 1585), Roakoke Inlet (historical), Roan Oak Barr (Maule 1718), Roanoake Inlet (historical), Roanoake Inlett (patent from Governor Howard to Mason, Jarvise (Jarves), and Willoughby, Currituck DB Miscellaneous, 1688), Roanoak Inlet (Speed 1676), Roan Oak Inlet (Currituck DB 11, 1811, 266—closed in this year), Roanock Inlet (Graffenried 1710), Roanokea Inlett (historical), Roanoke Einfahrt (Lucas 1826—*einfahrt*, inlet in German; labeled *versandet*, silted up, on map), Roanoke Inlett (Barnwell-Hammerton 1721), Roanoke River Inlet (Purcell 1788—only known use of "River," possibly since Roanoke River is principle river creating Albemarle Sound [estuary], though technically almost 100 miles e in Albemarle Sound), Roanok Inlett (Fisher et al. 1689, chart 11—small-scale, inconclusive application; also applied incorrectly to Ocracoke Inlet, same chart), Roanook Inlet (Wimble 1733), Ronoake Inlet (historical), Ronoak Inlet (Lawson 1709), Rounoak Inlet (Wimble 1738), Vieu Passage (several French maps late 1600s; *vieu*, French for old), View Passage (Stick 1958, 9—error misinterpreting "Vieu" from French maps).

Roanoke Island, island, 12 mi. long, 3 mi. wide, Dare County, Nags Head Township (USGS 2013: Manteo, Roanoke Island NE, Wanchese, Oregon Inlet). Between Albemarle Sound (n) and Pamlico Sound (s) separated from mainland by Croatan Sound and from Bodie Island by Roanoke Sound 45 mi. nw of Cape Hatteras. Roanoke only 16th-century name still referring to same place as 16th century (slightly different orthography). Most names given 16th and 17th centuries have numerous spellings because no standard orthography until early 19th century. The accounts of the Roanoke voyages 1584–90 used different spellings of same word in same sentence. For example, forms Roanoack and Roanocke were used in same sentence by John Smith (Jamestown fame) in recounting original Roanoke voyages.

"Roanoke" is reportedly of Indian origin (probably Algonquin word) with many variations of spelling thought to have multiple meanings; two are paramount. One meaning is reportedly "northern people," referring to Indians living on n Roanoke Island or possibly to their migration to Roanoke Island from the n. A second meaning reportedly refers to money (Ronoak [*sic*]; Lawson 1709, 194) or Indian's use of beads made of conch shells as form of money, and many argue this is first meaning of the word. The many meanings and uses of "Roanoke" result from metonymic process of word substitution for different meanings. For example, Roanoke, original inhabitants, meaning later transferred to objects of barter or money and then later to the place itself.

Original usage on early maps was Roan Oak or Roan-Oak, prompting a very few uninformed individuals to suggest Roanoak is not of Indian origin but merely combination of roan (brownish colored horse or soft leather-colored brown) and "oak." This is complete fabrication as it is clear in original manuscripts and logs of the "Voyages to Roanoak" that use by the English was for an Indian term. Some ask about William Faulkner naming (or renaming) his house in Oxford, Mississippi, Rowan Oak, which he did after the historical practice in Scotland of placing rowan wood over a door for symbolic protection. "Rowan" refers to wood of ash trees (in North Carolina native only in Appalachian Mountains); unknown really why Faulkner chose "oak" rather than "ash" other than it probably suggests a better image. Speculation is he mixed the two tree types because rowan (ash) is supposed to have magical and protective powers and oak symbolizes strength. He had no links to Roanoke Island or the Outer Banks and no association with the word "Roanoke."

Roanoke Island is site of first attempted English colony in North America 1585 (not Lost Colony), a military colony composed solely of 107 soldiers and intended as temporary since harbors were not deep enough to serve as a base for privateering and harassing the Spanish. The lower Chesapeake was to be the more permanent colony and the stated destination of what became Lost Colony 1587 (*see* website for complete information: OBXplacenames. com). Soldiers of first attempted colony and settlers of second attempted colony certainly assigned names to features as a means of communicating. Recall function of naming is communication and to do so by identifying landmarks in an otherwise undifferentiated environment. However, first colony of soldiers lasted only a year (before returning to England with Sir Francis Drake's ships) with no maps, other than White's 1585 map, and any names they assigned or used are lost except for a few such references in Lane (1585) and White's map. The second colony (1587) was the Lost Colony, which disappeared leaving no maps or papers (only "CRO" carved into a tree and "Croatoan" on a post were found, with no indication of the distress signal, a cross pattée similar to Maltese cross), so no names from that ill-fated colony are known. Theories abound regarding the fate of the colonists (*see* OBXplacenames.com). Colonists (and White, colony's leader) had no intention of staying at Roanoke, only checking on 15 soldiers left from relief ship for first colony (1585) before proceeding to the Chesapeake

area, but intrigue from the pilot (Simon Fernandez) interceded, with the captains strangely quiet (implication is White was captain of the flagship but with Spicer and Stafford as captains of companion ships, although Fernandez really in charge) (*see* OBXplacenames.com for additional material). Virginia Dare, first English child born in now U.S., documented before White's return to England, also male child born few days later, surname Harvie (given name unknown). The 100-year hiatus before people returned here has created several name problems, especially with inlet names near Roanoke Island (*see* Roanoke Island historical inlets).

Attempts were made to settle the island and establish a town (*see* Carteret) in 1676 to control commerce in Albemarle Sound region, but settlement never materialized for numerous reasons, including Roanoke Inlet was shoaling (mid-1700s) and was not ever really a deep inlet with a dependable channel (most inlets are not dependable). By 1700, settlement appeared on the island in scattered fashion, mostly for grazing. Six subdivisions named for feature.

Other names: Croonoake (Cheeseman 1982, 193), Iland of Roanoak (Haklyut 1589), Ile de Magdelena (Keulen 1682), Ile de Raonack (DeLisle 1718), Ile de Roanoack (L'Isle 1703), Ile of Raonoak (Haklyut 1589), Ile Raonoake (historical), Ile Roanoak (Haklyut 1589), Island of Roan-Oak (Maule 1718), Island of Roanoak (Currituck DB 6, 1789, 256–57), Isle de Rannock (L'Isle 1703), Isle of Roanoak (Haklyut 1589), Paonack Island (Coxe 1722—transcribing error), Raonack Island (historical), Raonoak (Haklyut 1589 from logs, Amadas and Barlowe), Raonoke Island (Currituck DB 5, 1787, 238), Rawliana (Ferrar 1667—added by his daughter apparently honoring Sir Walter Raleigh, vague reference to Roanoke Island or possibly surrounding area), Rawrenoke (Cheeseman 1982, 193), Rhoanoke Island (Trebellas and Chapman 1999, 2), Roanaac (Cheeseman 1982, 193), Roanoac (DeBry 1590), Roanoac Island (White 1585), Roanoack (Smith 1624, map), Roanoacke (Smith 1624, map), Roanoak (Smith 1624, map), Roanoake (Haklyut 1589), Roanoake Iland (Ogilby 1672), Roanoake Island (1585), Roanoak Iland (Comberford 1657), Roanoak Island (maps and charts since 18th century; Lawson 1859), Roanocke

(Willard 2008, 30, from Zúñiga 1612), Roanock Iland (Comberford 1657), Roanoke Ile (historical), Roanoke Isla (early Spanish reference), Roanoke Isle (historical), Roanok Ile (Bland 1651), Roanok Island (d'Anville 1756), Roanonck (Blaeu 1640), Roenoac (Cheeseman 1982, 193), Roenoke (Cheeseman 1982, 193), Roenoque Island (Gascoyne 1682), Roenok Island (Fisher et al. 1689, Chart 15, 1689; Moll 1729), Roneoake Island (Currituck DB 7, 1796, 351–52), Ronoack Island (historical), Ronoak Island (Lawson 1859), Ronoque (explorer Marmaduke Raynor voyage 1620 Albemarle Region), Roonock (Zúñiga from Smith 1608), Ronock Island (Currituck DB 5, 1787, 265–66), Ronoke Island (Currituck DB 9, 1808, 414), Roonok (Zúñiga from Smith 1608).

Roanoke Island historical inlets, clarification of four historical inlets, Dare County, Nags Head Township. Each inlet has a separate entry. Port Ferdinando, 2 mi. n of Oregon Inlet was open from before 1585 to 1798; from about 1700 to 1798 was known as Gunt Inlet. Port Lane was 3 mi. n of Port Ferdinando and open before 1585 to around 1660 and became Roanoke Inlet or closed. Port Lane's closed site was also what a few cartographers labeled as Old Roanoke Inlet. Port Lane then migrated n and became Roanoke Inlet, or a new inlet opened shortly after Port Lane closed. Trinety Harbor was open pre-1585 to around 1660. This summarizes the problem of names of inlets in Roanoke Island area 1585 to approx. 1730. The first Roanoke voyage (Amadas and Barlowe 1584) includes no mention of inlet names, referring only to Hatrask vaguely near what would be Port Ferdinando (Gunt Inlet) by 1585. White published the first map of the Outer Banks (1585), on which no inlets are named. Port Ferdinando and Port Lane are shown correctly but not named. Hatrask is labeled at what is now Pea Island and not near enough to Port Ferdinando to indicate a named inlet. Trinety Harbor is not shown or named. A later version of White's map (year unknown) appears with Port Ferdinando mysteriously labeled at that inlet, and Trinety Harbor added at the appropriate location, though the inlet itself is not shown.

DeBry's 1590 map, based on White's 1585 map, shows location of Port Ferdinando but with no name, which seems strange because the inlet had been named since at least 1585.

The name Hatrask now appears opposite inlet named Port Ferdinando, leading some authors to indicate the inlet as Hatrask. Hondius and Mercator (collaborated 1606, 1607, 1610, and 1630) show the locations of Port Ferdinando and Port Lane correctly but unnamed. However, Blaeu late as 1640 uses Hantaraske (sic) for the area s of Port Ferdinando (no longer an island). DeBry, Mercator, and Hondius all show and name Trinety Harbor. Blaeu's 1640 map is one of the few that depicts and labels each of the inlets correctly. Blaeu's map also offers a clue as to probable relationship between closing Port Lane and newly developing Roanoke Inlet; Port Lane shown at almost future location of what would become Roanoke Inlet. Ogilby (1672) labels Roanoke Inlet at former Port Lane migrating or newly opened.

Gascoyne's 1682 map indicates Port Ferdinando (Gunt Inlet) is beginning to close; labels the inlet Old Inlet, while what was once Port Lane had closed or migrated n. Latter now labeled New Inlet, perhaps indicating a new inlet that would later be named Roanoke Inlet. Trinety Harbor is no longer shown, having closed 1660. By 1685, Fisher et al, with Moll 1708, show Old Inlet incorrectly at a location opposite Colington Island (corroborated by Cumming 1969, 23—**see** Gunt Inlet), prompting others to believe an inlet was here (**see** Kill Devil Hills Inlet); no evidence to support that notion. Furthermore, New Inlet is labeled at approximate former Trinety Harbor, which had closed 1660, or at Caffeys Inlet, which did not open until 1770. Occasionally, maps late as 1718 (DeLisle 1718) portray this incorrect information.

So, inlets in Roanoke Island area were Port Ferdinando, open from before 1585 until 1798 and rarely labeled on maps, before becoming Gunt Inlet by around 1700 and closing 1798. Gunt Inlet, or Gun Inlet, first appeared on Bowen's 1747 map, based on 1745 data, itself based on 1733 data, and Roanoke Inlet is depicted correctly. A smaller companion inlet to Port Ferdinando was Port Lane, open from before 1585; this name was used sparingly until the mid-1600s, when the inlet migrated and became larger (Fisher 1962) or closed, while a new inlet opened slightly n of Port Lane's location and became known as Roanoke Inlet.

Roanoke Island Marshes, extensive marsh, 2 mi. long, 1 mi. wide, Dare County, Nags Head Township (N.C. Wildlife Resources Commission 2016a). Now from US 64 and 264 (n), e of NC 345 s to just n of Baumtown Road (just n of Wanchese), e to Roanoke Sound, including peninsula of Broad Creek Point (though game-land preserve does not include marshes of the peninsula of Broad Creek Point immediately along Roanoke Sound), center 3.5 mi. sse of Manteo. Historically, merely descriptive reference to all marshes s of Manteo and n of Wanchese, so slightly larger than presently defined by game-land preserve using these highways as boundaries. Usage has become place name by references to game-land preserve. Roanoke Island Marshes should not be confused with historical Roanoke Marshes, completely inundated by Roanoke Inlet closing and water being forced through Croatan Sound. *See* Roanoke Island and Roanoke Marshes. *Other names:* Roanoke Island Juncus Marsh (Sorrie 2014, map, 160—juncus [sedge, *Juncus* spp.] not true grass but resembles grass, often referenced as "sedge" on the Outer Banks).

Roanoke Marshes, former marsh, Dare County, Nags Head and Croatan Townships (18th- and early 19th-century sources). Originally marsh islands in Croatan Sound w to mainland from sw Roanoke Island. In 17th and 18th centuries form they no longer exist; a substantial barrier until early 19th century. Roanoke Inlet's closing (1811) forced a greater volume of water through Croatan Sound, submerging the marshes. Remnants of Roanoke Marshes can be seen at shoreline of mainland and as shoals in Croatan Sound. Evidence of Roanoke Marshes in Croatan Sound still visible as late as 1850s. *See* Roanoke Island, Eastern Channel, Roan Oak Narrows, and Ship Channel (Dare County). *Other names:* Daniels Marches (recording error), Daniels Marshes (Collet et al. 1770), The Marshes (usually historical spoken use because of significance).

Roanoke Sound, strait, 17.2 mi. long, Dare County, Nags Head Township (USGS 2013: Manteo, Roanoke Island NE, Oregon Inlet). Trends nnw–sse from Albemarle Sound to Pamlico Sound, separating Roanoke Island from Bodie Island. Name known, used, and mentioned by Ralph Lane as early as 1585. Variant Sandersons Channel, used only temporarily, for an original landowner 18th century when smaller. *See* Roanoke Island. Subdivision named for feature. Now spanned by double version of Washington Baum Bridge built 1994. Original single-span version of Washington Baum Bridge built 1962 and named in his honor because he led efforts to build first bridge 1929, as most agree but exact date is debated. First bridge named Roanoke Sound Bridge and connected Roanoke Island to Nags Head supporting tourism. *Other names:* Narrows (Finley and Young 1827), Ocoan River (misspelling and application error of Occam or Ocam, Indian name for Albemarle Sound, maybe including some of s Currituck Sound), Sandersons Channel (Maule 1718; Currituck DB 2, 1770, 294—95), Walter Rawleigh Sound (Collet et al. 1770).

Roanoke Sound Channel, channel, 11 mi. long, Dare County, Nags Head Township (USGS 2013: Manteo, Oregon Inlet). In Roanoke Sound just e of Roanoke Island from just nw of Oregon Inlet through Roanoke Sound to a point just ne of Manteo at Shallowbag Bay. Dredging and maintenance began around 1910. *See* Roanoke Island and Carolina Cays (hummocks). Made official by USBGN 1975. *Other names:* Manteo-Oregon Inlet Channel (ACE 1948).

Roanoke Wharf, former landing, Dare County, Nags Head Township (Cobb 1905, 8). Was presumably just ne of Cedar Island and The Causeway near soundside of former Roanoke Inlet (Cobb's reference as Nags Head Inlet), where small cargo offloaded for lightering (transferring cargo to smaller, shallow-draft vessels). Only reference found to this probable landing; some names in Cobb 1905 are not well documented and based on peculiar conjectures. *See* Roanoke Island.

Roanoke Woods, woods, Dare County, Nags Head Township (local use). Historically applied to pines on most of n Roanoke Island, today to remaining wooded areas. *See* Roanoke Island. *Other names:* Croatan Woods (limited use—proximity, Croatan Sound).

Robbs Creek. *See* Mill Creek.

Robbs Salt Marsh, former marsh, Dare County, Hatteras Township (Covey 2018, 47). Was in Frisco just e of Brigands Bay subdivision at w edge of former Indian Town (q.v.) 2 mi. w of Buxton. Now encompassed by much larger marsh, Brigands Bay. *Other names:* Davis Salt Marsh (less use).

Roberson Creek, small stream, Dare County, Atlantic Township (Census Block maps). Trends n-s just n of Sound Landing to Avery Pond at Kitty Hawk Landing subdivision, 2 mi. w of original Kitty Hawk. *Other names:* Robersons Creek (Currituck DB 6, 1791, 237–38), Robertson Creek (Currituck DB 7, 1795, 176–77), Robertsons Creek (Currituck DB 11, 1811, 92), Robinsons Creek (Harris 2017; unknown, 1787).

Robbies Way, path, Hyde County, Ocracoke Township (signage). Just s of Windmill Point, e of Teaches Hole Channel and w of Silver Lake in e Ocracoke (village—Pointers area; *see* Ocracoke Village Areas). Maintained pathway for Pamlico Sound access (swimming dangerous, not advised); legacy from Charles and Robbie Runyon helping to maintain Ocracoke's way of life (clever application with double meaning; preservation intent and pathway).

Rockhall Creek, cove, 0.3 mi. wide, Dare County, Nags Head Township (USGS 2013: Roanoke Island NE). In Roanoke Sound at nw end Headquarters Island 5 mi. s of Nags Head (center). One channel remnant of Roanoke Inlet. Meaning unknown locally, and no information has been found. First shown C&GS 1876a.

Rock Point, point, Carteret County, Morehead Township (USGS 2013: Salter Path). On Bogue Banks (soundside) in Indian Beach, 9.8 mi. w of Atlantic Beach (town). Should not be confused with more recently named Rocky Point 4 mi. w of here. *Other names:* Rocky Point (CS 1852).

Rocky Point, point, Carteret County, White Oak Township (local use). Protrudes into Core Sound in e Emerald Isle 3.5 mi. w of Indian Beach (town, w part). Should not be confused with older-named Rock Point in Indian Beach (town) 4 mi. e of here. Subdivision named for feature.

Rodanthe, village, Dare County, Kinnakeet Township (USGS 2013: Rodanthe). On Hatteras Island just n of Waves 27 mi. s of Nags Head. At e-most point North Carolina (former Cape Kenrick [q.v.]; subdivision here named East Point Reef, but developer's name, no evidence of a reef here by that name). Post office est. 1873 but Post Office Department refused to accept original name of Chicamacomico, supposedly too difficult to spell and pronounce. Original meaning or choice of Rodanthe has been lost. Chicamacomico was original reference to a broader area including Waves and Salvo, and Rodanthe was often North Chicamacomico (for some). Specific meaning of "rodanthe" (Greek *rhodon*, rose) seems to have no meaning here. Rosebush Marsh is 2.5 mi. s in s Waves but is minor and with no known relationship. Comparing this selection of post office name with Corolla might be interesting but can only be coincidental. The reason Corolla was chosen as post office name is lost or never known (except for local stories), yet both Corolla and Rodanthe are related to flowers; however, Corolla post office est. 21 years *after* Rodanthe. Also, reportedly postmaster of new post office in Salvo (1901) suggested Phlox, after flower found in e North Carolina, but rejected as post office name; not documented or substantiated. In each case only a functionary at Post Office Department then and original postmasters would have known reasons for choice. Some newer arrivals mention the meaning of Rodanthe to be related to winds or windy. No evidence suggests any such relationship.

Rodanthe is one of the few remaining communities in U.S. to celebrate "Old Christmas" on January 5 or 6. England adopted new Gregorian calendar (1752 to adjust inconsistencies in old Julian calendar) introduced by Pope Gregory XIII (1582) to replace the Julian calendar. The change was resisted by certain isolated groups of Protestants, including parts with English colonies such as Chicamacomico. Subdivision named for feature.

Other names: Big Kinnakeet (misapplication, applied to now Avon, 18 mi. s), Chicamacomico (numerous sources, most accepted spelling before Rodanthe), Chicamicomico (MacNeill 1958, 2), Chichinock-cominock (Outer Banks Visitors Bureau 2016), Chicimacomico (benchmark labeled at Rodanthe, USGS 1943: Roanoke Island 1:125,000 scale), Chickamacomick (Stick 1958, 76), Chickamacomico (Hill 1983, 11), Chickamicomico (historical), Chicomicomio (Bishop 1878), Chiconocomick (early 18th-century maps), Chicky (MacNeill 1958, 201), Kinnakeet (misrecording, indigenous name for Avon, 18 mi. s), Midgett Town (MacNeill 1958, 11—surname prevalent here), North Chicamacomico (Outer Banks Visitors Bureau 2016; Dunbar 1958, 205), Northard Woods (Outer Banks Visitors Bureau 2016—could be direct recording of "Northern Woods" from local pronunciation or misinterpretation of "n," but also said by most merely dropping apostrophe from "n'ard" derived from "northward"), North Chicamacomico (Dunbar 1958, 205), Northern Woods (reference to small wooded area here disappeared by 20th century; Dunbar 1958, 205), North Rodanthe (NCDOT 1936), Old Chicamacomico (historical), Rodantha (sic) (personal letter between acquaintances there, November 5, 1979, schooner Two Sisters, 1902 [White et al. 2017, 24]—both cases written as pronounced).

Rodanthe Beach, beach, 1.5 mi. long, Dare County, Kinnakeet Township (USGS 2013: Rodanthe). Term "beach at Rodanthe" was originally descriptive and used to describe oceanside beach, today used more frequently as named beach. Rodanthe, Waves, and Salvo known historically as Chicamcomico; some resurgence of use for this name here at Rodanthe Beach and s to Salvo. See Chicamacamico Banks, Chicamacomico Beach, and Rodanthe. *Other names:* Chicamacomico Beach (historical, but resurgent use with promotion for tourism), North Beach (sometimes used, as South Beach is used for Salvo Beach).

Rodanthe Breach, former water passage, Dare County, Kinnakeet Township (NCDOT 2013, 4–5). Was on Hatteras Island just se of Round Hammock Bay, 2 mi. n of Rodanthe. Created August 2011 by Hurricane Irene, same storm reopening New Inlet (Pea Island Inlet) 4.5 mi. n of here. Almost exactly same position as former Chickinacommock Inlet (open middle to late 17th century). Not as severe as reopening of New Inlet (Pea Island Inlet) so NCDOT quickly filled this breach with material brought in from a site in Avon (20 mi. s). Breaches during storms are common here in S Curves (q.v.), resulting in authorization and funding of a bridge (known as The Jug Handle) bypassing this area (3 mi. long) under construction (2020). See Rodanthe. *Other names:* Irene Breach (NCDOT 2013, map, B-91—informal report reference since breach created by Hurricane

Irene), Mirlo Breach (local reference, proximity to Mirlo Beach), Mirlo Inlet (limited local use).

Rodanthe Channel, channel, Dare County, Kinnakeet Township (White et al. 2017, fig. 13, 20). Dredged by ACE just n of Chicamacomico Channel trending from Rodanthe Harbor nw 1 mi. then sw 0.5 mi. to connect with Pughs Channel accessing open waters of Pamlico Sound. Also, serves emergency ferry service to Stumpy Point on mainland in cases where access by vehicle might be temporarily interrupted. *Other names:* Rodanthe Emergency Channel (state and local reports), Rodanthe Harbor Channel (local use).

Rodanthe Harbor, harbor, Dare County, Kinnakeet Township (Outer Banks Scenic Byway 2008, 48). At Rodanthe, e terminus Blackmar Gut (harbor approach), 4 mi. n of Salvo. Dredged 1936 and 1937 by U.S. Coast Guard (only such activity on the Outer Banks not accomplished by ACE). *See* Rodanthe. *Other names:* Black Mar Cut (early local use), Black Mar Gut (early use), Blackmar Gut (some local use), Black Mire Gut (early use), Rodanthe Boat Harbor (Dare County Planning Department 2009, map 12 F, 72), The Creek (first half 20th century, especially 1930s and 1940s), The Harbor (local use), The Landing (early usage mostly around the harbor but also the actual harbor).

Roespock Run, former stream, 2 mi. long, Dare County, Atlantic Township (early maps). Began just ne of former Otila (community), flowed s through Loving Canal into Kitty Hawk Bay at Hog Island 1.6 mi. sw of original Kitty Hawk. Newfoundlin Gut, used on Census Block maps, is unusual and found on no other source, a misinterpretation of Newfoundland Gut (Town of Kitty Hawk 2007). No connection to Newfoundland in Canada, though some suggest it might be recorded instance of spoken language referring to the breed of dog from Newfoundland; however, no relationship or connection and no documentation found. According to Harris (2017), Newfoundland was used as early as 1769, which clouds further original name origin. So, just descriptive term for "new found land."

The generic term "run" was used a few times on n Outer Banks (*see* The Run) for a flowing stream (flowing streams are mostly absent); unusual use in tidal creek areas. "Creek" was (is) an English generic used originally for application to tidal streams. So, to distinguish from flowing streams, "run" appeared in colonial America for swift-flowing streams (descriptively) applied to such streams extensively throughout middle Atlantic, especially Virginia, Maryland, parts of Pennsylvania, parts of Kentucky, and parts of (now) West Virginia.

Almost 15 variations of Roespock found thus far, with Rowspock and Roespock most common forms. Application mostly in Kill Devil Hills, though a few forms found applied here to a couple of streams as variant names and, in one case (this feature), legacy name in s Kitty Hawk ridge-and-swale system (q.v.; *see also* Rowspock Point). Name and variations believed by many authors to be of indigenous origin but are **not**. Variations are really corruptions referring to "roebuck," prevalent name given by early colonists (17th and early 18th centuries) applied for profusion of deer here historically. "Roe" refers to roe deer, European (*Capreolus capreolus*) and Asian (*Capreolus pygargus*) varieties of deer known to European colonists ("roebuck," male roe; "buck," male of antlered animals). "Roe deer" is from Old English *rāhdēor*, morphed simply into roe deer. "Buck" was corrupted into "pock." Colonists saw similarity with North American white-tailed deer (*Odocoileus virginianus*) and used familiar "roe deer." Variations of the name were used by early colonists in se Virginia; a contemporary example is popular Buck Roe Beach in Hampton Roads, Virginia.

Other names: Newfoundland Gut (lower portion only—Town of Kitty Hawk 2007; Harris 2017; unknown, 1769), Newfoundlin Gut (Census Block maps), Roanpock Run (Currituck DB 1, 1712, 198), Roasepock Run (misinterpretations), Roesepock Run (early deeds).

Rollinson Channel, channel, 2.7 mi. long, Dare County, Hatteras Township (local use). In Pamlico Sound trending nnw from Hatteras (village), 4 mi. ne of Hatteras Inlet with e-w extension along s tip Hatteras Island. E-w extension used by Ocracoke-Hatteras Ferry to approach South Ferry Channel until shoaling forced new, longer route through

Barney Slue. Used temporarily from 2013, now is more permanent because South Ferry Channel is shoaling beyond maintaining (U.S. Coast Guard 2015). Origin is for John Rollinson, who lived here most of 19th century and served as Collector of Port (Hatteras) 1859–61. He also kept a thorough if unconventional journal (unpublished). Confusing spelling Rawlinson appears on USGS 2013: Hatteras, though all previous USGS maps use Rollinson and the 2013 map still labels navigational aids in the channel as Rollinson. A man mentioned by Smith (1624) associated with some voyages was named Rawlinson, but no evidence of any connection with this channel or this area, named much later. Use of Rawlinson likely a misinterpretation by cartographers. There were several variations in spelling the name, but most family members prefer Rollinson. *Other names:* Oliver Channel (in part), Rawlinsons Channel (USGS 2013: Cape Hatteras), Rocky Rollinson Channel (some use), Rollison Channel (error on internet sites).

Rollinsons Mill, former mill and windmill, Dare County, Hatteras Township (MacNeill 1958). Commercial venture in Frisco (Trent). Exact location reportedly now 100 yards or more offshore. There were about 100 such windmills on the Outer Banks at high point of use and operation. Some such mills were larger and more popular, such as this one and Baums Mill. *See* Rollinson Channel. *Other names:* Frisco Mill (NPS 2005B: NPS 1, 279–80), Rollinson Windmill (historical local use).

Roosevelt Beach, beach, 2 mi. long, Carteret County, Morehead Township (some use). Just w of Pine Knoll Shores 5 mi. w of Atlantic Beach (town). Name of recent origin applied and used because beach is opposite Theodore Roosevelt Natural Area. *See* Pine Knoll Shores for information regarding involvement of the Roosevelt family here. Small subdivision named Roosevelt Beach 3.5 mi. w, but only relationship is for family name.

Rosebush Marsh, small marsh, Dare County, Kinnakeet Township (Garrity-Blake 2010, 492). Soundside on s tip Davids Point in s Waves 2.5 mi. s of Rodanthe.

Rose Harbor, linear approach harbor, Carteret

County, Harkers Island Township (N.C. Marine Fisheries, 2019, E7, map 27). Just w of Bayview Harbor Marina on northern Harkers Island (private business area).

Roses Path, former settlement, Carteret County, White Oak Township (local informants). Was in w Emerald Isle near Emerald Landing subdivision 3.2 mi. e of Bogue Inlet. *See* Bogue Banks historical paths.

Rotten Rock, former shoals, Carteret County, Harkers Island Township (Price and Strother 1798). Was in Atlantic Ocean just se of Cape Point 8.5 mi. sse of Harkers Island (village). No known use today, and configuration is different, but on 1798 map name refers to five shelly shoals (as described). Reason for name unknown other than hazardous nature ("rotten" sometimes used for dangerous in 18th century).

Round-About Hills, large sand dunes, Dare County, Atlantic and Nags Head Townships (Stick 1958, 264). Complex of dunes between Kill Devil Hills (n) and Jockeys Ridge (s), 4 mi. s of Kill Devil Hills (town). Somewhat stabilized, and composed of complex, distorted, continuously changing sand dunes, making it difficult to navigate originally. Name is descriptive. *Other names:* Nags Head Dunes (NPS 1952, 4).

Round Hammock, sand dunes, Dare County, Hatteras Township (CS 1849b). Rounded high dunes just e of Hatteras Inlet, 3 mi. se of Hatteras (village). Variants Round Hammock and Ourdsleys Hammock used interchangeably 19th century when more prominent, but names fallen into disuse. Ourdsleys Hammock originally applied to much larger sand dune than the more distinctive feature named Round Hammock, applied to smaller more distinct part of Ourdsleys Hammock. Both less defined today than last half 19th and early 20th centuries. Variant Baileys Hammick (*sic*) never used by many. "Hammick" a variation of "hummock" (locally spelled "hammock") and used rarely. Similarly, use of generic term "hommock" is rare variation of "hummock." *See* Black Hammock. *Other names:* Baileys Hammick (CS 1861), Ballances Hill (Hooker 1850), Colline Ronde (Blanchard 1856—"Mouillage" [map title] means wet and refers to "recent" [1846] opening of Hatteras Inlet; "colline," small hill), Round Hommock (*sic*) (CS 1853), West

Mount (Blunt 1857, 343—reference to w tip of Hatteras Island).

Round Hammock, hummock, Dare County, Kinnakeet Township (local use). Small peninsula of Hatteras Island at n Round Hammock Bay; nw point is Round Hammock Point just sw of former Loggerhead Inlet 4 mi. n of Rodanthe. *See* Black Hammock.

Round Hammock Bay, bay, 0.3 mi. wide, Dare County, Kinnakeet Township (USGS 2013: Pea Island, Rodanthe). In Pamlico Sound just sw of former Loggerhead Inlet 2.7 mi. n of Rodanthe. *See* Black Hammock. *Other names:* End of Hills Bay (Farrow to Meekins bill of sale, 1771).

Round Hammock Point, marsh point, Dare County, Kinnakeet Township (USGS 2013: Pea Island). Nw point of Round Hammock on Hatteras Island 2.9 mi. nnw of Rodanthe. *See* Black Hammock.

Round Island, former island, Carteret County, Beaufort Township (C&GS 1889b). Was highest point (n end) of unnamed crescent-shaped shoal between Pivers Island (n) and Town Marsh (s) 0.5 mi. ssw of Beaufort (mainland). Existed last half 19th century. Descriptive name. *Other names:* Round Rock (C&GS 1899b).

Round Pond, lake, Dare County, Kinnakeet Township (Covey 2018, 12). Listed by Covey as descriptive name example possibly in Little Kinnakeet or South'ard Water (q.v.) or maybe Cape Hatteras "bulge."

Round Shoal, shoal, Hyde County, Swan Quarter Township; and Pamlico County, Township Number 4 (CS 1862a). Centered on Brant Island Shoal 20 mi. w of Ocracoke (village). More prominent middle to late 19th century; while still occasionally not covered, name has fallen into disuse.

Rowspock Point, point, Dare County, Atlantic Township (probably) (Currituck DB 3, 1739, 33–34). Exact location unknown beyond somewhere on the barrier island side of Lemors Bay, since that name is almost always mentioned with forms of Rowspock, generally in Kill Devil Hills. Reference 1739 deed merely indicates "on North Banks running to Lemors Southern Creek" (*see* Lemors Bay). Name also used for stream in s Kitty Hawk ridge-and-swale system (q.v.) just n of Kitty Hawk Bay (*see* Roespock Run), so slight possibility of that location, though somewhere on Lemors Bay more likely. *See* Roespock Run for name origin. *Other names:* Rancepock (Currituck DB 11, 1810, 124–25), Roscows Point (Currituck DB 11, 1811, 91 — misinterpretation of Rowspock), Rowney Pock Point (Harris 2017; unknown, 1773).

Royal Channel, small channel, Carteret County, Morehead Township (Carteret County GIS 2019). Trends e-w, approach to entrance to Canals at Atlantic Beach (w section Atlantic Beach Isles subdivision), 1.2 mi. s of Morehead City (mainland).

Royal Point, point, Carteret County, Portsmouth Township (USGS 1950: Portsmouth). On small unnamed marsh island in Pamlico Sound at n entrance Royal Point Bay 7.8 mi. sw of Ocracoke (village). *See* Royal Point Bay.

Royal Point Bay, small cove, 0.1 mi. wide, Carteret County, Portsmouth Township (USGS 1950: Portsmouth). In Pamlico Sound just sw of The Haulover, 7.7 mi. sw of Ocracoke (village). No relationship found of this bay with large feature named Royal Shoal (since early 1700s) 7 mi. n of here (though there could be relationship).

Royal Shoal, shoal, Carteret County, Portsmouth and Cedar Island Townships; and Hyde County, Ocracoke Township (NOS 11508, 2014b). In Pamlico Sound forming an arc from Beacon Island 8 mi. nw of Ocracoke Inlet, 8.2 mi. nw of Ocracoke (village). The shoal is a massive continuation of Bluff Shoal (q.v.) but always considered separately. Used since early 1700s; feature changed little since then. Variant Roll Shoal is from spoken use, with no known formal documentation, only notes, etc. — misinterpretation of local pronunciation of "royal." *Other names:* Roll Shoal (spoken usage), Royal Shoal Rock (limited historical use), Royal Shoals (Wimble 1738), Royal Shol (Wimble 1733), Royal Shole (Collet et al. 1770), Ryals Shoal (Moseley 1733), Ryals Shoal Rock (based on Moseley's 1733 map), The Royal Shoals (Hooker 1850).

Royal Shoal Harbor, former anchorage, Carteret County, Portsmouth and Cedar Island Townships; and Hyde County, Ocracoke Township (ACE 1893). Former place ships anchored in deeper water inside crescent-shaped Royal Shoal, 8 mi. nw of Ocracoke (village). Feature no longer used. *See* Royal Shoal. *Other names:* Bight of Royal Shoal (White 2012, 240), The Straddle (local slang q.v.).

Royal Shoal Rock, rock, Carteret County, Cedar Island Township (NOS 2014i). Usually exposed high point of Royal Shoal, 10 mi. nw of Ocracoke (village). *See* Royal Shoal.

Royal Tern Canal, small canal, Dare County, Atlantic Township (Town of Southern Shores 2015). In Southern Shores just e of Great Blue Heron Canal 5 mi. n of original Kitty Hawk. Names of Southern Shores canals are for shorebirds (except Gravey Pond Canal). The royal tern (*Thalasseus maximus*) is here during summer and s of Cape Hatteras year-round.

Rudder Canal, canal, 0.5 mi. long, Dare County, Nags Head Township (PC HOA 2016). Trending s-n loop, then n-s, then e-w 1.3 mi. se of Sandy Point at Roanoke Island Festival Park, 2.5 mi. w of Whalebone Junction and Nags Head. One of seven named canal segments interconnected throughout Pirates Cove subdivision, named portions corresponding with limits of adjacent named subdivisions.

Rum Cove, cove, 0.2 mi. across, Currituck County, Fruitville Township (USGS 2013: Knotts Island). Ne corner Fresh Pond Bay, 2.5 mi. e of Knotts Island (village). Not noted for illegal rum production or rum running early 20th century. *See* Bottle Run Point.

Rumleys Hammock, marsh hummock, Carteret County, Harkers Island Township (USGS 2013: Horsepen Point). On Core Banks just s of Try Yard Creek, 4.2 mi. e of Harkers Island (village). *See* Black Hammock.

Run, The, former small stream, Dare County, Atlantic and Nags Head Townships (historical local use). Formerly connected "Fresh Ponds" (now Fresh Pond) to Roanoke Sound before 1900. Course previously uncertain and might have exited "Fresh Ponds" at n end and flowed through small break in dune configuration where now several small remnant ponds exist, and emptied into Panters Creek (cove; named since colonial times) and then into Buzzard Bay, ostensibly corroborated by the name Run Hill appearing just n of this location. Another reported possibility was The Run flowed out of s portion "Fresh Ponds" through what was in late 1800s a trough-like passage through sand dunes into Roanoke Sound just s of

Mann Point. Based on historical topography, both routes seem plausible.

However, clue is found in Currituck DB 11 (1810, 124–25), which reads "a tract of land on the North Banks known as Rancepock [*see* Rowspock Point] on Collonton [*sic*] Creek. Beginning at mouth of Fresh Pond various courses along water of Colonton [*sic*] Creek." Colington (Colonton) Creek ends at its s end between Deep Ditch Point and Buzzard Point and extends only n from that location. These two points are just n of Panters Creek, where the n route would have been. So, it can be concluded the route of The Run was this n route from Fresh Pond (Ponds) to the sound water.

The generic term "run" was used a few times on the n Outer Banks for a flowing stream, unusual in this tidal creek area. "Creek" is an English generic used for application to tidal streams, so to distinguish from flowing streams "run" was applied. "Run" was coined in colonial era for swift-flowing streams and used extensively throughout middle Atlantic, especially Virginia, Maryland, parts of Pennsylvania, parts of Kentucky, and parts of (now) West Virginia. Rarely used on the Outer Banks and only on the n portion, usually restricted to Kitty Hawk and Kill Devils Hills. During colonial period, "creek" was used in the traditional English sense of a generally open tidal creek (also today), while smaller ditch-like and sluggish water was often referenced as "gutt" or "gut." In 18th-century deeds used terminology such as "running the creek then up the gutt to a branch." "Run" was infrequently used and often later than 18th century.

Other names: Fresh Pond Branch (Currituck DB 7, 1795, 391), Fresh Pond Run (Harris 2017; unknown, 1787), Fresh Pon Runn (Currituck DB 7, 1793, 167–68), Struls Run (Harris 2017; unknown, 1798—probable transcription error for Steeles that had been misapplied—*see* Tillmans Creek), The Fresh Pon (*sic*) Run (Currituck DB 8, 1798, 267).

Run Hill, sand dune, 80 ft. high, Dare County, Atlantic Township (USGS 2013: Kitty Hawk, Manteo). On Currituck Banks, 3 mi. n of Kill Devil Hill, 4.6 mi. sse of original Kitty Hawk. Associative name from stream named The Run (q.v.), formerly from Fresh Pond to Buzzard Bay. Big Kill Devil Hill (Kill Devil Hill), Little Kill Devil Hill, West Hill, Run Hill, and other small sand dunes known collectively as Kill Devil Hills.

Runnells Creek, narrow water passage, 0.5 mi. long, Currituck County, Fruitville Township (Cox 1906). E-w passage separates Walk Island from Runnells Marshes, 2 mi. ene of Knotts Island (village).

Runnells Marshes, marsh, 0.7 mi. long and wide, Currituck County, Fruitville Township (Cox 1923). Extensive marsh maze just s and e of Walk Island just n of Fresh Pond Bay, 1.8 mi. ene of Knotts Island (village). *Other names:* Pine Island (Currituck Deeds, miscellaneous, 1719).

Rush Creek, former small tidal cove, Carteret County, Harkers Island Township (historical). Sw Harkers Island 4.5 mi. ese of Beaufort (mainland). Now private boat basin; name not used.

Rush Creek Harbor, harbor, Carteret County, Harkers Island Township (local use). Boat basin created by former Rush Creek sw tip Harkers Island 5 mi. ese of Beaufort (mainland). *Other names:* Coats Landing Harbor (N.C. Marine Fisheries 2019, E7, map 27—unknown, not used).

Rush Hog Island Point, point, Dare County, Atlantic Township (Town of Kitty Hawk 2007). Just ne of Hog Island 1 mi. wsw of Poor Ridge Landing, 2 mi. sw of original Kitty Hawk. Unusual mixture of two names (perhaps applied in error originally) used for nearby Hog Island (Rush Island) and applied to a point across from and w from Hog Island. *Other names:* Rush Point (occasional use).

Rush Island, marsh island, 0.2 mi. long and wide, Carteret County, Harkers Island Township (USGS 2013: Horsepen Point). In Core Sound at entrance Hogpen Bay 3.6 mi. e of Harkers Island (village). Refers to common rush plant (*Juncus effuses*) native to much of U.S. and the Outer Banks, though is used sparingly and mostly on s Outer Banks.

Rush Point, point, Carteret County, Harkers Island Township (USGS 2013: Harkers Island). Sw point of Harkers Island 1.6 mi. wnw of Harkers Island (village). *See* Rush Island.

S

Sage Island, small marsh island, Currituck County, Poplar Branch Township (unknown, ca. 1900). In n entrance Neals Creek just s of Little Narrows, 8.8 mi. sw of Corolla. Probably no relationship, but an island named Sledge Island (q.v.) is 2 mi. s. Could have been an application problem by misinterpretation of pronunciation. If a relationship exists, speculation would be name from 1900 map (Sage Island) is more likely correct since sage (*Salvia* spp.) is known here. "Sledge" is a heavy hammer, with probably no relationship, and certainly not a reference to sled known as "sledge." However, while "sage" is known, more common reference throughout the Outer Banks is to sedge (*Carex* and *Juncus* spp.), marsh grasses (accounting more for application of "sledge" as a misspelling of "sedge" to nearby feature). So, name could also be a misinterpretation of "sedge" (grass). "Sage" and "sedge" are similar in pronunciation, especially with the Outer Banks spoken accent. It would be unusual to name two islands just 2 mi. apart the same name, so likely Sage is correct here and Sedge correct 2 mi. s.

Sage Path, former area, Carteret County, Morehead Township (Zaenker 2014). Was on Bogue Banks in central Pine Knoll Shores 3.3 mi. w of Atlantic Beach (town). "Paths" often used to access temporary fishing camps and other related reasons. However, Sage Path was a specific access way from Alice Hoffman's Shore House (residence soundside—*see* Pine Knoll Shores) to her Tea House (oceanside), where she entertained in early days of her life at Bogue Banks. Today it would cross Pine Knoll Waterway, not there during Alice Hoffman's residence. "Sage" is known on the Outer Banks and used, but "sedge" is also more prevalent as a type of grass (*Carex* or *Juncus* sp.),. "Sage" simply could be a misinterpreted pronunciation of "sedge." "Sage" and "sedge" are similar in pronunciation, especially with the Outer Banks spoken accent. Still, Ms. Hoffman

(Roosevelt) probably would have used sage. *See* Bogue Banks historical paths.

Sage Swamp, small swamp, Dare County, Atlantic Township (Town of Kitty Hawk 2007). Just w of Ash Swamp 1 mi. ene of Sound Landing, 1.5 mi. nw of original Kitty Hawk. In nw Kitty Hawk Woods Swamps (q.v.). "Sage" is known throughout North Carolina, but "sedge" is a common reference to marsh grass (*Carex* and *Juncus* spp.), in swampy and tidal areas. So, the name might be a misinterpretation of "sedge," which could be corroborated by Harris (2017) since he notes use of Sedge Swamp here as early as 1855, while Sage Swamp does not appear until 1859. "Sage" and "sedge" are similar in pronunciation, especially with the Outer Banks spoken accent. *See* Kitty Hawk ridge-and-swale system. *Other names:* Sedge Swamp (Harris 2017; unknown, 1855).

Sailfish Beach. *See* Whalehead Beach (subdivision).

Sailfish Canal, canal, 0.2 mi. long, Dare County, Nags Head Township (PC HOA 2016). Trends e-w 1.5 mi. se of Sandy Point at Roanoke Island Festival Park, 2.5 mi. w of Whalebone Junction. One of seven named canal segments interconnected throughout Pirates Cove subdivision, named portions corresponding with limits of adjacent named subdivisions.

Sailfish Point, point, Dare County, Nags Head Township (PC HOA 2016). In Pirates Cove subdivision 3 mi. se of Manteo (center). Recent name applied only with development of Pirates Cove subdivision around 1987.

Saint Clair Landing landing, Dare County, Kinnakeet Township (local use). At campground on s edge of Aunt Phoebes Marsh at The Drain just n of Waves 1.3 mi. s of Rodanthe. Saint Clair was a given name used by the Midgett family (*see* Saint Clair Midgetts Camp, Saint Clair Lump, and Saint Clairs Island). *Other names:* Saint Clairs Landing (local use).

Saint Clair Lump, marsh island, 0.1 mi. long and wide, Dare County, Kinnakeet Township (USGS 2013: Pea Island). In Pamlico Sound just w of Goulds Lump 4.9 mi. nnw of Rodanthe. *See* Dorland Lump and Saint Clair Landing.

Saint Clair Midgetts Camp, former camp, Dare County, Kinnakeet Township (historical local use). Was near bridge ruins (1930s) across remnants of New Inlet near Saint Clair Lump and Beach Slue. *See* Camp Cass Williams and Saint Clair Landing. *Other names:* Mr. Sinclairs Fish Camp (Brown 2015—might have been separate, though likely verbal misinterpretation), Saint Claire Midgetts Camp (Garrity-Blake 2010, 90), Saint Clair's Hunting and Fishing Camp (Covey, 2018, 13).

Saint Clairs Island, island, Dare County, Nags Head Township (local informant). In n Oregon Inlet just se of Duck Island 4.5 mi. se of Wanchese. Description provided by informant not precise and possibly could apply to nearby island. *See* Saint Clair Landing. *Other names:* Clairs Island (local use).

Sally Bells Slew, channel, Carteret County, White Oak (probably) or Morehead Township (Stephens 1984, 94). Distance of several mi. from Salter Path (probably w), no additional locative information provided. *See* Allen Slough.

Salt Creek, small tidal stream, 0.5 mi. long, Dare County, Hatteras Township (local use). In Frisco 1 mi. ne of Joe Saur Creek 4 mi. ene of Hatteras (village). Subdivision named for feature.

Salter Path, village, Carteret County, Morehead Township (USGS 2013: Salter Path). On Bogue Banks 9.2 mi. w of Atlantic Beach (town). Developed as temporary fishing camp and became permanent settlement around 1900. Stephens (1984) reports that in 1880s Riley Salter arrived and built a house. Developed as path for carrying fish from oceanside to soundside for transporting. Stephens (1984, 42–43) indicates then "settlers named it Salters Path." Conflicting reports believed by some named from fisherman Tom Salter. Story is he walked to and from ocean to fish, so known as Salter Path. Some indicate named for Owen Salter. Since Riley Salter was first reported settler, more agree named for Riley. Residents sometimes used informally Eastern (Easterd) and Western (Westerd) Salter Path when giving locations. Two areas separated by The Ditch (q.v.); there was reportedly good-natured competition between the two.

"Path" was used frequently on w Bogue Banks for temporary fishing camps and trails. "Path" is not found on n Outer Banks (except Jacks Cabin Path [q.v.]). Post office opened 1918 and discontinued 2011. Post office here

1915–18 named Gillikin, and village known also by this name for a while. Gillikin, named for Bettie Gillikin (Zaenker 2014), surname from family who came here from Diamond City on e Shackleford Banks late 1890s after Diamond City was abandoned because of devastating hurricanes. Somehow might have been selected as post office name, though Gillikin was recent name when post office opened. Salter Path, only remaining place using term "path" still existing, though Rice(s) Path still shown on some maps. Occasionally on some local early maps road from Atlantic Beach depicted as Salt Path Road, but use of Salt Path for Salter Path is unknown. *See* Hoffman Beach and Rice(s) Path. *Other names:* Gilliken (Stick 1958), Gillikin (Stick 1958, 193), Salterpath (NCDOT 1944, 1953), Salters Path (local use, Zaenker 2014).

Salters Creek, water passage, 0.5 mi. long, Carteret County, Portsmouth Township (White 2012, 168). Trends n-s from Casey Bay in Pamlico Sound to Portsmouth Flats, just se of Portsmouth (village), 7 mi. se of Ocracoke (village). *Other names:* Evergreen Slough (USGS 1950: Portsmouth), Wallace Creek (NPS 2007, A-4).

Salters Lumps, marsh islands, 0.5 mi. long, Carteret County, Davis Township (USGS 2013: Davis). In Core Sound just se of mainland, 2.5 mi. ne of Davis (mainland). *See* Dorland Lump and Piney Point Shoal. *Other names:* Cotton Hammock (secondary), Salters Lump (local use).

Salt Flats, area, Dare County, Kinnakeet Township (F&WS 2016). Evaporation area creating salt flats in n Pea Island National Wildlife Refuge, 10 mi. n of Rodanthe. Originally descriptive, became name through usage.

Salt House Bay, linear bay, Currituck County, Poplar Branch Township (C&GS 1852). N-s-trending bay adjacent to Doxeys Salthouse 6.5 mi. nw of Duck. Some applications extend Baums Creek into Salt House Bay. Doxeys Salthouse, marsh just se, could be related in naming process.

Salt Pond. *See* Lighthouse Pond.

Salvage Ile. *See* Portsmouth Island.

Salvo, village, Dare County, Kinnakeet Township (USGS 2013: Rodanthe). On Hatteras Island 13 mi. n of original Avon. Name origin interesting, with heaps of circumstantial evidence, though likely apocryphal. Substantiation derived from residents perpetuating following story. Original name was Clarks, but name apparently did not appear on maps or charts. During Civil War, Union forces proceeding n after securing Fort Clark and Fort Hatteras; commander of a vessel noticed village and asked its name. He was informed chart had no name for the village. His remark reportedly was "give it a salvo anyway," and notation "salvo" was arbitrarily entered onto chart, though this chart has yet to produce itself. "Salvo," simultaneous firing of cannon. Salvo (nor Clarks) actually not labeled on any charts from Civil War (first shows on maps in early 1900s—Geologic map 1909, C&GS not until 1920). Post office est. 1901, closed for a time, reopened 1939, then ceased continuous operation 1992, finally closed 2004. Salvo apparently had been perpetuated somehow but not on maps and charts but was therefore chosen by Post Office Department as the name because Clarks (too close in spelling to Clark) was already used in North Carolina. K. R. Pugh, first postmaster, for reasons unknown reportedly requested the name Phlox (indigenous flower), rejected by Post Office Department. Phlox might have been suggested because it is a flower and might have been suggested relating to Rodanthe (also could refer to part of a flower) for name of post office in that nearby village, but purely a guess. Name of post office eventually became village name. *Other names:* Cape Kenrick (Stick 1970, never used for village), Chicamacomico (in part, Rodanthe, Waves, Salvo original name), Chicimacomico (Chicamacomico variation), Clark (Outer Banks Visitors Bureau 2016), Clarks (numerous sources), Clarksville (numerous brochures, Dunbar 1958, 202), South Chicamacomico (Dunbar 1958, 205), Southern Woods (Dunbar 1958, 205), South Rodanthe (Stick 1970).

Salvo Beach, beach, Dare County, Kinnakeet Township (local use). Oceanside 4 mi. s of Rodanthe. *See* Salvo. Subdivision named for feature. *Other names:* Clarks Beach (historical local use, Bishop 1878—Clarks, original name of Salvo), South Beach (some local use, s-most beach area in Tri-Villages area).

Salvo Harbor, small harbor, Dare County, Kinnakeet Township (Dare County Planning Department 2009, map 12 F, 72). Dredged harbor at Salvo just n of Opening Marshes 3.7 mi. s of Rodanthe. *See* Salvo. *Other names:* Salvo Marina (Dare County GIS), The Harbor (Garrity-Blake 2010, map, 136).

Salvo Holes, area, Dare County, Kinnakeet Township (local use). Deep holes interspersed throughout s Wimble Shoals (q.v.) and n Five Fathom Bank (q.v.) 4 mi. s of Salvo. Name known to local folk and fishermen only; where fish reportedly gather. *See* Salvo.

Sam Pete Cove, small cove, Dare County, Nags Head Township (local use). Is 1 mi. se of Mann Point, 1 mi. w of Jockeys Ridge.

Sam Smiths Point point, Carteret County, Morehead Township (Stephens 1984, 57). Soundside at Salter Path just ne of Indian Beach (town) 4 mi. w of original Emerald Isle. *Other names:* Sam Smith Point (Zaenker 2014).

Samuel Butler's Wharf, former landing, Dare County, Kinnakeet Township (Stick 1958, 76). Was somewhere in Salvo (Clarks) or Waves (South Rodanthe) or Rodanthe (Chicamacomico). The three villages together were Chicamacomico, though Rodanthe was best known by this name. (Samuel) Butler's Wharf reported by Stick as a quote from an announced vendue sale. "Vendue" is from Latin *vendere* (to sell) through French *vendre* into English as "vendue." These auctions were held for owners and investors to receive some sort of compensation for their loss from a shipwreck and were held quickly because it was difficult protecting remains of cargo and ship. By 1800, North Carolina had established wreck districts each with a commissioner to take charge of wreckage and its cargo, and eventually to hold a vendue. So, Stick reports an announced vendue from "State Gazette for May 2, 1794" to be held "on Captain Samuel Butler's Wharf . . . also the hull of the schooner Success, as she lies on Gull Shore [*sic*], within five miles of Chickamacomick." Gull Shore refers to present Gull Island, named Gull Shore on many 18th-century maps, 5 mi. sw of Salvo. Samuel Butler's Wharf must have been in Salvo area of Chickamacomick (*sic*) or Chicamacomico. *Other names:* Butler's Wharf (Stick 1958, 76).

Sand Banks, sand dunes, Dare County, Atlantic Township (USGS 2013: Jarvisburg). At Sanderling 3.3 mi. n of Duck. Originally descriptive, applied on historical maps, but these pronounced dunes have acquired the term as a name.

Sand Beach Creek, water passage, 0.9 mi. long, Dare County, Nags Head Township (USGS 2013: Manteo, Wanchese). Trends s-n on Roanoke Island from near Broad Creek to Johns Creek 1.3 mi. n of Wanchese. *Other names:* Great Sandy Beach Creek (Currituck DB 13, 1814, 52–55), North Sandy Beach Creek (Currituck DB 1786, 5, 235—apparent directional to Broad Creek), Sandy Beach Creek (Currituck DB 2, 1768, 94–95).

Sand Cove, cove, 0.2 mi. wide, Currituck County, Poplar Branch Township (USGS 2013: Mossey Islands). In Currituck Sound just n of Lone Oak Channel, 5.4 mi. s of Corolla.

Sand Cove, cove, Dare County, Atlantic Township (local use). In e Kill Devil Hills (town) just n of Oyster Point at Jack Neck Island 3 mi. se of original Kitty Hawk. Should not be confused with Sand Cove on e shore Les Island 1 mi. w (*see* next entry). Difficult to determine if folk mean the same feature or two different features.

Sand Cove, small cove, Dare County, Atlantic Township (local use). On e shore Les Island in Kitty Hawk Bay Islands (q.v.) complex, n open water of Colington Creek, 2.5 mi. s of original Kitty Hawk. Should not be confused with Sand Cove at Oyster Point 1 mi. e (*see* previous entry). Difficult to determine if folk mean the same feature, just differing in description, or two different features.

Sand Dollar Island, recent very small island, Carteret County, Harkers Island Township (local use).

Sanderling, subdivision, Dare County, Atlantic Township (signage). On Currituck Banks 1 mi. s of former Caffeys Inlet, 3.4 mi. nnw of Duck (center). Resort development from mid-20th century and now in n Duck. Reportedly named for sanderling (*Calidris alba*), bird found during winter on the Outer Banks, similar to a sandpiper except it has no back toe. Of note, Sanders is surname here, and several names use Sanders. Sanderlen surname found in Currituck DB 8 (1797, 13; 1798, 59–60). Sanderling as surname appears in Currituck DB 9 (1807, 289–90). Also, Sanderlin (no "g") appears numerous times as surname in Currituck DB 11–27. These deed references are mostly to Sanderlin(s) witnessing deeds of transfer around Powells Point (mainland), but references to Sanderlin's location are vague. The deed references are late 1790s to mid-1800s then disappear. Also, noted in Currituck DB 28 (1861, 486) is reference to Sanderlin Swamp (mainland at Powells Point). Further, Sanderlin (no "g") occurs in subdivision Sanderlin Shores in Kitty Hawk. Two Life-Saving Service members stationed at Kitty Hawk late as 1900 were Robert Fulton Sanderlin and Thomas Nelson Sanderlin. Local folk served at these life-saving stations; numerous occurrences of Sanderlin in Kitty Hawk. Additionally, one local informant indicated around former Caffeys Inlet (this area) historically was known as Sanderlin (no "g"). Stick (1958, 255) indicates a historical community (name implied as Caffeys Inlet) near Caffeys Inlet, but if so, not recorded as such on any older maps and was likely scattered families known historically here. Reference possibly could have been Poyners Hill community (q.v.) 3 mi. n; more likely this location known locally for short time as Sanderlin and perhaps perpetuated. So, perhaps these scattered families living here did have a community name. In either case, no known documentation (Stick provides no additional reference). Preponderance of circumstantial evidence indicates an origin perhaps from some form of surnames Sanders or Sanderlin (no "g"). Still, name origin is thought/believed by most to be shore bird, which might seem plausible form of folk etymology since naming for surname might have been forgotten.

Sanderling Ridge, small sand ridge, 0.5 mi. long, Dare County, Hatteras Township (local use). An offshoot n-s ridge of Crooked Ridge in Buxton 3 mi. n of Cape Point. Named for small subdivision there. Sanderling (*Calidris alba*) is a small shore bird here in winter only. *See* Sanderling.

Sanders Bay, cove, 0.9 mi. wide, Currituck County, Poplar Branch Township (USGS 2013: Mossey Islands). In Currituck Sound just n of Mossey Islands complex at Currituck Banks 3.8 mi. s of Corolla. *Other names:* Brock Bay (soundside e and n of Sanders Bay known locally as Brocks early 20th century), Sandersons Bay (18th-century maps), Saners Bay (C&GS 1913b), Saunders Bay (misinterpretation).

Sanders Creek, water passage, 0.7 mi. long,

Currituck County, Poplar Branch Township (USGS 2013: Mossey Islands). Between Mossey Islands complex and Currituck Banks at Three Dunes separated from Wells Creek by Sedge Island, 4.5 mi. s of Corolla. *Other names:* Saunders Cove (local use), Wells Creek (local use applied to include Wells Creek).

Sandersons Channel. *See* Roanoke Sound.

Sanderson Swamp, swamp, Dare County, Nags Head Township (Currituck DB 8, 1799, 165–66). On w Roanoke Island, unclear if s Roanoke Island (Wanchese) or n Roanoke Island (Manteo), most likely the former.

Sanders Point, point, Carteret County, Morehead Township (local use). Into Bogue Sound, 1 mi. ne of Indian Beach (town), 3.5 mi. w of Pine Knoll Shores.

Sand Flats **(South Shoal)**, former shoal, 2.5 mi. long, Dare County, Nags Head and Kinnakeet Townships (USGS 1943: Roanoke Island 1:125,000 scale). Was in Pamlico Sound just inside Oregon Inlet, 10 mi. se of Manteo. Ceased to exist from natural erosion and artificial dredging, recently reappeared as South Shoal. Originally applied as descriptor; with continued use developed into name, used until disappeared.

Sand Hill, distinct man-enhanced sand dune, Hyde County, Ocracoke Township (local informants). On small peninsula just w of ferry landing, 0.5 mi. n of Styron Hills, 12.5 mi. ene of Ocracoke (village). Some houses built here.

Sand Hill Crane Canal, canal, 0.5 mi. long, Dare County, Atlantic Township (Town of Southern Shores 2015). In Southern Shores 4 mi. n of original Kitty Hawk. Names of Southern Shores canals are for shorebirds (except Gravey Pond Canal). The sandhill (usual spelling) crane (*Antigone canadensis*) is not prevalent here, only during migration stops.

Sand Hills, sand ridges, Carteret County, Harkers Island Township (Mackay 1756). Descriptive name applied collectively to sand ridges on South Core Banks on some 18th-century maps, from historical Old Drum Inlet near Rumleys Hammock sw to Cape Lookout.

Sand Hole Creek, cove, 0.05 mi. wide, Hyde County, Ocracoke Township (USGS 2002 Howard Reef). In Pamlico Sound, 3.2 mi. ne of Ocracoke (village). *Other names:* Sandhole Creek (occasional).

Sand Hummocks, historical sand dunes,

formerly 2 mi. long, Hyde County, Ocracoke Township (Blunt 1809). Ne-sw to Ocracoke Inlet on sw terminus of Ocracoke Island. Was farther ne than today as inlet has migrated sw. Descriptive term applied as geographic name. Unusual for "hummock" to be used as local spelling is "hammock." The correct but unusual spelling is result of early usage and application by the cartographer. *See* Black Hammock.

Sand Island, island, 1.6 mi. long, Carteret County, Portsmouth Township (USGS 2013: Wainwright Island). Small barrier beach part of North Core Banks between Cricket Island and Sand Island Inlet 11.2 mi. sw of Portsmouth (village).

Sand Island, small island, Currituck County, Fruitville Township (N.C. Wildlife Resources Commission, 2016b). "Vegetation covered" just w of Knotts Island Ferry Dock, 2.5 mi. ssw of Knotts Island (village).

Sand Island, island, Dare County, Nags Head Township (CS 1877). At sw end Roanoke Island just s of Baum Creek 1.3 mi. w of Wanchese.

Sand Island Inlet, water passage, 0.3 mi. long, Carteret County, Portsmouth Township (C&GS 1945). Connects Core Sound with Atlantic Ocean separating Sand Island from Old House Beach 18 mi. sw of Ocracoke (village). Open periodically since mid-1800s, now mostly closed, though carries water on occasion. Use of Pillintary Inlet by Bishop (1878) is interesting because Bishop indicates clearly the name Pillintary Inlet was offered by and used by local folk with whom he spent "close time" sharing their houses and meals. Indication is inlet opened around 1858, 16.5 mi. s of Portsmouth (village), and was short-lived, yet no mention of inlet by this name in any documents, on any maps, by any barrier island and inlet specialists (except two possible exceptions below), and residents now have no recollection of such an inlet except for a few vague recollections that might or might not be relevant. "Pillintary" is form of "pilontary," general local spelling for "pellitory" (*see* Pilontary Islands, 8 mi. ne). Based on Bishop's description as relayed by local residents then, this inlet breached about 1858, which could coincide with Drum Inlet, opened and closed throughout 1800s. Fisher (1962) only expert to mention a possible inlet using a form of "Pilontary," Pilentary Cubhouse

Inlet, but only mentions (if existed) was pre-1900s and existed only briefly. Fisher notes Pilentary (Pilontary) Clubhouse Inlet named in congressional report from late 1800s but indicates he could find no other reference (must have been near clubhouse). Pilontary Clubhouse Inlet is mentioned in N.C. Fisheries (1923, 27). No reference by research but believe name must be variant name referencing Swash Inlet because Pilontary Islands (reportedly Pilentary [sic] Club location) is just sw of Swash Inlet, though is 7.5 mi. ne of the location reported by Bishop. Also, this inlet, Sand Island Inlet, is only 3 mi. ne of reported location by Bishop, was open and closed off and on during later 19th century. So, this Pillintary Inlet "discovered" by Bishop could have been Drum Inlet, Sand Island Inlet, or was probably Swash Inlet. Pilentary Inlet was applied for a short time (locally) to Drum Inlet, Sand Island Inlet, or probably Swash Inlet, or was short-lived, small breach possibly between Drum Inlet and Sand Island Inlet opened so short a time not reported anywhere. Short-lived breaches were commonplace all along Core Banks because of narrowness of barrier ridge here. *Other names:* New Inlet (U.S. Congress 1876), Normans Inlet (Fisher 1962, 102), Old Sand Inlet (Whisnant and Whisnant 2010, map, 490), Sand Inlet (Fisher 1962, 102).

Sand Lead, water passage, Currituck County, Poplar Branch Township (C&GS 1852). Separates Middle Burris Islands (s) from North Burris Island (n), 6.2 mi. s of Corolla. *See* Buzzard Lead.

Sand Lump Island, small island, Dare County, Nags Head Township (Dare County tax records). In s Roanoke Sound 1 mi. wsw of Theoff Point, 3.5 mi. nw of Oregon Inlet, 2.5 mi. se of Wanchese. Curious use of terms "lump" "and" island together—*see* Dorland Lump.

Sandpiper Canal, small canal, Dare County, Atlantic Township (Town of Southern Shores 2015). In Southern Shores e shore Jeanguite Creek 4 mi. n of original Kitty Hawk. Names of Southern Shores canals are for shorebirds (except Gravey Pond Canal). The least sandpiper (*Calidris minutilla*) here during winter, with several other sandpiper species stopping on both summer and fall migrations.

Sand Point, point, Currituck County, Fruitville Township (Cox 1923). Just nw of Sand Pond 3.2 mi. se of Knotts Island (village).

Sand Point, marsh point, Dare County, Nags Head Township (USGS 2013: Manteo). On sw Roanoke Island 1.8 mi. ssw of Manteo.

Sand Point Beach, former beach, Hyde County, Ocracoke Township (Blunt 1809). Descriptive name applied early 19th century at sw end Ocracoke Island; had migrated sw and name no longer used.

Sand Pond, small cove, 0.2 mi. across, Currituck County, Fruitville Township (Cox 1923). Se terminus of Alberts Pond 1 mi. e of Middle Marsh, 3.5 mi. se of Knotts Island (village). *See* Adams Pond.

Sand Ridge, sand dunes, 4 mi. long, Currituck County, Fruitville Township (USGS 2013: Knotts Island Overedge East). Continuous ridge on Currituck Banks at Carova 3.5 mi. e of Knotts Island (village).

Sand Ridge, sand dunes, 5 mi. long, Dare County, Kinnakeet Township (numerous maps, charts, reports). Forms almost continuous ridge just s of New Inlet 1.5 mi. n of Rodanthe. Example of descriptive term, through use, becoming name. Popular hunt club bearing this name near center until middle to late 20th century. *Other names:* Sandy Ridge (older local use).

Sands, The, beach, 1.5 mi. long, Carteret County, Portsmouth Township (USGS 2013: Wainwright Island). On North Core Banks just sw of Old House Beach, 14.7 mi. sw of Portsmouth (village).

Sand Wave of Hatteras, former sand ridge, Dare County, Kinnakeet Township (Stick 1958, 286). Developed partly from rapid denuding here during 19th century for boat-building industry centered around Kinnakeet (Avon) and partly from epic hurricane that created Oregon Inlet and Hatteras Inlet. Resulted in sand dunes developing, some coalescing into larger dunes that moved rapidly across the island covering much of what remained of maritime forests (Stick 1958, 286). Contrived name to describe a process, never really used outside of a few published references. Today not relevant.

Sandy Bay, bay, 1.1 mi. wide, Dare County, Hatteras Township (USGS 2013: Cape Hatteras). In Pamlico Sound 0.9 mi. ne of Hatteras (village). *Other names:* Durant Bay (CS 1852), Durants Bay (CS 1861).

Sandy Bay Shoal, shoal, Dare County, Croatan

SANDY BAY SHOAL / 263

Township (CS 1862a). In Pamlico Sound just e of entrance Sandy Bay 12 mi. e of Rodanthe. Name fallen into disuse today.

Sandy Cove, cove, 0.4 mi. wide, Currituck County, Fruitville Township (USGS 2013: Barco). In extreme ne Bellows Bay at se Great Marsh, just w of s Knotts Island, 2.2 mi. s of Knotts Island (village).

Sandy Creek, water passage, 0.2 mi. long, Dare County, Atlantic Township (USGS 2013: Jarvisburg). Just s of Sandy Creek Island, 4.5 mi. nw of Duck.

Sandy Creek Island, marsh island, 0.2 mi. long, Dare County, Atlantic Township (USGS 2013: Jarvisburg). Just n of Sandy Creek, 4.6 mi. nw of Duck.

Sandy Hell Creek, water passage, 1.5 mi. long, Currituck County, Fruitville Township (Cox 1923). Trends n-s separating Little Skinner Island from Currituck Banks, 6.5 mi. se of Knotts Island (village). Graphically descriptive of navigating the water passage. *Other names:* Sandy Hall Creek (Currituck DB 14, 1819, 42), Sandy Haul (F&WS 1999, map—misinterpretation).

Sandy Point, point, Carteret County, Harkers Island Township (USGS 2013: Harkers Island). S tip of small marsh island 0.1 mi. s of Browns Island, 2.1 mi. ene of Harkers Island (village).

Sandy Point, point, Currituck County, Fruitville Township (USGS 2016: Creeds). On w Morse Point (large Peninsula), 4.3 mi. w of Knotts Island (village).

Sandy Point, point, Dare County, Hatteras Township (NPS 2005b: NPS 2, 294). Protrudes into central Sandy Bay 1 mi. e of Hatteras (village). *Other names:* Pamlico Point (sometimes, mostly because subdivision here), Roberts Point (recent use, name of rental house here).

Sandy Point, point, Dare County, Nags Head Township (USGS 2013: Manteo). On nw shore Shallowbag Bay 0.4 mi. e of Manteo. *Other names:* Doughs Point (historical local use), North Point (Currituck DB 2, 1770, 294–95), Tom Doe Point (misinterpretation, surname Dough), Tom Doughs Point (historical local use).

Sandy Ridge, sand ridge, Dare County, Atlantic Township (local use). In Sandy Ridge subdivision in n Duck, 3 mi. s of Sanderling. Unclear whether name was used before subdivision established or if name came into use after subdivision est. last quarter 20th century. If latter, example of reversed usage, natural feature acquiring name of man-made feature.

Sandy Ridge, small sand ridge, Dare County, Nags Head Township (Gray 2009, 31). On Roanoke Island just e of Skyco 2 mi. sse of Manteo.

Sandy Run, small stream, 0.5 mi. long, Dare County, Atlantic Township (Currituck DB 6, 1789, 36). Begins just n of Sandy Run Swamp, flows s through Sandy Run Park and Sandy Run Swamp to Duck Pond Creek 1 mi. nw of original Kitty Hawk. The name has been used since the late 1700s. Bridge apparently somewhere across this stream named Sandy Run Bridge (Currituck DB 23, 1840, 30–31). *See* The Run. *Other names:* Sandy Run Creek (Harris 2017).

Sandy Run Ditch, linear stream, 2.5 mi. long, Dare County, Atlantic Township (Town of Kitty Hawk 2007). In Kitty Hawk ridge-and-swale system (q.v.) in Kitty Hawk beginning just n of Sandy Run Swamp trending s to Kitty Hawk Bay at Hay Point 1 mi. s of original Kitty Hawk. Harris (2017) notes in Kitty Hawk "drain" was pronounced as "drean" and "dream." Variant Drean verified and indeed (former) local pronunciation and known as a dialectical variation of "drain," though there is no known written application today. However, variant Dream has not been validated despite efforts, so perhaps really is meant to be "stream" or "dreen." Names were spelled as sounded or as folk (many without organized education) thought the name *ought* to be spelled. *See* The Run. *Other names:* Sandy Run Branch (Harris 2017; unknown, 1814), Sandy Run Drain (Harris 2017; unknown, 1825), Sandy Run Dream (*sic*) (Harris 2017; unknown, 1790—maybe "stream" not "dream," though "stream" not used on Outer Banks), Sandy Run Gut (Harris 2017; unknown, 1831).

Sandy Run Swamp, linear swamp, Dare County, Atlantic Township (Town of Kitty Hawk 2007). In Sandy Run Park, 0.8 mi. ne of original Kitty Hawk, 2.5 mi. n of Poor Ridge Landing. In nw Kitty Hawk Woods Swamps (q.v.). *See* Kitty Hawk ridge-and-swale system and The Run.

Sarahs Hole, water passage, Dare County,

Atlantic Township (local use). Deeper water separating Bobs Island (s) and Great Gap Island (n), 4 mi. nw of Duck.

Sassafras Island. *See* Big Skinner Island.

Sassafras Marsh, marsh, Currituck County, Fruitville Township (Currituck DB 7, 1782, 405–6). On Big Skinner Island just s of South Channel, primary remnant channel of New Currituck Inlet, 5 mi. n of Corolla. Sassafras was an important export from America 1600s and early 1700s, believed to be cure-all for all sorts of maladies, so important to know where sassafras was found. Sassafras grew more on mainland but tolerates sandy soil so also grew on larger islands, not entirely marsh, soundside of barrier islands.

Sawmill Ridge, sand ridge, 0.5 mi. long, Dare County, Hatteras Township (Garrity-Blake 2010, 211). Trends e-w just s of Middle Ridge just n of Flowers Ridge and w extension of Great Ridge, 1 mi. s of Buxton.

Sawyers Landing, small landing, Dare County, Nags Head Township (limited local use). Limited access landing at end of an unnamed canal (*see* Canals at Manteo) in Mother Vineyard just n of downtown Manteo. Named for Sawyer family who developed adjacent subdivision, Sawyer's Landing.

Scarboro, former settlement, Dare County, Kinnakeet Township (historical local use). Was on Hatteras Island 1.7 mi. n of original Avon just ne of n Avon (The North'ard). Named for an extended family here but no trace of this former settlement today other than redevelopment. Scarboro and The North'ard often considered as together or adjacent. *Other names:* Scabbertown (Stick 1958, 154—indelicate term sometimes used), Scarborotown (Stick 1958, 286), Scarborough (CS 1852), Scarborough City (occasionally used historically in an amusing manner with few families here), Scarboroughtown (NPS 2005b: NPS 1, 162), Scarsborough (Bishop 1878—misinterpretation).

Scarboro Creek, cove, 0.3 mi. wide, Dare County, Nags Head Township (USGS 2013: Manteo). In Shallowbag Bay 0.7 mi. sse of Manteo (center). Subdivision named for feature. *Other names:* Scarborough Creek (Dare County Planning Department 2009, map 1, 56—earlier spelling of surname Scarboro).

Scarboro Point, point, Dare County, Nags Head Township (USGS 2013: Manteo). N point Scarboro Creek just s of Shallowbag Bay, 0.6 mi. se of Manteo (center). *Other names:* Scarboros Point (Fulton 1820).

Schooner Ridge, sand dune, Currituck County, Poplar Branch Township (local use). Oceanside just e of The Currituck Club, just ne of s-most dune of Three Dunes, 6 mi. s of Corolla. Recent usage after man-disturbed development and road naming, example of reversed usage, natural feature acquiring name of man-made feature (subdivision).

Schooner Ridge. *See* Powder Ridge.

Scotch Bonnet Canal, canal, Dare County, Hatteras Township (N.C. Marine Fisheries 2019, H4, map 8). Approach from Pamlico Sound to Scotch Bonnet Marina, 3.5 mi. w of Buxton. *See* Scotch Bonnet Marina.

Scotch Bonnet Marina, harbor, Dare County, Hatteras Township (signage). In Frisco 0.5 mi. sw of Brigands Bay, 3.5 mi. w of Buxton. Scotch bonnet (*Semicassis granulata*) is an indigenous sea snail named because shape and color resemble a Scottish cap (tam o'shanter). *Other names:* Frisco Marina (sometimes Frisco Cove and Marina—name Frisco Cove never used locally, with no pronounced cove, only very small tidal inlet; marina access dredged 1970s).

Scotts Marsh, former marsh, Dare County, Kinnakeet Township (Covey 2018, 12). Was soundside at Oregon Inlet now 13 mi. n of Rodanthe.

Scotts Muck, former area, Dare County, Kinnakeet Township (Covey 2018, 12). Low-lying often flooded mud and debris in Scotts Marsh at now Oregon Inlet 13 mi. n of Rodanthe.

Scotts Reef, shoal, Dare County, Kinnakeet Township (Garrity-Blake 2010, 492). In Pamlico Sound just nw of Sheeps Head Shoal, 5 mi. w of Waves. "Reef" in Outer Banks geographic names usually refers to oyster colonies.

Scrag Cedar Hills, sand dunes, 3.6 mi. long, 30 ft. high, Hyde County, Ocracoke Township (local use). On ne Ocracoke Island 8.8 mi. ne of Ocracoke (village). Use of "scrag" refers to sparse vegetation here and generally prevalent (now) throughout the Outer Banks. "Scrag" also refers to small whale with no dorsal fin but merely protuberances on dorsal ridge near the tale. Reference to this specific type of whale (now extinct, similar to gray whale) is possible, but lack of vegetation is local preference for name origin. Some evidence of Outer Banks–style whaling indicated by nearby Try Yard Creek, but this activity was early historically, and most Outer Banks whaling was s of Ocracoke near Cape Lookout and Shackleford Banks (*see* Cape Lookout Grounds). *Other names:* Scrag Cedar Hill (Weslager 1954).

Scrag Cedars, former woods, 0.5 mi. long, 5 ft. high, Hyde County, Ocracoke Township (historical local use). Formerly wooded dunes on ne Ocracoke Island just sse of The Great Swash 8.6 mi. ne of Ocracoke (village). "Scrag" used here in its 18th-century English reference to stumps, likely indicating scrub trees originally. *See* Scrag Cedar Hills. *Other names:* Scraggly Cedars (O'Neal et al. 1976, 26).

Scraggly Oak Hills, sand dunes, Dare County, Nags Head Township (Stick 1958, 264). Somewhat stabilized dunes just s of Round-About Hills just w of Jockeys Ridge, 2 mi. nnw of original Nags Head. Refers to scrub trees.

S-Curves, area, Dare County, Kinnakeet Township (NCDOT 2013). Just n of Mirlo Beach, 1.5 mi. n of Rodanthe, 10 mi. s of Oregon Inlet. Coined and used by NCDOT referring to small "hot spots" prone to overwash and breaches; site of Rodanthe Breach August 2011 (Hurricane Irene) and also Chickinacommock Inlet, open 1650s to 1680s and then periodically thereafter. Hurricane Arthur (2014) created significant overwash here. Has become common usage, though is really only one elongated S curve. Early 2017, North Carolina approved construction of a bridge (3 mi. long) in Pamlico Sound to bypass this overwash-prone area (known locally as the "Jug Handle" for its designed shape). *Other names:* S-Turns (popularized by NCDOT).

Seagull, former village, Currituck County, Fruitville Township (postal service). On Currituck Banks just s of Swan Beach 1.5 mi. s of New Currituck Inlet site, 3.5 mi. n of Corolla at Pennys Hill. Known locally as Currituck Inlet as the village's location was near former New Currituck Inlet, closed by 1828, but remnants still visible as South Channel. So, late as 1900, Currituck Inlet still used with qualifier "New" dropped (Wescott 1958, 3). Post office named Seagull established at Pennys Hill (village) 1908 and as other communities, post office name was eventually adopted. Reason for post office name was arbitrary and for prevalence of (sea)gulls here. "Seagull" is used extensively everywhere but is not really a valid word applied to these birds collectively; simply "gulls" is appropriate term. Post office was discontinued 1924. Late as 1950 about 25 people here, but today no trace of former village, now covered by Pennys Hill (q.v.) migrating sw though Seagull; is still known by locals. Also, new, very small subdivision established recently just ne using name Seagull Beach. *Other names:* Currituck Inlet (Wescott 1958—two churches here), Old Currituck Inlet (some local use), Pennys Hill (historical local use), Sea Gull (Norfolk and Southern Railway 1881).

Seagull Beach, beach (former application), Currituck County, Fruitville Township (local informants). Was at former Seagull village (q.v.) now near Swan Beach (q.v.) 3.5 mi. n of Corolla. Name of beach when former Seagull village existed, but former village is now covered by Pennys Hill sand dune. Newer community, Swan Beach, is approx. same location (just n) of where Seagull was located; beach's name today is mostly known as Swan Beach, though some usage of Seagull Beach for just s of Swan Beach by real estate agents, from small subdivision. Seagull Beach as a beach is mostly remembered by older residents.

Sea Holly Ridge, isolated sand dune, 20 ft. high (historically higher), Dare County, Atlantic Township (local use). Lower after alteration by development, in Kill Devil Hills (town) 1.5 mi. n of Wright Brothers Monument, 2 mi. s of original Kitty Hawk. Circular and more dune-like than ridge-like. Named for profusion of herbaceous sea holly here; most varieties are not native to North America, but one variety (*Eryngium yuccifolium*) is native to much of e U.S. Subdivision here named for feature.

Sea Isle Hills, sand dunes, Dare County, Kinnakeet Township (limited new local use). In Waves, 2.2 mi. s of Rodanthe. Recent origin, selected for real estate development to be attractive, not sort of name used historically on the Outer Banks. New seasonal residents sometimes use the name.

Sea Isle Marina, harbor, Carteret County,

Morehead Township (signage). In Sea Isle Plantation (subdivision) at Salter Path 3.5 mi. w of Pine Knoll Shores.

Sea Isle Point. *See* Cannon Point.

Sea Ridge, short sand ridge, Currituck County, Poplar Branch Township (local use). In Monteray Shores, 3.5 mi. s of Corolla. Unclear whether name used before community established or if name came into use afterward in last quarter of 20th century; if latter then reversed usage, natural feature acquiring name of man-made feature.

Sea Side Hills, former sand dunes, Dare County, Kinnakeet and Hatteras Townships (historical deeds). Found in numerous deeds from 18th and early 19th centuries; was original dune system on Pea Island and Hatteras Island.

Sea Side Plains, The, historical, Dare County, Kinnakeet Township (Covey 2018, 20). Reference was to beach from Cape Creek n to The South'ard Water at Long Point 3 mi. s of original Avon.

Sea Water Marina, dock, Carteret County, Morehead Township (signage). E side Atlantic Beach Causeway just n of Atlantic Beach 1.3 mi. s of Morehead City (mainland).

Second Creek, tidal stream, Dare County, Kinnakeet Township (Garrity-Blake 2010, 169). Just s of First Creek, two streams almost join at mouths, 0.7 mi. s of Peters Ditch (Avon Harbor entrance), 6 mi. n of Buxton. Derived from being second major tidal stream s of original Avon. *See* First Creek.

Second Grass, point, 10 ft. high, Hyde County, Ocracoke Township (USGS 2013: Ocracoke). On Ocracoke Island 2.3 mi. sw of Ocracoke (village). Same principle of naming applied as described in entry First Grass. *Other names:* Little Grass (Weslager 1954 — confirmed by interviews with Ballance [2017, 2018] and Howard [2017, 2018]).

Second Hill, sand dune, Carteret County, White Oak Township (local use). Just w of Yellow Hill in original Emerald Isle, 8.2 mi. w of Pine Knoll Shores. *See* Yellow Hill.

Second Pond, man-enhanced pond, Currituck County, Poplar Branch Township (local use). In s Dews Island, 4.3 mi. nw of Duck. Derived being second of three large man-enhanced ponds from n to s on the island.

Second Slough, natural channel, 15 mi. long, Dare County, Nags Head and Kinnakeet Townships (local use). Trends n-s just e of Platt Shoals 6 mi. e of Oregon Inlet.

Descriptive, second deep area e of Oregon Inlet used primarily by fishermen (not shown on official or local maps).

Sedge, The, former grass, Dare County, Hatteras Township (Urias O'Neal estate map, 1954, from Covey 2018, 33). Was in Frisco just s of Brigands Bay subdivision, just s of present NC 12, 3 mi. w of Buxton.

Sedge Island, small marsh island, less than 0.1 mi. across, Currituck County, Fruitville Township (USGS 2013: Knotts Island). In North Graven Creek between Graven Island and sw Walk Island, 1.3 mi. e of Knotts Island (village). Sedges (*Carex* and *Juncus* spp.) are grass-like plants forming marshes and grow throughout the Outer Banks.

Sedge Island, island, 0.3 mi. long, 0.2 mi. wide, Currituck County, Poplar Branch Township (USGS 2013: Mossey Islands). N end Wells Creek just w of Three Dunes, 5 mi. s of Corolla. North Piney Island and West Piney Island now joined on n side by Sedge Island. *See* Sedge Island above. *Other names:* Buzzard Island (across Wells Creek from Sedge Island, often misapplied).

Sedge Island, marsh island, Dare County, Atlantic Township (local use). In Currituck Sound 1 mi. w of Station Bay, 4 mi. nnw of Duck. *See* Sedge Island.

Seeder Hammock, hummock, Dare County, Atlantic Township (Currituck DB 5, 1787, 216). Exact location unknown and not remembered; Harris (2017) and Stick (1958, 264) provide only general reference to being one of numerous hummocks somewhere in Kitty Hawk ridge-and-swale system (q.v.) 2 mi. w of original Kitty Hawk. "Seeder" form of "cedar"; spelling oddities were common 1700s here and elsewhere—names were spelled as sounded or as folk thought the name ought to be spelled. Use of "seeder" for "cedar" appears several times in Currituck deeds (1700s). *See* Cedar Hammock.

Seeder Hammock Gut, tidal stream, Dare County, Atlantic Township (Currituck DB 5, 1787, 216). Exact location unknown and not remembered; Harris (2017) and Stick (1958, 264) provide only general reference to being one of the numerous tidal streams somewhere in Kitty Hawk ridge-and-swale system (q.v.) 2 mi. w of original Kitty Hawk. *See* Seeder Hammock and Alligator Gut. *Other names:* Ceder (*sic*) Hammock Gut (Harris 2017).

Seeder Hammock Ridge, sand ridge, Dare County, Atlantic Township (Currituck DB 5, 1787, 216). Exact location unknown and not remembered; Harris (2017) and Stick (1958, 264) provide only general reference to being one of the numerous ridges somewhere in Kitty Hawk ridge-and-swale system (q.v.) 2 mi. w of original Kitty Hawk. *See* Seeder Hammock. *Other names:* Seder Hammock Ridge (Currituck DB 6, 1788, 142), Seeder Hammack Ridge (Currituck DB 5, 1787, 216).

Serenity Ridge, sand ridge, 0.5 mi. long, 20 ft. high, Dare County, Hatteras Township (local use). Soundside sand ridge on e-w–trending largest part s Hatteras Island. Disagreement exists whether name preceded housing subdivision (same name) or named from the housing subdivision; probably latter, example of reversed usage, natural feature acquiring name of man-made feature.

Set Net Creek, narrow water passage, 0.5 mi. long, Currituck County, Fruitville Township (Cox 1923). N-s trending in w Runnells Marshes, arm of Fresh Pond Bay, 1.6 mi. ene of Knotts Island (village).

Set Net Creek Point, point, Currituck County, Fruitville Township (local use). At sw Set Neck Creek opening into Knotts Island Bay, sw tip Runnells Marshes 1.5 mi. e of Knotts Island (village). Associative from Set Net Creek.

Sevenfoot Patch, shoal, 1.9 mi. long, Hyde County, Lake Landing Township (NOS 2014i). In Pamlico Sound on Bluff Shoal, 9 mi. nnw of Ocracoke (village). Reportedly descriptive of water depth. *Other names:* Seven Foot Patch (C&GS 1899b).

Seven Sisters, sand dunes,70 ft. high, Dare County, Nags Head Township (USGS 2011: Manteo and USGS 2013: Roanoke Island NE). Seven dunes, 0.4 mi. se of Sound Side in Nags Head (center) ; not as prominent as 100 years ago. Legend relates story of humane owner of seven ill slave girls whom he sent to the seaside to cure their illness. Folk etymology, name is merely descriptive. *See* Bay Tree. Subdivision named for feature. *Other names:* Seven Sisters Dunes (historical written references).

Sextant Canal, canal, Dare County, 0.3 mi. long, Nags Head Township (PC HOA 2016). Trends nw-se 1.2 mi. se of Sandy Point at Roanoke Island Festival Park, 3.3 mi. w of Whalebone Junction. One of seven named canal segments interconnected throughout Pirates Cove subdivision, named portions corresponding with limits of adjacent named subdivisions. Sextant, navigation instrument used to measure angle between two visible objects. Hence, instrument used from invention early 18th century until more modern devices to determine ship's position.

Shackleford Banks, barrier island, 9.2 mi. long, 0.3 mi. wide, 35 ft. high, Carteret County, Harkers Island Township (USGS 2013: Harkers Island, Beaufort). Trends se-nw from Barden Inlet to Beaufort Inlet, separated from Harkers Island and mainland at Beaufort by Back Sound. Named for John Shackleford, who purchased land 1713 (with Enoch Ward), originally Porter Grant (portion) and included Shackleford Banks and s Core Banks portion. Shackleford and Ward divided the purchase, with Shackleford acquiring w part (basically Shackleford Banks) and Ward e part. W tip a spit (created by moving sand by longshore or littoral drift) deposited mostly between 1949 and 1971. Stanford Islands (q.v.) was applied collectively to Bogue Banks and Shackleford Banks (reason for plural) in colonial period. Wades Shore on w Shackleford Banks was village at Mullet Pond; sometimes Wades Shore and Mullet Shore used informally for the island, before mid-20th century. Local residents use "shack" in informal spoken language but does not appear on maps. Early colonial period Shackleford Banks mostly covered with maritime forest but was deforested by mid-18th century mostly for shipbuilding in Beaufort. Made official by USBGN 1892. *Other names:* Cape Banks (in part—also Cape Lookout n-ward; Stephens 1989, 84—pronounced "cay" by residents of Salter Path), Cape Lookout Island (Moseley 1733, inset), Core Sound Banks (Wimble 1738), Mullet Shore (local slang), Shackleford Bank (Binkley 2007, 200), Shackelfords Bank (Kell 1777), Shackleford Island (G. Colton 1861), Shacklefords Bank (CS 1857a), Shacklefords Banks (CS 1860), Stanford Island (18th-century applications), Stanford Islands (Romans 1776), Wades Shore (sometimes used for entire w end, settlement by that name there).

Shackleford Beach, beach, 8 mi. long, Carteret County, Harkers Island Township (local use). Corresponds to Shackleford Banks from Barden Inlet (se) to near Shackleford Point. Used historically, but after several decades of little use has experienced increased usage with more tourists visiting here via passenger-only ferry service provided by NPS. *Other names:* Shackleford Banks Beach (Runyon et al. 2005, 74).

Shackleford Point, point, 10 ft. high, Carteret County, Harkers Island Township (USGS 2013: Beaufort). Near w end Shackleford Banks 2.4 mi. s of Beaufort (mainland). Was w-most point on Shackleford Banks, but w-most point is 0.9 mi. farther w from deposition from longshore drift (sand and other materials being advanced along shore by oblique or angled waves, culminating in a spit or hook at terminus of land). *See* Shackleford Banks. *Other names:* Shackleford Spit (sometimes used from curved formation made by longshore drift this end Shackleford Banks, classic spit formation), Shacklesford Point (Angley 1982, 28).

Shackleford Slue, channel, 3.5 mi. long, Carteret County, Harkers Island, Beaufort Townships (USGS 2013: Harkers Island, Beaufort). Trends ese-wnw in Back Sound from Middle Marshes to Beaufort Inlet 2.4 mi. se of Beaufort (mainland) and separates Horse Island, Carrot Island, and Middle Marshes from Shackleford Banks. *See* Shackleford Banks and Allen Slough. *Other names:* Shackleford Bank Channel (alternate usage), Shackleford Slough (C&GS 1968).

Shackleford Spit Breakers, breakers, Carteret County, Beaufort and Harkers Island Townships (local use). Breakers in shoal-water off tip Shackleford Point (Shackleford Spit) on Shackleford Banks, 2.5 mi. s of Beaufort (mainland). *See* Shackleford Banks.

Shad Hole, cove, Hyde County, Ocracoke Township (USGS 2013: Howard Reef). In Pamlico Sound at Hammock Woods 4.5 mi. ne of Ocracoke (village). Shad (*Alosa sapidissima*), type of anadromous fish (spawns upstream) common to the Outer Banks, and name origin. Also, shad boat was common to the Outer Banks with shallow draft for navigation in shallow sounds. First shad boat built in Manteo by George Washington Creef, 1870s. *See* Hattie Creef Landing and Piliauga Creek.

Shad Hole Creek, tidal stream, 0.5 mi. long, Hyde County, Ocracoke Township (USGS 2013: Howard Reef). Trends n from unnamed sand dunes to Pamlico Sound at Quokes Point, 4.8 mi. ne of Ocracoke (village). *See* Shad Hole.

Shallowbag Bay, bay, 1.2 mi. wide, Dare County, Nags Head Township (USGS 2013: Manteo). In Roanoke Sound at Manteo 4.2 mi. sw of Nags Head. Name origin, while apparent as totally descriptive, is not known for sure or remembered, but name appears unchanged from earliest maps to present. "Shallow" refers to feature's overall depth and known problematic, as evidenced by frequent use of Ballast Point to drop ballast. "Bag" refers to feature's shape and was common 17th-century feature reference. Also, "bag" common descriptive reference to slack part in center of gill net frequently used here. Name used by Johnson (1863), Shallow Back Bay, is misinterpretation. Variant Shalon-bas Bay on a few (French) maps 19th century, reported as Chalon-bas, meaning a low trawling net. Not found in modern French usage, corruption of older French term *chalut*, referring to trawling, and *bas* is low, so "low trawling." Exactly how and why this term would be applied to Shallowbag Bay is unknown. Two parts often referenced in reports and development papers but are not actual names—Outer Shallowbag Bay and Inner Shallowbag Bay (Town of Manteo 2007, fig. 4, 40).

Other names: Gaskins Creek (local surname used only by few for short time historically), Gibs Creek (short form of Gibson), Gibson Creek (Moseley 1733), Lanes Harbor (vague reference in Lane's 1585 discussions with Drake), Manteo Bay (rare spoken reference; Angley 1985, 12), Manteo Harbor (Stick 1958, 183n), Shallow Back Bay (CS 1882), Shallow Bag Bay (NPS 1952, 4), Shallowbags Bay (misrecordings), Shallowbay Bay (C&GS 1862—misinterpreted decision based on lack of knowledge), Shalolog Bay (Currituck DB 1815, 14, 12–13), Shalon-bas Bay (Martin 1829, 35), Town Creek (sporadically used for Doughs Creek, flows into Shallowbag Bay, sometimes applied to Shallowbag Bay—Maule 1716).

Shallowbag Bay Marina, harbor, Dare County, Nags Head Township (signage). In Manteo at extreme se Shallowbag Bay just w of entrance Scarboro Creek. *See* Shallowbag Bay.

Shallow Point, point, Dare County, Kinnakeet Township (local use). Mouth of Askins Creek with heavy amounts of accumulated sand, 2 mi. s of original Avon.

Shannons Island, marsh island, 0.1 mi. across,

Dare County, Atlantic Township (local use). In Currituck Sound, 2.8 mi. nw of Duck.

Shark Shoal, former shoal, 1 mi. long, Carteret County, Beaufort Township (USGS 2013: Beaufort). Was just nw of Beaufort Inlet, 1.2 mi. w of Beaufort (mainland). *Other names:* Shark Shoals (Tompson and Albert 1854).

Shark Shoal, former shoal, Carteret County, Portsmouth Township (ACE 1893). Was at entrance Ocracoke Inlet, 3.5 mi. sw of Ocracoke (village). Extension of Dry Sand Shoal, today completely awash.

Shark Shoal, shoal, 1.4 mi. long, Dare County, Hatteras Township (USGS 2013: Hatteras Overedge North). In Pamlico Sound 3.3 mi. e of Clam Shoal, 3.4 mi. n of Hatteras (village).

Shark Shoal Channel, channel, 2 mi. long, Dare County, Hatteras Township (local use). Trends sse–nnw in Pamlico Sound just w of Shark Shoal, 4 mi. nnw of Hatteras (village). Extension of Rollinson Channel.

Sharp Island, small marsh island, 0.1 mi. wide, Dare County, Atlantic Township (local use). In Blount Bay at extreme s tip Kitty Hawk Bay Islands (q.v.) complex just off sw tip Baum Point Island, 3.5 mi. s of original Kitty Hawk.

Sheep Creek, narrow water passage, 0.4 mi. long, Currituck County, Poplar Branch Township (USGS 1982: Jarvisburg). Through unnamed marsh islands just s of Little Yankee Pond, 0.6 mi. w of Currituck Banks, 6.1 mi. nw of Duck.

Sheephead Marsh, marsh, 1 mi. across, Carteret County, Beaufort Township (USGS 1997: Harkers Island). Between Shep Shoal (not typographical error) and North River Marsh 2.6 mi. wnw of Harkers Island (village). Name origin is for the channel bass (*Sciaenops ocellatus*) another name for red drum fish off coast here.

Sheep Island, marsh island, 0.1 mi. long, Carteret County, Harkers Island Township (USGS 2013: Harkers Island). Junction Core Sound and Back Sound, 3.4 mi. sse of Harkers Island (village).

Sheep Island, island, 0.6 mi. wide, Carteret County, Portsmouth Township (former local use, various publications). Between Salters Creek and The Haulover (and Piliauga Creek), 1 mi. sw of Portsmouth (village), 7 mi. sw of Ocracoke (village). S-most Portsmouth inhabited area. This part Portsmouth Island referred to as "up the banks" (though s)

because land higher here. Remnants here of Salter Battle Fishing and Hunting Lodge. *See* Sheep Island (former community). USGS (1950: Portsmouth) labeled incorrectly in marsh named Bay Marsh just w of Portsmouth (village), 6.8 mi. sw of Ocracoke (village). *Other names:* Evergreen Island (in part—USGS 1950: Portsmouth).

Sheep Island, former community, Carteret County, Portsmouth Township (White 2012, 168; NPS 2007, 29). S-most community of Portsmouth Island, 1 mi. sw of Portsmouth (village), 7.2 mi. sw of Ocracoke (village). Connected to main Portsmouth (village) by "the straight road" also known as "old straight road" and several rudimentary bridges. On Sheep Island, referenced as "up the banks" though s-ward because it was higher land. A practice on Portsmouth Island when the island was inhabited was to indicate n end of the island as "down the banks" and the s end of the island as "up the banks," peculiar to a nonlocal person because one uses (generally) "up" for n and "down" for s since maps of n hemisphere always have n at top or "up." Opposite was case at Portsmouth because higher ground was s end of the island. No one remained after 1933 hurricane. All named outlying communities part of Portsmouth (village) just clusters of houses separated by marsh and open area and referenced by separate names for convenience and clarity of location (*see* East Portsmouth, Middle Portsmouth, Portsmouth, and South Portsmouth). *See* Sheep Island (island—Carteret County, Portsmouth Township).

Sheep Island, island, Currituck County, Poplar Branch Township (unknown, ca. 1900). At w side of Big Narrows separated from Narrows Island by Negro Creek, 7.5 mi. sw of Corolla. *Other names:* Negro Creek Island (older local use), Nigger Creek Island (C&GS 1852).

Sheep Island Bay. *See* Casey Bay.

Sheep Island Creek, small cove, Carteret County, Portsmouth Township (C&GS 1866). In Pamlico Sound at n end Sheep Island just sw of Portsmouth (village), 7 mi. sw of Ocracoke (village). *Other names:* Sheep Island Bay (Olszewski NPS, 33).

Sheep Islands, islands, 0.2 mi. wide, Carteret County, Sea Level Township (USGS 2013: Styron Bay). In Core Sound 0.7 mi. ne of Big Marsh, 3.4 mi. s of Atlantic (mainland).

Sheep Island Shoal, extensive shoal, 1.5 mi. long, 0.5 mi. wide, Carteret County, Portsmouth Township (USGS 1950: Portsmouth; USGS 2013: Wainwright Island Overedge North). In Pamlico Sound, just nw Sheep island 5.5 mi. sw of Ocracoke (village). N one-third often bares at low water, much larger historically.

Sheep Island Slue, channel, 0.9 mi. long, Carteret County, Harkers Island Township (USGS 2013: Harkers Island). Junction Back Sound and Core Sound between Cedar Hammock and Morgan Island separated from Light House Channel by Morgan Island and Sheep Island, 3.3 mi. sse of Harkers Island (village). *See* Allen Slough.

Sheep Island Slue, channel, 4 mi. long, Carteret County, Portsmouth Township (USGS 1950: Portsmouth). Trends e-w in Pamlico Sound from Wallace Channel just ene of Sheep Island Shoal. Just nw of Portsmouth (village) 6.2 mi. sw of Ocracoke (village). *See* Allen Slough. *Other names:* George Gilgos Slough (White 2012, 30: "it was George Gilgo's Slough when you first went into it"), Mount Vernon Slue (just ne of Mount Vernon Rock; ACE 1893), Sheep Island Slough (White 2012, 30).

Sheep Marsh, shoal, Currituck County, Fruitville Township (C&GS 1913a). On e approach to entrance Knotts Island Bay, surrounds Sheep Marsh Island just nw of Swan Island 2.3 mi. se of Knotts Island (village). More shoal than marsh, though more marsh mid-19th century. Big Sheep Marsh sometimes applied to s part and Little Sheep Marsh then to n part. *Other names:* Big Sheep Marsh (local use—s part), Little Sheep Marsh (local use—n part).

Sheep Marsh Island, small marsh island, Currituck County, Fruitville Township (C&GS 1913a). In Currituck Sound at s entrance Knotts Island Bay 2 mi. se of Knotts Island (village). Associative with Sheep Marsh.

Sheep Pen, former area, 1 mi. long, Currituck County, Poplar Branch Township (Codman, Crowninshield, and Lawrence 1925). Was soundside in Peters Quarter just w of Monteray Shores subdivision 3.5 mi. s of Corolla. Historical descriptive reference used during late 19th and early 20th centuries.

Sheep Pen, former area, Dare County, Atlantic Township (Harris 2017). Was just s of original Kitty Hawk near More Shore at e end Kitty Hawk Bay 1 mi. e of Hay Point. Descriptive of activity in former large grazing area.

Sheep Pen Creek, cove, 0.1 mi. long, Carteret County, Sea Level Township (USGS 1951: Styron Bay). In Core Sound 3.4. mi. s of Atlantic (mainland). *Other names:* Sheeppen Creek (occasionally written historically).

Sheep Pen Creek, cove, 0.6 mi. long, 0.3 mi. wide, Carteret County, Smyrna Township (USGS 2013: Horsepen Point). In Core Sound just s of Cowpen Island 5 mi. e of Harkers Island (village). *Other names:* Sheep Creek (C&GS 1888b), Sheeppen Creek (occasionally written historically).

Sheep Pen Island, former island, Currituck County, Poplar Branch Township (CS 1852). Was just ese of Teals Island 2.5 mi. s of Monteray Shores. Part of Teals Island since end 1800s.

Sheep Pen Point, point, Currituck County, Poplar Branch Township (USGS 2013: Mossey Islands). Ne point of Narrows Island 6.8 mi. sw of Corolla.

Sheep Ridge, low sand ridge, 5–10 ft. high, Dare County, Hatteras Township (local use). Barely discernable because covered in vegetation between Back Creek and Muddy Creek in n Hatteras (village) 4.3 mi. ne of Hatteras Inlet.

Sheeps Head Shoal, shoal, Dare County, Kinnakeet Township (Garrity-Blake 2010, 492). In Pamlico Sound just s of Franks Reef, 2 mi. e of Salvo.

Shellbank, shore, 1 mi. long, Dare County, Atlantic Township (USGS 2013: Kitty Hawk). At Currituck Sound between Shellbank Point and Long Point just n of entrance to Kitty Hawk Bay, 2.4 mi. wsw of original Kitty Hawk. Descriptive for many shells here and shifted application over years, was historically applied (18th century) to large mound (midden) of oyster shells at entrance Kitty Hawk Bay. *Other names:* Shell Bank (Colton and Fillmore 1862).

Shellbank Landing. *See* Kitty Hawk Landing.

Shellbank Point, point, Dare County, Atlantic Township (USGS 2013: Kitty Hawk). In sw Kitty Hawk ridge-and-swale system (q.v.) in Kitty Hawk Landing subdivision, 2.2 mi. w of original Kitty Hawk. *Other names:* Alford Point (given name appears here on numerous deeds from 1700s), Allfords Point (colonial deeds), Shellbank (Harris 2017), Shell Bank Point (NCDOT 1938).

Shellbank Ridge, short sand ridge, Dare

County, Atlantic Township (Harris 2017). Almost nonexistent now in n Kitty Hawk Landing subdivision, 0.7 mi. n of Shellbank Point, 2 mi. w of original Kitty Hawk. Named for close proximity to Shellbank Point and Shellbank (shore). *Other names:* Shell Bank Ridge (Harris 2017).

Shellbank Slew, channel, Dare County, Atlantic Township (local use). In e end Albemarle Sound at Shellbank (shore) just n of Shellbank Point, just w of Kitty Hawk Landing subdivision, 2.5 mi. w of original Kitty Hawk. *See* Allen Slough. *Other names:* Shell Bank Slew (Harris 2017; unknown, 1878).

Shell Castle, island, 0.1 mi. wide, Carteret County, Portsmouth Township (USGS 1950: Portsmouth). In Pamlico Sound at w end Ocracoke Inlet 7 mi. w of Ocracoke (village). Former names Old Rock and Shell Castle Island were changed to Shell Castle by owners John Wallace and John Gray Blount 1789. Was part of Oyster Rocks (q.v.), with smaller application 18th century and smaller now than 20th century. "Castle" first used by merchants 1790 (McGuinn 2000, 60—reason not provided). Federal government (1794) authorized construction of a wooden lighthouse on Shell Castle, completed 1798. Owners reportedly operated several commercial activities here, including a windmill, preliminary stop for Portsmouth (village) and inland ports serving as a lightering point, or place for redistributing cargo to smaller vessels for more efficient travel in shallow sounds and estuaries. Place for refreshment (tavern) and several warehouses were available. Interestingly, Blunt's 1809 map labeled Shell Castle as "The Domain of Shell Castle," which is the only known occurrence; presumably reference to activities here. No trace remains of commercial activities or lighthouse.

Other names: Castle (historical spoken reference), Castle Island (CS 1856), Castle Rock (historical), Old Rock (Stick 1958, 77), Shell Castle Island (e.g., CS 1856; Miller 1974; MacNeill 1958; Williamson 1992), Shell Castle Islands (NPS 2007, 140), Shell Castle Rock (Goerch 1956—original usage), Shell Island (Torres 1985, 61), Shell Island Castle (CS 1852–82), The Castle (Price 1795, 630), Upper Anchorage (NPS 2007, 27, 28).

Shell Castle Harbour, former harbor, Carteret County, Portsmouth Township (historical sources). Was at Shell Castle 7 mi. w of Ocracoke (village). Was commercial harbor at Shell Castle (q.v.). Variant Crib Wharf was sometimes used because docks made from logs creating crib-like structures, named from an original meaning of "crib," to restrain. Crib wharves were necessary rather than cobb wharves (cobblestones) because more resistant to erosion. Spelling of "harbour" is legitimate from time period. *Other names:* Crib Wharf (McGuinn 2000, 401), Eastend (McGuinn 2000, 401), Shell Castle Wharf (McGuinn 2000, 19).

Shell Castle Point, point, Carteret County, Portsmouth Township (CS 1854). W tip of midden (pile of shells) with sand and marsh (*see* Shell Castle) 8 mi. w of Ocracoke (village). *See* Shell Castle.

Shell Castle Shoal, former small shoal, Carteret County, Portsmouth Township (Price 1795, 629). Was just n of Shell Castle, small channel separating it from Beacon Island Shoal 5.3 mi. wsw of Ocracoke (village). *See* Shell Castle. *Other names:* Shell Castle Reef (Weslager 1954), Shell Castle Shoals (Price 1795, 630).

Shell Castle Shoal Channel, former channel, 1 mi. long, Carteret County, Portsmouth Township (McGuinn 2000, 212). Was an approach to Shell Castle between Shell Castle Shoal and Beacon Island Shoal 6 mi. w of Ocracoke (village).

Shell Castle Swash, shoal, Carteret County, Portsmouth Township (McGuinn 2000, 19). At Shell Castle Shoal just ne of Shell Castle 5 mi. w of Ocracoke (village). Relevant when Shell Castle was an economic concern in late 18th century. *See* Daniel Swash.

Shell Castle Windmill. *See* Shell Castle.

Shell Cove, small cove, Dare County, Atlantic Township (Currituck DB 6, 1789, 34–35). Just s of Shellbank Point and Kitty Hawk Landing subdivision 1 mi. n of Long Point, 2 mi. wsw of original Kitty Hawk.

Shell Hall, island, Currituck County, Fruitville Township (Cox 1923). Just n of Crow Island (Big Raymond Island) at s entrance South Channel, 4 mi. se of Knotts Island (village). Sometimes attached to Crow Island (Big Raymond Island). *See* Guys Hall.

Shell Island, elongated island, Carteret County, Cedar Island Township (USGS 2013: Wainwright Island). In Core Sound 0.8 mi.

nw of Wainwright Island, 2.5 mi. w of Swash Inlet, 15.5 mi. sw of Ocracoke (village).

Shell Point, point, Carteret County, Harkers Island Township (USGS 2013: Harkers Island). Se point Harkers Island 2.1 mi. ese of Harkers Island (village). Named for large mound (midden) of shells left here by Indians over a long period.

Shell Point, former point, Carteret County, Portsmouth Township (U.S. War Department 1895). Was s point of Shell Castle (island—highest part) 6.5 mi. w of Ocracoke (village).

Shell Point Landing, dock, Carteret County, Harkers Island Township (local use). NPS facility for ferry service 4.2 mi. to Cape Lookout Lighthouse and Shackleford Banks, 8 mi. ese of Beaufort (mainland).

Shell Rock, rock, Currituck County, Poplar Branch Township (Codman, Crowninshield, and Lawrence 1925). Just offshore at Great Beach 0.3 mi. n of Great Beach Pond, 1.5 mi. s of Corolla.

Shell Rock, rock, Currituck County, Poplar Branch Township (local use). In Currituck Sound 8.8 mi. ssw of Corolla.

Shell Rock Point, point, Currituck County, Fruitville Township (Cox 1923). At se entrance Fresh Pond Bay, 2.4 mi. ese of Knotts Island (village).

Shelly Island, former shoal-island, 1 mi. long, 0.2 mi. wide, Dare County, Hatteras Township (multiple media sources). Former crescent-shape ne-nw just s of Cape Point at Cape Hatteras (about 50 yards), 3.5 mi. sse of Buxton. Was exposed portion Hatteras Shoals (q.v.), June 2017 (lasted just less than one year), innermost of three shoals of Diamond Shoals. Hypsography (land formations even if covered by water) of these shoals are constantly changing and often bare during storms but are later covered. This occurrence is attributed to major storms increasing longshore drift, or movement of sand laterally followed by period of calm, allowing deposition. Appeared April 2017 as mere speck and grew into exposed island 1 mi. long and 0.2 mi. wide (about 20 acres). Name given reportedly by youngster with family exploring island for shells. In March 2018, battered by storms, the island was divided, with half attaching to Cape Hatteras and other portion lasting only a few days before disappearing and again becoming part of Hatteras Shoals. Whatever the present situation of this former island (should it reappear), and according to officials at Cape Hatteras National Seashore, no attempt should be made to access it by walking or swimming (true of all such places at the Outer Banks) as passage between Cape Point and former Shelly Island was fraught with danger, including but not limited to sharks, stingrays, hazardous debris, and unpredictable, swirling currents.

Shelor Canal, canal, 0.5 mi. long, Carteret County, Morehead Township (Carteret County GIS 2019). Next canal n of Smith Canal in Atlantic Beach Isles subdivision (w part of Canals at Atlantic Beach q.v.), 1.4 mi. s of Morehead City (mainland). Shelor is a surname.

Shep Shoal, shoal, 0.2 mi. across, Carteret County, Beaufort Township (USGS 2013: Harkers Island). Junction Back Sound and entrance North River 2.4 mi. wnw of Harkers Island (village). Appeared on maps since 1949 as Shep; if typographical error, persisted for over 60 years. Just s of Sheephead Marsh (suggesting an application error). However, interviews confirm named for Shep Willis, also confirmed by road sign here displaying name. *Other names:* Sheep Shoal (N.C. Marine Fisheries 2019, E5, map 29).

Shingle Creek, cove, 0.1 mi. wide, Hyde County, Ocracoke Township (USGS 2013: Green Island). In Pamlico Sound 4.2 mi. sw of Hatteras Inlet, 12.5 mi. ne of Ocracoke (village). "Shingle" refers to beach type specifically composed of varying grades of gravel or pebbles; some faint remnant evidence might have been the case here. Making shingles (for roofs) was also an industry for a while, historically, in Kitty Hawk (*see* Bermuda Island), but not here. Also, story told of a ship carrying roofing shingles wrecked nearby (Weslager 1954 cites this explanation as merely a story—folk etymology). However, numerous loads of shingles passed through lightering services at Shell Castle (q.v.) in Ocracoke Inlet, so might be possible for name origin.

Shingle Landing, former landing, Dare County, Atlantic Township (historical local use). Was on s shore nw Colington Island, 4.1 mi. s of original Kitty Hawk. Post office for Colington (community) est. 1889 at Shingle Landing. "Shingle" refers to beach type specifically made up of varying grades of gravel or pebbles. However, here refers to point from where shingles for houses were loaded for export; shingle making was an early industry here (*see* Bermuda Island).

Shingle Point, point, Carteret County, Davis Township (USGS 2013: Davis). W point two unnamed marsh islands in Core Sound 0.3 mi. n of Goose Island, 2.7 mi. s of Davis (mainland). "Shingle" refers to beach type specifically made up of varying grades of gravel or pebbles, rare on the Outer Banks.

Ship Channel, former channel, Carteret County, Harkers Island Township (CS 1850a). Was ne approach to Beaufort Inlet between former breakers and Shackleford Point 3.5 mi. s of Beaufort (mainland). Existed in second half 19th century, example of how descriptive terms became place names.

Ship Channel, former channel, 4 mi. long, Carteret County, Portsmouth Township (historical local use). Was in Pamlico Sound just w of Middle Ground from Blair Channel (just after backside Ocracoke Inlet) nw-ward in arc around North Rock to former Flounder Slue, 4 mi. w of Ocracoke (village). Se channel portion still partially open but remainder closed. *Other names:* Common Channel (McGuinn 2000, 19), Old Ship Channel (ACE 1893).

Ship Channel, former channel, Dare County, Croatan Township (CS 1862a). Was between mainland and remnants of Roanoke Marshes just e of mainland across from s end Roanoke Island 6 mi. sw of Wanchese (Currituck DB 11, 1810, 56–57; ACE 1843). Existed (opened) a couple of decades, allowing small boats to pass from Albemarle Sound through the increasingly disappearing Roanoke Marshes. Interestingly, Narrow of Rone Oake Marshes and Ship Channel were used as descriptors in same deed 1810. So, names used together for short while until Roan Oak Narrows (and variations) disappeared. Process of inundating Roanoke Marshes and forming Croatan Sound had begun by end 18th century, when Roanoke Inlet began to close. Name used locally and never in prominent usage. Portion previously Roan Oak Narrows, fell into disuse becoming completely unknown when more flooding from closing of Roanoke Inlet had opened this channel further. *See also* Eastern Channel, Roan Oak Narrows, and Roanoke Marshes. *Other names:* Narrow of Rone

Oake Marshes (Currituck DB 11, 1810, 56–57), Roanoke Marshes Channel (Stick 1958, 142), The Thoroughfare (Collet 1770).

Ships Bay, cove, 0.5 mi. wide, Currituck County, Poplar Branch Township (USGS 2013: Corolla). In Currituck Sound, 0.7 mi. n of Raccoon Bay, 1.6 mi. nnw of Corolla. *Other names:* Ship Bay (Currituck DB 24, 1842, 104; Codman, Crowninshield, and Lawrence 1925), Shipps Bay (local brochures).

Shitty Point, point, Hyde County, Ocracoke Township (NPS 2005b: NPS 2, 488). Location unknown exactly but thought just e of Horsepen Point (Hyde County), undeveloped containing hummocks (treed islands) surrounded by marsh creating difficult approaches, probable name explanation.

Shoal Point, point, Dare County, Hatteras Township (local use). Just ne of Hatteras Inlet, n point of unnamed shoals (s point Inlet Peninsula), 3 mi. sw of Hatteras (village). Awash at high tide. *Other names:* Hatteras Point (Covey, 2018, 89), South Point (Garrity-Blake, 2010, 19).

Shoal Waters, The, marsh and shoal, 0.5 mi. wide, Carteret County, White Oak Township (local use). Soundside at w end Bogue Banks and Emerald Isle (town) trends e-w, just s of Banks Channel 1 mi. w of entrance Langston Bridge. Descriptive term becoming a name through usage.

Shoehole Bay, bay, 0.3 mi. across, Currituck County, Poplar Branch Township (local use). In Currituck Sound 1.6 mi. w of Currituck Banks in small marsh 5.8 mi. nnw of Duck. *Other names:* Shoe Hole (local maps), Shoe Hole Bay (USGS 2013, 2010, 1982: Jarvisburg), The Shoehole (some local use).

Shooting Hammock, marsh island, 0.3 mi. long, Carteret County, Harkers Island Township (USGS 2013: Harkers Island). In Back Sound at ne entrance Bald Hill Bay 2.1 mi. s of Harkers Island (village). Reference to hunting activity here. *See* Black Hammock. *Other names:* Bells Island (Mason 2000, NPS map, 1987, 38—*see* Bells Island).

Short Creeks, tidal streams, Hyde County, Ocracoke Township (local use). Descriptive reference to several small tidal streams soundside 0.7 mi. ne of Hammock Hills, 4 mi. e of Ocracoke (village). *Other names:* Shorts Creek (some spoken use).

Signpost, The, former area, Dare County, Atlantic Township (Angley 1995, 6; Harris

2017). Was surrounding intersection of The Woods Road and Twiford Road just w of Duck Pond and Duck Pond Swamp where small school existed. Old School Lane still extends s from this intersection to West Kitty Hawk Drive, 1 mi. nw of Kitty Hawk (center). The "signpost" here might have related to the school or something else entirely; no one knows or remembers the name.

Silver Lake, harbor, 0.5 mi. wide, Hyde County, Ocracoke Township (USGS 2013: Ocracoke). At Ocracoke (village). Original name, Cockle Creek, from prominence of cockles or clams here at Ocracoke (village). Local residents, then and still, reference it simply as The Creek. Dredged into a harbor early 1900s–1940s. Name persistently reported in sources changed to Silver Lake, descriptive of appearance, reportedly given by visitor 1920s or 1930s. Incorrect—name was known perhaps as early as 1885 when the Spencer brothers, owners of Ocracoke Hotel, reportedly used that "description" as referent, which became the name (*Daily Journal* [New Bern], 1890, reported in *Ocracoke Island Journal*, June 2, 2014). Before dredging Cockle Creek into Silver Lake, three small creeks at se part toward Pamlico Sound for 0.3 mi.; each filled in eventually. Collectively they were known as Old Guts (q.v.). *See* Big Gut and Little Gut. Made official by the USBGN 1922.

    Other names: Cockle Creek (C&GS 1905—original name), Cockle Creek Harbor (used sparingly before dredging), Cockrel Creek (Garrity-Blake 2010, 356), Cockrel Pond Creek (some older local use), Ocracoke Creek (Weslager 1954, 44), Ocracoke Harbor (Williamson 1992), Silver Creek (Garrity-Blake 2010, 362—must be mistake, not encountered elsewhere and not used locally), Silver Lake Harbor (ACE 1939), The Branch (Garrity-Blake 2010, 363), The Creek (older local use before dredging), The Ditch (Garrity-Blake 2010, 355—name of access from Pamlico Sound to Silver Lake), The Harbor (O'Neal et al. 1976, 26), The Pond (early local use).

Simon Island, elongated island, 0.5 mi. long, Currituck County, Fruitville Township; and City of Virginia Beach. Mostly in Virginia (USGS 2013: Knotts Island). Small portion in North Carolina 3 mi. ne of Knotts Island (village).

Simpson Neck, peninsula, 0.9 mi. long, Currituck County, Fruitville Township (USGS

2013: Knotts Island). Separates Capsies Creek and Porpoise Slough 2.2 mi. n of Knotts Island (village). "Neck" applied by early settlers to interfluves (land between rivers or water bodies) or peninsulas. Used extensively in Virginia and Maryland, but rarely used on the Outer Banks, except near North Carolina–Virginia boundary. *Other names:* Pinte of Land (Currituck DB 12, 1814, 354–55).

Simpson Hole, small area, Currituck County, Fruitville Township (local use). Deeper than surroundings at e shore s end of peninsula Simpson Neck, in extreme nw Knotts Island Channel 2.5 mi. n of Knotts Island (village).

Simpsons Creek. *See* Capsies Creek and Porpoise Slough.

Sinkers Island, former island, Currituck County, Poplar Branch Township (C&GS 1852). Was in Jarvis Channel just se of South Burris Island, 8.2 mi. s of Corolla. Name origin speculation to do with fishing or disappearance of island, but no one knows.

Six Mile Channel, channel, 2 mi. long, Hyde County, Ocracoke Township (local use). Separates Six Mile Hammock Reef from significant soundside tidal flats from Horsepen Point just e of Ocracoke Island to near Little Swash Opening, 5 mi. ene of Ocracoke (village). Associative name with Six Mile Hammock and Six Mile Hammock Reef.

Six Mile Hammock, hummock, Hyde County, Ocracoke Township (USGS 2013: Howard Reef). High ground on Ocracoke Island 6 mi. ne of Ocracoke (village). Named for distance from Ocracoke (village). Naming practice used because of importance knowing location of vegetation. Named early as 1795 (Price). *See* Black Hammock.

Six Mile Hammock Reef, shoal, Hyde County, Ocracoke Township (local use). At Ocracoke Island 3 mi. nnw of Six Mile Hammock, 6 mi. ne of Ocracoke (village). E end Howard Reef, sometimes local use is for Six Mile Hammock Reef because Howard Reef is long and a more precise reference required. Named for its proximity to Six Mile Hammock, named for distance from Ocracoke (village). "Reef" in Outer Banks geographic names usually refers to oyster colonies.

Skinners Landing, former landing, Dare County, Nags Head Township (historical local use). Was on sw Roanoke Island just sw of Wanchese. Still numerous access canals in heavy marsh, and historically numerous landings here: Davis Landing, Hookers Landing, Pugh Landing, etc. Exact location is unknown, but near Skinners Landing subdivision.

Skull Island, island, Carteret County, Harkers Island Township (local informants). Junction of Back Sound and Core Sound 1 mi. s of Shell Point (se tip Harkers Island), 2.5 mi. se of Harkers Island (village). After numerous interviews, no one really sure of name origin, but presume descriptive of island shape: like a skull as if top of skull oriented ne.

Skyco, community, Dare County, Nags Head Township (signage). On s-central Roanoke Island at Ashbee Harbor 2.2 mi. s of Manteo. Original name Ashbees Harbor, but when post office opened 1892 name was Skyco. Originally spelled Skiko, named for son of a Choanoke Indian chief who was held hostage by early military party of English soldiers (first Roanoke colony) for their own protection against unfriendly Indians. The spelling "Skico" also used but never used for the village. Eventually adopted name of post office but retained Ashbee as harbor name. Decline of steamship industry decreased relative importance of Skyco, and post office discontinued 1913. Today only a few people live here, but resurgence in name usage reflected by sign "Welcome to Skyco," applying to larger area now. *Other names:* Ashbee Harbor (original name), Ashbees Harbor (some use), Ashbees Landing (Downing 2013, 100), Ashbees Wharf (steamship use), Ashby Harbor (occasional spelling), Ashbys Harbor (occasional spelling), Ashbys Landing (Wise 2010, 276), Skiko (occasionally written, never used).

Slash, The, water passage, 1 mi. wide, Dare County, Hatteras Township (USGS 2013: Cape Hatteras). Trends e-w, one of two tidal streams (other is The Creek) in Hatteras (village center) 4 mi. w of Frisco. Descriptive of appearance. *Other names:* Big Ditch (some local use), Slash Creek (NPS 2005B: NPS 1, 47).

Sledge Island, island, 0.3 mi. across, Currituck County, Poplar Branch Township (USGS 2013: Mossey Islands). In Currituck Sound just sw of Mossey Islands complex 8.7 mi. sw of Corolla. Name appeared on maps since early 1980s, but likely a misrecording perpetuated. Also an island named Sage Island (q.v.) 2 mi. n, though likely no relationship. However, sage (*Salvia* spp.) is known here

and use of "sledge" is unknown as a place name. Likely corruption of "sedge," common reference used on the Outer Banks for marsh grasses (*Carex* and *Juncus* spp.). No relation to type of sled by this name.

Slippery Pine Branch. *See* Pine Creek.

Sloop Channel, channel, 2.5 mi. long, Hyde County, Ocracoke Township (local use). In w Hatteras Inlet 5.5 mi. w of Hatteras (village), used for Ocracoke-Hatteras Ferry. *See* Sloop Creek.

Sloop Creek, water passage, 0.4 mi. long, Dare County, Atlantic Township (USGS 2013: Kitty Hawk). Nw part of water passage trending sw from Colington Creek to Dog Point Creek, connects to Blount Bay just n of Colington (community), 3 mi. s of original Kitty Hawk. "Sloop" usually refers to fore-and-aft rigged boat with mainsail or single mast.

Sloop Inlet, canal, Dare County, Atlantic Township (local use). At Colington Harbour, 2.5 mi. wsw of Kill Devil Hills (town). "Inlet" not used in traditional sense on the Outer Banks as barrier island breach. Indicative of dredging allowing water inward for access by boats to open water (Albemarle Sound). Canal naming scheme at Colington Harbour is ships or nautical terms. *See* Sloop Creek.

Sloop Island, island, 0.8 mi. long, 0.5 mi. wide, Dare County, Atlantic Township (USGS 2013: Kitty Hawk). In Kitty Hawk Bay just s of Burnt Island in Kitty Hawk Bay Islands (q.v.), 2.4 mi. s of original Kitty Hawk. *See* Sloop Creek. *Other names:* Frying Pan Island (reportedly resembles distorted inverted frying pan, not now but late 20th century).

Slue, The, former channel, 1 mi. long, Carteret County, Morehead Township (CS 1850a). Separated two unnamed shoals in Atlantic Ocean, 2.5 mi. sw of Beaufort Inlet 3.2 mi. s of Morehead City (mainland). Disappeared by 20th century. *See* Allen Slough.

Smith Canal, canal, 0.5 mi. long, Carteret County, Morehead Township (Carteret County GIS 2019). S-most of nine canals in Atlantic Beach Isles subdivision (w part of Canals at Atlantic Beach q.v.), 1.5 mi. s of Morehead City (mainland).

Smith Creek, water passage, 0.3 mi. long, Dare County, Nags Head Township (USGS 2013: Oregon Inlet). Trends n-s in Roanoke Sound separating Smith Island from Hog Island 3.6 mi. sse of Wanchese.

Smith Inlet. *See* Caffeys Inlet.

Smith Island, marsh island, 0.1 mi. wide, 0.2 mi. long, Currituck County, Fruitville Township (USGS 2013: Knotts Island). In marsh islands just w of Manns Islands at n end Knotts Island Channel 2.3 mi. ne of Knotts Island (village).

Smith Island, marsh island, 0.3 mi. long, Dare County, Nags Head Township (USGS 2013: Oregon Inlet). In Roanoke Sound just se of Roanoke Island, 1.5 mi. w of Duck Island, 3.6 mi. s of Wanchese.

Smith Ridge. *See* Blind Ridge.

Smiths Creek. *See* Hog Hill Creek.

Smiths Ridge, sand ridge, Dare County, Atlantic Township (Currituck DB 1a, 1763, 147–48). Exact location unknown but described as on "Bank Land on Kitty Hawk Bay." Was most likely one of the numerous ridges in Kitty Hawk ridge-and-swale system (q.v.) just w of and up to 3 mi. w of original Kitty Hawk.

Snake Island. *See* Long Island (Carteret County, White Oak Township).

Snake Pit Landing. *See* Percys Landing.

Snake Run, stream, Dare County, Atlantic Township (Currituck DB 5, 1787, 273). Exact location unknown and not remembered; Stick (1958, 264) provides only a general reference to being one of the streams somewhere in Kitty Hawk ridge-and-swale system (q.v.) 2 mi. w of original Kitty Hawk. Deed (1787) indicates beginning at a "sipress" (*sic*) swamp; there are (were) many here and continuing across to Kitty Hawk Ridge. *See* The Run.

Snow Goose Canal, canal, 1 mi. long, Dare County, Atlantic Township (Town of Southern Shores 2015). E-w trending, connecting junction of Snowy Egret Canal (s) and Sand Hill Crane Canal (n) with Jeanguite Creek (w) 4 mi. n of original Kitty Hawk. Names of canals at Southern Shores are for shorebirds (except Gravey Pond Canal). Snow goose (*Chen caerulescens*) frequents the Outer Banks during winter.

Snowy Egret Canal, canal, 2.5 mi. long, Dare County, Atlantic Township (Town of Southern Shores 2015). In Southern Shores 3.5 mi. n of original Kitty Hawk. Names of Southern Shores canals are for shorebirds (except Gravey Pond Canal). Snowy egret (*Egretta thula*) here year-round.

Snug Harbor, small cove, Carteret County, Beaufort Township (local use). At nw Radio Island just s of causeway carrying US 70, 1.7 mi. w of Beaufort (mainland). Radio station WMBL was on n shore Snug Harbor when radio station existed, name origin for Radio Island.

Solomon Harbor. *See* Ashbee harbor.

Sound Landing, former landing, Dare County, Atlantic Township (USGS 2013: Kitty Hawk). Was on Currituck Banks 0.7 mi. n of Shellbank Point, 2.1 mi. w of original Kitty Hawk. Historically, steamboat landing for vacationers at Nags Head, one of earliest places on the Outer Banks for spending a holiday. During early 20th century also used by timber industry. Today unimportant, with modern highway access. *Other names:* Baums Wharf (Patterson 2008, 87—reference vague but believed to docks at Sound Landing), Botilla (occasional mistaken written reference), Otilla (historical local use), Shellbank (Warner and Beers 1875—small-scale map, not much detail, uses community symbol here).

Sound Side, former community, Dare County, Nags Head Township (USGS 2013: Manteo—still labeled). In Nags Head 3.6 mi. ne of Manteo. Original settlement around Nags Head and served as landing for Nags Head vacationers. Mattie's Store here 1914 to 1930s, when moved to oceanside. *See* Nags Head Cove. *Other names:* Nags Head Woods (occasional locational reference, s portion), Old Nags Head (Miller 1974).

South'ard, The, area, Dare County, Kinnakeet Township (NPS 2005b: NPS 1, 166). Extreme s original Avon (Kinankeet), 1 mi. s of original Avon center, 5.5 mi. n of Buxton. Directional term contracting "southward," used in conjunction with The North'ard (q.v.). Five or six families here, and isolated; eventually these families moved to original Avon.

South'ard Channel, small channel, Dare County, Kinnakeet Township (Garrity-Blake 2010, 492). In Pamlico Sound 3 mi. sw of Rodanthe, 2 mi. s of Chicamacomico Channel, also known as North'ard Channel. *See* The South'ard.

South'ard Hunting Grounds, historical area, Dare County, Kinnakeet Township (Garrity-Blake 2010, 210). Historically applied to water, marsh, open areas, and low vegetation at and just s of small settlement (a few houses) known historically as The South'ard (q.v.), 1.5 mi. s of original Avon.

South'ard Reef, shoal, Dare County, Kinnakeet

Township (Garrity-Blake 2010, 493). Just se of Gull Island and Gull Island Shoal 2.7 mi. w of Bay Point, 8 mi. sw of Salvo, 3 mi. s of North'ard Reef, each a directional name. "Reef" in Outer Banks geographic names usually refers to oyster colonies. *See* The South'ard.

South'ard Water, historical area, Dare County, Kinnakeet Township (Garrity-Blake 2010, 210). Historical, surrounding Long Point Creek; still a complex maze of tidal creeks and water passages with Long Point Creek as principal tidal creek 2.5 mi. s of original Avon. Tidal streams here canalized 1930s by extensive diking, remnants of which remain. *See* The South'ard. *Other names:* Northard Water (Garrity-Blake 2010, map, 211—directional related to Cape Hatteras area 4 mi. s; some question whether was Southard or Northard, indication is South'ard relating to The South'ard area 2 mi. n though term unknown to most), The Creeks (several deeds early 1800s).

South Bar, former shoal, Carteret County, Portsmouth Township (Price et al. 1808). At s approach to Ocracoke Inlet 4 mi. sw of Ocracoke (village).

South Bar, shoal, Hyde County, Ocracoke Township; and Dare County, Hatteras Township (CS 1853). S side of primary channel for Hatteras Inlet 4.5 mi. wsw of Hatteras (village). *Other names:* South Breaker Head (Coles and Price 1806).

South Beach, beach, 2 mi. long, Carteret County, Harkers Island Township (NPS 2000). W side Cape Lookout 7.5 mi. s of Harkers Island (village). Only known occurrence, hand-annotated on map, and is used only by NPS. Peculiar South Beach due w of East Beach (q.v.) and on w side Cape Lookout.

South Beach, beach, 2.5 mi. long, Dare County, Hatteras Township (Goldstein 2000, locs. 3022 and 3033). At Cape Hatteras, e-w adjacent to and just w of Cape Hatteras Lighthouse Beach 2.5 mi. ssw of Buxton, 2.5 mi. se of Frisco.

South Beach, beach, Dare County, Nags Head Township (Goldstein 2000, loc. 2869). Oceanside, n shore Oregon Inlet just s of North Beach, 1.5 mi. sse of Coquina Beach, 10 mi. s of Whalebone Junction. Relatively new name associated with s migration of Oregon Inlet used mostly by local folk, fishermen, and off-road enthusiasts.

South Beach Drain, very small ditch, Dare County, Hatteras Township (NPS 2006a, 11). At South Beach 1.5 mi. nw of Cape Point 2.5 mi. s of Buxton. Trends n-s from complex of small dunes to ocean.

South Beach Drain Pond, small pond, Dare County, Hatteras Township (NPS, 2006a, 11). At n end South Beach Drain 1.5 mi. nw of Cape Point 2.5 mi. s of Buxton.

South Birch Island, marsh island, Dare County, Nags Head Township (local informant). Off sw Roanoke Island just s of Birch Island 1.5 mi. sw of Wanchese. *See* Birch Island.

South Bitterswash Creek, cove, 0.1 mi. long, Hyde County, Ocracoke Township (USGS 1950: Green Island). In Pamlico Sound, 0.4 mi. sw of North Bitterswash Creek 11 mi. ne of Ocracoke (village). Today, collective name Bitterswash Creeks used more than the individual names North Bitterswash Creek and South Bitterswash Creek.

South Breakers, breakers, Dare County, Hatteras Township; and Hyde County, Ocracoke Township (CS 1850b). At entrance Hatteras Inlet, 4.5 mi. sw of Hatteras (village). *Other names:* Southern Breakers (Blunt 1857, 343).

South Breakers, former breakers, Hyde County, Ocracoke Township (historical). Were at s approach to Old Hatteras Inlet near Scrag Cedars 10.3 mi. sw of Hatteras (village).

South Breakers, former breakers, Hyde County, Ocracoke Township (Moseley 1733). Was s of Middle Ground (not larger shoal named Middle Ground inside Ocracoke Inlet) n side Ocracoke Inlet (18th century before deposition filled it) 2.9 mi. s of Ocracoke (village). *Other names:* South Breaker (Price 1795, 627), South Breaker Head (Coles and Price 1806—shallows causing breakers).

South Buckle Island, marsh island, 0.3 mi. long, 0.2 mi. wide, Currituck County, Fruitville Township (USGS 2013: Knotts Island). In marsh islands at n end Knotts Island Channel 2.5 mi. ne of Knotts Island (village). N part still sometimes referenced as Mon Island (q.v.). Mon, misinterpretation by mapping crews of Mann (surname here) from local accent in pronunciation, and also historically applied to incorrect island (*see* Mann Island). So, 2006, with local assistance and state approval, rectified by USBGN by removing the name Mon Island, applying South Buckle Island. Original name was Buckle Island, but Buckle Island had for decades been applied to an island in Virginia 1 mi. n of this island. So, proposed to rename Buckle Island in Virginia North Buckle Island and this feature Buckle Island (original name); however, proposal rejected by Virginia State Name Authority as creating confusion since Buckle Island had been applied for decades to the feature in Virginia, so this island was then named South Buckle Island. *Other names:* Buckle Island (local use), Buckles Island (local use), Bucket Island (external misinterpretation), Mon Island (q.v.—local use), Porpoise Island (some local use, proximity to Porpoise Slough).

South Burris Island, irregular marsh island, 0.7 mi. across, Currituck County, Poplar Branch Township (USGS 2013: Mossey Islands). Separates Currituck Sound and Burris Bay 0.7 mi. s of North Burris Island, 7.2 mi. s of Corolla. *See* Burris Islands. *Other names:* Cedar Island (isolated 18th-century references; also used for North Burris Island), South Burrus Island (spelling variation), West Burows Island (C&GS 1852).

South Channel, water passage, 1.6 mi. long, Currituck County, Fruitville Township (USGS 2013: Corolla, Barco). In Currituck Sound just w of former New Currituck Inlet, 8.5 mi. nnw of Corolla. Most prominent remnant of s-most channel leading from former New Currituck Inlet. Generally, inlets exhibit two distinct channels while open; some channels remain in different forms for some time after an inlet closes. *Other names:* Old Inlet (Fisher 1962, 103—primary remnant channel former New Currituck Inlet).

South Core Banks, barrier beach, 20 mi. long, Carteret County; Atlantic, Sea Level, Stacy, Davis, Smyrna, Harkers Island Townships (local use). S part Core Banks, ne end at Drum Inlet (now closed) sw to Cape Lookout. Name evolved 21st century from a more descriptive term to place name usage on maps. Mallinson et al. (2008, 12) and others consider Ophelia Inlet n terminus of South Core Banks because after opening of Ophelia Inlet, name Middle Core Banks has been applied generally from Ophelia Inlet to former Drum Inlet, though not used locally. Historical and continued local usage extends South Core Banks from Cape Lookout ne-ward to Drum Inlet (now closed). NPS applies the name in brochures from Ophelia Inlet

(ne) to Cape Point at Cape Lookout. Use of Davis Island and sometimes Davidsons Island for South Core Banks by some local residents is confusing (local informants) because small island exists in Core Sound 2.5 mi. sw of Davis (mainland) named Davis Island, but is practiced locally. Use of Davidsons Island is not (cannot be) explained by anyone but occasionally used with decreasing frequency. *See* Core Banks. *Other names:* Cape Banks (in part—included Shackleford Banks; Stephens 1989, 84—pronounced "cay" by residents of Salter Path), Davidsons Island (local informants), Davis Island (local informants), Portsmouth Island (misapplication from hand-drawn map depicting CCC location e Bogue Banks; Hobson 1935 presented in PKS 2016), Southern Core Bank (Goldstein 2000, map, loc. 4518).

South Core Beach, beach, 20 mi. long, Carteret County; Atlantic, Sea Level, Stacy, Davis, Smyrna, Harkers Island Townships (local use). Corresponds to South Core Banks from near New Drum Inlet to Cape Point at Cape Lookout. Ne part overlaps Ophelia Beach and Middle Core Beach, 21st-century applications not much used locally. *See* Core Banks, Ophelia Banks, and Middle Banks.

South Creek, canalized tidal stream, 1 mi. long, Dare County, Nags Head Township (local use). Mouth at Roanoke Sound just e of Bells Island, runs w to e onto Bodie Island 1.7 mi. s of Whalebone Junction. Subdivision uses name.

South Dike, dike, Dare County, Kinnakeet Township (Garrity-Blake 2010, 493). Just ne of No Ache at Flag Creek in s Salvo 4.3 mi. s of Rodanthe. *See* North Dike.

South Drain, stream, Dare County, Kinnakeet Township (local use). In n Waves just s of North Drain just n of Aunt Phoebes Marsh 1 mi. s of Rodanthe. Named in comparison to North Drain.

Southeast Point, point, Currituck County, Poplar Branch Township (C&GS 1852). On se South Burris Island 8 mi. nnw of Duck.

Southeast Point, distinct point, Currituck County, Poplar Branch Township (local use). At Currituck Sound 0.6 mi. n of s tip Dews Island, 4.2 mi. nw of Duck.

Southeast Point, point, Dare County, Kinnakeet Township (Garrity-Blake 2010, 168). Se point Big Island just n of original Avon, 8 mi. n of Buxton. Only three points on Big Island named with ordinal (interdirectional as opposed to cardinal or prime directional) directions; ne point (direction) not used.

Southeast Slew, former channel, Carteret County, Portsmouth Township (Blunt 1809 and Hooker 1850). Was there early to mid-19th century as "southeast" approach through shoals at Ocracoke Inlet 4 mi. sw of Ocracoke (village). But was actually sw approach to inlet when considering true n, but from a mariner's point of view, channel was s and e of point of Portsmouth Island on which one would take a bearing, hence name. *See* Haulover Slew and Allen Slough.

South End, area, Currituck County, Fruitville Township (local use and road sign). References housing and built-up area at s end Knotts Island, including ferry docks at Knotts Landing, 2 mi. ssw of Knotts Island (village).

South End, area, Hyde County, Ocracoke Township (local use). References beach and dunes beginning halfway between Second Grass and Ocracoke Point (South Point), 2.5 mi. s of Ocracoke (village). Though at sw end Ocracoke Island, named for direction from Ocracoke (village).

Southerne Virginia Sea, sea. Was applied to portion of Atlantic Ocean between the Outer Banks and Gulf Stream, generally from Cape Hatteras n to Cape Henry in Virginia (Comberford 1657). Appeared on early maps of the New World but never became established and name eventually disappeared. *Other names:* Sea of Virginy (Visscher 1717), Southern Virginia Sea (Saunders 1886, 21–23), Southern Virginia Seas (Lawson 1709, 240), The Southerne Virginia Sea (Comberford 1657), The Virginian Sea (Smith 1624, map), Virginian Sea (historical), Virginia Sea (Saunders 1886, 21–23).

Southern Islands. *See* Kitty Hawk Bay Islands.

Southern Shores, town, Dare County, Atlantic Township (signage). S Currituck Banks 3 mi. n of original Kitty Hawk. Began as real estate development (subdivision) 1947, incorporated 1979, now well-established town. Name selected as marketing tool, but according to David Stick (Board of Realtors n.d.), most prospective purchasers were likely from more n states; it seemed an acceptable name and "nobody came up with anything better." Thought odd, name was Southern Shores

yet near n-most Outer Banks, especially part accessible by automobile. *Other names:* Jeanguite (slang usage).

Southern Shores Marina, small harbor, Dare County, Atlantic Township (signage). In Southern Shores at ne point of entrance to Jeanguite Creek, 4.5 mi. nnw of original Kitty Hawk. *See* Southern Shores. *Other names:* Southern Shores Landing (occasional use never officially applied; used for small subdivision along US 158).

Southern Shores Woods, woods, Dare County, Atlantic Township (local use). Much of central and s parts of town wooded originally and now. Contemporary term after town established (1947). *See* Duck Woods.

Southern Woods, former woods, Dare County, Kinnakeet Township (historical documents). Was maritime forest near Salvo. Historically, a few wooded areas along soundside between Cape Hatteras and Rodanthe but by 20th century had been depleted for numerous uses. *See* Northern Woods. *Other names:* The Great Woods (Cobb 1905).

South Ferry Channel, dredged channel, Dare County, Hatteras Township; and Hyde County, Ocracoke Township (State reports). Was route of Ocracoke-Hatteras Ferry between Hatteras (village) and w tip Ocracoke Island, center 20 mi. ene of Ocracoke (village). This shorter route used Rollinson Channel extension and this dredged channel until it began to shoal heavily. Ferry route was switched to Barney Slue 2013 while this channel was dredged. However, futility was realized and longer route through Barney Slue used (U.S. Coast Guard 2015). Dredging continues 2020, but still problematic. *Other names:* Connecting Channel (US Coast Guard), South Ferry Cut (local use), South Ferry Cross Over Channel (local media).

South Flats, flat, Currituck County, Fruitville Township (F&WS 1999, map 11). On Currituck Banks 1 mi. ne of South Channel (remnants New Currituck Inlet) 6.5 mi. n of Corolla. Confusion locally regarding this reference since mostly known in F&WS reports to differentiate from Swan Island Flats, hardly known locally. *Other names:* The Flats (F&WS 1999, map 16).

South Graven Creek, small water passage, Currituck County, Fruitville Township (Cox 1923). At s end Graven Island, separating

Graven Island (n) from Point of Marsh Island (s) 0.3 mi. s of North Graven Creek, 1.5 mi. e of Knotts Island (village).

South Hatteras Beach, reference, Dare County, Hatteras Township (brochures). Wsw from Cape Point to Hatteras Inlet. Some local use, mostly scientific reports.

South Hatteras Island, reference, Dare County, Hatteras Township (brochures). Wsw from Cape Point to Hatteras Inlet. Some local use, mostly scientific reports.

South Hog Island, island, Currituck County, Poplar Branch Township (C&GS 1852). In Beasley Bay, s-most in Hog Islands complex, 7.7 mi. s of Corolla. *See* Hog Islands.

South Island, island, 0.5 mi. long, 0.3 mi. wide, Carteret County, Cedar Island Township (local use). At n end Cedar Island Bay 2 mi. e of Cedar Island Ferry landing, 12.8 mi. sw of Ocracoke (village).

South Johnson Marshes, marshes, Currituck County, Fruitville Township (F&WS 1999, map 16). References marsh s Johnson Island and marsh (mostly with individual names) between Johnson Island (w) and Currituck Banks (e) between South Marsh (s) and Swan Island Marshes (n) just nw and n of South Channel (remnant New Currituck Inlet) 5 mi. nnw of Corolla.

South Jones Island, marsh island, Currituck County, Poplar Branch Township (Codman, Crowninshield, and Lawrence 1925). Just s of North Jones Island 1 mi. nnw of Whale Head Bay, 1 mi. wsw of Corolla. *Other names:* Southwest Jones Island (historical local use).

South Marsh, marsh complex, 2 mi. wide, 1.5 mi. long, Currituck County, Fruitville Township (F&WS 1999, map). Just s of South Channel (remnant New Currituck Inlet) 5 mi. nw of Corolla. Not well known and has come into usage mostly from use by F&WS. Numerous large and small, named and unnamed marsh islands, including Big Skinner Island, Little Skinner Island, Crow Island, Walkers Island, Raymond Island, other smaller unnamed islands, including maze of named and unnamed tidal waterways. *Other names:* Church Islands (misapplied, Church Island at mainland).

South Nags Head, area, Dare County, Nags Head Township (signage). In Nags Head (town) and originally just n of Whalebone Junction at what is now The Village at Nags Head, but now (and for some time, though as late as 2007 a notation of Whalebone Beach being in South Nags Head was noted) refers to developed area with numerous named subdivisions just s of Whalebone Junction 8.5 mi. sse of Nags Head (center). Subdivision named for feature. *See* Nags Head. *Other names:* Bodie Island (real estate brochures), Bodie Island Beach (real estate brochures).

South Point, area, 0.1 mi. long and wide, Currituck County, Poplar Branch Township (local use). S part Monteray Shores subdivision, 4 mi. s of Corolla. Not a natural point, but referent to extreme s Monteray Shores formed by NC 12 (Ocean Trail) (e) and Monteray Drive (w).

South Point, point, Dare County, Kinnakeet Township (USGS 2013: Oregon Inlet). N-most point of Pea Island at Oregon Inlet 15 mi. n of Rodanthe. Use is for same feature named North Point (Kinnakeet Township) middle to late 19th century, then descriptive of n point of Pea Island, though joined with Hatteras Island at times when New Inlet is closed. Name North Point fell into disuse when South Point (more e point from inlet migration) came into use for same point, indicating change in naming process, focusing on inlet reference rather than land reference. *See* North Point New Inlet.

South Point, point, Dare County, Nags Head Township (local use). S tip Bodie Island (former) n side Oregon Inlet 9.5 mi. s of Whalebone Junction. Both South Point and North Point are used for this feature depending on user and perspective. If inlet reference is more important, then North Point is used; otherwise South Point is used. *See* North Point. *Other names:* North Point (local use).

South Point, point, Dare County, Nags Head Township (Abbott 1866 and Battle of Roanoke Island maps). Applied vaguely to entire s portion Roanoke Island s of Wanchese and inland from marsh accretion on s end Roanoke Island over past 150 years. Never really been used locally but applied during Civil War. *See* Wanchese Canals, Ditches, Guts, and Water Passages.

South Point. *See* Ocracoke Point.

South Point of Ocracock (sic) ***Island***, former point, Hyde County, Ocracoke Township (Blunt 1809). Used by Blunt to indicate terminus of Ocracoke Island in 1809, extended 2 mi. sw since then. Not used today, so presented in original form, only form known to have been used.

South Point of Ocracock (*sic*) **Woods**, former woods, Hyde County, Ocracoke Township (Coles and Price 1806). Was s terminus former Ocracock Woods just n of former Ocracoke Point (South Point), extended 1 mi. se over past 100 years. Unusual form used as an important descriptor and defined where former woods ended at the bare beach.

South Point South Jones Island, point, Currituck County, Poplar Branch Township (Codman, Crowninshield, and Lawrence 1925). South Jones Island sw island tip, 1.5 mi. wsw of Corolla.

South Pond, man-made lake, Dare County, Kinnakeet Township (F&WS 2015). In Pea Island Wildlife Refuge 7.5 mi. nnw of Rodanthe. With North Pond, constructed by CCC to enhance and preserve stopover feeding areas for migrating birds along Atlantic Flyway. *Other names:* South Pool (occasional references).

South Portsmouth, former community, Carteret County, Portsmouth Township (CS 1856; Colton 1861). Just s of Portsmouth (village). All named outlying communities part of Portsmouth (village) just clusters of houses separated by marsh and open area and known by separate names for convenience and clarity of location. Mostly used on maps but more often considered locally as Middle Portsmouth (Middle Community). *See* East Portsmouth, Middle Portsmouth, Portsmouth, and Sheep Island. *Other names:* South Community (White 2012, 30).

South Prong Deep Creek, former water passage, Dare County, Kinnakeet Township (Currituck DB 23, 1840, 48). Was tributary Deep Creek on n tip Pea Island at site of first Bodie Island Lighthouse, now inundated by Oregon Inlet 14 mi. n of Rodanthe. Use of "prong" with water passages or streams at the Outer Banks is unusual. "Prong" as a generic term more used in w U.S. *See* Deep Creek (Dare County, Currituck DB, 23).

South Ridge, sand dune, Dare County, Nags Head Township (signage). Distinct n-s linear dune in Nags Head (village) s end Jockey's Ridge.

South Rodanthe, area, Dare County, Kinnakeet Township (USGS 2013: Rodanthe—still labeled). Really is Waves just s of Rodanthe 16 mi. s of Oregon Inlet. Included because

USGS 2013: Rodanthe and NCDOT (1936) maps show this name applied about halfway between Rodanthe and Waves; more applied to Waves locally. *Other names:* South Chicamacomico (NPS 2005b, 72).

South Shoar, former point, Hyde County, Ocracoke Township (Lawson 1709, 65). Was 3.7 mi. sw of Ocracoke (village), and *was* former s approach to Ocracoke Inlet. S shore (and inlet) through shoaling have migrated 1 mi. sw during 18th century, so what is now n shore was then s shore of the inlet. Reference to avoid approach to narrow channel on then s side of inlet so marked on maps and charts. "Shoar" an earlier spelling of "shore." *Other names:* South Cape (Lawson 1709, 65).

South Slough, small channel, Dare County, Kinnakeet Township (Garrity-Blake 2010, 492). In Pamlico Sound just s of Mullet Shoal 3.5 mi. sw of New Inlet 6 mi. nw of Rodanthe.

South Virginia, historical region. Applied historically to the Albemarle region but fell into disuse early 18th century. Southern Plantation sometimes substituted because colonists themselves were known as planters. The society was agrarian; planters gradually evolved into the elaborate plantation system of the antebellum s U.S.—this reference is 17th century and is to settled or "colonized area."

Southwest Beach, beach, Carteret County, Harkers Island Township (scientific reports). Sw area Cape Lookout from Cape Point to Power Squadron Spit; not used locally.

Southwest Breakers, breakers, Carteret County, Morehead Township (limited use, boating community). These shoals and therefore breakers are changeable and shift continuously; was along sw Beaufort Inlet Channel, main entrance Beaufort Inlet, 3.5 mi. se of Morehead City (mainland). *Other names:* Bar Breakers (Blunt 1857, 345), SW Brakers (Williamson 1992, 192), Western Breakers (Blunt 1857, 345).

Southwest Island, marsh island, Currituck County, Fruitville Township (Cox 1923). In North Channel 0.5 mi. before sw terminus North Channel joining South Channel at Currituck Sound, 6 mi. se of Knotts Island (village).

Southwest Island, island, Currituck County, Poplar Branch Township (C&GS 1852). Just se of Northwest Island in w portion Mossey Islands complex 5.5 mi. ssw of Corolla (village).

Southwest Point, point, Currituck County, Poplar Branch Township (C&GS 1852). S-most point in Burris Islands complex and sw tip South Burris Island, 9 mi. s of Corolla.

Southwest Point, point, Dare County, Kinnakeet Township (Garrity-Blake 2010, 168). Sw point of Big Island just n of original Avon, 8 mi. n of Buxton. Only three points on Big Island (Dare County, Kinnakeet Township) named with ordinal (interdirectional as opposed to cardinal or prime directional) directions; ne point (direction) not used.

Southwest Point, point, Hyde County, Lake Landing Township (NOS 2014i). On sw tip of Great Island 22 mi. nw of Ocracoke (village).

Southwest Point Pughs Reef, point of shoal, Dare County, Kinnakeet Township (shipwreck reports, 1907). Sw-most point on Pughs Reef, 5 mi. wnw of Rodanthe. Directional names necessary for functional actions, here describing location of stranded members of shoal-bound vessel. *Other names:* Southwest Point Pugh Reef (launch, *Mabel E. Horton*, 1907 [White et al. 2017, 56]).

Southwest Point Shoal, shoal, Carteret County, Cedar Island Township (Williamson 1992, 101). At extreme sw point Royal Shoal at Southwest Straddle (also named Southwest Point—White 2012, 133) 7.5 mi. w of Ocracoke (village). Uses associative name Southwest Point at better-known feature Southwest Straddle. *Other names:* Southwest Point Royal Shoal (historical use), South West Point Royal Shoal (historical), Southwest Royal Shoal (historical), SW Point Shoal (Williamson 1992, 101).

Southwest Spit, point, Dare County, Hatteras Township (CS 1850b). At Fort Clark ruins, 2.9 mi. sw of Hatteras (village). Formerly s tip Hatteras Island, but by deposition, 0.6 mi. from Hatteras Inlet. Spit is a hooked deposition created by longshore or littoral (means shore) drift, movement of sand along the shore.

Southwest Straddle, submerged point, Carteret County, Cedar Island Township (Hooker 1850). Underwater point at sw point of arch-shaped Royal Shoal in Pamlico Sound, 8 mi. w of Ocracoke (village). *See* Northwest Straddle. *Other names:* South Swash Straddle (Price 1795, 631), South West Point (Williamson 1992, 131), Southwest Point (C&GS 1945), Southwest Point Royal Shoal (NPS 2012, 18), SW Straddle (unknown, 1807).

Spencer Creek, cove, 0.1 mi. wide, Dare County, Kinnakeet Township (USGS 1950 Buxton). On Hatteras Island 2 mi. n of original Avon. End of 20th century, canalized, altered, expanded to create canals for a development in what was originally a marsh. Named for Thomas Spencer, colonial landowner. *Other names:* Island Creek (some local use, subdivision using name), Spencers Cove (from nearby housing subdivision), Spencers Creek (Currituk DB 8, 1745, 29–30).

Spencers Woods, small woods, Dare County, Hatteras Township (local use). Just s of Brigands Bay 3 mi. wsw of Buxton. Separately named in w Buxton Woods. *Other names:* Frisco Woods (sometimes considered in Frisco Woods), Spencers Wood (road sign and subdivision).

Spinnaker Canal, canal, 0.2 mi. long, Dare County, Nags Head Township (PC HOA 2016). Trending e-w 1.5 mi. se of Sandy Point at Roanoke Island Festival Park 2.7 mi. w of Whalebone Junction. One of seven named canal segments interconnected throughout Pirates Cove subdivision, named portions corresponding with limits of adjacent named subdivisions. Spinnaker, special type of sail used for sailing with wind that balloons out when filled.

Spot Shoal Island, island, Currituck County, Fruitville Township (Cox 1923). At ne terminus North Channel, 5.5 mi. se of Knotts Island (village). Indicates good place to fish because fish gather at shoals to feed (origin, "shoal" of fish—not "school," which is incorrect), and "spot" is often local usage on the Outer Banks for good fishing place. Alternatively could be for spot fish (*Leiostomus xanthurus*) here.

Sprig Point. *See* Pettys Pond Point.

Springers Point, point, Hyde County, Ocracoke Township (USGS 2013: Ocracoke). On Ocracoke Island 0.9 mi. sw of Ocracoke (village). Reportedly original settlement here, but semitemporary quarters for Blackbeard and his associates (*see* Teaches Hole). Near this point Lieutenant Robert Maynard dispatched from Virginia defeated and beheaded Blackbeard. Named Springer since 1883, when Springer family acquired land around the point from other owners. The Springers were from Pamlico Peninsula (mainland), not permanent residents of Ocracoke. There is a trail in the area, and

Howard (July 22, 2018) reports in the 1960s Loop Road here was referred to by young folk as Moonlight Valley Road for its allure and propitious qualities, but no real valley here. *Other names:* Blackbeards Point (well-known name used to promote tourism where Blackbeard was known to reside for periods; Weslager 1954, 47), Howards Point (Angley 1984—original name, original resident, William Howard, late 1700s, later his grandson acquired the point [1814], name again used), Singers Point (transcribing error), Springer Point (Outer Banks Scenic Byway 2008), Teachs Castle (Weslager 1954, 47), The Point (local use), Williams Point (1759–1814—Howard 2017).

Springers Point Oaks, woods, Hyde County, Ocracoke Township (local use). Stand of live oaks (*Quercus virginiana*) at Springers Point 0.5 mi. sw of Ocracoke (village). *See* Springers Point. *Other names:* Widgeon Woods (sometimes used since n section in this section of Ocracoke Village areas).

Springers Point Well, former well, Hyde County, Ocracoke Township (local use). At Springers Point 0.8 mi. sw of Ocracoke (village). Disagreement regarding when and by whom well was dug. Most believe or assume it was built early 1800s (perhaps when brick was added), but some researchers believe much older, and might have been dug by Indians or be an enhanced natural well, which may explain why Blackbeard made this a temporary headquarters. Moseley (1733) map clearly indicates a well by symbol and the word "well," not specifically at Springers Point but nearby. However, given grossness of scale and known shifting shorelines here, this is the well to which Moseley referred, predating early 1800s to early 1700s. Sealed shut but can be viewed along nature hike trail at Springers Point. *See* Springers Point.

Spry Creek, small tidal stream, Currituck County, Poplar Branch Township (local informants). Just nw of historic village of Corolla, connects to Raccoon Bay 2.5 mi. se of Monkey Island. Fishermen at Corolla used this waterway to access Raccoon Bay and Currituck Sound. *Other names:* Sprys Cove (Currituck DB 28, 1859, 298).

Spy Hill, historical, Dare County, Kinnakeet Township (probably) (Covey 2018, 18). *See* Lookout Cedar.

Standard Point Shoal, large shoal, Carteret County, Portsmouth Township (Williamson 1992, 121). In Pamlico Sound, bare spots at low water 8 mi. w of Ocracoke (village).

Stanford Islands, former islands, Carteret County (Romans 1776). Was collective reference vaguely applied to what is now portion of e Bogue Banks, sometimes some of w Shackleford Banks during colonial period, and also included several smaller islands (now disappeared). Usually from former Cheeseman Inlet to Beaufort Inlet, often included all of Bogue Banks and Shackleford Banks from Bogue Inlet to what is now Barden Inlet at Cape Lookout, though the barrier island configuration then was different. Person or persons from whom this name derived unknown—name unknown locally except by a few historians as appearing only on colonial maps. *Other names:* Sanford Island (Fisher, 1962), Stamfords Islands (Pinkerton et al. 1809), Stanford Banks (Mouzon 1775), Stanford Isles (Anderson 1796).

Stanton Canal, canal, 0.25 mi. long, Carteret County, Morehead Township (Carteret County GIS 2019). Just n of The Pond (q.v.) trending e-w in Atlantic Beach Isles subdivision (w part of Canals at Atlantic Beach q.v.), 1 mi. s of Morehead City (mainland).

Station Bay, bay, Dare County, Atlantic Township (local use). In Currituck Sound just ne of Sanderling, 4 mi. n of Duck. Use and application historically to much smaller gradual embayment just w of Sanderling but today used for larger water. Derived from former Caffeys Inlet Life Saving Station nearby on Currituck Banks at Sanderling.

Station Bay Cove, cove, 0.2 mi. wide, Currituck County, Poplar Branch Township; and Dare County, Atlantic Township (County GIS). Just n of Station Bay at Currituck Banks, 5 mi. nnw of Duck. Subdivision named for feature. *Other names:* Station Bay (sometimes used considered part of Station Bay q.v.).

Station Bay Marina, dock, Dare County, Atlantic Township (signage). Very small facility rarely used, at Sanderling 4.3 mi. n of Duck (center).

Station Creek, cove, Dare County, Kinnakeet Township (Garrity-Blake 2010, 493). Soundside in Pamlico Sound 1.5 mi. s of No Ache, 6.5 mi. s of Rodanthe. Named for close proximity to Gull Shoal Coast Guard Station.

Station Landing, former landing, Currituck County, Fruitville Township (historical use). Was soundside just w of North Swan Beach (originally Wash Woods community). No trace today. Named for Wash Woods (Deals) Life Saving Station located beachside here (refurbished commercially).

Station Landing, former landing, Dare County, Atlantic Township (historical local use). Was soundside at Station Bay at Sanderling, 3.5 mi. n of Duck. Used when Caffeys Inlet Life Saving Station operated here (*see* Caffeys Inlet).

Station Landing, former landing, Dare County, Atlantic Township (local informant). Was specifically to serve Bias Shores (q.v.) and Hargraves Beach (q.v.) 1930s, small developments developed by three men, Bias, Hargraves, and Jenkins, from Elizabeth City specifically as vacation place for African Americans. Dance hall was here. Generic application to transportation destination and not related to nearby Paul Gamiels Hill Life Saving Station near Paul Gamiels Hill 1 mi. se. *See* Bias Shores. *Other names:* Bias Landing (some reported use by vacationers 1930s), Hargraves Landing (some reported use by vacationers 1930s).

Station Landing, former landing, Dare County, Kinnakeet Township (Garrity-Blake 2010, 169). Was soundside, junction First Creek and Second Creek, 0.5 mi. w of former Big Kinnakeet Coast Guard Station (hence name), 7 mi. n of Buxton. Served Big Kinnakeet Coast Guard Station. *Other names:* Old Station Landing (Garrity-Blake 2010, map, 210).

Station Landing Marsh, marsh, Currituck County, Fruitville Township (F&WS 2006, map, 64). Extensive marsh just w of North Swan Beach, 2.5 mi. e of Knotts Island (village). *See* Station Landing (Currituck).

Steels Creek, former small stream, Dare County, Nags Head Township (Currituck DB 6, 1791, 170–71). Flowed into Tillmans Creek (originally Francis Creek, cove-like feature) near junction Albemarle Sound and Roanoke Sound in nw Nags Head just n of Mann Point 1.3 mi. w nw of Jockeys Ridge. Was slightly larger historically and exact location not certain as topography here has changed. *Other names:* Steeles Gutt (Currituck DB 1719, unnumbered,), Steuts Gut (Currituck DB 1798, 8, 103–4).

Steep Point, point, Carteret County, Beaufort Township (USGS 2013: Harkers Island). High point at n terminus of unnamed marsh island at n entrance Steep Point Channel 3.8 mi. nw of Harkers Island (village). Some infer name might be Sheep Point as Sheephead Marsh is less than 1 mi. ese and nothing remarkable about appearance or elevation here (less than 5 ft.). Still local preference is Steep.

Steep Point, point, Currituck County, Fruitville Township (Cox 1923). At se entrance to Fresh Pond Bay, 2.3 mi. e of Knotts Island (village). Not to be confused with Steep Point, 5 mi. w, at mouth of Back Creek.

Steep Point, point, Currituck County, Fruitville Township (F&WS 1984, map, 74). Separates mouth of Back Creek (n) and Duckpond (s) on n Mackay Island 3.5 mi. w of Knotts Island (village). Not to be confused with Steep Point, 5 mi. e, at entrance to Fresh Pond Bay.

Steep Point Channel, channel, 3 mi. long, Carteret County, Beaufort Township (USGS 2013: Harkers Island). Trends n-s 1 mi. n of North River Marsh separating mainland and unnamed marsh islands from North River Marsh 3.6 mi. wnw of Harkers Island (village). *See* Steep Point (Carteret County).

Steer Island, small marsh island, less than 0.1 mi. across, Currituck County, Poplar Branch Township (USGS 2013: Mossey Islands). In Beasley Bay at ne end Jarvis Channel, 11.3 mi. s of Corolla. *See* Hog Islands.

Steer Island Pond, small cove, Currituck County, Poplar Branch Township (local use). On s end Steer Island (q.v.) in Hog Islands complex, 7 mi. s of Corolla. *See* Adams Pond.

Stetson's Fishing Station, area, Dare County, Nags Head Township (Oppermann 2005, map, 135). Was some sort of processing place for fish (1878) oceanside 1.3 mi. e of Tommy Hammock, 4 mi. s of Whalebone Junction.

Stevensons Marsh, marsh, Currituck County, Poplar Branch Township (C&GS 1852). Just n of Great Beach Pond at s end Whale Head Bay near center Corolla Light subdivision 2 mi. s of Corolla. Considerably altered by development.

Sticky Bottom, area, Dare County, Hatteras Township (Garrity-Blake 2010, 493). In Hatteras (village) just sw of center, 3 mi. ene of Hatteras Inlet. Acquired name from marsh and quagmire of same name. Reported there were only a few houses historically and boards laid for walking and small wooden footbridges connecting numerous small hummocks ("hammocks"—known very locally as "hamlets"—did not occur outside Hatteras village). *Other names:* Down the Road (Garrity-Blake 2010, 290).

Sticky Bottom, marsh, 0.5 mi. wide, Dare County, Hatteras Township (local informant). Just sw of Hatteras (village center) 3 mi. ene of Hatteras Inlet. References thick layer of mud and muck here. Much was filled by WPA project 1930s.

Still Island former marsh island, Carteret County, Beaufort Township (local informants). Largest in Reids Marsh just e of Still Island Creek, just w of Beaufort (mainland), 3 mi. e of Morehead City (mainland). No longer exists as island, resulting from enhancing causeway carrying US 70 Business.

Still Island Creek, former tidal stream, Carteret County, Beaufort Township (C&GS 1888a). Was in former Reids Marsh just w of Gallants Channel 1 mi. nw of Beaufort (mainland). Name fallen into disuse and configuration of tidal stream changed since late 19th century.

Stillwater Cove, small cove, Carteret County, White Oak Township (local use). In Bogue Sound at historical Plum Orchard 1.5 mi. w of entrance Archer Creek (cove) 5.5 mi. w of original Emerald Isle. Subdivision named for feature.

Stillwater Landing, landing, Currituck County, Fruitville Township (local use). In ne Knotts Island (village), just sw of Cason Point, 3.5 mi. sw of Carova. Subdivision named for feature.

Stingray Point, point of shoal, Hyde County, Ocracoke Township (local use). E point of Legged Lump 15 mi. e of Ocracoke (village). Bluntnose stingray (Say's stingray, *Dasyatis say*) is indigenous to se Atlantic coast from Chesapeake Bay to Florida, the Caribbean, and Texas.

Stone Island, marsh island, 0.6 mi. wide, Dare County, Atlantic Township (Town of Kitty Hawk 2007). At n entrance Kitty Hawk Bay 2.5 mi. wsw of original Kitty Hawk. Name used mostly Stone Island though Stove Island is known since recorded on USGS maps and other maps copied from USGS (a known practice). *Other names:* Stanley Island (occasional local use), Stove Island (USGS 2013: Kitty Hawk).

Stone Island Point, point, Dare County, Atlantic Township (Town of Kitty Hawk 2007). Ne tip of Stone Island, 2 mi. wsw of original Kitty Hawk. *See* Stone Island. *Other names:* Stove Island Point (USGS 2013: Kitty Hawk).

Stone Point, point, Carteret County, Davis Township (local use). On an unnamed marsh island 0.3 mi. e of Douglas Point, 3.1 mi. sse of Davis (mainland).

Stone Rock, rock, Hyde County, Ocracoke Township (Weslager 1954—confirmed by interviews with Ballance [2017, 2018] and Howard [2017, 2018]). Collection of ballast stones (carried in ships to increase stability) just w of Springers Point 1 mi. sw of Ocracoke (village center). Ballast rocks (and other material) formerly used in stabilizing ships are often discarded near entrance of harbors.

Stove Island. *See* Stone Island.

Stowe Landing, former landing, Dare County, Hatteras Township (local historical use). Was in Hatteras (village) 1 mi. s of Durant Point. Used mostly 19th and early 20th centuries, but today is private. Stowe, surname prevalent at Hatteras (*see* Stowes).

Stowes, former community, Dare County, Hatteras Township (historical local use). Was just w of Hatteras (village), 4 mi. ne of Hatteras Inlet. Only a windmill and general store at this small 19th-century cluster. Became more of a gathering point than most mills, which just sold grain. Stowe well-established surname here. *See* Stowes Windmill. *Other names:* Stowe (CS 1855).

Stowes Hills, large sand dunes, 3 mi. long, Dare County, Hatteras Township (Price 1795, 626). Three lengthy and prominent sand dunes between Buxton and Frisco, most prominent is Creeds Hill, 3 mi. sse of Buxton. General reference used more 19th and early 20th centuries. Creeds Hill used now in more expanded reference, though still a specific sand dune. Stowe well-established surname here. *Other names:* Stows Hills (Price and Strother 1798), Styron Hills (Garrity-Blake 2010, 13—possible confusion with Styron Hills e end Ocracoke Island), The Three Hillocks (Holland 1794—descriptive—former use but secondary).

Stowes Windmill, former mill and windmill, Dare County, Hatteras Township (historical use). Was at Stowes just w of Hatteras (village), 4 mi. ne of Hatteras Inlet. Stowe, surname prevalent here. *See* Stowes. *Other names:* Stowes Mills (historical local use).

Straddle, The, area, Carteret County, Portsmouth and Cedar Island Townships; and Hyde County, Ocracoke Township (historical sources). Created by arc shape of Royal Shoal between Southwest Straddle and Northwest Straddle. *See* Northwest Straddle. *Other names:* Royal Shoal Harbor (historical q.v.).

Straddle, The. *See* Royal Shoal Harbor.

Straight Creek, narrow water passage, 1 mi. long, Currituck County, Poplar Branch Township (USGS 1982: Jarvisburg). Through unnamed marsh islands, 0.3 mi. e of Pine Island Bay, 5.8 mi. nw of Duck. *Other names:* Pettys Creek (local use), Potteets Creek (C&GS 1852).

Straight Creek, narrow tidal stream, 0.6 mi. long, Currituck County, Poplar Branch Township (USGS 2013: Mossey Islands). In s part Mossey Islands complex 0.9 mi. w of Three Dunes, 5.3 mi. s of Corolla. *Other names:* Strate Creek (C&GS 1852).

Straight Creek Island, marsh island, Currituck County, Poplar Branch Township (local use). In central Mossey Islands complex just ne of Straight Creek 5 mi. ssw of Corolla. Variant Strait Creek Island recorded on C&GS 1852 coast chart incidentally next to Strate Creek. Unclear intent in variant name since use of generic term "strait" usually refers to much wider water passage, though it could have been so, and "strate" is rare 19th-century alternate spelling. Whether by misuse over years or by original intent, today use is for "straight" for both island and water passage. *Other names:* Strait Creek Island (C&GS 1852—adjacent to Strate [sic] Creek).

Strait Creek, small water passage, 0.3 mi. long, Currituck County, Poplar Branch Township (USGS 2013: Mossey Islands). Connects s portion Neals Creek (sometimes Neels Creek) to n Dowdy Bay near Gaffey (sic) Landing 8.7 mi. sw of Corolla. "Strait" used in unusual manner for this small water passage as "strait" usually signifies passage with some degree of width. So, could merely be a misspelling of "straight." Gaffey Landing (q.v.) might be misapplication of Caffey. *Other names:* Straight Creek (spelling difference).

Straits, The, water passage, 4 mi. long, 0.5 mi. wide, Carteret County, Harkers Island Township (USGS 2013: Harkers Island). Separates Harkers Island and Browns Island from mainland and connects Core Sound and North River 1.4 mi. n of Harkers Island (village). *Other names:* Core Sound (misapplication; The Straits is w extension of where Core Sound ends), Core Straits (limited local use combining both "Core" and "Straits"—descriptive initially), Straights (Brazier 1833, county map 1962), Straits (Hooker 1850), Streight (obsolete spelling of "strait"—Price and Strother 1798).

Stumpy Cove cove, 0.5 mi. wide, Currituck County, Poplar Branch Township (USGS 2013: Mossey Islands). In Currituck Sound just s of Indian Gap at unnamed marsh island, 8.5 mi. s of Corolla.

Sturgeon Beach. *See* Whalehead Beach (subdivision).

Styron Hills, three sand dunes, 25 ft. high, Hyde County, Ocracoke Township (USGS 2013: Green Island). At ne end Ocracoke Island, 1.4 mi. sw of Hatteras Inlet, 15 mi. ne of Ocracoke (village). *Other names:* Stowes Hills (probable misuse from nearby Cape Hatteras, where Stowes Hills is located, though Dunbar [1958, 74], reports this as the original name here), Styrons Hill (Weslager 1954).

Sues Cabin, area, Currituck County, Poplar Branch Township. Is 5.2 mi. nnw of Duck (Currituck deeds). Cabin here reported existing as early as 18th century, still used as reference.

Sues Cabin Ridge, sand ridge, Currituck County, Poplar Branch Township (Currituck DB 7, 1794, 124–25). Just n of former Caffeys Inlet, 1.5 mi. n of Sanderling, 6 mi. n of Duck (center). Altered considerably by development, not remembered by anyone; not used today. Associative with Sues Cabin. *Other names:* Sues Cabben Ridge (Currituck DB 7, 1796, 338–39).

Sugar Creek, small tidal stream, 0.1 mi. long, Dare County, Nags Head Township (local informants). At e end of The Causeway from Whalebone Junction to Roanoke Island 5 mi. s of Nags Head (center). According to local residents, name derived from large cargo of sugar accidentally falling into the creek (belief was sugar for making rum, though no evidence rum made here then), which served as small landing area for offloading cargo. Some accounts merely indicate ship wrecked, losing its cargo. CS (1854) chart makes cryptic reference here to "Sugar Wreck," adding credence to the story; no other documented proof of this origin, but widely believed.

Sugarloaf Island, island, 0.5 mi. long, 0.2 mi. wide, Carteret County, Morehead Township (USGS 2013: Beaufort). Just n of Bogue Banks, 1.5 mi. ne of Atlantic Beach (town) at docks and port facility of Morehead City (mainland). Originally smaller natural island but man-enhanced considerably with spoil (material from dredging) from continuous dredging and improvement of harbor at Morehead City (mainland). Descriptive; sugarloaf originally sort of tall cone-like structure with a flat top but later a loaf-like structure with a flat top, and how sugar was sold until granulated and cube sugar introduced early 20th century. Development of port at Morehead City began in earnest 1850s, by early 20th century island well established and acquired the name. *Other names:* Sugar Loaf Island (C&GS 1953).

Sunnyside, former community (now subdivision), 10 ft. high, Dare County, Nags Head Township (signage). On nw Roanoke Island 0.8 mi. nw of Dare County Regional Airport, 2.4 mi. nw of Manteo (center). Originally one family used Sunny Side descriptively because ideally receives afternoon sun. Today, well-established subdivision with numerous houses.

Sunset Landing, small landing, Carteret County, White Oak Township (signage). Private landing area and docks for subdivision Sunset Landing just e of barrier island causeway to Langston Bridge.

Suples Hill, small hill, 6 ft. high, Dare County, Nags Head Township (Wise 2010, map, 12). Just s of Midway Intersection, US 64, US 264, and NC 345, junction of Water Plant Road and NC 345, 1.5 mi. s of Manteo (center). Highest point along The Causeway (Roanoke Island, n-s carrying NC 345), site of historic temporary Fort Russell and short battle resulting in fall of Roanoke Island to Union forces. Today, this high ground is known to most local residents, but not the name.

Surf Landing Cove, canal, 0.1 mi. long, Carteret County, White Oak Township (local use). In central Emerald Isle from Bogue Sound into Surf Landing Cove subdivision. Greatly man-

enhanced tidal stream is soundside, rather than oceanside as name suggests.

Swan Beach, beach, Currituck County, Fruitville Township (local use). At Swan Beach (community) on n Currituck Banks 5 mi. n of Corolla. Name is recent origin from establishment of the community Swan Beach and overlaps usage in s part (historically) with Seagull Beach (recent subdivision, not to be confused with former Seagull village).

Swan Beach, community, Currituck County, Fruitville Township (local maps). On n Currituck Banks just n of former Seagull village (q.v.) 4.7 mi. n of Corolla, access only by 4-wheel-drive vehicles. Name is recent origin. *Other names:* Pennys Hill (sometimes albeit rarely used in real estate references for proximity to Pennys Hill), South Swan Beach (ecosystem pamphlets—used by some in response to North Swan Beach, but locally is Swan Beach), Swan Beach Estates (local real estate pamphlets).

Swan Island, former island, Pamlico County, Township 4 (C&GS 1888c). Just se of Brant Island (Pamlico County) 25 mi. wsw of Ocracoke (village). Often inundated.

Swan Island, mostly marsh island, 0.4 mi. long, 0.3 mi. wide, Currituck County, Fruitville Township (USGS 2013: Barco). In Currituck Sound 6.9 mi. nnw of Corolla. Swan Island Hunt Club, one of numerous such clubs, here early 20th century (originally Crow Island Hunt Club, sometimes Crow used). A few families lived on the island during hunt club period. Early records indicate originally (historically) sometimes Swan Island referenced as Crow Island (possibly because of club name). Sometimes Swan Island, Johnson Island referenced as Swan Islands; occasionally Crow Island, Raymond Island might be included. Crow Island, larger island 1.5 mi. sse, where it was always applied on maps since 1700s. *Other names:* Crow Island (C&GS 1913a).

Swan Island, marsh island, 0.1 mi. across, Currituck County, Poplar Branch Township (USGS 2013: Mossey Islands). In Sanders Bay just n of Mossey Islands complex, 4 mi. s of Corolla.

Swan Island Flats, flat area, Currituck County, Fruitville Township (F&WS 1999, map 23). Open area on Currituck Banks near Swan Island Estates subdivision, 1 mi. n of South

Channel, remnants of New Currituck Inlet, 7 mi. n of Corolla. Local folk are not too familiar with the name and disagree on any exact location. Listed in F&WS (1999, map, 23), but no precise location provided; 2 mi. e of sizable island in Currituck Sound (just w of Currituck Bay) named Swan Island. Confusion between this name and application with South Flats just s; South Flats considered to be part of Swan Island Flats by few who know the names. *Other names:* The Flats (F&WS 1999, map, 16).

Swan Island Landing, landing, Currituck County, Fruitville Township (local use). Was at nw shore of Swan Island 3.5 mi. s of Knotts Island (village). Used for the few residents of the island and when the Swan Island Hunt Club was here early 20th century. *See* Swan Island (Fruitville Township).

Swan Island Lead, water passage, Currituck County, Fruitville Township (local use). Trends n-s to ne Swan Island at nw Currituck Bay (not Currituck Sound) 3 mi. s of Knotts Island (village). *See* Buzzard Lead.

Swan Island Marshes, area of marsh, Currituck County, Fruitville Township (F&WS 1999, map 16). Between Swan Island and Currituck Banks just n of South Johnson Marshes, 1 mi. n of South Channel (remnants New Currituck Inlet) 7 mi. nnw of Corolla.

Swan Quarter Narrows. *See* Great Island Narrows.

Swash, The, former shoal, Carteret County, Portsmouth Township (Price 1795, 628). Was in Pamlico Sound at The Bulk Head, junction of three channels, Old Swash Channel, Ship Channel, and Bulkhead Channel, 4.5 mi. w of Ocracoke (village). *See* Daniel Swash.

Swash, The, cove, 0.8 mi. long, 0.4 mi. wide, Carteret County, Smyrna Township (USGS 2013: Davis). In Core Sound between Horse Island and Core Banks 3.8 mi. e of Davis (mainland). *See* Daniel Swash. *Other names:* Great Swash (Piggott 1894b), Horse Island Bay (some local use, adjacent ne to Horse Island).

Swash Channel, former channel, Dare County, Hatteras Township (Foster 1866b). Trended s-n then e-w in Pamlico Sound just s of Egg Shoal, 3 mi. n of Hatteras (village). No longer used. *See* Daniel Swash.

Swash Channel, water passage, 0.2 mi. long, Hyde County, Ocracoke Township (C&GS 1945). In Pamlico Sound between Big

Foot Slough Channel and Nine Foot Shoal Channel 1.3 mi. nw of Ocracoke (village). *See* Daniel Swash.

Swash Inlet, water passage, 0.8 mi. long, Carteret County, Portsmouth Township (USGS 2013: Wainwright Island). Connects Core Sound and Atlantic Ocean separating Portsmouth Island from Pilontary Islands 13.5 mi. sw of Ocracoke (village). Open before 1585 until 1722 reopened 1939, and mostly shoaled up by 1961, though awash periodically. Descriptive because mostly "shoaled up," completely awash only at high tide. Fisher (1962, 109) notes a separate inlet as New Inlet according to 1948 congressional report and indicates only the inlet is between Sand Inlet (Sand Island Inlet) and High Hills Inlet, but no other known reference to separate inlet named New Inlet here, so reference must have been to Swash Inlet, halfway between High Hills Inlet (Whalebone Inlet) and Sand Island Inlet. Additionally, Fisher notes Pilentary (Pilontary) Clubhouse Inlet in a Congressional report from late 1800s but then indicates he could find no other reference. N.C. Fisheries (1923, 27) mentions Pilentary Inlet near this location, the name must be a variant name referencing Swash Inlet since Pilentary Islands (reportedly Pilentary [sic] Club location) is just sw of Swash Inlet. *See* Drum Inlet, Sand Island Inlet, and Daniel Swash.

Other names: Bare Inlet (Wimble 1733), Bare Rever (Wimble 1733), Bare Rever Inlet (Wimble 1733), New Inlet (Fisher 1962, 102), Nord Entré (Nolin 1783), Okok Inlet (confused application with Ocracoke Inlet), Old Swash Inlet (Whisnant and Whisnant 2010, map, 490), Pilentary Clubhouse Inlet (Fisher 1962, 108), Vokokon Inlet (confused application with Ocracoke Inlet), Whalebone Inlet (confused application with High Hills Inlet or Whalebone Inlet 2.5 mi. ne).

Sweetgum Swamp, swamp, Dare County, Atlantic Township (Nature Conservancy). In Nags Head Woods just se of Panler Creek, 2 mi. nw of Jockeys Ridge, 4 mi. s of original Kitty Hawk. Sweetgum tree (*Liquidambar styraciflua*) native here and named for "sweetish" resin exuded when cut. *Other names:* Sweet Gum Swamp.

T

Tar Branch, former stream, Dare County, Nags Head Township (Currituck DB 1786, 5, 241). Former small stream flowing into (n) Broad Creek from e side. Current condition unknown. *See* Tar Cove Marsh.

Tar Cove, small cove, Currituck County, Poplar Branch Township (local use). Sw end Tar Cove Marsh where Deep Neck (q.v.) enters southern Beasley Bay just n of Pine Island, 6.7 mi. n of Duck (center). Used more early to mid-20th century. *See* Tar Cove Marsh.

Tar Cove Marsh, marsh, 0.5 mi. wide, Currituck County, Poplar Branch Township (USGS 1982: Mossey Islands). Recent deposition soundside Currituck Banks 2.9 mi. s of Three Dunes, 7.8 mi. s of Corolla. Use of "tar" on the Outer Banks usually indicates site where local fishermen tarred their boats and nets, but here descriptive from deposition.

Tar Cove Point, point, Currituck County, Poplar Branch Township (local use). Sw point Tar Cove Marsh at ne Tar Cove Bay just n of Pine Island, 7 mi. n of Duck (center). *See* Tar Cove Marsh.

Tar Hole Beach, beach, Hyde County, Ocracoke Township (USGS 2013: Green Island). Oceanside on ne Ocracoke Island at Tar Hole Plains 2.1 mi. sw of Hatteras Inlet. Reportedly indicates where local fishermen tarred their boats and nets. *See* Tar Hole Plains.

Tar Hole Inlet, cove, 0.1 mi. wide, Hyde County, Ocracoke Township (USGS 2013: Green Island). In Pamlico Sound 1.6 mi. w of Hatteras Inlet, 13 mi. ne of Ocracoke (village). Use of "inlet" is unclear, no evidence historically of breach in barrier island here, the normal use on the Outer Banks. Only other known such use is Gap Inlet, also Ocracoke Island. *See* Tar Hole Beach. *Other names:* The Tar Hole (local use).

Tar Hole Plains, flat, 1 mi. long, Hyde County, Ocracoke Township (USGS 2013: Green Island). Just behind Tar Hole Beach on Ocracoke Island near Styron Hills 1.7 mi. sw of Hatteras Inlet. Reportedly named from tar washing ashore from a ship's cargo during a storm (Weslager 1954); or, where

local fishermen tarred their boats and nets. *Other names:* Tar Hole Plain (Weslager 1954), Tar-Hone (*sic*) Plains (O'Neal et al. 1976, 26—transcribing error).

Tarkle Creek, water passage, 0.8 mi. long, Dare County, Atlantic Township (Town of Kitty Hawk 2007). Trends nw-se from Albemarle Sound through Tarkle Ridge Cove to Flag Cove (some indicate ending in Tarkle Ridge Cove), 1 mi. s of Kitty Hawk Landing subdivision, 1.5 mi. sw of original Kitty Hawk. Tarkle, local surname.

Tarkle Ridge, sand ridge, 1 mi. long, Dare County, Atlantic Township (Town of Kitty Hawk 2007). Trends n-s 0.5 mi. e of Kitty Hawk Landing subdivision 2 mi. w of original Kitty Hawk. Tarkle, local surname. *See* Kitty Hawk ridge-and-swale system.

Tarkle Ridge Cove, cove, 0.1 mi. wide, Dare County, Atlantic Township (local use). Just n of Stone Island, 1.9 mi. wsw of original Kitty Hawk. Tarkle, local surname.

Tar Landing, landing, Carteret County, Morehead Township (local use). At Tar Landing Bay on e Bogue Banks, 2 mi. e of Atlantic Beach (town). *See* Tar Landing Bay.

Tar Landing Bay, cove, 0.4 mi. long, Carteret County, Morehead Township (USGS 2013: Beaufort). In Bogue Sound at e end Bogue Banks 2 mi. e of Atlantic Beach (town). Activities for tarring (waterproofing) boats took place here. Variant Farlanding on a few maps depicting Civil War 1860s, only known occurrences and are recording errors. *Other names:* Farlanding Bay (George Colton 1861, transcribing error).

Tarpon Ridge, sand ridge, Dare County, Atlantic Township (Harris 2017). Just ne of High Ridge, 2 mi. wnw of original Kitty Hawk. Tarpon refers (usually) to nonfood fish (*Megalops atlanticus*) ubiquitous to s Atlantic Ocean; though tarpon as name is well known as far n as Cape Hatteras and occasionally slightly n, an unusual name, especially on the Outer Banks. Only known occurrence in an Outer Banks place name.

Tar Shack, area, Currituck County, Fruitville Township (F&WS 1999, map 4). Was at se end of Swan Island 3.5 mi. se of Knotts Island (village). Descriptive reference to shack used as a reference point, in some instances used for se tip Swan Island.

Tartan Inlet, canal, Dare County, Atlantic Township (local use). Main entry canal just s of Colington Harbour for canal system at Colington Harbour, 2.5 mi. wsw of Kill Devil Hills (town). "Inlet" not used in the traditional sense on the Outer Banks as barrier island breach because indicative of dredging allowing water inward for access by boats to open water (Albemarle Sound). Not from familiar Scottish design of lines crossing at right angles in multicolored designs but nautical term—canal names of Colington Harbour have a ship or nautical theme. Specifically, "tartan" refers to a fore-and-aft (front and back)–rigged triangular sail (termed lateen sail) on small coastal ships in Mediterranean Sea. *Other names:* Tarten Inlet (occasional misspelling).

Tater Patch Cove, cove, 0.3 mi. wide, Dare County, Atlantic Township (local use not much remembered now). In Colington Creek, 3.2 mi. s of original Kitty Hawk. Descriptive, and "tater" is rural colloquialism (spoken language) for potato. *Other names:* Potater Pach [sic] (Currituck DB 1799, 8, 152–53).

Taylor Creek, water passage, 2.6 mi. long, Carteret County, Beaufort Township (USGS 2013: Beaufort, Harkers Island). Separates Carrot Island from mainland 4.4 mi. e of Harkers Island (village). Stanford (2015) reports Carrot Island Channel was original name; not so, because Taylor Creek is shown on maps as early as 1770 (Sauthier 1770). Further, original name 1770s for Carrot Island was reportedly Cart Island—*see* Carrot Island. *Other names:* Carrot Island Channel (Stanford 2015, 83), Taylors Creek (ACE 1969, Carteret County GIS 2019).

Taylor Creek, water passage, 0.4 mi. long, Currituck County, Poplar Branch Township (USGS 2013: Mossey Islands). In Currituck Sound just n of Bearhead 5.6 mi. ssw of Corolla. *Other names:* Taylors Creek (Currituck DB 16, 1822, 220).

Taylor Creek Channel, channel, 3 mi. long, Carteret County, Beaufort Township (USGS 2013: Beaufort, Harkers Island). In Taylor Creek, separates Town Marsh and Carrot Island from mainland at Beaufort (mainland) 2.2 mi. nnw of Beaufort Inlet. *Other names:* Taylors Creek Channel (ACE 1983).

Teaches Breakers, breakers, Hyde County, Ocracoke Township (Blunt 1809). Was just inside Ocracoke Inlet at Teaches Hole Bar sw end Teaches Hole Channel 3.5 mi. sw of Ocracoke (village). Blunt (1809) shows The Bulk Head (shoal) farther toward Ocracoke Inlet, with these breakers here at s end of The Bulk Head, but later The Bulk Head was much smaller, remnants were Teaches Hole Bar. *See* Teaches Hole. *Other names:* Teaches Breakers (Cole and Price 1806).

Teaches Hole, deep area, Hyde County, Ocracoke Township (local use). In Pamlico Sound at entrance to Blair Channel and Teaches Hole Channel just n of Ocracoke Inlet 3 mi. sw of Ocracoke (village). The "notorious" pirate Blackbeard—Edward Drummond most likely his original name (also Edward Teach, Teech, Thatch, Tach, Tache, or Tatch)—was killed near here on November 22, 1718, by Lieutenant Robert Maynard, dispatched by Governor Spotswood of Virginia specifically to rid the Carolina coast of Blackbeard and his pirates (North Carolina Governor Eden had pardoned Blackbeard and obvious they had an agreement). A nearby channel is known as Teaches Hole Channel, and shoal is known as Teaches Hole Bar. *Other names:* Teache Hole (Ocracoke Island History 2016), Teachs Hole (Ocracoke Island History 2016), Teeches Hole (Hooker 1850), Thatches Hole (Angley 1984, 84, from Quinn 1955—reportedly Thatch one version of Blackbeard's actual surname), Thatchs Hole (Teach is accepted spelling but Thatch found recorded occasionally; Moseley 1733).

Teaches Hole Bar, shoal, Hyde County, Ocracoke Township (ACE 1893). Just sw of Teaches Hole just before entrance to Teaches Hole Channel 3.5 mi. sw of Ocracoke (village). Highly changeable with different sizes over the years. *See* Teaches Hole. *Other names:* Peaches Hole Swash (Blunt 1857, 343—misinterpretation), Teaches Hole Swash (Angley 1984, 47), Teachs Hole Bar (ACE 1883).

Teaches Hole Channel, channel, 1.8 mi. long, Hyde County, Ocracoke Township (USGS 2013: Ocracoke, Portsmouth). In Pamlico Sound from Ocracoke Inlet to Silver Lake at Ocracoke (village). *See* Teaches Hole. *Other names:* Teaches Hole (Powell 1968), Teachs Hole Channel (O'Neal et al. 1976, 64).

Teachs Castle. *See* Springers Point.

Teachs Lair Marina, harbor, Dare County, Hatteras Township (signage). At sw Hatteras (village) just ne of Austin Creek (Hatteras-Ocracoke Ferry landing). Used for marketing and to be attractive since notorious pirate

Blackbeard (Edward Drummond, or Edward Teach) frequented Ocracoke (Springers Point) and has become a folkloric figure. Blackbeard did not use Hatteras—no Hatteras village during Blackbeard's time at the Outer Banks, and no Hatteras Inlet in its modern location, only small and unpredictable Old Hatteras Inlet a short distance farther w along what is now Ocracoke Island. Unusual spelling of Teaches. *See also* Teaches Hole.

Teal Island, island, 0.2 mi. long, Carteret County, Harkers Island Township (USGS 2013: Horsepen Point). In Core Sound 0.5 mi. n of Hogpen Bay 3.7 mi. e of Harkers Island (village). Teal (*Anas* spp.) are surface-feeding ducks common on the Outer Banks, but could also be surname.

Teals Island, marsh island, Currituck County, Poplar Branch Township (C&GS 1852). In central Mossey Islands complex just n of Buzzard Lead 5.5 mi. ssw of Corolla. Name origin unclear; normally, with migrating fowl in Atlantic Flyway and duck hunting, one would presume named for blue-winged teal (*Anas discors*) and green-winged teal (*Anas carolinensis*) frequently here. However, possible use of possessive form might suggest surname.

Ten-Fathom Ledge, shoal, Carteret County, Harkers Island Township (ACE 2013). With steep precipice in Cape Lookout Shoals at Cape Lookout. Name is descriptive of depth (60 ft.).

Ten Feet Channel, former channel, Carteret County, Harkers Island Township (Mouzon 1775). Was in Cape Lookout Shoals just off of what was then Cape Point 3.5 mi. ssw of Cape Lookout Lighthouse. Does not exist today from highly changeable nature of these shoals but was apparently a useful descriptive name indicating deep (for the time period) channel e-w through inner portion Cape Lookout Shoals; important enough to appear on Mouzon's 1775 map. Plural form used, despite such distance statements usually singular and hyphenated (e.g., 10-Foot Channel), but no real grammatical or orthographic rules until early 19th century.

Terrapin Creek, cove, 0.3 mi. long, 0.05 mi. wide, Dare County, Kinnakeet Township (USGS 1983: Pea Island). Trends ene to wsw in Pamlico Sound to Terrapin Creek Bay 8 mi. nnw of Rodanthe. Reportedly an Anglicized

version of an Algonquian word referring to any North American turtles inhabiting fresh or brackish waters.

Terrapin Creek, cove, Dare County, Kinnakeet Township (Garrity-Blake 2010, 493). In Pamlico Sound 2 mi. e of Gull Island, 4.5 mi. s of Salvo. *See* Terrapin Creek.

Terrapin Creek Bay, bay, 1.2 mi. wide, Dare County, Kinnakeet Township (USGS 2013: Pea Island). In Pamlico Sound, 7.5 mi. n of Rodanthe. *See* Terrapin Creek.

Terrapin Creek Point, point, Dare County, Kinnakeet Township (USGS 2013: Pea Island). N point Terrapin Creek Bay and s point Pea Island Bay on marsh island 8.1 mi. nnw of Rodanthe. *See* Terrapin Creek.

Terrapin Island, island, Carteret County, Portsmouth Township (C&GS 1900). In soundside islands in s portion Portsmouth Island 7.5 mi. se of Portsmouth (village). Changed form over the years and will continue to do so. In last half 20th century became two islands, but is shoaling back into one island. *See* Terrapin Creek.

Terrapin Island, small island, Hyde County, Ocracoke Township (local use). Between Shingle Creek and Terrapin Shoal 9.2 mi. ne of Ocracoke (village). *See* Terrapin Creek.

Terrapin Point, marsh point, Dare County, Kinnakeet Township (USGS 2013: Little Kinnakeet). On Hatteras Island just nw of former Little Kinnakeet 4.4 mi. n of original Avon. *See* Terrapin Creek.

Terrapin Shoal, shoal, 0.9 mi. long, Hyde County, Ocracoke Township (USGS 2013: Green Island). In Pamlico Sound at Ocracoke Island, 6.7 mi. ne of Ocracoke (village), near Old Hatteras Inlet (q.v.). Use of Great Swash and The Great Swash were confused applications with that named feature 2 mi. sw. *See* Terrapin Creek. *Other names:* Great Swash (misapplication), The Great Swash (misapplication).

Terrapin Shoal Point, shoal, Hyde County, Ocracoke Township (local use). E tip Terrapin Shoal just nw of Quork Hammock 9 mi. ne of Ocracoke (village). Reference is necessary when navigating this curved portion Terrapin Shoal. *See* Terrapin Creek. *Other names:* Point of Terrapin Shoal (local use), Terrapin Shoals (O'Neal et al. 1976, 44).

Theodora Creek, cove or tidal creek, Currituck County, Poplar Branch Township (local use). Off s Raccoon Bay 1 mi. nw of Corolla. Some insinuation, because of similarity, named for Theodosia Burr Alston, daughter of Aaron Burr, and by inference then possibly "the wreck site" of the ship *Patriot* on which Ms. Alston was traveling from Charleston, South Carolina (left December 31, 1812), to New York City (her husband, Joseph Alston, was governor of South Carolina). After leaving Charleston, the ship and Ms. Alston were never seen again. There are many stories (some ostensibly deathbed confessions) mostly implicating the *Patriot*'s capture by pirates and all aboard then being murdered, and including "walking the plank" stories. Whatever happened could have been anywhere along the route, including one confession ostensibly placing some emphasis on the Nags Head legend (*see* Nags Head) of "Bankers" walking a horse with a lantern around its neck along the beach to lure ships—not true. Also, story of a resident (historical) having painting of Mrs. Alston she was taking to New York (either washed ashore or given), told to me firsthand by direct descendent, but evidence is sketchy. Fate of the *Patriot* could have been pirates or British blockade (War of 1812), but most likely a severe storm. According to a British ship's logbooks there was a severe storm in Cape Hatteras area January 2, 1813, could have been reason for loss of the *Patriot*. Still, no connection here to Theodosia Burr Alston and no documentation or any reason to believe any relationship with this feature. Name is merely a local given name.

Theoff Point, marsh point, Dare County, Nags Head Township (USGS 2013: Oregon Inlet). On se Bodie Island just n of Cedar Island 3.8 mi. ese of Wanchese. Contraction and reference to nearby water passage known as The Cutoff. One-word form probably transcribing error. *See* Off Island and The Cutoff.

Thicket Lump, marsh island, Dare County, Nags Head Township (local use and road sign). On se tip Roanoke Island, intense marsh just s of Mill Landing, 1.5 mi. ese of Wanchese. *See* Green Lump and Wanchese Marshes.

Thicket Lump Marina, harbor, less than 0.1 mi. across, Dare County, Nags Head Township (signage). On se Roanoke Island, just se of Wanchese 6.5 mi. se of Manteo. *See* Thicket Lump.

Thickety Point. *See* Mill Point.

Thickety Ridge, sand ridge, Dare County, Atlantic Township (local use and NCDOT). In original Kitty Hawk near mouth former Jacks Cabin Creek (Penny Toler Ditch—Town of Kitty Hawk 2007), descriptively applied at North Cove, ne Kitty Hawk Bay, 3 mi. nw of Kill Devil Hills (town). Not well known and not on any sources other than street maps in NCDOT database. Those interviewed think the name is most likely used from name of short e-w street from this point to Elijah Baum Road. Dare County GIS uses Thickety Point Road, implying application to the nearby point; if so, historical Mill Point.

Thick Island, former island, Dare County, Nags Head Township probably (Currituck DB 11, 1811, 90). Described as "a parcel of land & marsh on the North Banks near Nags Head. Beginning on the Sound side opposite the N. W. end of Thick Island" Tempting to declare this island must have been one of what is now Penguin Islands, though a few miles s of original Nags Head (there were no appreciable islands soundside here). Possibly in former Green Islands (q.v.) complex at what is now The Causeway. The problem is these islands are at or just s of former Roanoke Inlet, the s limit of North Banks and n limit of Bodies Island. Still, reference to North Banks could have been a general reference, or since "near Nags Head" was stated and Nags Head itself was on North Banks, perhaps one of these islands qualifies. Anyway, Thick Island was soundside somewhere in Nags Head, perhaps former name of Nags Head Island.

Thick Ridge, sand ridge, 0.2 mi. long, Dare County, Atlantic Township (Town of Kitty Hawk 2007). Trends n-s 1.3 mi. w of original Kitty Hawk. Descriptive of short length and wide appearance. *See* Kitty Hawk ridge-and-swale system.

Third Pond, man-enhanced, Currituck County, Poplar Branch Township (local use). On s Dews Island 0.3 mi. n of s tip Dews Island, 4 mi. nw of Duck. Derived from third of three large man-enhanced ponds from n-to-s on the island.

Thomas Island, small marsh island, Currituck County, Fruitville Township (Cox 1923). W entrance to North Graven Creek between Graven Island and sw tip Walk Island, 1 mi. e of Knotts Island (village).

Thomas Paines Landing, former landing,

Dare County, Kinnakeet Township (references early documents). Soundside near Rodanthe possibly at Blackmar Gut. Paine (and other spellings) an established surname (numerous 1700s deeds) here and directly across Pamlico Sound at Stumpy Point on mainland. *See* North Drain. *Other names:* Thomas Paines Wharf (vendue announcement).

Thompsons Hammock, hummock, Carteret County, Portsmouth Township or Atlantic Township (Stick 1958, 308). Somewhere on s Portsmouth Island near High Hills or Merkle Hammock, possibly on North Core Banks near Pilontary Islands.

Thorofare, The, water passage, 0.6 mi. long, Currituck County, Poplar Branch Township (USGS 2013: Mossey Islands). In Currituck Sound between Thorofare Island and Brant Island, 3.5 mi. ssw of Corolla. *Other names:* Thorofare (USGS 2013: Mossey Islands), Thorofare Lead (C&GS 1852—*see* Buzzard Lead), Throufare Creek (local spelling).

Thorofare Island, island, 0.3 mi. long, Currituck County, Poplar Branch Township (USGS 2013: Mossey Islands). In Currituck Sound just n of The Thorofare, 5.3 mi. ssw of Corolla. *Other names:* Throufare Island (C&GS 1852), Thoroughfare Island (C&GS 1860).

Thoroughfare, The, water passage, 1.7 mi. long, Dare County, Atlantic Township (local use). Trends n-s separating Sloop Island from Burnt Island, 1.5 mi. w of Kill Devil Hills (town). *Other names:* Thoroughfare (local use), Thoro Fare (written locally), Thorofare (some use).

Thoroughfare Marsh, former marsh, Carteret County, Beaufort Township (CS 1850a). Is 1 mi. w of Town Marsh, 1.5 mi. wsw of Beaufort (mainland). Now marsh on e side of Radio Island, though extent of application is unknown. Name origin is result of being at sw entrance to Lewis Thoroughfare.

Three Dunes, sand dunes, 60 ft. (n dune), 70 ft. (center dune), 50 ft. (s dune), Currituck County, Poplar Branch Township (USGS 2013: Mossey Islands). On Currituck Banks 1 mi. e of Mossey Islands complex, 5 mi. sse of Corolla. Appeared on maps since 1700s, at The Currituck Club subdivision, and altered considerably by building golf course. *Other names:* The Hammocks (in part—n area, recent reference from section in subdivision The Currituck Club), The Sand Hills (Anderson

1796), The Three Dunes (18th-century maps), The Three Sand Hills (Mouzon 1775), Three Sand Hills (Collet et al. 1770), Three Sisters (colonial maps).

Three Hats Channel, former channel, Carteret County, Portsmouth Township (vague historical references). Was in Core Sound, from Three Hats Shoal toward High Hills Inlet. References are general from historical documents, and though shoal appeared named on a few early 19th-century charts, channel did not appear named on maps or charts. *See* Three Hats Shoal. *Other names:* Crab Slough (Wimble).

Three Hats Creek. *See* High Hills Inlet.

Three Hats Shoal, shoal, 1.5 mi. across, Carteret County, Portsmouth Township (Price 1795). In Pamlico Sound, 3.5 mi. w of Portsmouth (village). Shape on early charts bore some resemblance to three 18th-century tricorne hats. *Other names:* Three Hat Shoal (Ocracock [sic] Harbour [sic], 1807).

Tillets Camp, former camp, Dare County, Atlantic Township (historical local use). Was just n of Jockeys Ridge 2 mi. nnw of Nags Head (center). *See* Camp Cass Williams. *Other names:* Tillets Fish Camp (earlier use).

Tillets Cove, cove, Dare County, Atlantic Township (local use). In n Kitty Hawk Bay at Poor Ridge Landing, 1 mi. sw of original Kitty Hawk. *Other names:* Tillett Cove (local use).

Tillets Landing Areas, former area, Dare County, Nags Head and Kinnakeet Townships (Stick 1949). Was two areas, n and s shores Oregon Inlet where Tillet operated a ferry 1920s (3 cars, later 10 cars). No specific location or dock as the location on both sides of the inlet varied because of the constantly changing shoals requiring a landing ramp attachment on the ferries.

Tillmans Creek, cove, Dare County, Nags Head Township (local use). On w shore of barrier island in Roanoke Sound, 1.3 mi. wnw of Jockeys Ridge 1.8 mi. wnw of Nags Head (center). Contains a short stream-like portion extending 0.2 mi. inland. Original name, first 150 years or more was Francis (Frances) Creek, appearing on early maps in that form in all early deeds but changed over the years. *Other names:* Frances Creek (Currituck DB 3, 1739, 283–84), Francis Creek (Currituck DB 3, 1784, 286–87), Padricks Creek (Currituck DB 7, 1794, 46), Patricks Creek (possibly—Currituck DB 30, 1869, 285), Patrix Creek (Currituck

DB 1862, 29, 81), Steeles Gutt (18th-century maps), Struls Gut (Harris 2017; unknown, 1798—probable transcription error for Steeles).

Tobacco Point, former point, Hyde County, Ocracoke Township (Blunt 1857, 344). Was somewhere between Ocracoke (village) and Royal Shoal (8.5 mi.). Blunt is unclear on exact location but implication is probably somewhere on Royal Shoal's distinctive formation; name unknown and not found in any other sources.

Tombstone Point, point, Carteret County, Morehead Township (USGS 2013: Beaufort). On e end of Bogue Banks 2.9 mi. e of Atlantic Beach (town).

Tom Curles Ridge, small sand ridge, Dare County, Atlantic Township (Harris 2017). In s original Kitty Hawk just n of ne corner of North Cove, ne Kitty Hawk Bay, just e of Old Landing Ridge. *Other names:* Tom Curls Ridge (Harris 2017).

Tom Fishers Creek, tidal stream, Dare County, Kinnakeet Township (Covey 2018, 57). In Waves just n of Waves Landing 2 mi. s of Rodanthe. *Other names:* Tom Fisher Creek (some use).

Tom Gilgo Hammock, dune, Carteret County, Portsmouth Township (NPS 2007, A5). Small irregular sand hill in South Portsmouth just n of Sheep Island 1 mi. s of central Portsmouth (village).

Tom Kings Creek, stream, Dare County, Hatteras Township (Covey 2018, 50). In Frisco just s of Brigands Bay subdivision extending inland from Pamlico Sound 3 mi. to just w of Buxton. Wallaces Ditch occupies lower part w of NC 12. *Other names:* Wallaces Ditch (lower part—Farrow map, Covey 2018, 44).

Tommies Creek, small tidal stream, Dare County, Kinnakeet Township (Garrity-Blake 2010, 168). In The North'ard part of Avon and former Scarboro 0.5 mi. e of Big Island, and 8 mi. n of Buxton. Canalized and altered beyond recognition by development.

Tommy Hammock, hummock, 0.2 mi. wide, 5 ft. high, Dare County, Nags Head Township (USGS 2013: Oregon Inlet). On sw Bodie Island 2.9 mi. nw of Bodie Island Lighthouse, 2.9 mi. nne of Wanchese. *See* Black Hammock. *Other names:* Tommys Hammock (CS 1852), Tommys Hummock (Stick 1958, 173).

Tom Smith's Camp, temporary former fishing camp, Carteret County, Morehead Township (White 2012, 229). Was on Bogue Banks near or just e of Salter Path.

Topsail Inlet. *See* Beaufort Inlet.

Torpedo Junction. *See* Diamond Shoals.

Tower Beach, beach, 1 mi. long, Dare County, Hatteras Township (local use). From Buxton Beach (s) to where NC 12 turns due w 1.3 mi. ese of Buxton. References temporary steel tower used for Cape Hatteras Light 1935 until 1942 while CCC and WPA worked to reclaim land encroached upon by sea, accomplished only for a while. Cape Hatteras Lighthouse was moved (1999) 0.5 mi. w and inland to save it from the sea. *See* Old Tower Hill.

Town Creek. *See* Doughs Creek.

Town Marsh, marsh, 0.4 mi. long, 0.2 mi. wide, Carteret County, Beaufort Township (USGS 1951: Beaufort). Just s of Beaufort (mainland) 3 mi. e of Morehead City (mainland).

Town Marsh Channel, former channel, 1 mi. long, Carteret County, Beaufort Township (historical local use). Separated Town Marsh from Bird Island Shoal, 1.2 mi. s of Beaufort (mainland).

Trade Winds Marina, harbor, Carteret County, Morehead Township (signage). In Indian Beach (town) just w of Salter Path in Paradise Bay (mobile homes), 5 mi. w of Pine Knoll Shores. Fanciful name because the belt of Trade Winds lies between 30° N and 30° S latitude, the n limit about 500 mi. s of here.

Trail Ridge, short ridge, 0.5 mi. long, Dare County, Nags Head Township (limited local use). Heavily vegetated ridge about 25–30 ft. high e central Roanoke Island, 3 mi. w of Manteo. Name unknown generally and only 2 people indicated they had heard the name. Limited use from subdivision (six lots) by this name adjacent se.

Trees Point, point, Carteret County, Morehead Township (Holland 1794). Ne point of then Stanford Islands and today ne point Bogue Banks on Bogue Point 1.3 mi. s of Beaufort (mainland). Used only colonial period and only on Holland's map.

Trench, The, cove, 0.3 mi. long, Dare County, Kinnakeet Township (USGS 2013: Pea Island). Between Goose Island Point and Pea Island Point 8.7 mi. nne of Rodanthe.

Trent. *See* Frisco.

Trent Church Camp, former military camp, Dare County, Hatteras Township (historical documents). Temporary small Union camp in Frisco during Civil War. *Other names:* Trent Church Picket (Covey 2018, 117).

Trent Lake, lake, Dare County, Hatteras Township (local use). Just s of Brigands Bay 5 mi. ne of Hatteras (village). Trent was original name of Frisco before post office established and named Frisco because already post office in North Carolina named Trent. Trent, local surname. *See* Frisco. *Other names:* Lake Trent (Brooks 2010).

Trent Windmill, former windmill, Hyde County, Ocracoke Township (Howard, January 21, 2013). Was somewhere in Up Trent area about 1 mi. east of Ocracoke (village center) soundside possibly near Horsepen Point. The name was likely that of the miller but is not known.

Trent Woods, former woods, Hyde County, Ocracoke Township (Garrity-Blake 2010, 356). Was just s of Horsepen Point in Trentwood, 1 mi. e of Silver Lake and Ocracoke (village center). Not to be confused with former Trent Woods, now Frisco Woods, in Frisco on Hatteras Island. On Ocracoke not nearly as distinct as early 20th century. *See* Trent Lake.

Trinety Harbor, former water passage, Dare County, Atlantic Township (DeBry 1590; Hondius 1606). Connected Currituck Sound to Atlantic Ocean 3 mi. nw of Duck (center). Open before 1585 (Lane 1585, second letter to Walsingham, August 1585), closed before 1660. Religious name, unknown specifically by whom it was named, though seemingly by Thomas Hariot during Grenville's voyage (second Roanoke voyage). Lane indicates in his second letter August 12, 1585, "There bee only, in all, three entryes and portes: the one which wee have named Trynytye Harborough" Also, Lane indicates, Thomas Hariot (illustrator on the voyage) had a Bible and often religious terms were used in dealing with Indians (Lane 1585, second letter to Walsingham). Unusual "harbor" used not "harbour," but "harbor" is clearly form used on DeBry's 1590 map and subsequent maps. "Harbour" was usual spelling then, but no orthographic rules.

Inlet location is controversial, and many different locations are given by authors who have written about the Outer Banks. The most frequently selected sites are Jeanguite Creek (e.g., Stick 1958, 262), Caffeys Inlet, and a site 5 mi. n of Caffeys Inlet at Beasley Bay selected by Fisher (1962, 110) based on his analysis. However, many (including me after examination of historical maps) conclude the inlet to have been 1 mi. s of former Caffeys Inlet—fits distances reported by Amadas and Barlowe (first Roanoke voyage). Use of generic term "harbor" referring to an inlet was common until 18th century and indicates ships rode at anchor just off beach near inlet. Some authors believe this to be inlet through which Amadas and Barlowe passed on the initial voyage of reconnaissance (1584) searching for sites to establish a colony. Not certain because of ambiguities from Amadas and Barlowe's logs, Lane's letters, and Butler's deposition. However, distances indicated in logs of the voyage by Amadas and Barlowe seem to support this inlet for initial entry rather than Port Ferdinando (Gunt Inlet); English sailings from Trinety Harbor toward Roanoke Island also shown in later versions of DeBry's 1590 map. *See* Roanoke Island historical inlets and Gunt Inlet for detailed explanation and analysis.

Other names: New Inlet (late 17th-century maps), Port Trinitie (some modern spoken usage from subdivision of same name), Porto della Trinita (Dudley 1647), Port Trinity (Lane, governor of first colony 1585, letter to Secretary Walsingham, August 12, 1585, acknowledging existence of inlet and naming it), The Haven (Haklyut 1589), Trinite Habor (Blaeu 1640), Trinite Harbor (Homann 1714), Trinite Harbour (Keulen 1690; Hondius 1606), Trinitie Harbor (map and text interpretive references), Trinitie Harbour (Torres 1985, 21, 22; Keulen 1690), Trinitie Harbro (Quinn 1975—misrecording), Trinity Harbor (Cobb 1905; Miller 1974), Trinity Harbor Inlet (Frankenberg 1995, loc. 152, 3—"Inlet" added, no other known occurrence), Trinity Harbour (Cheeseman 1982, 21), Trinityherber (misspelling, or perhaps not, since origin of word is Old English *herebeorg*), Trinity Inlet (Hyde County Planning 2008, 5), Trynytye Harboroughe (Lane 1585, letter 2), Wercester Inlet (variation of Worcester), Worcester Inlet (Smith 1624, map—possible tribute to First [Henry] or Second [Edward] Somerset, Marques of Worcester, England—name appeared only short time).

Triple S Marina, harbor, Carteret County, Morehead Township (signage). At Triple S Marina Village subdivision on e end Bogue Banks just ne of Money Island Beach, 1.5 mi. e of Atlantic Beach (town). Marina (and subdivision) named for Triple S Pier formerly Oceanside (across highway from marina). Reportedly, the pier was named for three doctors each of whose surname began with the letter S, and by whom the pier was developed.

Tri-Villages, area, Dare County, Kinnakeet Township (modern local tourism support). Used 21st century for (n-s) Rodanthe (and South Rodanthe), Waves, and Salvo villages because they are adjacent to one another. Not used except occasionally in brochures. *Other names:* The Northern End (sometimes used commercial brochures—reference to n end Hatteras Island).

Trout Creek, short water passage, 0.5 mi. long, Carteret County, White Oak Township (Williamson 1992, 201). In Bogue Sound just sw of Trout Creek Reef Shoal separating marsh islands 2.5 mi. sse of Swansboro (mainland). References spotted or speckled seatrout (*Cynoscion nebulosus*) prevalent here; some place names throughout the Outer Banks use the reference.

Trout Creek Reef Shoal, small shoal, Carteret County, White Oak Township (Williamson 1992, 201). In Bogue Sound, ne end of Trout Creek near junction of Banks Channel and Main Channel, 2 mi. w of Langston Bridge, 2.5 mi. se of Swansboro (mainland). "Reef" in Outer Banks geographic names usually refers to oyster colonies. Triple generic term use, "creek reef shoal," means name was associative with Trout Creek and this was likely expired oyster colony now covered with sand. *See* Trout Creek.

Trout Hole, deep, Currituck County, Poplar Branch Township (C&GS 1895b). Just e of n Dowdy Bay 6.5 mi. nw of Duck. The name was more prevalent in the 19th century. *See* Trout Creek.

Trout Slue, channel, Hyde County, Ocracoke Township (local informants). In Pamlico Sound adjacent to Trout Slue Shoal 1.5 mi. nw of Silver Lake (Ocracoke village). Most folk have no recollection or knowledge, and name rarely if ever used. *See* Trout Creek and Allen Slue.

Trout Slue Shoal, small shoal, Hyde County, Ocracoke Township (local informants). In Pamlico Sound 1.5 mi. nw of Silver Lake (Ocracoke village). Most folk have no recollection or knowledge, and the name rarely if ever used. Associative with Trout Slue. *See* Trout Creek.

Try Yard Creek, water passage, 0.3 mi. long, Carteret County, Smyrna Township (USGS 2013: Horsepen Point). In Core Sound, separates Core Banks from unnamed marsh island 4.4 mi. e of Harkers Island (village). Name origin unclear to anyone (except a few historians); some believe a nautical term as in "bring to" or "coming about." However, "try yard" formerly indicated place where beached whale (in some cases porpoises) was processed, resulting from former Outer Banks method of whaling (*see* Cape Lookout Grounds), relying on occasional beached whale or later by attacking the whale from longboats launched through the surf. Name applied historically when now obsolete meaning of word "try" meant to render good from bad, eventually meant render oil from blubber or fat. This style of whaling was concentrated around Cape Lookout but existed as far north as Cape Hatteras early in colonial period (and Ocracoke Island—*see* Try Yard Creek [Hyde County]).

Try Yard Creek, cove, 0.2 mi. wide, Hyde County, Ocracoke Township (USGS 2002: Howard Reef). In Pamlico Sound, 6.1 mi. ne of Ocracoke (village). *See* Try Yard Creek (Carteret County).

Tuna Beach. *See* Whalehead Beach (subdivision).

Turkells Gut, water passage, 0.1 mi. long, Currituck County, Poplar Branch Township (USGS 2013: Mossey Islands). Connects n Neals Creek (sometimes Nells Creek) to Big Pond, 9 mi. sw of Corolla. *See* Alligator Gut.

Turtle Bay, bay, Carteret County, Harkers Island Township (NPS 2000). Se Lookout Bight between Wreck Point (e) and Power Squadron Spit (w) 2.5 mi. n of Cape Point (Cape Lookout), 6 mi. s of Harkers Island (village).

Turtle Pond, small pond, Dare County, Atlantic Township (local use and street sign). In s-central Southern Shores (town), 1 mi. e of Jeanguite Creek; almost disappeared.

Turtle Pond, small lake, Dare County, Hatteras

Township (Sorrie 2014, 175). At Cape Hatteras 1.3 mi. se of Buxton 2.5 mi. n of Cape Point. *Other names:* Entrance Road Pond (NPS, Water Quality Report 2006, 11).

Turtle Pond, small man-made lake, Dare County, Kinnakeet Township (F&WS 2016). Just s of Pea Island National Wildlife Refuge Visitors' Center at entrance North Pond Nature Trail, 9 mi. n of Rodanthe. Descriptive of use.

Turtle Pond, small man-made lake, Dare County, Nags Head Township (signage). Near entrance to Pirates Cove subdivision, 2 mi. se of central Manteo. Named for large amount of turtles in pond, specifically yellow-bellied sliders, *Trachemys scripta scripta* (signage).

Uncle Bates Ditch, small canalized tidal stream, Dare County, Kinnakeet Township (Garrity-Blake 2010, 169). Soundside in s original Avon (between Dog Ridge and Pothead) halfway between Peters Ditch (Avon Harbor entrance) and First Creek, 0.3 mi. from each, 7 mi. n of Buxton.

Uncle Dicks Creek, tidal stream, Dare County, Kinnakeet Township (Garrity-Blake 2010, 493). Just n of No Ache e end Clarks Bay at North Dike 0.7 mi. s of Salvo.

Uncle Jimmys Landing, landing, Dare County, Kinnakeet Township (USGS 2013: Rodanthe). Reportedly 0.4 mi. ne of Greens Point, 0.5 mi. nw of Rodanthe, though Covey (2018, 13) indicates actually what is now Waves Landing (q.v.) — local opinion is mixed.

Uncle Johns Path, former path, Carteret County, Morehead Township (Stephens 1989, 13). In central Salter Path near Methodist Church, used for foot traffic through area until 1950s. *See* Bogue Banks historical paths.

Upper Dune, small sand dune, Dare County, Atlantic Township (local use). Isolated outlier dune 1.7 mi. n of center Kill Devil Hills sand dunes complex between Wright Brothers Monument and Avalon Beach subdivision, 3 mi. sse of original Kitty Hawk. References position in large Kill Devil Hills sand dunes complex (nearby road named Upper Dune).

Upper Hobbs Marsh, marsh, Currituck County, Poplar Branch Township (C&GS 1852). At se Sanders Bay, just n of Hobbs Marsh 4.5 mi. s of Corolla. *See* Hobbs Marsh.

Upper Landing, former landing, Currituck County, Poplar Branch Township (C&GS 1852). On Currituck Banks just w of Piper Hill, 8 mi. nnw of Duck. Derived from being just n of A. Baums Landing.

Upper Middle, shoal, 2.2. mi. long, Hyde County, Swan Quarter Township (NOS 2014i). On nw part Middle Ground in Pamlico Sound 20 mi. nw of Ocracoke (village).

Upper Roads, former anchorage, Carteret County, Portsmouth Township (Hooker 1850). Was in Ship Channel just n of North Rock, 8 mi. w of Ocracoke (village). *See* Beacon Island Roads.

Upper Roads Shoal, shoal, 2 mi. long, Carteret County, Portsmouth Township (Weslager 1954). Trends ese to wnw from historical Upper Roads, was just n of North Rock 8.5 mi. w of Ocracoke (village). Still shallow with depths less than 3 ft. *See* Beacon Island Roads. *Other names:* Upper Road Shoal (Weslager 1954).

Up the Road, former area, Dare County, Atlantic Township (Harris 2017). Referenced w Kitty Hawk in Kitty Hawk ridge-and-swale system (q.v.) n of Shellbank s of Sound Landing just w of Kitty Hawk Landing subdivision. Unlike same reference used in Salvo, n-s orientation on narrow barrier island there, this reference was e-w, differentiating original Kitty Hawk (Down The Road [q.v.]) from here.

Up the Road, former area, Dare County, Kinnakeet Township (Garrity-Blake 2010, 136). Historical in n Salvo differentiating from other parts of the village. "Up" is common usage for n because n is top on most maps of n hemisphere. Also used in Buxton, Hatteras, most communities between Oregon Inlet and Hatteras Inlet.

Up Trent, area, Hyde County, Ocracoke Township (local sources and Howard 2017 and 2018). One of three major areas in Ocracoke (village) defining historic parts within the village. Each generated mild form of competition first half 20th century (and bit beyond) as there were three major focal points of dwellings: w side of Silver Lake (Cockle Creek [q.v.]), Pointers (Springers Point reference); around s, n, and e sides Silver Lake, Creekers; and ne part of village near

Pamlico Sound, Trenters (this entry). *See also* Ocracoke Village areas. *Other names:* Trent (Garrity-Blake 2010, 403), Trentwood (earlier local use), Upland Trent (O'Neal et al. 1976, map, back cover).

Vanes Pole, historical, Dare County, Kinnakeet Township (probably) (Covey 2018, 18). *See* Lookout Cedar. Additionally, Covey suggests there could be a relationship with the pirate Charles Vane, who reportedly spent some weeks collaborating and carousing with Blackbeard at Ocracoke. The meeting did likely take place, though evidence is mostly circumstantial.

Vera Cruz Shoal, former shoal, 0.4 mi. long, Carteret County, Portsmouth Township (USGS 1950: Portsmouth). Was in Ocracoke Inlet 2.1 mi. e of Portsmouth (village), 4.2 mi. sw of Ocracoke (village). Originally larger and named Dry Sand Shoal or Dry Shoal Point 18th and 19th centuries because covered with water only during storms. Name changed early 20th century when it became increasingly inundated, and renamed after ship *Vera Cruz VII*, stranded here on May 8 and 9, 1903. All passengers, crew (except for captain and first mate, who mysteriously disappeared), and cargo were saved; remnants of the *Vera Cruz* are still on the shoal (now totally inundated). Local tales indicate captain disappeared because he was attempting to smuggle a large number of people from Cape Verde into U.S.—neither proven nor discounted. By late 20th century, shoal had become completely inundated. *Other names:* Dry Sand Shoal (historical maps; White 2012), Dry Shoal Point (historical maps; White 2012), Vera Cruz Shoals (sometimes used when appearing as more than one shoal).

Village at Nags Head, The, subdivision, 1.5 mi. long, 1 mi. wide (between mileposts 13.5 and 15), Dare County, Nags Head Township (signage). Large development in s Nags Head (early 20th century was South Nags Head, though that name has now shifted to development s of Whalebone Junction). Numerous subdivisions at The Village at Nags Head (many with signage, some without): Atlantic Watch, Bay Meadow, Beach Haven North, Beach Haven South, Captains Watch, Coastal Cove, Craig End, Dolphin Run, Duneridge Estates, Duneridge North, Elliot Estates, Heron Cove, Leeward Shores, Linkside, Marsh Links, Moongate, North Seaside (Clubside), Oceanwatch (Oceans Watch), Reflections, Sand Castle Village (Sand Castle), Sawgrass, Seapointe Duplexes, Seaside, Sea Watch, Seven Sisters, Sunset Greens, The Quay, The Masters, The Ridges, The Wedges, Watersedge Village (Watersedge), and Whispering Sands (PC HOA 2016). (Use of "end" for community, neighborhood, part of town, city, or subdivision generally referred to place, places, or cluster at end of road, path, etc. Original Middle English referenced "quarter" [*see* Hunting Quarter] or undefined region; over years morphed into current meaning. Used in Craig End is an "attractive" albeit archaic use for a small named cul-de-sac.) *Other names:* Epstein Tract (historical name at first development before being sold by Epstein family—Town of Nags Head 2000, 16), Nags Head Village (real estate listings), The Village (Town of Nags Head 2000, 18), Village at Nags Head (local usage), Village of Nags Head (real estate listings).

Village Marina, harbor, Dare County, Hatteras Township (signage). In Hatteras (village), 0.7 mi. ne of Austin Creek (Hatteras-Ocracoke Ferry docks).

Virginia, historical region. Before settlement of Jamestown, in and around Roanoke Island and all English lands in North America were named Virginia in honor of Queen Elizabeth I of England, the "virgin queen." The Roanoke Island colonies failed, and first successful colony was farther n at Jamestown; name Virginia applied to that colony area eventually. Between 36° N lat. and 31° N lat. was granted to the eight Lords Proprietors in 1663 by Charles II of England, named Carolina (Latin form) in honor of Charles I, father of Charles II (*see* Carolina). Area n of former Currituck Inlet remained Virginia.

Virginia Dare Shores Dock, former landing, Dare County, Atlantic Township (historical documents). Was in Kitty Hawk Bay in Kill Devil Hills (town) in Virginia Dare Shores subdivision 2 mi. s of original Kitty Hawk. Housed facilities for entertaining, another building was pavilion for concerts, etc.

Vista Lake, man-made lake, Dare County, Nags Head Township (local use). In s Manteo 1.5 mi. w of Pirates Cove subdivision. Subdivision named for feature.

Wades Hammock, hummock, Carteret County, Harkers Island Township (Stick 1958, 188). Was on w end Shackleford Banks at Mullet Pond 3 mi. sse of Beaufort (mainland). Small community of Wades Shore was here and also known sometimes as Wades Hammock. *See* Black Hammock and Wades Shore (former community).

Wades Shore, shore, Carteret County, Harkers Island Township (Mason 2000; NPS 1987, map, 38). On w Shackleford Banks adjacent to and n of former scattered community of Wades Shore 4 mi. wsw of Harkers Island (village).

Wades Shore, former community, Carteret County, Harkers Island Township (historical local use). About 100 people on n or soundside w Shackleford Banks near Mullet Pond. Not as large as Diamond City (e Shackleford Banks), Wades Shore was principal community on w Shackleford Banks for fishing and whaling Outer Banks style (*see* Cape Lookout Grounds). Abandoned early 20th century; however, many "fishing" cottages and "shacks" were maintained here until Shackleford Banks incorporated into Cape Lookout National Seashore; by early 1986 by direction of NPS all buildings were razed or removed (floated to mainland). *Other names:* Mullet Pond (historical, settlement was at Mullet Pond), Mullet Shore (Stick 1958, 187), Shackleford (occasional historical local use), Shackleford Banks (Stick 1958, 187), Shacklefords (occasional historical local use), Wade Shore (Williamson 1986), Wades Hammock (Stick 1958, 189).

Wades Shore. *See* Shackleford Banks.

Wading Point, point, Carteret County, Harkers Island Township (USGS 2013: Harkers Island). Nw point of Browns Island 1.3 mi. ne of Harkers Island (village).

Wahabs Causeway, area, Dare County, Kinnakeet Township (probably) (Covey 2018, 12). Covey lists this name as an example of feature named for family or person. Name associated with Farrow family of Avon but also with families on Ocracoke. Covey does not elaborate on specific location or whether this was man-made or natural causeway. Name unknown today. *See* Farrows Creek.

Wahabs Windmill, former windmill, Hyde County, Ocracoke Township (Howard, January 21, 2013). On Windmill Point w side of Silver Lake in Ocracoke (village). Believed to be the windmill for which Windmill Point is named since Job Wahab owned the land and reportedly operated a windmill.

Wainwright Island, island, 0.3 mi. wide, Carteret County, Cedar Island Township (USGS 2013: Wainwright Island). In Core Sound 3.3 mi. e of Harbor Island 16.2 mi. sw of Ocracoke (village). Named for James Wainwright, who settled nearby. As an aside, "wainwright" (same as a "cartwright"— "wain" means wagon) is a wagon maker. "Wright," older English, one who makes or builds something, though usage today survives only in surnames. *Other names:* Wainwrights Island (Hooker 1850).

Wainwright Shoals, small shoal, Carteret County, Cedar Island Township (former signage). Surrounds much of Wainwright Island mostly on e side, 6 mi. e of Cedar Island Ferry landing, 13.5 mi. se of Ocracoke (village). Late as 1990s sign in Pamlico Sound near its junction with Core Sound identifying the location along Cedar Island–Ocracoke Ferry route. *See* Wainwright Island.

Wainwright Slue, channel, 1 mi. long, Carteret County, Cedar Island Township (NOS 2014b). In Core Sound junction with Pamlico Sound just e of Wainwright Island 12.7 mi. s of Ocracoke (village). *See* Wainwright Island and Allen Slough. *Other names:* Wainwright Channel (Goerch 1956), Wainwright Slough (alternate use).

Walker Bay. *See* Baum Bay.

Walker Island, island, 0.6 mi. long, 0.3 mi. wide, Dare County, Atlantic Township (older local use). Separates Colington Creek from Deep

Ditch 4.5 mi. nw of Nags Head (center). *Other names:* Walkers Island (alternate historical use).

Walkers Island, irregular marsh island, 1 mi. across, Currituck County, Fruitville Township (Cox 1923). Just se of Crow Island (Big Raymond Island), 5 mi. se of Knotts Island (village).

Walks Island, islands, 1 mi. long and wide, Currituck County, Fruitville Township (Cox 1906). W-most maze of marsh islands separated from Knotts Island by Knotts Island Channel, 2 mi. ene of Knotts Island (village). *Other names:* Pine Island (Currituck Deeds, miscellaneous, 1719—historical use sometimes included Franks Island and Runnells Marshes just w of Walk Island), Walk Island (Currituck DB 25, 1849, 387).

Walks Island Cove, small cove, 0.2 mi. wide, Currituck County, Fruitville Township (local use). At nw Walks Island just e of Knotts Island Channel, 1.5 mi. ne of Knotts Island (village). Associative with Walks Island. *Other names:* The Cove (some usage).

Wallace and Blount Docks, former landing, Carteret County, Portsmouth Township (Stick 1958, 77). Former docks and port facilities on Shell Castle (q.v.) operating 1790 until around War of 1812 when channel approach began to shoal up. At its height, facilities were busy allowing cargo to be transferred to smaller boats (lightering) for easily navigating tricky channels and shallow waters of the sounds. Today no trace of any of these former docks or buildings.

Wallace Channel, channel, Carteret County, Portsmouth Township (USGS 1950: Portsmouth). In Ocracoke Inlet just w of Blair Channel 3.7 mi. sw of Ocracoke (village). Dredging began 1895. Some confusion regarding name origin; named for John W. Wallace, "governor" or part owner of Shell Castle late 18th and early 19th centuries, or David Wallace Jr., whose house on Portsmouth Island, used as sighting point by pilots using channel when entering Ocracoke Inlet from Atlantic Ocean. Opinion and evidence slightly favor John Wallace. Beacon Island Road(s) early usage because channel served Beacon Island ("roads" used for places where ships could anchor safely—*see* Beacon Island Roads). *Other names:* Beacon Island Road (Torres 1985, 49), Beacon Island Roads

(in part—at Beacon Island), Flounder Slue (nw part—historical use), Middle Channel (Johnson 1872), Old Ship Channel (Whisnant and Whisnant 2010, 110), Walaces Channel (typographical error), Wallaces Channel (Whisnant and Whisnant 2010, 125), Wallases Channel (Hooker 1850), Wallico's Channel (CS 1857c text), Walliss Channel (colonial maps).

Wallace Channel Dock, former landing, Carteret County, Portsmouth Township (NPS 2007, table, B-9). Indicated somewhere "along road to beach" from former Portsmouth Coast Guard Station. Wallace Channel offshore with "possible" remnants of former dock visible 0.5 mi. ene of beach road halfway to beach along sand trail, unusual place for dock. No other known reference and specific location not provided. *Other names:* Wallace Dock (NPS brochures).

Wallace Channel Swash, shoal, Carteret County, Portsmouth Township (McGuinn 2000, 22). Swash along parts of Wallace Channel 4 mi. sw of Ocracoke (village). *See* Daniel Swash. *Other names:* Wallaces Channel Swash (McGuinn 2000, 22).

Wallace Point, point, Carteret County, Portsmouth Township (White 2012, 269). Believed just n of Daniel Swash 3.5 mi. ssw of Portsmouth (village). From an interview in secondary source, exact location not provided. Conversation suggests this location.

Wallaces Ditch, canal, Dare County, Hatteras Township (Covey 2018, Farrow map, 44). Historically, canalized lower end Tom Kings Creek (q.v.) in Frisco at Brigands Bay, part w of NC 12.

Walter Island. *See* Pond Island.

Walter Perry's Camp, former camp, Dare County, Atlantic Township (exact location unknown—historical local use). Fish and hunting camp was just s of Sanderling, 3 mi. n of Duck (center). *See* Camp Cass Williams.

Walter Slough, channel, 0.8 mi. long, Dare County, Nags Head Township (USGS 2013: Oregon Inlet). In Pamlico Sound just n of Old House Slough, just nw of Oregon Inlet, 5.6 mi. se of Wanchese. Walter, surname of early 18th-century homesteader just n of here.

Wanchese, village, 10 ft. high, Dare County, Nags Head Township (signage). Scattered village on s Roanoke Island 5 mi. s of Manteo. Named for one of two Indians taken to

England by Amadas and Barlowe 1584 (first Roanoke voyage), chief of subgroup of Algonquian Indians residing on Roanoke Island. After his return from England, unlike Manteo (from Croatoan or Hatteras Indians), Wanchese became belligerent toward the English, partially from colonists' behavior (first attempted military colony, 1585) and partially from misunderstanding. Wanchese (village) sometimes referenced as Lower End and Manteo as Upper End for relative locations on Roanoke Island, but many felt this reference improper and Lower End fell into disuse. Wanchese was commercial fishing center for n Outer Banks when commercial fishing was profitable. Post office est. 1886. *Other names:* Island Long Settlement (Maule 1718), Lower End (local use), South End (Wise 2010, 37; Joshua Judson Davis Papers, 1888, from Smith 2001, 100).

Wanchese canals, ditches, guts, and water passages, system of water passages, marshes, and occasional hummocks, Dare County, Nags Head Township (general reference). Complex of canals, ditches, guts, and water passages interspersed with marshland and occasional hummocks. Large area on s Roanoke Island, begins just s of Baumtown, and is sort of semicircle from Croatan Sound (nw) then se then e to Roanoke Sound, going around large hummock containing Wanchese. S end Roanoke Island historically and presently mostly marsh and swamp, except for hummock containing Wanchese. Interlaced with water passages mostly canalized. Each of these numerous canals and ditches have names informally, not published or documented, and generally are some form of landowner's surname or given name of his or her family. Not a place name—provided for general reference.

Wanchese Harbor, harbor, Dare County, Nags Head Township (local use and media use). At Mill Landing Creek 1.3 mi. e of Wanchese. Originally known by both Mill Landing Creek Harbor and Wanchese Harbor, over years Wanchese Harbor became used more, easier to say and identified with the town. Fish processing began in mid-1930s and expanded through 1960s, then by 1990s specialized and began moving processing facilities to Norfolk because of continuous shoaling problems at Oregon Inlet. Turning basin completed 1979. Name Wanchese Inner Harbor sometimes used for docking facilities. *See* Wanchese. *Other names:* Mill Landing Creek Harbor (historical local use), Wanchese Wharf (historical use).

Wanchese Marina, harbor, Dare County, Nags Head Township (signage). At w Wanchese Harbor, 1.7 mi. e of Wanchese. *See* Wanchese.

Wanchese Marshes, marsh, Dare County, Nags Head Township (ACE 2013). Extensive marsh in s Roanoke Island Marshes (q.v.) generally on s and se Roanoke Island s of Midway Intersection. *See* Wanchese.

Wards Creek, former stream, Dare County, Hatteras Township (Covey 2018, 12). Was in former Lambards Marsh at Cape Hatteras 2 mi. s of Buxton. Today streams here are not identifiable, and Covey (2018) indicates exact location never known.

Ware Creek, tidal stream, 0.7 mi. long, Currituck County, Poplar Branch Township (USGS 1982: Mossey Islands). In marsh soundside Currituck Banks, 0.7 mi. s of Three Dunes, 6 mi. s of Corolla. Spelling of "ware" probable misspelling of "weir." Wire Creek (q.v.) labeled on C&GS (1852) applied to smaller tidal stream adjacent (w), and Piney Creek applied to what is now Ware Creek. Hydrographic configuration was different then and was different late as 1980s. *See* Weir Point. *Other names:* Piney Creek (C&GS 1852).

Ware Point, point, Currituck County, Poplar Branch Township (Currituck DB 5, 1784, 73). Nw point Dews Island at head of Dews Island Bay 7 mi. wnw of Duck. Described in an early deed, though name is unknown today. "Ware" is a variation of "weir." *See* Weir Point.

Warren Gilgos Creek, cove, 0.2 mi. long, Carteret County, Portsmouth Township (USGS 1950: Portsmouth). Is 0.5 mi. sw of center (The Crossroads) of Portsmouth (village), 6.5 mi. sw of Ocracoke (village). Separated Middle Portsmouth (Middle Community) from South Portsmouth. *Other names:* Warren Creek (NPS 2007, 29).

Warrens Island, island, 0.3 mi. across, Dare County, Nags Head Township (C&GS 1895a). In Roanoke Sound at Bodie Island just n of Headquarters Island, 5.2 mi. se of Manteo. *Other names:* Warren Island (from NPS Director Conrad Wirth, letter in *Coastland*

Times, October 27, 1952, in NPS 2005b: NPS 1, 587).

Warxes (Island). *See* Hermitage Island.

Wash Creek, tidal stream, Dare County, Nags Head Township (Currituck DB 30, 1869, 290–91). Described as soundside somewhere on Bodie Island. The two deeds provide no clues to exact location; then name Bodie Island was applied as far s as New Inlet and possibly as far n as Mann Point (deed descriptions, anyway), a few miles n of former Roanoke Inlet, historical boundary of Bodie Island. Descriptive name indicates tidal stream was subject to frequent flooding, still could have been at any location. Variant "Wase" must be spelling variation of "wash." None of adjacent property owners' names are same in the two deeds (deeds are 59 years apart, could account for different names). No reason to believe "wase," as used here, is in anyway related to British definition of cloth to protect while carrying items, or archaic meaning of small amount of straw or hay. *Other names:* Wase Creek (listed only as on Bodies [*sic*] Island, Currituck DB 8, 1800, 215).

Washing Yard Marsh, small marsh, Dare County, Hatteras Township (Brooks 2010). At Buxton Landing 1 mi. sw of Bald Point, 3.5 mi. e of Frisco.

Wash Woods former woods, Currituck County, Fruitville Township (historical local use). Was at Deals (Wash Woods), now North Swan Beach 9.5 mi. nnw of Corolla. Named from many tree stumps awash at low tide, remnants of sea encroachment on former woods (maritime forest) hundreds of years old. Historically much larger, extending into Virginia. *See* Deals and North Swan Beach (community). *Other names:* The Wash Woods (Brazier 1833), Wash Wood (brochures misprint), Wish Woods (GNIS—typographical error).

Wash Woods. *See* Deals.

Water Bush Island. *See* Goose Island (Dare County, Atlantic Township).

Waterfield Point, point, Currituck County, Fruitville Township (F&WS 1984, map, 74). At sw Barleys Bay on se Morse Point 3 mi. wnw of Knotts Island (village). *Other names:* John Waterfield Point (Cox 1923).

Watering Place, The, former area, Carteret County, Portsmouth Township (NPS, map, 27 and 28, 2007). At Haulover Point just n of Portsmouth (village) 6 mi. sw of Ocracoke

(village). Major place for collecting surface water for watering livestock. Numerous such places were on Portsmouth Island, but this one was significant enough to acquire the definite article "the," becoming place name. For drinking water, almost every house at Portsmouth had a cistern for collecting rainwater, or a "water box," wooden box used to collect rainwater, since surface water had to be boiled, and wells were not possible.

Waves, village, Dare County, Kinnakeet Township (signage). On Hatteras Island, 2 mi. n of Salvo. Post office est. 1939, closed 2004. Name Waves chosen for no apparent reason other than environment reference, though indicated proposed by local postmaster Anna Midgette to promote tourism. Also, Chicamacomico was broad reference, and Waves was sometimes referenced as South Chicamacomico, though originally Waves was considered to be in broader application of Chicamacomico. *Other names:* Chicamacomico (Stick 1958, 154), Chickamicomico (historical maps), Chicomicomio (Bishop 1878), Clarks (Stick 1970), South Chicamacomico (Outer Banks Visitors Bureau 2016; Dunbar 1958, 205), Southard (could be direct recording of Southern Woods from local pronunciation or misinterpretation of "south," but also said by most to be merely dropping apostrophe from "south'ard" derived from "southward"), Southard Woods (contrast to Rodanthe as Northern Woods), Southern Woods (reference to small wooded area disappeared by 20th century: Rodanthe was Northern Woods, Salvo was Southern Woods, though sometimes Waves known by the name—Dunbar 1958, 205), South Rodanthe (NCDOT 1936), The Hump (used mostly from mainland, appearance-based from Pamlico Sound, use never popular).

Waves Landing, landing, Dare County, Kinnakeet Township (USGS 2013: Rodanthe). Just w of Waves 1.9 mi. n of Salvo. Originally, main landing at Midyett (Midgett) Plantation. *See* Waves and Uncle Jimmys Landing. *Other names:* ID's Harbor (Garrity-Blake 2010, 492—use of upper case "D" indicates someone's initials), Midyettes Landing (for vast holdings of Midgett family at Midgett Plantation; Midyette original form), Uncle Jimmys Landing (Covey 2018, 13).

Webster Pond. *See* Muskrat Pond.

Websters Island. *See* Hammock Island.

Weir Marsh Island, small elongated marsh island, Dare County, Atlantic Township (local use). In Currituck Sound, 3.2 mi. n of Duck. Originally two distinct small islands, now one marsh island. *See* Weir Point.

Weir Point, point, Dare County, Nags Head Township (USGS 2013: Manteo). On nw Roanoke Island 2.7 mi. nw of Manteo. A weir is a net, stake, or some kind of enclosure set in water for catching fish. Original meaning was simply fishing place (often created by small dam), evolved to include many mechanisms employed at the "fishing place." Descriptive of activity near here. *Other names:* Fort Point (short usage during Civil War, Fort Huger here), Wear Point (Brazier 1820), Weirs Point (C&GS 1895b), Wier Point (ACE 1843—recording error), Wiers Point (recording error—Foster 1866a).

Weir Stake Point, point, Currituck County, Poplar Branch Township (Codman, Crowninshield, and Lawrence 1925). S-most point of ne-sw–trending island, Holy Island, separating Jenkins Cove (n) and Ships Bay (s) 1.7 mi. nw of Corolla. *See* Weir Point.

Wells, The. *See* Wells Creek Inlet.

Wells Bay, bay, 1 mi. wide, Currituck County, Poplar Branch Township (USGS 2013: Mossey Islands). In Currituck Sound just w of Mossey Islands complex, 4.5 mi. ssw of Corolla. *See* Wells Island. *Other names:* Wells Creek (alternate use), Wills Bay (CS 1852).

Wells Creek, water passage, Currituck County, Poplar Branch Township (USGS 2013: Mossey Islands). In Currituck Sound just se of Mossey Islands separated from Sanders Creek by Sedge Island, 1 mi. sw of Three Dunes, 5.5 mi. s of Corolla. *See* Wells Island. *Other names:* Sanders Creek (local use).

Wells Creek. *See* Sanders Creek.

Wells Creek. *See* Shingle Creek.

Wells Creek Inlet, former water passage, Hyde County, Ocracoke Township (CS 1852). Was 9.5 mi. ne of Ocracoke (village). Open about 10 years mid-19th century, mostly mid-1840s to mid-1850s (open 1852), shown on only a few maps. Reportedly reopened a short time in late 1930s and early 1940s, but no documented evidence to support this. Little information available for this feature, but evidence and local opinion supports location near Shingle (Hyde County). Variant West

Inlet was used for a short time while this inlet was open simultaneously with Hatteras Inlet (opened 1846) as distinguishing descriptive name. Weslager (1954) included this in his list of "creeks" or tidal streams, remnant channel of Wells Creek Inlet. *Other names:* Wells Creek (CS 1862a), The Wells (Garrity-Blake 2010, 357–58), Wells Inlet (USGS 1986, 17), West Inlet (CS 1852).

Wells Island, former small island, Currituck County, Poplar Branch Township (local use). Just s of Oyster Creek Island in n Wells Bay 4.7 mi. ssw of Corolla. No longer exists, recorded in deeds and on C&GS 1852 as Wills Island, as was Wills Island Pond; however, name of other features were recorded as Wells. Today, preferred spelling in local use is Wells. *Other names:* Wills Island (Currituck DB 24, 1845, 406–7; C&GS 1852).

Wells Island, island, Dare County, Kinnakeet Township (ACE 2013). Sw-most of seven exposed sandy spoil or disposal islands of Bird Islands (q.v.), exposed Bulkhead Shoal at w end Oregon Inlet 10 mi. s of Whalebone Junction.

Wells Pond, cove, 0.2 mi. wide, Currituck County, Poplar Branch Township (USGS 2013: Mossey Islands). Just n of Wells Bay, 4.2 mi. s of Corolla. *See* Wells Island. *Other names:* Wills Pond (typographical error), Wills Island Pond (C&GS 1852).

Wells Shoal, small shoal, Hyde County, Ocracoke Township (local use). Just offshore, just w of Green Island 3.2 mi. sw of Hatteras Inlet, 13 mi. e of Ocracoke (village). Barely 1 ft. of water covers this shoal.

Wenberg Ridge, small sand ridge, Dare County, Kinnakeet Township (Covey 2018, 28). Eroded ridge in Waves at Waves Landing 1 mi. ne of Great Island, 2 mi. s of Rodanthe. Covey indicates he coined the name from surname of person who owns property where ridge is located (location verified Dare County GIS). Covey uses this ridge in support of his findings to indicate this, not Rodanthe, as site of Civil War–era Live Oak Camp (q.v.). Name not used.

West Burris Island, former island, Currituck County, Poplar Branch Township (local use). Was distinct w portion South Burris Island, 7.8 mi. nnw of Duck. *See* Burris Islands. *Other names:* West Burows Island (C&GS 1852).

West Canal, canal, 3 mi. long, Carteret County, Morehead Township (Carteret County GIS

2019). Largest and w-most canal trending n-s in Sound View Isles subdivision (e-part Canals at Atlantic Beach q.v.). Connects canals at Sound View Isles subdivision to Bogue Sound.

West Dike, dam, Currituck County, Fruitville Township (F&WS 1984, 32). On sw Mackay Island in Mackay Island Wildlife Refuge from just s of Bay Tree Point near the shore to near Live Oak Point 4 mi. wsw of Knotts Island (village). Constructed 1984 by F&WS with Parallel Dike and Long Dike to create West Pool to enhance wildlife protection. "Dike" is wall, embankment, or similar structure to function as a dam to prevent flooding or, as here, to contain and control water level. *Other names:* West Pool Dike (F&WS 1984, 32).

Western Rocks, rocks, Carteret County, Portsmouth Township (Hooker 1850). W portion North Rock (q.v.) and Oyster Rocks complex, 1 mi. n of Shell Castle 8 mi. w of Ocracoke (village). Probable former oyster colony, as variant Western Reef was also used; "reef" in Outer Banks geographic names usually refers to oyster colonies. *Other names:* Great Shell Rock (historical usage), Western Reef (Weslager 1954).

West Hill, hill, 60 ft. high, Dare County, Atlantic Township (USGS 2013: Kitty Hawk). Stabilized dune on Currituck Banks, 0.4 mi. wnw of Kill Devil Hill, 3.9 mi. se of original Kitty Hawk. Big Kill Devil Hill (Kill Devil Hill), Little Kill Devil Hill, West Hill, Run Hill, and other small sand dunes known collectively as Kill Devil Hills.

West Hog Island, marsh island, Carteret County, Cedar Island Township (local use). Part of Hog Island 2 mi. e of Cedar Island Ferry landing separated from East Hog Island by Hog Island Narrows. Actually nnw of East Hog Island.

West Mount Swash, former swash, Dare County, Hatteras Township (Blunt 1857, 343). Was turbulent shoal area just e of West Splt near former False Channel, 1 mi. wsw of Round Hammock (sometimes West Mount), 2.7 mi. sw of Hatteras (village). Area is turbulent still as Hatteras Island is in accretion process here.

West Mouth, former cove, Carteret County, Portsmouth Township (historical use). Was in s Western Rocks (w part of North Rock complex), 5.5 mi. wsw of Ocracoke (village).

Westmouth Bay, bay, 1 mi. wide, Carteret County, Harkers Island Township (USGS 2013: Harkers Island). In The Straits, separates n Harkers Island from Browns Island, 0.8 mi. n of Harkers Island (village). Both one-word and two-word forms used; one-word form more prevalent on official sources. *Other names:* Westbay (from subdivision name near here), West Mouth Bay (real estate brochures from nearby subdivision name).

West Mouth Swash, former shoal area, Carteret County, Portsmouth Township (Blunt 1857, 344). Was between Old Swash Channel and Western Rocks (part of North Rock complex), 5 mi. wsw of Ocracoke (village).

West Piney Island, island, Currituck County, Poplar Branch Township (C&GS 1852). Just e of North Piney Island 0.7 mi. w of Three Dunes, 6.5 mi. ssw of Corolla. North Piney Island and West Piney Island changed and merged with Sedge Island (Poplar Branch Township) (n).

West Point, point, Dare County, Nags Head Township (Goldstein 2000, loc. 2869). Distinct point jutting into Pamlico Sound on spit of land created over past 50 years by s migration of Oregon Inlet; 0.5 mi. nw of Oregon Inlet, 9 mi. s of Whalebone Junction. Relatively new name associated with s migration of Oregon Inlet, used mostly by local folk, fishermen, and off-road enthusiasts.

West Pool, man-enhanced, Currituck County, Fruitville Township (F&WS 1984, map, 74). Stages of marsh, dry land, and open water, w-most of three such areas in Mackay Island National Wildlife Refuge at sw Mackay Island 3 mi. w of Knotts Island (village). Created 1984 by establishing West Dike, Parallel Dike, and Long Dike; status of composition can be controlled in accordance with situation. *Other names:* Small Impoundment (original name, F&WS 1984, 10), West Impoundment (F&WS 1984, 10), West Pools (F&WS 1984, 10).

Westport Marina, landing, Carteret County, Morehead Township (local use). At Westport (section, Beacons Reach) on central Bogue Banks, 3 mi. w of Pine Knoll Shores. *Other names:* Beacons Reach Marina (some use since in Beacons Reach community, Carteret County GIS 2019), Westport Port (limited use because point just n named Westport Port Pointe).

Westport Port Pointe, point, Carteret County, Morehead Township (PKS 2016). Man-enhanced n side of Westport Marina (q.v.) in Beacons Reach 2.7 mi. w of Pine Knoll Shores, undeveloped area. Cumbersome name because generic term "port" is embedded in Westport and then repeated. Also, so-called "quaint" 16th- and 17th-century form "pointe" used.

West Roanoke Island Marshes, extensive marsh, 1.3 mi. across, Dare County, Nags Head Township (Sorrie 2014, map, 179). On w Roanoke Island n-ward from Virginia Dare Bridge just beyond First Creeks to Deep Wear Point, 1.3 mi. s of Manteo (center). Not place name per se but used in scientific reports; useful in describing this extensive marsh. *Other names:* Back Marsh (descriptive in Currituck DB 9, 1805, 44–45).

West Spit, former shoal, Hyde County, Ocracoke Township (CS 1853). More exposed 19th century (hence name), extreme w tip small shoals from tip of Inlet Peninsula (w terminus Hatteras Island). Mostly inundated now from shifting hydrography. "Spit" refers to end (curling) formed by sand moving by the process of longshore drift, or movement of sand along the shore from the action of waves obliquely striking beach. *Other names:* Southwest Spit (CS 1850b).

Whalebone Beach, beach, 2 mi. long, Dare County, Nags Head Township (local use). In Nags Head nnw-ward from Whalebone Junction 4.7 mi. e of Manteo. Used sporadically since 1930s when Whalebone Junction (also Whalebone) established, more used today with increased tourism and numbers of residents. Subdivision named for feature. *Other names:* Epstein Beach (for central part from named access—original owners), South Beach (local slang based on location in Nags Head, not to be confused with South Beach at Oregon Inlet).

Whalebone Hills. *See* The High Hills.

Whalebone Inlet. *See* High Hills Inlet.

Whalebone Island, island, 0.5 mi. long, Carteret County, Portsmouth Township (USGS 1950: Portsmouth). In Pamlico Sound just s of High Hills Inlet (Whalebone Inlet), 4.9 mi. sw of Portsmouth (village).

Whalebone Junction, area, Dare County, Nags Head Township (signage). Small locality grew around intersection, now in Nags Head (s)

2.5 mi. s of Nags Head (center). Applied to junction of US 64, US 264, US 158, and NC 12 because owner of service station here displayed skeleton of whale washed ashore 1930s; removed by 1940. Now short form, Whalebone, has often crept into written material. *Other names:* The Junction (some verbal local use), Whalebone (USGS 2013: Roanoke Island NE; NCDOT 1960), Whale Bone (NPS 2005b: NPS 1, 586), Whale Bone Junction (occasional written use).

Whale Creek, cove, 0.3 mi. wide, Carteret County, Harkers Island Township (USGS 2013: Harkers Island). In Back Sound just off central Shackleford Banks at Cabs Creek, 2.5 mi. ssw of Harkers Island (village).

Whale Creek, former settlement, Carteret County, Harkers Island Township (local stories). Several families at central Shackleford Banks at Whale Creek 19th century 2.5 mi. ssw of Harkers Island (village). Supported fishing and Outer Banks–style whaling (*see* Cape Lookout Grounds). *See* Guthries Lump, Winsors Lump, and Whale Hill.

Whale Head. *See* Corolla.

Whale Head Bay, bay, 1.2 mi. wide, Currituck County, Poplar Branch Township (USGS 2013: Mossey Islands). In Currituck Sound 1 mi. s of Corolla, 2.7 mi. n of Mossey Islands complex. Subdivision soundside here with views of both Whale Head Bay and Great Beach Pond known as Views at Corolla Bay subdivision or simply Corolla Bay. Unknown what is meant by Corolla Bay since there is not now or historically a feature named Corolla Bay. Developers perhaps meant Whale Head Bay or Great Beach Pond or both as nearby reference; apparently toponymic liberties were taken. Additionally, Cruz Bay sometimes used because n-s road here named Cruz Bay Lane (reason unknown other than developer's choice); entrance road is inexplicably Devils Bay. *Other names:* Whalehead Bay (Carr 2016, 107), Whales Head Bay (C&GS 1852), Wholehead Bay (perpetuated typographical error on some maps), Whole Head Bay (error—Google Maps).

Whalehead Beach, beach, Currituck County, Poplar Branch Township (signage). At The Whaleshead, just e of Currituck Lighthouse just se of Corolla. Part of Currituck Beach, this part also known locally as Whalehead

Beach reportedly because local resident drove his wagon through jaws of a beached whale's skeleton head—questionable (picture exists but might be fake). With increased visitors here, Currituck Beach at The Whaleshead, and Whalehead Beach subdivision, this beach has come to be known as Whalehead Beach. *Other names:* Currituck Beach (historical local use), Whalehead (Currituck County website, real estate brochures).

Whalehead Beach, subdivision, Currituck County, Poplar Branch Township (signage). Just s of Corolla Light subdivision, 0.5 mi. s of Corolla, s 3.2 mi. to Buck Island subdivision (Currituck County website; real estate brochures; spoken use) and Whale Head Beach (brochures). Nine named beach accesses here using "beach" in the name, causing some, especially transient tourists, to use specific beach access name for that particular small Whalehead Beach section. These names are not named parts of Whalehead Beach, but through usage might become more common. These accesses are listed here only as cross-references, not separate entries: Perch Beach, Sailfish Beach, Coral Beach, Bonito Street Beach (Atlantic bonito [*Sarda sarda*], smaller relative of tuna, not Spanish *bonito* for beautiful), Mackerel Beach, Herring Beach, Barracuda Beach, Sturgeon Beach, and Tuna Beach. Theme for named beach accesses is fish, with exception of Coral Beach (*see* Coral Ridge—sand ridge). *Other names:* Whalehead (based on stories this is local term for large sand dunes—unsubstantiated).

Whalehead Beach. *See* Currituck Beach.

Whale Head Hill, sand dune, 13 ft. high, Currituck County, Poplar Branch Township (USGS 2013: Mossey Islands). Is 0.7 mi. s of Currituck Beach, 1 mi. s of Corolla. Variant Whales Head Barchane (and Whaleshead Barchane) used by some authors in studies of barrier island geomorphology because some dunes here are (or were) crescent-shaped (barchane dune); some suggest these dunes are known locally as Whales Heads or Whaleheads—not locally substantiated. *Barchane* (or *barchan*), Turkish term meaning moving forward, adapted for application to sand dunes worldwide, indicating mobility of these particular sand dunes, tending to move mostly ne-sw until intervention by man (many still do move—*see* Pennys Hill). Dunbar (1958, 238) reports Murphy (1951) indicated "barchane" was introduced by shipwrecked Turkish sailor, who named a sand dune Barchane Hill (no doubt where he shipwrecked), but neither Murphy nor Dunbar provides additional information, and location of this so-named dune not provided. No supporting evidence, likely just a story—folk etymology (story to explain something for which no information is available). Barchane most likely simply from scientific reports. Whale Head Hill is sand dune complex 1.5 mi. s-n, terminating in highest part, named separately The Whaleshead (descriptive). The sand dune considerably altered by development of subdivision Whalehead Beach. *Other names:* Whaleback (CS 1873), Whalehead Hill (local use), Whaleshead (local use), Whales Head (local use), Whaleshead Barchane (local use), Whales Head Barchane (local use), Whales Head Hill (C&GS 1879), Whaleshead Hills (CS 1862a).

Whale Hill, sand dune, 10 ft. high (higher late 19th century), Carteret County, Harkers Island Township (Mason 2000; NPS 1987, 38). On central Shackleford Banks just s of Bald Hill Bay, 1 mi. se of former community of Winsors Lump, 6 mi. nw of Cape Point. Also were a few families here. *See* Whale Hill (former settlement). Used for subsistence whale watching (*see* Lookout Dune).

Whale Hill, former settlement, Carteret County, Harkers Island Township (historical stories). A few families on central Shackleford Banks at shore Bald Hill Bay at small tidal stream just n of Whale Hill (sand dune) 2 mi. se of Harkers Island (village). Fishing and shore-based Outer Banks–style whaling community (*see* Cape Lookout Grounds). *See* Whale Creek, Guthries Lump, and Winsors Lump.

Whale Point, point, Carteret County, Portsmouth Township (White 2012, 269). Just n of former High Hills Inlet (Whalebone Inlet) 5 mi. ssw of Portsmouth (village). From an interview in secondary source; exact location not provided. Conversation suggests this location.

Whalers Camp Point, former point, Carteret County, Harkers Island Township (Stick 1958,

308). Was just s of Cape Hills, or possibly on Shackleford Banks near Whale Creek, or somewhere else on Core Banks n of Cape Lookout. Stick is not clear, though suggests feature was on Core Banks, Cape Lookout location. Included because illustrates numerous temporary, some semipermanent whale camps where captured whales (*see* Cape Lookout Grounds) were "tried" (processed—*see* Try Yard Creek). Most of these camps were in Cape Lookout area or e Shackleford Banks. Middle (originally Middel) Whales Camp just west of Whalers Camp. *Other names:* Whale Camp Point.

Whalers Ridge, sand ridge, 0.5 mi. long, Carteret County, Harkers Island Township (local use). W end Harkers Island just e of Rush Point n-s 1.5 mi. wnw of Harkers Island (village center). In 19th century, shore-based whaling was major activity here (*see* Cape Lookout Grounds). Lookouts would watch for whales from high dunes at Cape Lookout and on Shackleford Banks; most lived at Diamond City. Name transferred to Harkers Island with people moving from Shackleford Banks. Subdivision named for feature.

Whalers Ridge, former settlement, Carteret County, Harkers Island Township (local use). Small settlement was on w Harkers Island at Whalers Ridge about 1.7 mi. w of the center of Harkers Island (village). *See* Whalers Ridge (sand ridge).

Whaleshead, The, sand dune, 25 ft. high, 1.5 mi. long, Currituck County, Poplar Branch Township (local use). Just e of Currituck Beach Lighthouse 0.3 mi. se of Corolla (village). Highest point, and n terminus of sand dune complex named Whale Head Hill, s-n. Considerably altered by developing Whalehead Beach subdivision. *See* Whale Head Hill. *Other names:* Wales Head Hill (misrecording).

Wheat Patch, historical, Dare County, Kinnakeet Township (Covey 2018, 111). Was at Farrow Scarborough Landing (q.v.), n Avon where there was a mill (*see* Farrow Scarborough Windmill). Apparently descriptive—while wheat was processed at these mills, commodity most often ground was corn. Unknown why this term was used; perhaps this mill specialized in wheat. Name unknown today.

Whidbee Swamp, swamp, Dare County, Atlantic Township (Harris 2017). Just e of center of Whidbee Swamp Ridge, 0.6 mi. n of Kitty Hawk Landing subdivision, 2 mi. wnw of original Kitty Hawk. W-most swamp in Kitty Hawk Woods Swamps (q.v.), periodically and alternately pond-like and swamp-like. *See* Kitty Hawk ridge-and-swale system. *Other names:* Whidby Swamp (Harris 2017; unknown, 1802), Whitbys Swamp (Currituck DB 11, 1811, 92).

Whidbee Swamp Ridge, sand ridge, 0.5 mi. long, Dare County, Atlantic Township (Harris 2017). Just n of Shellbank Ridge, 0.7 mi. n of Kitty Hawk Landing subdivision, 1.8 mi. wnw of original Kitty Hawk. Associative with nearby Whidbee Swamp. *Other names:* Whibity Swamp Ridge (Harris 2017—recorded correctly as Whidbee, but includes spelling variation on hand-annotated map).

Whistling Swan Canal, canal, 0.5 mi. long, Dare County, Atlantic Township (Town of Southern Shores 2015). In Southern Shores 4 mi. n of original Kitty Hawk. Names of Southern Shores canals are for shorebirds (except Gravey Pond Canal). The whistling swan, or tundra swan (*Cygnus columbianus*), winters along the Outer Banks.

White Ash Swamp, swamp, 1 mi. wide, Carteret County, Morehead Township (USGS 2013: Mansfield). Just w of Hoop Pole Woods 5.1 mi. w of Atlantic Beach (town). Descriptive of vegetation here since earliest maps were published.

Whitehurst Island, marsh island, 0.3 mi. long, Carteret County, Harkers Island Township (USGS 2013: Harkers Island). Junction Core Sound and Back Sound, 3.7 mi. sse of Harkers Island (village).

White Ibis Canal, small canal, Dare County, Atlantic Township (Town of Southern Shores 2015). In Southern Shores 5 mi. n of original Kitty Hawk. Names of Southern Shores canals are for shorebirds (except Gravey Pond Canal). The white ibis (*Eudocimus albus*) here year-round.

White Point, marsh point, Carteret County, Harkers Island Township (USGS 2013: Harkers Island). At n entrance Henry Jones Creek on Harkers Island 0.5 mi. nne of Harkers Island (village).

White Point Shoal, shoal, Carteret County, Atlantic Township (Williamson 1992, 147). In Core Sound just sse of White Point, on mainland 1 mi. e of Atlantic (mainland).

White Rock, rock, Carteret County, Portsmouth

Township (NPS, map, 27 and 28, 2007). In Pamlico Sound 2 mi. w of Ayers Rock, 8 mi. w of Ocracoke (village).

Whites Creek, short water passage, Currituck County, Fruitville Township (Cox 1923). E-w trending in s Eastern Marsh just n of Currituck Bay (not Currituck Sound), just ne of Swan Island 3 mi. s of Knotts Island (village). *See* Whites Neck.

Whites Hill, sand dune, Dare County, Hatteras Township (Garrity-Blake 2010, 232). Just s of Buxton Landing, 4.5 mi. e of Frisco.

White Shoal, shoal, Carteret County, Portsmouth Township (diminished use). In Pamlico Sound, 5.4 mi. wsw of Ocracoke (village).

White Shoal Marsh, marsh island, 0.2 mi. long, Carteret County, Harkers Island Township (USGS 1997: Harkers Island). Is 2.1 mi. s of Harkers Island (village).

Whites Neck, peninsula, Currituck County, Fruitville Township (local use, road sign). At se Knotts Island, tip is Bay Point, 2 mi. s of Knotts Island (village). Originally named for Patrick White and family, who received land patent here. *See* Deep Neck.

Whites Nole, former small hummock, Currituck County, Fruitville Township (Currituck DB 23, 1841, 156). On s Knotts Island at Indian Creek probably 2.5 mi. sw of Knotts Island (village). Abbey Nole, Jesse Nole, and Long Nole also here, according to deed, where named are "in Knotts Island . . . at an angle of Indian Creek." Only distinctive angle today is halfway between Indian Pond and Sandy Cove, no knolls or hummocks there. Topography could change considerably over 200 years, and features might no longer exist or could be short distance ne on e side of Indian Pond, where some hummocks exist. "Nole" is variation of "knoll."

Whites Point, small marsh point, Currituck County, Poplar Branch Township (local use). Distinctive, just s of Piney Pont just w of center runway Pine Island Airport, 6 mi. n of Duck (center).

Widgeon Island, small island, Currituck County, Poplar Branch Township (C&GS 1852). In w portion Mossey Islands complex just e of Wells Bay 6 mi. ssw of Corolla. American wigeon (*Mareca americana*; "wigeon" alternate spelling more popular 19th century), type of duck frequent here during winter.

Wilets Creek, tidal stream, Currituck County, Poplar Branch Township (CS 1852). Just e of Piney Cove, ne end Beasley Bay 6.5 mi. s of Corolla. *Other names:* Valets Bay (Currituck DB 1769, 2, 247).

Willets Hill. *See* Poyners Hill.

Williams Island, island, Currituck County, Fruitville Township (Cox 1923). Just e of n Crow Island (Big Raymond Island) at n end Little Walkers Creek, 5.8 mi. se of Knotts Island (village).

Williams Point, former point, Hyde County, Ocracoke Township (appeared locally in otherwise illegible papers). Was former terminus Ocracoke Island, 2.5 mi. sw of Ocracoke (village). Today, Ocracoke Island extends 1 mi. beyond original application of name Williams Point (former landowner).

Williams Point. *See* Springers Point.

William White Pond, small man-made lake, Dare County, Nags Head Township (signage). In Sextant Village section (center) of Pirates Cove subdivision 2 mi. se of Manteo (center).

Willis Canal, canal, 1 mi. long, Carteret County, Morehead Township (Carteret County GIS 2019). Central canal trending e-w then n-s in Atlantic Beach Isles subdivision (w part of Canals at Atlantic Beach q.v.) 1.2 mi. s of Morehead City (mainland).

Willis Creek, cove, 0.1 mi. long, Carteret County, Portsmouth Township (historical local use). Joins Bill Salters Creek in se Casey Bay just sw of Portsmouth (village) 7.2 mi. sw of Ocracoke (village).

Willis Creek, tidal passage, Carteret County, Portsmouth Township (CS 1866). S Portsmouth Island, 0.75 mi. s of Sheep Island 2 mi. s of Portsmouth (village).

Willis Dock. *See* Community Square Docks.

Willis Landing, landing, Carteret County, Morehead Township (USGS 2013: Mansfield). On Bogue Banks (oceanside) at Hoop Pole Woods, 2.2 mi. w of Atlantic Beach. Unusual for a landing to be oceanside, as most are soundside in calmer water, but in this case probably related to Alice Hoffman estate (*see* Pine Knoll Shores), 0.5 mi. nw of here.

Willis Landing, landing, Dare County, Hatteras Township (signage). In se Hatteras Harbor in Hatteras (village) just e of Hatteras Harbor Marina, 3.2 mi. ne of Hatteras Inlet.

Willis Lump, marsh island(s), Carteret County, Harkers Island Township (local informants). Along n shore central Shackleford Banks between Cabs Creek (s) and Winsors Lump (n) 4 mi. wnw of Barden Inlet, 2 mi. se of Harkers Island (village). Unclear exact extent or location; only general reference made. *See* Dorland Lump.

Willow Pond, flat, Carteret County, Harkers Island Township (USGS 1997: Harkers Island). Drained area on sw Harkers Island, just nw of Shell Point, just w of National Park Headquarters, 1.7 mi. ese of Harkers Island (village).

Willows, former area, Currituck County, Poplar Branch Township (Codman, Crowninshield, and Lawrence 1925). Small area used for hunting fowl named descriptively for trees.

Wimble Shoals, shoals, Dare County, Kinnakeet Township (Wimble 1738). In Atlantic Ocean, 3 mi. se of Rodanthe, 15 mi. s of Oregon Inlet, and 20 mi. nne of Cape Hatteras. Remnants of Cape Kenrick (q.v.; prominent during Roanoke voyages), named by James Wimble, who charted the shoals 1730s. First appeared on Wimble's chart 1738. USGS incorrectly and inexplicably labels Wimble Shoals in Pamlico Sound on USGS 2013: Rodanthe map, unfortunately "copycat" websites and applications are perpetuating this error. Three subdivisions named for feature. *Other names:* Chickinnacomoc (Lawson 1709), Five Fathoms Bank (considered by some as s Wimble Shoals), Wimble Shoal (Price and Strother 1798), Wimble Sholes (Austin 1984), Wimple Shoals (Fry et al. 1775 — misrecording).

Windhaven Shores Canal, canal, Dare County, Hatteras Township (N.C. Marine Fisheries 2019, H4, map 8). Access from Pamlico Sound to Windhaven Shores subdivision just sw of Brigands Bay, 3.2 mi. w of Buxton. Recent, named for subdivision of same name.

Windmill Island, former island, Dare County, Kinnakeet Township (Covey 2018, 126). Was connected to the barrier island by muck just n of Blackmar Gut in Rodanthe where Green Point Windmill (Midyett's [sic] Windmill) was located.

Windmill Point, small point, Dare County, Nags Head Township (local use). Juts into Roanoke Sound, in s Nags Head just nw of Whalebone Junction, 4 mi. e of Manteo. Still some question whether this name is reversed usage, natural feature acquiring name of man-made feature. Restaurant was here named Windmill Point Restaurant

displaying authentic windmill, now moved to Island Farm Park just n of Manteo. Unclear whether an actual windmill here historically; probably was one in this area as there were over 100 windmills on the Outer Banks at one time. Still, usage might have stemmed from restaurant name, as stories are now muddled. Restaurant, est. early 1970s, fell into disrepair with no interest in restoration, destroyed 2011 in fire-training exercise for Nags Head Fire Department.

Windmill Point, point, Hyde County, Ocracoke Township (USGS 2013: Ocracoke). On Ocracoke Island at s entrance Silver Lake 0.4 mi. w of Ocracoke (village center). Named because windmill at one time here. Windmills were prominent throughout the Outer Banks 18th and 19th centuries; only a few place name references indicate their previous use. Dunbar (1956, 113) and Torres (1985, 57) believe this to be Howards Windmill, but Howard (January 21, 2013) reports this is likely Wahabs Windmill since he owned the property, with Howards Windmill at Springers Point supported by Howard owning that land. Also, neighborhood name (*see* Ocracoke Village areas). *Other names:* The Point (occasional local use).

Winslows Wharf, former landing, Hyde County, Ocracoke Township (ACE 1896 or 1897). According to ACE was on Ocracoke Island at Springers Point 1 mi. sw of Ocracoke (village center). No other references found to this feature (could be Winstons — map not clear).

Winsors Lump, island, 0.2 mi. long, Carteret County, Harkers Island Township (local stories and USGS 2013: Harkers Island). In Back Sound in marsh islands, n from central Shackleford Banks into Back Sound 1.9 mi. ssw of Harkers Island (village), 4.5 mi. nw of Barden Inlet. Named for original resident near here. *See* Dorland Lump and Winsors Lump (former settlement). *Other names:* Sam Windsors Lump (spelling variation), Sam Winsers Lump (spelling variation), Sam Winsors Lump (USGS 2013: Harkers Island), Sam Winter Lump (USGS 1951: Harkers Island), Sam Winters Lump (historical local use), Windsors Lump (spelling variation).

Winsors Lump, former settlement, Carteret County, Harkers Island Township (local stories). Several families on central Shackleford Banks 1 mi. s of marsh island Winsors Lump, 2 mi. ssw of Harkers Island (village), 4 mi. nnw of Barden Inlet. No one here by early 20th century after everyone left Shackleford Banks after great hurricane of 1899. Clear from scores of interviewees some folk had heard of the place, none (including older folk) knew exact location beyond somewhere on central Shackleford ("I think," they commented—*see* Guthries Lump). Other small settlements on Shackleford Banks included Wades Shore (w end) and Diamond City (Lookout Woods—e end) with Guthries Lump (central). Whale Creek and Whale Hill were s and just se of community of Winsors Lump, settled for fishing and shore-based whaling (Outer Banks style—*see* Cape Lookout Grounds). Also some families were around Wreck Point (*see* Fish Wharf) as wharf was there for processing and transferring fish catches. Numerous interviews with local residents have not clarified successfully whether Winsors Lump or Winters Lump (both names appear on official USGS map, albeit cumbersomely and one in error). Those familiar with the name (not necessarily exact location) are divided 50/50 whether Winsors or Winters. Further, examination of census records and cemetery records for Carteret County (strangely) yields no occurrence of either surname (three people named Windsor in Beaufort late 19th to mid-20th centuries, otherwise no records). Firmest of informants insist Winters Lump, but majority of written documentation uses Winsors Lump. *See* Dorland Lump. *Other names:* Sam Windsors Lump (*see* above), Sam Winsers Lump (*see* above), Sam Winsors Lump (Stick 1958, 188–89; USGS 2013: Harkers Island), Sam Winter Lump (USGS 2013: Harkers Island), Sam Winters Lump (some local use), Windsors Lump (*see* above).

Winter Marsh, marsh, 0.5 mi. across, Currituck County, Poplar Branch Township (local use). Just w of Currituck Banks, 5.3 mi. nnw of Duck.

Wire Creek, small tidal stream, Currituck County, Poplar Branch Township (C&GS 1852). Between Piney Cove and Ware Creek (Piney Creek) at se West Piney Island, 6.5 mi. s of Corolla. Probable misrecording of Weir Creek; Wire Creek an unusual name on the Outer Banks (*see* Ware Creek and Weir Point). Hydrographic configuration different then and late as 1980s.

Wises Creek, former tidal stream, Dare County,

Kinnakeet Township (NOS field notes 1930s). Was on Pea Island 1.5 mi. se of Oregon Inlet, 8 mi. se of Wanchese.

Wishes Hammock, elongated marsh island, 0.7 mi. long, Currituck County, Fruitville Township (Cox 1906). Trends se-nw, just ne of Walk Island, 2.3 mi. ene of Knotts Island (village).

Wishes Hammock Creek, water passage, 1.5 mi. long, Currituck County, Fruitville Township (Cox 1906). Trends s-n connecting upper Fresh Pond Bay and Buzzard Bay, 2.2 mi. e of Knotts Island (village). Associative with Wishes Hammock. *Other names:* John Davis Creek (Currituck Deeds, miscellaneous, 1719).

Wokokon, former island. Was applied on early maps from just e of present Ocracoke village (sometimes as far as where Old Hatteras Inlet would later open) sw to Ocracoke Inlet, but usually including much of Portsmouth Island (Haklyut 1589; DeBry 1590). Misapplied by many early mapmakers. Reportedly means fort or enclosed place and referenced a specific site in or near present Ocracoke (village). If so, was temporary indigenous peoples campsite, as no permanent village was here. Also reports indicate named from name of Indians in area, though difficult to determine who copied from whom, and if so, more likely subgroup of Hatteras or Hatarask Indians. Notably, Brickell's (1743) lists of Indian tribes, providing English equivalent of some words, includes Woccon as tribal name (mainland). Grenville, second Roanoke voyage (1585), stopped here for over two weeks on his way to delivering Lane and his soldiers as the first colony at Roanoke Island (not second, Lost Colony). Wokokon is the name from which Ocracoke evolved. *See* Ocracoke Island for more information. *Other names:* Gordens Ile (Smith 1624, map—probable gesture to acquaintance or friend in England; Smith's names did not last), Ile of Wokokon (Smith 1624, map), Ococan (Cheeseman, 1982, 195), Ococon (Cheeseman 1982, 195), Okok (Speed 1676), Vokokon (DeLisle 1718), Vokoton (variation), Wococon (Haklyut 1589), Wocohon (historical), Wococok (historical), Wocokon (Haklyut 1589), Wocotan (historical), Wocoton (Keulen 1690), Wokocon (Haklyut 1589), Wokokan, Wokoken (Visscher 1680), Wosoton (Sanson 1696).

Wokokon Inlet, possibly historical inlet,

Carteret County, Portsmouth Township; implied in various historical renditions, including Cheeseman (1982, 195). No real evidence exists indicating this inlet existed other than shown on small-scale, partially contrived maps from the early 1600s, with Wokokon variously placed and presumed since the area vaguely marked the s limit of Wokokon. Some authors speculate that this might be the initial passage used by Grenville (1585), but not likely since if there was an inlet here it was small, shallow, and probably just awash. Grenville used Ocracoke Inlet.

Woodall Way Neighborhood, area, Dare County, Hatteras Township (local use). In se Hatteras (village) just e of Hatteras-Ocracoke Ferry docks, 5 mi. wsw of Frisco. General term applied to collection of subdivisions, including Teachs Lair Estates (entrance), Ballance Division (four sections), Dunes East, Sutton Place, Paquiac Pines, and Sea Breeze. Derived from principal street in neighborhoods, unofficial and not listed in Dare County tax records (except by street name).

Woodhouses Island, island, Currituck County, Poplar Branch Township (CS 1852). W-most island in Mossey Islands complex 7 mi. ssw of Corolla. *Other names:* Long Point Marsh Island (Currituck DB 16, 1822, 220).

Wood Island, island, 0.4 mi. long, Carteret County, White Oak Township (USGS 2013: Salter Path). In Bogue Sound just n of original Emerald Isle 4.5 mi. w of Salter Path. Former bombing range, could be hazardous so is off-limits. *Other names:* Cat Island (often confused with former Cat Island 1 mi. w).

Woodlands Fish Camp, former camp, Carteret County, Morehead Township (Stephens 1984, 148–49). Was just w of Salter Path, 3.5 mi. e of Pine Knoll Shores. Several fish camps, but in 1920s this was large commercial operation with sleeping bunks, kitchen, etc., built by J. E. Woodland. It included tramway for easier movement of large quantities of fish oceanside to soundside for transport.

Woodlands Hill, sand dune, Carteret County, Morehead Township (local informants). Was used for for short time in 1920s when J. E. Woodland operated a large commercial fish camp here. Name no longer used.

Woodleigh, community, Currituck County, Fruitville Township (USGS 2013: Knotts

Island). Scattered community on Knotts Island 1.1 mi. nne of Knotts Island (village). Post office operated 1900–1934 with sporadic activity until 1944.

Woods, The, small distinct hummock, Carteret County, White Oak Township (original subdivision plat Emerald Isle By The Sea). Fully wooded at w end of large, apparently unnamed marsh created by The Canal (Carteret County, White Oak Township) just n of Emerald Isle By The Sea subdivision (Bogue Sound subdivision) in original Emerald Isle 5.7 mi. w of Indian Beach (town).

Worcester Inlet. *See* Trinety Harbor.

Wreck Creek, cove, 0.7 mi. long, 0.1 mi. wide, Dare County, Kinnakeet Township (USGS 2013: Pea Island). Trends e-w in Pamlico Sound separating Cedar Hammock from Goulds Lump 4.9 mi. nnw of Rodanthe.

Wreck Hill, sand dune, Dare County, Nags Head Township (vague reference in fishing reports). On Bodie Island near and e of Tommy Hammock 3 mi. e of Wanchese. Only remnants of original dune remain today.

Wreck Point, point, Carteret County, Harkers Island Township (USGS 2013: Cape Lookout). W point on projection of sand from Catfish Point (e point is Fishermans Point) into Lookout Bight partly submerged at times (second ne point occasionally bare referenced sometimes as New Wreck Point). Is 1 mi. n of former Cape Lookout (village), 5.2 mi. s of Harkers Island (village). Historically, some families just s of here periodically (*see* Fish Wharf and Guthries Lump).

Wright Brothers Monument, park, Dare County, Atlantic Township (Downing 2013, 50–51). Small obelisk monument at original camp of Wright Brothers in Kitty Hawk before they moved 4 mi. s to Kill Devil Hills national monument location. Was solely effort of local people who thought original site where Wright brothers worked initially (Kitty Hawk) should be commemorated. Money collected locally, and monument erected 1927, dedicated six months before national monument at Kill Devil Hill (Big Kill Devil Hill).

Wright Brothers National Memorial, monument, 90 ft. high, Dare County, Atlantic Township (signage). On Currituck Banks at summit of Kill Devil Hill 3.7 mi. sse of original Kitty Hawk. The first flight was launched from n-side base of Kill Devil Hill (Big Kill

Devil Hill then). Memorial renamed to its present name 1953, fiftieth anniversary. Note, name of stabilized hill bearing monument now just Kill Devil Hill, but for historical correctness, NPS in its displays uses Big Kill Devil Hill, name when Wright brothers completed experiments and flights. There was also Little Kill Devil Hill, now almost nonexistent—why Big Kill Devil Hill is now just Kill Devil Hill. *See* Kill Devil Hill. *Other names:* Kill Devil Hill Monument National Memorial (original name when built 1927), Kill Devil Hills Monument National Memorial (Stick 1958, 270), Kill Devil Hills National Memorial (Downing 2013, 47), Wright Brother Monument (commercial maps), Wright Brothers National Monument (USGS 2010: Kitty Hawk), Wright Memorial (numerous abbreviated references), Wright Memorial Monument (USGS 1940: Kitty Hawk, 1:62,500 scale), Wright Monument (USGS 1940: Kitty Hawk, 1:62,500 ; NOS 2014e), Wright National Monument (some usage, reference to actual monument).

Y, The, intersection, Dare County, Hatteras Township (Outer Banks Scenic Byway 2008, 8). Junction of several roads in Hatteras (village center), 3.8 mi. ne of Hatteras Inlet.

Yankee Ponds, open water, Currituck County, Poplar Branch Township (local use). Two ponds just w of Pine Island Airport, just n of Straight Creek, 5.5 mi. n of Duck. Collective name includes Big Yankee Pond (q.v.) and Little Yankee Pond (q.v.). USGS map shows only Yankee Pond for Little Yankee Pond, not name for Big Yankee Pond. Local use has become just Yankee Pond, though difficult to determine to which feature referred to. Names Big Yankee Pond and Little Yankee Pond are becoming less used.

Yaupon Hammock Gut, cove, 0.2 mi. wide, Carteret County, Atlantic Township (USGS 2013: Styron Bay). In Core Sound 5 mi. s of Atlantic (mainland). Yaupon (*Ilex vomitoria*—though it has no emetic properties), member of holly tree family in s U.S., especially on the Outer Banks, has been used as substitute for tea when tea was too expensive. Yaupon tea also known as "the black drink" with strong taste and pungent odor. Name dahoon (origin unknown) often used for this holly, but unknown in place names of the Outer Banks. Yaupon reportedly originates from an indigenous term (supposedly Catawba Indians in the interior) from *yop*, meaning tree, and diminutive suffix *pa* or *pon*, likely referring to a leaf. *See* Black Hammock. *Other names:* Yaupon Hammock Bay (Carteret County GIS 2019).

Yaupon Point, point, Carteret County, Morehead Township (local use). Soundside of Bogue Banks at nw edge Pine Knoll Shores 3 mi. w of Atlantic Beach (town). *See* Yaupon Hammock Gut. *Other names:* Bockle Point (CS 1852), Bullock Point (Zaenker 2014—1943 Army Map Service map, actually survey marker, named anything by surveyors, sometimes the natural feature, friends, made up, etc., so not another name), Yeopon Point (unusual alternate spelling).

Yellow Hill, sand dune, Carteret County, White Oak Township (PKS 2016). Adjacent to Yellow Hill Landing in original Emerald Isle, 2.5 mi. w of Rice(s) Path, 8 mi. w of Pine Knoll Shores. Descriptive name for color of dune.

Yellow Hill, former community, Carteret County, White Oak Township (Stephens 1984, 36). Was soundside at Yellow Hill Landing in original Emerald Isle just n of Yellow Hill (sand dune), 3.5 mi. w of Indian Beach (town). Various reports, including reproduced newspaper article (no dates or credit), indicate Bell Cove and Yellow Hill same, but separate 2 mi. apart. As with small communities w of Salter Path, families eventually moved to Salter Path by early 20th century for various reasons. Named for nearby Yellow Hill dune (q.v.).

Yellow Hill Landing, landing, Carteret County, White Oak Township (USGS 2013: Salter Path). Bogue Banks (soundside) in original Emerald Isle 5 mi. w of Salter Path at former community Yellow Hill. *See* Yellow Hill (former community).

Yellow Shoal. *See* Great Shoal (Smyrna Township).

Yopon Hill, sand dune, Dare County, Atlantic or Nags Head Township (Stick 1958, 264). Exact location or present condition unknown and not remembered now; Stick provides only general reference to being one of the sand dunes somewhere in Kill Devil Hills complex, Round-About Hills complex, Scraggly Hills complex, or Jockeys Ridge complex; these sand dunes extend n-s from n Kill Devil Hills (town) to n Nags Head (town). Spelling unusual and rarely encountered; accepted spelling is "yaupon." *See* Yaupon Hammock Gut.

Z

Zack Creek, water passage, 0.6 mi. long, Carteret County, Smyrna Township (USGS 2013: Horsepen Point). In Core Sound separating unnamed marsh island from Cowpen Island 4.9 mi. e of Harkers Island (village). Reportedly, several inlets here before and just after European arrival. There could have been as inlets could exist just about anywhere along Core Banks throughout pre-European history of Core Banks, because these barrier beaches are low and narrow.

Zeb Millers Landing, former landing, Dare County, Kinnakeet Township (Garrity-Blake 2010, 169). Was in original Avon halfway between Peters Ditch and Uncle Bates Ditch 0.2 mi. between each, 6 mi. n of Buxton.

Zeb Millers Windmill, former mill and windmill, Dare County, Kinnakeet Township (Garrity-Blake 2010, 169). Was at former Zeb Millers Landing in original Avon halfway between Peters Ditch and Uncle Bates Ditch 0.2 mi. between each, 6 mi. n of Buxton. Some question whether this was same mill and windmill as Barnes Mill (q.v.); locations are almost identical, and there were only two windmills in Avon—this one and Farrow Scarborough Windmill 1 mi. n. Zeb Millers Windmill is most remembered, with no mention of Barnes Landing. Windmills changed ownership and therefore names 18th and 19th centuries. *See* Farrow Scarborough Windmill and Barnes Mill.

Acknowledgments

A study of geographic place names requires assistance from many and varied people. First and foremost are the scores of people who have spent considerable time answering questions about specific locations and name origins. Fortunately, "Bankers" are congenial people and take great pride in the Outer Banks, which has made fieldwork a good deal easier. It is with deepest appreciation I extend thanks to the hundreds who assisted me in this study by agreeing to interviews and spending time answering questions.

Additional and notable recognition is extended to Tama Creef and staff at the Outer Banks History Center; Greg Ball, director of GIS for Dare County; Randy Campbell, historian in Carteret County; Anja Collette, GIS specialist at Carteret County; Nick D'Amato in Kitty Hawk; Michael O'Dell and Tanya Young in Kill Devil Hills; Ted Kinni and Donna Kinni in Corolla; and Phillip Howard and Gene Ballance, historians at Ocracoke. Each of these individuals, with patience and interest, answered many questions utilizing their skills and expertise, greatly enhancing the contents of this book. Also, the editing skills of noted toponymist Jenny Runyon were paramount and her suggestions critical. Additionally, editing and advice on publication from Lucas Church, Jay Mazzocchi, Andrew Winters, and Trish Watson was essential in the success of the book. A special recognition is for Sonny Williamson from Down East, an author and true expert in many things, for our special meetings and conversations at Cape Lookout.

Mention must also be made of the effective influence on me and the remarkable advice of four well-known and respected scholars of toponymy, cartography, and linguistics—friends and colleagues Meredith "Pete" Burrill, Lewis L. McArthur, Donald J. Orth, and Richard R. Randall.

A special recognition and appreciation are extended to Anne, my wife; Jennifer, my daughter; and Matt, my stepson, for their constructive comments and their patience.

Glossary

This list relates specifically to the Outer Banks and might not necessarily apply in the same way in other regions (no official sets of terms or definitions exist by any government or any organization—such matters are application driven). "Former" indicates feature no longer exists.

Anchorage. Protected place, little or no facilities, ships can safely anchor; generally used on the Outer Banks in historical context.

Area. Used to describe feature with vague, poorly defined, or implied boundaries that does not readily conform to another category.

Barrier beach. Offshore, single, elongated sand ridge rising above high tide level, with one or more coves and separating open water body (ocean) from enclosed water body (lagoon or sound).

Barrier chain. A string of barrier islands, barrier beaches, barrier spits.

Barrier island. Complex barrier formation composed of multiple sand ridges, dunes, overwash fans, and tidal marshes above high tide level; separates open water body from enclosed water body in same manner as barrier beach.

Barrier spit. Barrier connected to mainland at one end conforming to definition of barrier beach or barrier island.

Bay. Indentation of water body into land; generally wider than cove but smaller than bight or gulf.

Beach. Sloping accumulation of material along water body washed by waves or tides.

Bight. Wide, shallow curve or indentation of water body into coast where width greater than indentation.

Breakers. Violent, turbulent water created by waves from deep water passing over shoals or shallows.

Camp. Temporary place used for variety of commercial, recreational, or military activities.

Canal. Artificial water course constructed for navigation by watercraft; used on the Outer Banks previously in historical context; also for dredged waterways in subdivisions for access to open water.

Cape. Prominent projection of land into water body, usually open sea.

Channel. Linear deep part of water body, natural or dredged, through which main volume of water flows; used for navigation by watercraft in shallow or shoal waters.

Civil division. Political division or subdivision formed for administrative purposes.

Community. Unincorporated (no legal boundaries), well-known places with scattered mostly full-time residents.

Cove. Small indentation of water body into land.

Estuary. Drowned river mouth or valley where tides ebb and flood, created by general rise in sea level.

Flat. Relatively level place within greater relief; generally references flat expanses of sand within high sand dunes or hummocks, or expanses of water.

Fort. Enclosed or fortified place displaying some barrier of defense, usually equipped with guns; now only historical context on the Outer Banks.

Harbor. Protected water where ships and boats can dock; also marina; usually has shipping or boating facilities.

Hill. Elevation rising steeply from surroundings; sand dunes generally stabilized by vegetation.

Hummock (hammock). Drier land rising slightly above surrounding swamp or marsh; might reference marsh island in water body; usage on the Outer Banks "hammock" not "hummock."

Indian village. Formerly permanent or temporary place of residence for tribe or portion of tribe of Indians; used totally in historical sense because Indians of the Outer Banks and neighboring mainland were decreased to only few mainland villages by middle 18th century, extinct or assimilated by beginning 19th century.

Island. Dry or relatively dry land completely surrounded by water or wetlands.

Lagoon. Water body, brackish or fresh, separated from larger water body (open sea) by barrier islands and barrier beaches.

Lake. Water body completely surrounded by land but frequently with stream as an outlet, often contains freshwater.

Landing. Originally referenced place where ships or boats loaded or unloaded; now also includes other activities; built-up dock area.

Marsh. Wet, low places with standing water, possibly fresh, usually brackish, containing variety of grasses; extensive marsh often results from deposition creating overwash fans during ocean storm surges.

Ocean current. Distinct large stream of ocean water moving continuously in same path, usually with marked difference in temperature and color from surrounding water.

Peninsula. Large projection of land surrounded on three sides by water, connected on one side to land.

Point. Protuberance of land into a water body; less prominent than cape.

Region. Defined unit on Earth's surface, differentiated by one or more similar characteristics or activities.

Rock. Usually submerged in water and visible at low tide; shell middens (piles).

Sand dune. Dynamic or changing ridge or hill of sand piled up by wind action.

Sand dunes. Complex of sand dunes referenced collectively or as a unit.

Sea. Large open saltwater body.

Settlement. Mostly former, small community areas where people lived mostly full-time.

Shoal. Accumulation of sand, mud, and other materials in water creating shallows surrounded by deeper water.

Strait. Narrow water body of some magnitude representing major feature connecting two larger water bodies.

Stream. Linear flowing water body on Earth's surface, used here infrequently because references freshwater features.

Subdivision. Defined and bounded area where people live full-time or part-time or designated for such activity, named and recognized as legal entity by county—not incorporated city, town, or village; not a township.

Swamp. Poorly drained wetland, freshwater or saltwater, and associated vegetation.

Tidal flat. Mud and sand covered by water at high tide, exposed at low tide.

Tidal stream. Linear feature, ebbs and floods with tides, often originates in marsh, swamp, or similar feature in the interior; gradually opens or trends toward larger water body.

Town. Incorporated places with legally defined boundaries and chartered by state government where people reside mostly full-time.

Village. Unincorporated (no legal boundaries) coalesced and well-known places where people reside mostly full-time.

Water passage. Waterway (inlet), ebbs and floods with tides, connects larger water bodies or other waterways.

Woods. Area covered with dense growth of trees in contrast to lack of trees surrounding.

Current and Historic Inlets

This table provides quick reference to and information about current and historical inlets at the Outer Banks, in order from north to south (see also map of inlets). Each named inlet has a complete detailed entry in the gazetteer. All variant names (other names), including minor spelling variations found, are included in the main gazetteer entry, along with name origin and other relevant information.

Inlet	Location	Open/Close Dates
Currituck Inlet (historical)	Just south of N.C.–V.A. boundary	Pre-1585–1731
New Currituck Inlet (historical)	At South Channel 6 miles north of Corolla	1713–1828
Musketo Inlet (historical)	Just north of Corolla	Pre-1585–1680s
Caffeys Inlet (historical)	4.5 miles north of Duck (center)	1770–1810
Trinety Harbor (historical)	3 miles north of Duck (center)	Pre-1585–1660
Kill Devil Hills Inlet (probably did not exist)	Kitty Hawk Bay area (possibly)	Early 1700s (claimed)
Roanoke Inlet (Port Lane) (historical)	Southern Nags Head	Pre-1585–1811; 1660s–1811 known as Roanoke Inlet (see Port Lane)
Old Roanoke Inlet (historical — might not have existed; probable cartographic contrivance accounting for Port Lane)	2 miles south of Roanoke Inlet	Unknown, maybe late 1600s; mistaken for what was Port Lane
Port Lane (historical)	3 miles north of Gunt Inlet migrating northward	Pre-1585–mid-1600s closed, maybe captured by what became Roanoke Inlet; some labeled as Old Roanoke Inlet (incorrectly)
Gunt Inlet (Port Ferdinando) (historical)	2 miles north of Oregon Inlet	Pre-1585–1790s
Oregon Inlet	15 miles north of Rodanthe	1846–present
New Inlet	6 miles north of Rodanthe	Open and closed periodically since 1650s, reopened 2011 to present
Loggerhead Inlet (historical)	2 miles north of Rodanthe	1843–70
Chickinacommock Inlet (historical)	1.5 miles north of Rodanthe	1657–83, possibly 1700s, 1862–65
Keneckid Inlet (historical)	probably 3 miles south of Salvo	Illusive, late 1600s–early 1700s
Buxton Inlet (historical)	2.5 miles northeast of Buxton	1962–63
Chacandepeco Inlet (historical)	1 mile east of Buxton	Pre-1585–early 1670s
Isabel Inlet (historical)	3 miles east of Hatteras (village)	2003 (2 months)
Little Inlet (historical)	2 miles southwest of Hatteras (village)	Periodic temporary breaches historically, including 2003 and 2016
Hatteras Inlet	4 miles southwest of Hatteras (village)	1846–present
Wells Creek Inlet (historical)	9.5 miles northeast of Ocracoke	1840s–1850s
Old Hatteras Inlet (historical)	7 miles southwest of Hatteras Inlet	1650s–1764

Current and Historic Inlets (cont.)

Inlet	Location	Open/Close Dates
Nigh Inlet (historical)	Just southeast of Ocracoke (village)	Possibly existed; dates unknown
Ocracoke Inlet	3.6 miles southwest of Ocracoke (village)	Pre-1585–present
High Hills Inlet (Whalebone Inlet) (historical)	10 miles southwest of Ocracoke (village)	1865–1916, 1942–61
Swash Inlet (historical)	13.5 miles southwest of Ocracoke (village)	Pre-1585–1722, 1939–61, awash periodically
Sand Island Inlet	18 miles southwest of Ocracoke (village)	Mid-1800s–occasionally awash to present
Long Point Inlet (historical)	5 miles east of Atlantic (mainland)	Early 1800s
Drum Inlet (historical) (Old Drum Inlet)	3.5 miles east of Atlantic (mainland)	Periodically open 1700s–1920, 1933–71, 1999–2008
New Drum Inlet	Just northeast of Ophelia Inlet	1971–72, 2011–merging with Ophelia Inlet
Ophelia Inlet	3.5 miles south of Atlantic (mainland)	2005–present
Cedar Inlet (historical)	4 miles south of Atlantic (mainland)	1729–55, 1770–1865
Old Drum Inlet (historical)	8 miles south of Davis (mainland)	1722–80
Barden Inlet (The Drain) (at Cape Lookout)	5 miles south of Harkers Island (village)	1770–1860 (The Drain), 1933–present (Barden)
Beaufort Inlet	2 miles south of Beaufort (mainland)	Pre-1585–present
Cheeseman Inlet (historical)	1.5 miles west of Atlantic Beach (town)	1700–1750 awash, closed 1816, 1800s–1850 awash
Bogue Inlet	3.3 miles south of Swansboro (mainland)	Pre-1585–present

Selected Annotated Bibliography

Books, Magazines, Papers, Theses, and Online Sources

ACE (U.S. Army Corps of Engineers). 2013. *Manteo, Old House Channel, NC Section 204 Beneficial Use of Dredged Material Restoration Project*. Wilmington, N.C.: ACE.

Angley, F. Wilson. 1982. *Historical Overview of Beaufort Inlet, Cape Lookout Area of North Carolina*. Raleigh: N.C. Historical Commission, Division of Archives and History, Research Branch.

————. 1984. *History of Ocracoke Inlet and the Adjacent Areas*. Raleigh: N.C. Division of Archives and History, Research Branch.

————. 1985. *Historical Overview of Oregon Inlet*. Raleigh: N.C. Division of Archives and History, Research Branch.

————. 1994. *Brief History of Kitty Hawk Woods, Dare County, North Carolina*. Raleigh: N.C. Division of Archives and History, Research Branch.

Balash, Andrew M. 2008. "How Maps Tell the Truth by Lying: An Analysis of Delisle's 1718 Carte de la Louisiane." Master's thesis in history, University of Texas at Arlington.

Barlowe, Arthur. 2002. *The First Voyage to Roanoke 1584*. Chapel Hill: University of North Carolina Academic Affairs Library. Full title: *The First Voyage Made to the Coasts of America, with Two Barks, wherein Were Captains M. Philip Amadas and M. Arthur Barlowe, Who Discovered Part of the Countrey Now Called Virginia, anno 1584. Written by One of the Said Captaines, and Sent to Sir Walter Ralegh, Knight, at Whose Charge and Direction, the Said Voyage Was Set Forth*.

Binkley, Cameron. 2007. *The Creation and Establishment of Cape Hatteras National Seashore: The Great Depression through Mission 66*. Atlanta: NPS.

Bishop, Nathaniel H. 1878. *Voyage of the Paper Canoe: A Geographical Journey of 2,500 Miles from Quebec to the Gulf of Mexico during the Years 1874–1875*. Boston: Lee and Shepard Publishers.

Bland, Edward. 1651. *The Discovery of New Brittaine* (reprint). London. New Brittaine was a proposed new "colony" in what is now south-central Virginia and north-central North Carolina; an expedition was made, promotional pamphlet published, but no results were realized particularly because Bland died shortly afterward. New York: Readex Great Americana 1966.

Blunt, Edmund, and G. W. Blunt. 1857. *American Coast Pilot*. New York. Eighteenth Edition. Coast pilots were published with useful information for boating along shipping routes and especially later the Intracoastal Waterway.

Boone, Jim. 1988. *Birds of the Bodie Island Lighthouse Pond and the Roadside Ponds and Marshes, Cape Hatteras National Seashore, North Carolina*. CPSU Technical Report 46. Athens: University of Georgia. Cooperative effort with School of Forestry Resources and NPS.

Bratton, Susan, and Kathryn Davison. 1985. *The Disturbance History of Buxton Woods, Cape Hatteras, North Carolina*. CPSU Technical Report 16. Athens: University of Georgia.

Brereton, John. 1602. *A Brief and True Relation of the Discoverie of the North Part of Virginia*. London. Description of a voyage to what is now Virginia based on discoveries of "Captaine Bartholomew Gosnold and Captaine Bartholomew Gilbert under permissions of the honourable knight Sir Walter Raleigh." New York Readex Great Americana, 1966.

Brickell, John. 1743. *The Natural History of North Carolina*. Dublin and London.

Brown, Marvin A. 2015. *Before They Opened the Valve: Dare County's Outer Banks 1865–1963*. Raleigh: NCDOT.

Burke, Kenneth E., Jr. 1958. "The History of Portsmouth, North Carolina, from Its Founding 1753 to Its Evacuation in the Face of Federal Forces 1861." Honors thesis, paper 408, University of Richmond.

Burkholder, Jo Ann, Elle H. Allen, Carol A. Kinder, and Stacie Flood. 2017. *Natural Resources Condition Assessment, Cape Lookout National Seashore*. Natural Resources Report NPS/SECN/NRR-2017/1434. Fort Collins, Colo.: NPS.

Burney, D. A., and L. P. Burney. 1987. *Recent Paleoecology of Nags Head Woods on North Carolina's Outer Banks*. Torrey Botanical Club. Vol. 114, no. 2, 156–68. Durham, N.C.: Duke University Press.

Byrd, William. 1728. *Histories of the Dividing Line betwixt Virginia and North Carolina.* Repr., North Carolina Historical Commission edition, 1929; repr., New York: Dover, 1967. Detailed description of establishing and fixing the boundary between Virginia and North Carolina, with attendant detailed descriptions, including place names of the barrier island at the boundary and Knotts Island.

Carr, Dawson. 2016. *NC 12: Gateway to the Outer Banks.* Chapel Hill: University of North Carolina Press.

Charlet, James D. 2020. *Shipwrecks of the Outer Banks.* Lanham, Md.: Rowman & Littlefield Publishers (Globe Pequot Press).

Cheeseman, Bruce S. 1982. *Four Centuries and Roanoke Island: A Legacy of Geographical Change.* Raleigh: N.C. Division of Archives and History, Research Branch.

Click, Patricia C. 2001. *Time Full of Trial: The Roanoke Island Freedman's Colony 1862–1867.* Chapel Hill: University of North Carolina Press.

Cobb, Collier. 1905. "Some Changes in the North Carolina Coast since 1585." *North Carolina Booklet* 4, no. 9: 3–13.

Corbitt, David Leroy. 1950. *The Formation of the North Carolina Counties 1663–1943.* Raleigh, N.C.: Division of Archives and History, Research Branch.

Covey, Mel. 2018. *Indian Town Revealed: William Elks and the Rest of the Hatteras Indians 1759 Land Patent and Interpreted Survey.* This online book provides a wealth of information on selected names in support of its topic.

Cumming, William P. 1969. *Captain James Wimble: His Maps and the Colonial Cartography of the North Carolina Coast.* Raleigh, N.C.: State Department of Archives and History, Research Branch.

———. 1998. *The Southeast in Early Maps.* 3rd ed., rev. and enl. by Loui D. Vorsey Jr. Chapel Hill: University of North Carolina Press.

Currituck County. 2013. *Connecting Corolla: Bike, Pedestrian, Access and Wayfinding Plan.*

Darden, Mark Fielding. 2016. *Will This Town Survive: Songs and Stories from Salter Path, North Carolina?* http://www.salterpathnc .com/history-content.htm.

Dare County Board of Commissioners. 2015. *Meeting Minutes, October 5, 2015.* Manteo, N.C.: Dare County Board of Commissioners.

Dare County Planning Department. 2009. *Dare County Land Use Plan Update.* Manteo, N.C.: Dare County.

Deaton, Anne S., et al. 2012. *North Carolina Coastal Habitat Protection Plan.* Raleigh: N.C. Division of Marine Fisheries.

Downing, Sarah. 2013. *Hidden History of the Outer Banks.* Charleston, S.C.: History Press.

———. 2008. *Vintage Outer Banks: Shifting Sands and Bygone Beaches.* Charleston, S.C.: History Press.

Dunbar, Gary S. 1956 and 1958. *Historical Geography of the North Carolina Outer Banks.* Coastal Studies Series 3 (ltd. circ.). Baton Rouge: Louisiana State University Studies.

F&WS (U.S. Fish and Wildlife Service). 1984. *Mackay Island National Wildlife Refuge: Annual Report,* 1983 and 1984. Washington, D.C.: National Wildlife Refuge System, F&WS. Includes numerous maps.

———. 1999. *Currituck National Wildlife Refuge: Annual Narrative Report.* Washington, D.C.: F&WS.

———. 2002. *Bogue Inlet and Bogue Sound as Bird Islands.* Washington, D.C.: F&WS.

———. 2006. *Draft Comprehensive Conservation Plan and Environmental Assessment Currituck National Wildlife Refuge.* Atlanta: F&WS.

Federal Writers Project. 1940. *Currituck County, North Carolina.* Washington, D.C.: Government Printing Office. The Federal Writers Project was established 1935 as part of the New Deal recovery program in the Great Depression with writers employed to compile local histories, oral histories, ethnographies, children's books, and other works.

Fink, Paul M. n.d. *Early Explorers in the Great Smokies.* Knoxville: East Tennessee Historical Society.

Fisher, John J. 1962. "Geomorphic Expression of Former Inlets along the Outer Banks of North Carolina." Master's thesis, University of North Carolina at Chapel Hill, Department of Geology and Geography. Detailed with excellent analyses of inlets of the Outer Banks up to publication date.

Fisher, William, John Thornton, and Coolie Verner. 1689. *The English Pilot: The Fourth Book 1689).* Repr., Theatrum Orbis Terrarum Atlases in Facsimile, ser. 4, vol. 5, Amsterdam: Theatrvm Oribs Terrarvm, 1967. Vol. 5 described the "Sea-Coasts; Capes,

Head-Lands, Rivers, Bays, Roads, Havens, Harbours, Streights [sic], Islands, Depths, Rocks, Shoals, Sands, Banks, and Dangers from River Amazon to New-found-Land; with all West-India Navigation, and Islands therein, as Cuba, Hispagniola [sic], Jamaica, Barbados, Porto [sic] Rico, and remaining Caribbe Islands. With A New Description of New-found-Land, New-England, Virginia, Mary-Land, &c. shewing the courses and distances from one place to another, the ebbing and flowing of the Sea, the settings of the tides and currents, &c." Charts referenced are numbers 2 and 12 and 15 pertaining to the Outer Banks. Widely used from its publication until early 18th century accounting for distinct errors of inlet locations and names in vicinity of Roanoke Island because, as was common practice historically, many cartographers copied other sources because there was a lack of readily available information, thereby perpetuating errors. For detailed information, see entry for Roanoke Island Historical Inlets.

Frankenberg, Dirk. 1995. *The Nature of the Outer Banks: Environmental Processes, Field Sites, and Development Issues, Corolla to Ocracoke.* Chapel Hill: University of North Carolina Press.

Garrity-Blake, Barbara J. 2010. *Ethnographic Study Analysis of Cape Hatteras National Seashore.* Manteo, N.C.: NPS. Two distinct publications referenced as nos. 1 and 2. Each makes use of hand-stylized maps from which most names from these sources are taken. *See also* NPS 2005. *Final Technical Report,* vol. 1: *Ethnohistorical Description of the Eight Villages Adjoining Cape Hatteras National Seashore and Interpretive Themes of History and Heritage.* Manteo, N.C.: NPS.

Godfrey, Paul J., and Melinda M. Godfrey. 1976. *Barrier Island Ecology of Cape Lookout National Seashore and Vicinity, North Carolina.* NPS Scientific Monograph Series 9. Amherst: NPS Cooperative Research Unit, University of Massachusetts, Amherst.

Goerch, Carl. 1956. *Ocracoke.* Winston-Salem, N.C.: Blair.

Goldstein, Robert J. 2000. *Coastal Fishing in the Carolinas: From Surf, Pier, and Jetty.* 3rd ed. [online]. Winston-Salem, N.C.: Blair. The online version features location numbers (loc.) rather than page numbers.

Gray, R. Wayne. 2009. *A History of Bethany United Methodist Church.* Wanchese, N.C.: Daisy Publishing.

Haklyut, Richard. 1589. *The Principall Navigations, Voiages [sic] and Discoveries of the English Nation Made by Sea or Over Land to the Most Remote and Farthest Distant Quarters of the Earth, at Any Time within the Compass of These 1500 years.* Repr., London: Everyman's Library, 6:121–227, 1962. 8 vols. No mention of any name origins.

Harrington, J. C. 1962. *Search for the Cittie of Ralegh [sic]: Archeological Excavations at Fort Raleigh National Historic Site, North Carolina.* Washington, D.C.: NPS.

Heitman, Francis B. 1903. *Historical Register and Dictionary of USA Army.* Vol. 2. Washington, D.C.: Government Printing Office.

Hill, Michael R. 1983. *Historical Overview of Hyde County, North Carolina.* Raleigh: N.C. Division of Archives and History, Research Branch.

Hitchcock, Susan. 2014. *Bodie Island Light Station; Cultural Landscape Report.* Atlanta: NPS.

Holland Consulting Planners. 2006. *Town of Atlantic Beach Core Use Plan.* Wilmington, N.C.: Holland Consulting Partners.

Howard, Bernard James. 2016. "Navigating Historical Waters: A Study of the Pilots and Original Residents of Ocracoke Island." Master's thesis, East Carolina University.

Howard, Phillip. 2001. *Fannie Pearl MacWilliams Wahab.* Ocracoke: Village Craftsmen Newsletter. May 4.

———. 2007. *The Black Squall.* Ocracoke: Village Craftsmen Newsletter. July 27.

———. 2012. *Hurricane Boards.* Ocracoke: Village Craftsmen Newsletter. July 21.

———. 2013. *A History of the United States Post Office at Ocracoke.* Ocracoke: Village Craftsmen Newsletter. April 21.

———. 2013. *Windmills on Ocracoke.* Ocracoke: Village Craftsmen Newsletter. January 21.

———. 2014. *From Philadelphia to Ocracoke, 1951.* Ocracoke: Village Craftsmen Newsletter. April 21.

———. 2018. *Ocracoke Street Names.* Ocracoke: Village Craftsmen Newsletter. July 22.

Hyde County Planning. 2008. *Hyde County, NC, Coastal Area Management Authority (CAMA) Core Land Use Plan.* Wilmington, N.C.: Holland Consulting Planners.

Lawrence, Richard W. 2008. *Overview of North Carolina Shipwrecks with an Emphasis on Eighteenth-Century Vessel Losses at*

Beaufort Inlet. Raleigh: N.C. Office of State Archaeology, Department of Natural and Cultural Resources, Underwater Archaeology Branch.

Lawson, John. 1709. *A New Voyage to Carolina Containing the Exact Description and Natural History of That Country Together with the Present State Thereof and a Journal of a Thousand Miles Travel'd thro' Several Nations of Indians Giving a Particular Account of Their Customs, Manners, etc.* London. John Lawson was the first surveyor general of North Carolina.

MacNeill, Ben Dixon. 1958. *The Hatterasman*. Winston-Salem, N.C.: Blair. Narrative format with "researched" histories.

Mallin, Michael A., Matthew R. McIver, and Virginia L. Johnson. 2006. *Assessment of Coastal Water Resources and Watershed Conditions at Cape Hatteras National Seashore, North Carolina*. Technical Report NPS/NRWRD/NRTR-2006/351. Washington, D.C.: NPS.

Mallinson, David J., et al. 2008. *Past, Present, and Future Inlets of the Outer Banks Barrier Islands*. Greenville, N.C.: Department of Geological Sciences, Thomas Harriot College of Arts and Sciences, and Institute for Coastal Science and Policy, East Carolina University.

Mallinson, David J., Stanley R. Riggs, Stephen J. Culver, and Dorothea Ames. 2009 *The North Carolina Outer Banks Barrier Islands: A Field Trip Guide to the Geology, Geomorphology, and Processes*. Greenville, N.C.: East Carolina University. Results of field investigations. Year not provided, but post-2008.

Martin, Francois-Xavier. 1829. *History of North Carolina from the Earliest Period*. New Orleans: A. T. Penniman.

McGuinn, Phillip Horne. 2000. "Shell Castle, a North Carolina Entrepôt, 1789–1820: A Historical and Archaeological Investigation." Master's thesis, East Carolina University, Department of History.

McMullan, Phillip. 2009. *A Role for Sassafras in the Search for the Lost Colony*. Lost Colony Research Group. www.lost-colony.com.

McMullan, Philip, and Fred Willard. 2015. *The Search for the Lost Colony of Roanoke: Hidden Maps, Hidden Cities*. Williamston, N.C.: Lost Colony Center for Science and Research. The particular citation used is "Anonymous Map" in one of the letters written by Ralph Lane (head of first attempted Roanoke Colony) to Sir Francis Walsingham (reportedly Queen Elizabeth I's spy; see Lane 1585). Published previously in Quinn 1955: 847; Anonymous, *A Description of the Land of Virginia*, Colonial Papers, vol. 1, no. 42, 1660. The map has illegible hand annotations, including islands of the Outer Banks; one relevant to place names is an apparent variant name for Ocracoke Inlet. Hand annotations are interpreted and clarified in relevant gazetteer entries.

Miller, Helen Hill. 1974. *Historic Places around the Outer Banks*. Charlotte, N.C.: McNally and Lofton.

Montoya, Liliana Velasquez. 2018. "Observation and Modeling of the Morphodynamics of Tidal Inlets in the Northern Outer Banks of North Carolina." Ph.D. diss., North Carolina State University, School of Engineering.

Murphy, I. 1951. *The Outer Banks*. Kill Devil Hills, N.C.: Surfside Press.

N.C. Division of Coastal Management. 1998. *Kitty Hawk Woods Reserve Management Plan*. Raleigh, N.C.: Coastal Reserve Program.

NCDOT (N.C. Department of Transportation). 2013. *NC 12 Rodanthe Breach Long-Term Improvements, Bonner Bridge Replacement Project Phase IIb, Federal-Aid no. BRNHF-0012(56), NCDOT Project Definition: 32635, STIP no. B-2500B, Dare County, North Carolina: Administrative Action, Environmental Assessment*. Raleigh: NCDOT Project Development and Environmental Analysis.

NPS (U.S. National Park Service). 1987. *Little Kinnakeet Life Saving and Coast Guard Station: Historic Structure Report*. Denver, Colo.: NPS.

NPS (U.S. National Park Service) [Crow and Svenson]. 2000. *Cape Lookout Village Historic District Registration Form*. Washington, D.C.: NPS.

NPS (U.S. National Park Service). 2004a. *Cape Lookout Coast Guard Station Boat House: Historic Structure Report*. Atlanta: NPS, Historical Architecture, Cultural Resources Division, Southeast Regional Office.

———. 2004b. *Cape Lookout Lighthouse Keeper's Dwelling (1907): Historic Structure Report*. Atlanta: NPS.

———. 2004c. *Wash Roberts House Historic Structure Report*. Atlanta: NPS.

———. 2005a. *Cape Lookout Village Cultural Landscape Report*. Washington, D.C.: NPS.

———. 2005b. *Final Technical Report*, vol. 1, *Ethnohistorical Description of the Eight Villages Adjoining Cape Hatteras National Seashore and Interpretive Themes of History and Heritage*. Manteo, N.C.: NPS. Two volumes referenced in the entries as NPS 1 and NPS 2. The eight villages are, north to south (1) Rodanthe, (2) Waves, (3) Salvo, (4) Avon, (5) Buxton, (6) Frisco, (7) Hatteras, and (8) Ocracoke. Vol. 1 includes villages 1–4; vol. 2 includes villages 5–8.

———. 2006a. Issues Related to Water Quality Cape Point Area. Harpers Ferry.

———. 2006b. *Portsmouth Life-Saving Station: Historic Structure Report*. Atlanta: NPS.

———. 2007. *Portsmouth Village Cultural Landscape Report*. Harkers Island. Atlanta: NPS.

———. 2010. *Fort Raleigh National Historic Site: Cultural Landscapes Inventory*. Manteo, N.C.: NPS.

———. 2011. *Secrets in the Sand: Archeology at Fort Raleigh, 1990–2010*. Manteo, N.C.: NPS.

NPS (U.S. National Park Service) [Herbert W. Stanford III]. 2012. *Cape Lookout Lighthouse: North Carolina's Coastal Icon—1812–2012—200 Years Lighting the Way*. Washington, D.C.: NPS.

Oldmixon, John. 1708. *The British Empire in America*, vol. 1, *Containing the History of the Discovery, Settlement, Progress and State of the British Colonies of the Continents and Islands of America*. Repr., London: Brotherton, 1741.

Olszewski, George G. (national park historian). 1970. *History of Portsmouth*. Washington, D.C.: NPS. Preliminary version with editorial notes. The number listed is the online count.

O'Neal, Calvin J., Alice K. Rondthaler, and Anita Fletcher. 1976. *The Story of Ocracoke Island: A Hyde County Bicentennial Project*. Charlotte, N.C.: Eaton Publishing and Hyde County Historical Society.

Oppermann, Joseph K. 2005. *Bodie Island Life-Saving Station and Boat House: Historic Structure Report*. Winston-Salem, N.C.: NPS.

Outer Banks Scenic Byway Advisory Committee. 2008. *Corridor Management Plan for the Outer Banks Scenic Highway*. Rodanthe.

Patterson, Bryan E. 2008. "The 'Beach People' Take Flight: Inventing the Airplane and Modernizing the Outer Banks of North Carolina, 1900–1932." History honors paper no. 5, Connecticut College.

Payne, Roger L., and Donald J. Orth. 1997. *Principles, Policies, and Procedures: Domestic Geographic Names*. Reston, Va.: USBGN.

PK Association (Pine Knoll Association [sic—without Shores]). 2016. Parks and Marinas. http://pineknollhistory.blogspot.com/.

PKS (Pine Knoll Shores History Committee). 2016. *Pine Knoll Shores History*. Website with various online blogs and vignettes regarding the history of Pine Knoll Shores and other relative aspects, including history and development of central Bogue Banks.

Portinaro, Pierluigi, and Franco Knuisch. 1987. *The Cartography of North America 1500–1800*. New York: Facts on File.

Powell, William S. 1968. *Place Names of North Carolina*. Chapel Hill: University of North Carolina Press. A later edition was published in 2010.

Quinn, David B. 1975. *North America from Earliest Discovery to First Settlements*. New York: Harper and Row.

———, ed. 1971. *North American Discovery circa 1000–1612*. Columbia: South Carolina Press.

Rivers and Ball, eds. 1955 and 1961. *Pine Knoll Shores, a Subdivision of Roosevelt Property on Bogue Banks Island [sic] off the Coast of Morehead City, N.C.* Revised edition (1961) is from original for original Pine Knoll Shores eastern part (east of Pine Knoll Waterway).

Runyon, Timothy J., et al. 2005. *Ocracoke Shipwreck Database and Remote Sensing Survey*. Greenville, N.C.: East Carolina University, University of North Carolina Coastal Studies Institute.

Sainsbury, W. Noel. 1860. *Calendar of State Papers: Colonial Series, America and West Indies, 1574–1674 and 1674–1676*. This volume includes copies of the five letters from Lane (governor of the 1st colony—2nd voyage). Second letter is mysterious in its passage (to several researchers) regarding mention of Port Scarborough, which never existed. *See* the Gunt Inlet entry for explanation.

Salley, Alexander S., Jr., ed. 1911. *Narratives of Early Carolina 1650–1708*. New York: C. Scribner's Sons.

Sandbeck, Penne Smith. 2003. *Currituck Banks, North Banks, and Roanoke Island*. Manteo, N.C.: State Historic Preservation Office, Natural and Cultural Resources. Architectural survey report.

Simpson, Marcus B., Jr., and Sallie W. Simpson. 1988. "The Pursuit of Leviathan: A History of

Whaling on the North Carolina Coast." *North Carolina Historical Review* 65, no. 1: 1–51.

Skeat, Walter W. 1888. *An Etymological Dictionary of the English Language.* Oxford: Clarendon Press.

Smith, John. 1624. *The Generall Historie of Virginia, New-England, and the Summer Islaes [sic] with the Names of the Adventurers, Planters, and Govenours from Their First Beginning Ano 1584 to This Present 1624.* London: Michael Sparker. Repr., Hinesville, Ga.: Nova Anglia Press. John Smith's "Generall Historie" concentrated mostly on what is now Virginia. "Summer Islaes [sic]" refers to Bermuda, sometimes referenced as Somers Isles or Summer Isles. Also, *Ould Virginia,* 1624—Smith's names on this map used only here or occasionally another isolated application; Smith's names on the Outer Banks never permanently applied.

Smith, Penne. 2001. *The Etheridge Homeplace: A History.* Outer Banks Conservationists. https://obcinc.org/wp-content/uploads /2019/06/etheridge_homeplace.pdf.

Sorrie, Bruce A. 2014. *Inventory of the Natural Areas of Dare County, North Carolina.* Raleigh, N.C.: N.C. Natural Heritage Program, Department of Natural and Cultural Resources.

Stanford, Herbert W., III. 2015. *Carteret County Historical Gazetteer: Guide to the History of Important Sites and Events That Have Shaped Carteret County, North Carolina.* Web page.

The State (Greensboro, N.C.). 1954. Advertisement for Emerald Isle By-the-Sea. July 3, p. 41.

Stephens, Kay Holt Roberts. 1984 and 1989. *Judgement Land: The Story of Salter Path.* Bks. 1 and 2. Havelock, N.C.: Bogue Sound Books.

———. 2007. *Salter Path: A Brief History.* Repr. from *Judgement Land: The Story of Salter Path,* Core Sound Waterfowl Museum and Heritage Center website, 1993.

Stick, David. 1949. "Toby Tillett and His Ferry." *The State,* vol. 17, no. 3, June 18.

———. 1952. *Graveyard of the Atlantic: Shipwrecks of the North Carolina Coast.* Chapel Hill: University of North Carolina Press.

———. 1958. *Outer Banks.* Chapel Hill: University of North Carolina Press. David Stick was the noted expert on the Outer Banks and wrote prolifically.

———. 1970. *Dare County: A Brief History.* Raleigh: N.C. Historical Commission, Division of Archives and History.

———. 1998. *Outer Banks Reader.* Chapel Hill: University of North Carolina Press.

———. n.d. *The Dare County Board of Realtors History (1962–1973).* Nags Head, N.C.: Outer Banks Association of Realtors. Online version.

Throop, George Higby. 1850. *Nags Head, or Two Months among the "Bankers."* Philadelphia: A. Hart, T. K. and P. G. Collins Printers.

Torres, Louis. 1985. *Historic Resource Study of the Cape Hatteras National Seashore.* Denver, Colo.: NPS.

Town of Manteo. 1987. *Land Use Development Plan for the Town of Manteo.* Manteo, N.C.: Town of Manteo.

———. 2007. *Core CAMA Land Use Plan Update.* Manteo, N.C.: Town of Manteo.

Town of Nags Head. 2000. *Town of Nags Head Land and Water Use Plan.* Nags Head, N.C.: Town of Nags Head.

Trebellas, Christine, and William Chapman 1999. *Fort Raleigh National Historic Site: Historic Resource Study.* Atlanta: NPS.

Turner, William R. [William C. Overman Associates]. 2000. *Town of Kill Devil Hills Land Use Plan Update.* Kill Devil Hills, N.C.: Kill Devil Hills Board of Commissioners.

U.S. Coast Guard. 2015. *Atlantic Coast: Shrewsbury River, New Jersey to Little River, South Carolina—Light List.* Washington, D.C.: Government Printing Office.

USGS (U.S. Geological Survey). 1986. *The Outer Banks of North Carolina.* USGS Professional Paper 1177-B. Reston, Va.: USGS.

Van Zandt, Franklin K. 1976. *Boundaries of USA and the Several States.* Professional Paper 909. Reston, Va.: USGS. This publication superseded USGS Bulletin 1212 (1966). Page 97 references Kerr, N.C. Geological Survey, 1875, vol. 1, pp. 2–4, explains error in original assumption of location of Currituck Inlet at 36°30'00" N and error of 1728 survey placing it at 36°31'00" N when actually at 36°33'00" (and a few seconds).

Vincent, Susan Hart. 2003. *Cape Hatteras Light Station: Cultural Landscape Report.* Charlotte, N.C.: NPS.

Weslager, C. A. 1954. "Place Names on Ocracoke Island." *North Carolina Historical Review* 31, no. 1: 41–49. Unfortunately, locations are vague at best and most names are merely listed with no additional information. Approximately 40 percent of the names in this article were already known and recorded. Another 40 percent or so have been verified through avenues of research including numerous local interviews and use of additional materials. Many of the remaining 20 percent have been identified as variants of existing names, and the other few have been included with location as approximate based upon local information.

Whisnant, David E., and Anne Mitchell Whisnant. 2010. *Cape Lookout National Seashore Historic Resource Study*. Atlanta: Organization of American Historians and NPS.

White, James E., III. 2012. *Paradise Lost: An Oral History of Portsmouth Island*. Trent Woods, N.C.: Mount Truxton Publishing Company.

White, Nancy, et al. 2017. *Research to Support Design and Siting of Deposition Areas for Dredged Material from the Rodanthe Emergency Channel*. NCDOT Project 14-0790, in 3 pts. Greenville, N.C.: East Carolina University, UNC Coastal Studies Institute.

Willard, Fred. 2008. "A Reassessment of the Zuniga [*sic*] Map." History Paper 5150. https://www.lost-colony.com/Zuniga.pdf.

———. 2007. *Migration Patterns of Coastal N.C. Indians*. Web page.

Williamson, Sonny. 1986. *The Cousin Shamus Dictionary of Down East Words and Sayings*. Marshallberg, N.C.: Grandma Publications.

———. 1992. *Unsung Heroes of the Surf: The Life Saving Services of Carteret County*. Marshallberg, N.C.: Grandma Publications. Sonny Williamson had a wealth of knowledge of the "lower" banks, from Ocracoke Inlet south to Barden Inlet and west to Beaufort Inlet, and it was a delight to listen to his stories and for him to share his knowledge of the toponymy of the area.

Willis, James, III (Cap'n Jim). n.d. *A Brief History of Atlantic Beach, N.C.* Website. General information, history.

Wise, Harold Lee. 2010. *The Battle of Roanoke Island North Carolina: A History*. Amazon Digital Service. Online version featuring location numbers rather than page numbers.

Wiss and Milner. 2005. *Cape Lookout Village Cultural Landscape Report*. Atlanta: NPS.

Essays, Pamphlets, Brochures, Legal Documents, Letters, Newspapers, and Interviews

Austin, James. 1984. *Hatteras Island's Croatoan: Was the Lost Colony Really Lost?* Hatteras: Austin Jones Publications.

Ball, Greg. 2017 and 2018. Email and conversations. Director GIS, Dare County.

Ballance, Gene. 2017 and 2018. Email and interviews. Noted expert on Ocracoke history.

Butler, Richard. 1596. *Deposition Given to Spanish Authorities*. Simancas, Spain. Provides conflicting information about the Amadas and Barlowe 1594 voyage but seems to suggest naming of Port Ferdinando on the 1st Roanoke voyage, although inconclusive. *See* Gunt Inlet entry.

Campbell, Randy. 2017 and 2018. Email and conversations. Noted historian, Carteret County.

Carteret County GIS Database. 2019. Tax Maps. Carteret County Government. Online mapping service.

Carteret County Planning Board. 2006. *Minutes of the Meeting August 28, 2006*. Beaufort, N.C.: Carteret County Planning Board. Approval to establish Bell Cove Village subdivision.

Charles I, King of England, etc. 1629. *Carolina Charter 1629* (facsimile). In *The Colonial Records of North Carolina*, vol. 1, *1662–1712*, by William Laurence Saunders. Raleigh: P. M. Hale State Printer, 1886. This charter to Sir Robert Heath (1629) was ruled invalid by the interim government (Cromwell and the Commonwealth, 1649–60) after Charles I was defeated, convicted of treason, and executed. Charles II was restored 1660.

Charles II, King of England, etc. 1663. *Carolina Charter 1663* (facsimile). In *The Colonial Records of North Carolina*, vol. 1, *1662–1712*, by William Laurence Saunders. Raleigh: P. M. Hale State Printer, 1886. Charles II issued the second charter three years after his restoration to the throne of England (1660) to the eight lords proprietors: Edward Earl of Clarendon, George Duke of Albemarle, William Lord Craven, John Lord Berkley, Anthony Lord Ashley, Sir George Carteret, Sir William Berkley, and Sir John Colleton.

Collette, Anja. 2017. Email. GIS specialist, Carteret County.

Creef, Tama. 2017 and 2018. Email and conversations. Chief archivist, Outer Banks History Center, Dare County.

Currituck County Board of Adjustments. 2013. *Meeting January 10, 2013.* Currituck County Board of Adjustments.

Currituck County Register of Deeds, Currituck Court House. Numerous books, including first 60 books (a few missing) prior to 1870 when Currituck County ceded land with other counties for Dare County formation. Names are mentioned, and they are added accordingly, but this source is mostly good for adding variant names because locational references are vague: descriptions mostly indicate common landmarks such as trees, posts, etc., and features only generically, so many names are mentioned with no possibility of determining even a general location. Where possible, location was determined and associated with existing entries or occasionally resulting in a new entry.

D'Amato, Nick. 2017 and 2018. Email. President of Kitty Hawk Landing HOA, Dare County.

Dare County Register of Deeds, Dare County Government Center. Manteo, N.C. Various records and GIS access.

F&WS (U.S. Fish and Wildlife Service). 2016. *Pea Island National Wildlife Refuge.* Manteo, N.C.: F&WS.

———. 2018, 2001. *Mackay Island Brochure with Map.* Knotts Island.

George II, King of England, etc., 1753. *Tract of Land Containing Six Hundred and Forty Acres Lying and Being in the County of Carteret.* Records of the Secretary of State, N.C., Book 10, page 362, file 246.

Harper's Weekly. 1862. New York: Harper & Brothers. Published 1857–1916.

Harris, Bill. 2017. Bill Harris Collection. Manteo, N.C.: Outer Banks History Center. Papers from the historical research of Bill Harris (8 pp. plus three hand-drawn maps), based on his extensive local interviews. Unfortunately, these papers represent only a list of names with dates (presumably date of first use or first noted use), with three hand-drawn and hand-annotated maps that provide general and coarse representation of each feature's location. All names have been investigated and researched, and included as variant names (other names) for existing official names or entries added accordingly.

Howard, Phillip. 2017 and 2018. Email and interviews. Noted expert on Ocracoke history.

Jarvis, Samuel. *Public Comment Representing the Currituck Area of North Carolina during the Colonial Period* (Google Books facsimile).

Lane, Ralph. 1585. *Letters to Sir Francis Walsingham (advisor to the Queen).* London: State-Paper Office and British Museum. Three letters: two to Sir Walsingham and one to Sir Sidney, on Sir Walter Raleigh's first American colonies and colony at Jamestown.

———. 1589. Ralph Lane's [own] narrative, in Haklyut 1589.

N.C. General Assembly. 1716. *An Act for Settling and Maintaining Pillotts [sic] at Roanoke and Ocacock Inletts [sic]* (facsimile). November 17, 1715–January 19, 1716, vol. 25, pp. 159–61, no. 23, Act of 1715. Little River, N.C. (in what is now Perquimans County and what was then Albemarle County): N.C. General Assembly. In the early years, with no specific capital, the General Assembly often met where the governor lived or at some prominent member's house. The capital was established in Edenton 1722, but nothing substantial ever happened there. New Bern(e) selected as capital 1766.

———. 1753. *An Act Creating Town on Core Banks.* April 11, 1753, vol. 23, p. 282, no. 91.

NPS (U.S. National Park Service). 1952. *Fort Raleigh Historical Site.* Historical Handbook no. 16. Washington, D.C.: NPS.

———. 2000. *Cape Lookout Village Historic District Registration Form.* Washington, D.C.: NPS. The form and accompanying justification material is 40, pp. with two maps and one satellite image.

———. 2006. *Cape Lookout National Seashore Brochure.* Manteo, N.C.: NPS.

———. 2007. *Portsmouth Village Reports.* Manteo, N.C.: NPS. Cultural landscape reports: site history, analysis and evaluation, and treatment recommendations, each with some information and map content provided to NPS by John Milner Associates.

———. 2015. *Fort Raleigh Brochure.* Manteo, N.C.: NPS.

———. 2016. *Cape Hatteras Brochure.* Manteo, N.C.: NPS.

———. 2018. *Cultural Landscape Inventory: Portsmouth Village Historic District.* Atlanta: NPS.

Ocracoke Island History. 2016. *Ocracoke: Outer Banks This Week*.

Outer Banks Visitors Bureau. 2016. *Outer Banks Brochure*. Rodanthe, N.C.: Waves, Salvo Civic Association. Welcome brochure.

Rollinson, John. 1884. "Portions Provided by the North Carolina GenWeb Project Website." Personal journal, originally presented in *The Island Breeze*, April 1993, by Daniel C. Couch.

Sanderson, Richard. 1733. Richard's Will (facsimile reference). Little River (presently Perquimans County). Richard Sanderson had acquired all of Ocracoke Island.

Saunders, William Laurence. 1886. *The Colonial Records of North Carolina*, vol. 1, *1662–1712*. Raleigh, N.C.: P. M. Hale State Printer.

South Carolina and American General Gazette. 1775. Facsimile reference. Charleston, S.C., Newspaper operated 1764–81.

Town of Emerald Isle. 2006. *Planning Board Meeting Minutes, August 16, 1999, and January, 23, 2006*. Emerald Isle: Town of Emerald Isle. Preliminary plat of Rocky Point subdivision, p. 1. Approval of the separate subdivision, Shell Cove North, p. 2. Also, board of commissioners special meeting, March 12, 2004, p. 2.

Town of Southern Shores. 2015. *"Beach Parking."* Southern Shores, N.C.: Town of Southern Shores.

USBGN (U.S. Board on Geographic Names). Secretariat, staff files, etc. Reston, Va.: USBGN.

U.S. Congress. 1876. *Executive Documents. Forty-Fourth Congress (First Session)*. Washington, D.C.

U.S. House of Representatives. 1895. The Executive Documents of the House of Representatives of the Fifty-Third Congress 1893–1894. Washington, D.C.: Government Printing Office, 1300–1500.

U.S. Postal Service. 2015. *Internet Services and Websites (Historical Post Offices)*. Washington, D.C.: U.S. Postal Service. https://about.usps.com/publications/pub119/pub119_v03_toc.htm.

Verrazzano, Giovanni da. 1524. *Del Viaggio del Verazzano Nobile Fiorentino al Servizio di Francesco I, Ri de Francia, fatto nel 1524 all'America Settentrionale (Letter to King Francis 1 of France 8 July 1524)*. Repr., Research Triangle Park, N.C.: National Humanities Center, 2006. Reprinted letter with comments.

Wescott, Mattie Sanderlin. 1958. *A Brief History of the Kitty Hawk Methodist Church*. Kitty Hawk, N.C.: Kitty Hawk Methodist Church Centennial Committee.

White, John. 1590. *Narrative facsimile*.

Willard, Fred, and Barbara Midgett. 2007. *The Roanoke Sagas, Lane's Fort and Port Ferdinando*. Williamston, N.C.: Lost Colony Center for Science and Research.

Wilmington Gazette. n.d. *We Have been Favored with the Following Account of the Last Storm, Shell Castle, September 29*. Wilmington, N.C. Relayed by Howard, noted Ocracoke historian, wreck of schooner *Mount Vernon*.

Wingfield, Edward Maria. 1608. *Discourse of Virginia*. Jamestown, Virginia. Repr., with edits, Boston: Charles Deane, 1860.

Maps

Aa, Pieter van der. 1729. *La Floride, Suivant les Nouvelles Observations de Messrs. de l'Academie Royale des Sciences, etc.* Scale: 1:9,313,920. Leiden: Pieter van der Aa Publisher.

Abbott, John S. C. 1866. *Map of Roanoke February 1862*. Scale: 1:633,600. Originally published in *Harper's New Monthly Magazine* (with article), vol. 32, Dec. 1865–May 1866, p. 575.

ACE (U.S. Army Corps of Engineers). 1879. *Blueprint (Wanchese)*. Scale not provided. Washington, D.C.: ACE.

Anderson, Alexander. 1796. *An Accurate Map of USA of America According to the Treaty of Paris of 1783*. Scale not provided. New York: Smith, Reid, and Wayland Publishers.

Andrews, Lieutenant. 1862. *Roanoke Island Battlefield Map*. Washington, D.C.: Office of the Secretary of War, Office of the Chief of Engineers.

Asbury, G. P. n.d. *Lord Carteret's Grant*. Scale not provided. London. Original map by Tom.

Bachman, John. 1861. *Birds Eye View of North and South Carolina, and Part of Georgia*. Scale not provided (not to scale). New York: John Bachman and Co.

Baldwin, R. 1755. *North Carolina, South Carolina, Georgia, Virginia, Maryland, and Part of New Jersey*. Scale not provided. *London Magazine*, vol. 24, July.

Barnwell-Hammerton. 1721. *Southeast North America (Northeast Quadrant)*. Scale unknown.

Bellin, Jacques Nicolas. 1757. *Carte de la Caroline and Georgie: Pour Servir a la l'Histoire*

Generale des Voyages. Scale: 1:4,000,000. Paris.

———. 1764. *La Caroline dans l'Amerique Septentrionale Suivant les Cartes Angloise*. Scale: 1:2,000,000. Paris.

Bew, John, and John Ladge. 1780. *A New and Accurate Map of North Carolina and Part of South Carolina with the Field of Battle between Earl Cornwallis and General Gates*. Scale: 1:1,140,480. London: J. Bew.

Blaeu, Willem Janszoon. 1640. *Virginia Partis Australis et Floridae Partis Orientales, Intejacentiumque Regionum Nova Descriptio*. Scale: 1:2,280,960.

Blanchard, A. 1856. *Mouillage du Cap Hatteras*. Scale: 1:124,000. U.S. coast survey from Dépôt Général de la Marine, Paris. (*Mouillage*, "wet" in French, refers to the "recent" opening of Hatteras Inlet 1846.)

Blome, Richard. 1672. *A Generall Mapp of Carolina*. Scale unknown.

Blunt, Edmund M. 1809. *Ocracock [sic] Bar Including Shell Castle*. Scale unknown. New York: Blunt Publishing.

Bowen, Emanuel. 1747. *A New and Accurate Map of the Provinces of North and South Carolina, and Georgia, &c*. Scale: 1:2,487,760. London. Repr. from Bowen's *A Complete Atlas or Distinct View of the Known World*. Based on Popple 1733.

Bowen, Emanuel, and Thomas Bowen. 1754. *A Map of the British American Plantations: Extending from Boston in New England to Georgia; Including all the Back Settlements in the Respective Provinces, as far as the Mississippi*. Scale: 1:6,336,000.

Brazier, Robert H. (Assistant State Engineer). 1833. *North Carolina*. Scale unknown. Raleigh, N.C.

Brooks, Baylus. 2010. *Map of Hatteras Island Place Names*. Manteo, N.C.: Lost Colony Research Group.

Burgess, Daniel, and Roswell Chamberlain Smith. 1841. *Map of the Middle States Designed to Accompany Smith's Geography for Schools*. Scale: 1:2,851,200. New York: Paine and Burgess Publisher.

Burr, David H. 1834. *North and South Carolina*. Scale: 1:2,851,200. New York: Illman and Pilbrow Publisher.

Cantino, Alberto. 1502. *La Carta del Cantino* (facsimile). Scale varying. Portugal.

Codman, Crowninshield, and Lawrence. 1925. *Map of a Part of Currituck Sound Showing the Shooting Points of the Light-House Club*. n.p.: Light-House Club. The map is compiled from *Charts of the Coast and Geodetic Survey* with assistance from the Light-House Club, Monkey Island Club, and Currituck Club.

Coles, Thomas, and Jonathan Price. 1806. *Ocracock [sic] Bar Including Shell Castle*. Scale not provided.

Collet, John, I. Bayly, and Samuel Hooper. 1770. *A Compleat Map of North Carolina from an Actual Survey*. Scale not provided. London: S. Hooper Publisher.

Colton and Company. 1887. *Map Showing the Albemarle and Pantego Railroad and Its Connections*. New York: G. W. & C. B. Colton & Co. Scale: 1:1,267,000.

Colton, George Woolworth. 1861. *The War in North Carolina Map of the Entrance to Beaufort Harbor, North Carolina Showing the Position of Fort Macon, etc*. New York: G. Woolworth Colton. Scale: 1:48,000.

———. 1863. *New Guide Map of USA and Canada, with Railroads, Counties, etc*. Scale: 1:3,168,000. Chicago: Rufus Blanchard Publisher.

Colton, Joseph Hutchins. 1854 and 1860. *Map of North Carolina and South Carolina*. Scale: 1:3,100,000. New York: J. H. Colton and Co.

———. 1857. *North Carolina*. New York.

———. 1861. *Topographical Map of North and South Carolina; A Large Portion of Georgia and Part of Adjoining States*. Scale: 1:1,550,000. New York: Lang and Laing Publishers.

———. 1870s. *North Carolina*. Scale: 1:2,027,000. New York: J. H. Colton and Co.

Colton, Joseph Hutchins, and Millard Fillmore. 1862. *Map of the Seat of War in Virginia: Showing Minutely the Interesting Localities in the Vicinity of Richmond*. Scale not provided. New York: J. H. Colton and Co.

Comberford, Nicholas. 1657. *The South Part of Virginia Now the North Part of Carolina*.

Cox, David [surveyor]. 1906. *Property of the Deals Island Shooting Club*. Scale: 1:7,920. Hertford, N.C. Survey for the shooting club.

———. 1923. *Currituck Sound Shooting Club's Property*. Scale: 1:1,320. Currituck Courthouse: Register of Deeds.

Coxe, Daniel. 1722. *A Map of Carolana and of the River Meschacebe*. Scale: 1:7,476,480. London: Rose and Crown Publisher.

Cram, George Franklin. 1889. *New Railroad and County Map of North Carolina*. Scale: 1:1,584,000. Chicago: George F. Cram and Co.

————. 1896. *North Carolina and South Carolina.* Scale not provided. Chicago: George Cram and Co.

Cram, Thomas Jefferson, and Charles Worret. 1861. *S. E. Portion of Virginia and N. E. Portion of N'th Carolina.* Scale: 1:400,000.

Crisp, Edward. 1711. *A Complete Description of the Province of Carolina in 3 Parts. A New Chart of the Coast of Carolina from Cape Henry to the Havana in the Iland of Cuba.* London: John Harris engraver.

Currituck County. 2015. *Visitors Map of the Outer Banks—Currituck.* Currituck County.

D'Anville. 1756. *America Septentrionalis a Domino d'Anville in Galliis Edita Nunc in Anglia. Coloniis in Interiorem Virginiam Deductis Nec non Fluvii Ohio Cursu aucta Notisque Geographicis et Historicis Illustrata et Ad Bellum Praesentis Temporis Accomodata.* Library of Congress. Scale: 1:6,300,000.

DeBry, Theodor. 1590. *Americae Pars Nunc, Virginia Dicta Primum: ab Anglis Inuenta, Sumtibus Dn. Walteri Raleigh, Equistrus, Ordinis Viri, Anno Dńi. MDLXXXV Regni Vero Sereniss. Nostrae Reginae Elizabethae XXVII, Hujus Vero Historia Peculiari Libro Descripta est, Additis etiam Indigenarum Inconibus.* Library of Congress. Scale not provided.

DeLisle. 1718. *Carte de la Louisiane et du Cours du Mississippi.* Scale: 1:4,700,000. Paris: Chez Delisle.

Denison, J., Amos Doolittle, and Jedidiah Morse. 1796. *Map of North and South Carolina.* Scale: 1:3,484,800. Boston: I. Thomas and E. T. Andrews Publisher.

Dudley. 1647 and rev. 1661. *Carta Particulaire della Costa di Floridae di Virginia.* Scale not provided.

Faden, William, and Charles Cornwallis (Marquis). 1787. *The Marches of Lord Cornwallis in the South Provinces, Now States of North America; Comprehending the Two Carolinas with Virginia and Maryland and the Delaware Counties.* Scale: 1:500,000. London: William Faden, Geographer to the King.

Ferrar, John. 1667, 1651. *A Mapp of Virginia Discovered to Ye Hills, and in Its Latt. From 35 deg. & Neer Florida to 41 deg. Bounds of New England.* Scale not provided. London: John Overton Publisher. Reportedly the mapmaker's daughter later enhanced the map adding some names.

Finley, Anthony, and James Hamilton Young.

1827. *North and South Carolina and Georgia, Constructed from the Latest Authorities.* Scale: 1:1,774,000. Philadelphia: A. Finley Publisher.

Foster, John Gray. 1866a. *A Sketch of Roanoke Island February 8, 1862.* Scale not provided. Washington, D.C.: Government Printing Office. From U.S. Congress, Joint Committee on Conduct of the War. *Suppl. Rep. of the Joint Committee on Conduct of the War,* 2 vols. Supplemental to Senate rep. no. 142, 38th Cong., 2nd sess., vol. 2, folio p. 16.

————. 1866b. *Sketch Showing Route of the Burnside Expedition to Roanoke Island, N.C., February 6, 1862.* Scale not provided. Washington, D.C.: Government Printing Office. From U.S. Congress, Joint Committee on Conduct of the War. *Suppl. Rep. of the Joint Committee on Conduct of the War,* 2 vols. Supplemental to Senate rep. no. 142, 38th Cong., 2nd sess., vol. 2, folio p. 16.

Frédéric, François-Alexandre-, duc de La Rochefoucauld-Liancourt. 1807 and 1808. *Carte des Provinces Méridionales des Etats-Unis.* Scale: 1:2,534,400. Paris: Chez du Pont. From 1807 French edition of John Marshall's *Life of Washington* (1849) but originally published in *Voyage dans les Etats-Unis d'Amerique, Fait en 1795, 1796 et 1797* (Paris, 1799) by Francois Alexandre Frédéric, duc de La Rochefoucauld-Liancourt.

Fry, Joshua, Peter Jefferson, Thomas Jeffereys, and Robert Sayer. 1775. *A Map of the Most Inhabited Part of Virginia, Containing the Whole Province of Maryland with Part of Pensilvania [sic], New Jersey, and North Carolina.* Scale: 1:660,000. London.

Fulton, Hamilton (State Engineer). 1820. *Plan of Croatan and Roanoke Sounds Shewing the Proposed Situations of the Embankments and Inlet.* Scale: 1:15,840. Depicts embankments, locations, etc., to assist in reopening Roanoke Inlet.

Gascoyne, Joel. 1682. *A New Map of the Country of Carolina.* Scale not provided. London: Signe of the Platnere Mapping and The Rose and The Crown.

Graffenried, Christoph von. 1710. *Relation du Voyage d'Amerique.* Scale not provided.

Gray, Ormando Willis. 1872. *Gray's Atlas Map of North Carolina.* Scale: 1:2,027,000. Philadelphia.

Henry, Mathew Schropp. 1860. *North Carolina, South Carolina, and Virginia Map outlining*

Sir Walter Raleigh's Expeditions. Scale not provided. Representation of 1584 map. Some orthography might have been altered to mid-19th-century spellings.

Holland. 1794. *Coastal Carteret County*. Scale not provided. n.p.

Homann, Johann B. 1714. *Virginia, Marylandia, et Carolina*. Scale unknown.

Hondius, Jodocus. 1606. *Virginiae Item et Floridae America Provinciarum Nova Descriptio*. Amsterdam: 1632 Latin edition Mercator's Atlas Outer Banks History Center. Scale not provided.

Hooker, William. 1846 and 1850. *Coast of USA of North America from Cape Hatteras to Cape Fear North Carolina*. Scale not provided. New York: E. and G. W. Blunt.

Huber, Johannes Henry. 1711. *Die Provintz Nord und Sud Carolina. Bern, Switzerland*. Scale: 1:1,600,673. Based on Lawson's 1709 map.

Imlay, Gilbert. 1795. *A Map of the Western Part of the Territories Belonging to USA of America*. Scale not provided. London: Debrett.

Johnson, A. J. 1863 and 1872. *North Carolina and South Carolina*. Scale: 1:1,584,000. New York: A. J. Johnson and Co.

Kell, Jean Bruyere. 1777. *Plan of Old Topsail Inlet and the Harbour of Beaufort*. Scale not provided.

Kerr, W. C. 1882. *Map of North Carolina*. Scale not provided. Raleigh, N.C.: Office of State Geologist.

Keulen, Johannes Van. 1682 and 1690. *Pas Kaart Van de Kust von Carolina*. Scale: 1:1,774,080. Amsterdam: Johannes van Keulen Publisher.

Kilian, Georg Cristoph. 1764. *America Septentrionalis oder Mitternachtiger Theil von America*. Scale not provided. Augsberg, Bavaria (Germany).

Kitchen, Thomas. 1765. *A New Map of North and South Carolina and Georgia*. Scale: 1:6,336,000. London.

Lathrop, John (Albemarle and Chesapeake Canal Co.). 1858. *Map of the Albemarle and Chesapeake Canal Connecting Chesapeake Bay with Currituck, Albemarle, and Pamlico Sounds and Their Tributary Streams*. Scale not provided. New York: Hosford and Co. Publisher.

Lawson (Surveyor General of North Carolina). 1859. *The Western Ocean (facsimile of a map) of the Inhabited Parts of N. Carolina 1709*. Scale not provided. Fayetteville, N.C.: E. J. Hale and Son Publisher.

Lea, Philip. 1690. *A New Map of Carolina*. Scale: 1:1,330,500. London.

Leffers, John (County Surveyor). 1896. *Plat of an Island of Marsh [Little Wade Island] in Smyrna Township, Carteret County, State of North Carolina, Lying on Northeast Side of Johnsons Creek, East of Davis Island and Southeast from Davis Shore*. Scale: 1:1,200. Carteret County.

Leslie, Frank. 1861. *Map of the Atlantic Coast from Fortress Monroe, Va., to Fort Macon, N.C., Showing the Theatre of Present Naval Operations—Number 237*. New York: Leslie Publishing.

Lewis, Samuel, and Francis Shallus. 1807. *A Map of Those Parts of Virginia, North Carolina, South Carolina, and Georgia, which Were the Scenes of the Most Important Operations of the Southern Armies*. Scale: 1:1,900,800. Philadelphia: C. P. Wayne, G. G. Robinson, and John Robinson Publisher.

Lewis, Samuel, John Vallance, and Mathew Carey. 1795, 1814. *The State of North Carolina from the Best Authorities, &c*. Scale: 1:1,267,200. Philadelphia: Mathew Carey Publisher.

L'Isle, Guillame de. 1703. *Carte du Mexique et de la Floride des Terres Angloises et des Isles Antilles: du Cours et des Environs de la Riviere de Mississipi [sic], Dressée sur Ungrand Nombre de Memoires Principalemt. sur Ceux de M.rs d'Iberville et le Sueur*. Scale not provided. Paris: Chez l'auteur sur le Quai de l'Horloge.

Lodge, John, and James Adair. 1775. *A Map of the American Indian Nations, Adjoining to the Mississippi, West and East Florida, Georgia, S. and N. Carolina, Virginia, &c*. Scale not provided. London: Dilly Publishers.

Lok, Michael. 1582. *Illvstrivir, Domino Philippo Sidnaeo/Michael Lok Civis Londinensis/Hanc Chart Amdedicabat*. London: Thomas Woodcocke.

Lost Colony Center for Science and Research. n.d. *Map Depictions Online*. Williamston, N.C. A display of maps at the website where the White-DeBry map has been annotated ostensibly to enhance identification, but without explanation of sources.

Lucas, Fielding. 1826. *Geographisch-statistische und historische Charte von Nordcarolina*. Scale: 1:1,650,000. Weimar: Verlage des Geographishen Instituts.

Mackay, Arthur. 1756. *A Survey of the Coast about*

Cape Lookout in North Carolina. Scale not provided. n.p.

Mallinson et al. 2008. *Map in Past, Present, and Future Inlets of the Outer Banks Barrier Islands*, p. 6. Scale not provided. Greenville, N.C.: East Carolina University.

Mason, Connie. 2000. *Shackleford Banks; 1850–90.* Scale not provided. Washington, D.C.: NPS. Cape Lookout Village Historic District registration form, with accompanying justification material, 40 pp. with two maps and one satellite image.

Mast, Crowell and Kirkpatrick. 1890. *Map of North and South Carolina.* Scale: 1:2,534,400. Springfield, Ohio: Mast, Crowell and Kirkpatrick.

Maule, William (Surveyor General of North Carolina). 1718. *The Plane as Here Delineated and Layed Out Represents the Island of Roan-Oak in North Carolina Containing Twelve Thousand Acres of Land and Marsh.* Scale: 1:31,680. Division of land depicted with other miscellaneous known and useful information.

Meyer, Joseph, and Henry Schenke Tanner. 1849. *Neueste Karte von Nord Carolina mit Seinen Canaelen, Strassen, Eisenbahnen, Entfernungen der Hauptpunkte und Routen für Dampfschiffe.* Scale: 1:2,500,000. Amsterdam: Aus der Graviranstalat des Bibliographisch. Instituts zu Hildburghausen.

Moll, Hermann. 1708 and 1729. *Carolina.* Scale: 1:4,750,000. London: H. Moll.

———. 1720. *A New Map of the North Parts of America Claimed by France under Ye Names of Louisiana, Mississipi [sic], Canada, and New France with Ye Adjoining Territories of England and Spain.* Scale not provided. London: H. Moll.

———. 1730. *A Map of the West Indies, etc., Mexico or New Spain.* Scale: 1:21,874,016. London: Thomas and John Bowles Publisher.

Moll, Hermann, John Bowles, and Thomas Bowles. 1731. *A New and Exact Map of the Domain of the King of Great Britain on Ye Continent of North America, Containing Newfoundland, New Scotland New England, New York, New Jersey, Pensilvania [sic], Maryland, Virginia, and Carolina.* Scale: 1:3,168,000. London: T. Bowles, J. Bowles, and I. King.

Morden, Robert. 1688. *A New Map of Carolina.* R. Morden.

Morse, Jedidiah. 1794. *A Map of North Carolina from the Best Authorities.* Scale not provided. London: Stockdale Publishers.

Moseley, Edward. 1733 and 1737. *A New and Correct map of the Province of North Carolina.* Scale: 1:633,600. London: J Cowley surveyor; UNC Maps, N.C. State Archives.

Mouzon, Henry. 1775. *An Accurate Map of North and South Carolina with Their Indian Frontiers, Shewing in a Distinct Manner All the Mountains, Rivers, Swamps, Marshes, Bays, Creeks, Harbours, Sandbanks and Soundings on the Coasts; with the Roads and Indian Paths; as well as the Boundary of Provincial Lines, the Several Townships and Other Divisions of the Land in Both the Provinces.* Scale: 1:552,500. London: Bennett and Sayer.

Mouzon, Henry, and George Louis La Rouge. 1777. *Carolina Septentrionale et Meridionale en 4 Feuilles.* Scale: 1:570,000. Paris: Chex La Rouge.

Nature Conservancy. 2019 *Nags Head Woods Preserve Trail Guide.* Scale not provided. Arlington, Va.: Nature Conservancy.

NCDOT (N.C. Department of Transportation). 1936, 1938, 1953, 1960, 1963. *Dare County Highway Map.* Scale: 1:126,720. Raleigh: N.C. Department of Transportation,

———. 2005. *Dare County Bicycle Map.* Raleigh: N.C. Department of Transportation.

N.C. Fisheries Commission. 1923. *Additional Inlets of the North Carolina Coast.* Morehead City: Fisheries Commission Board. Report of the Special Committee on Inlets, which investigated the proposal(s) to construct additional inlets.

N.C. Marine Fisheries. 2013 *Descriptive Boundaries for Coastal-Joint-Inland Waters.* Scale: 1:187,165. Raleigh: N.C. Marine Fisheries. Series of maps.

———. 2019. *Shellfish Sanitation Maps.* Various scales. Morehead City.

N.C. Wildlife Resources Commission. 2016a. *Roanoke Island Marshes Gameland.* Raleigh: N.C. Wildlife Resources Commission.

———. 2016b. *Currituck Banks Game Land.* Raleigh: Nature Conservancy, N.C. Wildlife Resources Commission.

NOAA (National Oceanic and Atmospheric Administration). 1988. *Submerged Aquatic Vegetation Study.* National Ocean Service: Rockville, Md.

Nolin, Jean Baptiste. 1783. *Partie Méridionale des*

Possessions Angloises en Amérique. Scale not provided. Paris.

Norfolk and Southern Railway. 1881. *Norfolk and Southern Routes*. Norfolk, Va.: Norfolk and Southern Railway Company.

Ocracoke Civic and Business Association. 2015. *Ocracoke Island*. Scale: 1:800. Ocracoke, N.C.: Ocracoke Civic and Business Association.

Ogilby, John, and James Moxon. 1671 and 1676. *A New Discription [sic] of Carolina by the Order of the Lords Proprietors (First Lords Proprietors' Map; New Description of Carolina)*. Scale: 1:710,720. London: John Ogilby Publisher.

Ortelius, Abraham. 1587. *Americae Sive Novi Orbis Nova Descriptio*. Scale not provided. Outer Banks History Center.

PC HOA (Pirates Cove Home Owner's Association). 2016. *Map of Pirates Cove*. Manteo, N.C.: PC HOA.

Piggott, Cull (County Surveyor). 1894a. *Plat of Tract of Land, Carteret County, State of North Carolina, Known as East Wicar Island and Situated in Great Island Bay, Southwest from Great Island*. Scale: 1:600. Carteret County.

———. 1894b. *Plat of Tract of Land, Carteret County, State of North Carolina Known as Horse Island and Situated in the Southeastern Side of Core Sound Adjoining the Banks about 4½ Miles East by North East from Davis Island and about Opposite to Davis Shore*. Scale: 1:6,000. Carteret County.

Pinkerton, John, Samuel John Neele, and L. Herbert. 1809. *United States of America Southern Part*. Scale: 1:2,154,240. London: Cadell and Davies Publisher.

Prang, L. 1863. *Prang's War Map: North Carolina Coast*. No scale. Boston: Prang Publishing.

Price, Jonathan. 1795. *A Description of Occacock [sic] Inlet; and of Its Coasts, Islands, Shoals, and Anchorages: with the Courses and Distances to and from the Most Remarkable Places, And Directions to Sail over the Bar and thro' the Channels*. New Bern, N.C.: Francois X. Martin Publisher. Reprinted in *North Carolina Historical Review* (1926): 624–34.

Price, Jonathon, and John Strother. 1798. *Chart of the Coast from Cape Henry and the Albemarle Sound to North Santee Bay or Virginia South to South Carolina*. New Bern, N.C.: W. Johnston.

Price, Jonathon, John Strother, and William Harrison. 1808. *First Actual Survey of North Carolina*. Scale: 1:506,880. Philadelphia.

Purcell. 1788, 1792, 1797. *A New Map of the States of Georgia, South and North Carolina, Virginia and Maryland, Including the Spanish Provinces of West and East Florida*. Scale: 1:6,336,000. New York: Cornelius.

Quinn, David B. 1955 and 1977. *Raleigh's Virginia 1584–90*. Scale not provided. In *North America from Earliest Discovery to First Settlements*, p. 336. New York: Harper and Row.

Rand McNally. 1890. *North Carolina and South Carolina*. Chicago. Repr. from *World Atlas* (1884). Interestingly, in 1884 a conference (22 countries attending) in Washington, D.C., established the Prime Meridian or 0° longitude at Greenwich near London, but this map published 1890 still uses longitude "west from Washington"—French continued using Paris until 1911.

Romans, B. 1776. *A General Map of the Southern British Colonies, in America. containing North and South Carolina, Georgia, East and West Florida, with the Neighbouring Indian Countries*. Scale: 1:3,168,000. London: Bennett and Sayer. The map is based upon previous work by Collet, Mouzon, and others.

Russell, F. 1795. *Map of the Southern States of America*. Scale not provided. London: (publisher's name unclear).

Russell, John. 1799. *Map of the Southern Provinces of USA circa 1787*. Scale: 1:2,534,400. London: R. Phillips Mapmaker.

Russell, William, and John Lodge. 1778. *An Exact Map of North Carolina, South Carolina, and Georgia*. Scale not provided. In *History of America . . .*, vol. 2, by William Russell. London: William Russell Publisher.

Sanson, Nicolas. 1696. *Carte Generale de la Caroline*. Scale: 1:1,300,00. Amsterdam, Pierre Mortier.

Sauthier, C. J. 1769a. *Plan of the Town and Port of Bath*. Scale not provided. n.p.

———. 1769b. *Plan of the Town and Port of Edenton*. Scale not provided. n.p.

———. 1770. *Plan of the Town and Port of Beaufort*. Scale not provided. n.p.

Schroeter, George. 1859. *Carolina Described* (facsimile). Scale not provided. Fayetteville, N.C.: E. J. Hale and Son. This map is based on a pamphlet published by Robert Horne, 1666.

Seller, John. 1682. *Carolina Newly Described*. Scale: 1:6,000,000. London: A. Godbid and J. Playford Publisher.

Smith, John 1608. *Zúñiga Map*. Smith is listed

as cartographer, although true cartographer could have been Nathaniel Powell, cartographer who accompanied Smith on his explorations. The map is known as the *Zúñiga Map* or *Zúñiga Chart*, named for Don Pedro de Zúñiga, Spanish ambassador to England from Spain, who purloined the map and sent it to Spain, where it was discovered at Archivo General de Simancas, M.P.D., IV-66, XIX-15. The interpretation is by Alexander Brown (1890), who discovered the map in Simancas while doing research.

———. 1612. *Map of Virginia with a Description of the Countrey [sic], the Commodities, People, Government and Religion*. Scale not provided. Oxford: Joseph Barnes. Repr., Ben C. McCary, Charlottesville, Va.: University Press of Virginia, 1957.

Sneden, Robert Knox. 1862. *Map of Roanoke Island Showing Rebel Forts*. Scale not provided. Hand annotated.

Speed. 1676. *A New Description of Carolina*. Scale: 1:1,710,720. London: Basset and Chiswell.

Tanner, Henry Schenck. 1855. *A New Map of Nth. Carolina: with Its Canals, Roads and Distances from Place to Place, along the Stage and Steam Boat Routes*. Scale not provided. Philadelphia: Thomas, Cowperthwait and Co.

Tardieu, Pierre Francois. ca. 1800. *Carta delle Provincie Meridionali degli Stati-Uniti*. Scale: 1:2,534,000. Italy.

Tompson, W. Beverhout, and T. Albert. 1854. *Sketch of Beaufort Harbor, North Carolina (authorized by) the U.S. Coast Survey of Superintendent Bache together with an Addition by Actual Survey from the Mouth of Newport River and Continued up that River to Include Shepherd's Point and Gallants Point North Carolina*. Scale: 1:21,000. New York: John F. Trow Publisher. Based on the chart published by U.S. Coast Survey.

Town of Atlantic Beach. 2016. *Planning, Zoning, and Inspections* (various maps). Atlantic Beach, N.C.: Town of Atlantic Beach.

Town of Kitty Hawk. 2007. *Official Zoning Map*. Scale: 1:12,000. Kitty Hawk, N.C.: Town of Kitty Hawk.

Town of Nags Head. 2000. *Land and Water Use Plan*. Nags Head, N.C.: Town of Nags Head.

Town of Southern Shores. 2015. *Map of Canals*. Southern Shores, N.C.: Town of Southern Shores.

Unknown. 1779. *A New and Accurate Map of North Carolina in North America*. Scale not provided. London.

Unknown. 1806. *Carte des Deux Carolines et Géorgie*. Scale not provided.

Unknown. 1807. *A Plan of the Harbour of Ocracock [sic] and the Entrance into Pamtico [sic] Sound*. Scale unknown. n.p.

Unknown. 1870. *A New Map of the State of North Carolina Constructed from Actual Surveys, Actual Public Documents, and Private Contributors*. Scale not provided. Pearce and Best Publisher.

Unknown. 1891. *B Sketch Showing Route of the Burnside Expedition*. Scale not provided. In *The Atlas to Accompany the Official Records of the Union and Confederate Armies*, pl. 40, no. 3, ser. 1, vol. 9. Washington, D.C.: Government Printing Office.

Unknown. ca. 1900. *Narrows Island and Surroundings*. Scale not provided. A local survey of property holdings in The Narrows (Currituck County).

Unknown. n.d. *Mean Westerly Limits of the Gulf Stream*. Scale not provided. Blunt Publisher.

U.S. War Department. 1895. *General Map III*. Scale: 1:633,600. Washington, D.C.: Government Printing Office.

Vaugondy, Robert. 1753. *Carte de Pays Connus Sous le Nom de Canada, dans Laquelle Sont Destinguées les Possesions Françoise et Angl*. Scale: 1:4,000,000. Paris: Ministre Sécrétaire d'Etat.

———. 1755. *Carte de la Virginie et du Maryland*. Josué Fry and Pierre Jefferson.

Verrazano, Gerolama da. 1529. *World Map (Florida and Southeast North America Coast)*.

Vespucci, Juan. 1526. *World Map (Caribbean and Southeast North America)*.

Village at Nags Head. 2016. *Map of the Village at Nags Head*. Nags Head, N.C.: Village at Nags Head Home Owners' Association.

Visscher, Nicolaes. 1680. *Insulae Americanae in Oceano Septentrionali*.

Visscher, Nicolaes, and Luggart van Anse. ca. 1717. *Nova Tabula Geographica Complectens Borealiorem Americae Partem. In Qua Exacte Delinetae Sunt Canada Sive Nova Francia, Nova Scotia, Nova Anglia, Novum Belgium, Pensylvania [sic], Virginia, Carolina, et Terra Nova cum omnibus Littorum Pulvinorumque Profunditatibu*. Scale not provided. Amsterdam.

Walton, D. S. 1861 and 1867. *Dismal Swamp Canal*

Connecting Chesapeake Bay with Currituck, Albemarle, and Pamlico Sounds and Their Tributary Streams. Scale not provided. New York: Hosford and Sons.

Warner and Beers. 1875. *North Carolina, South Carolina, Georgia, and Florida*. Scale Unknown. In *The Atlas of USA*. Chicago, 1875.

White, John. 1585. *La Virginea Pars (facsimile)*. With Thomas Harriot. Scale not provided. British Museum. More than one version with different names appearing on each, including DeBry 1590.

Wildey, George, and John Thornton. 1685. *A New Map of Carolina*. Scale: 1:1,330,560. London: Wildey Publisher. Republished by Robert Morden and later by Phillip Lea without acknowledging the original compilers.

Wimble, Captain James. 1733 and 1738. *Chart of His Majesties Province of North Carolina*. Scale: 1:570,240. London: William Mount and Thomas Page Publishers. Wimble was notorious for peculiar and unconventional orthography (spelling) even in this time before standardized orthography.

Wright. 1599. *A chart of the World (Southeastern North America)*. Haklyut, 1600.

Zaenker, Walt. 2014. *Annotated Contemporary Maps Depicting Pine Knoll Shores*. Pine Knoll Shores, N.C.: Pine Knoll Shores Historical Committee.

Charts of U.S. National Oceanic and Atmospheric Administration

The U.S. Coast Survey (CS) was established in 1807 generally to define and manage the national coordinate system, essential for communication and transportation. As responsibilities increased, and to reflect these additional responsibilities, the name was changed 1878 to U.S. Coast and Geodetic Survey (C&GS). C&GS briefly became part of the newly organized Environment Sciences Services Administration 1965–70 when the larger and expanded National Oceanic and Atmospheric Administration was formed and National Ocean Service (NOS) established. Responsibility for charting the nation's coasts and water bodies has been responsibility of these organizations since 1807.

U.S. Coast Survey (CS), Washington, D.C.

CS. 1848. *Currituck Sound, Jew Quarter Island to Collington Island and North River, N.C.* Scale: 1:20,000.

CS. 1849a *Bodies Island*. Scale unknown.

CS. 1849b. *Navigation Chart for Hatteras Inlet, Coast of North Carolina*. Scale: 1:20,000.

CS. 1850a and 1876. *Navigation Chart of Beaufort Harbor N.C.* Scale: 1:40,000.

CS. 1850b. *Reconnoissance [sic] of Hatteras Inlet, Harbor of Refuge (Wainwright, Richard)*. Scale: 1:20,000.

CS. 1850c. *Sketch D Number 5 Showing the Progress of the Survey in Section Number 5 Beaufort Harbor (Dallas), N Carolina*. Scale: 1:60,000.

CS. 1852. *Map of the Coast of North Carolina from Whales Head Hill to Thorofare (Hassler)*. Scale: 1:21,120.

CS. 1852–82. *Sketch D, Showing the Progress of Section IV 1845–52 (and 1854, 1855, 1856, 1867, 1873, 1877, 1882)*. Scale: 1:600,000.

CS. 1853. *Reconnaissance of Hatteras Inlet*. 4th ed. Scale: 1:20,000.

CS. 1856. *Preliminary Chart of the Sea Coast of North Carolina from Cape Hatteras to Ocracoke Inlet (Wadsworth)*. Scale: 1:200,000.

CS. 1857a. *Comparative Chart Showing Changes to the Entrance of Beaufort Harbor North Carolina*. Scale: 1:10,000.

CS. 1857b. *Preliminary Chart Number 2 of the Sea Coast of USA from Cape Hatteras to Ocracoke Inlet and from Cape Lookout to Bogue Inlet North Carolina*. Scale: 1:200,000.

CS. 1857c. *Preliminary Survey of Hatteras Inlet (Wadsworth)*. Scale: 1:20,000.

CS. 1860. *The Coast of USA, Sheet No. 2: from Cape Lookout to Cape Carnaveral [sic] (Blunt)*.

CS. 1861. *Sketch of the Coast of North Carolina from Oregon Inlet to Ocracoke Inlet*. Scale: 1:200,000.

CS. 1862a. *Coast of North Carolina and Virginia (Lindenkohl)*. Scale: 1:200,000.

CS. 1862b. *Navigation Chart for Oregon Inlet*. Scale: 1:20,000.

CS. 1865. *Map of Part of South-Eastern Virginia*. Scale: 1:644,158.

CS. 1865. *North Carolina and South Carolina. Lindenkohl and Krebs*. Scale: 1:633,600.

CS. 1866. *Parts of Portsmouth and Core Banks, North Carolina*. Scale: 1:20,000.

CS. 1870. *From Killdevil Hills to Loggerhead Inlet N.C.* Scale: 1:40,000.

U.S. Coast and Geodetic Survey (C&GS), Washington, D.C.

CS/C&GS. 1860, 1877, 1889a, 1892, and 1895a. *Albemarle Sound North Carolina Eastern Part (Dallas)*. Scale: 1:80,000.

CS/C&GS. 1876a and 1895b. *Chart no. 40, Albemarle Sound North Carolina Eastern Part from the Atlantic Ocean to the Pasquotank River (Dallas)*. Scale: 1:80,000.

CS. 1876b. *Navigation Chart of Core Sound and Straits*. Scale: 1:40,000.

C&GS. 1878. *From Cape Henry to Currituck Beach (Hassler)*. Scale: 1:80,000.

C&GS. 1879. *Chart Number 138 from Currituck Beach to Oregon Inlet (Dallas)*. Scale: 1:80,000.

C&GS. 1882. *North Landing River (Head of Currituck Sound) Virginia and N. Carolina*. Scale: 1:40,000.

C&GS. 1883. *General Chart of the Coast Number V from Cape Henry to Cape Lookout*. Scale: 1:400,000.

C&GS. 1883. *Pamplico [sic] Sound North Carolina Eastern Sheet*. Scale: 1:80,000.

C&GS. 1888a (CS) and 1889b. *Beaufort Harbor, North Carolina (Colonna)*. Scale: 1:40,000.

C&GS. 1888b, 1896, 1905, and 1915a. *Chart Number 147 Core Sound to Bogue Inlet Including Cape Lookout North Carolina*. Scale: 1:80,000.

C&GS. 1888c. *Pamplico [sic] Sound North Carolina*. Scale: 1:80,000.

C&GS. 1899a and 1913a. *From Cape Henry to Currituck Beach Including the Albemarle and Chesapeake Canal*. Scale: 1:80,000.

C&GS. 1899b. *Chart Numbers 142, 143, and 144 Pamlico Sound North Carolina* (middle sheet). Scale: 1:80,000.

C&GS. 1899c. *East Coast North Carolina Core Sound and Straits*. Scale: 1:40,000.

C&GS. 1900 and 1910a. *Chart Number 146 Ocracoke Inlet to Beaufort Including Core Sound North Carolina*. Scale: 1:80,000.

C&GS. 1910b. *Chart Number 145 Cape Hatteras to Ocracoke Inlet North Carolina*. Scale: 1:80,000.

C&GS. 1910c. *Croatan and Roanoke Sounds and Part of Pamlico Sound, North Carolina (Meekins, Rude, and Tittmann)*. Scale: 1:80,000.

C&GS. 1913b and 1923. *East Coast North Carolina Currituck Beach to New Inlet*. Scale: 1:80,000.

C&GS. 1915b. *East Coast North Carolina Portsmouth Island to Beaufort including Cape Lookout Shoals*. Scale: 1:80,000.

C&GS. 1916a, 1918, and 1928. *East Coast North Carolina Cape Hatteras Wimble Shoals to Ocracoke Inlet*. Scale: 1:80,000.

C&GS. 1916b. *East Coast Cape May to Cape Hatteras*. Scale: 1:415,000.

C&GS. 1931 and 1938. *Core Sound*. Scale: 1:40,000.

C&GS. 1932 and 1969a. *East Coast North Carolina Currituck Beach Light to Wimble Shoals*. Scale: 1:80,000.

C&GS. 1937. *Neuse River to New River Inlet*. Scale: 1:40,000.

C&GS. 1945. *East Coast North Carolina Ocracoke Inlet*. Scale: 1:20,000.

C&GS. 1947. *East Coast North Carolina Beaufort Inlet and Part of Core Sound*. Scale: 1:40,000.

C&GS. 1953. *Morehead City Harbor*. Scale: 1:2,500.

C&GS. 1968. *Portsmouth Island to Beaufort*. Scale: 1:80,000.

C&GS. 1969b. *Chart Number 1229 East Coast North Carolina Currituck Beach Light to Wimble Shoals*. Scale: 1:80,000.

U.S. National Ocean Service (NOS), Department of Commerce, Washington, D.C.

NOS. 1985. *East Coast North Carolina, Cape Hatteras, Wimble Shoals to Ocracoke Inlet*. Scale: 1:80,000.

NOS. 2012. *Cape Lookout to New River Chart 11545*. Scale: 1:80,000.

NOS. 2013. *Neuse River to Myrtle Grove Sound Chart 11541*. Scale: 1:40,000.

NOS. 2014a. *Beaufort Inlet and Part of Core Sound Chart 11545*. Scale: 1:40,000.

NOS. 2014b. *Cape Hatteras, Wimble Shoals to Ocracoke Inlet Chart 11555*. Scale: 1:80,000.

NOS. 2014c. *Cape Henry to Currituck Beach Light Chart 12207*. Scale: 1:80,000.

NOS. 2014d. *Cape May to Cape Hatteras Chart 12200*. Scale: 1:419,706.

NOS. 2014e. *Currituck Beach Light to Wimble Shoals Chart 12204*. Scale: 1:80,000.

NOS. 2014 f. *Morehead City Harbor Chart 11547*. Scale: 1:5,000.

NOS. 2014g. *[Cape Henry to Pea Island with Albemarle Sound Chart 12205]*. Scale: 1:80,000.

NOS. 2014h. *Ocracoke Inlet and Part of Core Sound Chart 11550*. Scale: 1:40,000.

NOS. 2014i. *Pamlico Sound, Western Part Chart 11548*. Scale: 1:80,000.

NOS. 2014j. *Portsmouth Island to Beaufort Inlet including Cape Lookout Shoals Chart 11544.* Scale: 1:80,000.

Charts by U.S. Agencies

ACE (U.S. Army Corps of Engineers) (Graham). 1843. *Survey of Roanoke Inlet and Sound, 1829.* Scale: 1:63,360. Washington, D.C.: ACE.

ACE (U.S. Army Corps of Engineers) (Fillmore). 1862. *Eastern Portion of the Military Department of North Carolina.* Scale: 1:316,800. Washington, D.C.: ACE.

ACE (U.S. Army Corps of Engineers) (Farquahr). 1864. *Hatteras.* Scale unknown. Washington, D.C.: ACE.

ACE (U.S. Army Corps of Engineers). 1891. *Inland Waterway: Beaufort to New Berne [sic].* Scale: 1:101,376. Washington, D.C.: ACE.

ACE (U.S. Army Corps of Engineers) (Lucas). 1893. *Ocracoke Inlet Showing Velocity Stations, Tide Gauges, and Level Lines.* Scale: 1:36,000. Washington, D.C.: ACE.

ACE (U.S. Army Corps of Engineers) (Stanton). 1895. *Cape Lookout Harbor of Refuge Known as Lookout Bight.* Scale not provided. Wilmington, N.C.: ACE.

ACE (U.S. Army Corps of Engineers) (Heap). 1896 or 1897 (data 1891–96). *Ocracoke Inlet.* Scale unknown. n.p.: ACE.

ACE (U.S. Army Corps of Engineers). 1939. *Silver Lake Harbor.* Wilmington, N.C.: ACE.

ACE (U.S. Army Corps of Engineers). 1948. *Oregon Inlet and Connecting Channels.* Scale unknown. Wilmington, N.C.: ACE.

ACE (U.S. Army Corps of Engineers) (Heap). 1950. *Ocracoke Inlet.* Scale unknown. n.p.: ACE.

ACE (U.S. Army Corps of Engineers). 1969 and 1983. *Map of Beaufort Harbor.* Scale not provided. Washington, D.C.: ACE.

F&WS (U.S. Fish and Wildlife Service). 1999. *Currituck National Wildlife Refuge.* Manteo, N.C.: F&WS.

F&WS (U.S. Fish and Wildlife Service). 2015. *Pea Island National Wildlife Refuge (map).* Scale not provided. Manteo, N.C.: F&WS.

Soil Conservation Service. 1978. *Map, Hyde County.* Scale not provided. Washington, D.C.: U.S. Department of Agriculture.

U.S. Navy. 1839. *Beaufort Harbour, North Carolina,* Scale: 1:9,600. December 9th. Washington, D.C.: Naval Department.

U.S. Navy. 1862. *Naval Battle of Roanoke Island.* Scale: 1:95,040. Washington, D.C.: Government Printing Office.

U.S. Navy (Gray). 1918. *Property of Radio Direction Station Cape Hatteras, NC Surveyed by the Navy.* Scale: 1:1,200. Washington, D.C.

U.S. Geological Survey Topographic Maps

Maps from the U.S. Geological Survey (USGS) are topographic maps, meaning basically a general map showing hydrography, topography, culture, transportation, and toponymy (geographic names). These maps show contour lines to depict elevation, connecting points of equal elevation (isohypse), thereby simulating landform depiction two dimensionally, hence "topographic." USGS maps are based solely on geographic grids (latitude and longitude). Each map covers about 60 square miles and is typically named for the most prominent feature on the map, often the largest town or village. For example, Nags Head is on USGS Manteo and Roanoke Island NE maps but is not in Manteo or on Roanoke Island and is a separate incorporated town merely within boundaries of the maps that bear those names.

These maps are mostly large scale (mostly 1:24,000, or one inch equals 24,000 inches on the ground or 2,000 feet), showing much detail, so they are a good base from which to compile geographic names to which others can be added from nautical charts of different scales (and dates), local and state official maps and documents, and historical maps and documents, and a wide array of other source materials, including vetted websites with provenance identified. So, feature locations could be identified relatively precisely. In all cases (especially the internet sources), the names have been verified with more than one source of proven provenance (quality and stability of source).

If a name is referenced to a USGS map in the gazetteer, reference is "USGS year date: map name." Some maps are relatively current, and some are historical. If no scale number appears, then the scale is 1:24,000; if the scale differs from 1:24,000, then the scale is included with the reference. To download digital versions of USGS topographic maps, use https://store.usgs .gov/.

CPSIA information can be obtained
at www.ICGtesting.com
Printed in the USA
LVHW091531080321
680887LV00012B/2869